THE BIGGEST
PUB
QUIZ
BOOK

Ever!

1 85868 808 6

Executive Editor: Tim Dedopulos
Production: Garry Lewis

Questions set by The Puzzle House

Printed and bound in Great Britain

THE BIGGEST
PUB
QUIZ
BOOK

Ever!

CARLTON

Contents

INTRODUCTION

Quizzes are a strange thing. If you were to stroll up to some poor bloke on the street – let's say it's a Saturday lunch time, and he's out with the wife doing the weekly shopping, trying to get it over and done with so he can make it back home for kick-off – and started firing questions at him, one after the other, he'd probably take it pretty badly. He'd be nervous, irritated, and looking for quick ways to escape the maniac that's latched on to him. If you take a moment to picture it ("Quick, mate, what would you ride in a velodrome? What colour is an aubergine?"), you'll see how ludicrous it sounds. If he doesn't lamp you one, he'll probably run off screaming.

However, get the same bloke later on the same Saturday, down the pub with his mates after the match, and then you leap up and start firing the same questions at him, at the very least he's going to rise to the challenge and prove he's the equal of your questions. If you've taken the time to sort things out with the landlord in advance, and you're asking the whole pub, you'll have a crowd of people enthralled, hanging on your every word, and not just our bloke. Even if – and this is the best part – there's absolutely no prize at the end of it. We all love glory, after all, and what could be more glorious than proving you've got the keenest mind in the bar? It beats getting onto a horse and charging at a cannon hands down.

Way back in 1996 The Best Pub Quiz Book Ever! was first published; it was followed, rather rapidly, by the tongue-twisting The Best Pub Pop Quiz Book Ever! and then by the soccer-mad The Best Football Quiz Book Ever!. That the public cannot get enough of their quizzes and that the idea of doing them in a pub is not a fad but an institution is now a fact that manifests itself in the fabulous The Biggest Pub Quiz Book Ever! Welcome.

The aim of this fine tome is to guide you through the pitfalls of pub quizzardry to the land of Pub Facts (and I'm not talking warm beer) where you can safely head up a quiz at your local hostelry and thereby gain the undying gratitude of the stout yeoman of the bar and love of the locals.

There is a guide to the rear of the book that will show you the way forward but some initial pointers for you to note are that the whole ideal of the pub quiz is one of entertainment. It may engender well-placed pedantry and overzealous Zimmer rattling but it will be fun, fun, fun. Keep this as your philosophy and you won't go far wrong.

Talk the idea through with your landlord and have the quiz at your local where you know everyone and everyone knows you and where you can escape home all the quicker if the locals fall upon you with cries and hollers and flaming torches. Start slowly and build up your quiz nights carefully, controlling and feeding the voracious appetites of the regulars until you have them eating quiz out of the palms of your hands. Finally and quite seriously. No, really. When setting a quiz make sure you note down all the questions and then the answers and then double check that everything is present and correct. If an answer gives you pause to think then double-check it and make sure it's the right answer and moreover the *only* right answer. Also while every effort has been undertaken to ensure that the answers given are the correct answers there is a possibility, however slight, that the answer given is incorrect. If, however, you have checked this then you can begin your quiz with quiet confidence, or even loud and booming confidence. At any rate, you can begin.

The best of luck.

Easy Questions

Let's look at the facts for a minute:

easy adj. **1** not difficult. **2** free from pain, care, or anxiety. **3** tolerant and undemanding; easy-going **4** readily influenced; pliant: an *easy victim*.... We'll leave the dictionary definition there. You should have got the message, but just in case you haven't I'll underline it, metaphorically of course, in double-line puce ink. This section of the quiz book is not difficult: it is, like, so many pub regulars, simple. Not hard. If this section were an aeroplane it would be made out of balsa wood, driven by an elastic band and piloted by a five-year-old. People who find difficulty in this section should be asked to leave the pub because they're under age (by around 17 years) or over the limit (by about 30 units). To further clarify: people who cannot answer the following questions should not be asked to participate in the quiz AT ALL:

What is your name?
How old are you?
$2 + 2 = ?$
Fill in the missing number: 1, 2, 3, ?, 5
Finish this sentence: "Mine's a..."

As Shirley Crabtree (AKA 'Big Daddy', grapple fans) sang: Easy!...Easy!...Easy!...Easy!...Easy!...Easy!...Easy!...Easy!... Easy!...(*repeat to fade*)

LEVEL 1

1 Who married Patsy Kensit in April 1997?
2 Which singer's daughter is called Lourdes Maria?
3 Who has a backing group called the Waves?
4 Who took "Wannabe" to No. 1 in 1996?
5 Who is lead singer with Wet Wet Wet?
6 Who won the Eurovision Song Contest with "Puppet on a String"?
7 Who sang "Strangers in the Night"?
8 Who is the brother of the late Karen Carpenter?
9 Who wrote "Words", a 90s hit for Boyzone?
10 Which singer/songwriter received a knighthood in January 1997?
11 Who was Bernie Taupin's most famous songwriting partner?
12 Who is Mick Jagger's second wife?
13 Who changed his name from Gordon Sumner to top the charts?
14 Who was the only female singer managed by Brian Epstein?
15 Who was the female vocalist with the Pretenders?
16 Who co-starred with Whitney Houston in *The Bodyguard*?
17 Who wrote the music for *Jesus Christ Superstar*?
18 Who were known on TV as Dave Tucker and Paddy Garvey?
19 Who sang that they were "Back For Good" in 1995?
20 Whose "new" single, "Free As A Bird", charted in 1995?
21 The title from which TV drama gave Jimmy Nail a hit in 1994?
22 Who was the subject of the biopic *What's Love Got to Do With It?*?
23 Whose first solo No. 1 was "Sacrifice/Healing Hands"?
24 Who was the British Monkee?
25 Who played Wimbledon's Centre Court without a racket in 1996?
26 Who had a hit with "Radio Ga Ga"?
27 Who was the father of the former Mrs Lisa Marie Jackson?
28 Which 80s duo included Andrew Ridgeley?
29 Who had his first UK solo No. 1 with "I Just Called To Say I Love You"?
30 Who was lead singer with Culture Club?

1　On which day are hot cross buns traditionally eaten?
2　How many signs of the zodiac are there?
3　In which decade of the 20th century was Muhammad Ali born?
4　What word can go after "hobby" and before "radish"?
5　How is Maurice Cole better known?
6　Which soccer club has had Royal and Woolwich as part of its name?
7　Who wrote the novel Lucky Jim?
8　On a Monopoly board, what colour is Old Kent Road?
9　Who invented Braille?
10　In song, who was born "on a mountain top in Tennessee"?
11　What is Kampuchea now called?
12　Which Richard starred in "The Good Life"?
13　Lance Cairns played cricket for which country?
14　What word can go before "draft", "flow" and "shadow"?
15　Traditionally, what colour is willow pattern?
16　In which country is the city of Addis Ababa?
17　Which Boys recorded "Barbara Ann" in the 60s?
18　Which cartoon character has an anchor tattooed on his arm?
19　What is the square root of 4?
20　Iceberg and Dorothy Perkins are examples of what?
21　Ivor Allchurch is associated with which sport?
22　Which film ends with "tomorrow is another day"?
23　A revolving firework is named after which saint?
24　Who murdered Abel?
25　In 1974, parts of Somerset and Gloucestershire made which new county?
26　Which Italian phrase used in English means in the fresh or cool air?
27　In which TV series did the characters Edina and Saffron appear?
28　Which Ben won an Oscar for Best Actor in Gandhi?
29　How many degrees in a right angle?
30　Which group had a No. 1 with "Hey Jude"?

Answers

Around the UK (see Quiz 4)
1 Strathclyde. 2 Leeds. 3 Clwyd. 4 M1. 5 Anglesey. 6 Northern Ireland.
7 One - Devon. 8 Lake District. 9 Scarborough. 10 Scotland. 11 Humber.
12 Birmingham. 13 Edinburgh. 14 East. 15 M11. 16 Regent's Park.
17 M4. 18 Isle of Wight. 19 Bognor, Lyme. 20 Ealing, Enfield.
21 Liverpool. 22 Guernsey. 23 The Mall. 24 Blackpool. 25 Fife.
26 Dartford. 27 M6. 28 Suffolk. 29 Glasgow. 30 North.

LEVEL 1

1 Who left "EastEnders" for France with two of her three children?
2 What is the name of Maureen's mum in "Coronation Street"?
3 Who is the Street's repetitive butcher?
4 In which soap did Dave Glover perish in a fire?
5 Which "Coronation Street" MacDonald twin went to prison?
6 In which soap does Sinbad appear?
7 What is EastEnder Tiffany's daughter called?
8 What was Ivy Tilsley's surname when she died?
9 Former members of which soap starred in a BT ad in 1997?
10 In "Neighbours" what was the surname of Scott, Paul, Lucy and Julie?
11 Who was Frank Tate's murdered wife in "Emmerdale"?
12 What is the name of Jack and Vera Duckworth's wayward son?
13 Where was David Wicks heading for when he left "EastEnders"?
14 Who is Bianca's mum in "EastEnders"?
15 Who married Shane in "Home and Away"?
16 What is the name of the Barbara Windsor character in "EastEnders"?
17 In the Street what is Curly's real name?
18 Where was Curly's wife Raquel heading for on leaving Weatherfield?
19 Which Street character had a fling with gangster Fraser Henderson?
20 Which soap pub is famous for its Newton & Ridley beer?
21 "Home and Away" is set near which Australian city?
22 What is Phil and Kathy Mitchell's son called?
23 Who is the most senior of the Archer family?
24 In which soap would you see the character Tinhead?
25 Which soap is set in Erinsborough?
26 What was the name of Joan Collins's character in "Dynasty"?
27 Who sponsored "Coronation Street" in 1997?
28 Which soap is "Knot's Landing" a spin off from?
29 Which soap is set in Borsetshire?
30 Which dish is the Rover's Return's Betty Williams famous for?

Quiz 4 Around the UK

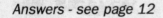

Answers - see page 12

Answers - see page 12

LEVEL 1

1 Glasgow is the administrative centre of which Scottish region?
2 Which is further north, Liverpool or Leeds?
3 What before the 1996 reorganization was the only Welsh county to begin with C?
4 Which motorway would you travel on from London to Leeds?
5 How is the Welsh island Ynys Mon also known?
6 In which part of the UK is Newry?
7 How many counties have a border with Cornwall?
8 In which District are Ullswater and Bassenthwaite?
9 Which resort beginning with S lies between Whitby and Bridlington?
10 In which country is Prestwick Airport?
11 On which river does Hull lie?
12 Which city's major station is New Street?
13 In which city is Princes Street a major shopping thoroughfare?
14 On which coast of Scotland is Dundee?
15 Which motorway would you travel on from London to Cambridge?
16 London Zoo is in which Park?
17 Which motorway stretches from the outskirts of London into Wales?
18 On which island are Shanklin and Sandown?
19 Which two south-coast resorts include the name Regis?
20 Which two London Boroughs begin with E?
21 In which city is Lime Street station and the Albert Dock?
22 On which Channel Island is St Peter Port?
23 Which road leads from Trafalgar Square up to Buckingham Palace?
24 St Annes lies to the south of which major seaside resort?
25 Which is the only Scottish region beginning with F?
26 Which tunnel is a major link around the M25?
27 Which motorway would you travel on from Birmingham to Lancaster?
28 Which county lies between Norfolk and Essex?
29 In which city is Sauciehall Street?
30 Does London's Euston station serve the north, south, east or west of the country?

Answers

Pot Luck 1 (see Quiz 2)

1 Good Friday. 2 12. 3 40s. 4 "Horse". 5 Kenny Everett. 6 Arsenal.
7 Kingsley Amis. 8 Brown. 9 Louis Braille. 10 Davy Crockett.
11 Cambodia. 12 Briers. 13 New Zealand. 14 "Over". 15 Blue.
16 Ethiopia. 17 The Beach Boys. 18 Popeye. 19 2. 20 Rose. 21 Football.
22 *Gone With The Wind*. 23 Catherine. 24 Cain. 25 Avon. 26 Al fresco.
27 "Absolutely Fabulous". 28 Kingsley. 29 90. 30 The Beatles.

Quiz 5 Pot Luck 2

1   Which UK car manufacturer produced the Cambridge?
2   Which Welsh comedian was a member of the Goons?
3   Gubby Allen is associated with which sport?
4   What word can go after "roller" and before "board"?
5   In which country is the city of Acapulco?
6   How many millimetres in three centimetres?
7   Who wrote the novel *Jane Eyre*?
8   The character Elsie Tanner appeared in which TV soap?
9   Who had an 80s No. 1 with "You Win Again"?
10 In which decade of the 20th century was Woody Allen born?
11 Al is the chemical symbol for which element?
12 In which TV series did the characters James, Siegfried and Tristan appear?
13 What title did the eldest son of the king of France hold?
14 Ben Gurion airport is in which country?
15 How is Sophia Scicoloni better known?
16 Which Tim became Britain's most expensive soccer keeper in 1993?
17 Bob Cratchit appears in which Charles Dickens novel?
18 What does the C stand for in ACAS?
19 What is the administrative centre for the county of Avon?
20 Which quizmaster says, "I've started so I'll finish"?
21 What colour appears along with white on the Polish flag?
22 Which Glenda starred in "Elizabeth R"?
23 What is 3 cubed?
24 DEAR CASH is an anagram of which indoor game?
25 What is measured in amperes?
26 What is the study of the earth's crust and rocks called?
27 What term describes instruments that produce sound when struck?
28 Which Tony had a 50s hit with "Stranger In Paradise"?
29 What was the name of the painter and decorator in "Brush Strokes"?
30 How many sides does a trapezium have?

Answers

Pot Luck 3 (see Quiz 7)
1 Parlophone. 2 Logie. 3 40s. 4 "Cracker". 5 Dirk Bogarde. 6 Aston Villa. 7 Agatha Christie. 8 Golf. 9 Queen Elizabeth I. 10 "Hound Dog". 11 Caffeine. 12 Dennis the Menace. 13 Rossiter. 14 "Show". 15 Rouge. 16 Stephen Sondheim. 17 Déjà vu. 18 1,000. 19 Canada. 20 "'Allo 'Allo". 21 Tuesday. 22 Hanks. 23 Grey and red. 24 Salvation Army. 25 Fred Flintstone. 26 Eyes. 27 Police. 28 Egypt. 29 Lent. 30 Dark blue.

Quiz 6 Hobbies & Leisure 1

Answers - see page 18

LEVEL 1

1   How many different coloured squares are there on a chessboard?
2   What would you buy from a Gibbons' catalogue?
3   Whose three-dimensional cube became a 70s and 80s craze?
4   If 3 is on the top side of a dice, what number is on the hidden side?
5   What does a snorkel help you do?
6   What is the art of knotting cord or string in patterns?
7   In Scrabble what is the value of the blank tile?
8   What does the musical term largo mean?
9   What fairground attraction did George Ferris construct in the 1890s?
10 Jokers apart, how many red cards are there in a standard pack?
11 What does a twitcher look for?
12 Which game features Miss Scarlet and the Reverend Green?
13 What do we call the art of paper-folding, which originated in Japan?
14 How many discs does each player have to start with in draughts?
15 What type of dancing was originally only performed by men, usually dressed in white, with bells and garlands?
16 If you practise calligraphy what do you do?
17 If you're involved in firing, throwing and glazing what do you do?
18 Which game has a board, cards and wedges?
19 In which leisure pursuit might you do a Turkey Trot or a Bunny Hug?
20 How many people can you normally fit in a go-kart?
21 What is a John Innes No. 1?
22 If you combined k and p to make cables what would your hobby be?
23 What was developed to experience the excitement of surfing on land?
24 Which exercises are designed to increase oxygen consumption and speed blood circulation?
25 What is a whist competition or tournament called?
26 A Royal Flush is the best hand you can get in which card game?
27 Which British game is known as checkers in the USA?
28 Which card game has a pegboard used for scoring?
29 Where on your body would you wear flippers?
30 Which playing card is the Black Lady?

Answers

Living World (see Quiz 8)
1 Elm. 2 Fish. 3 Constriction. 4 Eagle. 5 Two. 6 Breed of terrier.
7 Snake. 8 Below. 9 Its colour. 10 Tree. 11 Southern. 12 Beaver.
13 Vixen. 14 Its tail. 15 Caterpillar. 16 Canada. 17 Deer. 18 Fungus.
19 America. 20 Skunk. 21 Shark. 22 White. 23 Liver. 24 Red.
25 Venom. 26 Fish. 27 Two. 28 Kangaroo. 29 Swim - type of tuna fish.
30 Australia.

Quiz 7 Pot Luck 3

Answers - see page 15

LEVEL 1

1 On which label did the Beatles have their first hit record?
2 What was the television pioneer John Baird's middle name?
3 In which decade of the 20th century was Paddy Ashdown born?
4 What word can go after "nut" and before "jack"?
5 How is Derek Jules Gaspard Ulrich Van Den Bogaerde better known?
6 Which soccer team does Nigel Kennedy support?
7 Who wrote the novel *The Murder Of Roger Ackroyd*?
8 Peter Allis is associated with which sport?
9 Who is the US state of Virginia name after?
10 Which Elvis song has the words "you ain't never caught a rabbit"?
11 Which stimulant is found in tea and coffee?
12 Who has a dog called Gnasher?
13 Which Leonard starred in "The Rise And fall Of Reginald Perrin"?
14 What word can go before "down", "jumping" and "off"?
15 Which make-up item is the French word for red?
16 Who wrote "Send In The Clowns"?
17 Which French phrase used in English means already seen?
18 What number is represented by the Roman numeral M?
19 The airline Labrador Airways is from which country?
20 In which TV series did the character René Artois appear?
21 Which day of the week is Shrove once a year?
22 Which Tom won an Oscar for Best Actor in *Forrest Gump*?
23 What two colours of squirrel are found in Britain?
24 The *War Cry* is the magazine of which organization?
25 Whose catchphrase is "Yabba-dabba-doo!"?
26 In Cockney rhyming slang what are mince pies?
27 Who had a 70s No. 1 with "Message In a Bottle"?
28 In which country is the city of Alexandria?
29 Ash Wednesday is the first day of which period of fasting?
30 On a Monopoly board, what colour is Mayfair?

Quiz 8 Living World

Answers - see page 16

1 Which tree can be Dutch, English or wych?
2 What type of creature is a stingray?
3 How does a boa kill?
4 Which bird can be bald, golden or harpy?
5 How many humps does a Bactrian camel have?
6 What sort of animal is a Dandie Dinmont?
7 What is a mamba?
8 Would a tuber grow above or below the ground?
9 What is a chameleon famous for being capable of changing?
10 What is a monkey puzzle?
11 To which hemisphere do penguins belong?
12 Which creature constructs dams and lodges?
13 What is a female fox called?
14 What does a rattlesnake rattle when it is disturbed?
15 What is the larva of a butterfly or moth called?
16 Which country were Newfoundland dogs originally from?
17 The moose or elk are species of which creature?
18 What sort of plant is a common puffball?
19 On which continent is the opossum found in its natural habitat?
20 Which American creature is renowned for its foul-smelling defence mechanism?
21 What can be great white, tiger or whale?
22 What colour is a West Highland terrier?
23 Bile is a secretion of which organ of the body?
24 What colour are the bracts of a poinsettia?
25 What is snake poison called?
26 A shoal is a group of what type of creatures?
27 How many sets of teeth do most mammals have?
28 Which is larger, the wallaby or the kangaroo?
29 Does a skipjack, jump, skip or swim?
30 Where are emus found in their natural habitat?

Quiz 9 Pot Luck 4

Answers - see page 21

LEVEL 1

1 In which month is Epiphany?
2 Who went with Christopher Robin to Buckingham Palace?
3 In which TV series did Mrs Slocombe and Mr Humphries first appear?
4 What word can go after "sand" and before "account"?
5 In which country is the city of Amritsar?
6 Which Amateur Association has the abbreviation AAA?
7 Who wrote the novel *Rebecca*?
8 The characters Jason and Sable appeared in which TV soap?
9 Moving clockwise on a dartboard what number is next to 1?
10 In which decade of the 20th century was Richard Attenborough born?
11 What is the name of Del Trotter's local?
12 How many yards in a chain?
13 The zodiac sign Pisces covers which two calendar months?
14 Steve Backley is associated with which branch of athletics?
15 How is Charles Holley better known?
16 Who was the first German to be *Football Writers'* Player of the Year?
17 In the Bible, which Book immediately follows Genesis?
18 What is 80 per cent of 400?
19 Frigophobia is the fear of what?
20 In the 80s, who had a No. 1 with "Eternal Flame"?
21 Charles de Gaulle airport is in which country?
22 Which Andrew starred in "Fawlty Towers"?
23 What device goes across a guitar fretboard to raise the pitch?
24 In printing, uppercase are what type of letters?
25 Beta is the second letter of which alphabet?
26 In which game would you find a night watchman?
27 Which Italian dictator was the founder of Fascism?
28 Which UK car manufacturer produced the Anglia?
29 Who played the characters of Simon Templar and Maverick?
30 In song, in which Row was Mother Kelly's doorstep?

Answers

Pot Luck 5 (see Quiz 11)

1 Grandma. 2 Sepia. 3 40s. 4 "Cup". 5 Rocky Marciano. 6 Spurs.
7 Charles Kingsley. 8 Brown. 9 Victory In Europe. 10 Choux. 11 Doo-Dah
Band. 12 Lyndhurst. 13 Belgium. 14 180. 15 Whitney Houston. 16 Geoff
Hamilton. 17 Monday. 18 Pacino. 19 Countess. 20 "House". 21 Cricket.
22 Jamboree. 23 20th. 24 Kenneth Williams. 25 Gold. 26 Familiarity.
27 Faux pas. 28 "The Avengers". 29 3. 30 Confederation.

1 Which Steve scored Leicester's 1997 League Cup Final winner?
2 What was Daniel Amokachi's first English league club?
3 Who followed Ossie Ardiles as manager of Spurs?
4 Who was Arsenal's regular keeper in the 1970-71 double season?
5 Which player was nicknamed "The Divine Ponytail"?
6 Which was the first English club to install an artificial pitch?
7 Who was Blackburn's benefactor of the 90s?
8 Robins, Valiants and Addicks are all nicknames of which team?
9 How many England caps did Steve Bruce win?
10 What colour are Colombian international shirts?
11 Who moved from Aston Villa to Bari for over £5 million in 1991?
12 What was Darren Anderton's first league club?
13 Which Ted scored nine goals in an FA Cup game for Bournemouth?
14 Keeper Chris Woods set a British record for clean sheets at which club?
15 Who became the first female football club managing director?
16 Who was manager when Ipswich first won the FA Cup?
17 Stan Collymore won his first England cap while at which club?
18 Which former Manchester United star also turned out for Fulham and Hibs?
19 Peter Schmeichel plays for which country?
20 What was Gazza's first London club?
21 Which Marco was three times European Footballer of the Year?
22 Tony Parkes was caretaker manager of which Premiership club?
23 Which Premiership team had three points deducted in 1996-7?
24 What has been Bolton's home ground for most of the 20th century?
25 Vinny Jones has played for which country?
26 At which club did Alan Shearer start his league career?
27 Who was Celtic's boss when they first won the European Cup?
28 Which Italian side did Gazza play for?
29 Which club did Alex Ferguson leave to go to Manchester United?
30 Which Spurs keeper scored in a 60s Charity Shield game?

1   St Winifred's School Choir sang about which relative?
2   Which colour describes Victorian photographs?
3   In which decade of the 20th century was Joan Baez born?
4   What word can go after "egg" and before "board"?
5   How is Rocco Marchegiano better known?
6   In the 90s, which London club had the "Famous Five" strike force?
7   Who wrote the novel *The Water Babies*?
8   What colour is a female blackbird?
9   What does VE stand for in VE Day?
10 What type of pastry is used to make profiteroles?
11 In the group's name, what comes after Bonzo Dog?
12 Which Nicholas starred in "Goodnight Sweetheart"?
13 In which country is the city of Antwerp?
14 How many degrees in a semicircle?
15 In the 80s, who had a No. 1 with "One Moment In Time"?
16 Which BBC TV gardener died suddenly of a heart attack in 1996?
17 If Boxing Day is a Friday what day is December 1?
18 Which Al won an Oscar for Best Actor in *Scent Of A Woman*?
19 What is the female equivalent of the rank of Earl?
20 What word can follow "light", "green" and "slaughter"?
21 Dennis Amis is associated with which sport?
22 What is a scout rally called?
23 Puccini died in which century?
24 Whose catchphrase was "Stop messing about"?
25 Au is the chemical symbol for which element?
26 What, according to proverb, breeds contempt?
27 Which French phrase used in English means a false step or mistake?
28 In which TV series did the characters Steed and Emma Peel appear?
29 What is the square root of 9?
30 What does the C stand for in the business organization the CBI?

Quiz 12 50s films

Answers - see page 20

LEVEL 1

1 Which film told of Moses leading the Israelites to the Promised Land?
2 Who starred as Moses in the film?
3 What or who is Lady in *Lady and the Tramp*?
4 Which film of J.M. Barrie's book was described as "a painful travesty"?
5 Which 11-Oscar-winning film of 1959 cost four million dollars?
6 Who was the star of *Around the World in Eighty Days*?
7 Which film company released *Sleeping Beauty*?
8 The action of *South Pacific* takes place during which war?
9 Which Welsh actor Richard starred in *The Robe*?
10 Which 1957 film had the whistled "Colonel Bogey" as its theme?
11 Who played the pop star in *Jailhouse Rock*?
12 What completes the line from "All About Eve", "Fasten your _____, it's going to be a bumpy night"?
13 What was the surname of film the director Darryl F?
14 Which Maurice starred in *Gigi*?
15 Which US singer had an acting role in *From Here to Eternity*?
16 Which actress starred in *From Here to Eternity* and *The King and I*?
17 Who played the starring role of Terry in *On the Waterfront*?
18 Which film catapulted James Dean to stardom?
19 Which French star appeared in *And God Created Woman* set in St Tropez?
20 Which dancer/singer was the "American in Paris"?
21 Which entertainment features in *The Greatest Show on Earth*?
22 Which Ealing comedy Mob organized a bullion robbery?
23 Which future Princess starred in Hitchcock's *Rear Window*?
24 Which Hitchcock film features a detective who was afraid of heights?
25 Who played the boozy Charlie Allnut in *The African Queen*?
26 Which British actor was Simon Sparrow in the Doctor films?
27 Which musical told of the life of Annie Oakley?
28 Which singer/actress starred opposite Rock Hudson in *Pillow Talk*?
29 Which film featured "You'll Never Walk Alone"?
30 How many Oscars did *High Society* win?

Quiz 13 Pot Luck 6

LEVEL 1

1   If it's Friday and it's five o'clock, what else is it in children's TV terms?
2   Which two colours are most frequently confused in colour blindness?
3   In which decade of the 20th century was Roger Bannister born?
4   What word can go after "neighbour" and before "wink"?
5   In the 90s, who had a No. 1 with "Always On My Mind"?
6   Moving anticlockwise on a dartboard, what number is next to 4?
7   Who wrote the novel *Lady Chatterley's Lover*?
8   Dennis Andries is associated with which sport?
9   In which country is the city of Bulawayo?
10 In which TV series did Sharon, Tracey and Dorian appear?
11 How many pints in a gallon?
12 What was the name of Dick Turpin's horse?
13 In which decade did Radio 1 start?
14 Wilkins Micawber appears in which Charles Dickens novel?
15 How is Allen Konigsberg better known?
16 Who was the only Robbie in England's Euro 96 squad?
17 Which group of workers does ABTA represent?
18 The character Pete Beal appeared in which TV soap?
19 What can be cardinal or ordinal?
20 In *Cinderella*, what was the pumpkin turned in to?
21 What is the administrative centre for the county of Cornwall?
22 Which Henry starred in "Happy Days"?
23 The airline Luxair is from which country?
24 How does 7.20 p.m. appear on a 24-hour clock?
25 Which Frank created Billy Bunter?
26 In pre-decimal money how many farthings were in a penny?
27 The film *The Great Rock 'n' Roll Swindle* was about which group?
28 Whose catchphrase is "It's the way I tell 'em!"?
29 Which military tune is sounded at the start of the day?
30 How many sides has a rhombus?

Answers

Pop: The 60s (see Quiz 15)

1 The Beach Boys. 2 Monkees. 3 Elvis Presley. 4 Paperback Writer.
5 The Bee Gees. 6 The Kinks. 7 Supremes. 8 The Hollies. 9 Her feet.
10 Helen Shapiro. 11 Yes. 12 Springfield. 13 Matchstick. 14 Jim Reeves.
15 The Tremeloes. 16 Liverpool. 17 Frank Ifield. 18 Dozy. 19 Proby.
20 San Francisco. 21 Dave Clark. 22 Bob Dylan. 23 Faithfull. 24 US.
25 Martin. 26 Move. 27 Herman. 28 Lonnie Donegan. 29 John Lennon.
30 The Twist.

LEVEL 1

1 Who formed the Black Abbots and had a TV Madhouse?
2 Which Paula presented "The Tube" and "Big Breakfast"?
3 What is the profession of Miriam Stoppard?
4 What do Jilly Goolden and Oz Clarke of "Food and Drink" sample?
5 Which Jeremy has fronted "Newsnight" and "University Challenge"?
6 Which Gaby presented the first series of "Whatever You Want"?
7 Barry Norman fronts a long-running show on which subject?
8 Which Sue co-presented ITV's 1997 "Election Night" programme?
9 What are the first names of Wood and Walters?
10 Which David presents sports programmes such as skiing and snooker?
11 Which part of the UK is GMTV's Lorraine Kelly from?
12 Which Mr Whiteley presents "Countdown"?
13 Which Alan replaced the late Geoff Hamilton on "Gardener's World"?
14 What is the surname of the actor David and his brother, the newsreader John?
15 Which Michael has been from "Pole to Pole"?
16 Which outspoken American interviewed the Duchess of York?
17 Which Eamonn spoke the first words on GMTV?
18 Who is Mrs Lenny Henry?
19 Which talented cartoonist presents "Animal Hospital"?
20 Which knight presents a breakfast programme on Sundays?
21 Which Carol was the first woman on Channel Four?
22 Who presented "Blue Peter" and "Duncan Dares"?
23 Which Julia reads the news for ITN?
24 Which Terry helped present "Animal Magic" and "The Really Wild Show"?
25 Which Jill replaced Sue Cook on "Crimewatch UK"?
26 What type of programme is Sophie Grigson most likely to present?
27 Which Chris was on "Tiswas" and has been "on TV"?
28 Bill Giles provides information about what on TV?
29 Which Matthew presents "Stars in Their Eyes"?
30 Which Carol was the first presenter of the midweek Lottery?

1 Who went "Surfin' USA"?
2 Micky Dolenz found fame in which simian-sounding group?
3 Who was Crying In the Chapel?
4 Which Beatles hit starts "Dear Sir or Madam, will you read my book"?
5 Brothers Barry, Maurice and Robin formed which group?
6 Who mocked the clothes conscious with "Dedicated Follower of Fashion"?
7 Diana Ross fronted which Tamla group?
8 Which group loved Jennifer Eccles?
9 Which part of her body did Sandie Shaw bare on stage?
10 Who sang "Don't Treat Me Like A Child" while still at school?
11 Were the Everley brothers actually brothers?
12 Which Dusty was Going Back?
13 Status Quo first charted with Pictures of what type of Men?
14 Which country-style singer was known as Gentleman Jim?
15 Who backed Brian Poole?
16 Which city did the Searchers come from?
17 Which Australian yodelled "I Remember You"?
18 Who completed the line-up with Dave Dee, Beaky, Mick and Tich?
19 Which trouser splitting singer had the initials PJ?
20 Which city did the Flowerpot Men want to go to?
21 Whose Five were in Bits And Pieces?
22 Critics said Donovan was a British copy of which US performer?
23 Which Marianne was linked with Mick Jagger?
24 Which country did Roy Orbison come from?
25 Which George produced the Beatles' records?
26 Which group recorded "Flowers In The Rain"?
27 Who was backed by Hermits?
28 Who managed to get to No. 1 with a song about a dustman?
29 Which John wanted to Give Peace A Chance at the end of the 60s?
30 Which dance was Chubby Checker doing at the start of the 60s?

Answers

Pot Luck 6 (see Quiz 13)
1 "Crackerjack". 2 Red and green. 3 20s. 4 "Hood". 5 Pet Shop Boys.
6 18. 7 D.H. Lawrence. 8 Boxing. 9 Zimbabwe. 10 "Birds Of A Feather".
11 Eight. 12 Black Bess. 13 1960s. 14 *David Copperfield*. 15 Woody Allen.
16 Fowler. 17 Travel agents. 18 "EastEnders". 19 Numbers.
20 A coach. 21 Truro. 22 Winkler. 23 Luxembourg. 24 19.20.
25 Richards. 26 Four. 27 The Sex Pistols. 28 Frank Carson.
29 Reveille. 30 Four.

Quiz 16 Pot Luck 7

Answers - see page 24

LEVEL 1

1 What nationality was Herb Alpert's Flea?
2 What is alopecia?
3 Sue Barker played which sport?
4 What word can go after "lance" and before "punishment"?
5 How is Frederick Austerlitz better known?
6 Which defender won 43 England caps while with Blackpool?
7 Who wrote the novel *Tinker, Tailor, Soldier, Spy*?
8 On which lake was Donald Campbell killed?
9 Beauty of Bath and Discovery are types of what?
10 In which decade of the 20th century was Tony Benn born?
11 Who died after being wounded in the heel by an arrow from Paris?
12 Which Nick starred in "Heartbeat"?
13 Which of the Beatles was the shortest?
14 What word can go before "auction", "courage" and "uncle"?
15 Which duo had a 70s hit with "Welcome Home"?
16 The band leader Glen Miller died in what type of tragedy?
17 In which British cathedral is the Whispering Gallery?
18 Who was the first presenter of "Blockbusters"?
19 In rhyme, where do you go to see a fine lady on a white horse?
20 Warm weather in autumn is described as what type of summer?
21 On a Monopoly board, what colour is Trafalgar Square?
22 What type of play is performed at Oberammergau?
23 In the song "Aquarius" which planet does Jupiter align with?
24 Which French phrase used in English means each dish individually priced?
25 In which TV series did Tinker and Lady Jane appear?
26 In the 90s, who had a No. 1 with "Sacrifice"?
27 Which Anthony won an Oscar for Best Actor in *The Silence Of the Lambs*?
28 What term describes the highest point of a triangle?
29 In which country is the city of Casablanca?
30 Who loads his van "Early in the morning, Just as day is dawning"?

Answers

TV: Who's Who? (see Quiz 14)
1 Russ Abbot. 2 Yates. 3 Doctor. 4 Drink. 5 Paxman. 6 Roslin. 7 Films.
8 Lawley. 9 Victoria, Julie. 10 Vine. 11 Scotland. 12 Richard.
13 Titchmarsh. 14 Suchet. 15 Palin. 16 Ruby Wax. 17 Holmes.
18 Dawn French. 19 Rolf Harris. 20 Sir David Frost. 21 Vorderman.
22 Peter Duncan. 23 Somerville. 24 Terry Nutkins. 25 Dando.
26 Cooking. 27 Tarrant. 28 The weather. 29 Kelly. 30 Smillie.

Quiz 17 Food & Drink 1

Answers - see page 29

1 What colour is crème de menthe?
2 Which county does Wensleydale cheese traditionally come from?
3 What type of vegetable is a Maris Piper?
4 What are the two main ingredients of a vinaigrette dressing?
5 What is the fruit flavour of Cointreau?
6 What type of food is coley?
7 What is basmati?
8 Which food accompaniment is Dijon famous for?
9 What is a small segment of garlic called?
10 What is the main ingredient of a traditional fondue?
11 What type of food is pitta?
12 Which shellfish are in Moules Marinière?
13 What is the top layer of a Queen of Puddings made from?
14 What type of meat is brisket?
15 What colour is paprika?
16 What is the chief vegetable ingredient of coleslaw?
17 At which stage of a meal would you have an hors d'oeuvre?
18 What type of drink is Darjeeling?
19 If a coffee was drunk au lait, what would it have added to it?
20 What is a tortilla?
21 What is a vol-au-vent made from?
22 Is a schnitzel sweet or savoury?
23 What colour is the flesh of an avocado?
24 Which red jelly is a traditional accompaniment to lamb?
25 What type of drink is Perrier?
26 What is mulligatawny?
27 What is filo?
28 What sort of fish is a kipper?
29 If a drink was served "on the rocks" what would it have in the glass?
30 What colour is the sauce served over a prawn cocktail?

Quiz 18 Pot Luck 8

Answers - see page 30

LEVEL 1

1 In the 90s, who had a No. 1 with "Pray"?
2 In the Bible, which Book immediately follows Matthew?
3 In which decade of the 20th century was Stuart Pearce born?
4 What word can go after "pad" and before "smith"?
5 In which country is the city of Crakow (or Kraków)?
6 In which TV series did the character Margaret Meldrew appear?
7 Who wrote the novel *Polo*?
8 In which month is St David's Day?
9 "Bush bush!" are the last words of which song?
10 What colour is the wax covering Edam cheese?
11 How did Marc Bolan die?
12 At the rate of 17·5 per cent, what VAT would be added to a £100 item?
13 Thermophobia is the fear of what?
14 Trevor Bailey is associated with which sport?
15 How is John Barry Prendergast better known?
16 In the UK's first million-pound soccer deal, which club bought Trevor Francis ?
17 In South Africa what does ANC stand for?
18 What part of the body did Adam not have that all other men do?
19 In which decade did Channel 4 start?
20 C is the chemical symbol for which element?
21 Which UK car manufacturer produced the Imp?
22 Which Su stared in "Hi-De-Hi!"?
23 Who was Jan's singing partner?
24 RED ANGER is an anagram of which job?
25 How many ounces in a pound?
26 Who produced Ike and Tina Turner's "River Deep, Mountain High"?
27 Which country was Nerys Hughes born in?
28 Moving clockwise on a dartboard what number is next to 5?
29 The character Meg Richardson appeared in which TV soap?
30 What is a Pontefract cake made of?

Answers

The 50s (see Quiz 20)

1 Conservative. 2 Campbell. 3 George VI. 4 Agatha Christie. 5 Suez.
6 Miss World. 7 Graham. 8 Winston Churchill. 9 Richards. 10 Eden.
11 Golding. 12 Car crash. 13 Eva Péron (Evita). 14 Reaching Everest's
summit. 15 X certificate. 16 Marciano. 17 Dan Dare. 18 Australia.
19 Cuba. 20 Diamonds. 21 Smog. 22 London. 23 Anne Frank.
24 "The Goon Show". 25 Hutton. 26 Liberace. 27 Munich. 28 Gaitskell.
29 Kelly. 30 Wright.

1   In which decade did Prince Charles marry Lady Diana Spencer?
2   What was Sarah Duchess of York's maiden name?
3   Prince Michael's title is of which county?
4   Who is the elder of Prince Andrew's daughters, Beatrice or Eugenie?
5   What is Princess Anne's son's first name?
6   Which royal title do Princess Anne's children have?
7   What was the occupation of Princess Margaret's first husband?
8   What was the name of the king who abdicated in 1936?
9   What was the surname of the woman he married a year later?
10 What was the name of the first monarch of the 20th century?
11 Which Duchess comforted a weeping Jana Novotna at Wimbledon?
12 Which royal yacht will be out of service from the end of the 1990s?
13 What is the Queen's residence in Norfolk called?
14 Which school did Prince William attend in his teens?
15 Who is next in line to the throne after Prince William?
16 With which royal did Captain Peter Townsend have a romance?
17 What was the name of the king immediately before Elizabeth II?
18 Which royal has a daughter called Zara?
19 Which royal couple organized a large golden-wedding anniversary celebration in 1997?
20 Which royal highlighted the problems of landmines in Angola?
21 Who had a father called Prince Andrew and has a son called Prince Andrew?
22 In which cathedral did Charles and Diana marry?
23 In which decade did Elizabeth II come to the throne?
24 How many children did she have when she became Queen?
25 Whose country home is at Highgrove?
26 Which birthday did the Queen Mother celebrate in 1996?
27 How many grandchildren does she have?
28 Who is the Queen Mother's younger daughter?
29 Which Princess is married to Angus Ogilvy?
30 What was Lord Mountbatten's first name?

1 In 1959, which party was elected for the third time in a row in Britain?
2 Which Donald set a world water speed record in the Lake District?
3 Which monarch died at Sandringham in 1952?
4 *The Mousetrap* opened its London stage run, but who wrote it?
5 Colonel Nasser nationalized which canal?
6 The first of which contest was won by a woman from Sweden in 1951?
7 Which American evangelist Billy led a London crusade?
8 Which 77-year-old was returned as British Prime Minister?
9 Which Sir Gordon won the Derby for the first time?
10 Which Anthony became British Prime Minister in the 50s?
11 *Lord of the Flies* was written by which author William?
12 How did James Dean die?
13 Who died in the 50s and was played on film by Madonna in the 90s?
14 What was the peak of Edmund Hilary's achievements in 1953?
15 Which film classification was introduced to show films were unsuitable for the under 16s?
16 Which Rocky retired undefeated as a professional boxer?
17 Which character in children's comics was the "Pilot Of The Future"?
18 Robert Menzies was PM of which country throughout the 50s?
19 Fidel Castro seized power in which country?
20 What, according to Marilyn Monroe, were a girl's best friend?
21 What was a London pea-souper?
22 The 1951 Festival of Britain was centred on which city?
23 The diary of which young girl hiding from the Germans was published?
24 Which radio show featured Bluebottle and Eccles?
25 Which Len captained England as they won the Ashes?
26 Which entertainer said, "I cried all the way to the bank"?
27 Manchester United's Bobby Charlton survived a plane crash in which city?
28 Which Hugh became leader of the Labour Party?
29 Which Grace married Prince Rainier of Monaco?
30 Which Billy became the first English soccer player to win 100 caps?

Pot Luck 8 (see Quiz 18)

Answers

Pot Luck 8 (see Quiz 18)
1 Take That. 2 Mark. 3 60s. 4 "Lock". 5 Poland. 6 "One Foot In The Grave". 7 Jilly Cooper. 8 March. 9 "Down At The Old Bull And Bush".
10 Red. 11 Involved in a car crash. 12 £17.50. 13 Heat. 14 Cricket.
15 John Barry. 16 Nottingham Forest. 17 African National Congress.
18 Navel. 19 1980s. 20 Carbon. 21 Hillman. 22 Pollard. 23 Dean.
24 Gardener. 25 16. 26 Phil Spector. 27 Wales. 28 20. 29 "Crossroads".
30 Liquorice.

1   How many zeros in a million written in digits?
2   Which TV series featured the characters Raquel and Uncle Albert?
3   Packham's Triumph and Conference are types of what?
4   What word can go after "bottle" and before "manager"?
5   How is George Ivan Morrison better known?
6   Which footballing Jack was nicknamed the Giraffe?
7   Who wrote the novel *Rumpole of the Bailey*?
8   What is East Pakistan now called?
9   On which hill did Fats Domino find his thrill?
10 In which decade of the 20th century was Ian Botham born?
11 In which country is the city of Durban?
12 Which Kevin stared in "Inspector Morse"?
13 What note is written in the space above the bottom line of the treble clef?
14 What word can go before "brother", "orange" and "thirsty"?
15 Brian Barnes is associated with which sport?
16 Which is greater 2/3 or 1/2?
17 The character Sheila Grant appeared in which TV soap?
18 Who joins Ginger, Baby, Sporty and Posh to make up the Spice Girls?
19 Which French phrase used in English means have a good journey?
20 In 1974 parts of Durham and Yorkshire made which new county?
21 Bob Woolmer played cricket for which country?
22 What was advertised as "your flexible friend"?
23 Which British film won nine Oscars in 1997?
24 Which planet in our solar system has the fewest letters in its name?
25 Which Daniel won an Oscar for Best Actor in *My Left Foot*?
26 What is the square root of 16?
27 In which activity do you purl and cast off?
28 In the Bible, who was paid 30 pieces of silver?
29 What colour is the famous big book in "This Is Your Life"?
30 In the 60s, who had a No. 1 with "House Of The Rising Sun"?

Quiz 22 Technology & Industry

Answers - see page 34

1 What name is given to a small, portable computer?
2 COBOL is common business-orientated what?
3 A molecule of water contains how many atoms of oxygen?
4 The study of fluids moving in pipes is known as what?
5 What is the process by which plants make food using light?
6 In a three-pronged plug what is the colour of the live wire?
7 Which small portable tape players were introduced by Sony?
8 Frank Whittle first produced what type of engine?
9 What is the chemical symbol for lead?
10 What do the initials LCD stand for?
11 Gouache is a type of what ?
12 In the 30s the Biro brothers produced the first low-cost what?
13 What device produces the air/petrol mix used in internal combustion engines?
14 Which Alfred invented dynamite and gelignite?
15 Sellafield is in which county in England?
16 What name is given to a screen picture that represents a standard computer function?
17 Which vehicle did J.C. Bamford give his name to?
18 What fuel is used by a Bunsen burner?
19 Which Michael invented the dynamo and the transformer?
20 What sort of pressure does a barometer measure?
21 In which decade did colour programmes first go out on British TV?
22 Which Chicago tower built in the 70s became the world's tallest building?
23 Clarence Birdseye developed processes for doing what to food?
24 Where in the Ukraine did a nuclear reactor explode in 1986?
25 Coal is composed of which element?
26 Watt, a unit of power, is named after which scientist?
27 In computing, WYSIWYG stands for "what you see is …" what?
28 Which Bill founded Microsoft?
29 Which Sir Francis gave his name to a scale of wind force?
30 What does a Geiger counter measure?

Answers

Movies: Superstars (see Quiz 24)
1 Marlon Brando. 2 Anthony Hopkins. 3 Harrison Ford. 4 Nicholson.
5 Murphy. 6 Caine. 7 Lemmon. 8 Demi Moore. 9 Hepburn. 10 Barbra
Streisand. 11 Beatty. 12 Newman. 13 Australia. 14 Tom Hanks.
15 Meryl Streep. 16 80s. 17 Scotland. 18 Pacino. 19 Tom Cruise.
20 Purple. 21 Nolte. 22 Willis. 23 Clint Eastwood. 24 Dustin Hoffman.
25 Elizabeth Taylor. 26 Costner. 27 Charlton Heston. 28 Jodie Foster.
29 Redford. 30 Pfeiffer.

1   In the 70s, which future MP had a shaved head to play a Tudor monarch?
2   Who is Gail's second husband in "Coronation Street"?
3   In which decade of the 20th century was Cliff Richard born?
4   The zodiac sign Taurus covers which two calendar months?
5   In the Bible, which book immediately follows the first book of Samuel?
6   Wally Barnes is associated with which sport?
7   Who wrote the novel *Kidnapped*?
8   What word can go after "boxing" and before "puppet"?
9   The campaign ASH stands for Action on what?
10 In which TV series did Superintendent Jane Tennison appear?
11 How many centimetres in seven metres?
12 In the 80s, who had a No. 1 with "Who's That Girl"?
13 The character Scott Robinson appeared in which TV soap?
14 In which country is the city of Fez?
15 How is John Lydon better known?
16 Barry Venison and Dean Saunders played for which Turkish team?
17 On a Monopoly board, what colour is the Angel, Islington?
18 Which UK car manufacturer produced the Elan?
19 Which saint's day follows Christmas Day?
20 Who in "Coronation Street" died of a heart attack after a road-rage incident?
21 What is the administrative centre for the county of Bedfordshire?
22 Which Melvyn starred in "It Ain't Half Hot, Mum"?
23 What term describes a triangle with two equal sides?
24 Who originally recorded "Light My Fire"?
25 Entebbe airport is in which country?
26 Which rugby league team are the Eagles?
27 In which decade did the writer Laurie Lee die?
28 Moving anticlockwise on a dartboard what number is next to 19?
29 What is the name of Dot Cotton's nasty son in "EastEnders"?
30 What colour is quartz citrine?

Quiz 24 Movies: Superstars

Answers - see page 32

1 Who played the head of the Corleone family in *The Godfather*?
2 Which Welsh actor starred opposite Debra Winger in *Shadowlands*?
3 Who played Han Solo in *Star Wars*?
4 Which Jack starred with Shirley Maclaine in *Terms of Endearment*?
5 Which Eddie's most famous role is in *Beverley Hills Cop*?
6 Which British Michael won an Oscar for *Hannah and her Sisters*?
7 Which Jack's films vary from *Some Like It Hot* to *The Odd Couple*?
8 Which Mrs Bruce Willis starred in *Ghost*?
9 Which Katherine has received a record 12 Oscar nominations?
10 Who starred in and wrote the song "Evergreen" for *A Star is Born*?
11 Which Warren starred in *Dick Tracy* and *Bugsy Malone*?
12 Which Paul was in *The Sting* and *The Color of Money*?
13 Although born in the US, where was Mel Gibson brought up?
14 Who won Oscars for *Philadelphia* in '93 and *Forrest Gump* in '94?
15 Who was the female Kramer in *Kramer v Kramer*?
16 In which decade did Sylvester Stallone first play Rambo?
17 Which country was Sean Connery born in?
18 Which Al won an Oscar for his role in *Scent of a Woman*?
19 Who was in *Rain Man* and was one of Four Good Men?
20 What "Color" is in the title of Whoopi Goldberg's first major film?
21 Which Nick starred in *The Prince of Tides*?
22 Which Bruce is co-owner of "Planet Hollywood"?
23 Who starred in *Every Which Way But Loose* and *The Outlaw Josey Wales*?
24 Which superstar played the title role in *Hook*?
25 Who married her seventh husband in Michael Jackson's garden?
26 Which Kevin played the President in *JFK*?
27 Whose film and TV appearances range from *Ben Hur* to "The Colbys"?
28 Who was in *Bugsy Malone* and *Taxi Driver* as a child and went on to *The Accused*?
29 Which Robert starred with Dustin Hoffman in *All the President's Men*?
30 Which Michelle played Catwoman in *Batman Returns*?

Answers

Technology & Industry (see Quiz 22)
1 Laptop. 2 Language. 3 One. 4 Hydraulics. 5 Photosynthesis. 6 Brown.
7 Walkmans. 8 Jet. 9 Pb. 10 Liquid crystal display. 11 Paint. 12 Biro
(ball-point pen). 13 Carburettor. 14 Nobel. 15 Cumbria. 16 Icon. 17 JCB.
18 Gas. 19 Faraday. 20 Atmospheric. 21 60s. 22 Sears Tower.
23 Freezing it. 24 Chernobyl. 25 Carbon. 26 James Watt. 27 What you
get. 28 Gates. 29 Beaufort. 30 Radioactivity.

1   Which TV show has an anagram puzzle called the Conundrum?
2   Who were the first team to win the FA Premiership?
3   In which decade of the 20th century was Elton John born?
4   In which country is the city of Kathmandu?
5   In which TV programme did Florence and Zebedee appear?
6   Ca is the chemical symbol for which element?
7   Who wrote the novel *Dracula*?
8   What is 1/3 as a percentage to two decimal places?
9   The character Len Fairclough appeared in which TV soap?
10 Which song features "the girl with kaleidoscope eyes"?
11 Which fruit do Macintosh computers use as a logo?
12 Which Jan starred in "Just Good Friends"?
13 Ken Barrington is associated with which sport?
14 What word can go before "thorn", "sand" and "silver"?
15 Miss Havisham appears in which Charles Dickens novel?
16 Which instrument was Nat King Cole famous for playing?
17 Who won an Oscar for Best Actor in *Rain Man* in 1989?
18 Who sang "On The Good Ship Lollipop"?
19 Which present-day country do we associate with the Magyars?
20 Which Damon was BBC Sports Personality of the Year in 1994?
21 Doctors Jack Kerruish and Beth Glover appeared in which TV series?
22 What make of car was the 1906 Silver Ghost?
23 In which month is St Swithin's Day?
24 What word can go after "slip" and before "rage"?
25 How is the actor Michel Shalhoub better known?
26 What colour was Gazza's hair during Euro 96?
27 In the 70s, who had a No. 1 with "We Don't Talk Anymore"?
28 The Kalahari desert is in which continent?
29 Which magician hosted "Every Second Counts"?
30 Which duke is associated with Arundel Castle?

Answers

Pot Luck 12 (see Quiz 27)

1 Feet. 2 "EastEnders". 3 Ahead. 4 "First". 5 Gene Vincent. 6 Matt Busby. 7 J.R.R. Tolkein. 8 Rugby (Union). 9 Commander. 10 First decade. 11 "Bread". 12 72. 13 Black Box. 14 1996. 15 Mrs Merton. 16 *Hamlet*. 17 In a while. 18 Port Stanley. 19 Palmer. 20 2. 21 Ukraine. 22 Owen. 23 Fears. 24 MG. 25 Eddie Cochran. 26 Lancashire. 27 Ethelred. 28 10. 29 "One Man and His Dog". 30 Lamont.

Quiz 26 Sport: Who's Who?

Answers - see page 38

1 Which Ben won the US Masters in 1995?
2 Was Geoff Boycott left- or right-handed as a batsman?
3 Which Spaniard won the Tour de France from 1991 to 1995?
4 Which Chris was WBO super middleweight champion in 1991?
5 Who was the first jockey to go through a seven-race card?
6 Who is the Crafty Cockney?
7 Who was the manager that took Chesterfield to the FA Cup semis?
8 Which Nigel was Formula 1 world champion in the 80s?
9 Which country does Greg Norman come from?
10 Which Australian tycoon was responsible for World Series Cricket?
11 Who was West Indian skipper for the 1996 World Cup?
12 Who was the National Hunt champion jockey from 1986 to 1992?
13 Who was Smokin' Joe?
14 In the 90s, who tried to claim 5 per cent of his transfer fee from Forest to Liverpool?
15 Woodforde and Woodbridge are partners in which sport?
16 Which snooker star was born on August 22 1957 in Plumstead?
17 Which golfer Sandy won the British Open in the 80s?
18 Who was the jockey who rode Aldaniti to Grand National success?
19 Who succeeded Jack Charlton as soccer boss of the Republic of Ireland?
20 Which England captain had his name linked with the Princess of Wales?
21 Who announced in September '96 that he would race for the TWR Arrows?
22 Who was the first male Brit to make Wimbledon's last eight in the 90s?
23 Who retired aged 30 after winning the Premiership with Man. Utd?
24 Which Jo played Wightman Cup tennis for Britain through the 80s?
25 Who was manager of Nottingham Forest throughout the 80s?
26 In February '96, which English jockey suffered severe head injuries in a Hong Kong race?
27 Which unseeded MaliVai reached the 1996 Wimbledon men's final?
28 In 1997, who scored the quickest ever FA Cup Final goal?
29 Who was the England cricket skipper in the ball-tampering claims of 1994?
30 Which scrum-half Gareth forged a partnership with Barry John for Cardiff and Wales?

1   In Cockney rhyming slang, what are 'plates of meat'?
2   The character Michelle Fowler appeared in which TV soap?
3   Is France ahead of or behind Greenwich Mean Time?
4   What word can go after "safety" and before "aid"?
5   How is Eugene Vincent Craddock better known?
6   Who managed the first English side to win soccer's European Cup?
7   Who wrote the novel *The Hobbit*?
8   Bill Beaumont is associated with which sport?
9   What does the C stand for in CBE?
10 In which decade of the 20th century was Barbara Cartland born?
11 Nellie and Adrian Boswell appeared in which TV series?
12 How many inches in six feet?
13 In the 90s, who had a No. 1 with "Ride On Time"?
14 When did the Super League begin in rugby league?
15 As which outspoken pensioner is Caroline Aherne better known?
16 In which play does the skull of Yorick appear?
17 In Bill Hayley's "See You Later, Alligator" what three words come before crocodile?
18 What is the capital of the Falkland Islands?
19 Who made up the trio with Emerson and Lake?
20 What number is cubed to give the answer 8?
21 In which country is the city of Kiev?
22 Which Bill starred in "Last Of The Summer Wine"?
23 Phobophobia is the fear of what?
24 Which UK car manufacturer produced the Midget?
25 Who had a No. 1 with "Three Steps To Heaven" after his death?
26 Which county have Gallian and Fairbrother played cricket for?
27 Which English king was known as the Unready?
28 Moving clockwise on a dartboard what number is next to 6?
29 Which BBC programme features Sheepdog Championships?
30 Which ex-Chancellor Norman lost his seat in 1997's general election?

Answers

Pot Luck 11 (see Quiz 25)
1 "Countdown". 2 Man. Utd. 3 40s. 4 Nepal. 5 "The Magic Roundabout".
6 Calcium. 7 Bram Stoker. 8 33.33. 9 "Coronation Street". 10 "Lucy In The
Sky With Diamonds". 11 Apple. 12 Francis. 13 Cricket. 14 "Quick".
15 *Great Expectations*. 16 Piano. 17 Dustin Hoffman. 18 Shirley Temple.
19 Hungary. 20 Hill. 21 "Peak Practice". 22 Rolls-Royce. 23 July.
24 "Road". 25 Omar Sharif. 26 Blond. 27 Cliff Richard. 28 Africa.
29 Paul Daniels. 30 Duke of Norfolk.

1   Which Anne presents "Watchdog"?
2   Which David and Gary are team captains on "They Think It's All Over"?
3   What sort of TV programmes does Sophie Grigson present?
4   What is the profession of Frost in "A Touch of Frost"?
5   What is the BBC's long-running hymn-singing programme called?
6   In which programme do Mulder and Scully appear?
7   What is the occupation of Bramwell?
8   What is the surname of a presenter called Vanessa?
9   Which show about emergencies has the name of a phone number?
10 Which Dimbleby presents the BBC's "Question Time"?
11 What is the programme "Top Gear" about?
12 In 1997, how many episodes of "Coronation Street" were there each week?
13 Which Geoff presented "Gardener's World" until his death in 1996?
14 Which chairman of "A Question of Sport" retired in 1997?
15 Which programme features the doctors of Cardale?
16 What is the profession of Sam Ryan in "Silent Witness"?
17 In which city does "Inspector Morse" take place?
18 What is the setting for "ER"?
19 Which Angus chairs "Have I Got News For You"?
20 In which sitcom did Saffron and Bubble appear?
21 Which late-evening current-affairs programme does Jeremy Paxman often present?
22 Which Sean starred on TV as Sharpe?
23 What time is the late-evening weekday news on BBC1?
24 Whose famous catchphrase is "I don't believe it!"?
25 Which comedy series was about an English priest in Ireland?
26 How many times per week is "Blue Peter" broadcast?
27 Which Denis presents "It'll Be Alright on the Night"?
28 Is the weather forecast immediately before or after "News At Ten"?
29 Which John played Kavanagh QC?
30 In which county does "Heartbeat" take place?

1 Which Michael won an Oscar for Best Actor in *Wall Street*?
2 What sort of animal was Terry Hall's puppet Lennie?
3 In which decade of the 20th century was Jose Carreras born?
4 What word can go after "monk" and before "cake"?
5 In the 90s, who had a No. 1 with "Think Twice"?
6 How would 14 be written in Roman numerals?
7 Who wrote the novel *War And Peace*?
8 Who plays rugby union at the Recreation Ground, London Road?
9 In which UK No. 1 did Elvis Presley sing in German?
10 Whom did Margaret Thatcher follow as Conservative Party leader?
11 Quicksilver is another name for which element?
12 Which Jean starred in "Bread"?
13 Are the North Downs north of London?
14 In which country is the city of Kualalumpur?
15 How is Edward Stewart Mainwaring better known?
16 What colour are the shorts of Germany's international soccer side?
17 Dave Bedford is associated with which sport?
18 In the Bible, which book immediately follows St John's Gospel?
19 What word can follow "fruit", "rabbit" and "Suffolk"?
20 Where on the body could a cataract form?
21 Private Pike appeared in which TV series?
22 The airline Aeroflot is from which country?
23 Who wrote the Messiah?
24 What is the square root of 25?
25 Which planet is named after the Roman god of war?
26 Which scandal made US President Richard Nixon resign?
27 On a Monopoly board, what colour is Bond Street?
28 Which two brothers hosted BBC's and ITV's 1997 election-night coverage?
29 Kurt Cobain was in which grunge group?
30 The character Cliff Barnes appeared in which TV soap?

Answers

Pot Luck 14 (see Quiz 31)
1 Ethiopia. 2 "The Good Life". 3 60s. 4 "Blood". 5 Boxing. 6 France.
7 Quatro. 8 Morris. 9 Nitrogen. 10 1,760. 11 Copper. 12 Abba.
13 Bamber Gascoigne. 14 Agency. 15 Burl Ives. 16 Ryan Giggs. 17
Potato. 18 Salome. 19 Your troubles. 20 The monster. 21 Acute.
22 Barrie. 23 Guinevere. 24 Paul McCartney. 25 "Home and Away".
26 Decibels. 27 Topiary. 28 Carpenters. 29 "Countdown". 30 2.

Quiz 30 Euro Tour

Answers - see page 42

Answers - see page 42

LEVEL 1

1 Reykjavik is the capital of which country?
2 Which is farther south - Corsica or Sardinia?
3 Which river runs through Belgrade, Budapest and Vienna?
4 Which Peter spent a Year In Provence?
5 The Acropolis overlooks which capital city?
6 Which is the highest mountain in the Alps?
7 Do the stripes go horizontally or vertically on the Austrian flag?
8 Belgium's coast touches which sea?
9 What is the currency of Greece?
10 Which capital takes its name from a prince of Troy?
11 Which ocean is Europe's northern boundary?
12 Which mountains divide Spain from France?
13 Ankara is the capital of which country?
14 What is the currency of Denmark?
15 Which tiny European country has the European Court of Justice?
16 Which two colours make up the Greek flag?
17 Nero fiddled while which city burnt?
18 Which of the three Baltic states of the former USSR does not begin with L?
19 What is the tourist area of southern Portugal called?
20 What is the capital of Malta?
21 Which mountains are Europe's eastern boundary?
22 What is the currency of Austria?
23 The Black Forest is a mountain range in which country?
24 Which country has the regions Lazio and Calabria?
25 What is the colour of the middle of the French flag?
26 Which Sea is Europe's southern boundary?
27 Which two major European rivers begin with R?
28 What would an English-speaking person call Bretagne?
29 Sofia is the capital of which country?
30 Which country has the markka or finnmark as its currency?

Answers

Pop: No. 1s (see Quiz 32)

1 Yellow. 2 "Love Is All Around". 3 1950s. 4 "Earth Song". 5 Brother.
6 "White Cliffs Of Dover". 7 Freddie Mercury. 8 Your Daughter.
9 "Mr Blobby". 10 Kate Bush. 11 Man. Utd. 12 Blondie. 13 Elton John.
14 "Without You". 15 Cliff Richard. 16 Gabrielle. 17 Massachusetts.
18 Take That. 19 "Yellow Submarine". 20 Abba. 21 Paul Simon.
22 Country. 23 Wham!. 24 Scaffold. 25 Village People. 26 The Shadows.
27 Waltz. 28 David Bowie. 29 Rednex. 30 Two.

Quiz 31 Pot Luck 14

LEVEL 1

Answers - see page 39

1 Live Aid raised money for famine relief in which country?
2 Margo and Jerry Leadbetter appeared in which TV series?
3 In which decade of the 20th century was Kenneth Branagh born?
4 What word can go after "blue" and before "hound"?
5 Nigel Benn is associated with which sport?
6 In which country is the city of Nice?
7 In the 70s, which Suzi had a No. 1 with "Devil Gate Drive"?
8 Which UK car manufacturer produced the Oxford?
9 80 per cent of Earth's atmosphere is formed by which gas?
10 How many yards in a mile?
11 Cu is the chemical symbol for which element?
12 Agnetha Faltskog was a singer with which group?
13 Who first presented BBC 2's "University Challenge"?
14 What does the A stand for in CIA?
15 How is Burl Ivanhoe better known?
16 Who in 1991 became the youngest ever Welsh soccer international?
17 Romano and Desiree are types of what?
18 Who wanted the head of John the Baptist?
19 In song, what do you pack up in your old kit bag?
20 What part did Boris Karloff play in the 30s film *Frankenstein*?
21 What name is given to angles of less than 90 degrees?
22 Which Chris starred in "The Brittas Empire"?
23 In legend, who was the wife of King Arthur?
24 Which Beatle played guitar left-handed?
25 The character Donald Fisher appeared in which TV soap?
26 Which units are used to measure sound intensity?
27 What name is given to trimming hedges into shapes?
28 "(They Long To Be) Close To You" was the first hit for which group?
29 What was the first quiz to be seen on Channel 4?
30 Moving anticlockwise on a dartboard what number is next to 17?

Answers

Pot Luck 13 (see Quiz 29)
1 Douglas. 2 Lion. 3 40s. 4 "Fish". 5 Celine Dion. 6 XIV. 7 Leo Tolstoy.
8 Bath. 9 Wooden Heart. 10 Edward Heath. 11 Mercury. 12 Boht.
13 No. 14 Malaysia. 15 Ed Stewart. 16 Black. 17 Athletics. 18 The Acts
of the Apostles. 19 "Punch". 20 The eye. 21 "Dad's Army".
22 Russia. 23 Handel. 24 5. 25 Mars. 26 Watergate. 27 Green.
28 David and Jonathan Dimbleby. 29 Nirvana. 30 "Dallas".

Quiz 32 Pop: No. 1s

Answers - see page 40

LEVEL 1

1   What colour was Bombalurina's teeny-weeny polka-dot bikini?
2   *Four Weddings And A Funeral* made which song a No. 1?
3   In which decade did Elvis have his first UK No. 1?
4   Which Song was a UK Christmas No. 1 in 1995 for Michael Jackson?
5   Which relative features in a Hollies song title?
6   Which other song was on Robson and Jerome's "Unchained Melody"?
7   Whose death gave "Bohemian Rhapsody" a second visit to No. 1?
8   Whom should you bring to the slaughter, according to Iron Maiden?
9   What was the imaginative title of Mr Blobby's first No. 1?
10 Who charted with a song about Heathcliff and Cathy?
11 Which soccer team were involved in "Come On You Reds"?
12 Who had No. 1s with "Call Me" and "Atomic"?
13 Who sang with Kiki Dee on "Don't Go Breaking My Heart"?
14 Which song was a No. 1 for both Nilsson and Mariah Carey?
15 Which English Sir has had No. 1s in the 50s, 60s, 70s, 80s and 90s?
16 Who had Dreams in 1993?
17 Which US state was the title of a Bee Gees No. 1?
18 Which band were Back For Good in 1995?
19 Which Beatle No. 1 featured the word Yellow in the title?
20 "The Winner Takes It All" was yet another No. 1 for which group?
21 Who wrote Simon and Garfunkel's "Bridge Over Troubled Water"?
22 What type of House did Blur take to the top of the charts?
23 George Michael first hit No. 1 as a member of which duo?
24 Who took "Lily The Pink" to No. 1?
25 Who thought it was fun to stay in the YMCA?
26 Whose first UK No. 1 was "Apache"?
27 In psychedelic '67, which old-time dance gave Englebert Humperdinck a huge hit?
28 Who teamed up with Queen for "Under Pressure"?
29 Who had a No. 1 with "Cotton Eye Joe"?
30 In the Frankie Goes To Hollywood hit, how many tribes were there?

Answers

Euro Tour (see Quiz 30)
1 Iceland. 2 Sardinia. 3 Danube. 4 Mayle. 5 Athens. 6 Mont Blanc.
7 Horizontally. 8 North Sea. 9 Drachma. 10 Paris. 11 Arctic.
12 Pyrenees. 13 Turkey. 14 Krone. 15 Luxembourg. 16 Blue and white.
17 Rome. 18 Estonia. 19 The Algarve. 20 Valetta. 21 Urals.
22 Schilling. 23 Germany. 24 Italy. 25 White. 26 Mediterranean.
27 Rhine, Rhone. 28 Brittany. 29 Bulgaria. 30 Finland.

1   Which vitamin deficiency was responsible for scurvy?
2   Which Doctor had a dog called K9?
3   Gary and Yvonne Sparrow appeared in which TV series?
4   What word can go after "honey" and before "wax"?
5   How is the comedian Thomas Derbyshire better known?
6   Steve Ogrizovic set an appearance record at which soccer club?
7   Who wrote the novel *Pride and Prejudice*?
8   Roger Black is associated with which sport?
9   How many seconds in one hour?
10 In which decade of the 20th century was Prince Charles born?
11 Who tried to mend his head with vinegar and brown paper?
12 Which Karl starred in "Brush Strokes"?
13 Where does an arboreal creature live?
14 Which descriptive word is linked with the singer John Baldry?
15 Which Henry won an Oscar for Best Actor in *On Golden Pond*?
16 What kind of bomb contains hydrogen sulphide?
17 What is the flavour of Pernod?
18 Little Nell appears in which Charles Dickens novel?
19 What word can go before "leader", "main" and "master"?
20 In which month is Hallowe'en?
21 How many people make up the panel of BBC's "Question Time"?
22 Which is smaller 5/10 or 3/4?
23 What is a hora?
24 Who sang the theme from *Goldfinger*?
25 The character Brian Tilsley appeared in which TV soap?
26 In boxing, what is the maximum number of rounds in a contest?
27 The letter S is on which row of a keyboard?
28 In the 70s, who had a No. 1 with "Mama Weer All Crazee Now"?
29 In which country is the city of Palermo?
30 Which cartoon series features Pebbles and Bam Bam?

Answers

Pot Luck 16 (see Quiz 35)

1 Black. 2 Football. 3 60s. 4 Purple. 5 July and August. 6 Cumbria.
7 H.E. Bates. 8 "Heartbeat". 9 10. 10 The Beach Boys. 11 Nine.
12 Sleepy. 13 1960s. 14 Cocktail. 15 Big Daddy. 16 Paris St Germain.
17 Germany. 18 14. 19 The Beatles. 20 Rural England. 21 Majorca.
22 Craig. 23 Two. 24 Creedence Clearwater Revival. 25 Kiwi fruit.
26 "Neighbours". 27 Faldo. 28 Reliant. 29 Makepeace. 30 Jones.

1 Charles Dodgson wrote his classic children's story under what name?
2 Which Frederick wrote *The Day of The Jackal*?
3 Fitzwilliam Darcy appears in which novel?
4 Whom did Bertie Wooster have as his manservant?
5 Which Irving Welsh novel was about Scottish heroin addicts?
6 Which county in England did Laurie Lee come from?
7 Which Arthur wrote the children's classic *Swallows and Amazons*?
8 Which James became Britain's most read vet?
9 Who created Thomas the Tank Engine?
10 Which French detective was created by Georges Simenon?
11 What was the first name of the girl who went to live at Green Gables?
12 Who created the Discworld books?
13 Which Ian created James Bond?
14 Which creatures are the central characters in *Watership Down*?
15 Who wrote *Rebecca*?
16 What was the name of the boy in *The Jungle Book*?
17 What term is used for writing a novel that will go out under someone else's name?
18 Which novelist born in 1886 had the initials H.G.?
19 What is Joseph Heller's novel with a number in its catchy title?
20 Which children's publisher has a black-and-red insect as its logo?
21 Who created Inspector Adam Dalgleish?
22 Which Douglas wrote *The Hitch Hiker's Guide To The Galaxy*?
23 Brother Cadfael belonged to which order of monks?
24 What sex was Richmal Crompton, author of the William books?
25 Which fictional barrister referred to his wife as "she who must be obeyed"?
26 Which country was Stephen King born in?
27 Which Victor wrote the novel *Les Miserables*?
28 Which Tory fundraiser wrote *Not A Penny More Not A Penny Less*?
29 Who wrote *Murder On the Orient Express*?
30 John Grisham's novels centre on which profession?

Quiz 35 Pot Luck 16

Answers - see page 43

1 What colour was the contestant's chair in "Mastermind"?
2 Steve Bloomer is associated with which sport?
3 In which decade of the 20th century was Diana, Princess of Wales born?
4 On a Monopoly board, what colour is Pall Mall?
5 The zodiac sign Leo covers which two calendar months?
6 In 1974 parts of Cumberland and Westmorland made which new county?
7 Who wrote the novel *The Darling Buds Of May*?
8 Nick and Kate Rowan appeared in which TV series?
9 How many sides does a decagon have?
10 Which group featured Brian Wilson?
11 How many spaces in a noughts-and-crosses frame?
12 Which of the Seven Dwarfs was always feeling tired?
13 In which decade did man first land on the moon?
14 What word can go after "prawn" and before "dress"?
15 How is Shirley Crabtree better known?
16 David Ginola joined Newcastle from which team?
17 The airline Lufthansa is from which country?
18 Moving clockwise on a dartboard what number is next to 11?
19 In the 60s, who had a No. 1 with "Can't Buy Me Love"?
20 The CPRE is the Council for the Preservation of what?
21 In which country is the city of Palma?
22 Which Wendy starred in "Butterflies"?
23 How many pints in a quart?
24 Which group had Clearwater as their middle name?
25 What is another name for Chinese gooseberries?
26 Madge and Harold Bishop appeared in which TV soap?
27 Which Nick was BBC Sports Personality of the Year in 1989?
28 Which UK car manufacturer produced the Robin?
29 Who was the female half of Dempsey and Makepeace?
30 Which Tom led the most weeks in the singles chart list for 1968?

Quiz 36 Movies: Who's Who?

Answers - see page 44

1 Which actress married André Agassi in 1997?
2 Which Jenny played Roberta in *The Railway Children*?
3 In which country was Arnold Schwarzenegger born?
4 Which Sharon played opposite Michael Douglas in *Basic Instinct*?
5 What did Susan Weaver change her first name to?
6 Which Leslie stars in *The Naked Gun* series of films?
7 Which Superman actor was seriously injured in a riding accident?
8 In which country was Gerard Dépardieu born?
9 Who is Donald Sutherland's actor son?
10 Which Ms Turner was the speaking voice of Jessica Rabbit?
11 Who directed *Psycho* and *The Birds*?
12 What is the first name of Michael Douglas's father?
13 What is the first name of Ms Arquette, star of *Desperately Seeking Susan*?
14 Which Drew was in *E.T.* and *Batman Forever*?
15 Which chart-topper was in *Silkwood* and *Moonstruck*?
16 In which film did Val Kilmer play the rock star Jim Morrison?
17 Which star of *Evita* was the first wife of the actor Sean Penn?
18 Which Joanne is Mrs Paul Newman?
19 How is Mary Elizabeth Spacek better known?
20 Which Tony is the father of Jamie Lee?
21 Which actor/director was born Allen Konigsberg in 1935?
22 What is the surname of the father and son actors Lloyd, Jeff and Beau?
23 Which character did Liam Neeson play in *Schindler's List*?
24 Who is the Oscar-winning daughter of Ryan O'Neal?
25 Which actor Reeves starred in *Bram Stoker's Dracula*?
26 Which Kim was the Bond girl in *Never Say Never Again*?
27 Who is Bridget Fonda's actress/fitness fanatic aunt?
28 Which talented bridge player played the title role in *Doctor Zhivago*?
29 Which Lauren was married to Humphrey Bogart?
30 Which Richard starred opposite Julia Roberts in *Pretty Woman*?

Answers

Books (see Quiz 34)
1 Lewis Carroll. 2 Forsyth. 3 *Pride and Prejudice*. 4 Jeeves.
5 *Trainspotting*. 6 Gloucestershire. 7 Rackham. 8 Herriot. 9 Rev Awdry.
10 Maigret. 11 Anne. 12 Terry Pratchett. 13 Fleming. 14 Rabbits.
15 Daphne Du Maurier. 16 Mowgli. 17 Ghosting. 18 Wells. 19 *Catch-22*.
20 Ladybird. 21 P D James. 22 Adams. 23 Benedictine. 24 Female.
25 Horace Rumpole. 26 US. 27 Hugo. 28 Jeffrey Archer. 29 Agatha
Christie. 30 Legal profession.

1 In the 90s, who had a No. 1 with "Some Might Say"?
2 Ted Bovis and Gladys Pugh appeared in which TV series?
3 In which decade of the 20th century was Bobby Charlton born?
4 What word can go after "bowling" and before "house"?
5 Bill Voce is associated with which sport?
6 In which country is the city of Saragossa?
7 Who wrote the novel *Wuthering Heights*?
8 H is the chemical symbol for which element?
9 Which Joan had a 60s hit with "There But For Fortune"?
10 The letter W is on which row of a typewriter or computer keyboard?
11 In cooking, Florentine means garnished with which vegetable?
12 Which Edward starred in "Callan"?
13 What is the square root of 36?
14 Who had a little buddy called Boo Boo?
15 The character Reg Holdsworth appeared in which TV soap?
16 Who described a wine as "sweaty gym shoes on hot tarmac"?
17 What is the administrative centre for the county of Devon?
18 What word can go before "ball", "drunk" and "line?"
19 How is Dora Broadbent better known?
20 Which Scottish soccer keeper Andy played for Oldham in the 80s?
21 Which children's TV show is based on the Guinness Book of Records?
22 At 17·5 per cent, how much VAT is added to an item priced at £300?
23 Who was singer/songwriter with the Boomtown Rats?
24 Which Robert won an Oscar for Best Actor in *Raging Bull*?
25 What is the only English anagram of WRONG?
26 Which major battle took place between July and November 1916?
27 What is the term for written or recorded defamation?
28 What are the two colours of a standard "Blue Peter" badge?
29 What is 5/8 minus 1/4?
30 Who partnered Jennifer Warnes on "Up Where We Belong"?

Quiz 38 TV Game Shows

Answers - see page 50

LEVEL 1

1 Which Gaby Roslin game show has contestants aiming to fulfil an ambition?
2 Who co-presents "Through the Keyhole" with David Frost?
3 Which TV wine expert is the presenter of "The Great Antiques Hunt"?
4 Which show introduced by Fern Britton features celebrity chefs?
5 Where does Dale Winton organize a TV Sweep?
6 Which Shane hosts "Lucky Numbers"?
7 What does Bruce Forsyth say to Play Right in the game show?
8 Which transport was used in "Treasure Hunt" with Anneka Rice?
9 What did "Strike It Lucky" change its name to?
10 Who was host in the 90s revival of "Take Your Pick"?
11 In which show did Bruce Forsyth say "What's on the board Miss Ford"?
12 What Factor was the subject of the contest to find a "superperson"?
13 Which inter-town Euro contest was hosted by Eddie Waring and Stuart Hall?
14 What was the weapon used in "The Golden Shot"?
15 Which game show is based on snooker?
16 Who introduced the very first edition of "Countdown"?
17 Which game show was based on a whodunnit board game?
18 Which show saw famous folk in a giant noughts-and-crosses board?
19 Which Mr Walker introduces "Catchphrase"?
20 Which quiz game was built around the game of darts?
21 How many contestants appear on a single panel on "Blind Date"?
22 Which Terry was the first host of "Blankety Blank"?
23 Which magician presented "Every Second Counts"?
24 What is the subject of the panel game "Going For A Song"?
25 On which Channel is "The Great Garden Game" broadcast?
26 Which Bob has presented "Call My Bluff"?
27 Which Michael first presented "Blockbusters" with older contestants?
28 What is Today in the show with Martyn Lewis?
29 Who replaced Bruce Forsyth in the 1990s "Generation Game"?
30 How many are reduced to One in the show with William G. Stewart?

Answers

Pot Luck 18 (see Quiz 40)
1 *William Tell Overture*. 2 Ceefax. 3 40s. 4 "Clip". 5 Richard Burton.
6 Crewe. 7 Daniel Defoe. 8 Equestrianism. 9 Exchange Rate Mechanism.
10 "Just Good Friends". 11 Triumph. 12 Birmingham. 13 Open spaces.
14 U2. 15 20. 16 "EastEnders". 17 Doncaster. 18 Mendel.
19 "Amazing Grace". 20 Circumference. 21 Germany. 22 Lindsay.
23 *The Three Musketeers*. 24 Stars. 25 First and fifth (the last). 26 Six.
27 Crosby. 28 1,000. 29 Hairdresser. 30 D.

1 Which country does Ian Baker-Finch come from?

2 How many reds are there at the start of a snooker game?

3 What does BDA stand for?

4 What sport do the Buffalo Bills play?

5 In which sport is the Giro D'Italia - the Tour of Italy?

6 Which sport combines cross-country skiing and rifle shooting?

7 What is the nickname of the heavyweight James Douglas?

8 Which rugby league team are the Bears?

9 How often is golf's US Masters held?

10 James Whittaker captained which side to the County Championship?

11 How many people are there in a hurling team?

12 Shannon Miler is famous for which sport?

13 In golf, what is the term for one under par for a hole?

14 In boxing, what is the lowest weight category?

15 Hale Irwin is famous for which sport?

16 Which England captain helped set up Kerry Packer's cricket "circus"?

17 The Mackeson Gold Cup is run at which course?

18 Dave Whitcombe plays darts for which country?

19 In the 90s, who lost the two major English finals and were relegated?

20 In 1996, which country was expelled from rugby's Five Nations?

21 AXA Equity & Law League cricket games are played on which day?

22 Wentworth golf course is in which county?

23 Which newspaper supported a darts tournament from 1948 to 1990?

24 Which ball in snooker is worth seven points?

25 A cricket umpire raises both arms above his head to signal what?

26 On what day of the week is the Prix De L'Arc de Triomphe race held?

27 Aikido is the ancient Japanese art of what?

28 Which county cricket club has its home at Grace Road?

29 Was Bertie Blunt the name of the rider or the horse that won the 1996 Badminton Horse Trials?

30 In what decade did David Gower first play cricket for England?

Pot Luck 17 (see Quiz 37)

Answers

1 Oasis. 2 "Hi-Di-Hi!". 3 30s. 4 "Green". 5 Cricket. 6 Spain.
7 Emily Brontë. 8 Hydrogen. 9 Baez. 10 Top letters row. 11 Spinach.
12 Woodward. 13 Six. 14 Yogi Bear. 15 "Coronation Street".
16 Jilly Goolden. 17 Exeter. 18 Punch. 19 Dora Bryan. 20 Andy Goram.
21 "Record Breakers". 22 £52.50. 23 Bob Geldof. 24 de Niro. 25 Grown.
26 Somme. 27 Libel. 28 Blue and white. 29 3/8. 30 Joe Cocker.

Quiz 40 Pot Luck 18

Answers - see page 48

1 Which classical overture became the "Lone Ranger" theme?
2 What is the BBC's teletext service called?
3 In which decade of the 20th century was Bill Clinton born?
4 What word can go after "paper" and before "board"?
5 How was Richard Jenkins better known?
6 Gresty Road is the home ground of which soccer club?
7 Who wrote the novel *Robinson Crusoe*?
8 Caroline Bradley is associated with which sport?
9 In monetary terms, what does ERM stand for?
10 The characters Vince and Penny appeared in which TV series?
11 Which UK car manufacturer produced the Herald?
12 What is the administrative centre for the county of West Midlands?
13 Agoraphobia is the fear of what?
14 In the 90s, who had a No. 1 with "The Fly"?
15 Moving anticlockwise on a dartboard what number is next to 1?
16 The character Frank Butcher appeared in which TV soap?
17 Which rugby league added Dragons to their name in the 90s?
18 Which Gregor was noted for experiments in genetics?
19 In song, which two words go before, "how sweet the sound, That saved a wretch like me"?
20 What is the boundary of a circle called?
21 In which country is the city of Stuttgart?
22 Which Robert starred in "Citizen Smith"?
23 Which book includes the words "All for one and one for all"?
24 Which are there more of on the USA flag - stars or stripes?
25 In a limerick, which lines should rhyme with the second line?
26 How many pockets does a snooker table have?
27 Who sang with Stills, Nash and Young?
28 How many milligrams in a gram?
29 What is Fiona Middleton's job in "Coronation Street"?
30 In music, what note is written on the line above the middle line of the treble clef?

1 Who made the "wind of change" speech?
2 George Cohen was a member of the world's winners at which sport?
3 Which call-girl Christine was involved in a government scandal?
4 Which future Princess of Wales was born in the 60s?
5 Edwin Aldrin became the second person to walk where?
6 Who played piano while Peter Cook sang?
7 Whom did Anthony Armstrong-Jones marry in 1960?
8 How did the English comic Tony Hancock die?
9 Whom did Richard Burton marry in Canada in 1964?
10 Gaddafi seized power in which country?
11 Which D.H. Lawrence book from the 20s featured in an Old Bailey obscenity trial?
12 Bob Dylan starred at a 1969 rock Festival on which British isle?
13 Which doctor's report led to the cutting of the railway network?
14 George Blake gained notoriety as what?
15 Which Francis sailed solo round the world?
16 Who became the youngest ever USA President?
17 Who was involved with John Lennon in a "bed-in" for peace?
18 Which President originally blocked Britain's entry into the EEC?
19 Which country banned a tour by England's cricketers?
20 Which country made the first manned space flight?
21 The Torrey Canyon was what type of transporter?
22 George Brown was a prominent MP for which party?
23 Which Private magazine signalled the satire boom?
24 Which theatre that "never closed" finally did close?
25 US President Johnson was known by which three initials?
26 Nuclear war threatened in 1962 over Soviet missiles in which country?
27 Which English footballer retired in 1965 at the age of 50?
28 Which Anglo-French supersonic airliner took to the skies?
29 Who was manager of the Beatles until his death in 1967?
30 Which ex-Nazi leader Adolf was tried and hanged?

Answers

Time And Space (see Quiz 43)
1 Mercury. 2 Big Bang. 3 Ursa Major (the Great Bear). 4 Sharman.
5 Galaxy. 6 Space Shuttle. 7 Star. 8 Jupiter. 9 Comet. 10 It exploded.
11 Kennedy. 12 The Moon. 13 Gravity. 14 Satellites. 15 Cosmology.
16 Glenn. 17 Apollo. 18 Uranus. 19 First man in space. 20 A year.
21 Halley's comet. 22 USA. 23 The Dog Star. 24 Quasars. 25 Patrick
Moore. 26 Shakespeare. 27 Cheshire. 28 Light years. 29 A dog.
30 The Milky Way.

Quiz 42 Pot Luck 19

Answers - see page 54

LEVEL 1

1 Elvis Costello was born in which country?

2 What word can go before "ground", "pedal" and "water"?

3 Two US cops, Christine and Mary Beth, appeared in which TV series?

4 What is Abyssinia now called?

5 How is actor William Claude Dukinfield better known?

6 Johan Cruyff started his career at which club?

7 Who wrote the novel *Middlemarch*?

8 Cambridge Gage and Victoria are types of what?

9 Which French phrase in English means a road closed at one end?

10 In the 90s, who had a No. 1 with "Never Forget"?

11 Which is greater 1/3 or 4/8?

12 Which Clive starred in "Dad's Army"?

13 In which decade of the 20th century was Eric Clapton born?

14 What word can go after "fish" and before "print"?

15 Chris Brasher is associated with which sport?

16 On a Monopoly board, what colour is Bow Street?

17 In schools, what do the initials GCSE stand for?

18 In which country is the city of Tangier?

19 Which five words traditionally closed the original Sooty show?

20 Who recorded the album *Money For Nothing*?

21 Geoff Miller played cricket for which country?

22 Ornithophobia is the fear of what?

23 What is 4 cubed?

24 What note is written in the space below the middle line of the treble clef?

25 Which Jack won an Oscar for Best Actor in *One Flew Over The Cuckoo's Nest*?

26 Is Barbados ahead of or behind Greenwich Mean Time?

27 Pearl celebrates which wedding anniversary?

28 Which TV quiz show always pits one contestant against two?

29 Which Alice declared: School's Out?

30 The character Charlene Mitchell appeared in which TV soap?

Answers

Pop: Singers (see Quiz 44)

1 Madonna. 2 Donny. 3 Gilbert O'Sullivan. 4 Dana. 5 Stansfield. 6 Holder. 7 Enya. 8 Kenny Rogers. 9 Marc Bolan. 10 Smokey Robinson. 11 Pretenders. 12 John Denver. 13 Bryan Adams. 14 Phil Collins. 15 Cliff Richard. 16 Boy George. 17 Nick Berry. 18 "Reet Petite". 19 Chris de Burgh. 20 Sting. 21 Jason Donovan. 22 Moyet. 23 Wet Wet Wet. 24 Wales. 25 Nat King Cole. 26 M. 27 Englebert Humperdinck. 28 Bob Marley. 29 UB40. 30 Frank Sinatra.

LEVEL 1

1   Which planet is closest to the sun?
2   Which Big theory explains the formation of the universe?
3   What is another name for the star constellation the Plough?
4   Which Helen became the first Briton in space?
5   What is the term for a giant group of stars held together by gravity?
6   In 1981, *Columbia I* was the first flight of which distinctive craft?
7   What can be a red dwarf or a white dwarf?
8   Which planet is the largest in our solar system?
9   Who or what was Hale-Bopp?
10   In 1986, what happened to *Challenger 52* after take-off?
11   Cape Canaveral took on board the name of which US President?
12   Where is the Sea of Tranquillity?
13   What is the name of the force that keeps planets moving round the sun?
14   Tiros, Echo and Sputnik were types of what?
15   What is the name for the study of the structure of the universe?
16   Which John was the first American to orbit Earth?
17   What was the name of the project that first put man on the moon?
18   Alphabetically, which is last in the list of planets in our solar system?
19   What is Yuri Gagarin's famous first?
20   Approximately how long does it take the Earth to travel round the sun?
21   Which bright comet visits Earth every 76 years?
22   Which country launched the Pioneer space probes?
23   What is the popular name for the star Sirius?
24   Quasi-stellar sources are in short usually known as what?
25   Who is the long-time presenter of "The Sky At Night"?
26   The moons of Uranus are named after which playwright's characters?
27   Jodrell Bank is in which English county?
28   What units are used for measuring distance in space?
29   What was the first animal in space?
30   Our solar system lies in which galaxy?

1   Who sang "Like A Virgin"?
2   Which Osmond sang "Puppy Love" and "Young Love"?
3   Who was Alone Again (Naturally)?
4   Which Irish singer won Eurovision with "All Kinds of Everything"?
5   Which Lisa sang on the "Five Live EP"?
6   Which Noddy sang lead with Slade?
7   Which female singer went solo from Clannad?
8   Who sang "Coward Of The County"?
9   Who sang lead with T. Rex?
10 Under what name did high-voiced William Robinson Jnr sing?
11 Chrissie Hynde was lead singer with which group?
12 Which writer and guitarist sang "Annie's Song"?
13 "(Everything I Do) I Do It For You" was a monster hit for whom?
14 Who had a No. 1 with "A Groovy Kind Of Love"?
15 Who had a Christmas No. 1 with "Saviour's Day"?
16 Who sang lead with Culture Club?
17 Who sang "Every Loser Wins"?
18 Which song gave Jackie Wilson a No. 1 years after his death?
19 Who sang "The Lady In Red"?
20 Who was lead singer with the Police?
21 Who hit No. 1 with "Any Dream Will Do"?
22 Which Alison revived "Love Letters" and "That Old Devil Called Love"?
23 Marti Pellow sang lead with which group?
24 Which country does Shirley Bassey come from?
25 Who sang "Mona Lisa" and "When I Fall In Love"?
26 Heather Small sang lead with which people?
27 Who had a huge 60s hit with "Release Me"?
28 Who sang with the Wailers?
29 Ali Campbell sings lead with which group?
30 Which singer is known as Old Blue Eyes?

Quiz 45 Pot Luck 20

Answers - see page 57

1 Eric Clapton, Ginger Baker and Jack Bruce formed which group?
2 What are Maplin's entertainment staff called?
3 How many square feet in a square yard?
4 What word can go after "free" and before "corporal"?
5 In 1974 parts of Yorkshire and Lincolnshire made which new county?
6 He is the chemical symbol for which element?
7 Who wrote the novel *Dead Cert*?
8 Moving clockwise on a dartboard what number is next to 15?
9 Which cosmetic company had an ad which featured a distinctive doorbell?
10 Which rugby league team are the Blue Sox?
11 In the 80s, who had a No. 1 with "Karma Chameleon"?
12 Galileo Galilei airport is in which country?
13 In which decade of the 20th century was Steve Davis born?
14 David Broome is associated with which sport?
15 How is the actor James Baumgartner better known?
16 Who was Liverpool's regular soccer keeper throughout the 80s?
17 The letter E is on which row of a typewriter or computer keyboard?
18 Which Linford was BBC Sports Personality of the Year in 1993?
19 Mr Bumble appears in which Charles Dickens novel?
20 Which UK car manufacturer produced the Victor?
21 In which country is the city of Toulouse?
22 Which Pam starred in "The Darling Buds Of May"?
23 What is the administrative centre for the county of Berkshire?
24 How many degrees in a circle?
25 The zodiac sign Aquarius covers which two calendar months?
26 Who had a hit with "I Want To Know What Love Is"?
27 What term describes vegetables cut thinly and slowly cooked in butter?
28 What sport does Murray Walker commentate on?
29 The character Clayton Farlow appeared in which TV soap?
30 Which Holly was in Frankie Goes To Hollywood?

Quiz 46 Crime & Punishment

Answers - see page 58

 LEVEL 1

1　Jack the Ripper operated in which city?

2　What nationality was the fictional sleuth Hercule Poirot?

3　Who was Burke's body-snatching partner?

4　Who wrote the comic opera *Trial By Jury*?

5　What is the name of a secret crime society based in Hong Kong?

6　Al Capone was imprisoned in the 30s for what offence?

7　Which notorious American island prison closed in March, 1963?

8　How were the US outlaws Parker and Barrow better known?

9　Which criminal was released by Pontius Pilate instead of Jesus?

10　Which Myra was involved in the Moors Murders?

11　Policemen got the nickname Peelers from whom?

12　How did Frederick West take his life?

13　When did the Knave of Hearts steal the tarts?

14　In which city was John Lennon murdered?

15　Which Kray twin was the first to die?

16　What is the Flying Squad in cockney rhyming slang?

17　What name is given to the crime of deliberately burning someone else's property?

18　Which Nick got nicked for the Barings Bank scam?

19　In which decade was the Great Train Robbery?

20　Whom did Dr Crippen murder?

21　In the US, which Charles led his "family" in ritual killings?

22　Which Arsenal boss got the boot after a bung?

23　Why does Ruth Ellis have her place assured in British crime history?

24　Lee Harvey Oswald was accused of murdering which famous American?

25　Klaus Barbie became known as the Butcher of where?

26　In England and Wales how many people sit on a jury?

27　Peter Sutcliffe became known as what?

28　Ernest Saunders was involved with the fraud trial at which drinks company?

29　Rudolf Hess spent the last years of his life at which prison?

30　Sweeney Todd operated in which London Street?

Quiz 47 Pot Luck 21

Answers - see page 55

1   Which Mia married André Previn?
2   Which church appeared on the Thames TV logo?
3   David Bryant is associated with which sport?
4   What word can go after "beach" and before "gown"?
5   How is the singer Terrence Parsons better known?
6   Stan Cullis took which English soccer club to the championship?
7   Who wrote the novel *2001: A Space Odyssey*?
8   In which month is St Andrew's Day?
9   Who was the long-time leader of the Mothers Of Invention?
10 Which John won an Oscar for Best Actor in *True Grit*?
11 What number is represented by the Roman numerals XC?
12 Which Polly starred in "The Liver Birds"?
13 In which decade of the 20th century was Sophia Loren born?
14 What does the abbreviation GMT stand for?
15 For which county does Darren Gough play cricket?
16 What are farfalle, pansotti and rigati?
17 Which musician wrote and recorded "Stranger On The Shore"?
18 In which country is the city of Vancouver?
19 What word can follow "letter", "tool" and "witness"?
20 In the 90s, who had a No. 1 with "Never Forget"?
21 Lenny Henry was Gareth Blackstock in which TV series?
22 What is the square root of 49?
23 What is the dog called in a Punch and Judy show?
24 Tin denotes which wedding anniversary?
25 The character Karen Fairgate appeared in which TV soap?
26 Which group made the album *The Joshua Tree*?
27 What date is St George's Day?
28 In song, how many times is Happy Birthday referred to before naming the person?
29 Which Anton starred in *May To December*?
30 What is the only English anagram of HATTER?

1   In which series did the London copper say "Evening, all"?
2   Which veteran presented "Gardening Club" in the 50s and 60s?
3   Who had a sidekick called Tonto?
4   "All Gas and Gaiters" was one of the first sitcoms to poke fun at whom?
5   Who was the female half of Mork and Mindy?
6   Which blonde actress played Purdey in "The New Avengers"?
7   Which Pamela was a regular on "Not the Nine O'Clock News"?
8   What is the world's longest-running current-affairs programme?
9   Which sitcom featured Bernard Hedges of Fenn Street School?
10 In which century was "Poldark" set?
11 Which king was played by Keith Michell in 1970?
12 Was it Starsky or Hutch who started a trend for chunky cardigans?
13 Which series featured the Cartwrights of the Ponderosa?
14 Which 60s sitcom was about the oil rich Clampett family?
15 In "A Family at War" where did the Ashtons live?
16 Which show recreated the era of music hall?
17 Which Saga was the last the BBC produced in black and white?
18 What were the real-life surnames of Terry and June?
19 Which 50s/60s medical drama was set in Oxbridge General Hospital?
20 What breed of dog was Rin-Tin-Tin?
21 What type of programme did Fanny Cradock present?
22 Whose Half Hour featured "the lad himself"?
23 Which future James Bond starred as Ivanhoe in the 50s?
24 Which Irishman presented "This is Your Life" from the 1950s?
25 Which Hattie starred in sitcoms with Eric Sykes?
26 How many Goodies were there?
27 Which Irish comic finished his act with "May your God go with you"?
28 Why was "Mastermind" an incongruous title for the first three series?
29 In which sitcom did Lucille Ball and her husband Desi Arnaz play Lucy and Ricky Ricardo?
30 Which 60s pop singer played the title role in "Budgie" in the 70s?

Quiz 49 Pot Luck 22

Answers - see page 61

LEVEL 1

1 How many yards in an acre?
2 Which Alf became mayor of Weatherfield in 1973?
3 In which decade of the 20th century was Margaret Thatcher born?
4 In the 90s, who had a No. 1 with "Fairground"?
5 Who plays rugby union at Welford Road?
6 In the Bible, which book immediately follows Exodus?
7 Who wrote the novel *The Runaway Jury*?
8 In which country is the city of Sao Paulo?
9 Joe and Annie Sugden appeared in which TV series?
10 Moving anticlockwise on a dartboard, what number is next to 5?
11 Who sang with Dolly Parton on "Islands In The Stream"?
12 On a Monopoly board, what colour is Park Lane?
13 Charles Buchan is associated with which sport?
14 What word can go after "double" and before "section"?
15 What name is given to a yacht with two hulls?
16 In song, which road is taken to get to Scotland "afore ye"?
17 In theatre, what is traditionally the main colour in a Pierrot costume?
18 Which UK car manufacturer produced the Princess?
19 How is actor Ronald Moodnick better known?
20 "You don't win anything with kids" was Alan Hansen's quote about which team?
21 Who in the 50s had "Rock Island Line" as his first million-seller?
22 Which Harry starred in "Men Behaving Badly"?
23 The airline Qantas is from which country?
24 What is 75 per cent of 200?
25 What name is given to a thin Mexican pancake?
26 Which English city has Oxford Road, Victoria and Piccadilly railway stations?
27 What is the former Prime Minister John Major's constituency?
28 Who called his autobiography From *Drags To Riches*?
29 Which Cat sang "I Love My Dog"?
30 The character Hattie Tavernier appeared in which TV soap?

Quiz 50 60s Films

Answers - see page 62

LEVEL 1

1 Who won a BAFTA for his role in *Lawrence of Arabia* but not an Oscar?
2 Who starred in *Funny Girl* and *Lawrence of Arabia*?
3 Who starred in *Mary Poppins* and *The Sound of Music*?
4 What is the job of Bert, alias Dick Van Dyke, in *Mary Poppins*?
5 In which Disney film does "The Bare Necessities" appear?
6 Which daughter of Charlie Chaplin appeared in *Doctor Zhivago*?
7 Who was Butch Cassidy in *Butch Cassidy and the Sundance Kid*?
8 Which classic had the line "This is Benjamin. He's a little worried about his future"?
9 Who played Eliza Doolittle in *My Fair Lady*?
10 In which city does *One Hundred and One Dalmatians* take place?
11 Which 1963 BAFTA winner shared its name with a 60s Welsh singer?
12 How many "years BC" were in the title of the 1966 Raquel Welch film?
13 Which "The Upper Hand" actress starred in *Goldfinger*?
14 In which film does 007 seek a diamond smuggler?
15 How many were there in the Dirty band led by Charles Bronson?
16 Which Romeo and Juliet type of musical won most Oscars in the 60s?
17 In which 1968 musical did Bill Sikes murder Nancy?
18 What was Paul Scofield A Man For in 1966?
19 Who co-starred with Jon Voight as Ratso Rizzo in *Midnight Cowboy*?
20 Who is the incompetent Inspector in the *Pink Panther* films?
21 Which *Carry On* film tells of the all-female Glamcabs firm?
22 Who starred in *The Alamo* and *True Grit*?
23 In *Easy Rider* what are the riders riding?
24 In which 60s film did the deranged character Norman Bates appear?
25 Which Mrs Richard Burton starred in *Who's Afraid of Virginia Woolf*?
26 Which Goon starred in *Dr Strangelove*?
27 Who co-starred with Walter Matthau in *The Odd Couple*?
28 Tommy Steele sang the title song in Half a what in 1967?
29 Who was a GI and was the star of a film with that in the title?
30 Which blonde's last film was *The Misfits* in 1960?

Answers

The Media 1 (see Quiz 52)
1 The *Sun*. 2 Anglia Television. 3 Channel 5. 4 Central. 5 Associated Television. 6 Radio 4. 7 The *Mail on Sunday*. 8 British Broadcasting Corporation. 9 1930s. 10 BBC 2. 11 Prime Minister. 12 Welsh. 13 Channel 4. 14 British Sky Broadcasting. 15 Camcorder. 16 Sunday. 17 News. 18 Adverts. 19 Drama-documentary. 20 *Today*. 21 1960s. 22 BBC 2. 23 London Weekend Television. 24 GMTV. 25 "Today" 26 Granada. 27 HTV. 28 "New At Ten". 29 Independent. 30 BBC 1 and BBC 2.

Quiz 51 Pot Luck 23

Answers - see page 59

LEVEL 1

1 Who was the outgoing American President when Bill Clinton took office?
2 What word can go before "bag", "clip" and "tiger"?
3 Manuel and Sybil appeared in which TV series?
4 Love apple is an old-fashioned name for what?
5 How was the singer Edith Giovanna Gassion better known?
6 In which city was Kenny Dalglish born?
7 Who wrote the novel *The Thirty-Nine Steps*?
8 What is the administrative centre for the county of Merseyside?
9 Veteran rockers Rossi and Parfitt are in which group?
10 In which decade of the 20th century was Mary Quant born?
11 Which is smaller 3/8 or 1/3?
12 Which Don starred in "Miami Vice"?
13 The zodiac sign Aries covers which two calendar months?
14 What word can go after "farm" and before "stick"?
15 Joe Bugner is associated with which sport?
16 In HMSO what does SO stand for?
17 In which country is the city of Zürich?
18 "It's Not Unusual" was the first No. 1 for which singer?
19 Which chess piece can change direction in a normal move?
20 What is the inscription on a "Jim'll Fix It" medal?
21 Meteorophobia is the fear of what?
22 Which Cabinet member Michael lost his Enfield seat at the 1997 general election?
23 Which Paul won an Oscar for Best Actor in *A Man For All Seasons*?
24 What name is given to the longest side of a right-angled triangle?
25 Ni is the chemical symbol for which element?
26 The character Beth Jordache appeared in which TV soap?
27 Which country did the Righteous Brothers come from?
28 In song, what did my true love send me on the second day of Christmas?
29 Which sitcom was set in Walmington-on-Sea?
30 In the 90s, who had a No. 1 with "Ain't No Doubt"?

Answers

Pot Luck 22 (see Quiz 49)
1 4,840. 2 Roberts. 3 20s. 4 Simply Red. 5 Leicester. 6 Leviticus.
7 John Grisham. 8 Brazil. 9 "Emmerdale". 10 12. 11 Kenny Rogers.
12 Dark Blue. 13 Football. 14 "Cross". 15 Catamaran. 16 Low Road.
17 White. 18 Austin. 19 Ron Moody. 20 Man. Utd. 21 Lonnie Donegan.
22 Enfield. 23 Australia. 24 150. 25 Tortilla. 26 Manchester.
27 Huntingdon. 28 Danny La Rue. 29 Stevens. 30 "EastEnders".

Quiz 52 The Media 1

1 Which British daily paper was founded in the 1960s?
2 Which independent TV company serves East Anglia?
3 Which Channel began broadcasting in March 1997?
4 Which company took over ATV's Midlands broadcasting?
5 What did ATV stand for?
6 On which Radio station is "The Archers" broadcast?
7 What is the Daily Mail's sister Sunday paper called?
8 What does BBC stand for?
9 In which decade did the BBC begin a TV broadcasting service?
10 Which channel was the third UK terrestrial channel?
11 Which political role did the Italian TV magnate Silvio Berlusconi have in 1994?
12 S4C broadcasts in which minority UK language?
13 On which channel is "Brookside" broadcast?
14 What is BSkyB an abbreviation of?
15 What is a video recorder and a recording device in one unit called?
16 Which day of the week is the *Observer* published?
17 What type of information does CNN broadcast?
18 In early ITV what was shown in a "natural break"?
19 What kind of programme is a drama-doc?
20 Which daily UK paper was founded in the 80s and ceased in the 90s?
21 In which decade did colour broadcasting begin?
22 On which channel were colour broadcasts first seen in the UK?
23 In broadcasting what did LWT stand for?
24 Which 90s breakfast TV station was originally known as Sunrise TV?
25 What is Radio 4's early-morning news programme called?
26 Which TV company was named after a Spanish city loved by its founder?
27 Harlech Television's name was shortened to what?
28 What was the UK's first 30 minute TV news programme begun in '67?
29 What did I stand for in IBA before 1991?
30 Which TV channels does the TV licence fund?

Answers

60s Films (see Quiz 50)
1 Peter O'Toole. 2 Omar Sharif. 3 Julie Andrews. 4 Chimney sweep.
5 *The Jungle Book*. 6 Geraldine. 7 Paul Newman. 8 *The Graduate*.
9 Audrey Hepburn. 10 London. 11 Tom Jones. 12 One Million.
13 Honor Blackman. 14 *Diamonds Are Forever*. 15 Dozen. 16 *West Side Story*. 17 *Oliver!*. 18 All Seasons. 19 Dustin Hoffman. 20 Clouseau.
21 Cabby. 22 John Wayne. 23 Motorbikes. 24 *Psycho*. 25 Elizabeth Taylor. 26 Peter Sellers. 27 Jack Lemmon. 28 Sixpence. 29 Elvis Presley.
30 Marilyn Monroe.

Quiz 53 Famous Names

Answers - see page 65

LEVEL 1

1   Michael Hutchence dated which model Helena before Paula Yates?
2   What name did Pamela Anderson add to her own when she wed rock star Tommy?
3   Which Johnny's name was once linked to the model Kate Moss?
4   Which Mrs Carling publicly criticized the Princess of Wales?
5   Which former Pakistan cricket captain married Jemima Goldsmith?
6   Mandy Allwood's expectation of how many babies made the news in 1996?
7   Which Gareth's summer miss of 1996 made him a household name?
8   What is the first name of the TV presenter Ms Frostrup?
9   What is Mrs Michael Jackson II's first name?
10 In '97 Man. Utd's David Beckham was dating one of which pop band?
11 What is the profession of Claudia Shiffer's ex, David Copperfield?
12 Which actress married Richard Burton twice?
13 Which star of *Evita* married the actress Melanie Griffith?
14 Which Royal Prince's name was linked with photographer Koo Stark?
15 Which former son-in-law of the Queen remarried in 1997?
16 Which tenor left his wife for a Miss Mantovani?
17 Although a top model, Jerry Hall is also famous as which star's wife?
18 Which comedian Paul split with wife Caroline Quentin in 1997?
19 Which singer was the second Mrs Andrew Lloyd Webber?
20 What is the first name of David Emanuel's fashion designer ex-wife?
21 Nicky Clarke's name is famous in which fashion field?
22 Trudie Styler married which singer/rainforest conservationist in 1992?
23 Which star of "Minder" has been married to the actress Rula Lenska?
24 Which model Elle is an ex-flame of the actor Kevin Costner?
25 What is the first name of Tony Blair's wife?
26 Which Francesca partnered Robson Green on TV and Ralph Fiennes in real life?
27 Who has been the husband of Rachel Hunter and Alana Hamilton?
28 Who is the wife of Derek Redmond and mother of Elliot?
29 What is the first name of Chelsea Clinton's mother?
30 Which actress, a.k.a. Dorien, had a rose named after her at the 1997 Chelsea Flower Show?

Answers

Record Breakers (see Quiz 55)
1 Somerset. 2 Cycling. 3 Faldo. 4 Alan Shearer. 5 Hingis. 6 Wigan.
7 Swimming. 8 Javelin. 9 Clive Lloyd. 10 Glenn Hoddle. 11 Underwood.
12 Sampras. 13 Joe Davis. 14 Badminton. 15 Ian Rush. 16 Shriver.
17 Rhodes. 18 Connors. 19 Andrew. 20 Offiah. 21 Brazil. 22 147.
23 Brian Lara. 24 Hastings. 25 English Channel. 26 Nicklaus. 27 Mark
and Steve. 28 Scotland. 29 All Blacks. 30 Wales.

Quiz 54 Pot Luck 24

LEVEL 1

1 Who was the first female presenter of "Desert Island Discs"?
2 Which UK car manufacturer produced the Zodiac?
3 What is Formosa now called?
4 What word can go after "sea" and before "heart"?
5 In the 90s, who had a No. 1 with "Stay Another Day"?
6 The letter M is on which row of a typewriter or computer keyboard?
7 Who wrote the novel *Lord Of The Flies*?
8 What is a third of 1,200?
9 Gary, Tony, Deborah and Dorothy appeared in which TV series?
10 In which decade of the 20th century was Jimmy Connors born?
11 Which Noel wrote the play Hay Fever?
12 Who formed a trio with Paul and Mary?
13 The character Annie Walker appeared in which TV soap?
14 Who created the detective Miss Marple?
15 Which prime minister held office first - Wilson or Heath?
16 What is 1/2 plus 2/8?
17 What is the administrative centre for the county of Dorset?
18 With which event in athletics was Geoff Capes associated?
19 How is the TV personality Annie Rice better known?
20 Which keeper John won championships at Arsenal and Leeds?
21 How many metres in four kilometres?
22 Which George starred in "Minder"?
23 Who wrote the song recorded for Dunblane?
24 Adnams brewery is located in which county?
25 Which Liverpudlian grandfather told "Thomas The Tank Engine" tales on TV?
26 In which country is South America's highest mountain?
27 Moving clockwise on a dartboard what number is next to 9?
28 In which country is the city of Istanbul?
29 Who has presented "Through The Keyhole" with Loyd Grossman?
30 Which standard begins, "They asked me how I knew, my true love was true"?

1 Ian Botham first played for which county?

2 Eddie Merckx was a record breaker in which sport?

3 In 1977, which Nick became the youngest ever Ryder Cup player?

4 Who set a new transfer record when he was bought and sold by Blackburn?

5 In the 90s which Martina became Wimbledon's youngest ever senior champ?

6 Which team set a record run as rugby league champs in the 90s?

7 In which sport was Mark Spitz a record-breaker?

8 In which event did Fatima Whitbread set a 1986 world record?

9 Who holds the record for most games as West Indian cricket captain?

10 In 1996, who became England's youngest ever soccer boss?

11 Which Rory played rugby union 85 times for England?

12 In tennis, which Pete set a men's record season earnings in 1995?

13 Who won the first 15 World Pro Snooker championships?

14 Gillian Clark made record England appearances in which sport?

15 Which Liverpool record-scorer moved to Leeds in 1996?

16 Which Pam was Martina Navratilova's doubles partner in the 80s?

17 Which Wilfred set a record as England's oldest player of Test cricket?

18 Which Jimmy was first to 100 tennis singles titles in a career?

19 In 1994, which Rob scored a record 27 points in a rugby union game for England?

20 Which Martin left Widnes for Wigan in a record rugby transfer?

21 Which team won soccer's World Cup for a record fourth time in 1994?

22 What is the maximum break in snooker?

23 Who became the first player to score over 500 in first-class cricket?

24 Which Gavin became Scotland's most capped rugby union player?

25 Matthew Webb was the first person to swim what?

26 Which Jack was first to six triumphs in golf's US Masters?

27 What is the name of cricket's Aussie Waugh brothers?

28 Which country is Stephen Hendry from?

29 Sean Fitzpatrick played for which international team?

30 Billy Meredith was playing soccer for which country when aged 45?

LEVEL 1

1 In which country is the city of Albuquerque?
2 What word can go before "baked", "measures" and "time"?
3 In which decade of the 20th century was Doris Day born?
4 What colour is Noddy's hat?
5 How is the actor James David Graham Nevins better known?
6 Who did Denmark beat in soccer's '92 European Championship Final?
7 Who wrote the novel *Tess of the D'Urbervilles*?
8 In the 70s, who had a No. 1 with "Long-Haired Lover From Liverpool"?
9 Who won an Oscar for Best Actor in *The Godfather*?
10 Which rugby league side added Giants to their name in the 90s?
11 Which 20th-century novelist used a Suffolk river as a pen name?
12 Which Bruce starred in "Moonlighting"?
13 Which Simon was vocalist with Duran Duran?
14 What word can go after "paper" and before "lifter"?
15 Henry Cecil is associated with which sport?
16 In the royal address HIH what does I stand for?
17 The character Shannon Reed appeared in which TV soap?
18 In music, what note is written on the top line of the treble clef?
19 Timbuktu is on the edge of which desert?
20 What is the square root of 64?
21 Who was singer with Roxy Music?
22 The characters Fletcher and Godber appeared in which TV series?
23 Which general made a last stand at Little Big Horn?
24 The airline Iberia is from which country?
25 On a Monopoly board, what colour is Strand?
26 What was Sharron Davies's name in Gladiators?
27 What is the only English anagram of COULD?
28 What type of a rectangle has four equal sides and angles?
29 Who introduced "the eight who are going to generate"?
30 What is Frank Sinatra's middle name?

Quiz 57 The 70s

Answers - see page 69

LEVEL 1

1　Which Spaniard won a British Open at golf?
2　Whom did Ted Heath replace as British PM?
3　The tennis superstar Bjorn Borg came from which country?
4　In the UK, the age of majority was lowered from 21 to what?
5　The song "Bright Eyes" was about what type of animal?
6　Haile Selassie was deposed in which country?
7　Which rock legend died at his mansion Graceland?
8　D-Day in 1971 introduced what to Britain?
9　Which athlete Sebastian broke three world records in six weeks?
10　Which art historian Sir Anthony was revealed to be a spy?
11　Idi Amin became President of which country?
12　Who vanished after the murder of Lady Lucan's nanny?
13　The Ayatollah Khomeini drove the Shah from which country?
14　Which Princess was named Sportswoman of the Year?
15　Which legendary artist Pablo died in 1973?
16　Which organization bombed pubs in Guildford and Birmingham?
17　In 1971, 200,000 people demonstrated in the US against which war?
18　Bobby Fischer became a world champion in which game?
19　Olga Korbut delighted the world in what?
20　Whose Silver Jubilee celebrations led to a week of festivities in 1977?
21　In 1976 Jeremy Thorpe resigned as leader of which party?
22　Which Richard was re-elected as President of the US?
23　Which James became motor racing's Formula 1 world champion?
24　Who became the first female leader of a British political party?
25　Which former British monarch passed away?
26　The monarchy returned to Spain after the death of which general?
27　Whom did Princess Anne marry in 1973?
28　Which author Aleksandr was expelled from the USSR?
29　Which commodity quadrupled in price after Israeli-Arab conflict?
30　Second Division Sunderland beat which soccer giants to win the FA Cup?

Answers

Pop: Charts (see Quiz 59)
1　Elton John. **2**　Bowie. **3**　"My Way". **4**　Smokie. **5**　Stewart. **6**　Carey.
7　UB40. **8**　Jones. **9**　Young. **10**　Waterloo. **11**　"Unchained Melody".
12　Bee Gees. **13**　On The Block. **14**　Gary Glitter. **15**　Roy Orbison.
16　80s. **17**　Blondie. **18**　David Bowie. **19**　Newton-John. **20**　"Stand By
Me". **21**　Astley. **22**　Abba. **23**　"Amazing Grace". **24**　Beautiful South.
25　Lennon. **26**　Dusty Springfield. **27**　"Living Doll". **28**　The Bee Gees.
29　1960s. **30**　1950s.

Answers - see page 70

1 Tony Blair is MP for which constituency?

2 What is sauerkraut?

3 The characters Rigsby and Miss Jones appeared in which TV series?

4 What word can go after "pine" and before "turnover"?

5 Jeremy Bates is associated with which sport?

6 What's the fruity link with the name of William III of England?

7 Who wrote the novel *For Whom the Bell Tolls*?

8 In the Bible, which book immediately follows Luke?

9 How many pounds in a stone?

10 In which decade of the 20th century was George Best born?

11 Which Top group are destined to be last in an alphabetical list?

12 In history, which harbour in the US had a famous Tea Party?

13 Is Uruguay ahead of or behind Greenwich Mean Time?

14 The character Jenna Wade appeared in which TV soap?

15 On a dartboard what number is opposite 20?

16 Which UK car manufacturer produced the Avenger?

17 In which country is the city of Auckland?

18 On a Monopoly board, what colour is Piccadilly?

19 How is comic great Arthur Jefferson better known?

20 Glenn Hoddle finished his playing career with which club?

21 Sydney Carton appears in which Charles Dickens novel?

22 In which month is St Patrick's Day?

23 Which Annette starred in "One Foot in the Grave"?

24 What is a quarter of 180?

25 Dr Hook sang about whose mother?

26 In which series did a dog called Rowf play the piano?

27 Who was awarded a supper of brown bread and butter?

28 Which Steve was BBC Sports Personality of the Year in 1988?

29 On TV what sort of animal was Dylan?

30 In the 70s, who had a No. 1 with "Dancing Queen"?

1   Whose first chart success was "Your Song"?

2   Which David has charted with both Bing Crosby and Mick Jagger?

3   Which Frank Sinatra hit has charted on more than ten occasions?

4   Roy "Chubie" Brown charted with which group in 1995?

5   Which Rod has had over 50 chart hits?

6   Which Mariah spent most weeks in the charts in 1994?

7   "Red Red Wine" was the first No. 1 for which group?

8   Which Welsh singer Tom had most weeks in the chart back in 1968?

9   In the 80s, which Paul first charted with "Wherever I Lay My Hat"?

10   Where in London did the Kinks watch the Sunset?

11   Which song was No. 1 for Jimmy Young and Robson and Jerome?

12   Who were Alone in the charts, 30 years after their first hit?

13   Which New Kids had seven singles in the charts in 1990?

14   Who was the leader of the gang in the glam rock 70s?

15   Who was in the charts with "Crying" in 1961 and 1992?

16   In which decade did Belinda Carlisle first hit the UK charts?

17   Debbie Harry fronted which chart busters in the late 70s early 80s?

18   Whose first chart entry was "Space Oddity"?

19   Which Olivia charted with John Travolta and ELO?

20   Which Ben E. King classic made No. 1 25 years after it was recorded?

21   Which Rick went to No. 1 with his first hit "Never Gonna Give You Up"?

22   "Waterloo" was the first chart success for which group?

23   Which Judy Collins song amazingly charted eight times in the 70s?

24   "Song For Whoever" was the first hit for which Beautiful group?

25   Which John had three No. 1s following his murder?

26   Which 60s female vocalist came back in the 80s with the Pet Shop Boys?

27   Which early hit did Cliff Richard rerecord with the Young Ones?

28   Boyzone charted with "Words" in the 90s, but who made the original?

29   In which decade did Stevie Wonder first hit the UK charts?

30   In which decade did charts start to be compiled in the UK?

1 Which Elton John song includes the words "Goodbye Norman Jean"?
2 Which TV soap was described by Les Dawson as "Dallas with dung"?
3 The letter A is on which row of a keyboard?
4 What word can follow "band", "hat" and "grand"?
5 How is Ernest Wiseman better known?
6 Which Russian keeper was known as the Black Spider?
7 Who wrote the novel *The Fourth Estate*?
8 Which International Committee has the initials IOC?
9 Which Hoagy penned "Stardust"?
10 What is the distance from any point on the circumference to the centre of a circle?
11 Which John wrote the play *Look Back In Anger*?
12 Which Ronnie starred in "Open All Hours"?
13 In which decade of the 20th century was Spice Girl Emma born?
14 What word can go after "sand" and before "mason"?
15 Maurice Colclough is associated with which sport?
16 In which country is the city of Baghdad?
17 O is the chemical symbol for which element?
18 In the song title what goes after "Yester-Me Yester-You"?
19 Who won an Oscar for Best Actor in *My Fair Lady*?
20 From which fruit is the drink kirsch made?
21 In ten-pin bowling, how many pins are there in the back row?
22 What is Dick Dastardly's dog called?
23 The characters Paddy Garvey and Dave Tucker appeared in which TV series?
24 Who is Colin Dexter's most famous creation?
25 Who had a 1993 hit with "Dreams"?
26 Which media man and MP David lost his Putney seat in 1997?
27 In which series did Zebedee appear?
28 The character Dolly Skilbeck appeared in which TV soap?
29 The zodiac sign Capricorn covers which two calendar months?
30 On a Monopoly board, what colour is Whitechapel?

Answers

Pot Luck 26 (see Quiz 58)

1 Sedgefield. 2 Pickled cabbage. 3 "Rising Damp". 4 Apple. 5 Tennis.
6 Orange. 7 Ernest Hemingway. 8 John. 9 14. 10 40s. 11 ZZ Top.
12 Boston. 13 Behind. 14 "Dallas". 15 3. 16 Hillman. 17 New Zealand.
18 Yellow. 19 Stan Laurel. 20 Chelsea. 21 *A Tale Of Two Cities*.
22 March. 23 Crosbie. 24 45. 25 Sylvia's. 26 "The Muppets".
27 Little Tommy Tucker. 28 Davis. 29 Rabbit. 30 Abba.

1. In "Dad's Army" who called Sgt Wilson Uncle Arthur?
2. What is the nationality of Margaret Meldrew?
3. Which family lived in Nelson Mandela House, Peckham?
4. Which space-age sitcom stars Craig Charles and Chris Barrie?
5. Which Scottish pop star played Adrian Mole's mum?
6. Which Felicity was the star of "Solo"?
7. Who plays Jean, husband of Lionel, in "As Time Goes By"?
8. Where did Hester and William Fields head for in the 80s/90s sitcom?
9. Which 70s character wore a knitted tanktop, long mac and a beret?
10. Which sitcom featured Mimi La Bonc and a painting by Van Clomp?
11. What was the occupation of Gladys Emmanuel in "Open All Hours"?
12. In which show does Tracey have a husband Darryl and son Garth?
13. Where were Miss Tibbs, Miss Gatsby and Major Gowen permanent guests?
14. In the 80s how were Candice, Amanda, Jennifer and Shelley known?
15. On which birthday did Tom Good begin "The Good Life"?
16. Whose dreams of his mother-in-law featured a hippopotamus?
17. Which 70s sitcom saw Wendy Richard as Miss Brahms?
18. Which Birmingham comic starred as Bob Louis in "The Detectives"?
19. What was the profession of Tom and Toby in "Don't Wait Up"?
20. How were the mature Dorothy, Blanche, Rose and Sophia known?
21. How was Bombadier Beaumont known in "It Ain't Half Hot Mum"?
22. In which show did Paul Nicholas play Vince Pinner?
23. What is the first name of Mr Bucket in "Keeping Up Appearances"?
24. Which sitcom was set in HMP Slade?
25. Which blonde does Leslie Ash play in "Men Behaving Badly"?
26. "Drop the Dead Donkey" takes place in what type of office?
27. In which show did Baldrick first appear?
28. Which sitcom chronicled the life of Zoë and Alec Callender?
29. Which show's theme song was "Holiday Rock"?
30. Which decade does Gary return to in "Goodnight Sweetheart"?

On the Map (see Quiz 63)

Answers

1 England. 2 Mountain. 3 Bath. 4 Suez Canal. 5 Downing Street.
6 America. 7 Canterbury. 8 They're not surrounded by water. 9 Norwich.
10 K2. 11 The Cenotaph. 12 Belgium. 13 Washington DC. 14 Ayers Rock.
15 Halifax. 16 Munich. 17 Hadrian's Wall. 18 Red. 19 The Queen
Mother. 20 Antarctica. 21 New South Wales. 22 Japan. 23 Sicily.
24 Midlands. 25 Niagara. 26 Paris. 27 Arab. 28 Holland.
29 Sandwich. 30 Mediterranean.

Quiz 62 Pot Luck 28

Answers - see page 74

1 Who is R2D2's robot companion in *Star Wars*?
2 In the "Street" what was Betty Williams's surname before she married Billy?
3 In which decade of the 20th century was Tim Henman born?
4 What word can go after "pike" and before "nurse"?
5 How is the rock guitarist William Perks better known?
6 Martin Edwards is soccer chairman of which club?
7 Who wrote the novel *Three Men In A Boat*?
8 Arachnophobia is the fear of what?
9 The character Nick Cotton appeared in which TV soap?
10 What is Persia now called?
11 Which Daniel sang "I Just Want To Dance With You"?
12 Which comic got major stars to act in "a play what I wrote"?
13 How many grams in a kilogram?
14 Queen Anne Boleyn was said to possess an extra what on her body?
15 Who was Queen of the Greek Gods?
16 Which is greater 6/8 or 2/3?
17 Which Kylie topped the most weeks in the singles chart list for 1988?
18 Moving clockwise on a dartboard what number is next to 16?
19 Henry Cotton is associated with which sport?
20 What word can go before "hound", "pressure" and "vessel"?
21 Cambridge Favourite and Cambridge Vigour are types of what?
22 Which Amanda starred in "Peak Practice"?
23 In which country is the city of Bangalore?
24 Wayne Daniel played cricket for which country?
25 What is 5 cubed?
26 What is the only English anagram of CLERIC?
27 What note is written in the space above the middle line of the treble clef?
28 Which UK car manufacturer produced the Cowley?
29 The character Frank Spencer appeared in which TV series?
30 In the 90s, which comic duo had a No. 1 with "The Stonk"?

Answers

70s Films (see Quiz 64)
1 Pink Panther. 2 *Star Wars*. 3 *Jaws*. 4 Fifties. 5 *The Godfather*.
6 *Superman*. 7 Spielberg. 8 Chicago. 9 Gibb. 10 *The Muppet Movie*.
11 *Jesus Christ Superstar*. 12 Streisand. 13 *Towering Inferno*. 14 *Airport*. 15
Los Angeles. 16 King Kong. 17 Roger Moore. 18 *M*A*S*H*.
19 McQueen. 20 *One Flew Over the Cuckoo's Nest*. 21 Rocky. 22 *Poseidon
Adventure*. 23 Hall. 24 Glenda Jackson. 25 Alice. 26 *Cabaret*.
27 Dudley. 28 Vietnam. 29 On the Roof. 30 Cop.

LEVEL 1

1   If you were in France and crossed La Manche, where would you be?
2   In Scotland what does Ben mean in a place name?
3   Which Somerset city has a Spa railway station?
4   Which Canal links the Mediterranean and the Red Sea?
5   In which London street is the Chancellor of the Exchequer's official residence?
6   In which continent is the Hoover Dam?
7   In which city is England's oldest cathedral?
8   What do the Isle of Ely and the Isle of Dogs have in common?
9   In which city is the University of East Anglia?
10 By which letter and number is Mount Godwin-Austen known?
11 Which war memorial is in Whitehall?
12 Which country has the international vehicle registration letter B?
13 Which capital city stands on the Potomac river?
14 Which Australian rock is sacred to the aborigines?
15 The capital of Nova Scotia shares its name with which Yorkshire town?
16 Which German city hosted the 1972 Olympics?
17 What was manmade and stretches from Tyne and Wear to Cumbria?
18 On the London Underground what colour is the Central Line?
19 Glamis Castle was the childhood home of which royal?
20 Which continent is the iciest?
21 Which Australian state is made up of three words?
22 In which country is Mount Fuji?
23 On which island is the volcanic Mount Etna?
24 In which area of the UK is the Black Country?
25 On which river are the Niagara Falls?
26 In which city would you find the Champs Elysées?
27 What does A stand for in the Middle Eastern UAE?
28 In which country is the port of Rotterdam?
29 Which of the Cinque Ports shares its name with a snack food?
30 Which European Sea's name means "Middle of the earth"?

1   Which Pink character appeared in three top films of the 70s?
2   Which 1977 film was rereleased 20 years later?
3   Which film was described as 'shark stew for the stupefied'?
4   In which decade does the action of *Grease* take place?
5   Which 1972 movie detailed the career of the Corleone family?
6   In which film did Clark Kent combat the Spider Lady?
7   Which Steven directed *Close Encounters of the Third Kind*?
8   In which gangster city does the action of *The Sting* take place?
9   Which brothers wrote most of the songs for *Saturday Night Fever*?
10 Which 1977 Movie had a frog as one of its main stars?
11 Which was the first Rice/Lloyd Webber musical made into a film?
12 Which Barbra starred in *A Star Is Born*?
13 Which film was based on *The Tower* and *The Glass Inferno*?
14 Which disaster movie was described as "Grand Hotel in the sky ..."?
15 In which Californian city did *Earthquake* take place?
16 Which gorilla was the star of a 1976 remake of a 30s classic?
17 Who played James Bond in *Moonraker*?
18 Which 1970 war film led to a long-running TV spin off with Alan Alda?
19 Which Steve starred in *Papillon*?
20 Which 1975 Jack Nicholson film takes place in a mental hospital?
21 Which boxer did Sylvester Stallone create on the big screen?
22 Which disaster movie tells of a capsized luxury liner?
23 Which Annie was an Oscar winner for Woody Allen?
24 Which future British MP won an Oscar for *Women in Love* in 1970?
25 Who Doesn't Live Here Any More in the 1974 movie?
26 Which Liza Minnelli Oscar-winning film was set in pre-war Germany?
27 Which Mr Moore starred opposite Bo Derek in *10*?
28 Which Asian war was *The Deer Hunter* about?
29 Where was the Fiddler in the 1971 film?
30 What was the profession of "hero" Doyle in *The French Connection*?

1 June Croft is associated with which sport?
2 Which major landmark is seen at the start of "News At Ten"?
3 In the 90s, who had a No. 1 with "Vogue"?
4 Which Nigel was BBC Sports Personality of the Year in 1992?
5 Prince Michael of Moldavia appeared in which TV soap?
6 In which country is the city of Berne?
7 Who wrote the novel *Cider With Rosie*?
8 The zodiac sign Gemini covers which two calendar months?
9 What does the Q stand for in IQ?
10 In which decade of the 20th century was Bob Dylan born?
11 Who was the outgoing American President when George Bush took office?
12 Which Helen starred in "Prime Suspect"?
13 Indira Gandhi International airport is in which country?
14 What word can go after "top" and before "trick"?
15 How is John Ravenscroft better known?
16 What colour are Holland's international soccer shirts?
17 Who sang with Frederick about a Little Donkey?
18 What did Wigan's name become for the 1997 rugby league season?
19 What is the administrative centre for the county of Buckinghamshire?
20 The character Captain Kirk appeared in which TV series?
21 Is Turkey ahead of or behind Greenwich Mean Time?
22 What were the two colours of Andy Pandy's costume?
23 Who backed Buddy Holly?
24 What does 1/2 x 1/2 equal?
25 On a Monopoly board, what colour is Euston Road?
26 Which is closer to the sea - London or New York?
27 Who predicted that everyone would be famous for 15 minutes?
28 Who won an Oscar for Best Actor in *Ben Hur*?
29 What is the square root of 100?
30 "U Can't Touch This" was the first chart success for which rapper?

1   If you practised callisthenics what type of activity would you be doing?
2   If you were watching someone on a PGA tour what would you be watching?
3   Which board game has a Genus Edition?
4   Which toy was Hornby most famous for?
5   What do you hit with a racket in badminton?
6   What was the traditional colour for Aran wool?
7   What sort of toy was a Cabbage Patch?
8   In which board game do you draw the meaning of a word?
9   Which game is also the name of a gourdlike vegetable?
10   How many balls are used in a game of billiards?
11   How many members make up a water polo team?
12   What type of food would you get at Harry Ramsden's?
13   Which game has lawn and crown green varieties?
14   In which sport would you wear blades or quads?
15   In DIY, which is shinier - emulsion or gloss?
16   Which is normally larger, a pool table or a billiards table?
17   In Scrabble what colour are the double-word-score squares?
18   In which county is Alton Towers?
19   Which London museum is named after a queen and her cousin?
20   In which sport would you use a sabre, foil or épée?
21   Which is the most versatile piece on a chessboard?
22   Which game is called the national pastime in the USA?
23   Which Lancashire seaside resort has a famous Pleasure Beach?
24   Which Manchester TV studio became a tourist attraction in the 80s?
25   Which actress Jane pioneered her workout plans for others to use?
26   What type of tourist attraction is at Whipsnade Park?
27   What is Barbie's boyfriend called?
28   Which city boasts the Jorvik Viking Centre?
29   Which total is aimed for in pegging in a game of cribbage?
30   In snooker what is the white ball called?

1 The letter R is on which row of a typewriter or computer keyboard?
2 Which Gloria recorded "I Will Survive"?
3 Mg is the chemical symbol for which element?
4 What word can go after "flag" and before "cat"?
5 How is Eric Bartholomew better known?
6 Eusebio played for which Portuguese club?
7 Who wrote the book *Vet In A Spin*?
8 The airline Olympic is from which country?
9 What did Gordon Honeycombe do in his TV appearances?
10 How many feet in a dozen yards?
11 Who was leader of Iraq during the 1991 Gulf War?
12 In 1974 parts of Lancashire and Cheshire made which new county?
13 In which decade of the 20th century was Bob Monkhouse born?
14 Laura Davies is associated with which sport?
15 The character Bet Gilroy appeared in which TV soap?
16 Who is John Oates's musical partner?
17 Which is smaller 60/100 or 8/10?
18 How many zeros in a billion written in digits?
19 Which UK car manufacturer produced the Dolomite?
20 What word can follow "box", "cloak" and "waiting"?
21 In which country is the city of Bilbao?
22 Which Michael starred in "Boon"?
23 In music, what note is written on the middle line of the treble clef?
24 Paper celebrates which wedding anniversary?
25 In the 80s, who had a No. 1 with "A Groovy Kind Of Love"?
26 What is the administrative centre for the county of Norfolk?
27 Moving anticlockwise on a dartboard what number is next to 6?
28 What is the first name of Rodney Trotter's wife?
29 Bibliophobia is the fear of what?
30 The father and son Albert and Harold appeared in which TV series?

Quiz 68 History: Who's Who?

Answers - see page 76

LEVEL 1

1 Who was British monarch throughout the Second World War?
2 Which US President was assassinated at the theatre?
3 Which ruler was stabbed to death in Rome in March 44 BC?
4 Who was Queen Elizabeth I's husband?
5 Who led the British forces at the Battle of Waterloo?
6 Who was Queen of England for nine days?
7 Which monarch was forced to sign the Magna Carta?
8 Which teenage girl led the French army against the English in the 15th century?
9 Who was Henry VIII's first wife?
10 Who was the famous General killed at Khartoum?
11 Which King Henry ordered the murder of Thomas Becket?
12 Which unpleasant-sounding Ivan was crowned first Tsar of Russia?
13 What was the name of the first King of England and Scotland?
14 Who was the Younger PM who introduced income tax?
15 From 1714 to 1830 all British monarchs were called what?
16 Who had his tomb in the Valley of Kings discovered in the 1920s?
17 Who was the famous captain of the ship the *Golden Hind*?
18 Inigo Jones followed which profession?
19 Who were massacred by the Campbells at Glencoe?
20 Of British monarchs, have more been called William or Edward?
21 In which battle was Admiral Horatio Nelson fatally wounded?
22 Who took the rap for the failed pot to blow up James I?
23 By what name was Richard I known?
24 How did Charles I die?
25 Whom does the Albert Hall in London commemorate?
26 To which monarch did Nell Gwyn display her oranges?
27 Which William ordered the building of the Tower of London?
28 Which Queen Marie lost her head in the French Revolution?
29 King George II gave his name to which American state?
30 Which monarch has ruled longest in the UK?

1   Which German player effectively created the sweeper role?
2   Which country does Patrick Berger play for?
3   What is the colour of the strip of the Welsh national team?
4   Which Billy was Northern Ireland manager throughout the 80s?
5   Boca Juniors come from which country?
6   Which striker's England goal tally was one short of Bobby Charlton's?
7   Franco Baresi played 450 plus games for which Italian club?
8   What was the Brazil v. Italy 1994 World Cup Final score at full time?
9   Jan Ceulemans played for which country?
10 At which Dutch club did Denis Bergkamp start his career?
11 In October 1995, who was the first Brazilian to sign for Middlesbrough?
12 What is the nationality of the FA Cup Final's fastest ever goal-scorer?
13 Carlos Alberto was skipper of which World Cup-winning country?
14 George Weah plays for which country?
15 Which Lothar is Germany's most capped player?
16 Who followed Cruyff as coach at Barcelona?
17 Which country hosted the 1994 World Cup?
18 Which Republic star Liam played for Juventus and Sampdoria?
19 The Stadium Of Light is home of which Portuguese club?
20 What was the "colour" of the type of goal that decided Euro 96's Final?
21 Which Scottish boss died of a heart attack during a game against Wales?
22 In which country did Pele wind down his playing career?
23 Who scored England's first and last goals in Euro 96?
24 Which country does Faustino Asprilla play for?
25 Which national team was managed by Roy Hodgson?
26 Which country hosted the 1966 World Cup?
27 Alfredo di Stefano was a regular European Cup Final scorer for which club?
28 Which Russian winger played for Man. Utd and Everton?
29 Who was the first person to have been in charge of England and Australia?
30 Gazza has played club football in which three European countries?

Quiz 70 Pot Luck 31

Answers - see page 82

LEVEL 1

1   Which prime minister held office first - Eden or Macmillan?
2   Which Don made the album *American Pie*?
3   Who won an Oscar for Best Actor in *The King And I*?
4   Who plays rugby union at Kingsholm Road?
5   The character Mrs Mangel appeared in which TV soap?
6   Sharron Davies is associated with which sport?
7   Who wrote the novel *Animal Farm*?
8   What does the M stand for in MIRAS?
9   In the Bible, which book immediately follows the Acts of the Apostles?
10 Who had a No. 1 with "I'd Do Anything For Love (But I Won't Do That)"?
11 In which country is the city of Calgary?
12 Which Martin starred in "The Chief"?
13 In which decade of the 20th century was Sue Lawley born?
14 What word can go after "sign" and before "office"?
15 Which Marvin Heard It Through the Grapevine?
16 Which Virginia was BBC Sports Personality of The Year in 1977?
17 Which George wrote the play *Pygmalion*?
18 Uriah Heep appears in which Charles Dickens novel?
19 What colour is in Cilla Black's maiden name?
20 Which prime minister supported Huddersfield Town?
21 How would 71 be shown in Roman numerals?
22 Jack Regan and George Carter appeared in which TV series?
23 Joy, Babs and Teddy formed which sisters?
24 In which month is St George's Day?
25 Which bird gave Fleetwood Mac their first No. 1?
26 For which county does Mike Atherton play cricket?
27 Which lumbering animals appear in the *Fantasia* ballet dance?
28 What instrument did Fats Waller play?
29 What is the only English anagram of CAUTION?
30 In which decade did Labour gain its biggest parliamentary majority?

Answers

Pot Luck 32 (see Quiz 72)
1 "Till Death Us Do Part". 2 Bangles. 3 Wolseley. 4 "Fisher". 5 Lynda La Plante. 6 Roy Evans. 7 Ben Elton. 8 M. 9 Four. 10 40s. 11 Democrat, Republican. 12 Battenberg. 13 Germany. 14 The Everly Brothers. 15 Cowardly Lion. 16 Watch. 17 Butterfly. 18 Gloria Estefan. 19 Football. 20 "Public". 21 13. 22 Havers. 23 Equilateral. 24 Decanters. 25 Venus. 26 The Chipmunks. 27 Crudités. 28 Wet Wet Wet. 29 "Home And Away". 30 Enclosed spaces.

Quiz 71 Animal World

Answers - see page 79

1 In mammals, the Asian elephant is second but man has the longest - what?
2 A papillon is a breed of what?
3 What is the term for a group of beavers?
4 Alphabetically, which animal always comes first?
5 Dromedary and Bactrian are types of what?
6 What is a male fox called?
7 How many teats does a cow usually have?
8 In Britain, which is the only venomous snake?
9 What type of leaves does a koala feed on?
10 The cairn terrier was originally bred in which country?
11 What type of animal is a natterjack?
12 What type of "ology" is the study of animals?
13 What colour are the markings on a skunk?
14 A jenny is a female what?
15 What is the term for a group of elephants?
16 Which monkey has a blue and red face?
17 What type of animal is an ibex?
18 Which animal lives in an earth or sett?
19 What type of animal eats meat?
20 What name is given to a baby kangaroo?
21 Which creature provides a mole's main source of food?
22 What type of animal was Baloo in *The Jungle Book*?
23 The common and the grey are types of which creature that breed around the coast of Britain?
24 What kind of Naked creature did Desmond Morris write about?
25 A leveret is a young what?
26 Which animal's home is called a drey?
27 Which creature is the fastest land mammal?
28 Which is the largest land animal?
29 What is the term for a group of foxhounds?
30 The wild dog the dingo comes from which country?

Answers

World Soccer (see Quiz 69)

1 Franz Beckenbauer. 2 Czech Republic. 3 Red. 4 Bingham. 5 Argentina. 6 Gary Lineker. 7 AC Milan. 8 0-0. 9 Belgium. 10 Ajax. 11 Juninho. 12 Italian. 13 Brazil. 14 Liberia. 15 Matthaus. 16 Bobby Robson. 17 USA. 18 Brady. 19 Benfica. 20 Golden. 21 Jock Stein. 22 USA. 23 Alan Shearer. 24 Colombia. 25 Switzerland. 26 England. 27 Real Madrid. 28 Andrei Kanchelskis. 29 Terry Venables. 30 England, Italy, Scotland.

1   The characters Alf, Else and Rita appeared in which TV series?
2   Which all-girl group had a Manic Monday in 1986?
3   Which UK car manufacturer produced the Hornet?
4   What word can go after "king" and before "man"?
5   How is the TV writer Lynda Titchmarsh better known?
6   Which Liverpool manager was born at Bootle in October 1948?
7   Who wrote the novel *Gridlock*?
8   What is the Roman numeral for one thousand?
9   How many gills in a pint?
10 In which decade of the 20th century was Mick Jagger born?
11 What are the two main parties in the US?
12 What name is given to a two-coloured oblong cake covered with almond paste?
13 In which country is the city of Dresden?
14 Which Brothers sang about the Price of Love?
15 Who wanted to ask the Wizard of Oz for courage?
16 In past times, what would a gentleman keep in his fob pocket?
17 What kind of creature is a cabbage white?
18 Who sang with the Miami Sound Machine?
19 Peter Docherty is associated with which sport?
20 What word can go before "holiday", "relations" and "school"?
21 Moving clockwise on a dartboard what number is next to 4?
22 Which Nigel starred in "Don't Wait Up"?
23 What type of triangle has equal sides and angles?
24 What is locked up in a tantalus?
25 Which planet is also referred to as the morning star?
26 Alvin, Theodore and Simon formed which group?
27 What name is given to a starter dish of sliced raw vegetables?
28 In the 90s, who had a No. 1 with "Goodnight Girl"?
29 The character Shane Parrish appeared in which TV soap?
30 Claustrophobia is the fear of what?

LEVEL 1

1 Who recorded *Rubber Soul*?

2 What goes after "What's The Story" in the title of Oasis's album?

3 Which Phil recorded *No Jacket Required*?

4 Who recorded *Dark Side of the Moon*?

5 Which Rod had six consecutive No. 1 albums in the 70s?

6 Who recorded *Purple Rain*?

7 Which group had a Night at the Opera and a Day at the Races?

8 Who recorded *Blue Hawaii*?

9 Paul McCartney was in which group for *Band On the Run*?

10 Who called their greatest hits album *End Of Part One*?

11 Which legendary guitarist recorded *From The Cradle*?

12 Who recorded *Off The Wall*?

13 Mike Oldfield presented what type of Bells?

14 Who recorded *The Colour Of My Love*?

15 Which Cat spent most weeks in the album charts in 1972?

16 Who recorded *Breakfast In America*?

17 Which Abba album had a French title?

18 Neil Diamond's film soundtrack album was about what type of singer?

19 Which easy-listening bandleader James has made over 50 albums?

20 Who recorded *Brothers In Arms*?

21 Which group were of a Different Class in 1995?

22 In the 90s, who broke out with *The Great Escape*?

23 Which Bruce spent most weeks in the album charts in 1985?

24 Who recorded *Bridge Over Troubled Water*?

25 In the 70s who recorded *Goodbye Yellow Brick Road*?

26 Which Simply Red album featured "For Your Babies" and "Stars"?

27 *Rumours* provided over 400 weeks on the album chart for whom ?

28 Who recorded *Bat Out Of Hell*?

29 Which Michael - not Jackson - spent most weeks in the 1991 charts?

30 What was Definitely the first No. 1 album from Oasis?

Quiz 74 Pot Luck 33

1   Desmond Douglas is associated with which sport?
2   What is Siam now called?
3   In which decade of the 20th century was Bonnie Langford born?
4   In which country is the city of Faisalabad?
5   Audrey Fforbes-Hamilton appeared in which TV series?
6   Alicante and Marmande are types of what?
7   Who wrote the novel *Black Beauty*?
8   In France, what is the abbreviation for Monsieur?
9   Which Michael declared "Love Changes Everything"?
10 Which Nigel was BBC Sports Personality of the Year in 1986?
11 What is the square root of 121?
12 Which John starred in "Bergerac"?
13 The airline Aer Lingus is from which country?
14 What word can go after "paper" and before "reaction"?
15 What is the administrative centre for the county of Essex?
16 Is Bermuda ahead of or behind Greenwich Mean Time?
17 In the 80s, who had a No. 1 with "Imagine"?
18 The zodiac sign Sagittarius covers which two calendar months?
19 How is the Hollywood actor John Charlton Carter better known?
20 Which Spanish club did Mark Hughes play for?
21 On a Monopoly board, what colour is Regent Street?
22 The character Amy Turtle appeared in which TV soap?
23 Was Neptune a Roman or Greek god?
24 Who won an Oscar for Best Actress in *The Silence of the Lambs*?
25 What is the traditional accompaniment to haggis on Burns Night?
26 How many minutes in half a day?
27 Which trumpeter Kenny performed with his Jazzmen?
28 How many walls surround a squash court?
29 The resort of Morecambe is in which county?
30 A4 is a size of what?

1 Which Clive chaired "Whose Line is it Anyway"?
2 Which 80s drama centred on Liverpudlian Yosser Hughes?
3 In which US city did the action of "Cheers" take place?
4 Which Doctor abandoned his Casebook in the 90s revival of the series?
5 Who played Jeeves to Hugh Laurie's Bertie Wooster?
6 In "Neighbours" Erinsborough is a suburb of which city?
7 On which night does "Noel's House Party" take place?
8 What were Rita Garnett's parents called?
9 In which series did Richard de Vere buy Grantleigh Manor?
10 Which animals did Barbara Woodhouse usually appear with?
11 Which soap was a spin-off from "Dallas"?
12 What is "Jimmy's"?
13 Who plays the Chef at the Le Château Anglais in Oxfordshire?
14 Which British actress played Alexis Carrington in "Dynasty"?
15 Which two Michaels have hosted "Give Us A Clue"?
16 What was James's wife called in "All Creatures Great and Small"?
17 Which Kate is famous for her news reports from Tiananmen Square ?
18 What is Charlie Fairhead's job at Holby City Hospital?
19 In "Dallas" which character returned from the dead in the shower?
20 Which Doctor has had assistants called Vicki, Jo, Melanie and Ace?
21 Which 90s series featured Guy Lofthouse and Guy MacFadyean?
22 Where was "Harry's Game" set?
23 What is the House in TV's "House of Cards"?
24 Which drama features Claude Jeremiah Greengrass?
25 Which comedy show is TV's answer to radio's "News Quiz"?
26 Who is the male presenter of BBC TV's "Children in Need"?
27 Which two comedians were famous for their 'head-to-head' scenes?
28 Which TV war reporter became an MP in 1997?
29 Which all-round entertainer's catchphrase is "Awight!"?
30 Which soap was trailed as "sex, sun and sangria"?

LEVEL 1

1 Diaghilev was associated with which branch of the arts?

2 In which London lane is the Theatre Royal?

3 Guiseppe Verdi is most famous for which type of musical work?

4 In which city is the Bolshoi Theatre?

5 Who wrote *HMS Pinafore*?

6 What was the nationality of the pianist and composer Claude Debussy?

7 How many symphonies did Beethoven write after the ninth?

8 Which series of concerts is held in late summer at the Albert Hall?

9 Which dance band leader disappeared during World War II?

10 In which branch of the arts did Joan Sutherland achieve fame?

11 In which Italian city is La Scala?

12 Which musical instrument does Stephane Grappelli play?

13 What type of entertainment did the Americans call vaudeville?

14 If you receive a Tony you have been performing in which country?

15 What kind of entertainment did Barnum call "the Greatest Show on Earth"?

16 What do you wish a performer when you say "break a leg"?

17 What is the name of the music centre that is the capital of Tennessee?

18 Which playwright married the TV doctor, Miriam?

19 How many sisters were in the title of the play by Chekhov?

20 What were the first names of Nureyev and Fonteyn?

21 What was Elgar's nationality?

22 Which musical instrument does Larry Adler play?

23 Which actress Maureen is the wife of the playwright Jack Rosenthal?

24 The cornet belongs to which family of musical instruments?

25 In which city is Broadway?

26 A balalaika originates from which country?

27 Which composer had the first names Peter Ilyich?

28 What is New York's Metropolitan Opera more popularly called?

29 Which Australian city has an imaginatively designed Opera House ?

30 Which Arthur wrote *The Crucible*?

1   In rugby, what did Keighley add to their name in the 90s?
2   Dipsophobia is the fear of what?
3   In which decade of the 20th century was John Thaw born?
4   What word can go after "soap" and before "office"?
5   How is the 60s singer James Marcus Smith better known?
6   Kendall, Walker and Royle have all managed which club?
7   Who wrote the novel *Tom Sawyer*?
8   How many yards in a furlong?
9   The characters Bill and Ben Porter appeared in which TV series?
10 In the 80s, who had a No. 1 with "Papa Don't Preach"?
11 What is the only English anagram of TEND?
12 Edwina Currie represented which political party?
13 Which country does the drink ouzo come from?
14 How many times do you sing "jingle" in a chorus of jingle bells?
15 The character Doreen Corkhill appeared in which TV soap?
16 Moving anticlockwise on a dartboard what number is next to 15?
17 In which country is the city of Gothenburg?
18 Mal Donaghy is associated with which sport?
19 What word can follow "filter", "graph" and "rice"?
20 In which city did Tony Bennett leave his heart?
21 By what name is endive known in the US?
22 Which Nigel starred in "Yes Minister"?
23 Which UK car manufacturer produced the Prefect?
24 What is 60 per cent of 3,000?
25 Who was singing about his Ding-a-Ling in 1972?
26 What is the sum of a century plus a gross?
27 A mazurka is a type of what?
28 On the Swedish flag what is the colour of the cross?
29 The soldier Robert Clive has his name linked with which country?
30 Who led the Family Stone?

Quiz 78 80s Films

Answers - see page 90

1   Which Attenborough brother directed *Gandhi*?

2   What is the nationality of the hero of *Crocodile Dundee*?

3   Which Raging animal is in the title of the 1980 Robert De Niro film?

4   The Return of what was the third of the *Star Wars* trilogy?

5   Whose Choice won Meryl Streep an Oscar in 1982?

6   Which British film was about the 1924 Olympics?

7   The Adventures of which Baron proved to be one of the greatest cinematic flops in history?

8   Which Crusade featured in the title of the 1989 *Indiana Jones* movie?

9   In which city does *Beverly Hills Cop* take place?

10 What sort of People were the stars of the 1980 Donald Sutherland film?

11 Which Henry and Katharine won Oscars for *On Golden Pond*?

12 In which film did Bob Hoskins play opposite a cartoon character?

13 Who renewed his battle against the Joker in 1989?

14 How many Men starred with a baby in the 1987 movie?

15 In which 1982 film did Dustin Hoffman appear in drag?

16 In which US state was the Best Little Whorehouse in 1982?

17 Which organization is *Married to the Mob* about?

18 Which country did the DJ say Good Morning to in the 1987 film?

19 Which continent featured in the Robert Redford/Meryl Streep film about Karen Blixen?

20 Whom was the chauffeur Driving in the 1989 film?

21 Which financial location was the subject of a Michael Douglas film?

22 Which Warren Beatty film of the 80s was set in communist Russia?

23 The Kiss of whom provided William Hurt with an Oscar?

24 Who and her Sisters were the subject of a Woody Allen movie?

25 Which Kevin appeared in *A Fish Called Wanda*?

26 If Billy Crystal was Harry, who was Sally in 1989?

27 Where was the American Werewolf in the 1981 film?

28 *The Killing Fields* deals with events in which neighbour of Vietnam?

29 Which Helena starred in *A Room With a View*?

30 Where was the Last Exit to in 1989?

Answers

Celebs (see Quiz 80)
1 Christy. 2 Roger Moore. 3 Swedish. 4 Gaby Roslin. 5 Monaco.
6 Andrew. 7 Ekland. 8 Henshall. 9 Gazza. 10 None. 11 Max. 12 Boys
- in a Wonderbra ad. 13 Ivana. 14 Zandra. 15 Antonia. 16 The Spice Girls.
17 Tennis. 18 Japanese. 19 Versace. 20 Helvin. 21 Lumley. 22 Collins.
23 Laura Ashley. 24 Frost. 25 Tara. 26 The car keys. 27 Hugh Grant.
28 Jasper. 29 Ronald. 30 Princess of Wales.

1 Agar-agar is a type of gelatine made from what?
2 Who won an Oscar for Best Actress in *Moonstruck*?
3 What type of angles are greater than 90 but less than 180 degrees?
4 What colour goes before Sabbath and Box in group names?
5 Which Adam starred in "Love Hurts"?
6 Terry Downes is associated with which sport?
7 Who wrote the book *The Hitch Hiker's Guide To the Galaxy*?
8 What is a sheep-shank?
9 Who played Pussy Galore in *Goldfinger*?
10 How many portraits are carved into Mount Rushmore?
11 In the 70s, who had a No. 1 with "Knowing Me Knowing You"?
12 Which Ministry is the MoD?
13 In which decade of the 20th century was Paul Daniels born?
14 What word can go after "colour" and before "spot"?
15 The character Charlie Burrows appeared in which TV series?
16 Alphabetically, who is the first of the Apostles?
17 Which Oscar wrote the play *The Importance of Being Earnest*?
18 In which country is the city of Hanover?
19 How is Charles Aznavurjan better known?
20 Who was the first black soccer player to captain England?
21 The character Stan Ogden appeared in which TV soap?
22 The letter D is on which row of a typewriter or computer keyboard?
23 Which Michael sang "How Am I Supposed To Live Without You"?
24 Zr is the chemical symbol for which element?
25 How many Tory MPs were left in Scotland after the 1997 general election?
26 In "The House That Jack Built", who milked the cow with the crumpled horn?
27 The River Tay flows into which sea?
28 On TV what does Fern Britten say after "Ready Steady"?
29 What is the term given to a side of unsliced bacon?
30 "There's No Other Way" was the first top ten hit for which group?

Quiz 80 Celebs

Answers - see page 88

1   What is the first name of the supermodel Ms Turlington?
2   Which former James Bond parted from his wife Luisa in the 1990s?
3   Which language other than English does Ulrika Jonsson speak?
4   Who is the daughter of the veteran broadcaster Clive Roslin?
5   Royals Albert, Caroline and Stephanie are from which principality?
6   What is the first name of Mr Parker-Bowles?
7   Which Swedish Britt was married to Peter Sellers?
8   Which musical star Ruthie became engaged to the actor John-Gordon Sinclair?
9   Which controversial footballer married Sheryl Failes?
10 Of Paula Yates and Bob Geldof's three children, how many are boys?
11 What is the first name of the publicist Mr Clifford?
12 To whom did Eva Herzigova most famously say hello?
13 What is the first name of Ivanka Trump's mother?
14 What is the first name of the flamboyant fashion designer Ms Rhodes?
15 Which Ms Da Sancha's affair with David Mellor caused his resignation?
16 Which quintet first advertised Pepsi in mid-1997?
17 Brooke Shields and Tatum O'Neal both married which type of sporting stars?
18 What is the nationality of the fashion designer Kenzo?
19 Who designed Liz Hurley's infamous "safety pin" dress?
20 Which model Marie was married to the photographer David Bailey?
21 Which actress Joanna was a model for the designer Jean Muir?
22 Which four-times-married actress Joan wrote *My Secrets*?
23 What was the designer Laura Mountney's married and business name?
24 Which political interviewer David is married to the daughter of the Duke of Norfolk?
25 What is the first name of the royal skiing companion Palmer-Tomkinson?
26 When Paula Hamilton advertised VW cars what were the only possessions of her ex's she kept?
27 Which English actor was arrested in Hollywood in a Divine situation?
28 What is Sir Terence Conran's designer son called?
29 What is the first name of Fergie's dad?
30 Andrew Morton became a celeb due to a biography of whom?

80s Films (see Quiz 78)

Answers

1 Richard. 2 Australian. 3 Bull. 4 The Jedi. 5 Sophie's. 6 *Chariots of Fire*.
7 Munchhausen. 8 Last. 9 Los Angeles. 10 Ordinary. 11 Fonda, Hepburn.
12 *Who Framed Roger Rabbit?*. 13 Batman. 14 Three. 15 *Tootsie*. 16 Texas.
17 Mafia. 18 Vietnam. 19 Africa. 20 Miss Daisy. 21 Wall Street.
22 *Reds*. 23 The Spider Woman. 24 Hannah. 25 Kline. 26 Meg Ryan.
27 London. 28 Cambodia. 29 Bonham-Carter. 30 Brooklyn.

LEVEL 1

1 Clive Rice played cricket for which country?
2 James Grieve and Lord Lambourne are types of what?
3 Which UK car manufacturer produced the Hunter?
4 In which month is All Saints' Day?
5 How is Francis Avallone better known?
6 Which team did Coventry beat in their 80s FA Cup Final triumph?
7 Who wrote the novel *A Clockwork Orange*?
8 In which country is Ho Chi Minh City?
9 What word describes a straight line crossing the centre of a circle?
10 In which decade of the 20th century was Jim Davidson born?
11 Which Bill topped the most weeks in the chart list for 1956?
12 Which Tom starred in "Magnum PI"?
13 Richard Dunwoody is associated with which sport?
14 What word can go after "salad" and before "gown"?
15 How many square inches in a square foot?
16 In *Snow White*, what do the dwarfs tell you to do while you work?
17 Who was queen of the Roman Gods?
18 If February 1 is a Thursday in a non-leap year, what day is March 1?
19 The butler Hudson appeared in which TV series?
20 Haematophobia is the fear of what?
21 On a Monopoly board, what colour is Vine Street?
22 In the 60s, who had a No. 1 with "Honky Tonk Women"?
23 Which is greater 2/3 or 7/10?
24 What word can go before "all", "cast" and "take"?
25 What is South West Africa now called?
26 The character Lofty Holloway appeared in which TV soap?
27 Gazpacho is a type of what?
28 In which city does Batman operate?
29 Which Mike was the musical force behind the Wombles?
30 In ancient China, which precious green stone vase was buried with the dead?

1 The green jacket is presented to the winner of which event?

2 Which country did the cricketer Graham Roope play for?

3 In boxing, what weight division is directly below heavyweight?

4 In horse racing, in which month is the Melbourne Cup held?

5 The 1994 Winter Olympic Games took place in which country?

6 Who won the Wimbledon women's singles most times in the 80s?

7 Which two USA cities stage major marathons?

8 Phil Hubble is associated with which sport?

9 How often is cycling's Tour of Spain held?

10 The golfer Nick Price comes from which country?

11 A cricket umpire extends both arms horizontally to signal what?

12 The boxers Ray Leonard and Ray Robinson were both known as what?

13 In which sport did Michelle Smith find fame?

14 In golf, what is the term for two under par for a hole?

15 What sport do the Pittsburgh Steelers play?

16 The Harry Vardon Trophy is presented in which sport?

17 Which country won the 1996 cricket World Cup Final?

18 Which county cricket club has its home at Old Trafford?

19 What is the nickname of rugby union's William Henry Hare?

20 In horse racing, which of the five Classics is held at Doncaster?

21 In boxing, what do the initials WBA stand for?

22 Allison Fisher is connected with which sport?

23 At which French course is the Prix du Jockey-Club held?

24 Who captained the 1997 visiting Aussie cricket team?

25 LOVELY is an anagram of which tennis term?

26 Which sport takes place in a velodrome?

27 In equestrianism, which Nick won the Volvo World Cup in 1995?

28 Martine Le Moignay is associated with which sport?

29 The terms serve, dig and spike relate to which sport?

30 Which rugby league team are the Tigers?

Answers

The 80s (see Quiz 84)

1 Lester Piggott. 2 Argentina. 3 October. 4 Marathon. 5 Bob Geldof. 6 Poland. 7 Mike Gatting. 8 Shergar. 9 Ronald Reagan. 10 Brighton. 11 Whitbread. 12 Foot. 13 Yuppies. 14 London. 15 Steel. 16 Egypt. 17 McEnroe. 18 Terry Waite. 19 Democrat. 20 Grade. 21 Arthur Scargill. 22 Livingstone. 23 AIDS. 24 Greenham. 25 Extraterrestrial. 26 Lawson. 27 Conservative. 28 *Mary Rose*. 29 India. 30 William.

1   Gnocchi is a food from which country?
2   In the 50s, who had a No. 1 with "Great Balls Of Fire"?
3   In which decade of the 20th century was Jill Dando born?
4   What word can go after "ice" and before "cheese"?
5   What is the administrative centre for the county of Cheshire?
6   Liz Edgar is associated with which sport?
7   Who wrote the book *The Big Sleep*?
8   In 1974 parts of Northumberland and Durham made which new county?
9   Aunt Sally and Dolly Clothes-Peg appeared in which TV series?
10 In rugby league what did Warrington add to their name for 1997?
11 The letter X is on which row of a typewriter or computer keyboard?
12 Which gnawing Canadian animal has bright-orange teeth?
13 What is the square root of 144?
14 Jan Smuts airport is in which country?
15 How is the opera singer Maria Kalogeropoulos better known?
16 Frank Stapleton became highest scorer for which international side?
17 Wackford Squeers appears in which Charles Dickens novel?
18 In France, what is the abbreviation for Madame?
19 The twins Caroline and Christina Alessi appeared in which TV soap?
20 "Making Your Mind Up" was the first No. 1 for which group?
21 Which Liz was BBC Sports Personality of The Year in 1991?
22 Which Patrick starred in "The Avengers"?
23 In which country is the city of Khartoum?
24 What is the only English anagram of RUSTIC?
25 What term describes the measurement of height?
26 Who won an Oscar for Best Actress in *Cabaret*?
27 Who was the outgoing American President when Ronald Reagan took office?
28 What is the main ingredient in glass?
29 Is Zambia ahead of or behind Greenwich Mean Time?
30 What instrument did Eddie Calvert play?

Answers

Pot Luck 36 (see Quiz 81)
1 South Africa. 2 Apple. 3 Hillman. 4 November. 5 Frankie Avalon.
6 Spurs. 7 Anthony Burgess. 8 Vietnam. 9 Diameter. 10 50s. 11 Haley.
12 Selleck. 13 Horse Racing. 14 "Dressing". 15 144. 16 Whistle.
17 Juno. 18 Thursday. 19 "Upstairs Downstairs". 20 Blood. 21 Orange.
22 Rolling Stones. 23 7/10. 24 "Over". 25 Namibia. 26 "EastEnders".
27 Soup. 28 Gotham. 29 Batt. 30 Jade.

LEVEL 1

1 Which British jockey was jailed for tax evasion in 1987?
2 General Galtieri was ousted as president of which country?
3 In which month was the hurricane of 1987 that swept Britain?
4 Which London race was held for the first time?
5 Who was the founder of Band Aid?
6 The Solidarity movement opposed communists in which country?
7 Which England cricket captain rowed with a Pakistani umpire?
8 Which Derby winning horse was kidnapped while in Ireland?
9 Which ex-movie actor became President of the US?
10 The IRA bombed a Tory Party conference at which seaside venue?
11 Which Fatima won Olympic gold for Britain in the javelin?
12 Which Michael became leader of the Labour Party?
13 Young upwardly mobile persons became known as what?
14 In which city were Prince Charles and Lady Diana Spencer married?
15 Which David stood down as Liberal leader in 1988?
16 Army officers assassinated President Sadat of which country?
17 Which John ended Borg's Wimbledon dominance?
18 Who was the special representative of the Archbishop of Canterbury taken hostage in Beirut?
19 What did the D stand for in the newly formed political party?
20 Which Michael took over as head of Channel Four?
21 Who was leader of the NUM in the mid-80s strikes?
22 Which Ken emerged as leader of the Greater London Council?
23 "Don't Die Of Ignorance" was a slogan linked with which disease?
24 Which Common witnessed protest against nuclear cruise missiles?
25 What does ET stand for in the Spielberg movie?
26 Which Nigel resigned as Mrs Thatcher's Chancellor ?
27 Which party had a landslide victory in Britain in the 1983 elections?
28 Which Tudor ship was raised from the seabed?
29 There was a chemical leak at Bhopal - in which country?
30 Which Prince was the first-born child of the Princess of Wales?

Quiz 85 Pop: Superstars

Answers - see page 97

LEVEL 1

1 "You Can't Hurry Love" was the first No. 1 for which male singer?
2 Who is the Boss?
3 Which Eurovision Song Contest entry gave Cliff Richard a UK No. 1?
4 Who was a "Rocket Man" in the 70s?
5 Ziggy Stardust was the creation of which performer?
6 Whose autobiography was titled *Moonwalk*?
7 Who penned "Sultans Of Swing"?
8 The death of whose son inspired the song "Tears In Heaven"?
9 Which Peter was a founder member of Genesis?
10 Which supergroup took "Innuendo" to No. 1 in the UK?
11 Whose name had turned into a symbol for "Most Beautiful Girl In The World"?
12 Including membership of a group, which Paul has 20-plus UK No. 1s?
13 Which female star recorded "Chain Reaction"?
14 "Holiday" was the first hit in the UK for which solo performer?
15 Who created the fashion for wearing only one glove?
16 Which George sang "Careless Whisper"?
17 In the 80s, which Barbra was "A Woman In Love"?
18 Who was nicknamed the Pelvis in the 50s?
19 Who - after his death - had a No. 1 called "Living On My Own"?
20 Who was Tina Turner's first husband?
21 Who was Dancing in the Street with Dave Bowie for Live Aid ?
22 Who used to sing with the Faces?
23 Which country queen first hit the charts with "Jolene"?
24 Whose first UK Top Ten hit was "Dancing in the Dark" in 1985?
25 Elton John and who duetted on "Don't Let The Sun Go Down On Me"?
26 In which film did Madonna sing "Another Suitcase In Another Hall"?
27 In the 90s, who sang "I've Got You Under My Skin" with Bono?
28 Which group had a No. 1 with "Night Fever"?
29 What was the 1990 duet hit single for Tina Turner and Rod Stewart?
30 "Cracklin' Rosie" was the first hit of which singer/writer?

Answers

TV: Cops & Robbers (see Quiz 87)
1 "EastEnders". 2 "Cracker". 3 Hill Street. 4 Adam. 5 Chef. 6 New York.
7 Poirot. 8 "Prime Suspect". 9 He was a ghost. 10 Sherlock Holmes.
11 Pierce Brosnan. 12 East Anglia. 13 Juliet Bravo. 14 Jim. 15 "The Bill".
16 Kojak. 17 Hamish Macbeth. 18 Maigret. 19 Inspector Wexford.
20 "Miami Vice". 21 Bergerac. 22 Boon. 23 Ironside. 24 Red.
25 Miss Marple. 26 London. 27 Roderick. 28 Singing. 29 "Z Cars".
30 Jimmy Nail.

Quiz 86 Pot Luck 38

Answers - see page 98

LEVEL 1

1. Which Rik starred in "The New Statesman"?
2. What word can follow "clip", "dart" and "side"?
3. In which country is the city of Kingston?
4. Moving anticlockwise on a dartboard what number is next to 9?
5. How is Desmond Dacres better known?
6. What was the first Scottish soccer side that Chris Waddle played for?
7. Who wrote the novel *Tilly Trotter*?
8. Hippophobia is the fear of what?
9. Glen Campbell sang about what type of Cowboy?
10. Zn is the chemical symbol for which element?
11. The characters Peter and Annie Mayle appeared in which TV series?
12. Peter Elliott is associated with which sport?
13. In which decade of the 20th century was Anna Ford born?
14. What word can go after "Victoria" and before "tomato"?
15. How many cubic feet in a cubic yard?
16. "Vision Of Love" was the first Top Ten hit for which Mariah?
17. What other fruit is crossed with a plum to produce a nectarine?
18. What do you have a pocket full of if you play ring-a-ring-o'-roses?
19. What note is written in the space below the top line of the treble clef?
20. Ruby denotes which wedding anniversary?
21. Which UK car manufacturer produced the Viva?
22. What is the name of Queen Victoria's house on the Isle Of Wight?
23. Which Cockney duo sang "There Ain't No Pleasing You"?
24. Chapatti is unleavened bread originally from which country?
25. What is three eighths of 96?
26. Which old English coin was known as the tanner?
27. The River Mersey flows into which sea?
28. Alphabetically, which is the first of the days of the week?
29. In the 90s, who had a No. 1 with "I Will Always Love You"?
30. The character Derek Wilton appeared in which TV soap?

Answers

Pot Luck 39 (see Quiz 88)
1 The Christians. 2 June and July. 3 20s. 4 "Barrel". 5 "Yes [Prime] Minister". 6 The sea. 7 Conan Doyle. 8 Rugby (Union). 9 Reflex. 10 Ireland. 11 Vivien Leigh. 12 Scotland. 13 September. 14 Teaching. 15 Crystal Gayle. 16 Elton John. 17 Deuteronomy. 18 Japan. 19 Robson and Jerome. 20 Nelson's. 21 Batman. 22 Waterman. 23 Right Said Fred. 24 19th. 25 Conservative. 26 Australia. 27 1/4. 28 "EastEnders". 29 Petula Clark. 30 White.

1   Michael French left which soap to star as Slade in "Crime Traveller"?
2   Which series featured Eddie "Fitz" Fitzgerald?
3   Which police station's Blues were led by Captain Frank Furillo?
4   What is the first name of P.D. James's Commander Dalgliesh?
5   In "Pie in the Sky" which profession did Henry combine with policing?
6   In which city was "Cagney and Lacey" set?
7   Which European sleuth's assistant was Captain Hastings?
8   Which series about a woman detective was written by Lynda La Plante?
9   Why was Marty Hopkirk an unusual detective?
10 Which Victorian sleuth was portrayed on TV by Jeremy Brett?
11 Which future 007 played Remington Steele?
12 In which area of the UK was "The Chief" set?
13 In the 80s what was the call sign of Inspector Jean Darblay then Inspector Kate Longton?
14 What was the first name of Rockford of "The Rockford Files"?
15 Which show features "Tosh" Lines, Jim Carver and June Ackland ?
16 Which New York cop ate lollipops?
17 Which policeman had a West Highland terrier called Wee Jock?
18 Which French detective had a pipe, raincoat and trilby?
19 Which Ruth Rendell detective lived in Kingsmarkham?
20 Which Florida-based drama had a theme song by Jan Hammer?
21 In the 80s who was rooting out villains in Jersey?
22 Which Midlands troubleshooter had a sidekick called Rocky?
23 Which wheelchair-bound detective was played by Raymond Burr?
24 What colour is Inspector Morse's Jaguar?
25 Which elderly female sleuth was played by Joan Hickson from 1984?
26 In which city did the action of "Between the Lines" take place?
27 What is the first name of Inspector Alleyn, created by Ngaio Marsh?
28 What was unusual about the detective in the Dennis Potter drama?
29 "Softly Softly" was the sequel to which TV police classic series?
30 Which Geordie actor starred as "Spender"?

Quiz 88 Pot Luck 39

Answers - see page 96

LEVEL 1

1 The three Christian brothers founded which group?
2 The zodiac sign Cancer covers which two calendar months?
3 In which decade of the 20th century was Bruce Forsyth born?
4 What word can go after "biscuit" and before "organ"?
5 The characters Jim and Annie Hacker appeared in which TV series?
6 Poseidon was the Greek god of what?
7 Who wrote *The Hound of the Baskervilles*?
8 Mike Gibson is associated with which sport?
9 Which angles are more than 180 but less than 360 degrees?
10 Which country did Clannad come from?
11 Who won an Oscar for Best Actress in *Gone With The Wind*?
12 Shortbread is a speciality of which country?
13 Alphabetically, what is the last of the calendar months?
14 Which profession is represented by the NAS/UWT?
15 How is the country singer Brenda Gail Webb better known?
16 Who was the first rock star to become chairman of a soccer club?
17 What is the fifth book of the Old Testament?
18 In which country is the city of Kyoto?
19 In the 90s, who had a No. 1 with "I Believe"?
20 The *Victory* was whose flagship?
21 In comics, on TV and in film, how is Bruce Wayne better known?
22 Which Dennis starred in "On The Up"?
23 Who recorded "Deeply Dippy"?
24 In which century was the Manchester Ship Canal opened?
25 Prime Minister Stanley Baldwin represented which political party?
26 The airline Aus-air is from which country?
27 Which is smaller 2/3 or 1/4?
28 The character David Wicks appeared in which TV soap?
29 Who took "Downtown" into the charts in the 60s and the 80s?
30 What is the middle colour of the Italian flag?

Quiz 89 Food & Drink 2

Answers - see page 101

LEVEL 1

1   What colour wine goes into sangria?
2   Which country does Calvados come from originally?
3   What is the outer layer of a baked Alaska made from?
4   What colour is usually associated with the liqueur Chartreuse?
5   What is the main ingredient of a caramel sauce?
6   What are the two main vegetable ingredients of bubble and squeak?
7   What are large tubes of pasta called, usually eaten stuffed?
8   What is espresso?
9   Is Greek yoghurt thick, or does it have a pouring consistency?
10   Mozzarella cheese is used on top of which snack-food favourite?
11   Rick Stein's TV programmes are chiefly about which food?
12   Which nuts are used in marzipan?
13   Which county is traditionally famous for its hotpot?
14   Chapatti is an item from which country's cuisine?
15   Italian egg-shaped tomatoes are named after which fruit?
16   What colour is demerara sugar?
17   What sort of fruit would go into a Dundee cake?
18   What colour is an extra-virgin olive oil?
19   A crown roast would be made up from which meat?
20   Morel and oyster are which types of vegetable?
21   What sort of drink would fino or oloroso be?
22   What is a crouton made from?
23   Is green bacon smoked or unsmoked?
24   What is a Blue Vinney?
25   Which spice would a steak au poivre have on its outside?
26   Would a brut champagne be sweet or dry?
27   Which herb is used in pesto sauce?
28   Would a three-star brandy be very good, average or rather inferior?
29   Does a raw apricot have equal, more or fewer calories than a fresh one?
30   Which fruit could be honeydew or cantaloupe?

1 In which decade did the driving test introduce a written section?
2 What is an Eskimo canoe called?
3 Which is Germany's main airport?
4 What name is given to a cigar-shaped airship?
5 Which musical features a song about a "surrey with a fringe on top"?
6 The Montgolfier brothers flew in what type of craft?
7 Which motor company made the first production-line car?
8 What shape is the bottom of a punt?
9 E is the international vehicle registration letter of which country?
10 Whose 60s report axed many railway lines in Britain?
11 Orly airport is in which city?
12 In which country did the Toyota Motor Corporation originate?
13 Eurostar goes from which London station?
14 In song, "my old man said follow" which vehicle?
15 A Chinook is what type of vehicle?
16 What colour is the Circle Line on a London Underground map?
17 In which century was the Suez Canal opened?
18 What is the Boeing 747 usually known as?
19 What is the international vehicle registration letter of Germany?
20 The SNFC operates in which country?
21 What is the usual colour of an aeroplane's black box?
22 In the 1820s, who designed the locomotive the Rocket?
23 Which country does a sampan come from?
24 In which decade did Concorde enter commercial service?
25 What type of transporter was the ill-fated *Herald Of Free Enterprise*?
26 The major cargo port of Felixstowe is in which county?
27 Which Sir Freddie saw his airways company collapse in 1982?
28 What type of cars did the de Lorean factory produce?
29 Which brothers pioneered the first powered flight?
30 S is the international vehicle registration letter of which country?

Answers

Screen Greats (see Quiz 92)
1 Fred Astaire. 2 Humphrey Bogart. 3 Charlie Chaplin. 4 Shirley Temple.
5 Hepburn. 6 Marilyn Monroe. 7 Clark Gable. 8 Dorothy Lamour. 9 Bette
Davis. 10 Orson Welles. 11 John Wayne. 12 Rudolph Valentino.
13 Stanwyck. 14 Rooney. 15 Peck. 16 Bela Lugosi. 17 McQueen.
18 Leigh. 19 Laurel. 20 Rock Hudson. 21 England. 22 Garland.
23 Douglas. 24 Marlene Dietrich. 25 Bing Crosby. 26 Cagney.
27 Mitchum. 28 Stockholm. 29 Joan, Olivia. 30 Cooper.

Quiz 91 Pot Luck 40

Answers - see page 99

LEVEL 1

1 In verse, which bells said "You owe me five farthings"?
2 Which Rosemary had a 50s No. 1 with "This Ole House"?
3 The characters Rick, Neil and Vyvyan appeared in which TV series?
4 What word can go after "board" and before "service"?
5 How is the singer Thomas Woodward better known?
6 In 1995, which striker moved from QPR to Newcastle for £6 million?
7 Who wrote the novel *My Family and Other Animals*?
8 How many gallons in a bushel?
9 Who was Herge's most famous comic creation?
10 In which decade of the 20th century was Keith Floyd born?
11 In song what name follows "There's an old mill by a stream"?
12 Which David starred in "Poirot"?
13 Which Natalie sang "Miss You Like Crazy"?
14 The letter K is on which row of a typewriter or computer keyboard?
15 In America, what is the traditional Thanksgiving Day dessert?
16 How many of Henry VIII's wives were executed?
17 "Byker Grove" was set in which city?
18 The character Jacqui Dixon appeared in which TV soap?
19 How does 10.45 p.m. appear on a 24-hour clock?
20 What word can go before "frost", "knife" and "pot"?
21 Josh Gifford is associated with which sport?
22 On a Monopoly board, what colour is Leicester Square?
23 Which UK car manufacturer produced the Kitten?
24 Hydrophobia is the fear of what?
25 In which country is the city of Leipzig?
26 Moving clockwise on a dartboard what number is next to 17?
27 In the 80s, who had a No. 1 with "I Should Be So Lucky"?
28 Which athlete Brendan was BBC Sports Personality of the Year in 1974?
29 What is the only English anagram of OCHRE?
30 What type of apes live on the rock of Gibraltar?

Answers

Food & Drink 2 (see Quiz 89)
1 Red. 2 France. 3 Meringue. 4 Green. 5 Sugar. 6 Potatoes, cabbage.
7 Cannelloni. 8 Coffee. 9 Thick. 10 Pizza. 11 Fish. 12 Almonds.
13 Lancashire. 14 India's. 15 Plum. 16 Brown. 17 Raisins, currants,
sultanas. 18 Green. 19 Lamb. 20 Mushrooms. 21 Sherry. 22 Bread.
23 Unsmoked. 24 Cheese. 25 Peppers. 26 Dry. 27 Basil. 28 Very good.
29 Fewer. 30 Melon.

Quiz 92 Screen Greats

Answers - see page 100

LEVEL 1

1   Who was Ginger Rogers' most famous screen partner?
2   Who played Rick Blaine in *Casablanca*?
3   Which tramp's hat and cane were sold for £55,000 in the early 90s?
4   Who won an Oscar in 1934 when she was six years old?
5   Which Katharine starred in many films with Spencer Tracy?
6   Which blonde starred as Lorelei Lee in *Gentlemen Prefer Blondes*?
7   Who starred in *It Happened One Night* and *Gone With the Wind*?
8   Who was the female member of the Road films trio?
9   Who acted with her fourth husband in *All About Eve*?
10 Who played the title role in *Citizen Kane*?
11 Whose real name was Marion and was most famous for his westerns?
12 Which silent-movie star was born Rodolpho Alphonso Guglielmi di Valentina d'Antonguolla?
13 Which Hollywood star Barbara was in "The Thorn Birds" and "The Colbys" on TV?
14 Which diminutive star Mickey played a cigar-smoking midget in his first film at the age of seven?
15 Which Gregory won an Oscar for *To Kill a Mockingbird*?
16 Which Dracula star was born Bela Ferenc Denszo Blasko?
17 Which Steve of *The Great Escape* did his own racing stunts?
18 Which Vivien was once Mrs Laurence Olivier?
19 Which half of Laurel and Hardy was born in the Lake District?
20 Which famous co-star of Doris Day died of AIDS in 1985?
21 In which country was Cary Grant born?
22 Which Judy started out as part of the Gumm Sisters Kiddie Act?
23 What was the first name of the father and son actors Fairbanks?
24 Which Berlin-born star's first major film was *The Blue Angel* in 1930?
25 Which actor/singer in *High Society* died on a golf course?
26 Which James is credited with the catchphrase "You dirty rat!"?
27 Which Robert is known for his languid, sleepy eyes?
28 In which European capital city was Greta Garbo born?
29 What were the first names of sisters Fontaine and De Havilland?
30 Which Gary, of *High Noon* was the archetypal strong silent type?

Answers

Travel and Transport (see Quiz 90)
1 1990s. 2 Kayak. 3 Frankfurt. 4 Zeppelin. 5 *Oklahoma*. 6 Hot-air balloon. 7 Ford. 8 Flat. 9 Spain. 10 Dr Beeching. 11 Paris. 12 Japan. 13 Waterloo. 14 Van. 15 Helicopter. 16 Yellow. 17 19th. 18 Jumbo jet. 19 D. 20 France. 21 Orange. 22 George Stephenson. 23 China. 24 1970s. 25 Ferry. 26 Suffolk. 27 Laker. 28 Sports cars. 29 Wright Brothers. 30 Sweden.

Quiz 93 Pot Luck 41

1   Which pianist Russ had a 50s No. 1?
2   The character Dave Glover appeared in which TV soap?
3   In which decade of the 20th century was Michael Fish born?
4   Dusty Hare is associated with which sport?
5   Of which country is NBC a major broadcasting company?
6   What number is represented by the Roman numeral D?
7   Who wrote the novel *Dr No*?
8   What is the administrative centre for the county of Hampshire?
9   The characters Ted and Rita Simcock appeared in which TV series?
10 In the 90s, who had a No. 1 with "These Are the Days of Our Lives"?
11 Who plays rugby union at the Franklins Garden, Weedon Road?
12 In mythology, was Aphrodite a Greek or Roman goddess?
13 In music, what note is written on the line below the middle line of the treble clef?
14 What word can go after "trade" and before "Jack"?
15 How is Huey Louis Clegg better known?
16 Who were runners-up in soccer's 1994 World Cup?
17 Which Sam Cooke song includes the words "draw back your bow"?
18 What name is given to small cubes of fried bread served with soup?
19 Balaclava was a battle in which war?
20 What is the square root of 169?
21 In which country is the city of Malaga?
22 Which Robin starred in "Poldark"?
23 Which group backed Steve Harley?
24 Which boxer Barry was BBC Sports Personality of the Year in 1985?
25 Which constellation has three stars forming a "belt"?
26 What colour is umber?
27 Who won an Oscar for Best Actress in *Mary Poppins*?
28 What is 1/4 plus 1/8?
29 Which county does Alec Stewart play cricket for?
30 Which Elvis recorded "Oliver's Army"?

Quiz 94 Plant World

Answers - see page 106

1   Which green plant is widely seen on St Patrick's Day?
2   Which term describes a plant crossed from different species?
3   Where in London are the Royal Botanical Gardens?
4   If a leaf is variegated it has two or more what?
5   What is the flower truss of a willow tree called?
6   Which flower became the emblem of the Labour Party in the 80s?
7   Which part of a tree is cork made from?
8   Which former Tory minister shares his name with a type of tree?
9   Which Busy plant is also called Impatiens walleriana?
10 Which part of a plant may be called tap?
11 Which word describes a plant which can withstand the cold and frost?
12 Which "trap" shares its name with a planet?
13 What name is given to a plant which completes its life cycle in less than a year?
14 Are conifers evergreen or deciduous?
15 Which London borough hosts an annual flower show?
16 The thistle may be a weed to some but it's the symbol of which country?
17 What does a fungicide do to fungi?
18 Which garden vegetable - often used as a fruit - has edible stems and poisonous leaves?
19 What is the study of plants called?
20 A type of crocus produces which yellow spice or flavouring?
21 What are the fruits of the wild rose called?
22 Which holly trees are the only ones to bear berries?
23 Which plant associated with the seaside is used to make laver bread?
24 The cone or flower cluster of which plant is used to make beer?
25 Which tree can be white or weeping?
26 Archers made their bows from which wood commonly found in churchyards?
27 Does a crocus grow from a bulb or a corm?
28 On which continent did potatoes originate?
29 The maple is the national emblem of which country?
30 Is the cocoa tree native to North or South America?

The Media 2 (see Quiz 96)
1 Radio 2. 2 Pre-recorded. 3 South/South East. 4 Radio 4. 5 Australian.
6 National Broadcasting Company. 7 Outside broadcast. 8 Radio and TV.
9 4-Tel. 10 McKenzie. 11 Live. 12 Situation comedy. 13 South of
England. 14 Betamax. 15 Classic FM. 16 *Financial Times*. 17 *Radio Times*.
18 Radio 1. 19 Tabloid. 20 Greater London Radio. 21 5. 22 Sundays.
23 USSR. 24 Manchester. 25 BBC 1. 26 1960s. 27 Five. 28 Baker.
29 The Vatican. 30 Circular.

Answers

Quiz 95 Pot Luck 42

Answers - see page 103

LEVEL 1

1 Who sang with Elton John on "True Love"?
2 The character Patsy Stone appeared in which TV series?
3 In which country is the city of Mandelay?
4 What word can go after "kid" and before "kin"?
5 How is David Soulberg better known?
6 Who was the first manager to twice win the English soccer double?
7 Who wrote the novel *Airport*?
8 U is the chemical symbol for which element?
9 In the 90s, who had a No. 1 with "Saturday Night"?
10 In which decade of the 20th century was Ruby Wax born?
11 On a dartboard what number is opposite 19?
12 Which James starred in "The Likely Lads"?
13 Monophobia is the fear of what?
14 What is the administrative centre for the county of Hereford and Worcester?
15 Which term describes a way of representing a number as a fraction of one hundred?
16 Which UK car manufacturer produced the Toledo?
17 In which month is Thanksgiving Day in the USA?
18 Rachel Heyhoe Flint is chiefly associated with which sport?
19 What word can follow "milk", "summer" and "Yorkshire"?
20 The character Maud Grimes appeared in which TV soap?
21 Which comedian Ken sang "Love Is Like A Violin"?
22 In rugby league, what did Leeds add to their name in the 1990s?
23 Is Greece ahead of or behind Greenwich Mean Time?
24 Who was the outgoing PM when Edward Heath took office?
25 How many pounds in a hundredweight?
26 The airline Danair is from which country?
27 What is French for twenty?
28 Which RAF rank is the higher - Air Commodore or Group Captain?
29 In heraldry what is argent?
30 Which relaxed Irish singer recorded "Walk Tall"?

Answers

Pot Luck 41 (see Quiz 93)
1 Conway. 2 "Emmerdale". 3 40s. 4 Rugby (Union). 5 USA. 6 500.
7 Ian Fleming. 8 Winchester. 9 "A Bit Of A Do". 10 Queen.
11 Northampton. 12 Greek. 13 G. 14 "Union". 15 Huey Lewis.
16 Italy. 17 Cupid. 18 Croutons. 19 Crimean. 20 13. 21 Spain.
22 Ellis. 23 Cockney Rebel. 24 McGuigan. 25 Orion. 26 Brown.
27 Julie Andrews. 28 3/8. 29 Surrey. 30 Costello.

1   On which Radio station does Jimmy Young have a morning show?
2   If laughter is "canned" what is it?
3   Which part of the country does Meridian serve?
4   On which Radio station is "Desert Island Discs"?
5   What is the nationality of the media mogul Rupert Murdoch?
6   What does NBC stand for in the US?
7   In broadcasting what is an OB?
8   A simulcast is a simultaneous broadcast on which two media?
9   What is Channel 4's teletext service called?
10 Which Kelvin left the *Sun* to run Live! TV?
11 Which term describes a broadcast, transmitted as it takes place?
12 What is sitcom an abbreviation of?
13 TVS broadcasts in which part of the UK?
14 Which video format was outrivalled by the now established VHS?
15 Which independent radio station broadcasts classical music?
16 Which UK daily newspaper is printed on pink newsprint?
17 Which listings magazine was originally "the official organ of the BBC"?
18 What did Chris Evans leave because he didn't want to work on Fridays?
19 Which size of newspaper is smaller, tabloid or broadsheet?
20 Which radio station is known by the initials GLR?
21 Of Radios 1,2,3,4, and 5 which is broadcast only on medium wave?
22 Which day of the week has an omnibus edition of "The Archers"?
23 Which country had an official newspaper *Pravda*?
24 Which city's name was dropped from the *Guardian* in 1959?
25 On which channel is the National Lottery draw seen live?
26 In which decade did BBC 2 open?
27 How many nights per week is "Newsnight" normally broadcast?
28 Which Danny was sacked by the BBC for criticizing football referees?
29 Which country, population only 738, has only one newspaper *L'Osservatore Romano*, yet prints more than 70,000 copies?
30 What shape is the logo for Channel 5?

1 Which Pat was flat racing's champion jockey in 1993?
2 Mick the Miller was a champion in which sport?
3 Which Liz won the 1991 New York Marathon?
4 Which country did motor racing's Nelson Piquet come from?
5 Which Carl won Olympic 100 metre gold in 1984 and 1988?
6 The quick bowler Shaun Pollock plays for which country?
7 Mike Hazelwood is associated with which sport?
8 Which athlete Diane was cleared of charges of drugs taking in March '96?
9 Which snooker player was known as Hurricane?
10 Which Graham was Formula 1 World Champion in the 60s?
11 Which speed race goes from Putney to Mortlake?
12 Steve Cram comes from which town in the north-east?
13 Sanath Jayasuriya raced to a 48-ball century in '96 for which country?
14 Which country is Jacques Villeneuve from?
15 Which Kriss broke a British 20-year record in the 400m hurdles?
16 Where is the San Marino Grand Prix raced?
17 Which team scored in the first minute of the 1997 FA Cup Final?
18 In motor racing, who lost his place with the Williams team in the year he finished World Champion?
19 Which Barry was a 70s motorcycling world champion?
20 In what sport has Sarah Hardcastle won Olympic medals?
21 Which record-breaking athlete became a Tory MP in the 90s?
22 Which German won nine Grand Prix victories in 1995?
23 The Curragh race course is in which Irish county?
24 Which Zola controversially ran for Britain in the 80s ?
25 Which county does Sally Gunnell come from?
26 Which snooker player was nicknamed Whirlwind?
27 Which Ben was stripped of 100m Olympic Gold after a drugs test?
28 Which country did motor racing's Ayrton Senna come from?
29 Which sport takes place on the Cresta Run?
30 Who won Olympic 100 metres gold in 1992 for Britain?

Pop: Musicals (see Quiz 99)
1 *Cats*. 2 Travolta. 3 Crawford. 4 Barbara Dickson. 5 *Chess*. 6 Sensible.
7 *Carousel*. 8 Madonna. 9 Joseph. 10 "Don't Cry For Me, Argentina".
11 Grease. 12 Abba. 13 Banderas. 14 Cliff Richard. 15 Andrew Lloyd
Webber. 16 Townshend. 17 Tim Rice. 18 Technicolor. 19 Magaldi.
20 *Les Miserables*. 21 *Phantom of the Opera*. 22 Electric Light Orchestra.
23 Summer. 24 *Sunset Boulevard*. 25 Jason Donovan. 26 Paige. 27 Essex.
28 *Cabaret*. 29 *Oliver!*. 30 Ball.

Quiz 98 Pot Luck 43

Answers - see page 110

LEVEL 1

1. The warmth rating of what is measured in togs?
2. The character Von Klinkerhoffen appeared in which TV series?
3. In which decade of the 20th century was Chris Tarrant born?
4. Which book is known as the NEB?
5. In the 60s, who had a No. 1 with "Eleanor Rigby"?
6. Gold denotes which wedding anniversary?
7. Who wrote the novel *Schindler's Ark*?
8. Totnes and Tiverton castles are both in which county?
9. In architecture, what is a water spout carved as a grotesque face?
10. In the US, who was Senator McCarthy trying to identify in his "witch-hunts"?
11. In mythology, who had a face that launched a thousand ships?
12. In the 80s, who joined forces with the Dubliners for "The Irish Rover"?
13. Patsy Hendren is associated with which sport?
14. What word can go after "home" and before "house"?
15. How is the singer Paul Hewson better known?
16. In October 1995, Middlesbrough's club shop sold 2,000 shirts of which international side?
17. The zodiac sign Virgo covers which two calendar months?
18. What is the total if VAT at 15% is added to a £500 item?
19. In London what are Harlequins and Saracens?
20. In 1965, "Times They Are A-Changin'" was whose first Top Ten hit?
21. In which country is the city of Marrakesh?
22. Which Julia starred in "Fresh Fields"?
23. In economics, what does the B stand for in PSBR?
24. Gouda cheese comes from which country?
25. Which Henry claimed that "History is bunk"?
26. Who won an Oscar for Best Actress in *Sophie's Choice*?
27. What is the only English anagram of INCH?
28. Which Rod topped the most weeks in the chart list for 1976?
29. The character Annalise Hartman appeared in which TV soap?
30. With which sport is Dickie Jeeps associated?

Quiz 99 Pop: Musicals

Answers - see page 107

LEVEL 1

1. The song "Memory" comes from which musical?
2. Which John starred in the film of *Grease*?
3. Which Michael had a hit with "Music Of The Night"?
4. Who sang with Elaine Paige on the single "I Know Him So Well"?
5. Which musical did the song come from?
6. Which Captain had an unlikely No. 1 with "Happy Talk"?
7. The song "You'll Never Walk Alone" comes from which musical?
8. In the film *Evita*, who sang "You Must Love Me"?
9. Phillip Schofield and Jason Donovan have played which biblical character?
10. In which song are the words, "I kept my promise, Don't keep your distance"?
11. Which musical features Danny and Sandy in the rock 'n' roll 50s?
12. Tim Rice and writers from which supergroup wrote *Chess*?
13. Which Antonio featured in the film *Evita*?
14. Who starred in the 60s film *Summer Holiday*?
15. Who provided the music for *Cats*?
16. Which Pete wrote the rock/opera *Tommy*?
17. Who wrote the lyrics for *Jesus Christ Superstar*?
18. What word describes Joseph's Dreamcoat?
19. Which character did Jimmy Nail play in *Evita*?
20. Which Victor Hugo novel became a musical?
21. Which stage musical is set in the Paris Opera House?
22. Which Orchestra feature on the No. 1 hit "Xanadu"?
23. Which type of Nights are in the title of a No. 1 single from *Grease*?
24. In which musical does the character Norma Desmond appear?
25. Who had a UK No. 1 with "Any Dream Will Do"?
26. Which Elaine played Grizabella the Glamour Cat?
27. Which Cockney David played Che on stage in *Evita*?
28. Which musical does the song "Cabaret" come from?
29. "As Long As He Needs Me" comes from which musical?
30. Which Michael first starred in *Aspects Of Love*?

Answers

Speed Stars (see Quiz 97)
1 Eddery. **2** Greyhound racing. **3** McColgan. **4** Brazil. **5** Lewis. **6** South Africa. **7** Water skiing. **8** Modahl. **9** Alex Higgins. **10** Hill. **11** University boat race. **12** Gateshead. **13** Sri Lanka. **14** Canada. **15** Akabusi. **16** Imola. **17** Chelsea. **18** Damon Hill. **19** Sheene. **20** Swimming. **21** Sebastian Coe. **22** Michael Schumacher. **23** Kildare. **24** Budd. **25** Essex. **26** Jimmy White. **27** Johnson. **28** Brazil. **29** Bobsleigh. **30** Linford Christie.

LEVEL 1

1 How many feet in a nautical mile?
2 In which country is the city of Osaka?
3 Brian Huggett is associated with which sport?
4 What word can go before "hole", "pie" and "post"?
5 Hoss and Little Joe Cartwright appeared in which TV series?
6 Who was drummer with the Who?
7 Who told a tale in "A Whiter Shade Of Pale"?
8 If the first of June is a Monday what day is the 1st of July?
9 What sport is played by the San Francisco 49ers?
10 In the Bible, what is the first book of the New Testament?
11 How many minutes in a day?
12 Which June starred in "Happy Ever After"?
13 On a Monopoly board, what colour is Oxford Street?
14 Peggotty appears in which Charles Dickens novel?
15 Which UK car manufacturer produced the Cresta?
16 Which song mentions a jolly swagman?
17 The letter U is on which row of a typewriter or computer keyboard?
18 In legend, which bird rises from its own ashes?
19 In computing, what does the A stand for in RAM?
20 Alphabetically, what is the first sign of the zodiac?
21 What name is given to the horizontal bar of a window?
22 Which phrase from French is used for a false step or a gaffe?
23 What day of the week did the Boomtown Rats not like?
24 What does a misogynist hate?
25 Which Foreign Secretary lost his seat in the 1997 general election?
26 Moving clockwise on a dartboard, what number is next to 19?
27 Chris Old is associated with which sport?
28 Xenophobia is the fear of what?
29 The character Dennis Watts appeared in which TV soap?
30 In the 80s, who had a No. 1 with "True Blue"?

Quiz 101 Children's TV

1   Which series dealt with International Rescue and their super aircraft?
2   Where would you find a rabbit called Dylan and Ermintrude the cow?
3   In "The Muppets" what was Fozzie?
4   Which continent did Paddington Bear come from?
5   What sort of animals were Pinky and Perky?
6   Which programme began "Here is a house. Here is a door. Windows: one, two, three, four"?
7   What was the number plate on Postman Pat's van?
8   Which show featured Zippy, George plus Rod, Jane and Freddy?
9   Which show features the tallest, the fastest, the biggest of everything?
10   What sort of animal was Skippy?
11   Which Gerry and Sylvia pioneered supermarionation?
12   How was Granny Smith, played by Gudrun Ure, better known?
13   Which podgy cartoon Captain's ship was the *Black Pig*?
14   Which long-running programme did Tim Vincent leave in 1997?
15   Which Tank Engine is blue and has the number 1 on it?
16   Which Maggie co-presented "Multi-Coloured Swap Shop"?
17   Whose vocabulary was limited to words like "flobbalot"?
18   Whose friends were Teddy and Looby Loo?
19   Which show awarded cabbages to its losers?
20   Which school did Tucker, Zammo and Tegs attend?
21   Which country did Ivor the Engine come from?
22   Who was the first presenter of "Newsround"?
23   What was ITV's answer to "Blue Peter" called ?
24   In which show did Uncle Bulgaria, Tomsk and Tobermory appear?
25   Which Johnny was the first presenter of "Animal Magic"?
26   What was Worzel Gummidge?
27   What day of the week was "Live and Kicking" broadcast?
28   Which show featured Dill the dog and Parsley the lion?
29   What sort of creature was Basil Brush?
30   What form of entertainment are Hanna-Barbera famous for?

Answers

The 90s   (see Quiz 103)

1 The Queen. **2** Driving test. **3** Margaret Thatcher. **4** Mel and Kim. **5** Channel tunnel. **6** John McCarthy. **7** George Bush. **8** Hadlee. **9** The BBC. **10** Imran Khan. **11** Glasgow. **12** MPs. **13** Bobby Robson. **14** Comet. **15** David Mellor. **16** Michael Heseltine. **17** Ireland. **18** Atlanta in 1996. **19** Laura Davies. **20** The Referendum Party. **21** John Smith. **22** Ladies' public toilets. **23** Chris Patten. **24** Freddie Mercury. **25** O.J. Simpson. **26** Estée Lauder. **27** Carson. **28** Eric Cantona. **29** Windsor. **30** Camelot.

1 Which Bette won an Oscar for Best Actress in *Dangerous*?
2 What is 10 cubed?
3 What is the administrative centre for the county of Shropshire?
4 What word can go after "music" and before "mark"?
5 How is Marvin Lee Addy better known?
6 Duncan Ferguson moved to Everton from which soccer club?
7 Who wrote the novel *The Shining*?
8 Tom Thumb and Little Gem are types of what?
9 In France, what is the abbreviation for Mademoiselle?
10 In which decade of the 20th century was Michaela Strachan born?
11 Brian Jacks is associated with which sport?
12 What does the Y stand for in NIMBY?
13 C.J. Parker and Lt Mitch Bucannon appeared in which TV series?
14 In the 80s, who had a No. 1 with "West End Girls"?
15 What did Castleford's name become for the 1997 rugby league season?
16 The airline El Al is from which country?
17 Who was the outgoing American President when Jimmy Carter took office?
18 What is Ceylon now called?
19 Mike Proctor played cricket for which country?
20 What word can follow "clay", "racing" and "wood"?
21 In which country is the city of Poona?
22 Which Paul starred in "Just Good Friends"?
23 Which Donna sang "Love To Love You Baby"?
24 Which Paul was BBC Sports Personality of the Year in 1990?
25 Diamond denotes which wedding anniversary?
26 Which army rank is the higher - colonel or brigadier?
27 The character Kim Tate appeared in which TV soap?
28 What is the only English anagram of ACHES?
29 What was Lot's wife turned into?
30 A merino is what kind of creature?

Answers

World Tour (see Quiz 104)
1 Perth. 2 Beijing. 3 Emus don't fly. 4 Mediterranean. 5 South Africa.
6 Bay of Biscay. 7 Bulgarian. 8 Italy. 9 East Germany. 10 Jerusalem.
11 South. 12 Seven. 13 Italy. 14 Casablanca. 15 Germany. 16 Cocaine.
17 Nile. 18 Barcelona. 19 Colchester. 20 Jodhpurs. 21 France and Spain.
22 Japan. 23 Africa. 24 Paris. 25 Victoria. 26 Arizona. 27 Estonia.
28 Qatar. 29 America. 30 Rupee.

1   Who described 1992 as an "annus horribilis"?
2   Which widely taken test had a theory element introduced in 1996?
3   Who became the first Prime Minister to be made a baroness?
4   Dying of cancer at 22, Mel Appleby had been part of which pop duo?
5   In which tunnel was there a major fire in autumn 1996?
6   Which former Beirut hostage wrote a book with Jill Morrell?
7   Who lost when Bill Clinton first became US President?
8   Which New Zealander Richard became the first to 400 Test wickets?
9   Before he was elected an MP in 1997, who was Martin Bell's employer?
10 Which Pakistan cricketer was named in the Botham/Lamb libel case?
11 Which Scottish city was the Cultural Capital of Europe in 1990-1?
12 Who voted themselves a 26-per-cent pay rise in 1996?
13 Who managed England's soccer team in Italia 90?
14 Hale-Bopp hit the headlines in the 90s, but who or what was it?
15 Which former "Minister of Fun" resigned over a scandal with an actress?
16 Who was John Major's Deputy Prime Minister?
17 Which country dominated the Eurovision Song Contest in the 90s?
18 Which Olympics were blighted by the Centennial Park bomb?
19 Which golfer became the first British woman in history to earn a million from her sport?
20 Which Party did Sir James Goldsmith found before the 1997 election?
21 Who immediately preceded Tony Blair as leader of the Labour Party?
22 In 1997 the WI campaigned for more private space in which public places?
23 Who was the last British Governor of Hong Kong?
24 Which member of Queen died?
25 Which ex-footballer's trial was a long-running saga on US TV?
26 Which cosmetic house signed up Liz Hurley in 1995?
27 Which Willie announced his retirement from horse racing in 1997?
28 Which French footballer moved from Leeds to Man. Utd?
29 Which royal castle caught fire in 1992?
30 Which company won the contract for the National Lottery?

Quiz 104 World Tour

Answers - see page 112

LEVEL 1

1　The capital of Western Australia shares its name with which Scottish city?
2　How is Peking now more commonly known?
3　In which country would you see an emu fly?
4　Is French Provence nearer the Channel or the Mediterranean?
5　In which country do people speak Afrikaans?
6　Which bay to the west of France is notorious for its rough seas?
7　What is the principal language of Bulgaria?
8　If you were visiting the home of Parmesan cheese, in which country would you be?
9　Which country used to be called the DDR?
10　In which city is the Wailing Wall?
11　Is the Orinoco in North or South America?
12　How many consonants are there in Mississippi?
13　Which country has the international vehicle registration letter I?
14　Which major town of Morocco shares its name with a famous film?
15　In which country is Bavaria?
16　Which drug is Colombia's chief export?
17　On which long African river is the Aswan Dam?
18　Which Spanish city hosted the 1992 Olympics?
19　In which city is the University of Essex?
20　An Indian city gave its name to which style of riding breeches?
21　Andorra lies between which two countries?
22　Which country's national sport is Sumo wrestling?
23　The Cape of Good Hope is at the tip of which continent?
24　Which city has the cathedrals of Notre Dame and Sacre Coeur?
25　Which falls lie on the Zambesi river?
26　Which US state, capital Phoenix, is called the Grand Canyon state?
27　Which Baltic state has Tallinn as its capital?
28　Which is the only country in the world to begin with Q?
29　In which continent is Mount McKinley?
30　Which currency would you spend in Pakistan?

Answers

Pot Luck 45 (see Quiz 102)
1 Davis. 2 1,000. 3 Shrewsbury. 4 "Hall". 5 Meat Loaf. 6 Rangers.
7 Stephen King. 8 Lettuce. 9 Mlle. 10 60s. 11 Judo. 12 Yard.
13 "Baywatch". 14 Pet Shop Boys. 15 Castleford Tigers. 16 Israel.
17 Gerald Ford. 18 Sri Lanka. 19 South Africa. 20 "Pigeon". 21 India.
22 Nicholas. 23 Summer. 24 Gascoigne. 25 Sixtieth. 26 Brigadier.
27 "Emmerdale". 28 Chase. 29 Pillar of salt. 30 Sheep.

1   In the 70s, who had a No. 1 with "Bright Eyes"?
2   What word can go before "ache", "ring" and "wig"?
3   Mark James is associated with which sport?
4   Blake and Krystle Carrington appeared in which TV series?
5   In tennis, what name is given to a score of 40-40?
6   Maastricht airport is in which country?
7   Who wrote the novel *The Invisible Man*?
8   What is 4/10 minus 2/5?
9   In Greek mythology, who was god of the sun?
10 In which decade of the 20th century was Phillip Schofield born?
11 Which UK car manufacturer produced the Capri?
12 Which Paul starred in "The Good Life"?
13 How would 42 be shown in Roman numerals?
14 What word can go after "special" and before "line"?
15 How is the singer Kim Smith better known?
16 Which club did Roy Keane play for before his move to Man. Utd?
17 What does E stand for in PEP?
18 In which country is the city of Port Elizabeth?
19 In which month is Christmas in Australia?
20 The zodiac sign Scorpio covers which two calendar months?
21 How is Christopher John Mottram better known?
22 Ra is the chemical symbol for which element?
23 The character Jean Crosbie appeared in which TV soap?
24 What type of Love was a hit for Soft Cell in 1981 and 1991?
25 How many kilograms in seven tonnes?
26 Is Greenland ahead of or behind Greenwich Mean Time?
27 The letter Y is on which row of a typewriter or computer keyboard?
28 Who won ice figure skating gold for Britain in 1980?
29 What is the administrative centre for the county of Cleveland?
30 Moving anticlockwise on a dartboard what number is next to 11?

1 In which film did Hannibal Lecter feature?
2 Which Steven Spielberg film was described as "65 million years in the making"?
3 Which film gave Macaulay Culkin his first huge success?
4 Which English film swept the Oscar board in 1997?
5 In which film did Robin Williams dress as a Scottish housekeeper?
6 Which actor was the ghost in the film of the same name?
7 Who did Kevin Costner protect in *The Bodyguard*?
8 Which musical instrument was the title of a 1993 Oscar winner?
9 Which comedy was described as "Five good reasons to stay single"?
10 In which film was Robin Williams the voice of the genie?
11 Which hero was Prince of Thieves in 1991?
12 Which creatures had the prefix Teenage Mutant Ninja?
13 In which film is Peter Pan a father and a lawyer?
14 Which Disney film was about the heroine who saved Captain Smith?
15 In which movie did Nigel Hawthorne play an English monarch?
16 Which 1990 Western had Kevin Costner as actor and director?
17 Which Disney film included "The Circle of Life" and "Hakuna Matata"?
18 Who played Eva Duarte in a 1996 musical?
19 In which film did Susan Sarandon play a nun who visits a prisoner on Death Row?
20 Which Disney Story was the first to be wholly computer-generated?
21 Which 1993 Spielberg film was largely shot in black and white?
22 In which film did Mel Gibson play the Scots hero William Wallace?
23 Which Whoopi Goldberg film was subtitled "Back in the Habit"?
24 Which western actor directed and starred in *Unforgiven*?
25 Which British actor Jeremy won an Oscar for *Reversal of Fortune*?
26 Which Tom was the star of *Forrest Gump*?
27 Which film had the song "Streets of Philadelphia"?
28 Which Jamie starred in *Fierce Creatures*?
29 Who played James Bond in *Goldeneye*?
30 Which US President did Anthony Hopkins play on film in 1995?

Answers

Hobbies & Leisure 3 (see Quiz 108)
1 12. 2 Baseball. 3 108. 4 Pontoon. 5 Sonic. 6 Hampton Court.
7 Tower of London. 8 Blue. 9 Pottery. 10 Birmingham. 11 Duplo.
12 Gretna Green. 13 Safari Park. 14 Conley. 15 Great Yarmouth.
16 Double-knitting. 17 Rook/castle. 18 Seven. 19 Red. 20 Breast stroke.
21 Equestrian. 22 Dwarf plants. 23 Indoors. 24 Stamp collecting.
25 Water polo. 26 Bath. 27 Moths or butterflies. 28 Circular. 29 Paris.
30 Imperial War Museum.

Quiz 107 Pot Luck 47

1 Janet Sixsmith is associated with which sport?
2 J.R. Ewing and Miss Ellie appeared in which TV series?
3 In which decade of the 20th century was Rory Bremner born?
4 In which country is the city of Port of Spain?
5 How is the country singer Virginia Pugh better known?
6 In the initials FIFA, what does the first F stand for?
7 Who wrote the controversial novel *The Satanic Verses*?
8 Which country's stamps have featured the word Helvetia?
9 In the 80s, who had a No. 1 with "When The Going Gets Tough, The Tough Get Going"?
10 What is the only English anagram of CLOBBER?
11 Who was the outgoing PM when Margaret Thatcher took office?
12 Which Wilfred starred in "Steptoe And Son"?
13 What sport is played by the Miami Dolphins?
14 Alphabetically, what is the last of the days of the week?
15 A nepotist favours what type of people?
16 Billingsgate Market was famous for what sort of food?
17 What is 1/8 as a percentage to two decimal points?
18 Which Julie won an Oscar for Best Actress in *Darling*?
19 The character Denise Osbourne appeared in which TV soap?
20 Who or what was Genevieve in the classic film of the same name?
21 A lift for food in a restaurant is known as what kind of waiter?
22 The humerus is in what part of the body?
23 Countersunk, flat-headed and snap-head are common types of what?
24 Which country did Galileo come from?
25 In Australia what is a jumbuck?
26 What is the name of the "Magic Roundabout" dog?
27 On a Monopoly board, what colour is Fleet Street?
28 Which group were simply Holding Back the Years in the 1986 charts?
29 In May 1997 which cricket ground was given a £4 million grant?
30 Which Debbie married Paul Daniels?

1. How many court cards are there in a standard pack?
2. In which game would you have a pitcher's mound and an outfield?
3. How many cards are needed for a game of canasta?
4. Which card game is also called vingt-et-un?
5. What is the name of the hedgehog in Sega's computer game?
6. Which London Palace has a famous maze?
7. Where are the Crown Jewels housed?
8. What colour flag is awarded by the EC to beaches of a certain standard?
9. What would you collect if you collected Clarice Cliff?
10. Near which city is Cadbury World?
11. What is the junior version of Lego called?
12. Where in Scotland is an Old Blacksmith's shop a tourist attraction?
13. What type of wildlife attraction is Longleat famous for?
14. Which Rosemary is famous for her keep-fit books and videos?
15. Which Norfolk seaside resort has a famous Pleasure Beach?
16. In knitting, which yarn is thicker, double-knitting or four-ply?
17. In chess, which piece can be called two different things?
18. How many cards do you deal to each player in rummy?
19. In Scrabble what colour are the triple-word score squares?
20. Which is the oldest swimming stroke?
21. What type of competition might you watch at a gymkhana?
22. If you like bonsai what would you be interested in?
23. Is volleyball normally played indoors or outdoors?
24. What would your hobby be if you bought a first day cover?
25. Which sport was originally called "football in the water"?
26. Which UK city would you visit to see Roman Baths and a famous Pump Room?
27. If you collected lepidoptera what would you collect?
28. In ice hockey what shape is a puck?
29. Europe's first Disney theme park was built near which city?
30. What type of museum has Imperial in front of its name in London?

1 The airline Finnair is from which country?
2 If a price is £1,200 with VAT, what is the value minus VAT at 20 per cent?
3 In which decade of the 20th century was Shane Richie born?
4 Colin Milburn is associated with which sport?
5 In which month is VE Day?
6 Moving anticlockwise on a dartboard, what number is next to 16?
7 Who wrote the novel *A Town Like Alice*?
8 In which country is the city of Salonika?
9 Which UK car manufacturer produced the Alpine?
10 The character Alan B'Stard appeared in which TV series?
11 In the 90s, who had a No. 1 with "Do The Bartman"?
12 How many acres in a square mile?
13 In billiards how many points are scored for a cannon?
14 A car must have its first MOT by what age?
15 How is Richard Penniman better known?
16 What was the first English club that Matt Le Tissier played for?
17 Jacob Marley appears in which Charles Dickens novel?
18 What is an ampersand used to mean?
19 Which liberation organization had the initials PLO?
20 A cricket umpire raises his index finger above his head to indicate what?
21 Zoophobia is the fear of what?
22 Which Arthur starred in "Dad's Army"?
23 In heraldry what is or?
24 Gorgonzola cheese comes from which country?
25 In computing, what does the O stand for in ROM?
26 Which American city was devastated by the earthquake of 1906?
27 What name is given to the vertical bar of a window?
28 What did former US President Jimmy Carter grow on his farm?
29 Which county have Boycott and Illingworth played cricket for?
30 The character Henry Ramsay appeared in which TV soap?

1 What does 'e' stand for in e-mail?
2 What was the world's first stamp called?
3 Which country has most first-language speakers of English?
4 What does the abbreviation BT stand for?
5 If A is for Alpha and B is for Bravo, what is C for ?
6 What did Samuel Morse design for communications?
7 When a number of computers are connected what are they called?
8 Which punctuation mark and letters indicate a UK Internet user?
9 How much do you pay for phone calls which begin with 0800?
10 In speech how should you - officially, at least - address a pope?
11 The Braille alphabet is made up of raised what?
12 Oftel is an independent watchdog relating to which service?
13 What does Hon. mean in the form of address Right Hon.?
14 A physician is addressed as Doctor; how is a male surgeon addressed?
15 The Greek letter beta corresponds with which letter of our alphabet?
16 Sputnik 1 was the first artificial what?
17 Which country has *Le Monde* as a major national newspaper?
18 What is Reuters?
19 In communication terms what is the *Washington Post*?
20 In which city is the headquarters of the *Scotsman* newspaper?
21 On inland phone calls when does the cheaper evening rate begin, Monday to Friday?
22 Phone calls made to 0345 numbers are charged at what rate?
23 If a skull and crossbones is seen on a container what does it mean?
24 To use a French road called a "péage" what must you do?
25 Which BT number do you dial to find your last caller's number?
26 Is it possible for a fax and a phone line to have the same number?
27 On the Internet what does the abbreviation WWW stand for?
28 An autoroute in France and an autobahn in Germany is what?
29 Which BT number do you ring for operator services?
30 What is the smallest denomination of postage stamp you can buy?

1 Which boxer Henry was BBC Sports Personality of the Year in 1970?
2 The character Jackie Merrick appeared in which TV soap?
3 What are the words in the shortest verse of the Bible?
4 In the royal address HSH what does S stand for?
5 How is the guitarist Huddie Ledbetter better known?
6 Which Tom was the first player to be twice Footballer of the Year?
7 Who wrote the novel *Around The World In Eighty Days*?
8 Which Whitney led the most weeks in the singles chart list for 1993?
9 In which country is the city of Tijuana?
10 Which ancient calculator used a frame and beads?
11 Which Richard starred in "Dr Kildare"?
12 The zodiac sign Libra covers which two calendar months?
13 In which decade of the 20th century was Jimmy Nail born?
14 Doug Mountjoy is associated with which sport?
15 N is the chemical symbol for which element?
16 The character ARP Warden Hodges appeared in which TV series?
17 In the 90s, who had a No. 1 with "Things Can Only Get Better"?
18 What is the administrative centre for the county of Humberside?
19 Which Dennis wrote "The Singing Detective"?
20 Who was the British monarch at the start of the 20th century?
21 In which country did the 1992 Olympics take place?
22 What does 1/4 x 1/4 equal?
23 How many players are there in a hockey team?
24 What is the only English anagram of TEACHING?
25 What kind of animal is Sooty's friend Soo?
26 Who won an Oscar for Best Actress in *Funny Girl*?
27 Who plays rugby union at the Recreation Ground, London Road?
28 If March 1 is a Saturday, what day is April 1?
29 In the Royal Navy which rank is higher - commander or commodore?
30 Cotton denotes which wedding anniversary?

Quiz 112 TV Times 3

Answers - see page 120

1   Who was the first permanent female presenter of "Points of View"?
2   Which Team heroically helped those in trouble in the 80s?
3   Who replaced Leslie Crowther on "The Price is Right"?
4   In which country is "Prisoner Cell Block H" set?
5   Which quiz features a picture board and "what happens next"?
6   Which political programme is based on radio's "Any Questions"?
7   Which series focused on the King's Fusiliers Infantry Regiment?
8   What were the "Spitting Image" puppets made from?
9   Which racing driver was BBC Sports Personality of the Year twice in the 90s?
10 Which decade was the setting for "Tenko"?
11 Who was the main female presenter of "That's Life"?
12 Which "EastEnders" character died on his allotment?
13 Which country is Rab C. Nesbitt from?
14 Which former "Opportunity Knocks" presenter died in 1997?
15 Who is resident cook on "Food and Drink"?
16 Who always embarked on a long monologue in "The Two Ronnies"?
17 What did Denis Neville and Oz say to those they left behind in the North-East in the 80s?
18 In which series does Assumpta Fitzgerald appear?
19 In which decade did the action of "M*A*S*H" take place?
20 Which sort of containers are Yogi Bear's favourite?
21 In which sitcom did Private Secretary Bernard Woolley appear?
22 Which joker presents "You've Been Framed"?
23 On which day of the week is "The Antiques Roadshow" broadcast?
24 Which series features the firefighters of Blue Watch B25?
25 Who presents her programme "Through the Cakehole"?
26 Which cook presented a Winter and Summer Collection in the 90s?
27 Which former Olympic swimmer left "The Big Breakfast" in 1997?
28 What are the surname of Richard and Judy of "This Morning"?
29 Which Bob assists Cilla Black in "Surprise Surprise"?
30 Which comedy drama was dubbed "The Antiques Rogue Show"?

Quiz 113 Pot Luck 50

Answers - see page 124

LEVEL 1

1 Kelvedon Wonder and Little Marvel are types of what?
2 Which programme presented prizes on a conveyor belt?
3 In the 90s, who had a No. 1 with "I Believe"?
4 Arnold J. Rimmer BSc SSC appeared in which TV series?
5 On a Monopoly board, what colour is Pentonville Road?
6 Billy Liddell is associated with which sport?
7 Who wrote the novel *The Inimitable Jeeves*?
8 Which of Queen Elizabeth II's children was first to marry?
9 What is the administrative centre for the county of Suffolk?
10 In which decade of the 20th century was Joanna Lumley born?
11 Who went to sea with silver buckles on his knee?
12 How many fluid ounces in a pint?
13 The character David Hunter appeared in which TV soap?
14 What is 1/6 as a percentage to two decimal places?
15 How is the singer Concetta Franconero better known?
16 Who was England's manager for Gary Lineker's last international?
17 Which UK car manufacturer produced the Stag?
18 In music, what note is written on the bottom line of the treble clef?
19 On a dartboard what number is opposite 5?
20 RIBA is the Royal Institute of British what?
21 What is Lucinda Prior-Palmer's married name?
22 In which month is Independence Day in the USA?
23 Which Keith starred in "Duty Free"?
24 In which country is the city of Turin?
25 How are angles measured other than degrees?
26 The Battle of Waterloo was fought in which country?
27 The letter O is on which row of a typewriter or computer keyboard?
28 What colour is the centre of an archery target?
29 Pop and Ma Larkin appeared in which TV series?
30 Which kind of pear is usually served as a starter?

Answers

Nature: Animal World (see Quiz 116)
1 (African) elephant. 2 Wolf. 3 Warm blooded. 4 Tooth. 5 Voice box.
6 Alone. 7 Primate. 8 Duck. 9 Dog. 10 Sheep. 11 Sight. 12 Offensive
smell. 13 Brown. 14 (South) America. 15 Eye. 16 Hare. 17 Its ears.
18 Alaska. 19 Warm. 20 Carnivorous. 21 Cows. 22 Chimpanzee.
23 Neck. 24 Invertebrates. 25 One. 26 Tail. 27 Polar bear. 28 Milk.
29 Fingerprints. 30 Southern.

1 Which Nick won the US Masters in 1989?
2 Which England cricketer had the first names Ian Terrence?
3 What sport do the New York Yankees play?
4 Which Pete had a hat-trick of Wimbledon triumphs in the 90s?
5 What did Dionicio Ceron win in London in 1994, 95 and 96?
6 In which city did Linford Christie win Olympic 100-metres gold?
7 What sport does Michael Jordan play?
8 The businessman Samuel Ryder initiated a cup in which sport?
9 Which rugby league team are the Bulls?
10 What do the initials WBC stand for?
11 Gary Kasparov became world champion in which game?
12 Which major British racing event was postponed in 1997 after a bomb scare?
13 How often are showjumping World Championships held?
14 At which sport did Liz Hobbs find fame?
15 Which rugby union club moved to QPR's soccer ground in the 90s?
16 Which Lloyd was undisputed welterweight world champion in 1986?
17 What relation is the batsman Tom Graveney to the 90s England selector David Graveney?
18 What sport do the Dallas Cowboys play?
19 Horse racing's Belmont Stakes is run in which country?
20 In golf, what is a double bogey?
21 How many players a side are there in basketball?
22 A cricket umpire waves an arm from side to side to signal what?
23 Who was the Brown Bomber?
24 What did Emerson Fittipaldi break at Michigan in 1996?
25 Which team said goodbye to their home Baseball Ground in 1997?
26 Which Dan was the BBC's voice of tennis from the 50s to the 90s?
27 Anita Lonsbrough is associated with which sport?
28 In which decade was cricket's first World Cup Final played?
29 Where is the Horse of the Year show staged?
30 Which county cricket club has its home at Edgbaston?

1　In which film did Uma Thurman play Emma Peel?
2　What part of her did Demi Moore remove completely for G.I.Jane?
3　How many films had Barbara Streisand been in before being the star of Funny Girl?
4　Which crime writer did Vanessa Redgrave play in Agatha?
5　Is Nicole Kidman shorter or taller than husband Tom Cruise?
6　Which Sandra starred in Speed and The Net?
7　What is the name of Audrey Hepburn's cat in Breakfast at Tiffany's?
8　Which blonde was the star of Some Like It Hot?
9　Which English actress was the first to play M in the Bond movies?
10　During which war was Land Girls with Anna Friel set?
11　Which Audrey played Eliza Doolittle in My Fair Lady?
12　Which Tallulah was known for calling everyone "Dahling"?
13　Who played Rita in Educating Rita?
14　Which Ms Foster had a son Charles in 1998?
15　Which actress Vanessa is Natasha Richardson's mother?
16　Ingrid Bergman and Judy Garland had what type of flower named after them?
17　What was the nationality of Ingrid Bergman?
18　What was Julie Andrews' first film, about a nanny?
19　Is Shirley MacLaine left or right handed?
20　Which Ursula co starred with Elvis in Fun in Acapulco?
21　Which blonde French actress's real name is Camille Javal?
22　Which Jane was one of the first actresses to produce fitness videos?
23　Which item of Madonna's underwear made £4,600 at auction in '97?
24　Brigitte Bardot had a theatre named after her in which French city?
25　Which Marlene said, "I acted vulgar, Madonna IS vulgar"?
26　Which Irish TV personality was named after Gloria Swanson?
27　Which actress Debra served in the Israeli army?
28　Which Christina played the sinister Wednesday in the Addam Family films?
29　What is Goldie Hawn's real name?
30　Catherine Zeta Jones supports which South Wales soccer side?

Quiz 116 Nature: Animal World

LEVEL 1

1 Which land mammal has the largest ears?
2 Which wild animal is the domesticated dog descended from?
3 Are mammals warm blooded or cold blooded?
4 Which part of the body has a crown and a root?
5 What is another name for the larynx?
6 Do tigers hunt in packs or alone?
7 Which group of animals shares its name with an archbishop?
8 What type of creature is an Aylesbury?
9 What was the first animal to be domesticated?
10 Cheviot and Suffolk are both types of what?
11 Shrews have acute sense of smell and hearing to compensate for which weak sense?
12 The opossum and the skunk are famous for what?
13 What colour is a grizzly bear?
14 The llama is native to which continent?
15 Which part of a human's body has a cornea?
16 A leveret is a young what?
17 What part of a Basset Hound is particularly long?
18 Which northerly US state is famous for the brown bear?
19 Does the moose live in a warm or cold climate?
20 Are crocodiles carnivorous or herbivores?
21 Which farm animals chew the cud?
22 Which primate species is the closest genetic cousin to humanity?
23 Where is human's jugular vein?
24 Are most animals vertebrates or invertebrates?
25 How many young does a kangaroo usually produce at any one time?
26 What part of the body of a Manx cat is missing which is present on most other cats?
27 Which bear is the largest meat-eating land animal?
28 What do all mammals feed their babies on?
29 Which part of a human includes loops and whorls?
30 In which hemisphere do penguins live in the wild?

Quiz 117 TV: Cops & Robbers

Answers - see page 128

LEVEL 1

1   What is the surname of cop Maisie played by Pauline Quirke?
2   Michael French left which soap to become a Crime Traveller?
3   Who replaced Sue Cook as co presenter of Crimewatch UK?
4   Which series featured Ediie "Fitz" Fitzgerald?
5   Which early police serial is found at the end of the alphabet?
6   Which Yorkshire police series did Nick Berry leave in 1997?
7   In which US city was Cagney and Lacey set?
8   Dangerfield deals with what type of police personnel?
9   David Suchet played which Belgian Agatha Christie detective?
10 In which English county does Wycliffe take place?
11 Which assistant to Morse was missing from the show in 1998?
12 Michael Gambon played which French detective in the 90s?
13 How was The Bill's DC Lines, played by Kevin Lloyd, better known?
14 Which Glasgow detective was played by Mark McManus?
15 Which Hetty has a sidekick called Geoffrey?
16 What is the surname of detective Jack played by David Jason?
17 Which police station's blues were led by Captain Frank Furillo?
18 What is the first name of Commander Dalgliesh, created by PD James?
19 Which Jimmy starred in Evita and played Geordie Spender?
20 Which Victorian sleuth from Baker Street was played by Jeremy Brett?
21 WIn "Pie in the Sky", which profession did Henry combine with policing?
22 In which northern city was City Central set?
23 How is Cordelia Gray's creator Baroness James better known?
24 Which bald TV cop was Friends' Jennifer Aniston's godfather?
25 Where was the police sitcom Duck Patrol set?
26 Where did Sonny Crockett aka Don Johnson sort out Vice?
27 Who has played Jack Regan and Morse?
28 In which city was Cagney and Lacey set?
29 Which crime buster show shared its name with insects?
30 In which city did Maigret operate?

Answers

Pot Luck 51 (see Quiz 118)

1 Drinks. 2 Bread & cheese. 3 American. 4 The Sun. 5 Romantic. 6 Paris.
7 The Mouse Trap. 8 Waterloo. 9 Pyramids. 10 Sheep. 11 Gates.
12 Christmas. 13 Nile. 14 Dog. 15 October. 16 Lancashire.
17 Association. 18 Thistle. 19 Cattle. 20 80s. 21 Travel. 22 Wight.
23 Game. 24 Royals. 25 Hong Kong. 26 London. 27 Mont Blanc.
28 Pancakes. 29 29th. 30 Beijing.

Quiz 118 Pot Luck 51

Answers - see page 127

1 What is usually sold at reduced prices during a happy hour?
2 What are the two main ingredients of a ploughman's lunch?
3 What was Martina Navratilova's nationality when winning her last Wimbledon title?
4 Which UK daily newspaper has the shortest name?
5 Dame Barbara Cartland is famous for what type of fiction?
6 In which city is the Louvre Museum?
7 Which Agatha Christie play has run in the West End for over 45 years?
8 From which London railway station do Eurostar trains depart?
9 Which surviving tombs were built for the Pharaohs of Egypt?
10 What type of animal was the first successful adult cloning?
11 Which Bill is the world's richest businessman?
12 Twelfth Night marks the end of which festive season?
13 On which river does Cairo stand?
14 What type of animal is a Chihuahua?
15 In which month did the 1987 hurricane take place in the UK?
16 Which county does TV detective Hetty Wainthropp come from?
17 In motoring terms, what does the second A in AA stand for?
18 What is the national emblem of Scotland?
19 What type of animal does BSE affect?
20 In which decade of the 20th century was Prince William born?
21 What sort of tickets would a bucket shop sell?
22 On which Isle is Parkhurst prison?
23 What is hopscotch?
24 Which family receives a payment from the Civil List?
25 Which British colony returned to China in July 1997?
26 In which city did rhyming slang originate?
27 Which alpine peak's name means White Mountain?
28 Which food is traditionally eaten on Shrove Tuesday?
29 If August 31st was a Wednesday what date would August Bank Holiday Monday be in England?
30 In which city is Tiananmen Square?

Answers

TV: Cops & Robbers (see Quiz 117)
1 Raine. 2 Eastenders. 3 Jill Dando. 4 Cracker. 5 Z Cars. 6 Heartbeat.
7 New York. 8 Police surgeon. 9 Poirot. 10 Cornwall. 11 Lewis.
12 Maigret. 13 Tosh. 14 Taggart. 15 Wainthropp. 16 Frost. 17 Hill St.
Blues. 18 Adam. 19 Nail. 20 Sherlock Holmes. 21 Chef. 22 Manchester.
23 P.D. James. 24 Kojak (Telly Savalas). 25 River Thames. 26 Miami. 27
John Thaw. 28 New York. 29 Bugs. 30 Paris.

1 How is Jeremy John Durham Ashdown better known?
2 Raymond Blanc is famous for being what?
3 Which Betty became the House of Commons' first woman Speaker?
4 Which Melvyn stopped starting the week when he became a peer?
5 Which one time husband and wife actors were dubbed Ken and Em?
6 Which trendy homeware store did Terence Conran found in the 60s?
7 Which part of you would you ask Nicky Clarke to cut off?
8 How was Yorkshire based murderer Peter Sutcliffe better known?
9 Which celebrity daughter was named after the song Chelsea Morning?
10 Who released an album in 1975 called Uri Geller?
11 Which 90s PM was in a university pop group called Ugly Rumours?
12 Who is taller, Kylie Minogue or Naomi Campbell?
13 Who launched Virgin Cola and Virgin PEPs ?
14 Which singer Sarah was once Mrs Andrew Lloyd Webber?
15 Who is Michelle Lineker's famous husband?
16 Which Monica was intimately associated with Bill Clinton?
17 Was Joan Collins born in the 1920s, 1930s or the 1940s?
18 Which British Party leader has the same first names as Bill Clinton?
19 Which model Jerry had a cameo role in Batman?
20 What colour is Dame Edna Everage's hair?
21 Which London football club does David Mellor famously support?
22 Which Scot Andrew was the Sunday Times editor from 1983 to 1994?
23 John Prescott is Deputy Leader of which political party?
24 Which Prime Minister had twins called Mark and Carol?
25 The names Saatchi and Saatchi are associated with which industry?
26 Which Rolling Stone Bill was 34 years older than bride Mandy Smith?
27 What title does the brother of the late Princess Diana have?
28 What type of shops did Tim Waterstone found?
29 Which designer Vivienne is famous for her outrageous clothes?
30 What is the nickname of Royal 'nanny' Alexandra Legge-Bourke?

Quiz 120 Pot Luck 52

Answers - see page 129

LEVEL 1

1 What kind of animal is Eeyore in the children's classic?
2 Which country produces Parmesan cheese?
3 Where, according to the song, is it a long way to in Ireland?
4 What colour were all guests asked to wear at Mel B's wedding?
5 Which flower is linked with Remembrance Sunday?
6 How many sides are there in a dozen quadrilaterals?
7 Which note follows the musical note 'soh'?
8 What name is given to a young elephant?
9 In which country was acupuncture developed?
10 Which singer was known affectionately as 'Old Blue Eyes'?
11 Which flag in motor racing signals the end of the race?
12 In which country is the yen the unit of currency?
13 Which vitamin is found in oranges and lemons?
14 Which composer had the forenames Johann Sebastian?
15 Which Government department collects V.A.T?
16 What kind of fruit is a satsuma?
17 How many players are in a hockey team?
18 What colour is the shade of cobalt?
19 The Abbey Theatre is in which Irish city?
20 Which nurse was called 'The Lady with the Lamp'?
21 What was Cinderella's coach made from?
22 Who rocked around the clock in 1955?
23 Which zoo is found in Regent's Park?
24 Who wrote The Ugly Duckling?
25 What is the Zodiac sign Gemini also called?
26 Shrewsbury is the county town of which county?
27 Which fruit when dried produces raisins?
28 In which sport did Ivan Lendl achieve fame?
29 What is measured in decibels?
30 How many horns was a unicorn supposed to have?

1. Messrs Docherty, Atkinson and Ferguson have all managed which team?
2. Who was the first football boss to marry one of her former players?
3. Which Arsenal player's autobiography was called Addicted?
4. Which Stanley was first winner of the European Footballer of the Year award?
5. Which was the first Rovers side to win the Premiership?
6. Graham Taylor was likened to a turnip after a defeat in which Scandinavian country?
7. Who did Ruud Gullit replace as manager of Newcastle Utd?
8. In which Asian country did Gary Lineker play club soccer?
9. What colour are the stripes on Newcastle Utd's first choice shirts?
10. Which side moved from Roker Park to the Stadium of Light?
11. Was Alan Shearer sold to Newcastle for £5 million, £15 million or £25 million?
12. In which country was George Best born?
13. What is the nationality of Dennis Bergkamp?
14. Which ex Anfield goalie Bruce was charged with match fixing in '95?
15. How many clubs were in the Premier league in 1997/8?
16. Which Yorkshire side was involved in a plane crash in March 1988?
17. Which Paul was the first black player to captain England?
18. Who was known as El Tel when he managed Barcelona?
19. Who in 1997 became Arsenal's all-time leading goal scorer?
20. How is the Football Association Challenge Cup better known?
21. Which Welshman Ian said living in Italy was like "living in a foreign country"?
22. Which club Charlton were promoted to the Premier League in 1998?
23. Which colour links shirts at Liverpool, Middlesbrough and Southampton?
24. Which Brian managed Notts Forest for 18 years?
25. At which international stadium were the 1993/4 FA Cup semis held?
26. Which Charlton brother was the first to be knighted?
27. Which Eric was the first overseas PFA Player of the Year winner?
28. Who was dubbed Duncan Disorderly?
29. Which London side does ex PM John Major support?
30. From which group of islands does Graeme Le Saux hail from?

Quiz 122 Pot Luck 53

Answers - see page 131

LEVEL 1

1 Vienna is the capital of which European country?
2 What name is given to a young deer?
3 Which fruit when dried produces prunes?
4 Where was Achilles hit with a fatal arrow?
5 Which relation gave actor Clive Dunn a hit?
6 Which musical note follows ray?
7 What do you find in a bunker on a golf course?
8 Who wrote The Tale of Peter Rabbit?
9 Winchester is the county town of which county?
10 What is the name of the French National Anthem?
11 Which animal was Androcles very friendly with?
12 Which black wood is used for piano keys?
13 Which island is affectionately called the Emerald Isle?
14 In which sport is the Ryder Cup competed for?
15 What is the clock tower in the Houses of Parliament usually called?
16 Which animal is linked with the Zodiac sign Taurus?
17 Which town is home to the Bayeux Tapestry?
18 What kind of meat can be silverside and topside?
19 What is the unit of currency in Italy?
20 What is the name of the Queen's youngest son?
21 How many notes are there in an octave?
22 What do you measure with a protractor?
23 Ronan Keating heads which boy band?
24 What is it said an ostrich does, if it thinks it is in danger?
25 After a selling price, what do the initials O.N.O stand for?
26 Which type of soup is a consomme?
27 What colour is magenta?
28 What type of fruit is an Orange Pippin?
29 Which London based football club are known as 'The Hammers'?
30 In which county is Sherwood Forest?

1 The art of self defence aikido originated in which country?
2 Which Bank Holiday comes immediately before Easter Day?
3 Pools is a gambling game based on which sport?
4 Where might you be entertained by a redcoat?
5 Which reptiles feature in a popular board game?
6 Which is bigger Disneyland or Disneyworld?
7 What do you play baccarat with?
8 Which leisure park Towers are near Stoke on Trent?
9 In which game is the object to gain checkmate?
10 What is the minimum number of players in a cribbage game?
11 Which quiz board game involves the collection of coloured wedges?
12 Brass rubbing usually takes place in what type of building?
13 How much is it for one game in the weekly national Lottery draw?
14 In which English city could you watch Rovers and City play soccer?
15 Which part of a pub shares its name with an area of a law court?
16 Which End of London is famous for its theatres?
17 Microlighting takes place in what sort of craft?
18 What name is given to the hours that a pub can open to sell alcohol?
19 Which property board game had a World Cup version in 1998?
20 What colour is the L on a normal learner driver's L plate?
21 What sort of accommodation is provided in a B & B?
22 Knitting needs needles, what does crochet need?
23 Which pier is to the north of Blackpool's central pier?
24 What type of castle do young children enjoy jumping up and down on?
25 'The dogs' involves races of which breed?
26 What colour are the segments on a roulette wheel?
27 Which Planet is a celebrity-founded restaurant chain?
28 What colour are Scrabble tiles?
29 Which gambling game's best hand is Royal flush?
30 What colour is the M on the McDonalds logo?

Pot Luck 54 (see Quiz 124)
1 Green. 2 Fish. 3 Friar Tuck. 4 Coal. 5 Leo. 6 Motor racing. 7 Public Limited Company. 8 Switzerland. 9 Bear. 10 Alexandra. 11 April. 12 76. 13 Pancakes. 14 On board ship. 15 A snake. 16 Linda McCartney. 17 Yellow/orange. 18 Apple. 19 George Orwell. 20 Isle of Wight. 21 60s. 22 Before they're hatched. 23 Holland. 24 Saturday. 25 A pup. 26 Malta. 27 Bill Clinton. 28 Eucalyptus leaves. 29 White coffee. 30 The Tower of London.

1   If you mix blue and yellow paint what colour is made?
2   What is usually eaten with Tartare Sauce?
3   Who was Robin Hood's priest?
4   What is normally kept at home in a bunker?
5   Which sign of the Zodiac is normally shown as a lion?
6   Which sport is associated with Silverstone and Brands Hatch?
7   What do the initials plc stand for after a company name?
8   Berne is the capital of which European country?
9   What type of creature was Baloo in The Jungle Book?
10 Which London palace is also called 'Ally Pally'?
11 St George's Day is in which month?
12 How many trombones led the big parade according to the song?
13 What are Crepes Suzettes a type of?
14 Where does a purser usually work?
15 What is a black mamba?
16 Which member of Wings died in 1998?
17 What colour is ochre?
18 What kind of fruit is a russet?
19 Who wrote Animal Farm?
20 On which island is Osborne House, home of Queen Victoria?
21 In which decade did Yuri Gagarin become the first man in space?
22 When must you not count your chickens, according to the proverb?
23 Which country makes Gouda cheese?
24 What day of the week is the Jewish Sabbath?
25 What name is given to a young seal?
26 Which island was awarded the George Cross in 1942?
27 Kenneth Starr produced a report about which famous American?
28 What does a koala have for its main source of food?
29 What is cafe au lait?
30 Where are the Crown Jewels kept?

Answers

Hobbies and Leisure 1 (see Quiz 123)
1 Japan. 2 Good Friday. 3 Football. 4 Holiday camp (Butlin's). 5 Snakes (& ladders). 6 Disneyworld. 7 Cards. 8 Alton Towers. 9 Chess. 10 Two. 11 Trivial Pursuits. 12 Churches. 13 £1. 14 Bristol. 15 Bar. 16 West End. 17 Plane. 18 Licensing hours. 19 Monopoly. 20 Red. 21 Bed & breakfast. 22 Hook. 23 North pier. 24 Bouncy castle. 25 Greyhounds. 26 Red, black. 27 Hollywood. 28 Cream. 29 Poker. 30 Yellow.

Quiz 125 Pop: Musical Babes

Answers - see page 136

LEVEL 1

1 Which Spice Girl advertised Milky Bars as a child?
2 Was Billie Piper 10, 15 or 20 when she first went to No 1?
3 Which Tina sang the title song from Whistle Down the Wind?
4 Who put her famous Union Jack dress up for auction?
5 What is singing babe PJ Harvey's first name?
6 How many girls make up N-Tyce?
7 Janet and La Toyah are from which famous family?
8 What is the first name of the welsh babe from Catatonia?
9 Whose album Always and Forever gives a clue to their name?
10 Which 60s babe's first hit was written by the Rolling Stones?
11 Heather Small found fame with which band?
12 What is the surname of sister Kylie and Dannii?
13 How many girls make up Alisha's Attic?
14 Which Michelle left EastEnders to pursue a pop career?
15 Where do Scary Spice and Princess Anne's daughter have a stud?
16 Who share their name with an Egyptian queen?
17 Which Aussie soap did Natalie Imbruglia appear in?
18 How many babes make up B*witched?
19 How did the Bangles Walk?
20 Shaznay is in which all girl band?
21 Which 60s singer now hosts Surprise Surprise?
22 Which Capstan sang with the B52s and guested with REM?
23 Which babe was the lead singer for Blondie?
24 Which musical instrument is Vanessa Mae famous for?
25 Wendy James was the lead singer with which Vamp band?
26 Alanis Morissette and Celine Dion are from which country?
27 Who sang about Baboushka and Wuthering Heights?
28 In which decade did Bananarama have their first hit?
29 Miss Nurding dropped her surname and became known as whom?
30 Tracy Shaw's pop career began when she was in which soap?

Quiz 126 Pot Luck 55

Answers - see page 135

LEVEL 1

1 St Swithin's Day is in which summer month?
2 Who or what is an Aberdeen Angus?
3 What drink did writer Laurie Lee share with Rosie?
4 Where did Paddington Bear originally come from?
5 What are pretzels?
6 Did man first land on the moon in 1966, 1969 or 1972?
7 In which Italian city is St Mark's cathedral?
8 On which Mount is the resting place of Noah's Ark?
9 Which fruit tastes sweetest according to the proverb?
10 What does a testator make, in law?
11 Which country produces Camembert cheese?
12 Which football team is known as 'The Canaries'?
13 Which Dutch painter cut off his ear?
14 Which Zodiac sign is normally associated with the ram?
15 What is the study of handwriting called?
16 Which London street is associated with the medical profession?
17 Which wooden puppet was written about by Carlo Collodi?
18 Shermans, Grants and Cromwells are all types of what?
19 Which day of the week is the Muslim Holy Day?
20 What is a quail?
21 In which castle was the investiture of the Prince of Wales?
22 Which fruit is used to make kirsch?
23 How old should you be to apply for a car driving licence in the UK?
24 In what month is Michaelmas Day?
25 Which county has Exeter as its county town?
26 For which religious ceremony is a font normally used?
27 Was Lulu's first husband a Beatle or a Bee Gee?
28 Who wrote about Tigger, Eeyore and Piglet?
29 Which animal has a name which means 'river horse'?
30 What would you be eating if you ate a saveloy?

1   Which early Spielberg blockbuster was about a shark?
2   Who played the title role in the Orson Welles directed Citizen Kane?
3   In which 90s musical film did Madonna change costume 85 times?
4   What was the name of the movie based on TV's The X Files?
5   Scarlett O'Hara was heroine of which Atlanta based epic?
6   Who was the star of the Western The Alamo?
7   Which musical about Danny and Sandy was re-released in 1998?
8   Which creatures dominated Jurassic Park?
9   What was Crocodile Dundee's homeland?
10 Hook was based on which children's book?
11 Which lizard-like monster's name is a mix of the Japanese words for gorilla and whale?
12 Who left Kramer in the 70s movie with Hoffman and Streep?
13 From Here To Eternity is set before the Japanese attack on where?
14 Raging Bull was about which sport?
15 Which film was an abbreviation of Extra Terrestrial?
16 The Empire Strikes Back was a sequel to what?
17 Raiders of the Lost Ark was about which Mr Jones?
18 Robin Hood was Prince of what in the 1991 blockbuster?
19 Was Snow White and the Seven Dwarfs released before or after World War II?
20 Where was Gary Oldman Lost in the 1998 hit movie?
21 Which Caped Crusader was the subject of one of the top 80s films?
22 Which watery film succeeded Waterworld as the most costly to make?
23 Gene Kelly was An American ... where in the Vincente Minnelli movie?
24 Which star of Grease and Saturday Night Fever is a qualified pilot?
25 Was The Sting a hit in the 50s, 70s or 90s?
26 Which Disney animal movie was a 1994 blockbuster set in Africa?
27 Amadeus told the story of which composer?
28 Home Alone shot which child star to fame?
29 Was Schindler's List in colour or black and white?
30 Which Kevin played Mariner in Waterworld?

1 Which country produces Gruyere cheese?
2 Who was invested as Prince of Wales in 1969?
3 Francis Drake's ship Pelican was renamed what?
4 Which opera by Gilbert and Sullivan is set in Venice?
5 Did John Le Carre write thrillers or romantic fiction?
6 Which London Street was home to several British newspapers?
7 Which county has Ipswich as its county town?
8 What shape are the teeth on pinking shears?
9 Which Saint is commemorated on the 17th of March?
10 Which Zodiac sign is normally associated with two fishes?
11 What kind of food is borscht?
12 What is the minimum age for leaving school in England?
13 In snooker, how many points is the brown ball worth?
14 Which TV programme has the logo QS?
15 What kind of animals were Cupid, Donner and Blitzen?
16 In which sport would you use a caddie?
17 Which science looks at the planets and the stars?
18 According to the proverb, which Italian city was not built in a day?
19 What is the first letter of the Greek alphabet?
20 What is a Shih-Tzu?
21 Which country does the wine claret come from?
22 In tennis, what does the initial L in LTA stand for?
23 What kind of plants are sage, lovage and basil?
24 Which London park is the name of a colour?
25 Who were the UK's first Eurovision winners after Bucks Fizz?
26 If you bought Le Figaro in France what would you be buying?
27 An elver is a young what?
28 What is kelp?
29 Which film featured the Von Trapp Family?
30 What is the county town of Dorset?

Answers

The Movies: Blockbusters (see Quiz 127)
1 Jaws. 2 Orson Welles. 3 Evita. 4 The X Files. 5 Gone With the Wind.
6 John Wayne. 7 Grease. 8 Dinosaurs. 9 Australia. 10 Peter Pan.
11 Godzilla. 12 Kramer. 13 Pearl Harbor. 14 Boxing. 15 E.T.
16 Star Wars. 17 Indiana Jones. 18 Thieves. 19 Before. 20 Space.
21 Batman. 22 Titanic. 23 Paris. 24 John Travolta. 25 70s. 26 The Lion
King. 27 Mozart. 28 Macaulay Culkin. 29 Black & white. 30 Costner.

1 On which channel is Countdown broadcast?
2 What is the version of 100 Per Cent for the over 50s called?
3 Which show does Dale Winton present from a supermarket?
4 Eric Knowles is the resident expert on which antiques quiz?
5 Which game show with Jim Davidson is based on snooker shots?
6 Who was the first 'female' presenter of Blankety Blank?
7 Which Noel Edmonds show was originally called Telly Quiz?
8 What completes the culinary challenge show Can't Cook,_____?
9 Through the Keyhole looks at which celebrity possessions?
10 How many students make up one University Challenge team?
11 In Blind Date a choice is made from what number of the opposite sex?
12 Which Ms Jonsson was the first female presenter of Gladiators?
13 Which darts based show offered losers a 'bendy Bully'?
14 Who hosts Bruce's Price is Right?
15 In the first Blockbusters were the contestants students or OAP's?
16 In which show do celebrities try to find True and Bluff?
17 Who presented the celebrity version of Countdown?
18 Which half of Richard and Judy hosted Cluedo?
19 Who was the only presenter of Mastermind on TV?
20 Which Angus says Have I Got News For You??
21 Does Carol adjudicate over letters or numbers in Countdown?
22 What night of the week is the National Lottery midweek draw?
23 Which Des hosted Take Your Pick in the 90s?
24 How many people start out on William G Stewart's afternoon quiz?
25 Which Frank was a team captain on Call My Bluff?
26 Which Gaby offered contestants Whatever You Want?
27 Who would have fulfilled your request to "Give me a K please, Bob?"
28 Which magician first presented Wipeout?
29 Which show had a Big Ticket challenge with Anthea Turner and Patrick Kielty?
30 What were contestants Going For in Henry Kelly's TV quiz show?

1   What does T stand for in the initials V.A.T?
2   What does a Venus fly-trap trap?
3   Which movement was founded by Lord Baden-Powell?
4   What day precedes Ash Wednesday?
5   In snooker, is the pink ball or the brown ball of higher value?
6   Which sign of the Zodiac is pictured by an archer?
7   What is the principal county town of Buckinghamshire?
8   Which animal is often given the name Brock?
9   Who was Patsy Kensit's third husband?
10 Which Shakespeare play features the Capulets and Montagues?
11 Which country was called Albion by Greeks and Romans?
12 In which country is the battle site of El Alamein?
13 Great oak trees grow from what, according to the proverb?
14 Which town did Jesus grow up in?
15 What is the name of the dress worn by a ballerina?
16 Which TV show features the Yes/No Game?
17 Stratus, Cirrus and Cumulus are all types of what?
18 Where do mosquitoes lay their eggs?
19 What are clogs traditionally made from?
20 Which actor played Basil Fawlty in Fawlty Towers?
21 Toronto is the capital of which Canadian province?
22 Who wrote Mein Kampf?
23 Which football team plays at Stamford Bridge?
24 What do your arteries carry from your heart?
25 In which northern Italian city is the Doge's Palace?
26 If speech is silver, what is golden according to the proverb?
27 Which county cricket team plays at Edgbaston?
28 What is a natterjack?
29 Which Gladys sang the theme song to the 007 movie Licence to Kill?
30 Which Hampshire town has England's largest military camp?

1   Which detective did Dr Watson assist?
2   Which egg shaped nursery rhyme character appears in Alice Through the Looking Glass?
3   Mrs Beeton was most famous for writing on what subject?
4   Are Penguin books hardbacks or paperbacks?
5   Was St Trinian's a school for boys or girls?
6   What type of animal is Winnie the Pooh?
7   What relation was Charlotte to Emily and Anne Bronte?
8   Who is Agatha Christie's most famous female detective?
9   Which ex MP Edwina wrote A Parliamentary Affair?
10   How is crime writer Baroness James better known?
11   Who's Winter Collection of recipes sold 1.5 million copies in just eight weeks?
12   What sort of Factory is associated with Roald Dahl's Charlie?
13   In which book are there four accounts of Jesus's life called gospels?
14   Which African president's autobiography was called Long Walk to Freedom?
15   Which animal was Beatrix Potter's Mrs Tiggywinkle?
16   What was Schindler's Ark renamed when it was made into a film?
17   Where was Douglas Adams' Hitchhiker's Guide to?
18   What type of tales did the Grimm brothers write?
19   What is the nationality of novelist Maeve Binchy?
20   Which novelist Dame Catherine died in 1998?
21   Which Jilly penned The Man who Made Husbands Jealous?
22   Who was Ian Fleming's most famous secret agent creation?
23   Who did Laurie Lee write of Cider with...?
24   Which soccer coach's World Cup Story 1998 caused an outrage over breaches of confidentiality?
25   Which Stephen is famous for horror writing such as The Shining?
26   What was Dick Francis's profession before he turned to writing?
27   What was Bram Stoker's most famous monstrous creation?
28   In which century did Charles Dickens live?
29   Which comedian Ben wrote Gridlock and Popcorn?
30   Which Frederick's first success was The Day of the Jackal?

Pot Luck 58 (see Quiz 132)
1 November. **2** The tail. **3** Oprah Winfrey. **4** An alkali. **5** A small wood.
6 Hamlet. **7** Angels. **8** Conservatives. **9** Afrikaans. **10** Kenya. **11** Willow.
12 Seven. **13** An eyrie. **14** Threadneedle Street. **15** Doncaster.
16 Goodbye Yellow Brick Road. **17** £1. **18** Ballet. **19** Violet. **20** Adder.
21 Nepal. **22** Agoraphobia. **23** Mercury. **24** Pasta. **25** Spencer. **26** A
Minister/Clergyman. **27** Norwich. **28** A News agency. **29** Mars. **30** Four.

Answers

Quiz 132 Pot Luck 58

Answers - see page 141

1   In which month is Thanksgiving celebrated in America?
2   Where is the rattle in a rattlesnake?
3   Which talk show hostess looks back on founding Harpo Productions?
4   What is the opposite of an acid?
5   What is a spinney?
6   Who said, "To be or not to be, that is the question"?
7   In The Bible, what were seraphim and cherubim?
8   Which political party had Benjamin Disraeli as a leader?
9   Which South African language derives from the Dutch settlers?
10 Which country has Nairobi as its capital?
11 Cricket bats are traditionally made from which wood?
12 How many colours are in the spectrum?
13 What name is given to the home of an eagle?
14 On which Street is the Bank of England?
15 The St Leger is run at which Yorkshire race course?
16 The original Candle in the Wind was on which album?
17 Which coin was first introduced in the UK in 1983?
18 For what type of dancing did Anna Pavlova achieve fame?
19 What colour is an amethyst?
20 What is the only poisonous snake in Britain?
21 Which country is native homeland to the Gurkha troops?
22 Which phobia is the fear of open spaces?
23 Which chemical is also known as quicksilver?
24 Penne, rigatoni and tagliatelle are all types of what?
25 What did the initial 'S' stand for in Winston S Churchill?
26 Who lives in a Manse?
27 Which Norfolk city stands on the River Wensum?
28 What is Reuters?
29 Who was god of war in Roman mythology?
30 How many times does the letter 'S' appear in Mississippi?

Leisure: Books (see Quiz 131)

Answers

1 Sherlock Holmes. 2 Humpty Dumpty. 3 Cooking. 4 Paperbacks. 5 Girls.
6 Bear. 7 Sisters. 8 Miss Marple. 9 Currie. 10 P.D. James. 11 Delia
Smith. 12 Chocolate. 13 Bible. 14 Nelson Mandela. 15 Hedgehog.
16 Schindler's List. 17 The Galaxy. 18 Fairy tales. 19 Irish. 20 Cookson.
21 Cooper. 22 James Bond. 23 Rosie. 24 Glenn Hoddle. 25 King.
26 Jockey. 27 Dracula. 28 19th. 29 Elton. 30 Forsyth.

1   Mark Spitz won seven Olympic golds at record speeds doing what?
2   Which South American soccer team has won most World Cups?
3   Was Tessa Sanderson competing in her second, fourth or sixth Olympics in 1996?
4   Lyn Davies broke the British record in which jump event?
5   David Campese was leading try scorer for which country?
6   Which Sally was a world record hurdler and '92 Olympic champion?
7   Who was made England's youngest ever football coach in 1996?
8   Did Roger Bannister run the first four minute mile in Oxford or Cambridge?
9   Was Martina Hingis 13, 15 or 17 when she first won Wimbledon doubles?
10 Which ice dancers won a record six successive British championships between 1978 and 1984?
11 Which Nigel was the first to win both F1 and Indy Car world championships?
12 Which record breaker Sebastian went on to become a Tory MP?
13 Which Tony made the first televised hole in one in Britain?
14 Who won the 100m in Seoul in record time before being disqualified?
15 Which Steve was six times World Snooker Champion in the 80s?
16 For which former Iron Curtain country did Marita Koch break records?
17 Which English Steve won four Olympic golds between '84 and '96?
18 How many events were in Daley Thompson's speciality event?
19 Which Pete equalled Borg's five Wimbledon singles wins in 1998?
20 Which Gareth became Wales youngest ever Rugby captain in 1968?
21 Alain Prost was the first to win the F1 world title for which country?
22 Bob Beaman held which Olympic jump record for over 20 years?
23 Who was Britain's only Men's 100m world record holder between 1983 and 1993?
24 Which David did Graham Gooch overtake to become England's highest scoring Test player?
25 World record breaker Kip Keino is from which continent?
26 Did Nadia Comaneci first score a perfect Olympic 10 at 14, 18 or 21?
27 Which two Steves were record breaking middle distance runners of the 70s and 80s?
28 Colin Jackson was a world record holder in which event?
29 Who was the first player to score 100 goals in the Premiership?
30 Duncan Goodhew held British records in which sport?

Quiz 134 Pot Luck 59

LEVEL 1

1 In which Dickens' novel is the character Bill Sikes?
2 Which alcoholic drink contains juniper as a flavour?
3 By what name is the mausoleum at Agra, India normally known?
4 Which dogs are a serious pest in Australia?
5 What would your profession be if you were a member of Equity?
6 Which instruments did Antonio Stradivari produce?
7 Which country is famous for moussaka?
8 In which month is Father's Day in the UK?
9 Pontoon and suspension are both types of which construction?
10 What did the 'M' stand for in Louisa M. Alcott's name?
11 Which name did a fairytale Queen have to guess or lose her child?
12 What is a salary paid to a clergyman called?
13 What colour is cochineal?
14 The British Standards Institute uses what mark as a sign of approval?
15 Which American city is served by Kennedy Airport?
16 Which bird has the largest wing span?
17 What does a cooper make?
18 What kind of drink is Amontillado?
19 What does an early bird catch, according to the proverb?
20 Which Beatle's daughter is a dress designer?
21 Bloomers and baps are both types of what?
22 How many years are there in four and a half decades?
23 Where are your incisors?
24 Who, together with Tim Rice, wrote Evita?
25 Where is Lord Nelson buried?
26 On a staircase are the risers flat or vertical?
27 The Cambridge, Adelphi and Lyric in London are all what?
28 What are the two ingredients of marzipan?
29 Billy Graham is famous for which branch of Christianity?
30 Which black and white bird is usually accused of stealing?

Quiz 135 Communication

Answers - see page 146

LEVEL 1

1 Is 0171 the dialling code for central Manchester or central London?
2 Which mobile phone company shares its name with a fruit?
3 If you dial 1471 whose number are you given?
4 Which four letters preface access to an Internet website?
5 What is the normal size of a floppy disk?
6 What sort of cards can you use in a cardphone?
7 What is held in the hands to communicate through semaphore?
8 The fingertips represent which five letters in sign language?
9 112 is an alternative to which number?
10 A modem connects a computer to what?
11 Qantas Airways originated in which country?
12 Which cross Channel link has its French terminus at Coquelles?
13 Tresco airport links which Isles to the UK?
14 What is the regulatory body of the telecommunications industry called?
15 What did Le Shuttle change its name to in 1998?
16 What does D stand for in IDD?
17 Which character divides the person from the place in an email address?
18 Which type of clock works from shadows?
19 Numbers beginning with 0800 usually cost how much to the caller?
20 What do Demon and AOL offer access to?
21 Combinations of which two signs are used in Morse code?
22 What country are PanAm based in?
23 Before '81, telecommunications were under the authority of which Office?
24 Which number do you ring to contact a BT operator?
25 Which country's airline has the code PK?
26 What is the American version of the British post code?
27 With BT calls when does daytime end Monday to Friday?
28 What does 'I' stand for in IT?
29 Which two digits are the first to dial for an international number?
30 Ryan Air is a budget airline from which country?

Answers

Pot Luck 60 (see Quiz 136)
1 Pastry. 2 Mr Hyde. 3 Jewellery. 4 Red. 5 Loudspeakers. 6 Marriage. 7 Flamingo. 8 Table Mountain. 9 The Rank Organisation. 10 China. 11 Senorita. 12 Russia. 13 Hudson (Butler). 14 Disraeli. 15 Dame Edna Everage. 16 Hong Kong. 17 Church/Cathedral. 18 Agenda. 19 Andrew. 20 Three. 21 Pears. 22 Shrew. 23 The Mayflower. 24 Oil Rigs. 25 Green. 26 Wuthering Heights. 27 Bridgetown. 28 Sultana. 29 Penultimate. 30 Fern Britton.

1   Choux, puff and short are all types of what?
2   Who was the more unpleasant - Dr Jekyll or Mr Hyde?
3   Generally what is Hatton Gardon in London famous for?
4   What colour is carmine?
5   What are tweeters and woofers?
6   Which ceremony is associated with orange blossom?
7   Which pink bird sleeps on one leg?
8   Which mountain overlooks Cape Town, South Africa?
9   Which British film company used a symbol of a man striking a gong?
10 Which country is renowned for sweet and sour cooking?
11 What is the Spanish word for a young or single lady?
12 Where was the news agency Tass based?
13 Which part did Gordon Jackson play in Upstairs, Downstairs?
14 Who was the first Jewish Prime Minister in Britain?
15 Comedian Barry Humphries plays which female character?
16 Which colony ceased to be British in June 1997?
17 Where would you be if you were in a transept?
18 What is the list of the subjects to be discussed at a meeting called?
19 Which Prince served in the Falklands War?
20 In the old saying, how many makes a crowd if two are company?
21 Conference and Cornice are types of which fruit?
22 Which animal needs 'Taming' in the title of the Shakespeare play?
23 Aboard which ship in 1620 did the Pilgrim Fathers sail to America?
24 What type of rigs are Ekofisk, Forties and Frigg?
25 What colour is angelica?
26 What connects singer Kate Bush with novelist Emily Bronte?
27 What is the capital of Barbados?
28 What is a wife of a sultan called?
29 What word describes something being next to last?
30 Who first presented Ready Steady Cook?

1   Which country did Abba come from?
2   Which 70s pop movie with John Travolta was re-released in 1998?
3   Which band did Diana Ross leave at the start of the decade?
4   T Rex was led by which singer?
5   What colour was Debbie Harry's hair which named her band?
6   Maggie May provided who with his first No 1?
7   Kiki Dee's biggest 70s hit was with whom?
8   Where did Supertramp have Breakfast in 1979?
9   Who was lead singer with the Boomtown Rats?
10   Who cleaned Wimbledon Common and cleaned up in the charts in '74?
11   What went with Peaches in the 70s charts?
12   Who had a posthumous hit with Way Down?
13   Song for whom was Elton John's first instrumental hit?
14   Which World Cup football squad did Rod Stewart have a hit with?
15   Which Rollers had two No 1's in 1975?
16   Who had a single hit from their album Bat Out of Hell?
17   Izhar Cohen and Alphabeta won Eurovision for which country?
18   Which brothers included Wayne, Donny and Little Jimmy?
19   Whose first hit was Wuthering Heights?
20   Which 70s B side for Queen became a football anthem?
21   Which Abba hit became the name of an Alan Partridge spoof?
22   Which Gary's first hit was as Tubeway Army?
23   Which hostel did the Village People visit in the 70s?
24   How many performers made up The Carpenters?
25   Which soccer side had a hit with I'm Forever Blowing Bubbles?
26   Tubular Bells is credited with establishing which record label?
27   Which band were Part of the Union?
28   Which Bryan founded Roxy Music?
29   Who celebrated his Ding-A-Ling in song?
30   Who had the last 70s Xmas No 1 with Another Brick in the Wall?

1 Which Disney film is I Wanna be Like You from?

2 Which British sausage is traditionally sold in a coil?

3 Which pop megastar celebrated his 40th birthday on 29th August 1998?

4 Which profession is associated with Savile Row?

5 What colour is the flower of an oil seed rape plant?

6 How many packs of playing cards are needed to play Canasta?

7 Bewick, Black and Whooper are all types of what?

8 Which pop star is linked with blue suede shoes?

9 Which animals live in a holt?

10 With which type of dance was Nijinsky famous?

11 In which country is the Algarve Coast?

12 Which voice is higher - a tenor or a baritone?

13 What colour is the St Andrew's cross on the Scottish flag?

14 Which University is based in Milton Keynes?

15 Who in AD 434 was King of the Huns?

16 Who invented the dot system with which the blind can read by touch?

17 On whose feast day did King Wenceslas look out?

18 Which vegetable are people told to eat to help them see at night?

19 An abacus helps you do what?

20 Which actress sang A Spoonful of Sugar in Mary Poppins?

21 Which musical does Climb Every Mountain come from?

22 The anaconda is native to which continent?

23 How many legs does a spider have?

24 Who wrote the waltz called The Blue Danube?

25 Who was the most famous dancing partner of Fred Astaire?

26 What are Gorgonzola, Dolcelatte and Pecorino?

27 On which board game are The Strand, Mayfair and Park Lane?

28 At which Scottish school was Prince Charles educated?

29 What colour is the spot on the Japanese flag?

30 Which continent is native home to the tiger?

Answers

Pop: 70s (see Quiz 137)
1 Sweden. 2 Grease. 3 The Supremes. 4 Marc Bolan. 5 Blonde. 6 Rod Stewart. 7 Elton John. 8 America. 9 Bob Geldof. 10 The Wombles. 11 Herb. 12 Elvis Presley. 13 Guy. 14 Scottish. 15 Bay City Rollers. 16 Meat Loaf. 17 Israel. 18 Osmond. 19 Kate Bush. 20 We Are the Champions. 21 Knowing Me Knowing You. 22 Numan. 23 YMCA. 24 Two. 25 West Ham. 26 Virgin. 27 Strawbs. 28 Ferry. 29 Chuck Berry. 30 Pink Floyd.

Quiz 139 TV: Sitcoms

Answers - see page 150

1 What is the profession of Geraldine Grainger of Dibley?
2 How do Men Martin Clunes and Neil Morrissey behave in the sitcom?
3 Which Scottish pop star played Adrian Mole's mum?
4 Which Duchess made a cameo appearance in Friends as herself?
5 Whatever Happened to the Likely Lads? was the sequel to what?
6 Which sitcom classic was about self sufficiency in Surbiton?
7 How did Hyacinth pronounce 'Bucket' in Keeping Up Appearances?
8 Which show about Grace Brothers' store had a rerun in 1998?
9 What was the sequel to Yes Minister?
10 Which sitcom about the Trotters was originally to be called Readies?
11 Craig Charles was Dave Lister in which sci fi sitcom?
12 Which Penelope alias Audrey was To the Manor Born?
13 How many children feature in the sitcom about Bill and Ben Porter?
14 Which Ronnie played Arkwright in Open All Hours?
15 Ian McShane starred in which sitcom about a shady antiques dealer?
16 In which historical sitcom did Baldrick first appear?
17 Which show was originally to have been called Your Bottom?
18 Which Felicity was the star of Solo?
19 In which sitcom did Joanna Lumley play champagne swilling Patsy?
20 What are the names of the Birds in Birds of a Feather?
21 In Dad's Army, who called Sgt. Wilson Uncle Arthur?
22 Frasier was a spin off from which series based in a Boston bar?
23 What was the occupation of the stars of Common as Muck?
24 Which wartime sitcom featured Rene and Edith Artois?
25 Who played Jean, husband of Lionel, in As Time Goes By?
26 Goodnight Sweetheart is set in the 40s and which other decade?
27 Which series was based on Butlin's and Pontin's?
28 What was Anton Rodgers' legal job in May to December?
29 Which Family is a sitcom with ex Mrs Merton Caroline Aherne?
30 What is Mrs Victor Meldrew's first name?

1   Red Admirals, Fritillaries and Tortoiseshells are all what?
2   Which pie is Melton Mowbray renowned for?
3   Which has more rainfall the Sahara or Antarctica?
4   Which sport would you see at Chepstow?
5   Which brothers made the first manned powered aero flight in 1903?
6   Who is the main male character in the novel Lorna Doone?
7   What was sold in an apothecary?
8   From which Disney film is Give a Little Whistle from?
9   Which animals live in an earth or lair?
10   Along with white, what colours appear on the Italian flag?
11   Which snake is it said Cleopatra used to poison herself?
12   How many ships came sailing by according to the carol?
13   Which musical does Don't Cry for Me, Argentina come from?
14   What is chipboard made from?
15   What bean is made into a baked bean?
16   What is a poinsettia?
17   In the novel what kind of animal was Tarka?
18   Bruges is the capital of which part of Belgium?
19   Which characters sang The Bare Necessities in the Jungle Book?
20   Madonna's Like A Prayer advertised which soft drink?
21   How many wings does a bee have?
22   In which decade did Britain convert to decimal currency?
23   Sardinia is part of which country?
24   What are collected by a philatelist?
25   What colour is the background of the Scottish flag?
26   What flavour is creme de menthe?
27   What type of bird are Ring, Turtle and Collared?
28   On which horse race course are Becher's Brook and the Chair?
29   Which is the highest female singing voice?
30   Which sea is called La Manche by the French?

1 Which Rowan played a vicar in Four Weddings and a Funeral?
2 Which Carry On film was set on board the SS Happy Wanderer?
3 Who played the bowler hatted Tramp in The Kid?
4 Addams Family Values was the follow up to what?
5 Which west London borough is associated with classic comedies?
6 What age group are the performers in the gangster film Bugsy Malone?
7 Which cartoon set in Bedrock starred John Goodman in the human version?
8 What type of Adventure did Bill and Ted have?
9 What sort of farm animal was Babe?
10 Which Tom starred in Jerry Maguire?
11 What type of animals were Lady and the Tramp?
12 Who's World did Mike Myers and Dana Garvey live in?
13 A Fish Called ... what was a John Cleese & Jamie Lee Curtis classic?
14 What was Whoopi Goldberg disguised as in Sister Act?
15 Which group sang the theme song for Four Weddings and a Funeral?
16 Which Jim was the shy bank clerk in The Mask?
17 Forrest Gump said life was like a box of what?
18 Which Julia was the Pretty Woman in the film's title?
19 Which British comedy duo were the stars of The Magnificent Two?
20 What did Robin Williams in Mrs Doubtfire and Dustin Hoffman in Tootsie have in common?
21 What unusual handicap did Bernie have as a host in A Weekend at Bernie's?
22 Which film of a Book featured The Bare Necessities?
23 Which Sid's first Carry On was Carry On Constable?
24 To whom did someone say 'I Shrunk The Kids' in the film title?
25 Which spinach-loving cartoon character was played by Robin Williams?
26 Which 1980 film title suggests normal working hours?
27 Was Patrick Swayze or Demi Moore the Ghost in the 1990 film?
28 Look Who's Talking Too was the sequel to what?
29 Who was the Queen of the Desert in the transvestsite comedy?
30 Which Inspector played by Peter Sellers was in The Pink Panther?

Quiz 142 Pot Luck 63

Answers - see page 151

1 Along with black which colours appear on the German flag?
2 What is a tourniquet used for in First Aid?
3 Which musical is based on a book called Anna and the King of Siam?
4 The chipmunk is native to America and which other country?
5 Who was pop's first Knight?
6 Where in London is the ceremony of the keys held each night?
7 What colour is indigo?
8 Which East Anglian county is often called "Constable Country"?
9 In 1926 which General crisis happened in England?
10 Which sport links Ted Dexter, Peter May and Ray Illingworth?
11 What was the nationality of composer Rimsky-Korsakov?
12 Budgerigars are native to which country?
13 How many carats in pure gold?
14 Caviar comes traditionally from which fish?
15 What does a cardiologist study?
16 What colour are Aylesbury ducks?
17 Which football team plays at Maine Road for its home matches?
18 What is used to check something is level by a builder?
19 Who wrote Black Beauty?
20 What does the Queen give out on the day before Good Friday?
21 What are the sealskin boats used by Eskimos called?
22 What did Nell Gwyn sell when Charles II first saw her?
23 What was the motto of the Three Musketeers?
24 On which course is the horse race the St Leger run?
25 Which castle is in the royal county of Berkshire?
26 If a musical note is lowered by a flat, what raises it?
27 Who was the first presenter of Animal Hospital?
28 In which city is the River Cam?
29 Apart from blue, what two other colours appear on the Dutch flag?
30 In 1930 which female aviator flew from England to Australia?

Quiz 143 Geography: The UK

LEVEL 1

1 Is Holy Island off the east or west coast of England?
2 What is a native of Aberdeen called?
3 Is London's Docklands, north, south, east or west of the city?
4 Where do people go to spot Nessie?
5 Which English gorge takes its name from a nearby village famous for its cheese?
6 Which county has the abbreviation Beds?
7 St Anne's lies to the south of which British seaside resort?
8 Which Royal residence stands by the river Dee?
9 In which country is the UK's highest mountain?
10 What sort of an institution in London is Bart's?
11 On a London Tube map the Central Line is what colour?
12 In which Scottish city did you find the Gorbals?
13 Where is London's most famous Dog's Home?
14 Which Isle off the south coast of England is a county in its own right?
15 What is Britain's most southerly country?
16 Norwich is the administrative centre of which county?
17 In which city did the National Trust buy the childhood home of Paul McCartney?
18 Which motorway runs almost parallel to the A4?
19 With which profession is London's Harley Street associated?
20 What is Britain's largest international airport?
21 In which county is Land's End?
22 Would a Scotsman wear a sporran at the front or at the back of a kilt?
23 Which motorway goes from Lancashire to Yorkshire east to west?
24 In Ireland what is a lough?
25 In which part of the UK is Land of My Fathers a traditional song?
26 Winchester is the adminstrative seat of which county?
27 Aston University is near which Midlands city?
28 Most of the Lake District is in which county?
29 What red flower does Lancs have?
30 In which city is the Barbican Centre?

Quiz 144 Pot Luck 64

Answers - see page 153

LEVEL 1

1   Pongo and Perdita appear in which canine film?
2   Who composed the opera The Marriage of Figaro?
3   What type of fruit is a nectarine?
4   Which of the four Channel Islands is the smallest?
5   What colour is sepia?
6   Who, according to the proverb, laughs longest?
7   In which year was Everest conquered?
8   Which house furnishing is associated with the town of Kidderminster?
9   How does a bishop move in chess?
10 The drink sangria comes from which European country?
11 Who wrote The Old Curiosity Shop?
12 What two colours other than red appear on the Belgian flag?
13 What is a female fox called?
14 What is sold in a patisserie?
15 When You Wish Upon A Star comes from which Disney film?
16 In which sport would you need a foil or epee?
17 What can a chameleon lizard change?
18 The rocks called The Needles are close to which island?
19 What is a barracuda?
20 How many steps were there in the title of the novel by John Buchan?
21 A loganberry is a cross between a raspberry and what?
22 Which river are the Victoria Falls on?
23 Sardines and pilchards are part of which fish family?
24 Which French Queen was executed in the French Revolution?
25 What name was spiced ham given during wartime?
26 Who wrote The Hunchback of Notre Dame?
27 Which seabird is associated with Lundy Island?
28 What are the three primary colours in art?
29 How many wings does a moth have?
30 From which country does the football team Juventus come from?

Answers

Geography: The UK (see Quiz 143)
1 East. 2 Aberdonian. 3 East. 4 Loch Ness. 5 Cheddar. 6 Bedfordshire.
7 Blackpool. 8 Balmoral. 9 Scotland. 10 Hospital. 11 Red. 12 Glasgow.
13 Battersea. 14 Isle of Wight. 15 England. 16 Norfolk. 17 Liverpool.
18 M4. 19 Medical profession. 20 Heathrow. 21 Cornwall. 22 Front.
23 M62. 24 Lake. 25 Wales. 26 Hampshire. 27 Birmingham.
28 Cumbria. 29 Rose. 30 London.

1   Who was tennis star Martina Hingis named after?
2   Which lauded soccer-star was born Edson Arantes do Nascimento?
3   Which French footballer David advertised L'Oreal hair products?
4   Golfer Ernie Els is from which African country?
5   Which British tennis player was born on Greg Rusedski's first birthday?
6   Jonah Lomu plays for which international side?
7   Athlete Kelly Holmes was formerly a member of which armed service?
8   Which swimmer Sharron is married to athlete Derek Redmond?
9   Which snooker champ Ray was nicknamed Dracula?
10 What sort of eye accessory does Chris Eubank wear?
11 Who replaced David Coleman on A Question of Sport?
12 Which Monica was stabbed in the back by a fanatical Graf supporter?
13 Was tennis's Michael Chang from Hong Kong or the USA?
14 Which Irishman Alex won his last World Snooker Championship in 1982?
15 Which TV presenter ended her relationship with Stan Collymore during France 98?
16 Which four legged, three times Grand National winner died in 1995?
17 Which Greg rejected a maple leaf for a Union Jack in the 90s?
18 Who founded the book known as the cricketer's Bible?
19 Rachel Hayhoe Flint is a famous name in which sport?
20 Who was Ben Johnson running for when disqualified in Seoul?
21 Which Princess won the '71 European Three Day Event?
22 Who replaced Mike Atherton as England cricket captain?
23 Which temperamental tennis player was dubbed Superbrat?
24 Which Jenny was the first woman to train a Grand National winner?
25 Who was John Fashanu's late brother?
26 Which boxer's catchphrase was "Know what I mean 'Arry"?
27 Which disappearing horse last won the Derby in 1981?
28 Who founded the Stewart motor racing team?
29 What was cricket umpire Harold Bird's nickname?
30 Who became the first black manager of a Premiership club when he took over at Chelsea in 1996?

Quiz 146 Pot Luck 65

LEVEL 1

1 How many wings does a butterfly have?
2 Which river is the longest in France?
3 Who is older – Kristin Scott Thomas or Kate Winslet?
4 In which county is Bodmin Moor?
5 Which compass point is opposite North-north-west?
6 Which Thomas wrote The Mayor of Casterbridge?
7 Which trade was abolished in 1807 in the British Empire?
8 Which chess piece should be protected at all costs?
9 What two colours are on the Austrian flag?
10 In which country was there a North v South civil war from 1861-65?
11 How many players are in a netball team?
12 Where in Britain are the Royal Botanic Gardens?
13 Which ancient wall crosses England from Wallsend to Solway?
14 What colour is an aubergine?
15 Which mountain is the highest in the Alps?
16 The artist Canaletto was associated with which Italian city?
17 In which month is the Trooping of the Colour?
18 Which island is also called the George Cross Island?
19 Which children's show did Anthea Turner present?
20 Cox, Braeburn and Gala are all kinds of which fruit?
21 In legal terms, what do the initials QC stand for?
22 Which disaster struck England in the 1340s?
23 Where, in America, is jazz supposed to have been born?
24 What is the opposite of a neap tide?
25 Which country lies immediately east of Chile?
26 Who was asked to ride "a bicycle made for two" in the song?
27 In which English county is the town of Telford?
28 The National Homing Union is involved with which leisure pursuit?
29 What kind of fruit can be cantaloupe?
30 Which country as well as France is Lake Geneva in?

1 Who went straight to No 1 in 81 with Stand and Deliver?
2 What colour Door gave Shakin' Stevens an 80s hit?
3 Which ex Beatle had a hit with Stevie Wonder in 1982?
4 Whose album Thriller provided several hit singles?
5 Who was KC's backing Band?
6 Which Scot had chart success after Esther Rantzen's The Big Time?
7 Which BBC Radio station banned Relax?
8 Ravel's Bolero charted because of which skaters' Olympic success?
9 Which actor Robert was named in a Bananarama song title ?
10 Which Superstar Rat sang Love Me Tender?
11 Which Alison's nickname was Alf?
12 Which Elaine and Barbara topped the charts in 1985?
13 Which Mrs Andrew Lloyd Webber had a hit with Pie Jesu?
14 David Bowie and Mick Jagger had a hit after which Concert?
15 Elton John charted with Nikita at the same time as Sting had which coincidental hit?
16 Who had hits as part of Visage and Ultravox?
17 Who told you that you were In The Army Now?
18 Who fronted Culture Club?
19 Graham McPherson of Madness was known as what?
20 Which Kim reached No 2 in 1981, 24 years after dad Marty?
21 Which Spanish singer had the UK's first chart topper in Spanish?
22 David Sylvian was part of which Asian sounding band?
23 Who was the first ventriloquist in the charts with Orville?
24 Who teamed up with Annie Lennox in The Eurythmics?
25 Who was the then oldest man in the charts with New York New York?
26 Who joined Cliff Richard for his 80s Living Doll?
27 Which TV puppets sang The Chicken Song?
28 Which red haired Royal liked Lady in Red?
29 Which future England coach joined Waddle on Diamond Lights?
30 Who had a Xmas No 1 in 88 after 30 year in the charts?

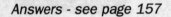

1 Which weatherman featured in a BT ad with the song Bring Me Sunshine?
2 Which cartoonist was the creator of The Snowman?
3 How many are there in a baker's dozen?
4 What would you find in a punnet?
5 In which county are Britain's Royal Botanic Gardens?
6 What is a speech or scene with only one actor called?
7 Douglas is the capital town of which Isle?
8 Who was wife to Prince Albert of Saxe-Coburg and Gotha?
9 The Spanish city of Seville is famous for which fruit?
10 What is the nationality of pianist Richard Clayderman?
11 Where does the Trooping of the Colour take place in London?
12 Pharmacology is the study of what?
13 Where, according to the song, should you pack up your troubles?
14 What is usually kept in a band-box?
15 What is the main ingredient in the drink mead?
16 In music, how many lines are there in a stave?
17 What name is given to the building where whisky is made?
18 According to the proverb, a bad workman always blames what?
19 Jesus Christ was baptised in which river?
20 What are inserted into the body during acupuncture?
21 According to rhyme which bird pecked off the maid's nose?
22 Which King was known as the 'Lionheart'?
23 Beluga, Sperm and Blue are all types of what?
24 Which sport is played on a grid iron?
25 Which Zodiac sign is known as the sign of the goat?
26 What is perry made from?
27 In which month is the State Opening of Parliament in England?
28 Who created sleuth Miss Marple?
29 With which sport do we associate Larry Holmes?
30 Which musical instrument is a national emblem of Ireland?

1 Which batter mix is an accompaniment to roast beef?
2 Which blackcurrant drink was advertised by Michael Portillo when he was a child?
3 What colour wine is Beaujolais Nouveau?
4 What colour is the flesh of an avocado?
5 What is the traditional colour for the outside of a stick of rock?
6 Would you eat or drink a Sally Lunn?
7 What type of egg is covered in sausage meat?
8 Scrumpy is a rough form of what?
9 Which mashed vegetable tops a shepherd's pie?
10 Which food has given its name to a road network near Birmingham?
11 Is a Spotted Dick a first course or a pudding?
12 Which fruit is associated with tennis at Wimbledon?
13 Champagne originated in which country?
14 Is a Melton Mowbray pie sweet or savoury?
15 What is a pistachio?
16 What sort of fruit is in a teacake?
17 What is a slice of bacon called?
18 Which is more substantial, afternoon tea or high tea?
19 If you ate al fresco would you be indoors or out of doors?
20 What is the usual shape of a Camembert cheese?
21 Which soft pulpy peas are eaten with fish and chips?
22 What type of food may be served clotted?
23 What would you make in a cafetiere?
24 What type of drink is Bristol Cream?
25 Is chowder a soup or a pudding?
26 A 'pinta' is usually a pint of what?
27 Should red wine normally be drunk chilled or a room temperature?
28 Is there milk in a cappuccino coffee?
29 Are you more likely to eat a croissant at breakfast or supper?
30 A gateau is a creamy type of what?

Pot Luck 67 (see Quiz 150)

Answers

1 Edward. 2 Staff/stave. 3 Everton. 4 Films. 5 Drowning Men. 6 Hillary Clinton. 7 Eyes. 8 A fool. 9 101 Dalmatians. 10 Baghdad. 11 B. 12 Four years. 13 Portugal. 14 Damon Hill. 15 Wood. 16 Fish. 17 Beta. 18 Ear, Nose & Throat. 19 Assisi. 20 Stitches. 21 Cancer. 22 Tammy Wynette. 23 Brown. 24 New Zealand. 25 St Bernard. 26 California. 27 21. 28 Michael and John. 29 Norway. 30 Roald Dahl.

1 Which English King was also called 'The Confessor'?
2 What are the lines called on which music is written?
3 Which football team play their home games at Goodison Park?
4 PG, 15 and 18 are all classifications for what?
5 According to the proverb, who clutches at straws?
6 How is US lawyer Hillary Roddam better known?
7 In Cockney rhyming slang, what are your mince pies?
8 According to the proverb, who is soon parted from his money?
9 From which Disney film does Cruella De Vil come from?
10 What is the capital of Iraq?
11 Which letter describes a soft lead pencil?
12 How long is an American president's term of office?
13 The Azores are a part of which European country?
14 Who, surprisingly, won the 1998 Belgian Formula 1 Grand Prix?
15 What are the bars on a xylophone made from?
16 What is a mud skipper?
17 What is the second letter of the Greek alphabet?
18 In medicine, what do the initials ENT stand for?
19 With which Italian town is Saint Francis linked?
20 Blanket, back and buttonhole are all types of what?
21 Which Zodiac sign is known as the sign of the crab?
22 Whose life story was called Stand By Your Man?
23 Which wire is live in modern three core electric cable?
24 From which country other than Australia did Anzac troops come from?
25 Who is the patron saint of mountaineers?
26 In which state of the US is the resort of Palm Springs?
27 How many consonants are in the English alphabet?
28 In Peter Pan what are names of Wendy's brothers?
29 The port of Bergen is in which European country?
30 Who wrote the original Tales of the Unexpected?

1   Which Coronation Street character had the names Fairclough and Sullivan?

2   In which country is The Sullivans set?

3   Characters from which UK soap went to the '98 World Cup Final?

4   What was Channel 5's first major soap called?

5   Which soap sparked the campaign to 'Free the Weatherfield 1'?

6   Lisa Riley was in which soap before You've Been Framed?

7   Danielle Brown of Emmerdale has a sister in which pop band?

8   In which soap were the Battersbys introduced as the family from hell?

9   In Albert Square did Sharon marry Grant or Phil Mitchell?

10   In which northern city was the docu soap Hotel set?

11   In Coronation Street is Spider a pet or an eco warrior?

12   Which soap has an omnibus edition on Sunday afternoons?

13   Gillian Taylforth's sister Kim joined which northern soap in 1998?

14   In which soap did Bobby come back from the dead?

15   The docu soap Lakesiders took place in what type of venue?

16   Which soap has featured aristocrat Lady Tara?

17   Who started soap life as Alma Sedgewick?

18   Which soap has a car repair business at The Arches?

19   What sort of road is Brookside?

20   What time does Coronation Street usually start?

21   Which actress Anna found fame as Beth Jordache in Brookside?

22   Who is Nick Cotton's long suffering mum in Albert Square?

23   How had the Carringtons made their money in Dynasty?

24   What is the first name of Phil and Grant Mitchell's mum?

25   Which Baldwin in Coronation Street hasn't a northern accent?

26   Which Jack and Vera took over the Rovers from the Bet Gilroy?

27   Which Ken has been in Coronation Street from the start?

28   Which soap is the BBC's most watched programme?

29   Which southern hemisphere country did Kathy go to when she left Albert Square?

30   In which city is Brookside set?

Quiz 152 Pot Luck 68

LEVEL 1

Answers - see page 161

1 What job was done by Peter and Andrew before they were disciples?
2 Ex MP David Owen previously followed which profession?
3 If you are in your birthday suit, what are you wearing?
4 Thailand was formerly known by what name?
5 Which letter describes a hard leaded pencil?
6 Which Zodiac sign is usually shown as a scorpion?
7 Osteoporosis affects which part of the body?
8 Where would you find an incisor?
9 Whose first UK No. 1 hit was Wherever I Lay My Hat?
10 According to the proverb, what happens if you spare the rod?
11 Stephane Grapelli is associated with which musical instrument?
12 What do vertebrates have that invertebrates do not?
13 Which vegetable can be dwarf, runner and broad?
14 Which Queen made a visit to Solomon in The Bible?
15 Who was Tony Blair's first Deputy PM?
16 Who wrote Lord of the Rings?
17 Which river is the longest in the British Isles?
18 On which date is Saint Andrew's Day?
19 Which is largest - cello, viola or double bass?
20 Which epic film had the theme tune Somewhere My Love?
21 Terry Wogan's daily show is on which radio station?
22 Buckingham Palace is at the end of which famous London road?
23 A muezzin is an official of which religion?
24 Who used the catch phrase, "Ooh, you are awful, but I like you"?
25 In which county is Salisbury Plain?
26 In Cockney rhyming slang, what is a tea leaf?
27 What colour is the skin of a kiwi fruit?
28 What does 'S' stand for in RSC?
29 What can be granny, sheepshank and bowline?
30 What do you need to sup with the devil, according to the proverb?

TV: Soaps (see Quiz 151)
1 Rita. 2 Australia. 3 EastEnders. 4 Family Affairs. 5 Coronation Street.
6 Emmerdale. 7 The Spice Girls. 8 Coronation Street. 9 Grant. 10 Liverpool.
11 Eco warrior. 12 EastEnders. 13 Brookside. 14 Dallas. 15 Shopping
centre. 16 Emmerdale. 17 Alma Baldwin. 18 EastEnders. 19 Close.
20 7.30 p.m.. 21 Friel. 22 Dot. 23 Oil. 24 Peggy. 25 Mike.
26 Duckworth. 27 Barlow. 28 EastEnders. 29 South Africa. 30 Liverpool.

LEVEL 1

1 Glaucoma affects which part of the body?
2 Which flightless bird lays the world's largest egg?
3 What is a puffball?
4 What happens to a female butterfly after it has laid its eggs?
5 In what type of environment do most crustaceans live?
6 Which natural disaster is measured on the Richter scale?
7 What is the main ingredient of glass?
8 Does a millipede have more, less or exactly 1,000 feet?
9 An ore is a mineral which contains a what?
10 Is the whale shark a mammal like the whale, or a fish like the shark?
11 Which bird is the symbol of the USA?
12 Are butterflies more colourful in warmer or cooler countries?
13 What sort of rock is lava?
14 Which is larger, the dolphin or the porpoise?
15 Which organ of the body has the aorta?
16 How many bones does a slug have?
17 Are worker ants male or female?
18 Altocumulus is a type of what?
19 What is the main source of energy in our ecosystem?
20 Which name for remains of plants and animals which lived on Earth means 'dug up'?
21 On which continent is the world's largest glacier?
22 Kelp is a type of what?
23 What order of mammals does the gibbon belong to?
24 What is the staple food of over half of the world's population?
25 Which creatures are larvae and pupae before being adults?
26 Are most bats visible at night or by day?
27 Which part of a jellyfish has stinging cells?
28 Natural rubber is obtained from what?
29 What is the mother of all the bees in a colony called?
30 The giant sequoia is the largest living what?

Quiz 154 Pot Luck 69

LEVEL 1

Answers - see page 163

1 Who appeared on The Cruise and became famous for her singing?
2 What is sugar added to, to make meringues?
3 Which poet laureate Sir John died in 1984?
4 What can pass through something if it is porous?
5 For which sport is Eddie Irvine famous?
6 How old should you be to marry without parental permission?
7 In The Bible, which angel foretold of the birth of Jesus?
8 What youth group took to wearing parkas?
9 What is the German word for the number three?
10 Which children's favourite bear said he had "very little brain"?
11 Which English king reputedly commanded the sea to retreat?
12 What is the letter "V" if A is Alpha and B is Bravo?
13 Whose is famous for saying, "Nice to see you, to see you nice"?
14 What is a popular name for the flower the antirrhinum?
15 Which Yorkshire city were Pulp from?
16 In music what does presto mean?
17 What object was invented by Lewis Waterman in 1884?
18 Tuscany is in which European country?
19 In the world of flying, what do the initials ETA stand for?
20 What is retsina?
21 Which Team featured Hannibal Smith?
22 Which monster first hit the headlines in 1933?
23 How many edges are there around a 20 pence coin?
24 What are the New Zealand rugby union team called?
25 According to the rhyme, who killed Cock Robin?
26 The Samba originated in which South American country?
27 Who wrote It Shouldn't Happen to a Vet?
28 The port of Gdansk is in which country?
29 Would you eat, play or sit on a sitar?
30 Which TV series included Sue Ellen and Miss Ellie?

Answers

Nature: Living World (see Quiz 153)
1 Eyes. 2 Ostrich. 3 Fungus. 4 It dies. 5 Water. 6 Earthquake. 7 Sand.
8 Less. 9 Metal. 10 Fish. 11 Eagle. 12 Warmer. 13 Volcanic rock.
14 Dolphin. 15 Heart. 16 None. 17 Female. 18 Cloud. 19 Sun.
20 Fossil. 21 Antarctica. 22 Seaweed. 23 Primates (also accept apes). 24
Rice. 25 Insects. 26 At night. 27 Tentacles. 28 Rubber Tree. 29 Queen.
30 Tree.

LEVEL 1

1 Which ex James Bond has 'Scotland Forever' tattooed on his arm?
2 Which Jools starred in Spiceworld: The Movie?
3 Which Irish born 007 starred in Tomorrow Never Dies?
4 Which Grease actor danced with Princess Diana at the White House?
5 Which sleuth did Albert Finney play in Agatha Christie's Murder on the Orient Express?
6 Which Attenborough brother is a film actor and director?
7 Who was the star of Moonwalker after being in The Jackson Five?
8 Which bespectacled US actor/director directed the musical Everyone Says I Love You?
9 What type of hat was Charlie Chaplin most famous for?
10 Who is Emma Forbes' actor/director dad?
11 Who was named after her home town of Winona?
12 Which knighted pop singer wrote the music for The Lion King?
13 Hayley Mills is the daughter of which knighted actor?
14 Who separated from husband Bruce Willis in 1998?
15 Which newspaper magnate bought 20th Century Fox in 1985?
16 Who was Sid played by Gary Oldman in Sid and Nancy?
17 What name usually associated with a schoolbag did Woody Allen give his son?
18 Which Welsh actor Sir Anthony bought part of Mount Snowdon in 1998?
19 Which pop star Tina starred in Mad Max Beyond the Thunderdome?
20 Which Ms Foster swapped her real first name from Alicia?
21 In rhyming slang what financial term is Gregory Peck?
22 Which child star was Shirley MacLaine named after?
23 Who appeared first at Madame Tussaud's, Harrison Ford or Hugh Grant?
24 Who starred as Steed in the film version of The Avengers?
25 Which boxer played himself in The Greatest?
26 Film buff Barry Norman is a member of which club with the same name as a Marx brother?
27 Who sang It's Not Unusual in Mars Attacks!?
28 Which racing driver Moss starred in Casino Royale?
29 Who are Cary, Katharine and James in The Philadelphia Story?
30 Whose real name is James Baumgarner?

Answers

Quiz 156 Pot Luck 70

Answers - see page 165

LEVEL 1

1 Which actress plays Ruth in the TV comedy Babes In The Wood?
2 Who wrote the novel You Only Live Twice?
3 Which English county has a border with only one other county?
4 What collective name is given to the structure of bones in the body?
5 The drink port takes its name from which town?
6 What colour is normally associated with ecological groups?
7 What is the hardest substance known to man?
8 Which people are associated with the Jolly Roger flag?
9 What is the French word for the number two?
10 Alphabetically, which is the second of the 12 calendar months?
11 With which sport do we associate a half nelson?
12 Which muscle is the largest - heart, biceps or buttocks?
13 Which actor played Che in Evita when Madonna was Eva Peron?
14 Which country did the paso doble dance originate in?
15 What type of food can be pilau?
16 In which American city is a 500 mile motor race run annually?
17 Which cartoon cat never manages to catch Tweetie Pie?
18 What is Britain's busiest ferry passenger port?
19 What kind of animal is a hind?
20 What can pass through something if it is translucent?
21 Which Tony first became MP for Sedgefield in 1983?
22 How many sides do seven hexagons have?
23 Was Crackerjack shown on BBC or ITV?
24 What is the letter "D" if A is Alpha and B is Bravo?
25 Which country does the drink sake come from?
26 For which sport is Pat Eddery famous?
27 What colour is saffron?
28 In children's books and on TV, what kind of animal is Babar?
29 Which group entered the UK charts in 1995 with Lifted?
30 What term is used in golf to indicate the stroke rating for each hole?

1   What is a bookmaker's licensed premises called?
2   What shape is the target in archery?
3   Where on a dartboard is the bull?
4   Which cubes are necessary for a game of craps?
5   Which direction do you go if you are abseiling?
6   What sort of Park is at Whipsnade?
7   Which locomotive identification hobby shares its name with a controversial 90s movie?
8   In which game do you aim to call "House!"?
9   Yoga was developed from which nation's religion?
10 Is scuba practised above or below the water's surface?
11 From which part of a vehicle might you sell goods to raise cash?
12 What name is given to a small piece of land rented for growing food?
13 In the UK most Bank Holidays fall on which day of the week?
14 Which commodities would you buy at a PYO centre?
15 What does E stand for in NEC?
16 What colour is the baize on a snooker table?
17 Which word precedes sport to describe killing animals for recreation?
18 What type of weapon is used in fencing?
19 What is the name of a coach trip where few know the destination?
20 If you practised on a pommel horse where would you probably be?
21 The Chamber of Horrors is in which London waxworks museum?
22 Which weekly draw is run by Camelot?
23 Are bonsai trees smaller or larger than average?
24 Which club moved to The Riverside in the 1990s?
25 What sort of establishment is a greasy spoon?
26 Who is a tied house usually tied to?
27 What is the type of billiards played in pubs called?
28 The Summer Bank Holiday takes place in which month in the UK?
29 Which name for an expert in a particular hobby is the same as a padded jacket?
30 What does Y stand for in DIY?

Answers

Pot Luck 71 (see Quiz 158)
1 70s. 2 Middlesborough. 3 Cuba. 4 Springfield. 5 Seven. 6 Toboggan.
7 Goliath. 8 On water - it's a boat. 9 Costner. 10 Elephant. 11 Tower
Bridge. 12 Their gills. 13 Meat. 14 Six. 15 Possession. 16 Green & Yellow.
17 Nephews. 18 Eins. 19 James Herriot. 20 Catherine Wheel. 21 Victoria.
22 Canaveral. 23 Mineral water. 24 Baldrick. 25 Pounds. 26 650.
27 Rome. 28 Yellow. 29 Moses. 30 Six.

Quiz 158 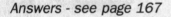 Pot Luck 71

Answers - see page 167

LEVEL 1

1 Did Britain join the EEC in the 60s, 70s or 80s?
2 At which club did Gazza and Paul Merson play in the same team?
3 The Rumba originated in which country?
4 Where do the cartoon Simpsons live?
5 How many edges are there around a 50 pence coin?
6 What type of vehicle is seen on the Cresta Run?
7 Which Biblical giant was killed by David?
8 Where would you find a useful junk?
9 Which Kevin was Wyatt Earp in the 1994 movie?
10 Which animal does ivory predominantly come from?
11 Which London bridge opens upwards to let tall ships through?
12 Fish breathe through what?
13 What was sold at London's Smithfield market?
14 How many noughts are there in the written number one million?
15 According to the saying, what is "nine points of the law"?
16 What colour is earth in modern three core electric cables?
17 What relation are Huey, Dewey and Louie to Donald Duck?
18 What is the German word for the number one?
19 Who wrote the novel All Creatures Great and Small?
20 Which firework is named after a saint?
21 Which Queen became Empress of India in 1876?
22 From which cape is the American Space Shuttle launched?
23 Vichy is famous for which drink?
24 Which Blackadder character had a fascination for turnips?
25 According to the saying, which money will look after itself?
26 How many centimetres are there in six and a half metres?
27 The Vatican City is within which other capital city?
28 What colour is the shade of jonquil?
29 In The Bible, who was found in the bulrushes?
30 How many points does a snowflake have?

Answers

Hobbies & Leisure 5 (see Quiz 157)
1 Betting shop. 2 Circular. 3 Centre. 4 Dice. 5 Downwards. 6 Animal Park.
7 Trainspotting. 8 Bingo. 9 Indian. 10 Below. 11 Car boot. 12 Allotment.
13 Monday. 14 Fruit and vegetables (Pick Your Own). 15 Exhibition.
16 Green. 17 Blood. 18 Sword. 19 Mystery tour. 20 Gym. 21 Madame
Tussaud's. 22 The National Lottery. 23 Smaller. 24 Middlesbrough. 25 Cafe.
26 Brewery. 27 Bar billiards. 28 August. 29 Anorak. 30 Yourself.

1   Which ice dance pair have the freedom of the city of Nottingham?
2   Which Frank Sinatra classic did Geoff Boycott choose on Desert Island Discs?
3   What sort of animal takes part in a point-to-point?
4   In snooker what colour ball scores least?
5   In which country did sumo wrestling originate?
6   What was the name of Damon Hill's racing driver father?
7   Mike Tyson was suspended for biting off which part of Evander Holyfield?
8   In which sport did Justin Rose become a pro after the '98 British Open?
9   In which Channel does the Admiral's Cup take place?
10   Which Scot Stephen won five successive snooker world championships in the 90s?
11   What do Redgrave and Pinsent race in?
12   Which Walter won the Derby on Lammtara in 1995?
13   In athletics what is the shortest outdoor track race?
14   What is the national sport of Spain known as corrida de toros?
15   How often is the Grand National normally run?
16   What would you ride in a velodrome?
17   Which sport has Australian Rules?
18   Which golfer Jack was known as the Golden Bear?
19   How long does the annual motor race at Le Man last?
20   The 'Golden Gloves' championship is in which sport?
21   The Fastnet Race is competed for on what type of surface?
22   Which youngsters run between the ends of the net during a tennis match ?
23   How does soccer player Dennis Bergkamp refuse to travel?
24   In which sport do you try to play below par?
25   Which Frankie had seven wins at Ascot at odds of 25,095 to 1?
26   How was Sir Garfield St Auburn Sobers known as a player?
27   Which sport do The Barbarians play?
28   Which game can be lawn or crown green?
29   Which two continents compete for the Ryder Cup?
30   Which jockey was jailed in the 80s for tax evasion?

1   Where are you if Mrs Goggins serves you in the post office?
2   Whose catchphrase was, "Didn't they do well"?
3   What percentage is half of a half?
4   Which late Michael was lead singer with INXS?
5   What happens if a bookie is "warned off Newmarket Heath"?
6   ABTA is concerned with which group of people?
7   In the body, which organ secretes bile?
8   In Switzerland, which famous soccer club has an insect name?
9   Which Julia starred as a waitress in Mystic Pizza?
10 What will Harvard University always be in America?
11 Which country was the first to use postage stamps?
12 Which part of his anatomy did Tony Bennett leave in San Francisco?
13 What does Bill Oddie like to go outside to watch?
14 Which Peter made the album Solsbury Hill?
15 Was the great racehorse Red Rum coloured red?
16 Traditionally, what colour is willow pattern?
17 How many members were there in the group The Carpenters?
18 Sauciehall Street is in which city?
19 Wasim Akram first played County Cricket for which county?
20 Which group was fronted by Bryan Ferry?
21 What is the distinctive pattern on Dennis The Menace's shirt?
22 In The Bible, who cut off Samson's hair?
23 The province of Manitoba is in which country?
24 Was Gazza's first foreign club based in France, Italy or Spain?
25 Which cowboy had a horse named Silver?
26 Is St Andrew's golf course on the east or west coast of Scotland?
27 Which Monica became intimately associated with Bill Clinton?
28 How many sides would four trapezium's have?
29 Which Liam married Patsy Kensit in 1997?
30 St Peter Port is on which island?

1   Who travelled from Pole to Pole and Around the World in 80 Days?

2   Which Newsnight interrogator has the nickname Paxo?

3   Clive James hails from which Commonwealth country?

4   Who was born John Cheese and changed his name by one letter?

5   Which Magnusson was given the first TV interview by Earl Spencer after his sister's death?

6   Which David and Jonathan hosted the 1998 Election coverage?

7   Which Gardener's World presenter wrote a novel Mr MacGregor?

8   Which Kate won an OBE for her reporting in Beijing and the Gulf?

9   Which famous part of her did Friends' Rachel advertise?

10 Anthony Worrall Thompson replaced Michael Barry on which food magazine show?

11 Which Sir David's catchphrase is "Hello, good evening and welcome"?

12 After 25 years at the BBC which football pundit went to Sky in 1998?

13 Which Paula gave interviews on her bed in The Big Breakfast?

14 Which Irishman has presented The Eurovision Song Contest?

15 Which practical joke Jeremy first hosted You've Been Framed?

16 Which 'big name' moved her talk show from ITV to BBC in 1998?

17 Is Paul Ross the brother, son or no relation of Jonathan Ross?

18 Whose catchphrase was 'Awight!'?

19 Which stock cube did Lynda Bellingham advertise?

20 How are TV cooks Clarissa and Jennifer better known?

21 What is Anthea Turner's TV presenter sister called?

22 Who was the footballing team captain on They Think It's All Over?

23 Who is actor Tony Britton's TV presenter daughter?

24 Ian McCaskill retired from presenting what in 1998?

25 Which Gloria presented an Open House on Channel 5?

26 In Ground Force is it Charlie or Tommy who has long red hair?

27 What are the first names of Reeves and Mortimer?

28 Which Judith did Anthea Turner replace on Wish You Were Here?

29 Which Match of the Day presenter took on a Radio 2 show in 1998?

30 What is Prime Suspect actress star Helen Mironoff's real name?

Pot Luck 73 (see Quiz 162)

Answers

1 Wherever I Lay My Hat. 2 13. 3 Hip. 4 Black Sea. 5 Carbon dioxide. 6 Hamlet. 7 Basketball. 8 Richard Branson. 9 Mary Poppins. 10 Seven. 11 June. 12 Gideons. 13 Shakespeare. 14 Member (of the Order) of the British Empire. 15 Country. 16 Jonah. 17 Motorcycling. 18 Louis Armstrong. 19 Primer. 20 Ludo. 21 Truro. 22 Anatomy. 23 Farming & Agriculture. 24 Time. 25 West Sussex. 26 Sherry. 27 Actual Bodily Harm. 28 Matador. 29 House of Commons. 30 Funf.

1   What was Paul Young's only UK No. 1 hit in 1983?

2   How many players are on a cricket field during normal play?

3   What fruit comes from the rose?

4   The River Danube flows out into which Sea?

5   Which gas puts the bubbles into bottled fizzy drinks?

6   Which Shakespeare character gave the "To be or not to be" speech?

7   The Harlem Globe Trotters are famous in which sport?

8   Who is older Richard Branson or William Hague?

9   "Supercalifragilisticexpialidocious" comes from which Disney movie?

10 How many noughts are there in the written number ten million?

11 Which month of the year in Britain includes the longest day?

12 Copies of The Bible are left in hotel rooms by which religious organisation?

13 Who wrote the play A Winter's Tale?

14 What do the initials M.B.E. stand for?

15 What have you betrayed if you commit treason?

16 Who was swallowed by a whale in The Bible?

17 For which sport is Mick Doohan famous?

18 Which musician had the nickname 'Satchmo'?

19 When decorating what name is given to the first coat?

20 What is the children's version of backgammon called?

21 What is the administrative headquarters of the county of Cornwall?

22 Which scientific word deals with the structure of the body?

23 The Royal Smithfield Show is connected to which industry?

24 What does a chronometer measure?

25 Chichester is the county town of which county?

26 Jerez in Spain is famous for which alcoholic drink?

27 In crime what do the initials A.B.H. stand for?

28 In a bull fight, what name is given to the person who kills the bull?

29 Which is the Lower House in British politics?

30 What is the German word for the number five?

LEVEL 1

1 Which pop band did Geri Halliwell leave in Spring 1998?
2 What is the married name of Cherie Booth QC?
3 Who was the fiancee of Michael Hutchence at the time of his death?
4 What is Caroline Aherne's showbiz pensioner persona?
5 Which London store did Mohammed Al-Fayed buy in 1985?
6 What is the first name of politician turned author Lord Archer?
7 Who is the man behind the Virgin group?
8 What type of adviser was subsequent bankrupt John Bryan to Fergie?
9 Which footballer married Sheryl and had a son called Regan?
10 Which Tory politician did Ffion Jenkins marry?
11 Which rock star did Texan model Jerry Hall marry in 1990?
12 In which country was Ulrika Jonsson born?
13 Which radio DJ has his own company, Ginger Productions?
14 Who left husband Peter Powell for Grant Bovey in 1998?
15 How is former Royal girlfriend Kathleen Stark better known?
16 Who founded the London nightclub Stringfellow's?
17 Which country did Earl Spencer move to in the mid 1990s?
18 Which Royal was Lord Snowdon married to?
19 What was Liz Hurley's infamous Versace dress held together with?
20 Which millionairess cook is a director of Norwich City Football Club?
21 Which chain of cosmetics shops did Anita Roddick found?
22 What was the sporting profession of Jemima Khan's husband?
23 What is Camilla Shand's married name?
24 What is Simon Le Bon's model wife called?
25 Which celebrity actor Grant's middle name is Mungo?
26 Which nightclub was named after Lady Annabel Goldsmith?
27 What does John Galliano design?
28 Which Nigel writes about celebs in his Daily Mail diary?
29 Which Foreign Secretary did Gaynor Regan marry in 1998?
30 What is the first name of PR man Mr Clifford?

Quiz 164 Pot Luck 74

Answers - see page 173

LEVEL 1

1 For which sport is Paula Radcliffe famous?
2 In the TV song, who was the 'Wonder Horse'?
3 Who wrote the novel "Let Sleeping Vets Lie"?
4 Which of Jacob's sons had a coat of many colours, in The Bible?
5 In crime what do the initials G.B.H. stand for?
6 According to the saying, how will March go out if it comes in like a lion?
7 Which Disney movie includes the song Whistle While You Work?
8 After how many years must an election be held in Britain?
9 Jamaica is in which sea?
10 Which country does the musical instrument the sitar come from?
11 Which kind of farming is arable farming?
12 Which famous film star gave her name to a life jacket?
13 Where would you wear an epaulette?
14 Which kind of spaniel was named after a king?
15 In the army what is an MP?
16 Is a jellyfish a mineral, vegetable or animal?
17 In the Sixties what was Biba?
18 In politics, what do the initials M.E.P. stand for?
19 In 1993, which horse race was made void after a false start?
20 Which two letters form the symbol for the element magnesium?
21 How many centimetres are there in twenty metres?
22 Which month of the year in Britain includes the shortest day?
23 Who killed the giant Goliath?
24 What is prepared in a tannery?
25 How many lines are there in a limerick?
26 Which member of the Beatles sang Imagine?
27 Which are the two main political parties in America?
28 What is the administrative headquarters of the county of Wiltshire?
29 What is the French word for the number ten?
30 Did Harry Corbett, Harry H Corbett or Ronnie Corbett work with Sooty?

Quiz 165 Children's TV

LEVEL 1

1   What mighty hero did Prince Adam turn into with the aid of Greyskull castle?
2   Where is Grange Hill Comprehensive?
3   What was the follow up to How!?
4   Tom Baker was the longest serving Doctor in which sci fi series?
5   Which children's favourite has the number plate PAT 1?
6   Which Linford presented Record Breakers?
7   Which Engine's friends were Terence the Tractor and Bertie the Bus?
8   Does Tom or Jerry have the furrier coat?
9   What cuddly creatures are Uncle Bulgaria and Orinoco?
10 What was Worzel Gummidge?
11 Are Smurfs blue or orange?
12 Which Street teaches about letters and numbers?
13 What sort of creature is Pingu?
14 Which family is headed by Homer?
15 What colour is Teletubby Laa Laa?
16 Which Bear was found in a London railway station?
17 What is Popeye's occupation?
18 What sort of creature is Children's BBC's Otis?
19 What is the most number of presenters Blue Peter has at once?
20 Matthew Corbett said goodbye to which puppet companion in 1998?
21 What sort of animal was Huckleberry?
22 Which Grove is a children's drama series?
23 Who is Dastardly's canine sidekick?
24 On Your Marks and Art Attack are about what subject?
25 Spot is chiefly what colour?
26 Which heroic earth organisation fought Spectra in Battle of the Planets?
27 What sort of animal is Garfield?
28 What is Casper?
29 What Sentinels were Mercury, Hercules and Astria?
30 What kind of prehistoric creature is Dink?

Pot Luck 75 (see Quiz 166)

Answers

1 Butterfly. 2 Two. 3 The eye. 4 Red rose. 5 Jamaica. 6 Tom Hanks.
7 Lisa Riley. 8 Alcohol. 9 Trois. 10 Animal. 11 Motor racing. 12 Fire.
13 Reveille. 14 Limerick. 15 John Smith. 16 Max Bygraves. 17 K.
18 Greece. 19 Mrs Laurence. 20 A brush. 21 El Salvador. 22 Etc.
23 A jellyfish. 24 Zoos. 25 A Tap. 26 U. 27 Tom. 28 Ulrika Jonsson.
29 Not speaking to them. 30 Three.

1 Which swimming stroke was introduced in the 1956 Olympics?
2 What's the greatest number of consecutive calendar months with 31 days?
3 What name is given to the calm area at the centre of a hurricane?
4 Which flower is the symbol of the Labour Party in Britain?
5 Kingston is the capital of which island nation?
6 Who played Forrest in the 1994 film Forrest Gump?
7 Who replaced Jeremy Beadle to present You've Been Framed!?
8 Complete the Oasis song title "Cigarettes and ....?
9 What is the French word for the number three?
10 Are sponges mineral, vegetable or animal?
11 For which sport is Jean Alesi famous?
12 According to the proverb, there's no smoke without what?
13 Which army bugle call is played to wake up the troops?
14 Which Irish town gives its name to a five line humorous verse?
15 Who preceded Tony Blair as Labour Party leader?
16 Who is renowned for saying, "I wanna tell you a story"?
17 Which letter of the alphabet is used as a measure of the size of a computer's memory?
18 Which country produces the pine scented wine called retsina?
19 What is the Princess Royal's married name?
20 What name is given to a fox's tail?
21 San Salvador is in which country?
22 Which abbreviation means "and so on"?
23 What is a Portuguese Man-o'-War?
24 What do Whipsnade, Chessington and London have in common?
25 What is the English equivalent of the American 'faucet'?
26 Alphabetically, which letter is the last of the vowels?
27 Which name links golfers Kite and Watson?
28 Who presents Gladiators with Jeremy Guscott?
29 What are we not doing if we send someone to Coventry?
30 How many balls are used in billiards?

1   Tikka is a dish in which country's cookery?
2   A strudel is usually filled with which fruit?
3   What relation is Albert to fellow chef and restaurateur Michel Roux?
4   Which pasta sauce originated in Bologna in Italy?
5   What is a frankfurter?
6   How are eggs usually cooked in the breakfast dish bacon and eggs?
7   What is fromage frais a soft type of?
8   Does an Italian risotto contain rice or pasta?
9   Over what would you normally pour a vinaigrette dressing?
10   Rick Stein's restaurant and cooking specialises in what?
11   What colour wine is a Valpolicella?
12   In which country did Chianti originate?
13   What is the main filling ingredient of a quiche?
14   Is a poppadum crisp or soft?
15   What sort of drink is espresso?
16   Is brioche a type of bread or a fruit?
17   What shape is the pasta used to make lasagne?
18   What is mozzarella?
19   What colour is fudge?
20   Which north of England county is famous for its hotpot?
21   Do you eat or drink a loyal toast?
22   What type of meat is found in a cock-a-leekie soup?
23   Which food links Gary Lineker and The Spice Girls?
24   What is the alcoholic ingredient of Gaelic coffee?
25   Which fruit is usually used in marmalade?
26   At what age can you legally drink alcohol in an pub?
27   What does G stand for in G and T?
28   What are the two main colours of liquorice Allsorts?
29   Would you eat or drink schnapps?
30   A Conference is what type of fruit?

Quiz 168 Pot Luck 76

LEVEL 1

1   According to the proverb, what plays when the cat's away?
2   Did Harry Vardon give his name to a disease, a sport's trophy or a fruit?
3   Which people wore moccasins originally?
4   Which Royal was born in 1900?
5   What is the main spoken language in Mexico?
6   In which year did Hong Kong revert to being part of China?
7   Who had hits with Magic Moments and Catch a Falling Star?
8   How many noughts are there in the written number fifty two million?
9   Which season comes just before Christmas in the Christian calendar?
10 Which long dress is traditionally worn by Japanese women?
11 In The Bible, on which mountain was Moses told the commandments?
12 Actor John Pertwee played which TV scarecrow?
13 At which Park is Princess Diana buried?
14 What does the Q stand for in IQ?
15 Where was the first atomic bomb dropped on 6th August 1945?
16 White Hart Lane is home to which football club?
17 Philippa Forrester and Peter Snow co-hosted which science based TV programme?
18 Hanover, Westphalia and Bavaria are all parts of which country?
19 For which sport is Chris Eubank famous?
20 What is the French word for the number nine?
21 Which animal in the poem by Blake was described as "burning bright"?
22 What do Americans call a dinner jacket?
23 In which battle was King Harold killed?
24 What type of animal can be Dutch, Angora and Chinchilla?
25 Who was a Beirut hostage with John McCarthy and Brian Keenan ?
26 What colour was the "itsy bitsy teeny weeny bikini" in the pop song?
27 What do the initials VE stand for in VE Day?
28 How many hours are there in a week?
29 Which part of the body can suffer from an astigmatism?
30 Which Jewish girl kept a diary whilst hidden in Amsterdam in 1942?

LEVEL 1

1   Which great screen dancer is on the cover of Sgt Pepper?
2   Which wartime classic starred Ingrid Bergman and Humphrey Bogart?
3   Who is Jamie Lee Curtis's actor father?
4   Cary Grant was born in which west country port?
5   Was Rita Hayworth a blonde or a redhead?
6   Was it Bob Hope or Bing Crosby who was born in south London?
7   Which monster was arguably Boris Karloff's most famous role?
8   How was dancer Eugene Curran Kelly better known?
9   Who was the original Candle in the Wind dedicated to?
10 Which Anthony starred as the lead character in Psycho?
11 Which Sir Alec starred in, and had a share of the profits of, Star Wars?
12 Who was taller, Rock Hudson or Mickey Rooney?
13 Which James starred in Harvey and The Philadelphia Story?
14 Which Italian born actor is best known for silent movies such as The Sheikh?
15 Which Citizen was the subject of Orson Welles' first film?
16 Lauren Bacall was the wife of which Humphrey?
17 Tough guy Frank J Cooper adopted which first name?
18 Which Joan starred in Whatever Happened to Baby Jane?
19 How was Ruth Elizabeth Davis better known?
20 Which Charlie was a founder of the film studio United Artists?
21 Bing Crosby had just finished a round of which game when he died?
22 William Claude Dunkenfield used his first two initials to become who?
23 Jane and Peter are the children of which screen great Henry?
24 Which Katharine enjoyed a long on and off screen relationship with Spencer Tracy?
25 Which Doris enjoyed popularity in films with Rock Hudson?
26 He was born John Uhler Lemmon III but how is he known in films?
27 Who is Michael Douglas's famous actor father?
28 In which German capital was Marlene Dietrich born?
29 Did Clark Gable die during his last film in the 40s, 50s or 60s?
30 Greta Garbo was born in which Scandinavian capital?

LEVEL 1

1 Sicily, Lombardy and Tuscany are all parts of which country?

2 What kind of wind blows no good according to the proverb?

3 Which Disney movie includes the song A Whole New World?

4 What type of animal can be Charolais, Galloway and Simmental?

5 Which is the largest castle in Britain?

6 Where did King John sign the Magna Carta?

7 In which capital is the Capitol Building?

8 Where would you wear a cummerbund?

9 What is the German word for the number nine?

10 Which country had eleven kings called Rameses?

11 What appears most as the initial letter in calendar month names?

12 According to the rhyme, who fixed his head with vinegar and brown paper?

13 What name is given to the Japanese craft of paper folding?

14 Billy Smart and Chipperfields provided what type of entertainment?

15 What was the nationality of diarist Anne Frank?

16 What was the name of Superman's home planet?

17 Who or what are Oxford Bags?

18 What part of your body is covered by orthodontics?

19 Paella is a traditional dish from which country?

20 How many seconds are in a quarter of an hour?

21 Which Friends star has advertised L'Oreal?

22 What are COBOL, FORTRAN and ALGOL?

23 What type of person was Laughing in the famous portrait?

24 Which festival follows Lent in the Christian calendar?

25 What colour is the Financial Times?

26 Brittany and Picardy are parts of which country?

27 Which phobia describes the fear of spiders?

28 In medicine, what does a dermatologist specialise in?

29 Suffolk Punch, Shires and Clydesdales are all types of what?

30 For which sport are Robbie and Henry Paul famous?

Quiz 171 Geography: Euro Tour

Answers - see page 182

LEVEL 1

1 In which country would you find Jerez?
2 How would you travel if you left for France from a hoverport?
3 Eurostar trains run from London to which Belgian city?
4 In which country is Cologne?
5 Does London or Rome have the higher population?
6 The province of Flanders is in which country?
7 Which landlocked country is divided into cantons?
8 In which city would you find the Parthenon?
9 Bohemia is part of which Republic, formerly part of Czechoslovakia?
10 Is Schiphol an airport or a river in the Netherlands?
11 In which country is Estoril?
12 Where is the Black Forest?
13 What type of country is Monaco?
14 Andorra lies between France and which other country?
15 In which Sea does Cyprus lie?
16 Belarus and Ukraine were formerly part of which huge republic?
17 What is the English name for the city known to Italians as Venezia?
18 Is Sweden a kingdom or a republic?
19 Vienna lies on which river?
20 Is Ibiza part of the Canaries or the Balearics?
21 In which Circle does about a third of Finland lie?
22 The Hague is the seat of government of which country?
23 Crete and Corfu belong to which country?
24 Which Scandinavian country is opposite Norway and Sweden?
25 Is Europe the second largest or the second smallest continent?
26 Which country marks the most westerly point of mainland Europe?
27 The Iberian Peninsula consists of Portugal and which other country?
28 Which French city is Europe's largest?
29 What are the Balkans, the Apennines and the Pyrenees?
30 Which island is known to the French as Corse?

Answers

Pot Luck 78 (see Quiz 172)
1 Film. 2 Born. 3 Brian Johnston. 4 Reed. 5 60s. 6 Muslim. 7 Michael Heseltine. 8 Enfield. 9 Bees. 10 Four. 11 Falk. 12 Golf. 13 Provence. 14 Devon. 15 Greek gods. 16 Flint. 17 John Le Mesurier. 18 Irish. 19 Noddy. 20 Triangular. 21 England. 22 Furniture. 23 Witch. 24 Harmonica. 25 Sport. 26 Keystone. 27 Forty. 28 Meat Loaf. 29 Celtic. 30 Dog.

1 Which came first the film or stage show of Phantom Of The Opera?
2 In Bruce Springsteen songs what goes before In The USA and To Run?
3 Which famous cricket commentator died of a heart attack in January 1994?
4 Which Lou wrote and sang A Perfect Day?
5 Was Liz Hurley born in the 50s, 60, or 70s?
6 Which religion has people called to prayer by a muezzin?
7 Which Tory MP earned the name Goldilocks?
8 Which Harry created the character of Frank Doberman?
9 Which insects include drones, queens and workers?
10 Has a violin four, six or eight strings?
11 Which actor Peter played crumple coated cop Columbo?
12 Fuzzy Zoeller was linked with which sport?
13 Where did Peter Mayle spend a year of his life?
14 In which county was the Plymouth Brethren founded?
15 Athena, Nike and Zeus were all what?
16 Which Keith is lead singer with the Prodigy?
17 As what name did John Elton Halliley act in Dad's Army?
18 Which Derby is run at the Curragh?
19 Who had a best friend with the politically incorrect name of Big Ears?
20 A lateen sail is what shape?
21 Revie, Robson, and Taylor have all managed which team?
22 Which valuable things were made by Thomas Sheraton?
23 On TV, Sabrina is the name of the Teenage... what?
24 Which musical instrument does Larry Adler play?
25 Tony Banks was Minister for what in Tony Blair's first Cabinet?
26 What type of crazy cops were created by Mack Sennett?
27 What do XL stand for in Roman numerals?
28 What's the foodie stage name of sizeable singer Marvin Lee Aday?
29 Brady, Macari and Stein have managed which Scottish soccer club?
30 What kind of animal is a fox terrier?

Answers

Geography: Euro Tour (see Quiz 171)
1 Spain. 2 Hovercraft. 3 Brussels. 4 Germany. 5 London. 6 Belgium.
7 Switzerland. 8 Athens. 9 Czech Republic. 10 Airport. 11 Portugal. 12 Germany. 13 Principality. 14 Spain. 15 Mediterranean. 16 USSR.
17 Venice. 18 Kingdom. 19 Danube. 20 Balearics. 21 Arctic Circle.
22 Netherlands. 23 Greece. 24 Denmark. 25 Second smallest.
26 Portugal. 27 Spain. 28 Paris. 29 Mountain ranges. 30 Corsica.

Quiz 173 Nature: Plant World

Answers - see page 183

LEVEL 1

1   Where is water stored in a cactus plant?
2   Are most conifers evergreen or deciduous?
3   Ceps and chanterelles are types of what?
4   Flax is grown to produce which fabric?
5   Which drug is obtained from the coca plant?
6   Bamboo is the tallest type of what?
7   Which Mexican drink comes from the agave plant?
8   Is it true or false that laurel has poisonous leaves?
9   The petiole is on which part of a plant?
10   What colour is cuckoo spit?
11   Juniper is the flavouring in which drink?
12   What colour are oil seed rape flowers?
13   What goes before lavender and holly to make another plant's name?
14   What can be obtained from the cassava plant which would have gone in a typical
     school dinner pudding?
15   Harebells are usually what colour?
16   Does a polyanthus have a single or several blooms?
17   Which ingredient in tonic water comes from the bark of the cinchona?
18   Which plants would a viticulturist grow?
19   Wild cornflowers are usually what colour?
20   Which paintbrush cleaner is found in the resin of a conifer?
21   Which pear has the most protein?
22   In the garden what would you use secateurs for?
23   Do peanuts grow on trees or low plants?
24   What colour is chlorophyll?
25   In which Gardens is the Princess of Wales Conservatory?
26   Cacti are native to which continent?
27   What would you find in an arboretum?
28   Which fast grower is nicknamed the mile-a-minute vine?
29   Which yellow flower is nicknamed the Lent lily?
30   Which trees carry their seeds in cones?

Answers

Pot Luck 79 (see Quiz 173)
1 A will. 2 Four. 3 Warwick. 4 Lewis Collins. 5 Zwanzig. 6 Bryan Adams.
7 A cactus. 8 Brazil. 9 Street-Porter. 10 Australia. 11 Eight. 12 Black.
13 Landscape Gardening. 14 A size of paper. 15 Edward Woodward. 16 A
herb. 17 River Niagara. 18 Snow White. 19 Horse racing. 20 Beef. 21 Purple.
22 Three. 23 Alaska. 24 Val Doonican. 25 Simple Simon. 26 Luke and Matt
Goss. 27 A kind of plum. 28 Fourteen. 29 Lizzie. 30 Flattery.

1 If you die intestate you have not made what?

2 What's the least number of Mondays that can occur in July?

3 Which Derek partnered John Cleland at the Vauxhall Touring Cars Team?

4 In the TV series The Professionals, who played Bodie?

5 What is the German word for the number twenty?

6 Who had a No. 1 UK hit with Everything I do, I do it for You?

7 What is a prickly pear?

8 Romario starred in the 1994 World Cup for which country?

9 Media person Janet Bull changed her last name to what in her search for 'yoof'?

10 Bob Hawke was prime minister of which country?

11 How many coins does Great Britain have?

12 What colour is sable in heraldry?

13 For what was Capability Brown famous?

14 What is foolscap?

15 On TV who played the Equaliser?

16 What kind of plant is marjoram?

17 On which River are the Niagara Falls?

18 Which Disney movie includes the song Heigh-Ho?

19 For which sport is Willie Carson famous?

20 Sirloin, Rump and Topside are all joints of which meat?

21 What colour is Tinky Winky in the Teletubbies?

22 How many leaves are on a shamrock?

23 Which American state is the largest in area?

24 Which singer was associated with a rocking chair?

25 According to the nursery rhyme, who met a pieman going to the fair?

26 Which two brothers made up the group Bros?

27 What is a bullace?

28 How many lines are in a sonnet?

29 A Model T Ford was nicknamed Tin what?

30 According to the proverb, imitation is the sincerest form of what?

Nature: Plant World (see Quiz 173)

Answers

1 Stem. 2 Evergreen. 3 Fungi. 4 Linen. 5 Cocaine. 6 Grass. 7 Tequila. 8 True. 9 Leaf stalk. 10 White. 11 Gin. 12 Yellow. 13 Sea. 14 Tapioca. 15 Blue. 16 Several. 17 Quinine. 18 Vines. 19 Blue. 20 Turpentine. 21 Avocado. 22 Cutting, pruning. 23 Low plants. 24 Green. 25 Kew. 26 America. 27 Trees. 28 Russian Vine. 29 Daffodil. 30 Conifers.

1   What type of sport is eventing?
2   Which international side did Diego Maradona play for?
3   Phidippides was the first runner of which 26 mile race?
4   Which Stephen was the then youngest ever winner of a professional snooker title in 1987?
5   Did Evander Holyfield box at heavyweight or welterweight?
6   Which country did Virginia Leng represent at the Olympic Games?
7   FC Porto play football in which country?
8   At the USA PGA Championships, what game is played?
9   If you saw Benny the Dip win, what would you be watching?
10 At which sport might you see the American Williams sisters play?
11 Does the Le Mans 24 hour race take place in summer or winter?
12 In swimming, is freestyle usually performed on the back or front?
13 Which country won the first 25 America's Cup trophies in yachting?
14 In which sport is there a Foil discipline?
15 How was boxer Rocco Francis Marchegiano better known?
16 Caber tossing is native to which country?
17 What is the slowest swimming stroke?
18 For which national rugby side did Gavin Hastings play?
19 Magic Johnson found fame at which US sport?
20 Which horse race is sometimes called just The National?
21 What was tennis's Billie Jean Moffitt's married name?
22 Which Jackie's record of Grand Prix wins did Alain Prost pass in '87?
23 Which heavyweight Mike knocked out 15 of his first 25 pro opponents in the first round?
24 Which first name is shared by jockeys Carson and Shoemaker?
25 In which sport is a ball hit through a hoop with a mallet?
26 What is Scottish long distance runner Liz Lynch's married name?
27 What does the first F in FIFA stand for?
28 F1 driver Jacques Villeneuve is from which country?
29 Which winter sport can be alpine or Nordic?
30 Is the Oaks a race for colts or fillies?

Answers

Pot Luck 80 (see Quiz 176)
1 Two. 2 Mean. 3 Lettuce. 4 A flag. 5 An even number. 6 Fan-dabi-dozi.
7 Avocado pear. 8 The mirror. 9 Half a pound of tuppenny rice. 10 Eight.
11 A Watermelon. 12 Penny Black. 13 Judas. 14 Half a crown. 15 Zulu.
16 One. 17 The Alps. 18 Gold. 19 Pepper. 20 Westminster Abbey. 21 A
knot. 22 Coffee. 23 Victory. 24 Bread. 25 Green. 26 The harp. 27 Blue.
28 White Star Line. 29 An element. 30 Queen Victoria.

1   How many people perform a pas de deux in a ballet?
2   If T is time what is M in G.M.T.?
3   Cos and Iceberg are varieties of which salad plant?
4   As well as being a TV programme, what is a Blue Peter?
5   What type of number will you always get if you add two odd numbers together?
6   What was the phrase associated with the duo the Krankies?
7   Which pear is usually served as a starter and is not sweet?
8   Who told the Queen that Snow White was the "fairest of them all"?
9   What is mixed with half a pound of treacle in Pop goes the Weasel?
10 How many furlongs are there in a mile?
11 Which melon has black pips and red juicy flesh?
12 What was the common name for the first postage stamp?
13 Which biblical character had the second name Iscariot?
14 What was the name for two shillings and sixpence?
15 What is the letter "Z" if A is Alpha and B is Bravo?
16 How many hooks do you use for crochet?
17 The Matterhorn is in which European mountain range?
18 What did Fort Knox originally store?
19 Steak au poivre is steak covered in what?
20 Where did the Queen's Coronation take place?
21 If you asked a Scout to make a sheep-shank, what would he make?
22 What drink is the main export from Brazil?
23 What was the name of Admiral Nelson's ship?
24 Chapatti is a kind of Indian what?
25 What colour is the door of the pub the Rovers Return?
26 Which stringed instrument has the most strings in an orchestra?
27 What colour is connected with the River Danube?
28 Which shipping line did Titanic belong to?
29 What is the name of the glowing curly wire in a light bulb?
30 At the start of the 20th century who was Queen of England?

Answers

Sporting Chance 5 (see Quiz 175)
1 Equestrian. 2 Argentina. 3 Marathon. 4 Hendry. 5 Heavyweight.
6 Great Britain. 7 Portugal. 8 Golf. 9 Horse racing. 10 Tennis.
11 Summer. 12 Front. 13 USA. 14 Fencing. 15 Rocky Marciano.
16 Scotland. 17 Breast stroke. 18 Scotland. 19 Basketball. 20 Grand
National. 21 King. 22 Stewart. 23 Tyson. 24 Willie. 25 Croquet.
26 McColgan. 27 Federation. 28 Canada. 29 Skiing. 30 Fillies.

1   Which Grease classic begins "I got chills, they're multiplyin'"?
2   What's the title of The Spice Girls hit which begins "I'll tell you what I want, what I really really want"?
3   What is the first line of Nessun Dorma?
4   What did Tina Turner sing after "Do I love you my oh my"?
5   What follows the Beatles "will you still need me, will you still feed me"?
6   Which song begins, "I feel it in my fingers, I feel it in my toes"?
7   In Candle in the Wind 98 " how are England's hills described?
8   How many times is "submarine" sung in the chorus of Yellow Submarine?
9   Which hit began "Oh my love, my darlin', I hunger for your touch"?
10 Which song's second line is "and so I face the final curtain"?
11 Which song begins "First I was afraid I was petrified"?
12 In which song did Tammy Wynette bemoan "Sometime it's hard to be a woman"?
13 Which Slade Xmas hit has the line "Everybody's having fun"?
14 In the Titanic song what follows, "Near, far, wherever you are, I believe..."?
15 What follows Bryan Adams "Everything I do"?
16 Which Dire Straits hit begins "Here comes Johnny"?
17 What follows "Two little boys had two little....."?
18 Which charity hit has the line "Feed the world"?
19 What follows The Spice Girls "swing it, shake it, move it, make it"?
20 Which Abba hit states "I was defeated you won the war"?
21 What do neighbours become in the Neighbours theme song?
22 What follows "I believe for every drop of rain that falls"?
23 Which football anthem speaks of "Jules Rimet still leaming"?
24 Which song's second line is "I just called to say I care"?
25 Which Evita song begins, "It won't be easy, you'll think it strange"?
26 What did Boy George sing after singing karma five times?
27 Which Lion King song began "From the day we arrive on the planet"?
28 Which Simon & Garfunkel hit begins "When you're weary, feeling small"?
29 Which traditional song has the line, "The pipes, the pipes are calling"?
30 What are the last three words of Queen's We Are the Champions?

1   If Dennis is the Menace what is Beryl?
2   Who had a huge UK hit in September 1998 with Crush?
3   Which sweet flavoured herb is often used to accompany roast lamb?
4   According to the rhyme, which two characters followed Tinker Tailor?
5   Which French port is closest to Britain?
6   To see which sport could you go to Towcester?
7   Lammas Day is in which month?
8   In which county is the Royal Military Academy at Sandhurst?
9   Which brass instrument has a sliding, adjustable tube?
10 Which day's child is "full of grace" according to the traditional rhyme?
11 Which current day tax replaced Purchase tax in 1973?
12 Is a snowdrop grown from a bulb or seed?
13 What colour is Laa Laa in the Teletubbies?
14 For which sport is David Gower famous?
15 Who composed the music for Cats?
16 What do we call a group of stars?
17 Which soup is made from a variety of vegetables and pasta?
18 What sort of drink is Moet & Chandon?
19 Maurice Chevalier "thanked heaven" for what?
20 Which has smaller cards, an ordinary pack or a patience pack?
21 What gives cause for concern about the seeds of a laburnum tree?
22 What colour is argent in heraldry?
23 The city of Calcutta stands on which river?
24 Tea contains which acid?
25 Which High Street chemists shop opened its first store in 1877?
26 What are you probably buying if you are gazumped?
27 What does the Italian "per favore" mean?
28 What colour, together with yellow, is the Spanish flag?
29 In which county was Lord Nelson born?
30 What kind of drink can be Bristol Cream?

Answers

Pop: Karaoke (see Quiz 63, page 70)
1 You're the One That I Want. 2 Wannabe. 3 Nessun dorma, nessun dorma.
4 River deep mountain high. 5 When I'm sixty four. 6 Love Is All Around.
7 Greenest. 8 Six. 9 Unchained Melody. 10 My Way. 11 I Will Survive.
12 Stand By Your Man. 13 Merry Christmas Everybody. 14 That the heart does go
on. 15 I do it for you. 16 Walk of Life. 17 Toys. 18 Do They Know It's
Christmas? 19 Who do you think you are?. 20 Waterloo. 21 Good friends.

1 Which is the female half of Mulder and Scully?
2 What is the profession of TV's Two Fat Ladies?
3 What is the subject of the Channel 4 show Hooked?
4 Football Focus is a part of which Saturday sports programme?
5 What colour is Channel 5's logo?
6 Which Ally is a zany US TV lawyer?
7 What would Peter Cockcroft talk about on TV?
8 Who took over Gardener's World from the late Geoff Hamilton?
9 Which Australian co presents Animal Hospital?
10 Maureen Rees found TV fame at what type of School?
11 GMTV is usually seen at what time of day?
12 Which letters does TV's Kavanagh have after his name?
13 What sex is the audience of Chris Tarrant's show Man O Man?
14 Who presents the celebrity version of Ready Steady Cook?
15 Which TV presenter is Johnny Ball's daughter?
16 Which Mary founded the Clean Up TV campaign in 1964?
17 Which female pop quintet launched Channel 5?
18 Does Food & Drink's Oz Clarke specialise in food or drink?
19 Which Jerry hosts a controversial talk show?
20 In which work location was the series The Hello Girls set?
21 Which Carol took over from Anne Robinson on Points of View?
22 What links Terry Wogan, Les Dawson and Lily Savage?
23 Which part of the country is served by Anglia Television?
24 Ground Force offered a viewer a makeover in which part of the home?
25 Who is presenter Julia Carling's ex-husband?
26 'It's good to talk' was the ad slogan of which phone company?
27 Who is taller, Michael Barrymore or Ronnie Corbett?
28 Which broadcasting corporation is known as Auntie?
29 On which channel is Panorama broadcast?
30 Who is the human half of Wallace and Gromit?

1 For which sport is Eric Bristow famous?

2 According to the nursery rhyme, who cut off the three mice tails?

3 Which is the largest musical instrument which has a keyboard?

4 What is mined at Kimberley in South Africa?

5 What does a German mean if he says something is "kaput"?

6 Who had a No. 1 UK hit in September 1998 with Bootie Call?

7 Which George Orwell novel has a year as its title?

8 Cider is made from which fruit?

9 What was the smallest county in England until 1974?

10 Which Disney movie includes the song He's A Tramp?

11 Which children's TV series was forty years old in October 1998?

12 What is dried in Kentish oast houses?

13 Which fruit can be served Belle Helene?

14 Which Day gave Cliff Richard a No. 1 for Christmas 1990?

15 Who is older Paul Merson or Paul Merton?

16 What colour along with red and blue is the Luxembourg flag?

17 What happened to Solomon Grundy on Wednesday, according to the rhyme?

18 Which Olympic ice skating duo danced to Ravel's Bolero?

19 On the Union Jack, how many blue triangles are there?

20 What does a choreographer plan?

21 What is a yucca?

22 In pop music, who is Jagger's long time writing partner?

23 What colour is Po in the Teletubbies?

24 Crossroads was set near which major city?

25 How many people are in a boat in a rowing coxed pair race?

26 What is sometimes called the 'Old Lady of Threadneedle Street'?

27 Which race meeting is known as 'Glorious'?

28 What was invented by Dom Peter Perignon, a French monk?

29 Is a tulip grown from seed or a bulb?

30 Which American city has the Yankees and Mets baseball teams?

1   What is the surname of German F1 drivers Ralph and Michael?
2   Which jump event did Carl Lewis specialise in as well as sprinting?
3   What colour is the cover of the Rothman's Football Yearbook?
4   Is professional badminton an indoor or outdoor game or both?
5   What was the professional name of boxer Joe Louis Barrow?
6   Who won the European Cup-winner's Cup in 1998?
7   Of the 197 teams invited to the 1996 Olympics, how many accepted?
8   At which sport did suspended Irish Olympic gold medal winner Michelle de Bruin compete?
9   Which horned animal name does Leeds' Rugby Super League team have?
10 In which sport might you hit another living thing with a crop?
11 Peter O'Sullevan commentated on which sport?
12 Which Rugby side shares its name with stinging insects?
13 Which red flower is the emblem of the England Rugby Union team?
14 In which country is the golfing venue Valderrama?
15 Which motoring Grand Prix is held at the Hungaroring?
16 What's the highest score in darts from three different doubles?
17 In which country is the oldest football league in the world?
18 Which area of New York has a Globetrotters basketball team?
19 Which Bin was introduced for Rugby League players in 1983?
20 How many disciplines are there in a biathlon?
21 In which Sheffield theatre were the World Snooker Championships first held in 1977?
22 In which country was judo coincidentally added to the Olympic programme?
23 In badminton what were goose feathers used for?
24 What is the usual surface of the lane in ten pin bowling?
25 Which German Men's Wimbledon champion was born on Billie Jean King's 23rd birthday?
26 Which positive statement did Magic Johnson make prior to temporary retirement?
27 On what surface is curling played?
28 Which animal is on top of Rugby's Calcutta Cup?
29 In which sport would you wear a judogi?
30 What type of sporting event was The Rumble in the Jungle?

Quiz 182 Pot Luck 83

Answers - see page 191

LEVEL 1

1   What colour is Michael Aspel's book on This is your Life?
2   What is a tam-o'-shanter?
3   Which organ is particularly affected by hepatitis?
4   Who played the title role in the film Educating Rita?
5   On which river estuary does Swansea stand?
6   The letters F.R.A.M. mean a Fellow of which Royal Academy?
7   For which sport was Duncan Goodhew famous?
8   The raven is traditionally associated with which Tower?
9   Who played Inspector Clouseau in the Pink Panther films?
10 In which country is the Big Apple?
11 What is a cockchafer?
12 Which animal isle is in the River Thames?
13 Where did a famous battle take place in 1066?
14 Which elephants are the largest - African or Indian?
15 Which English musician and comedian married Tuesday Weld?
16 Who released I Believe coupled with Up On The Roof?
17 What kind of mammal is a chamois?
18 Which fabric is produced from flax?
19 Does coq au vin contain red or white wine?
20 Which TV series is set in Sun Hill police station?
21 During the Gulf War, who was the leader of Iraq?
22 Which TV puppet programme makes fun of politicians?
23 Which car maker has the same name as a London bridge?
24 Which animal should you take by the horns, according to the proverb?
25 How many pins are in the back row of a ten pin bowling triangle?
26 Which city is furthest North - Bristol or Sheffield?
27 Which of Chippendale, Ming and Wedgwood is not a type of pottery?
28 How much gold is there in a one pound coin?
29 What are a pig's feet called?
30 Of which country's coast is the world's largest coral reef?

Quiz 183 Movies: The Brits

LEVEL 1

1   What was the Spice Girls' first film?
2   Who with The Shadows starred in The Young Ones?
3   Which movie told of redundant steel workers becoming strippers?
4   The Bridge on the River Kwai prisoners are imprisoned by whom?
5   Nick Hornby's Fever Pitch is about which game?
6   Which Kenneth directed and starred in Hamlet?
7   The Blue Lamp preceded which TV series about PC George Dixon?
8   A BAFTA is a British Award for film and what?
9   What nationality was The...Patient in the 1996 Oscar winner?
10 Which US food expert Loyd is the son in law of David Puttnam?
11 Mrs Blake Edwards won an Oscar for Mary Poppins; who was she?
12 What is the nationality of Sir Anthony Hopkins?
13 In which part of the UK was Trainspotting set?
14 Which British Transport Minister twice won an Oscar?
15 Which Sir Richard directed Chaplin?
16 Which 1994 British hit shot Hugh Grant to superstardom?
17 Which Emma wrote the screenplay for Sense & Sensibility?
18 Jenny Agutter found fame in which movie about an Edwardian family?
19 Is Helena Bonham Carter a British Prime Minister's or a US President's grand daughter?
20 Elizabeth Taylor was twice married to this Welsh actor; who was he?
21 Who was born Maurice Micklewhite but is perhaps best known as Alfie?
22 Which Julie was Oscar nominated in 1998?
23 Which Ewan plays the young Obi Wan Kenobi in Episode I of Star Wars
24 In which film did Tom Conti play Pauline Collins' Greek lover?
25 Which blonde bombshell was born Diana Fluck?
26 Linus Roache's father has played which Coronation Street character since the soap began?
27 Who or what was the film Wilde with Stephen Fry about?
28 In which film did Joanna Lumley play Shirley's old school friend?
29 In which part of the UK was Robert Carlyle born?
30 Hot Chocolate's You Sexy Thing was the theme for which 1997 film?

Answers

Pot Luck 84 (see Quiz 184)
1 France. 2 Windsor Castle. 3 Yogi Bear. 4 Lime. 5 Badminton. 6 Oysters.
7 Norman Watts. 8 Five. 9 Four. 10 Coronation. 11 Flock together.
12 Poet. 13 Ten shilling note. 14 Javelin. 15 Cornwall. 16 A catamaran.
17 Eeyore. 18 L. S. 19 An apple. 20 Europe, Asia. 21 Elizabeth I.
22 Yachting. 23 Yugoslavia. 24 Goat. 25 Leeds. 26 Peppermint.
27 The humming bird. 28 Cricket. 29 Michael & Janet. 30 Bottom.

Answers - see page 193

1   The Dauphin was heir to which European throne?
2   Which castle was partly damaged by fire in 1992?
3   Which bear had a friend called Boo Boo?
4   What is the another name for a linden tree?
5   Which sport is named after a place which is famous for horse trials?
6   The precious stone, a pearl, can be found in what?
7   What is Curly's proper character name in Coronation Street?
8   How many senior titles (excluding over 35 events) are contested each Wimbledon?
9   How many passenger terminals does Heathrow Airport have?
10 At which ceremony is a Monarch given their crown?
11 According to the saying, what do birds of a feather do?
12 Was Ted Hughes a dancer, painter or poet?
13 Which British bank note stopped being available in 1970?
14 For which sport is Tessa Sanderson famous?
15 Prince Charles is Duke of which English county?
16 What is a yacht with two hulls called?
17 Which character from Winnie The Pooh lost his tail?
18 What two initials did northern artist Lowry have?
19 What did William Tell shoot from his son's head with a crossbow?
20 Which continents are separated by the Urals?
21 Who was England's Queen when Shakespeare was alive?
22 Cowes on the Isle of Wight is famous for which sport?
23 Which country was formerly ruled by President Tito?
24 Which animal's milk is used to make cheese called Chevre?
25 Which city is furthest North – Lincoln or Leeds?
26 What flavour is Kendal's most famous cake?
27 Which is the only bird that can fly backwards?
28 What is John Major's favourite sport?
29 Which Jacksons recorded Scream?
30 Which part of your body is a character in Shakespeare's A Midsummer Night's Dream?

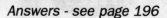

1 What sort of security device is a Chubb?
2 An Entryphone would normally be found at the entrance to what?
3 What in the bedroom would have a TOG rating?
4 What colour is Copydex adhesive?
5 What is the abbreviation for volt?
6 Is pine a soft or hard wood?
7 Which machine tool is used for turning wood?
8 Do weft fibres run across the width or the length of a fabric?
9 What goes between a nut and the surface to protect it?
10 Soldering joins two pieces of what?
11 Cushions, curtains etc. are referred to as what sort of furnishings?
12 Should silk be washed in hot or cool water?
13 Which tool can be band, hand or hack?
14 E numbers refer to additives to what?
15 Is an emery cloth rough or smooth?
16 Which device turns off an appliance when a temperature is reached?
17 A rasp is a type of what?
18 Is Araldite a strong or light glue?
19 In which sort of bank would you deposit waste glass?
20 Canning, bottling and freezing are types of what?
21 What would a bradawl produce in wood?
22 Batik is a type of dyeing on what?
23 What would you normally make in a percolator?
24 Where is the door on a chest freezer?
25 A bedsit usually consists of how many rooms?
26 What type of electrical devices are 'white goods'?
27 Is a kilogram less or more than two pounds in weight?
28 What colour does silver turn when it is tarnished?
29 Which wood is darker, mahogany or ash?
30 What does the ply of a yarn refer to?

Quiz 186 Pot Luck 85

Answers - see page 195

LEVEL 1

1   Who was the last President of the USA elected in the 1980s?
2   Which city is furthest North – Cardiff or Sheffield?
3   Which plant helps to take away the sting of a stinging nettle?
4   The River Forth flows into which Sea?
5   Which actress plays Jessica Fletcher in Murder She Wrote?
6   Which country was ruled by Chairman Mao?
7   What name is given to the imaginary lines drawn from north to south on a map?
8   Where in Britain can you spend paper £1 notes?
9   What is Rab C. Nesbitt's city?
10   Thomas Sheraton was a designer and manufacturer of what?
11   Which came first, zips, velcro or buttons?
12   Which horse named after a drink won the Grand National three times?
13   What was the name of Donald Duck's girlfriend?
14   What make of car was featured in the movie Back to the Future?
15   What is the fat of a whale called?
16   Which is the warmest sea in the world, The Red, Med or Dead?
17   Who wrote the pop anthem Knockin' On Heaven's Door?
18   Who or what flock together according to the saying?
19   What is the flavour of a Devil's Food Cake?
20   Which cowboy had a horse called Trigger?
21   For which sport is Daley Thompson famous?
22   Which King put his seal on the Magna Carta?
23   Which is nearest to Ireland, England, Scotland or Wales?
24   Abba-Esque wasn't a No. 1 for Abba, but it was for which group?
25   What is a horse rider's whip called?
26   What colour balls were used at Wimbledon before yellow balls?
27   Where would you expect to hear the prologue in a play?
28   Which of the following will not dissolve in water, salt, sugar or sand?
29   How many teats does a cow have normally?
30   Was the Flying Fortress a plane or a train?

Leisure: Home & D-I-Y (see Quiz 185)

Answers
1 Lock. 2 Block of flats. 3 Duvet. 4 White. 5 V. 6 Soft. 7 Lathe.
8 Width. 9 Washer. 10 Metal. 11 Soft furnishings. 12 Cool. 13 Saw.
14 Food. 15 Rough. 16 Thermostat. 17 File. 18 Strong. 19 Bottle bank.
20 Preserving. 21 Hole. 22 Fabric. 23 Coffee. 24 Top. 25 One.
26 Large kitchen appliances, such as freezers and washing machines. 27 More.
28 Black. 29 Mahogany. 30 Its thickness.

Quiz 187 Pop: The 90s

Answers - see page 198

LEVEL 1

1 Which football anthem was co written by Skinner and Baddiel?
2 What is the surname of Oasis brothers Noel and Liam?
3 Who was Candle in the Wind 1997 dedicated to?
4 Which Zoo sang Spaceman in 1996?
5 In which drama series did chart toppers Robson & Jerome find fame?
6 Isaac, Taylor and Zac make up which boy band?
7 Who said 'Eh Oh' on the their first smash hit?
8 Whose album of Urban Hymns hit the top spot?
9 Which 90s band were named after an area of London?
10 Knockin' On Heaven's Door was released after which 1996 tragedy?
11 Which single was released by Robson & Jerome and two years later by The Three Tenors?
12 Who was 'Older' in the 90s after a long running battle with Sony?
13 Who were Back For Good in 1995 before disbanding altogether?
14 Whose death propelled Bohemian Rhapsody back to the charts?
15 Which Peter had a No 1 with Flava?
16 Who had a No 1 with Nilsson's Without You?
17 Who backed Katrina on her 1997 Eurovision winner?
18 Which Damon fronted Blur?
19 Who starred in and sang on the soundtrack of The Bodyguard?
20 In September '98 Celine Dion released an album in which language?
21 Which toy provided Aqua with a No 1?
22 Which country singer John died flying his plane in 1997?
23 Who had a daughter Lourdes Maria in 1996?
24 Which band's name is a US emergency number?
25 Dana International won Eurovision 98 for which Middle East country?
26 Oasis were formed in which UK city?
27 Who had a huge hit with Drop Dead Gorgeous?
28 Which Darren appeared in the 90s version of Summer Holiday?
29 In which county were Blur formed?
30 My Heart Will Go On came from which smash hit film?

Quiz 188 Pot Luck 86

Answers - see page 197

1   Which Australian state is named after its discoverer Abel Tasman?
2   Which very soft wood is popular with model makers?
3   Which sport was played by Gabriela Sabatini?
4   According to the nursery rhyme, who joined the butcher and baker?
5   Do bananas grow pointing up or down?
6   Who wrote Charlie and the Chocolate Factory?
7   The River Ganges is sacred to the people of which religion?
8   Which Saint is the patron saint of Wales?
9   Which country was the 1994 football World Cup Final played in?
10 Was Terry Venables born in the 1940s, 1950s or the 1960s?
11 Which American hero wore a hat with a racoon tail hanging from the back?
12 Which sport is played on the largest pitch: cricket, football or polo?
13 What are or were winkle pickers?
14 Which part of an ocean shares its name with a musical?
15 Who was American president immediately before Bill Clinton?
16 Which metal is the FA Cup made from?
17 What did David throw from his sling to kill Goliath?
18 What do American children mean if they ask for candy?
19 Where was the person going, who met a man with seven wives?
20 Electricity comes into our homes at how many volts?
21 In the neck of a violin how many tuning pegs are there?
22 What were supporters of James II and his Stuart descendants called?
23 What is shouted by people when they make contact in fencing?
24 Which children's TV programme featured Bungle and Zippy?
25 Which English county shares its name with a beauty products range?
26 Which is the largest chain of chemist shops in the world?
27 What colour is Rupert the Bear's scarf?
28 For which sport was Fatima Whitbread famous?
29 How many players take part in a game of patience at any one time?
30 Which city is furthest north – Bristol or Chester?

Answers

Pop: The 90s (see Quiz 187)
1 Three Lions. 2 Gallagher. 3 Diana, Princess of Wales. 4 Babylon Zoo.
5 Soldier Soldier. 6 Hanson. 7 Teletubbies. 8 The Verve. 9 East 17.
10 Dunblane. 11 You'll Never Walk Alone. 12 George Michael. 13 Take
That. 14 Freddie Mercury. 15 Andre. 16 Mariah Carey. 17 The Waves.
18 Albarn. 19 Whitney Houston. 20 French. 21 Barbie. 22 Denver.
23 Madonna. 24 911. 25 Israel. 26 Manchester. 27 Republica. 28 Day.
29 Essex. 30 Titanic.

Quiz 189 People & Places

Answers - see page 200

1   In which World War was the Home Guard founded?
2   In which country were the Borgias a powerful family?
3   Benazir Bhutto was Prime Minister of which Muslim state?
4   Which Al was crime boss of Chicago during the Prohibition?
5   Which South African shared the Nobel Peace Prize with FW de Klerk in 1993?
6   What was President John F Kennedy's wife called?
7   What did Anthony Wedgwood Benn become known as?
8   In which country was Terry Waite imprisoned?
9   Roman Emperor Hadrian gave his name to what in Britain?
10 Which animals did Hannibal use to frighten the Romans?
11 Hirohito was Emperor of which country during WWII?
12 Which Russian word for Caesar was used by Russian monarchs?
13 Where was T.E. Lawrence involved in an independence struggle?
14 Which Russian revolutionary took his name from the River Lena?
15 When did Columbus discover America?
16 Which 11thC Scottish king was the subject of a Shakespeare play?
17 In which country of the UK was David Livingstone born?
18 Which British admiral Horatio was born in Norfolk?
19 Where is Botany Bay?
20 Which country put the first woman in space?
21 Which journalist John was imprisoned in Beirut with Brian Keenan?
22 What was Argentinean vice president Eva Duarte's married name?
23 Ho Chi Minh founded the Communist Party in which country?
24 Which English Quaker founded the colony of Pennsylvania?
25 Which African country was bombed on the orders of Ronald Reagan in 1986?
26 In which country was Joan of Arc born?
27 Where was the tomb of Tutankhamun discovered in 1922?
28 Which famous Indian monument was built by Shah Jahan?
29 Zulu leader Buthelezi became a government minister where?
30 Which nurse is famous for her work during the Crimean War?

Pot Luck 87 (see Quiz 190)

Answers

1 Golf. 2 Marzipan. 3 Rural England. 4 Two. 5 22. 6 Putty. 7 Roger Bannister. 8 Ballet. 9 Glasgow. 10 Eleven. 11 Des O'Connor. 12 A skateboard. 13 Carrot. 14 Gymnasts. 15 Billy Butlin. 16 The sea. 17 A fiddle. 18 Cookery. 19 Canada. 20 19th. 21 Collar bone. 22 Victoria. 23 The service. 24 Forget. 25 Grass. 26 Kill You. 27 A Swiss cheese. 28 Spain. 29 The knight. 30 Red and black.

LEVEL 1

1   Which sport is Sandy Lyle famous for playing?
2   What name is given to the almond coating often on a Christmas cake?
3   C.P.R.E. is the Council for the Protection of what?
4   How many Bank Holidays are there in May?
5   How many yards are there between the wickets in cricket?
6   What sticky paste usually holds glass in a window?
7   Who was the first person to run a mile in under four minutes?
8   What is performed by the Russian Bolshoi company?
9   Which Scottish city has the biggest population?
10 How many players can a team have on the field in American football?
11 Who invites contestants on the TV programme to Take Your Pick?
12 What has a kicktail and four wheels?
13 Which vegetable, high in vitamin A, is said to be good for the eyes?
14 What kind of athletes perform a flic-flac?
15 Who set up England's biggest chain of holiday camps?
16 Neptune was the god of what?
17 According to the saying, which instrument can you be as fit as?
18 What type of TV programmes are presented by Keith Floyd?
19 Which is biggest – the USA, Germany or Canada?
20 Was basketball developed in the 17th, 18th or 19th century?
21 What is the common name for the clavicle?
22 Africa's biggest lake is named after which British queen?
23 What is the name given to the first hit in a game of tennis?
24 What do elephants never do according to the saying?
25 Bamboo is a very large variety of what?
26 What will too much love do, according to Brian May?
27 What is Emmenthal?
28 In which country were the 1992 Summer Olympic Games held?
29 Which chess piece is shaped like a horse's head?
30 What two colours are Dennis the Menace's sweater?

LEVEL 1

1 On which type of show is Ainsley Harriott most likely to appear?
2 Which Carol was the first presenter of Changing Rooms?
3 Which washing up liquid did Nanette Newman famously advertise?
4 Which programme is often referred to simply as Corrie?
5 Which Zoe succeeded Gaby Roslin on The Big Breakfast?
6 Which impersonator Rory starred in Who Else?
7 Who is Mrs Richard Madely who appears on This Morning?
8 Which Fiona succeeded Anthea Turner on GMTV's morning sofa?
9 In which country is Ballykissangel set?
10 Scriptwriter Carla Lane is famous for campaigning on whose behalf?
11 Who was the BT housewife in the ads as played by Maureen Lipman?
12 In which show did David Jason call Nicholas Lyndhurst a plonker?
13 Which Rik was involved in a quad bike accident in 1998?
14 Which Have I Got News For You? star's real name is Paul Martin?
15 Which Helen appeared nude on the cover of Radio Times to celebrate her 50th birthday?
16 Who was the taller in the Peter Cook and Dudley Moore partnership?
17 Did Bob Monkhouse celebrate his 60th, 70th or 80th birthday in a TV special in 1998?
18 Who is Paul O'Grady's blonde, cigarette smoking alter ego?
19 What is the occupation of Bramwell in the TV series?
20 Who was the regular presenter of The Cook Report?
21 Who is Reeves' TV comedy partner?
22 In which show would you see the neighbour-from-hell Dorien Green?
23 Which TV cook went on tour on The Rhodes Show?
24 What is the first name of Prime Suspect writer La Plante?
25 Which morning show did Chris Evans and Gaby Roslin present?
26 Which TV astronomer was born Patrick Caldwell-Moore?
27 What is the surname of sister presenters Anthea and Wendy?
28 Who presented The Full Wax?
29 Which Victorian drama series has a hospital called The Thrift?
30 Laurence Lllewelyn-Bowen is a TV expert on what?

1   In 1959, what kind of vehicle crossed the Channel for the first time?
2   How many minutes are there per round in professional boxing?
3   Which animal built the hill that William III's horse stumbled on?
4   Which is female, Dempsey or Makepeace?
5   Which Channel Isle is famous for very creamy milk?
6   Which soccer boss left Arsenal following 'bung' allegations?
7   Which animals do sailors say desert a sinking ship?
8   Which triangle are ships and planes said to disappear in?
9   What were used on illegally parked cars for the first time in 1983?
10 The leaf from which tree is a logo for Air Canada?
11 Who was the legendary King Arthur's wife?
12 The TV series Byker Grove is set in which city?
13 Which Red Indian married Laughing Water?
14 What does a liquid turn into if it is heated up?
15 How many people take part in each heat of Blind Date?
16 A muster is a collection of what type of birds?
17 Who wrote about Noddy and Big Ears?
18 What is the proper name for a mouth organ?
19 Who is Paul Daniel's wife?
20 What is the start of a hockey match called?
21 What colour was Bobby Shafto's hair in the nursery rhyme?
22 Which popular drink was invented by Dr John Pemberton?
23 Which sport did Sam Snead play?
24 What is the Tigris?
25 In Starlight Express what do the performers wear on their feet?
26 Which sport is featured in the Rocky movies?
27 Which animal family do chipmunks belong to?
28 What colour is umber?
29 How many of Henry VIII's wives were called Catherine?
30 Which puppet show has two old men called Statler and Waldorf?

Answers

TV Times 5 (see Quiz 191)
1 Cookery. 2 Smillie. 3 Fairy liquid. 4 Coronation Street. 5 Ball. 6 Bremner. 7 Judy Finnegan. 8 Phillips. 9 Ireland. 10 Animals. 11 Beattie. 12 Only Fools and Horses. 13 Mayall. 14 Paul Merton. 15 Mirren. 16 Peter Cook. 17 70th. 18 Lily Savage. 19 Doctor. 20 Roger Cook. 21 Mortimer. 22 Birds of a Feather. 23 Gary Rhodes. 24 Lynda. 25 The Big Breakfast. 26 Patrick Moore. 27 Turner. 28 Ruby Wax. 29 Bramwell. 30 Home decorating.

1 Which sport are the Lord's Taverners famous for playing?
2 Which Denise won European gold in the heptathlon in '98?
3 Who was the last British Wimbledon champion?
4 Sergey Bubka has set a world record in which field event over 30 times?
5 Which British tennis star reached the Wimbledon semi finals in 1998?
6 Which summer sport did Kerry Packer revolutionise in the 70s?
7 Who has won moreMajor golf titles than any other player?
8 Chris Boardman suffered an accident riding what in summer 1998?
9 Which country staged the summer Olympics in 1984 and 1996?
10 Between 1990 and 1998 all Ladies Wimbledon Singles champions were born in which continent?
11 The summer Olympics are held every how many years?
12 In cricket, what must a ball not do to score six runs?
13 Jonathan Edwards specialises in what type of jump?
14 For which international side did Shane Warne play cricket?
15 Which golfer is known as the Great White Shark?
16 Which Martina did Martinez beat in the 1994 Wimbledon final?
17 Which Tour is the world's premier cycling event?
18 Which German tennis player's father Peter was jailed for tax fraud?
19 Sonia O'Sullivan races for which country?
20 How many runners are there in the 400m relay team?
21 Which Jana won Wimbledon 98 after her third final?
22 You would do a Fosbury flop in which athletics event?
23 Which country has the oldest cricket competition in the world?
24 How many balls an over are there in cricket?
25 Who told a Wimbledon umpire "You cannot be serious!"?
26 Which West Indian cricketer was called Vivian?
27 Who shattered Roger Maris's all-time Baseball home run record in '98
28 Which Jimmy won Wimbledon doubles with Ilie Nastase?
29 What was the nationality of tennis pin up Gabriela Sabatini?
30 Which team competes against America in the Ryder Cup?

1   With which sport is Hulk Hogan associated?
2   What are the metal loops that you place your feet in when horse riding?
3   Which bank is a dangerous sand bar in the North Sea?
4   How many players are there in a rounders team?
5   Whose official plane is Air Force One?
6   What does the letter P stand for in ESP?
7   Which group of countries did the Vikings come from?
8   How many Popes have been English – one, two or three?
9   What colour was Kojak's hair?
10 What kind of programmes are Hanna and Barbara famous for?
11 What is a man-made lake in which water is stored called?
12 What type of creature is a Black Widow?
13 Which overture has a date in its title and includes cannons and bells?
14 On what date did the St. Valentine's Day Massacre take place?
15 Winnie the Pooh lived in which wood?
16 Melbourne is the capital of which Australian State?
17 How many walls surround a squash court?
18 In The Bible, who parted the sea?
19 Fiji is in which ocean?
20 Which part of your body has a coating of enamel?
21 Which Mr Goldsmith promotes rock concerts?
22 Who milked the cow with the crumpled horn, in the rhyme?
23 Which part of the Venus de Milo's body are missing?
24 In which sport are Michael and John Whitaker famous?
25 Would a vermicide be used to kill worms or mice?
26 How many presidents' faces are carved into Mount Rushmore?
27 Which green stone was buried by the Chinese with their dead?
28 How many New Testament Gospels are there?
29 What word describes a picture made from sticking scraps onto a background?
30 Which English coin was nicknamed the tanner?

Quiz 195 Space

Answers - see page 206

LEVEL 1

1 What force makes the Earth orbit the Sun?
2 What colour is the Great Spot on Jupiter?
3 Is Jupiter larger or smaller than Earth?
4 Which gas is present in the Earth's atmosphere which is not present on any other planet?
5 A solar eclipse occurs when the Moon gets between Earth and what?
6 Which is the seventh planet from the Sun?
7 What is the layer around the Earth called?
8 What is the name given to matter so dense that even light cannot escape its pull?
9 Which planet's name comes nearest the end of the alphabet?
10 Herschel planned to name Uranus after the King; which one?
11 What would you find on a celestial map?
12 Is the science of celestial bodies, astrology or astronomy?
13 Which colour in the rainbow has the shortest name?
14 Which TV programme called space The Final Frontier?
15 Were the first US Shuttle flights in the 50s, 60s, or 80s?
16 Which show with Reeves & Mortimer shares its name with another term for meteors?
17 What is a group of stars which make a recognisable pattern called?
18 What does 'S' stand for in NASA?
19 In which decade was the US's first satellite launched?
20 What is the English name for the lunar sea Mare Tranquillitas?
21 Castor and Pollux are two stars in which constellation?
22 John Young ate which item of fast food in space in 1968?
23 Was Apollo a US or USSR space programme?
24 Prior to being an astronaut was John Glenn in the Air Force or the Marines?
25 How long does it take the Earth to orbit the Sun?
26 Mishka, the 1980 Olympic mascot was the first of which toy in space?
27 How is Ursa Major better known?
28 How many times did Gagarin orbit the Earth on his first space flight?
29 What travels at 186,272 miles per second?
30 Edward White was the first American to walk where?

Pot Luck 90 (see Quiz 196)
1 Nora Batty. 2 Green. 3 An earthquake. 4 Tennis. 5 Monday. 6 Barber.
7 Peron. 8 A sword. 9 West Ham. 10 Oxford. 11 Boxing Day. 12 Nine.
13 A bird (falcon). 14 Mo Mowlam. 15 Blue and White.
16 Boyzone. 17 Clint Eastwood. 18 A cherry. 19 Chess. 20 Nuclear.
21 Methane. 22 Nick Leeson. 23 Cain. 24 BSkyB. 25 Ena Sharples.
26 Annie. 27 Venice. 28 Eight. 29 Eiffel Tower. 30 Strawberry.

Answers

1 In Last of the Summer Wine, which part was played by Kathy Staff?
2 What colour is Dipsy in the Teletubbies?
3 An aftershock can sometimes follow what natural disaster?
4 For which sport was Sue Barker famous?
5 Which day's child is "fair of face" according to the traditional rhyme?
6 Which tradesman from Seville is featured in the title of an opera?
7 Which Argentinean president had wives called Eva and Maria Estela?
8 In legend, who or what was Excalibur?
9 Which London club did soccer's Ian Wright join from Arsenal?
10 Which university is the oldest in England?
11 St Stephen's Day is generally known by what other name?
12 How many players are in a baseball team?
13 What is a peregrine?
14 Who was Tony Blair's first Northern Ireland Minister?
15 What are the two main colours of the Argentinean flag?
16 Who had a No. 1 UK hit in September 1998 with No Matter What?
17 Which actor links Play Misty For Me and Pale Rider?
18 What type of fruit is a morello?
19 With which board game are Karpov and Kasparov associated?
20 Sizewell in Suffolk is associated with which form of power?
21 Which gas is the full name for marsh gas?
22 Who was Lisa Leeson's notorious husband?
23 In The Bible, who was Adam and Eve's firstborn son?
24 Which company acquired Manchester United Football Club in September 1998?
25 Which character in Coronation Street was played by Violet Carson?
26 The song Tomorrow comes from which musical?
27 In which Italian city is the Rialto Bridge?
28 How many noughts are in the written number one hundred million?
29 What is the most lasting symbol of the French Exhibition of 1889?
30 Royal Sovereign is a type of which soft fruit?

1   Which Oscar winner became a Labour MP?
2   Which sea disaster movie swept the Oscars at the 1998 ceremony?
3   Which Plasticine pair had six Oscar nominations by 1998?
4   Which Kevin won Best Director and starred in Dances With Wolves?
5   Braveheart was set in which country?
6   Who won Best Actor for The Silence of the Lambs?
7   Who directed Schindler's List?
8   Which British actor Jeremy was a winner with Reversal of Fortune?
9   Was it Tom Hanks or Tom Cruise who won in 1993 and again in '94?
10 Sonny's ex wife won Best Actress in Moonstruck; who was she?
11 Which Susan won for Dead Man Walking?
12 Which foot is named in the title of the movie with Daniel-Day Lewis?
13 Was Clint Eastwood Best Actor or Best Director for Unforgiven?
14 How often are the Oscars presented?
15 Which keyboard instrument gave its name to a film with Holly Hunter?
16 Kathy Bates won with Misery based on which Stephen's novel?
17 Which Kate was Oscar-nominated for Titanic?
18 Did Madonna receive one, two or no nominations for Evita?
19 What was Best Picture when Tom Hanks won Best Actor for Forrest Gump?
20 Which Al was Best Actor for Scent of a Woman?
21 Which Shirley won an Oscar at the age of five?
22 For which film did James Cameron win a 1997 Oscar?
23 Which British movie about the 1924 Olympics was an 80s winner?
24 Which Oscar winner based in India holds the record for most extras?
25 Which son of Kirk Douglas won for Wall Street?
26 Platoon was about which Asian war?
27 Which Ralph was an English Patient winner?
28 Talk To The Animals came from which movie about a Doctor?
29 When did the English Patient win Best Picture?
30 Dances With Wolves was the first film of what type to win Best Picture for 60 years?

Quiz 198 Pot Luck 91

LEVEL 1

Answers - see page 207

1   Which David directed the epic movie Lawrence of Arabia?
2   Which island is off the north-western tip of Wales?
3   The triple jump involves a run and then which three movements?
4   Which black boats sail along the canals of Venice?
5   Which bird was taken to work by miners to test for gas?
6   Mount Olympus is in which European country?
7   What colour hat is worn by Papa Smurf?
8   Which chocolate sweet bar is named after our galaxy?
9   For which sport was Gilles Villeneuve famous?
10 What colour did Dr. Banner become when he got angry?
11 How many legs does a fully grown insect have?
12 What can be discovered by counting the rings in a tree trunk?
13 Who or what is Sweet William?
14 What kind of creature is an anchovy?
15 What game are you playing if you hold a bat in a penholder grip?
16 In which sport would you see a Fosbury Flop?
17 Which word collectively describes all the stars and planets?
18 Which has the longer tail, a monkey or ape?
19 Who wrote the Peter Rabbit novels?
20 Which country produces Valencia oranges?
21 Where in your body would you find marrow?
22 Which tree does mistletoe grow on?
23 Who live at 342 Greasepit Terrace, Bedrock?
24 In which Dickens' novel does Jacob Marley's ghost appear?
25 Which islands were invaded in 1982 by the Argentineans?
26 What colour are the stars on the American flag?
27 In which country would you visit to kiss the Blarney Stone?
28 Which highwayman had a horse called Black Bess?
29 The TV series Take the High Road is set in which country?
30 How many strings are there on a Spanish guitar?

Answers

The Movies: The Oscars (see Quiz 197)
1 Glenda Jackson. 2 Titanic. 3 Wallace & Gromit. 4 Costner. 5 Scotland.
6 Anthony Hopkins. 7 Steven Spielberg. 8 Irons. 9 Hanks. 10 Cher.
11 Sarandon. 12 Left Foot. 13 Director. 14 Once a year. 15 The Piano.
16 King. 17 Winslet. 18 None. 19 Forrest Gump. 20 Pacino. 21 Temple.
22 Titanic. 23 Chariots of Fire. 24 Gandhi. 25 Michael. 26 Vietnam.
27 Fiennes. 28 Doolittle. 29 1996. 30 Western.

1   Which language other than English is an official language of the Channel Islands?
2   Which Tsar changed Russia's capital from Moscow to St Petersburg?
3   You would find Delphi on a map of which country?
4   What is farther north, Clacton or Brighton?
5   Which continent has an Ivory Coast?
6   On which island would you find the Giant's Causeway?
7   If you were on a French autoroute what type of road would you be on?
8   Which Gulf lies between Saudi Arabia and Iran?
9   Lake Superior is on the border of the USA and which other country?
10   Which tiny European landlocked state is a Grand Duchy?
11   Macedonia was formerly a part of which communist republic?
12   Which Himalayan kingdom has been called the world's highest rubbish dump because of waste left behind by climbers?
13   Which Australasian capital shares its name with a Duke and a boot?
14   Which river which flows through Germany is Europe's dirtiest?
15   Where would you be if you saw Nippon on the map?
16   Whose address is often referred to as Number Ten?
17   Which motorway goes past Stoke On Trent?
18   On which continent is the Basque country?
19   The Home Counties surround which city?
20   Malta is to the south of which island to the south of Italy?
21   The Ural Mountains mark the eastern frontier to which continent?
22   How is the London Orbital Motorway better known?
23   Is Moldova in Europe or Africa?
24   Which island republic lies to the north west of the UK?
25   Miami is a port in which US state?
26   Kew Gardens are next to which London river?
27   Which country has Lakes Garda, Maggiore and Como?
28   Is Madagascar an island or is it an African peninsula?
29   In which city is Red Square?
30   Which country's official languages are Hebrew and Arabic?

Quiz 200 Pot Luck 92

LEVEL 1

1 Actor Robert Carlyle led The Full Monty as which character?
2 What does a Catholic call the string of beads used when praying?
3 In 1851, what was invented by Isaac Singer?
4 In what type of educational establishment was Educating Rita set?
5 In The Bible, which King tried to get the baby Jesus put to death?
6 Which nurse returned to Casualty in the autumn 1998 series?
7 Who had a hit with the Titanic theme song My Heart Will Go On?
8 In cartoons, what type of animal is Sylvester?
9 Which letter represents 007's boss?
10 Which fish leap up river to get to their spawning grounds?
11 What do Americans usually mean by gas?
12 In which country did saunas originate?
13 A shuttlecock is used in which game?
14 What is measured by a pedometer?
15 How many creatures give their names to Chinese years?
16 Which domestic fuel has its charges calculated in therms?
17 How many decades are there in a millennium?
18 Who was disqualified from Wimbledon in 1995 after accidentally hitting a ball-girl?
19 What is the French word for the number eight?
20 In which part of London is there an annual famous carnival?
21 If put in an alkaline solution, what colour does litmus paper become?
22 Which animal lives in a drey?
23 If Dec 1st is a Tuesday, how many Wednesdays are in the month?
24 Did Beethoven come from Austria, Germany or Holland?
25 For which sport is Sam Torrance famous?
26 Belladonna is also known by which Deadly name?
27 Who hosts the TV entertainment programme The Moment of Truth?
28 The month March is named after which Roman god?
29 Leonardo da Vinci's religious painting featured The Last... what?
30 What colour is connected to neutral in modern three core electric cable?

1. What is normally the first Bank Holiday after Christmas Day?
2. Which sport would you watch at Aintree?
3. Are there more chairs at the start or end of a game of musical chairs?
4. What links a novice's ski slope and a garden centre?
5. What name is given to the promotional scheme to save points for cheaper plane travel?
6. Are boys or girls cubs?
7. What colour would a Sloane Ranger's wellies be?
8. The initials RSVP come from a request in which language?
9. What colour are most road signs on UK motorways?
10. In which UK county might you holiday on the Broads?
11. Are Open University courses usually followed by mature students or school leavers?
12. In which city is the exhibition centre Olympia?
13. What would you hire at Moss Bros?
14. Butlin's was the first type of what?
15. What is the flower shaped ribbon awarded at gymkhanas called?
16. What is a less formal name for a turf accountant?
17. Which magazine's title is the French word for 'she'?
18. On which summer bank holiday is the Notting Hill Carnival held?
19. Which public track can be used for horses but not traffic?
20. On which date in May was May Day traditionally?
21. Does a busker entertain indoors or out of doors?
22. In which month would you celebrate Hogmanay?
23. In golf, what is usually meant by the nineteenth hole?
24. What is a horse chestnut called when it's used in a children's game?
25. Which Scottish city hosts an annual arts festival?
26. What colour uniform do Guides wear?
27. Are seats in the circle of a theatre on the ground or first floor?
28. Where would a shopper be if they went to M&S?
29. If you wore jodhpurs you'd probably be about to do what?
30. On which ground in north west England do you watch Test cricket?

1   Who described 1992 as an 'annus horribilis'?
2   In which country would you see the Great and Little Orme?
3   According to Rudyard Kipling the female of what is deadlier than the male?
4   Which country hosted soccer's 1966 World Cup?
5   In EastEnders which Ethel had a dog called Willie?
6   What falls out if you have alopecia?
7   Which singer is Mrs Johnny Dankworth?
8   Who lives at Home Hill?
9   How does James Bond like his Martini served?
10 Which Richard was the first knighted New Zealand cricketer?
11 Europe's first motorway was built in which country?
12 What rude noise is the English equivalent of a Bronx Cheer?
13 What was Schindler's first name in the film Schindler's List?
14 In which South American country was Ayrton Senna born?
15 If January 1st was on a Thursday what day would February 1st be?
16 What colour was The Pimpernel created by Baroness Orczy?
17 Shanklin and Sandown are on which Isle?
18 Which Boys had a No.1 in the 1980s with Always On My Mind?
19 Who was the male half of the Torvill and Dean partnership?
20 What kind of animal was Korky from the Dandy comic?
21 Which Rory appeared with Gary Lineker in They Think It's All Over?
22 Which US tennis player married Brooke Shields?
23 Is Alberto Tomba a skier, a track athlete or an ice hockey player?
24 Which singer Michael had a No 1 with Earth Song?
25 Sodium chloride is better known as which condiment?
26 Was Brother Cadfael a fictional medieval or Victorian detective?
27 Which Prime Minister's son did Emma Noble become engaged to?
28 Which doll has a boyfriend called Ken?
29 According to The Comic Strip, in which county did Five Go Mad?
30 If Lions are playing Wallabies what sport are you watching?

1 Which day follows TFI on Chris Evans' show?
2 Who was the host of the variety show Lenny Goes To Town?
3 Which medical drama takes place in Holby's A & E department?
4 The Jerry Springer Show comes from which country?
5 At what time of day is Richard & Judy's magazine programme?
6 What is presented to the 'victim' at the end of This Is Your Life?
7 In ER, what is ER?
8 Which comedian John does LibDem Party Political Broadcasts?
9 How many rooms are changed in Changing Rooms?
10 Newsround is aimed at which group of viewers?
11 In which series set in Ireland did barmaid Assumpta meet a sad end?
12 Which near silent walking disaster was created by Rowan Atkinson?
13 Who is Mel Smith's TV comedy partner?
14 Which Geoff gardened at Barnsdale?
15 Which series was dubbed 'Barewatch' and 'Boobwatch'?
16 Which charity campaign has Pudsey Bear as its mascot?
17 Which Michael's 70s chat show was revived in 1998?
18 In which Practice have doctors Kerruish, Glover and Attwood worked?
19 Which was broadcast later, Newsnight or News at Ten?
20 Who is the host of GMTV's Lorraine Live?
21 Which phone number is the name of a series with Michael Buerk?
22 What follows Police, Camera..., in the show about awful drivers?
23 In which city is The Cosby Show set?
24 Which drama series where Robson and Jerome found fame is about army life?
25 On which day of the week does the so called God slot take place?
26 Which talent show features, 'Tonight Matthew I'm going to be....'?
27 Which Cilla Black series made dreams come true?
28 Which motor magazine now with Jeremy Clarkson began in 1978?
29 What is the hair link between Chris Evans and Nicholas Witchell?
30 Which Files feature Mulder and Scully?

1   Which comic did Dan Dare first appear in?
2   Golfer Ian Woosnam comes from which country?
3   Which song links Rolf Harris and Led Zeppelin?
4   Which inventor Michael is on a £20 note?
5   Gouache is a type of what?
6   The notorious Klaus Barbie was the Butcher of where in France?
7   Who is the mate of spoof DJ Smashy?
8   What shape is something if it is campanulate?
9   Boardman and Obree could clash in which sport?
10 Which Robin was the spoof film Men In Tights about?
11 Which word can go in front of BISCUIT, CLOSET and COLOUR?
12 As which character was Coronation Street actor Bruce Jones the neighbour from hell?
13 Which ticking instrument keeps perfect time for a musician?
14 Was the Automobile Association founded before or after World War I?
15 Which nation came back to international rugby in 1993?
16 Which is bigger A3 or A4 paper?
17 Which band featured Noddy Holder and Dave Hill?
18 The mesosphere and the stratosphere are layers of what?
19 With which country are Walloons associated?
20 What links a chocolate bar, a planet and a god of war?
21 Which Kevin was in the title of a hit for the Manic Street Preachers?
22 In which part of the body are the smallest bones?
23 In Greek legend, who had a bad hair day with snakes on her head?
24 Gubby Allen was linked with which sport?
25 What was the first name of Wacky Racer Mr Dastardly?
26 Was Chris Tarrant born in the 1940s or the 1960s?
27 Operation Overlord was the codename for the 1944 Allied invasion of where?
28 Who took a Careless Whisper to No. 1 in the 1980s?
29 Which country do golfers Nick Price and Mark McNulty come from?
30 What name is shared by actress Whittaker and the Webster she played in Corrie?

Quiz 205 Performing Arts

LEVEL 1

Answers - see page 216

1   Who sang a Barcelona duet with Freddy Mercury?
2   Which composer wrote the Four Seasons?
3   Which branch of performing is Michael Flatley famous for?
4   In which country was the Halle Orchestra founded?
5   Which dancer Wayne toured in 1998 to mark his 50th birthday?
6   Which instrument did Stephane Grapelli play?
7   Which writers of comic opera are referred to as G&S?
8   Which playwright was known as the Bard of Avon?
9   Billy Smart was associated with what type of entertainment?
10 In which country is an eisteddfod held?
11 Which Circle is a professional association of conjurors?
12 Which charity gala with many different performers is held in November and attended by the Royal Family?
13 Which Lord Andrew wrote the musical Whistle Down the Wind?
14 In Rodgers and Hammerstein who wrote the music?
15 In which country was the Bolshoi Ballet founded?
16 Which Vanessa is a famous young violinist?
17 Which London theatre shares its name with a half human, half fish mythical creature?
18 At what time of year would you go and watch a nativity play?
19 When faced with an orchestra, what does Sir Simon Rattle do?
20 The Last Night of the Proms takes place in which month?
21 A person playing a pantomime dame is usually which sex?
22 What type of singing made Maria Callas famous?
23 What was the surname of US musical composers George and Ira?
24 What is the final concert at the Promenade Concerts called?
25 Two out of the Three Tenors are which nationality?
26 Which Sir Noel wrote and starred in his plays and musicals?
27 What is the first name of Scarborough-based playwright Ayckbourn?
28 Opera singer Lesley Garrett is from which county?
29 Do you stand or sit for the Hallelujah Chorus from The Messiah?
30 In panto how do you respond to ' Oh yes it is!'?

(see Quiz 206)

Answers

Pot Luck 95 (see Quiz 206)
1 Fawlty Towers. 2 Middlesbrough. 3 Bill Wyman. 4 H.G. 5 Felicity.
6 The Young Ones. 7 Pottery. 8 Long haired. 9 James Bond. 10 Scarlett.
11 Wok. 12 The Archers. 13 Beef. 14 Horse. 15 Spoons. 16 Hello. 17 Nigel. 18 King Edward. 19 Crawford. 20 Arkansas. 21 Canada. 22 Etna.
23 Smoking. 24 Deer. 25 Outside. 26 Two (South Australia & New South Wales). 27 Moonlight Serenade. 28 New Testament. 29 Jeroboam. 30 Bronx.

1   Where did Polly work for Basil and Sybil?
2   Which English soccer side did Gazza make his debut for in a Wembley final?
3   Who is older Bill Wyman or the Prince of Wales?
4   What are the two initials of early 20th Century sci fi writer Wells?
5   Which Kendall starred in the sitcom Solo?
6   On which anarchic TV series did Neil, Mike, Rik and Vyvyan appear?
7   What did Clarice Cliff make?
8   Is an Afghan hound short haired or long haired?
9   Which secret agent was created by Ian Fleming?
10 Which Captain fought against the Mysterons?
11 What is a round bottomed Chinese cooking pan called?
12 In which radio series is there a pub called The Bull?
13 What sort of meat is usually in a hamburger?
14 What type of animal is a palomino?
15 What is Uri Geller famous for bending?
16 Would you say Bonjour to a French person when you say hello or goodbye?
17 Violinist Kennedy chose to drop which first name professionally?
18 Which monarch gave his name to a type of potato?
19 Which Michael created the Phantom in Lloyd Webber's musical?
20 Is Bill Clinton's home state Arkansas or Arizona?
21 In which country is Hudson Bay?
22 Which Sicilian mountain is Europe's highest volcano?
23 ASH is a pressure group against what?
24 Which animal might be fallow or red?
25 Would you find a gazebo inside or outside your home?
26 How many Australian states have South in their names?
27 Was Glenn Miller's theme tune Moonlight Sonata or Moonlight Serenade?
28 Is the book of Jude in the Old or New Testament?
29 Which is larger a magnum of champagne or a Jeroboam?
30 Which tough area of New York gives its name to a gin, vermouth and orange cocktail?

1 How often is the World Cup held?
2 Did Jimmy Greaves ever play in a World Cup Final?
3 Who won the last World Cup of the 20th century?
4 What colour shirts were England wearing when they won in 1966?
5 Who became known sarcastically as The Hand of God?
6 Who was sent off in France 98 and fled to Posh Spice in New York?
7 Which side from Great Britain did not make France 98?
8 Which 1966 World Cup veteran resigned as Eire manager in 1995?
9 Which British side did Brazil play in the first match of France 98?
10 Which European country did Berti Vogts manage?
11 Which TV pundit Jimmy spoke about every World Cup from 1966?
12 Who were beaten finalists in the last World Cup of the 20th century?
13 In France 98 which Caribbean side were called the Reggae Boys?
14 Who was axed from the England side in 98 after reports of kebab binges?
15 Was Sainsbury's or Tesco the official World Cup supermarket?
16 Is it true or false that Norway beat Germany in the 1995 World Cup?
17 In France 98 who did Suker play for?
18 Who was the only Englishman to lift the World Cup before 2000?
19 Which central American country was the first to host the World Cup twice, in 1986?
20 Which ex World Cup manager's autobiography is An Englishman Abroad?
21 What colour are Brazil's shirts?
22 Who were the only non Europeans to win the World Cup in the 90s?
23 Who was England's youngest player in France 98?
24 What colour coded hair was seen on the Nigerian team in France 98?
25 Which Gary was top scorer in the 1986 World Cup?
26 In which month did France 98 finish?
27 Which Scandinavian side was third in the 1994 US tournament?
28 Which South American side knocked England out of France 98?
29 In which city did France 98 begin and end?
30 On Top of the World was which country's World Cup anthem?

Quiz 208 Pot Luck 96

Answers - see page 217

LEVEL 1

1   Mike Atherton plays for which county cricket club?

2   Which were the initials of US President Johnson?

3   In which county is Ashford International station?

4   Does a Pina Colada contain rum or gin?

5   Which word for a duty doctor is a Latin name for place holder?

6   Which country's Rugby Union side are the Pumas?

7   Is a Dandie Dinmont, a dog, a cat or a horse?

8   In which county is the stately home of Althorp?

9   Which controversial author used the initials for his first names David Herbert?

10 What sort of fruit flavour does Calvados have?

11 In which country were BMW's first made?

12 St Francis of Assisi is patron saint of which country?

13 Who was the first Spice Girl to marry?

14 Which Sally was British women's team captain in the 1996 Olympics?

15 In which city is MP Diane Abbott's constituency?

16 Which country was once called Cathay?

17 Which Mr Ford starred in the 1990 movie Presumed Innocent?

18 Which Dennis created The Singing Detective?

19 Which Buddy did Alvin Stardust sing about?

20 Alec Stewart plays cricket for which English county?

21 Which bird lays its eggs in the nests of other birds?

22 Was the singer Mario Lanza a bass, baritone or tenor?

23 What name is given to the part of the bridle in a horse's mouth?

24 Wednesday and Pugsley are part of which family?

25 Christopher Davidson found fame as a singer as which Chris?

26 Maria Bueno was famous for which sport?

27 In fiction, which girl swam in a pool of her own tears?

28 A raglan forms which part of a garment?

29 Who had a huge 1995 hit with Think Twice?

30 Pram is an abbreviation of which word?

Answers

Sport: World Cup Fever (see Quiz 207)
1 Every four years. 2 No. 3 France. 4 Red. 5 Diego Maradonna. 6 David Beckham. 7 Wales. 8 Jack Charlton. 9 Scotland. 10 Germany. 11 Hill. 12 Brazil. 13 Jamaica. 14 Paul Gascoigne. 15 Sainsbury's. 16 True – Women's World Cup. 17 Croatia. 18 Bobby Moore. 19 Mexico. 20 Bobby Robson. 21 Yellow. 22 Brazil. 23 Michael Owen. 24 Green. 25 Lineker. 26 July. 27 Sweden. 28 Argentina. 29 Paris. 30 England's.

1   Which Yasser founded the PLO?
2   Which Kennedy announced he was running for President in 1960?
3   Nikita Krushchev was head of state of which Union?
4   In which Italian city were the 1960 summer Olympics held?
5   Whose Lover was the subject of a court case in book form?
6   The USSR sent its first man where in April 1960?
7   Which Russian dancer Rudolph defected to the West?
8   Across which former European capital was a Wall built?
9   Which drug taken by pregnant mothers caused abnormalities in babies?
10 Which Harold became Labour leader in 1963?
11 Of where did Neil Armstrong say, "The surface is like fine powder"?
12 What were mailbags containing over £1 million stolen from?
13 Caroline was the name of Britain's first off shore pirate what?
14 Which British WWII leader died in 1965?
15 What sort of champion was Arkle?
16 Which communist country had its famous Red Guards?
17 Which knighted soccer star retired aged 50?
18 Who launched the Queen Elizabeth II - QE2 - on Clydebank?
19 Which model Jean was called The Shrimp?
20 Which homeless charity was set up after TV's Cathy Come Home?
21 What product was banned from TV advertising on health grounds?
22 Which Rolling Stone singer was best man at David Bailey's wedding?
23 Which notorious East End gangland twins were jailed for murder?
24 Which rock star married Patricia Beaulieu?
25 Which capital was said to Swing in the 60s?
26 Which Martin famously gave his 'I have a dream' speech?
27 If Mods rode scooters, who rode motorbikes?
28 LBJ was President of which country?
29 How were Ian Brady and Myra Hindley known?
30 Which actress Marilyn was found dead in her bungalow near Hollywood?

1   Which John married actress Sheila Hancock?
2   Which pre decimal coin had the value of two shillings?
3   Which group revived a previous hit in the 90s with the help of Roy 'Chubby' Brown?
4   Which TV presenter's shows have had Toothbrush and Breakfast in their titles?
5   Were the Olympic Games last held in Russia in 1960, 1980 or 1988?
6   Who is Popeye's rival?
7   Was Sir Walter Scott Scottish?
8   Which English soccer side was managed by the late Bob Paisley?
9   What is the main language in Brazil?
10   Which Macaulay starred in the cartoon and live action film The Pagemaster?
11   Which is greater in distance a mile or a kilometre?
12   Which MP Harriet was axed in Tony Blair's first Cabinet reshuffle?
13   Which Billy Ray's Achy Breaky Heart helped establish line dancing?
14   How many red cards are there in a standard pack of cards?
15   Ray Davies was writer and singer with which band?
16   Adonis, Apollo and Poseidon were all what?
17   Who shares a flat with Gary in Men Behaving Badly?
18   Which dog is larger a borzoi or a corgi?
19   The Micra was made by which car company?
20   Which Stephen has been the TV partner of Dervla Kirwan?
21   A vixen is the female of which animal?
22   Which alphabet is used by Muscovites?
23   What links the names Chamberlain, Heath and Wilson?
24   Which jockey Bob fought back from cancer to win the Grand National?
25   Who is Simply Red's lead singer?
26   Which was the first antibiotic to be discovered?
27   Ian Smith played which Harold in Neighbours?
28   For which sport is Sunningdale famous?
29   A Muscovy is what type of bird?
30   Which musical Paul got involved with frogs and Rupert Bear?

Answers

Past Times: The 60s (see Quiz 209)
1 Arafat. 2 John. 3 Soviet. 4 Rome. 5 Lady Chatterley's. 6 Space.
7 Nureyev. 8 Berlin. 9 Thalidomide. 10 Wilson. 11 The Moon. 12 Train.
13 Radio station. 14 Churchill. 15 Horse. 16 China. 17 Sir Stanley
Matthews. 18 Queen Elizabeth II. 19 Jean Shrimpton. 20 Shelter.
21 Cigarettes. 22 Mick Jagger. 23 Kray twins. 24 Elvis Presley. 25 London.
26 Luther King. 27 Rockers. 28 USA. 29 Moors murderers. 30 Monroe.

1   Which actor was nicknamed 'Bogey'?
2   Which actor Marlon was paid $18 million for nine minutes in Superman in 1978?
3   Which western star John first acted as Duke Morrison?
4   Which Samuel starred as a gangster in Pulp Fiction?
5   Which Bruce starred in The Jackal?
6   Which soccer side does Evita actor Jimmy Nail support?
7   Tough guy Robert de Niro sang about New York in which film?
8   Which lager did Crocodile Dundee star Paul Hogan advertise?
9   Which Vietnam veteran Oliver directed Platoon?
10 Which star of The Godfather bought an island called Tetiaroa?
11 Which Martin was assigned to assassinate Brando in Apocalypse Now?
12 What did George C. Scott refuse to do about his Oscar for Patton?
13 Gene Hackman played cop Popeye Doyle in which classic thriller?
14 Which tough English actor Sean is the son of a former Dr. Who?
15 Which famous US family did Arnold Schwarzenegger marry into?
16 Was Charles Bronson one of ten or fifteen children?
17 Is Bruce Willis a cop or a soldier in the Die Hard movies?
18 Which hell raiser Oliver released a single Lonely For a Girl in 1965?
19 Lee Marvin headed a Dirty cast of how many in the 1967 movie?
20 Which singer who died in 1998 was the tough guy captain in Von Ryan's Express?
21 How many gunfighters were hired in The Magnificent film of 1960?
22 On what vehicle did Steve McQueen try to flee in The Great Escape?
23 Which Sylvester starred in Judge Dredd?
24 What is the first name of Reservoir Dogs director Tarantino?
25 Which tough guy Arnold has appeared on a postage stamp of Mali?
26 Which Mel starred in the Lethal Weapon series of films?
27 Which bare-headed actor was in The Magnificent Seven and The King and I?
28 Which Clint got the part in Dirty Harry when Sinatra pulled out?
29 Which James Bond has an actor son called Jason?
30 Was The Untouchables with Kevin Costner set in the 20s, 40s or 60s?

1　For which sport is Billie-Jean King famous?
2　According to the proverb, absence makes which organ grow fonder?
3　Who hosted ITVs Who Wants to be a Millionaire?
4　In which country is Ayer's Rock?
5　Which species of creature includes the most poisonous animal in the world?
6　Which figure advertised Bassetts Liquorice Allsorts?
7　If something is biodegradable, what will it do?
8　How many noughts are in the written number two hundred thousand?
9　Every how many years is a National Census taken in Britain?
10　Where are you if you visit the Granite City?
11　Which group had a No. 1 album in 1998 with Where We Belong?
12　In which country is the town of Spa?
13　What was the name of Dick Turpin's horse?
14　In the New Avengers, which character was played by Joanna Lumley?
15　Which guitarist is nicknamed 'Slowhand'?
16　In cricket, what does the initial M stand for in MCC?
17　Nassau is the capital of which group of islands?
18　In which Shakespeare play does Kate marry Petruchio?
19　Who was Tory leader immediately before John Major?
20　Which Lenny was the first genuinely black member of the Black and White Minstrel Show?
21　Which musical instrument does Tasmin Little play?
22　Which English county boasts the longest coastline?
23　In the TV series Minder, who played Arthur Daly?
24　Eden, Heath and Macdonald have all held which important position?
25　To the nearest mile, how long is the London Marathon?
26　What is the French word for the number twenty?
27　What are DC-10s and 747s?
28　See My Baby Jive was a 70s No 1 for which magic-sounding group?
29　What colour is azure in heraldry?
30　Which country is immediately south of Belgium?

1   In which country did black activist Steve Biko die in 1977?
2   Which US President was brought down by the Watergate scandal?
3   What did a policeman use to hide a streaker's embarrassment in a famous incident at Twickenham in 1974?
4   Which London born comic Charlie was knighted?
5   Which tree population was decimated by a Dutch disease?
6   Did Skytrain provide cut price tickets by air or rail?
7   Who succeeded John Paul I as Pope?
8   The New English version of which Book was published in 1970?
9   Which Czech tennis star Martina defected to the West?
10 In which country did Pol Pot conduct a reign of terror?
11 Which Sebastian was a record breaking middle distance runner?
12 Which father of twins was the husband of the British PM?
13 Which princess was sportswoman of the year in 1971?
14 The Queen celebrated how many years on the throne in her Jubilee?
15 Which Lord disappeared after his nanny was murdered?
16 Who beat four male candidates to become Tory leader in 1975?
17 Which war ended with the fall of Saigon in 1975?
18 Which country's athletes were murdered at the 1972 Olympics?
19 John Curry won Olympic gold on what surface?
20 In which county did a Ripper carry out horrific murders?
21 Which Lord and Royal uncle was murdered off Ireland?
22 Which Mother won a Nobel Peace Prize?
23 Charles de Gaulle died after being president of which country?
24 Were Sunderland in the first or second division when they won the FA Cup in 1973?
25 Where was the monarchy restored after the death of Franco?
26 In 1971 the first British soldier was killed in which British province?
27 Evonne Goolagong from which country won Wimbledon in 1971?
28 Which Chris was Jimmy Connors' fiancee when he first won Wimbledon?
29 Which James succeeded Harold Wilson as Prime Minister?
30 David Steel became leader of which political party in 1976?

Quiz 214 Pot Luck 99

LEVEL 1

1 In international soccer, what is the main colour of Holland's shirts?
2 Who is older – Ruby Wax or Jennifer Saunders?
3 Into The Groove gave a first UK No. 1 for which singer?
4 Which two cities were linked by the M1 when it first opened?
5 Which ex-Corrie actress Sarah shares her surname with an English county?
6 What is Britain's smallest bird?
7 How many sides are there in a pair of nonagons?
8 Which George was the main producer of The Beatles' hits?
9 E W Swanton wrote about which sport?
10 Was Joanna Lumley born in the 1940s,50s or 60s?
11 How is Eithne Ni Bhraonain better known in the music world?
12 Mohawk, Seminole and Sioux are all names of what?
13 Which star group was Jason Orange a member of?
14 Is Riesling a red or white wine?
15 How many Teletubbies are there?
16 What type of men gave Status Quo their first hit?
17 Who links the films Rebecca, Psycho and Vertigo?
18 What's the most number of Sundays that could occur in December?
19 Which author created the reclusive character Miss Havisham?
20 On TV, did David Soul play Starsky or Hutch?
21 What type of voice does opera star Lesley Garrett have?
22 What is England's most north easterly county?
23 Is Radio 5 Live broadcast on MW or FM?
24 What colour is verdigris which appears on copper or brass?
25 Who is killed if regicide is committed?
26 Ridings used to divide which county?
27 Is Robert Carrier linked with food, theatre or sport?
28 Pink gin is gin flavoured with what?
29 Which Judy starred in Meet Me In St Louis?
30 Brisbane is the capital of which Australian state?

LEVEL 1

1 What type of energy is generated by PowerGen?
2 What type of company can be found in Silicon Glen in Scotland?
3 In a car, what might be disc or drum?
4 Was the first modern cassette made in the 40s, 60s or 70s?
5 Which type of transport has rubber skirts?
6 A rotor propels what type of aircraft?
7 Did early TV have 405 or 625 lines?
8 The Manhattan Project in the early 40s was developing what?
9 Which substance, recently found to be dangerous, is called 'woolly rock'?
10 What is the lowest number on the Beaufort Scale?
11 Apples and Apricots were what in the technological world?
12 Is coal obtained from decayed animal or plant matter?
13 What produces bubbles in the making of champagne?
14 Is the empennage of a plane at the front or the tail?
15 William Morris, Lord Nuffield was the first UK manufacturer of mass produced what?
16 What does 'P' stand for in DTP?
17 Entrepreneur Ted Turner is a big name in which industry?
18 What ill-fated personal transport was invented by Sir Clive Sinclair?
19 Which letter is farthest left on a computer keyboard?
20 Which country is the world's largest exporter of grain?
21 Which metal is used thermometers?
22 Which colour identifies an ordinary diesel pump at a service station?
23 Nylon took its name from which two cities?
24 Which underground weapon did Whitehead develop in 1866?
25 Which boom is produced by breaking the sound barrier?
26 C-Curity was the first type of which fastener?
27 What does 'C' stand for in ASCII?
28 What sort of factory did Joseph Rowntree found?
29 What does a pluviometer measure?
30 Bournville was established for the workers of which company?

Quiz 216 Pot Luck 100

Answers - see page 225

LEVEL 1

1 Racing driver Niki Lauda was born in which country?

2 Which duo had hits with Mrs Robinson and America?

3 What is the fear of enclosed spaces called?

4 Which Sunday comes before Easter Day?

5 On TV, which night featured a show from the London Palladium?

6 Alphabetically, which is the last of the calendar months?

7 What would a palaeontologist study?

8 Which Disney creature nickname was given to Tony Blair?

9 What is the first name of New Baywatch star Hasselhoff?

10 When Eric Weiss escaped from his name he was known as who?

11 Which race course hosts the Ebor Handicap?

12 Which female presenter fronted the long running That's Life?

13 Which metal has the chemical symbol Fe?

14 Which Terry writes the best selling sci fi Discworld novels?

15 Which English county did Brian Lara first play for?

16 What's the sport if the Chicago Bears take on the Miami Dolphins?

17 What is the name of Sarah Ferguson's little helicopter?

18 In which country did golf originate?

19 Holly the computer appeared on which TV sci fi comedy?

20 Which is Australia's largest lake?

21 Who composed the New World Symphony?

22 Who presents Auntie's Sporting Bloomers on TV?

23 In which city does The Last Night of the Proms take place?

24 Vocalist Enya hails from which country?

25 Which Street is home for Leicester City?

26 Sugar Sugar was a one off number 1 for which group?

27 Which word can go in after BIRTHDAY, HEN, LABOUR and STAG?

28 Which Barrymore was in E.T. and Batman Forever?

29 What does the I stand for in ITV?

30 What would you be using if you needed a mouse mat?

Quiz 217 TV Gold

Answers - see page 228

1 Who was head of the family in Till Death Us Do Part?
2 Which house was Revisited in the classic 80s drama?
3 Where was the BBC's 1992 ill fated soap set?
4 On which weekend evening was Jim'll Fix It broadcast?
5 In Tenko the women were imprisoned by whom?
6 What was Lovejoy's occupation?
7 Which series was about a Mobile Army Surgical Hospital in Korea?
8 Which Michael played the hapless Frank Spencer?
9 What was unusual about Hopkirk in the Randall and Hopkirk agency?
10 What institution was Please Sir set in?
11 What was the rank of Phil Silvers' Bilko?
12 Who were the US TV equivalent of the Beatles?
13 Which Leonard Rossiter sitcom sounds like a problem with old houses?
14 How was Arthur Fonzerelli known in Happy Days?
15 Which animals did Barbara Woodhouse work with?
16 Who was June in Terry and June?
17 What sort of animal was Grizzly Adams?
18 What was Torquay's most famous hotel run by Basil and Sybil?
19 Jewel in the Crown was set in wartime where?
20 In which county was All Creatures Great and Small set?
21 What sort of performers were in Spitting Image?
22 Which father of Paula Yates presented Stars on Sunday?
23 What was the profession of Albert Steptoe and son Harold?
24 Which hero was "Riding through the glen, With his band of Men"?
25 Which classic sci fi series began in the 23rd century?
26 In which country was Van der Valk set?
27 What sort of statesman was Alan B'Stard?
28 Which Eric played Hattie Jacques' brother?
29 Was it Mork or Mindy who came from the planet Ork?
30 What sort of Men were Bill and Ben?

Quiz 218 Past Times: The 80s

Answers - see page 227

LEVEL 1

1   Which serving British PM survived an assassination attempt?

2   In which city did the SAS storm the Iranian embassy?

3   Edwina Currie resigned over a what type of farm food?

4   Which Ben was disqualified from the Seoul Olympics for drug taking?

5   In which Sea did the oil rig Piper Alpha catch fire?

6   Which north London Tube station was gutted by fire in 1987?

7   Who was Labour leader when Thatcher had her third election victory?

8   Which late Duchess's jewels were auctioned for over £30 million?

9   The Herald of Free Enterprise sank off which Belgian port?

10 President Marcos was ousted in a rebellion in which island country?

11 Desmond Tutu became an Archbishop in which country?

12 Who was the second of the Queen's sons to marry in the 80s?

13 Was Zola Budd a swimmer, a runner or a gymnast?

14 At which UK stadium was the Live Aid concert held?

15 Which Eric, half of a classic comedy duo died in 1984?

16 Which Tory minister Cecil resigned in a scandal in 1983?

17 In which Yorkshire city's football ground was there a fatal fire in '85?

18 What is the full name of the Lib Dems, formed in 1989?

19 Sally Ride became the USA's first woman where?

20 At which Common was there a camp against cruise missiles?

21 Outside which London store did a bomb explode in December 1983?

22 Which Swedish tennis star retired age 26?

23 In what type of accident was Princess Grace of Monaco killed?

24 Which soap asked the audience asked 'Who shot JR?'

25 Which war in the south Atlantic was Britain involved in?

26 Which Mike became the youngest heavyweight boxing champion?

27 Which Bob rode Aldaniti to a Grand National win in 1981?

28 Which US president was the victim of an assassination attempt?

29 In which city was Beatle John Lennon murdered?

30 Where was Lady Diana Spencer working when photographed in a seemingly see through skirt?

Answers

TV Gold (see Quiz 217)
1 Alf Garnett. 2 Brideshead. 3 Spain. 4 Saturday. 5 Japanese. 6 Antiques dealer. 7 M*A*S*H. 8 Crawford. 9 He was a ghost. 10 School. 11 Sergeant. 12 The Monkees. 13 Rising Damp. 14 The Fonz/Fonzie. 15 Dogs. 16 June Whitfield. 17 Human. 18 Fawlty Towers. 19 India. 20 Yorkshire. 21 Puppets. 22 Jess Yates. 23 Rag & bone merchants. 24 Robin Hood. 25 Star Trek. 26 Holland. 27 New Statesman. 28 Sykes. 29 Mork. 30 Flowerpot men.

1 Whose album True Blue was No 1 in 28 countries?
2 What was The Spice Girls' first No 1?
3 Whose charity hit included Something About the Way You Look Tonight?
4 Which of Madonna's two hits from Evita got highest in the charts?
5 Which Frank Sinatra hit has spent most weeks in the UK charts?
6 In which decade did the UK singles charts begin?
7 Who as well as The Troggs charted with Love Is All Around?
8 Which wartime song charted with Robson & Jerome's Unchained Melody?
9 Which father and daughter had a No 1 with Somethin' Stupid?
10 How was Roberto Milani known when he had Europe's '96 top seller?
11 Which soccer side charted with Come On You Reds?
12 Whose Release Me spent a record number of weeks in the charts?
13 Was Celine Dion's Power of Love the same as Jennifer Rush's or Frankie Goes to Hollywood's?
14 Who was the first all female band to have three consecutive No 1's?
15 How many weeks did Elvis spend in the charts duetting?
16 Who spent most weeks in the UK charts, the Stones or Status Quo?
17 Which musical did Boyzone's No 1 No Matter What come from?
18 Who is the most successful Australian female to have been in the UK singles charts?
19 Billboard is a list of best selling records where?
20 Which band were in the chart most weeks in 1995 and again in 1996?
21 Which family were at No 1 with Do the Bartman?
22 Which Scandinavian country do chart toppers Aqua come from?
23 Who accompanied Vic Reeves on his No 1 hit Dizzy?
24 Whose 96 No 1s were Firestarter and Breathe?
25 Which Boys' first No 1 was West End Girls?
26 Whose Cigarettes and Alcohol was their highest chart hit at the time?
27 Which solo Briton Cliff has spent most weeks in the UK singles charts?
28 Which female solo star has spent most weeks in the British charts?
29 Love Me For a Reason charted for The Osmonds and which band?
30 Who wrote the series Crocodile Shoes and its chart songs?

1   Who became US President in 1992 when Governor of Arkansas?
2   Which religious Army was founded by Catherine and William Booth?
3   Which scientist gave his name to the process of pasteurisation?
4   Who left $9 million to give prizes in five different fields?
5   Which King of England provided his children with most stepmothers?
6   Who lit the fuse for the 1605 Gunpowder Plot?
7   Was it John Ford or Henry Ford who manufactured cars?
8   During which war did Anne Frank write her diary?
9   Indira Gandhi was Prime Minister of which country?
10 John Paul Getty made his millions from which commodity?
11 Who was Labour leader Neil Kinnock's wife who became an MEP?
12 Who was the first 20th century Prince of Wales to be divorced?
13 How was Argentinean Ernesto Guevara de la Serna better known?
14 William Gladstone was Prime Minister under which monarch?
15 What was suffragette leader Emmeline Goulden's married name?
16 Who became President of Iraq in 1979?
17 How many English kings have been called Stephen?
18 What was the nationality of the Duchess of Windsor?
19 Which legendary cricketer had the first names William Gilbert?
20 How old was Hitler when he died, 46, 56 or 66?
21 By which name was silent movie star Joseph Keaton better known?
22 Which Nelson was the first black President of South Africa?
23 How was Mao Zedong also known?
24 Which Marx brother had a moustache, cigar and funny walk?
25 According to The Bible who was the mother of Jesus?
26 Which trombonist Glenn became a famous bandleader?
27 Who was Italian dictator between 1926 and 1943?
28 What was the nationality of inventor Marconi?
29 Which of Queen Elizabeth II's Prime Ministers was not even born when she came to the throne?
30 Who was the youngest US President to die in office?

1 Sir Paul McCartney was awarded the freedom of which city?
2 Which legendary band released The Wall?
3 Which soul star Ray has the nickname The Genius?
4 Which Shirley was dubbed the Tigress from Tiger Bay?
5 Supermodel Rachel Hunter married which superstar Rod?
6 Which ex Police singer founded the Rainforest Foundation in 1988?
7 Who does not use her surname Ciccone?
8 Which brother completes the Gibb trio with Maurice and Robin?
9 Which Billy toured with Elton John in 1998?
10 Which rock superstar was Lisa Marie Presley second husband?
11 Diana Ross is billed as who on her recording of I Will Survive?
12 Montserrat Caballe recorded Barcelona with which rock legend?
13 Which drummer's solo album No Jacket Required was a best seller?
14 Which Rolling Stone did not normally play an instrument on stage?
15 Which group was heard on the soundtrack of Saturday Night Fever?
16 Whose hits range from The Laughing Gnome to Space Oddity?
17 Who sang You Don't Bring Me Flowers with Barbra Streisand?
18 Which Queen of Soul sang the best version of Nessun Dorma according to Pavarotti?
19 Which band would you find The Edge and Bono in?
20 Who lived in a mansion called Graceland?
21 Which boys liked Califrnia Girls?
22 Whose Streets of Philadelphia was his highest hit at the time in 1994?
23 Which Stevie dropped the tag Little and had hits well into adulthood?
24 Which Tina recorded Bond theme Goldeneye?
25 Which superstar founded the Rocket record label?
26 All Lionel Richie's early hits were on which record label?
27 Which Scottish football fan has the first names Roderick David?
28 Which Roy charted with Crying with kd lang four years after his death?
29 Which Barbra did actor James Brolin marry in 1998?
30 Which Barry's song Copacabana became a musical?

Quiz 222 Leisure: The Media

LEVEL 1

Answers - see page 231

1   Which BBC radio and TV service broadcasts abroad?
2   Is The Spectator a programme to watch or a magazine to read?
3   The Sporting Life devotes itself to which sport?
4   Which radio and TV listings magazine is published by the BBC?
5   Which independent radio station specialises in classical music?
6   Is The Archers on Radio 1 or Radio 4?
7   Where does Capital Radio broadcast to?
8   What is the Sunday version of Daily Sport called?
9   Which BBC Radio station has Live after its number?
10 In which north of England city is Granada TV based?
11 What sort of Column tells of stories and rumours about celebrities?
12 What does M stand for in the pop paper NME?
13 Is GQ for men or women?
14 On which day is Grandstand always broadcast on BBC1?
15 On which shelf would someone buy an 'adult' magazine?
16 What does FT stand for in the name of the financial daily newspaper?
17 What is the Daily Mail's Sunday paper called?
18 On which day of the week is the News of the World published?
19 Which corporation is known as Auntie?
20 Which magazine about celebs is based on the Spanish mag Hola!?
21 Which Rupert founded Sky Television?
22 Which page in a newspaper is famous for its nude photos?
23 What does I stand for in ITV?
24 Which satirical magazine shares its name with the nickname for a detective?
25 Which newspaper is larger, a tabloid or a broadsheet?
26 Border TV serves the borders of which two countries?
27 What professional person would read The Lancet?
28 How often does the magazine Take A Break appear?
29 Which ex MP presented Late Night Currie on Radio 5 Live?
30 Which Sir David co founded LWT and TV-am?

Answers

Pop: Superstars (see Quiz 221)
1 Liverpool. 2 Pink Floyd. 3 Charles. 4 Bassey. 5 Stewart. 6 Sting.
7 Madonna. 8 Barry. 9 Joel. 10 Michael Jackson. 11 Diana. 12 Freddy
Mercury. 13 Phil Collins. 14 Mick Jagger. 15 Bee Gees. 16 David Bowie.
17 Neil Diamond. 18 Aretha Franklin. 19 U2. 20 Elvis Presley. 21 Beach
Boys. 22 Bruce Springsteen. 23 Wonder. 24 Turner. 25 Elton John.
26 Motown. 27 Rod Stewart. 28 Orbison. 29 Streisand. 30 Manilow.

1 Who is Julian Lennon's stepmother?
2 Which pop wife has Liam and a shamrock tattooed on her ankle?
3 Which George did not make a record for five years because of a dispute with Sony?
4 In which Irish city was Sinead O'Connor born?
5 Which Elaine changed her surname from Bickerstaff and went on to star in many West End musicals?
6 Which Stevie led the campaign to commemorate Martin Luther King's birthday in the US?
7 How is Katherine Dawn Lang better known?
8 Bernie Taupin collaborated with which performer for over 20 years?
9 Which Boys were famous for their surfing sound?
10 Whose real name is Charles Edward Anderson Berry?
11 In what type of tragic accident did John Denver meet his death?
12 Which composer of Boyzone's No Matter What appeared with them on Top of the Pops?
13 Andrew Ridgeley was the less famous half of which group?
14 Which band always comes last alphabetically?
15 Which ex Jackson 5 member was 40 in 1998?
16 The Spice Girls recorded their early hits on which label?
17 PJ and Duncan were also known as who?
18 Which soul star did Bryan Ferry name his son Otis after?
19 What are the first names of the Everly Brothers?
20 Was Bryan Adams born in Canada or the USA?
21 Who was left handed, Lennon or McCartney?
22 Which ex husband of Cher died in a skiing accident ?
23 Bjork hails from which country?
24 Who made the album Let's Talk About Love?
25 Which Olivia won a Hayley Mills look alike contest?
26 Who made the album 12 Deadly Cyns?
27 Which Mark co founded Dire Straits?
28 What name links Ant and Faith?
29 Which hit by D:Ream was used in the 97 Labour election campaign?
30 Who changed his name to a symbol?

1 Which famous actress Koo was romantically linked to Prince Andrew?
2 What relation is Prince Philip to Princess Margaret?
3 What did the Princess of Wales sell at auction in 1997?
4 What is the Princess Royal's real first name?
5 Which Prince's name was linked with PR girl Sophie Rhys-Jones?
6 What is the title of the wife of Prince Michael of Kent?
7 Which Princess was prevented from marrying divorced Peter Townsend in the 50s?
8 On which programme did Princess Diana say her marriage had been "a bit crowded"?
9 Prince Harry followed Prince William to which school in 1998?
10 Which dietary illness did Princess Diana allegedly suffer from?
11 Who is the mother of Princesses Beatrice and Eugenie?
12 Which son of Prince Charles has red hair?
13 Who is older, Prince Andrew or Prince Edward?
14 Which Royal is always referred to as Her Majesty?
15 Which Royal yacht was decommissioned in 1997?
16 Is Princess Anne's daughter a Princess, or a Miss?
17 Where is the Queen's holiday home north of the border?
18 What did the Queen Mother have replaced after a fall in 1997?
19 At which time of year does the Queen always make a TV broadcast?
20 What did Elton John sing at Princess Diana's funeral?
21 Which wife of Prince Rainier of Monaco was an Oscar winner?
22 What relation is the Queen Mother to Prince Charles?
23 In which Abbey did Prince Andrew and Sarah Ferguson marry?
24 Which 'Watchers' organisation did Fergie advertise?
25 Which profession is shared by Lords Snowdon and Lichfield?
26 In which city was Princess Diana tragically killed?
27 Which castle was reopened in 1998 after being damaged by fire?
28 Who was the last British monarch of the 19th century?
29 Before his marriage was Prince Philip in the army or the navy?
30 Which Princess was married to Captain Mark Phillips?

1   Which long river has White and Blue tributaries?
2   Which religious leader is head of state of the Vatican?
3   Is Perth on the west or east coast of Australia?
4   In which country is Calgary?
5   Does Bombay or Tokyo have the higher population?
6   What sort of Snowman is another name for the Himalayan yeti?
7   What is the world's smallest, flattest and driest continent?
8   Is Argentina in the northern or southern half of South America?
9   Pakistan and Bangladesh both border which country?
10 Which country's name is an anagram of PURE?
11 The West Indies lie in which Sea?
12 Zambia is a neighbour of which country which also begins with Z?
13 Which Egyptian canal links the Red Sea and the Mediterranean?
14 Is Ghana on the African coast or wholly inland?
15 Which ocean is the world's deepest?
16 In which country is the homeland of KwaZulu?
17 Who is commemorated at Washington's Lincoln Memorial?
18 Which US state has the zipcode (postcode) AZ?
19 New South Wales is in which country?
20 Which African desert is the world's largest?
21 Is Swaziland a monarchy or a republic?
22 Mount Kilimanjaro is the highest point of which continent?
23 Which US island state has the world's highest annual rainfall?
24 Which ocean lies to the east of South America?
25 Which Islamic Republic used to be called Persia?
26 Two thirds of Greenland lies in which Circle?
27 Is Namibia in northern or southern Africa?
28 Which country's head of state is Saddam Hussein al-Tikriti?
29 Which People's Republic has the world's largest population?
30 Alberta is a province of which country?

1 BA and Face were members of which alphabetically aware team?
2 Which opera singer gave a concert in Hyde Park in the pouring rain?
3 The discovery of what caused a rush to California in 1848?
4 What is the opposite of alkali?
5 In rhyme, who asked his way to Norwich when he came down too soon?
6 Which nutty chocolate is sold in triangular bars?
7 In which lane is the Great Fire of London said to have started?
8 Which lord was removed from the *Beano* in 1992?
9 In which game could an Australian's Chinaman beat an Englishman?
10 Which of the Wonders of the World was at Babylon?
11 In films, what kind of car is the "Love Bug"?
12 A bob was the popular name of which old English coin?
13 What was the Teenage Mutant Turtles' favourite food?
14 What comes after red, orange and yellow in the rainbow's colours?
15 Which soccer team does the DJ Ed Stewart support?
16 How many legs does a male insect have?
17 Which Greek Marbles are housed in the British Museum?
18 Which workhouse boy asked for more?
19 Which language does the word kitsch come from?
20 What is the state capital of Massachusetts?
21 How many strings does a Spanish guitar have?
22 What did Old Mother Hubbard keep in her cupboard?
23 What kind of creature is an anchovy?
24 Dad, kayak and rotavator are examples of what type of words?
25 Which juicy green fruit is named after a New Zealand bird?
26 What is the name for a blanket-like cloak with a slit for the head?
27 Most snow crystals have how many sides?
28 What does an entomologist study?
29 In Britain a general election must be held after how many years?
30 What sort of creature is a treecreeper?

Medium Questions

Welcome to the land of the bland, the grey area. Say hello to Mr Middle and Mickey Mean, who are all ruled by the law of averages and live in this the not-too-easy/not-too-hard world of the Medium section. Some of these questions will find your contestants sailing along, shrugging their shoulders and snubbing the opposition through a pall of thick smoke and nauseous self-confidence and others will leave them banging on the carpet (chance'd be a fine thing) and gurning like gargoyles.

The point is this: these questions should see the average contestant score about 50% to 80% and those they fail on will be subjects they happen to know absolutely nothing about. Still, a well-balanced team should have all the subjects covered by one member or another. And if they don't? Well, that's their lookout.

Sprinkle these questions liberally through your quizzes as you might sprinkle Parmesan on your spag boll.

1 Who had a 70s hit with "Feelings"?
2 Who had a "Pretty Good Year" in the charts in 1994?
3 Which Irish singer has made records with Clannad and Sinatra?
4 "Don't Worry" was the first solo success for which female singer?
5 Who was lead singer with the Animals?
6 Who did Nick Berry play in "EastEnders" at the time of his first No. 1?
7 Who did Marc Almond sing with for his first No. 1?
8 Who - in song - lived high on a mountain in Mexico?
9 Which group introduced Dina Carroll to the charts?
10 Who has recorded with Cliff Richard, Steve Harley and Jose Carreras?
11 Who was the "Wichita Lineman"?
12 What word added to Bells, Mink and Pearl completes group names?
13 Who was lead singer with the Bay City Rollers?
14 Which country did Aneka - who sang "Japanese Boy" - come from?
15 Who sang "Private Number" with William Bell?
16 Who was responsible for the English lyrics of "My Way"?
17 Who were Bobby, Mike, Cheryl and Jay?
18 Who did Chubby Checker sing with on the 80s twist revival single?
19 Who is Pat Boone's singing daughter?
20 Which female singer starred in the 80s video for "Ant Rap"?
21 Who was the Geno referred to in Dexy's Midnight Runners' No. 1?
22 Which Spice Girl comes from Leeds?
23 Who wrote and sang the original "Spirit In The Sky"?
24 Who took "Wonderwall" into the charts for the second time in 1995?
25 Who was the first female artist to have a No. 1 and wear an eye patch?
26 Who wrote "All By Myself"?
27 Who sang "Never On A Sunday"?
28 Who sang with Peabo Bryson on "A Whole New World"?
29 Our Cilla's "Anyone Who Had A Heart" was a cover of which singer's song?
30 Who was the guitar virtuoso who wrote "Albatross"?

Answers

TV Soaps (see Quiz 3)
1 Annie. 2 "Emmerdale". 3 April. 4 Sam Mitchell. 5 "Coronation Street".
6 Lisa Riley (Mandy Dingle, "Emmerdale"). 7 Letitia Dean (Sharon). 8 Chris
Collins. 9 The Queen Vic. 10 The Meal Machine. 11 Rosie, Sophie.
12 "Family Affairs". 13 Wellard. 14 "Brookside". 15 "The High Road".
16 Raymond. 17 Steph. 18 Helen Daniels. 19 Julia Brogan. 20 Fraser
Henderson. 21 Shane. 22 Martin Platt. 23 "Pacific Blue". 24 Hills.
25 Nigel Bates. 26 Steven and Peter. 27 Audrey Roberts. 28 Gary and Judy
Mallett. 29 Roy Evans. 30 In a fire.

LEVEL 2

1 Which moor is named after the county town of Cornwall?

2 Who laid the foundation stone at Coventry Cathedral?

3 In which city was Stephane Grappelli born?

4 Who had a No. 1 in the 60s with "Everlasting Love"?

5 Which tennis player was given the name "Ice Man" by the press?

6 Who cleaned at the Crossroads Motel?

7 Which does fibrin cause the blood to do?

8 What name links a former "EastEnders" actor and a radio DJ?

9 In which county are England's highest cliffs?

10 What is the Russian word for citadel?

11 In which century was George Frederick Handel born?

12 Which sportsman wrote the autobiography *Unleashed*?

13 What is John Gielgud's first name?

14 Who was the first female presenter of "Busman's Holiday"?

15 What is the Pentateuch?

16 In which sitcom did Sandra Hennessey appear?

17 What was the name of the first cloned sheep?

18 Which school did Billy Bunter go to?

19 Who wrote the books on which "The Jewel in the Crown" was based?

20 Who has advertised Brut, Patrick boots, Shredded Wheat and Sugar Puffs?

21 Allurophobia is a fear of what?

22 What do the letters P.S. stand for at the end of a letter?

23 Whose last words were "That was a great game of golf, fellas"?

24 In the Chinese calendar which year follows the year of the tiger?

25 Who was the first person to captain, coach and manage England at cricket?

26 Who was King of the Huns from 406 to 453?

27 What word can go after "tar" and before "gent"?

28 With which sport is Willie Wood connected?

29 In which decade of the 20th century was Eric Clapton born?

30 Which actor played the only Dirty Dozen member to survive?

Around the UK (see Quiz 4)

1 Four. 2 Portsmouth. 3 The Guild Hall. 4 Tobermory. 5 Sark.
6 Anglesey. 7 Cambridge. 8 Lloyd's of London. 9 Scillies. 10 Cheviots.
11 Glasgow. 12 Irish Sea. 13 Buckinghamshire. 14 York Minster.
15 Solway Firth. 16 Coventry. 17 Melton Mowbray. 18 The Backs.
19 Derbyshire. 20 Ermine Street. 21 Lytham St Annes. 22 Parkhurst.
23 Grosvenor Square. 24 The Great Fire of London. 25 The Solent.
26 Windsor. 27 Southend. 28 Downing Street. 29 Mermaid.
30 Northumberland.

1 What is the name of "EastEnders" club owner George Palmer's daughter?
2 Which soap was made in Esholt until 1997?
3 In "EastEnders" what was Carol Jackson's sister called?
4 Who was Ricky Butcher's first wife?
5 Tony Blair was seen on which soap set prior to the '97 General Election?
6 Which soap star modelled Etam clothes for larger ladies?
7 Which ex-EastEnder starred in "The Hello Girls" on BBC1?
8 The actor who was Danny Weir in "Emmerdale" played which "Coronation Street" character?
9 Eddie Royle was the landlord of which soap pub?
10 What was Ian Beale's catering business called?
11 In "Coronation Street" what are Kevin and Sally's daughters called?
12 Which was the first major UK soap on Channel 5?
13 What was the name of Robbie Jackson's dog in "EastEnders"?
14 Which soap did Lily Savage appear in?
15 In which soap does Mrs Mack appear?
16 What is the surname of Tiffany's brother Simon in "EastEnders"?
17 Who was Mrs Des Barnes when they moved into the Street ?
18 Which of the original "Neighbours" characters lasted the longest?
19 Who is Doreen Corkhill's mum in "Brookside"?
20 In the Street, what was the name of the gangster who had an affair with Liz McDonald?
21 In "Home and Away" what was Shane and Angel's daughter called?
22 Which male "Coronation Street" character trained to be a nurse?
23 Which Sky 2 soap was dubbed "Baywatch" on bikes?
24 What was "EastEnders" Kathy Mitchell's maiden name?
25 Who is Clare Tyler's stepfather in Albert Square?
26 Which children did Cindy Beale take with her to France?
27 Who is Martin Platt's mother-in-law in "Coronation Street"?
28 Who bought Jack and Vera's house in "Coronation Street"?
29 Which "EastEnders" character shares his name with a famous football manager?
30 How did Dave Glover die in "Emmerdale"?

Quiz 4 Around the UK

Answers - see page 241

1 How many faces has the clock on Big Ben's tower?
2 In which port were Dickens and Brunel both born?
3 In which London building is the Lord Mayor's banquet held?
4 Which Womble was named after the town on the Isle of Mull?
5 Which Channel Island is famous for having no cars?
6 Where is Beaumaris Castle?
7 Girton and Newnham are colleges of which university?
8 Where in London is the Lutine Bell?
9 Bryher is part of which islands?
10 Which Hills divide England and Scotland?
11 Cumbernauld is near which British city?
12 Which Sea joins the St George's Channel and the North Channel?
13 In which county is Chequers, the Prime Minister's country residence?
14 What is England's second largest cathedral?
15 Which Firth lies between south west Scotland and north west England?
16 Where is The Cathedral Church of St Michael, consecrated in 1962?
17 Which Leicestershire town is famous for its pork pies?
18 What are the canals in Cambridge called?
19 In which county is the southern end of the Pennine Way?
20 Which Roman road shares its name with a type of fur?
21 What is ERNIE's home town?
22 What is the high security prison on the Isle of Wight called?
23 In which London Square is the US Embassy?
24 Which disaster does London's Monument commemorate?
25 Which waterway divides the Isle of Wight from the mainland?
26 Which castle has St George's Chapel?
27 What is the nearest seaside resort to London?
28 Where in London are there gates named after Margaret Thatcher?
29 Which theatre was founded in 1959 at Blackfriars in London?
30 Dogger Bank is off which English county?

Answers

Pot Luck 1 (see Quiz 2)
1 Bodmin Moor. 2 Queen Elizabeth II. 3 Paris. 4 Love Affair. 5 Bjorn Borg. 6 Amy Turtle. 7 Clot. 8 Mike Reid. 9 Devon. 10 Kremlin. 11 17th. 12 Jack Russell. 13 Arthur. 14 Sarah Kennedy. 15 First five books of the Old Testament. 16 "The Liver Birds". 17 Dolly. 18 Greyfriars. 19 Paul Scott. 20 Kevin Keegan. 21 Cats. 22 Postscript. 23 Bing Crosby. 24 Rabbit. 25 Ray Illingworth. 26 Attila. 27 "Tan". 28 Bowls. 29 40s. 30 Charles Bronson.

Quiz 5 Pot Luck 2

Answers - see page 246

1   In medical terms, what are you if you are "DOA"?
2   In which crisis, in 1956, did England become involved?
3   What does Anno Domini mean?
4   Which Neil Diamond song was a No. 1 for UB40?
5   In which city is the area of Toxteth?
6   Who was the vocalist on Gary Moore's hit "Parisienne Walkways"?
7   In the farce, where did Charley's Aunt come from?
8   Over which sea was Glenn Miller lost?
9   Where is Britain's most southerly mainland point?
10   Which song title links Go West and Blondie?
11   What do W and S stand for in W.S. Gilbert's name?
12   Tony Doyle is connected with which sport?
13   In which century was Leonardo da Vinci born?
14   What was invented by Lewis E. Waterman?
15   Who wrote the novel *Emma*?
16   In which German town was "Auf Wiedersehen Pet" set?
17   Which birthstone is linked to January?
18   In which decade was the series "Agony" screened for the first time?
19   How is the General Purpose (GP) Vehicle commonly known?
20   Which poem begins, "Is there anybody there? said the Traveller"?
21   Who did George Bush defeat to become US President in 1988?
22   "The Town Of Titipu" is the subtitle of which light opera?
23   Which English cheese officially went on sale in 1982?
24   Which Japanese word means "divine wind"?
25   What did Fred Quimby produce so that his name is still seen today?
26   What was the live cargo on the *Mayflower* on its second trip to America?
27   Who played the title role in *Edward Scissorhands*?
28   What did both Johnny Haynes and Dennis Compton advertise?
29   Who had a 90s No. 1 with "Abba-Esque"?
30   In which county is Stonehenge?

Answers

Pot Luck 3   (see Quiz 7)

1 County of Swansea (was West Glamorgan till 1996). 2 Metal strips. 3 Brazil.
4 Abraham Lincoln. 5 Damascus. 6 Greater London. 7 A chef. 8 Eagle.
9 Olivia Newton-John. 10 Seville. 11 19th. 12 J.G. Ballard. 13 "Ring-a-ring-a Roses". 14 Benny Goodman. 15 Rocky Cassidy. 16 Hockey.
17 George Best. 18 Born same year (1935). 19 Died of syphilis.
20 Siamese. 21 *Prima facie*. 22 17. 23 Rick Parfitt. 24 Publishing (Writing).
25 Greek island of Kos. 26 Oldham. 27 30s. 28 Lady Chatterley.
29 Tropic of Cancer. 30 Tasmin Archer.

Answers - see page 247

LEVEL 2

1   Fountains Abbey is in which county?

2   In which museum would you see Constable's *Haywain*?

3   In what activity would you make a banjo cable or a leaf rib?

4   What moves when a chess player moves two pieces in one move?

5   Where would you go to see the Battle of the Flowers?

6   What would you have if you were a collector of Coalport?

7   How many tricks make up a grand slam in bridge?

8   What is the Viking Centre in York called?

9   What is the national game of the Basques?

10 In which seaside resort is Frontierland?

11 What is the value of the ace in baccarat?

12 What is the practice of creating replicas of animals from their dead skins called?

13 Which Cluedo weapon is nearest the beginning of the alphabet?

14 What is the minimum number of players in a game of bezique?

15 The aim is to knock down how many pins in a game of skittles?

16 What was the name of the first Rolls-Royce?

17 What is Brighton Pier called?

18 Which Essex town is famous for its Oyster Festival?

19 The Eurotunnel Exhibition Centre is nearest which port?

20 In pottery what is slip?

21 What is numismatics?

22 Alfred Wainwright wrote books on which leisure activity?

23 How many wheels are there normally on a skateboard?

24 In which month is the London-to-Brighton Veteran Car Run?

25 Where did bonsai gardens originate?

26 What would you be doing if you practised a strathspey and a pas de basque?

27 What is the practice of formal handwriting called?

28 In knitting what does psso mean?

29 In which city would you be if you went to the Fitzwilliam Museum?

30 What do British stamps not have on them which most other stamps do?

1 In which Welsh county is the Gower Peninsula?
2 What was first put into £1 notes in 1940?
3 Who were defending champions at the 1966 football World Cup?
4 Who was the first American president to be assassinated?
5 Which city in the book of Genesis is still in existence?
6 What did the City of London and 32 metropolitan boroughs become in 1965?
7 What did Ian Beale train to be in the early "EastEnders" episodes?
8 What bird is depicted over the door of the US Embassy in London?
9 Who has had hits with ELO, Cliff Richard and John Travolta?
10 In which city is Bizet's *Carmen* set?
11 In which century was Abraham Lincoln born?
12 Who wrote *Empire Of The Sun*?
13 Which children's rhyme was associated with the Black Death?
14 Who was known as the King of Swing?
15 Which character did Neil Morrissey play in "Boon"?
16 Vera Chapman played 66 times for England at which sport?
17 Which footballer's biography is *Where Do I Go from Here?*?
18 What do Johnny Mathis, Elvis Presley and Little Richard all share?
19 How did Al Capone meet his death?
20 Blue and seal-points are types of which cat?
21 Which Latin term - usually applied to legal evidence - means at first sight?
22 What is the next highest prime number above 13?
23 Which veteran rock star had a quadruple coronary heart bypass in May 1997?
24 What is Victor Gollancz particularly associated with?
25 Where did young Ben Needham mysteriously vanish in 1991?
26 Where in England was a railway station called Mumps?
27 In which decade of the 20th century was Sean Connery born?
28 Who had a lover called Mellors?
29 Which Tropic line goes through Taiwan?
30 Who had a 90s No. 1 with "Sleeping Satellite"?

1   What is the male honey bee known as?
2   Hermit and spider are types of what?
3   What is another name for an insect's feelers?
4   What name is given to the body a parasite feeds on?
5   How many eyes does a bee have?
6   Which beetle was sacred to the Egyptians?
7   What is the process of casting skin, hair or feathers called?
8   What is a gurnard?
9   Which bird is associated with Lundy Island?
10 What is a conch?
11 What sort of animal is a papillon?
12 What is the olfactory sense?
13 What does the term metamorphosis mean?
14 What is a hummingbird's hum caused by?
15 Which is the largest member of the crow family?
16 What and where is Minsmere?
17 What is another name for thunderflies or thunderbugs?
18 How many parts are there to an insect's body?
19 What do lugworms live in?
20 What is a dunnock?
21 Which system controls touch, sight and hearing?
22 From which language does the word budgerigar come?
23 What do the Americans call what the British call a ladybird?
24 How many wings does a flea have?
25 For whom is the Glorious Twelfth not glorious?
26 What is another name for cartilage?
27 How does a stoat's appearance change in the winter?
28 What is a mavis?
29 What is the smallest living unit called?
30 What do polled cattle not have?

Quiz 9 Pot Luck 4

LEVEL 2

1   Which London hospital took its first infant patient in 1852?
2   Which Cornish village claims to be the birthplace of King Arthur?
3   Which is the main river to flow through Hamburg?
4   Which band had a lead singer called Morrissey?
5   Who was jilted on her wedding day in *Great Expectations*?
6   What patent did Graham Bell file three hours before Elisha Gray?
7   What was the nickname given to V1 Flying bombs in World War II?
8   Which common British garden creature belongs to the locust family?
9   What damaged Alexandra Palace in both 1873 and 1980?
10 Which motel provides the setting in *Psycho*?
11 In which century was David Livingstone born?
12 Which character was the transvestite in "M*A*S*H"?
13 Who was the first female presenter of "Blue Peter"?
14 What does Genghis Khan mean?
15 Who wrote the book *Clayhanger*?
16 Which ocean liner, retired in 1967, became a hotel in Long Beach?
17 Paper sized 210mm x 297mm is known by which A number?
18 If it's 12 noon GMT what time is it in Berlin?
19 For Elton John's 50th birthday party who did Janet Street-Porter go dressed as?
20 Preston is on which river?
21 In which drama series did Frank Carver appear?
22 Which was the last Oxford University college to be made up of all female students?
23 Alan Minter was undisputed world boxing champion at which weight?
24 Who had a 90s No. 1 with "A Little Time"?
25 On a World War II battleship, what was called a Mae West ?
26 On record, who was the child with the talking magic piano?
27 Who had the only speaking part in Marcel Marceau's *Silent Movie*?
28 Charles Ross and Epicure are types of which fruit?
29 What time is it when Wee Willie Winkie runs through the town?
30 Who founded the Jesuits?

Answers

Pot Luck 5   (see Quiz 11)
1 Greater Manchester. 2 The Pope. 3 *The Pickwick Papers*. 4 Miami Beach.
5 Sinn Fein. 6 The Cresta Run. 7 Mandrills. 8 Richard Clayderman. 9 12.
10 Richard Nixon. 11 William Ewart. 12 Pet Shop Boys. 13 Sir James
Goldsmith. 14 God. 15 London Marathon. 16 Malcolm Bradbury.
17 Cribbage. 18 Comma. 19 15th. 20 *Dandy*. 21 Dog. 22 "Bar".
23 Androcles. 24 A contour line. 25 20s. 26 Chigwell. 27 None.
28 Ruby. 29 Champagne Charlie. 30 Aardvark.

Quiz 10 Football

Answers - see page 251

LEVEL 2

1 Who was the first boss to win the championship with separate English clubs?
2 How many FA Cup Finals did George Best play in?
3 Faustino Asprilla joined Newcastle from which club?
4 Which Scottish team are known as the Wee Roves?
5 Which club's ground has the Darwen End?
6 Which boss has won the League Cup for Sheffield Wednesday and Aston Villa?
7 Which country did Dennis Tuert play for?
8 John Collins made his debut at which Scottish club?
9 Where was John Barnes born?
10 Who was the first keeper to captain an FA Cup winning side?
11 Which Yorkshire club has its ground in Grove Street?
12 Which Spurs manager signed Ossie Ardiles?
13 Which Athletic side are known as the Wasps?
14 Which London team won the first Full Members' Cup in 1986?
15 Which footballing Danny refused to go on "This Is Your Life"?
16 Which Gary was crocked by Gazza's wild 1991 FA Cup Final tackle?
17 Who was the first black player/manager of an English league side?
18 To a year, how old was Karen Brady when she became managing director at Birmingham?
19 Which Scottish striker did Terry Venables take to Barcelona?
20 What did Bolton, Derby and Stoke all do in the summer of '97?
21 In which decade did Wales first reach the final stages of the World Cup?
22 Which was the first Belgian club to win a major European trophy?
23 Which England manager was born in Sacriston, Co. Durham?
24 Which country does the club Flamengo come from?
25 What was Stirling Albion's famous Scottish first for their ground?
26 In the 90s which player has played against and for Chelsea in FA Cup Finals?
27 Who were the only British team to win the UEFA Cup in the 80s?
28 Which team knocked the Republic out of the 1994 World Cup in USA?
29 David James joined Liverpool from which team?
30 Who play at Brockville Park?

Answers

Action Movies (see Quiz 12)
1 Blofeld. 2 Robert Aldrich. 3 *From Russia With Love*. 4 The Riddler.
5 Dante's Peak. 6 Bruce Lee. 7 Beer. 8 Boxing. 9 Doctor. 10 Bus.
11 Donnie Brasco. 12 San Francisco. 13 *Tomorrow Never Dies*. 14 *Die Hard With a Vengeance*. 15 Jane Seymour. 16 1930s. 17 *Heaven and Earth*.
18 Submarine. 19 Vietnam. 20 Frank Sinatra. 21 Sylvester Stallone.
22 *Terminator 2*. 23 Michelle Pfeiffer. 24 Barry Norman. 25 Francis Ford Coppola. 26 *Waterworld*. 27 Tina Turner. 28 Marseilles. 29 *Apollo 13*.
30 Sean Connery.

Quiz 11 Pot Luck 5

Answers - see page 248

LEVEL 2

1   In which county is Wigan?
2   Who sends encyclical letters?
3   Mr Wardle of Dingley Dell appeared in which Dickens book?
4   Where was the *Police Academy 5* movie set?
5   Which Party was introduced to Ireland in 1902 by Arthur Griffin?
6   Which world-famous European sporting track is rebuilt every year?
7   What name is given to the monkeys with red and blue bottoms?
8   What is French pianist Philippe Pages' stage name?
9   What is the highest number on the Richter scale?
10 Which US President had a wife called Thelma?
11 What do W and E stand for in W.E. Gladstone's name?
12 Who had a 80s No. 1 with "Heart"?
13 Who led the Referendum Party in 1997?
14 Theophobia is a fear of what?
15 Katrin Dorre had a hat-trick of wins in the 90s in which event?
16 Who wrote *The History Man*?
17 What card game can you peg out in?
18 Which punctuation mark has the same name as a butterfly?
19 In which century was Michelangelo born?
20 In which comic did Korky the Cat first appear?
21 1994 was the Chinese year of which creature?
22 What word can go before "gain", "row" and "tender"?
23 In legend, who removed the thorn from the lion's paw?
24 What line on a map connects points of the same height?
25 In which decade of the 20th century was Doris Day born?
26 In which suburb was "Birds of a Feather" set?
27 How many professional fights did Rocky Marciano lose?
28 Which birthstone is linked to July?
29 In song, who states that "Champagne drinking is my game"?
30 Alphabetically, which is the first creature in the dictionary?

Pot Luck 4 (see Quiz 9)
1 The Great Ormond Street Children's Hospital. 2 Tintagel. 3 The Elbe.
4 The Smiths. 5 Miss Havisham. 6 Telephone. 7 Doodlebugs. 8 The
grasshopper. 9 Fire. 10 The Bates Motel. 11 19th. 12 Corporal Klinger.
13 Leila Williams. 14 Universal ruler. 15 Arnold Bennett. 16 *Queen Mary*.
17 A4. 18 1 p.m. 19 Wonder Woman. 20 Ribble. 21 "Love Hurts".
22 St Hilda's College. 23 Middleweight. 24 The Beautiful South. 25 A life
jacket. 26 Sparky. 27 Marcel Marceau. 28 Apples. 29 Past 8 o'clock.
30 Ignatius Loyola.

Quiz 12 Action Movies

Answers - see page 249

1 Which Bond villain has been played by Telly Savalas and Donald Pleasence?
2 Who directed *Hustle* and *The Dirty Dozen*?
3 What was the second Bond film?
4 Which role did Jim Carrey play in *Batman Forever*?
5 In which 1997 film does Pierce Brosnan play a vulcanologist?
6 Whose film biography was called *Dragon*?
7 What does "Ice Cold" refer to in the John Mills film *Ice Cold in Alex*?
8 Which sport are *Kid's Return* and *Tokyo Fist* about?
9 What was the occupation of the Fugitive?
10 Which means of transport dominates in *Speed*?
11 Which 1997 Mafia film starred Al Pacino and Johnny Depp?
12 In which US city is *Metro* set?
13 What was Pierce Brosnan's second film as James Bond?
14 What was the third *Die Hard* film called?
15 Who played Bond girl Solitaire in *Live and Let Die*?
16 In which decade does the action of *Raiders of the Lost Ark* take place?
17 What was Oliver Stone's final Vietnam Trilogy film?
18 Which means of transport features in *The Hunt For Red October*?
19 Which country is the setting for Oliver Stone's *Platoon*?
20 Who plays the US captain escaping an Italian POW camp in *Von Ryan's Express*?
21 Who co-wrote and starred in *Cliffhanger* in 1993?
22 Which action movie is subtitled *Judgment Day*?
23 Who is the actress caught between an undercover cop and a drug dealer in *Tequila Sunrise*?
24 Which film critic's father produced *The Cruel Sea*?
25 Who directed the first three *Godfather* films?
26 Which 1995 film allegedly cost £1.3 million per minute screen time?
27 Which singer joined Mel Gibson for *Mad Max Beyond Thunderdome*?
28 Which city is the setting for *French Connection II*?
29 Which film's action begins with "Houston, we have a problem"?
30 Who played 007 in 1984 in *Never Say Never Again*?

Answers

Football (see Quiz 10)
1 Herbert Chapman. 2 None. 3 Parma. 4 Albion Rovers. 5 Blackburn Rovers. 6 Ron Atkinson. 7 England. 8 Hibs. 9 Jamaica. 10 Dave Beasant. 11 Barnsley. 12 Keith Burkinshaw. 13 Alloa. 14 Chelsea. 15 Blanchflower. 16 Charles. 17 Viv Anderson. 18 25. 19 Steve Archibald. 20 Moved grounds. 21 50s. 22 Anderlecht. 23 Bobby Robson. 24 Brazil. 25 First artificial pitch. 26 Mark Hughes. 27 Ipswich. 28 Holland. 29 Watford. 30 Falkirk.

1 What was a hit for Bobby "Boris" Pickett and the Crypt-Kickers?
2 What is the real name of the 90s road protestor Swampy?
3 Which former US president was born in Tampico, Illinois?
4 Which country signed the Waitangi Treaty with Britain?
5 What was the sequel to *Winnie the Pooh*?
6 What is the common name for inflamed sebaceous glands?
7 What kind of creature is a Queen Alexandra's Birdwing?
8 What returned to Piccadilly Circus in 1947 after being in hiding during the war?
9 What is the subject of Landseer's painting *The Monarch of the Glen*?
10 Which member of Queen wrote "Radio Ga Ga"?
11 What is the only English anagram of CROUTON?
12 Which English county was the home to the world's first iron bridge?
13 The Thomas Cup is awarded in which sport?
14 In woodwork, what does a tenon fit to form a joint?
15 Who was the hero of *The Camels Are Coming*, published in 1932?
16 What was Tonto's horse called?
17 What is the capital of Angola?
18 Who wrote the novel *The Tenant Of Wildfell Hall*?
19 What type of skate was invented in 1760 by Joseph Merlin?
20 Which Indian cricketer was nicknamed "Little Master"?
21 In fiction, where did Tom Brown graduate to?
22 In which century was Mozart born?
23 Which character did Laurence Olivier play in "Brideshead Revisited"?
24 What revolutionary fought with Castro and eventually died in Bolivia?
25 Who wrote the First World War poem "Anthem For Doomed Youth"?
26 In Scrabble, how many points is the letter R worth?
27 Who had an 80s No. 1 with "Doctorin' The Tardis"?
28 Who was Inspector Clouseau's manservant?
29 In which Dickens novel does John Jarndyce appear?
30 Which US city felt an earthquake for 47 seconds on April 18 1906?

1 Who presented "Crimewatch UK" with Nick Ross prior to Jill Dando?
2 Who were the two regulars on Gary Lineker and David Gower's teams in "They Think It's All Over"?
3 Who is the priest played by Stephen Tomkinson in "Ballykissangel"?
4 Who replaced Botham and Beaumont on "A Question of Sport"?
5 Who had a late-night chat show when Channel 5 was launched?
6 Who left "Blue Peter" to join the "Clothes Show" team?
7 Who is known as "Mr Trick Shot"?
8 Who starred as Blanco in "Porridge"?
9 Which TV star's first record release was "Extremis"?
10 What is the "Baywatch" star Pamela Anderson's son called?
11 Who were the stars of "A Close Shave"?
12 Who wrote "The Singing Detective" and "Pennies From Heaven"?
13 Which actress is married to John Thaw?
14 Who co-starred with Adam Faith in "Love Hurts"?
15 Who is Anthea Turner's TV presenter sister?
16 Who left "Peak Practice" for "Bliss"?
17 Whose TV wife was played by Teri Hatcher?
18 Who was known as the Green Goddess?
19 Who first presented the weather on BBC's "Breakfast Time"?
20 Who was known as the Galloping Gourmet?
21 Who became resident cook on GMTV in spring 1997?
22 Who first presented "The Antiques Roadshow" in 1981?
23 Who are team captains in Bob Holness's "Call My Bluff"?
24 Who hosted the retrospective quiz show "Backdate"?
25 Which TV star was flown in from the US to introduce the Spice Girls' first live UK performance?
26 Who is dubbed the King of Swing during election campaigns?
27 Who replaced Anthea Turner on GMTV's breakfast couch?
28 Who is Beverley Callard's actress daughter?
29 Who first presented "Nine O'Clock Live" on GMTV?
30 Which actress is married to the playwright Jack Rosenthal?

Answers

Pot Luck 7 (see Quiz 16)
1 Light blue. 2 Four years. 3 Winchester. 4 Lake Superior. 5 Darts.
6 Ermine Street. 7 Japan. 8 Elton John. 9 King's Oak. 10 It turns to stone.
11 16th. 12 Prince Philip. 13 Small Faces. 14 Andante. 15 Atlantic.
16 Bob Monkhouse. 17 Anthony Burgess. 18 Kansas. 19 "On the Up".
20 "Birds Of A Feather". 21 Hooves. 22 An Oscar. 23 Moon River.
24 Benjamin Jonson. 25 40s. 26 Jimmy Young. 27 American Football.
28 Haile Selassie. 29 Ruth. 30 Bashful.

1 Which all-girl group included Michael Steele?
2 Which country did A-Ha come from?
3 Mike D'Abo and Paul Jones sang with which group?
4 Tony McCarroll was the only non-family member of which group?
5 What was Blondie's first No. 1?
6 Who has had hits featuring Duane Eddy, Max Headroom and Tom Jones?
7 Which 60s group charted with "Tell Me When"?
8 What was the surname of Luke and Matt of Bros?
9 Who were Sarah Dullin, Siobhan Fahey and Keren Woodward?
10 Who was lead singer with Amen Corner?
11 What was in brackets in the title of Chic's "Dance Dance Dance"?
12 Which group featured Stewart "Woody" Wood?
13 Which group made records about an Arnold and an Emily?
14 Roger McGuinn and David Crosby were in which 60s band?
15 What was Wet Wet Wet's first No. 1?
16 Which 60s group featured Demis Roussos and Vangelis?
17 Thin Lizzy came from which country?
18 Steve Marriott and Ronnie Lane were in which band?
19 Which group were responsible for "Chirpy Chirpy Cheep Cheep"?
20 In the 60s who did the Roulettes back?
21 Who were "Going Underground" in 1980?
22 Who backed Bob Dylan on his late 60s and 70s tour?
23 Which Scottish group hit No. 1 after splitting up thanks to airplay from a Volkswagen ad in 1993?
24 Errol Browne is lead singer with which long-standing group?
25 Which group first charted with the Paul Simon classic "The Sound Of Silence"?
26 Who links Sakkarin, Bubblerock and Weathermen?
27 Which furry group were put together by Mike Batt?
28 Jacqueline Abbott and Briana Corrigan have sung with which group?
29 What is Blur's hometown?
30 Where were the Housemartins based?

Quiz 16 Pot Luck 7

Answers - see page 253

1   What is the background colour of the United Nations flag?
2   How old is a horse when it changes to a mare from a filly?
3   Which city is home to Britain's longest cathedral?
4   Which of the Great Lakes is the largest freshwater lake in the world?
5   The BDO is the UK governing body of which sport?
6   Which Roman road linked London to York?
7   What country are chrysanthemums native to?
8   Which former Watford chairman married Renate?
9   What was the name of the suburb in which "Crossroads" was set?
10 What happens to something if it is - literally - petrified?
11 In which century was William Shakespeare born?
12 Which Royal celebrates his birthday on June 10?
13 Who had a 60s No. 1 with "All Or Nothing"?
14 Which musical term means at a walking pace?
15 What does the A stand for in NATO?
16 Who was the first presenter of "Celebrity Squares"?
17 Who wrote the novel *A Clockwork Orange*?
18 Which American state is home to Dodge City?
19 In which sitcom did Sam and Mrs Wembley appear?
20 Which programme pushed "Panorama" out of its traditional 9.30 p.m. Monday slot in 1997?
21 What does an ungulate animal have?
22 What is 10 inches tall, gold-plated and weighs seven pounds?
23 In song, what river is wider than a mile?
24 In 1616, who became the first Poet Laureate?
25 In which decade of the 20th century was Robert de Niro born?
26 Which Radio 2 DJ used to finish his show with "TTFN" or "BFN"?
27 Emmitt Smith is associated with which sport?
28 How was Ras Tafari Makonnen better known?
29 In the Old Testament, the book of which woman directly follows Judges?
30 Alphabetically, who is the first of Snow White's Seven Dwarfs?

LEVEL 2

Answers - see page 258

1   Which type of wheat is used in gnocchi?

2   What type of meat is used in osso bucco?

3   What is the flavour of kummel?

4   Which cream has more fat, clotted cream or double cream?

5   What are suntinas?

6   What is special about porcini mushrooms?

7   How is Parmigiano Reggiano usually known in the UK?

8   Burtonwood Ales were originally based near which town?

9   What sort of meat is silverside?

10 What is the Italian equivalent of a French vin de table?

11 Which spirit is used in a Manhattan?

12 Which fruit flavour is used in crêpes suzette?

13 What are the two main ingredients of a coulibiac?

14 What is sake wine made from?

15 Which flavoured liqueur is used to make Kir?

16 What are the two main ingredients of kedgeree?

17 Which breeds of cow produce so-called gold-top milk?

18 Which liqueur is used in a sidecar?

19 Which type of pastry is usually bought frozen in wafer-thin slices?

20 Which two cheeses are layered in a Huntsman cheese?

21 How many standard bottles of wine are equivalent to a methuselah?

22 What is pancetta?

23 What type of flour is traditionally used in blinis?

24 What are flageolet and cannellini?

25 Which country does chorizo sausage come from?

26 From which part of France does Calvados originate?

27 What is focaccia?

28 Which two main ingredients would you add to spaghetti to make spaghetti alla carbonara?

29 What type of milk has a bottle with a blue-and-silver-checked cap?

30 What is arborio?

1   What was Disney's second animated feature film?
2   What is a glow worm as it is not a worm?
3   Where are the world headquarters of the Mormon Church?
4   Which Motown group featured Lionel Richie before he went solo?
5   What was the nickname of boxer Dave Green?
6   Which animal's name is Aboriginal and means "No drink"?
7   Which role did Phil Collins play in a stage version of *Oliver!*?
8   Which flowering plant family includes asparagus?
9   Which Irish county would you be in if you were in Tipperary?
10   Who was Muhammad Ali's first professional opponent outside the US?
11   Who wrote the children's classic *The Secret Garden*?
12   What was the nickname of Sir Arthur Travers Harris?
13   What genus and species is man classified as?
14   Which imaginary island was created in 1516 by Sir Thomas More?
15   Who had a 50s No. 1 with "The Story Of My Life"?
16   In which state was "Dynasty" set?
17   Which British school did Kurt Hahn found in the 1930s?
18   In which decade was the series "'Allo 'Allo" screened for the first time?
19   What word can go after "port" and before "seaman"?
20   In which continent is Lake Titicaca?
21   Who was asked for the bolt in the original "The Golden Shot"?
22   Which American Football team did Gavin Hastings first play for?
23   In which century was Charles Perrault collecting his fairy stories?
24   If the weather is calm what is wind force on the Beaufort scale?
25   What is the capital of Libya?
26   What was the name of the chess-playing computer that beat Kasparov?
27   Concorde and Louise Bonne are types of which fruit?
28   Who was the first winner on Wimbledon's new 1997 No. 1 court?
29   Who did Wimbledon players describe as a jellyfish?
30   What type of quadrilateral has all sides the same length but contains no right angles?

1   Who did Prince William invite to a parents' event at Eton in 1997?
2   Who is the first female in line to the throne?
3   Which King (name and number) was the subject of a 1995 film?
4   Who are the parents of Lady Helen Taylor?
5   Who played John Brown when Judi Dench was Victoria on TV?
6   Who interviewed Princess Diana for "Panorama" in 1995?
7   Princess Diana confessed to having had an affair with whom?
8   Who was Princess Anne's bridesmaid when she married Mark Phillips?
9   Who is Serena Linley's mother-in-law?
10 How many lots were there in the Christie's sale of Diana's dresses?
11 Who was Prince Charles's mother-in-law for 14 years?
12 Which Princess was married to the bodyguard Daniel Ducruet?
13 Emily Davison died under the hooves of which king's horse?
14 Which country did Princess Diana visit to publicize the dangers of landmines?
15 Who was Susan who accompanied Princess Elizabeth on her honeymoon?
16 Who was the first royal after Henry VIII to marry after a divorce?
17 Which letters did *Britannia* have before its name?
18 Who are the oldest royal bodyguards?
19 Reputedly how much was the Princess of Wales's divorce settlement?
20 Who presented the trophy at the 1997 Grand National?
21 What colour are "Princess of Wales" roses?
22 Who was Queen Elizabeth II's first prime minister?
23 In which church did Princess Anne's second marriage take place?
24 Who was the last Empress of India?
25 Which gardener's name was linked with Princess Margaret in the 70s?
26 In which month of the year is the Garter Service?
27 Which two Princes have birthdays in June?
28 Which Royal was an exhibitor at the 1997 Chelsea Flower Show?
29 Princess Diana is patron of which ballet company?
30 What role does Sir Robert Fellowes have amongst the Queen's staff?

1 Who was Richard Nixon's first vice-president?
2 In the 70s who did Idi Amin oust from power in Uganda?
3 Which Emperor of Japan ruled for over 60 years in the 20th century?
4 What was the first name of Mrs Gorbachev?
5 Who succeeded President Nasser in Egypt?
6 Bill Clinton has been governor of which state?
7 Who was the world's first woman prime minister?
8 In which decade did Juan Carlos I become King of Spain?
9 Robert Mugabe was prime minister and president of which country?
10 Who became Ireland's first woman president?
11 Who was president of Argentina from 1946 to 1955?
12 Which archbishop became the first president of an independent Cyprus?
13 Who was French president during the Paris student riots of the 60s?
14 In which country did Baby succeed Papa?
15 Which Israeli leader won the Nobel Peace Prize in 1978?
16 Which terrorist group murdered Italy's Aldo Moro?
17 In which decade did Indira Gandhi first become Indian prime minister?
18 How was Romanian dictator Ceaucescu executed?
19 Who was the first prime minister to give birth while in office?
20 Who was George Bush's vice president?
21 The former British PM James Callaghan became Baron Callaghan of where?
22 Which Australian PM got the push by the Governor General in the 70s?
23 Who ousted Khruschev in the Kremlin coup of the 60s?
24 Canan Banana was the first president of which country?
25 Nelson Rockefeller was vice-president to which USA president?
26 Who was president of South Africa before F.W. de Klerk?
27 Corazon Aquino was president of which country?
28 In which country did King Farouk abdicate after a military coup?
29 Who was the first president of the Fifth French Republic?
30 The splendidly named King Zog ruled which East European country?

Quiz 21 Pot Luck 9

LEVEL 2

1 Which is the third film of the *Star Wars* trilogy?
2 What is the diameter in inches of a standard competition dartboard?
3 Which children's programme had the sci-fi strip "Bleep and Booster"?
4 A beluga is a type of what?
5 Lent always begins on which day of the week?
6 Which royal told the press to "naff off" at the Badminton Horse Trials?
7 David Wagstaffe was the first British footballer to be shown what?
8 Which language does the word "anorak" come from?
9 Why did the catfish get its name?
10 What title did Billy Connolly give to the Village People's "In The Navy"?
11 Who wrote the novel *The Woman In White*?
12 What was the nickname of Arthur Marx?
13 In which century was Richard the Lionheart born?
14 Which US state is renowned for its Black Hills?
15 What kind a school was run by Pussy Galore?
16 Photophobia is a fear of what?
17 What relation, if any, was Pitt the Elder to Pitt the Younger?
18 Who had a 80s No. 1 with "Never Gonna Give You Up"?
19 Which character did Emma Samms play in "Dynasty"?
20 Which countries share the world's longest frontier?
21 Bruce Woodcock was connected with which sport?
22 On what part of the body are mukluks worn?
23 Which film from 1970 tells of a relationship of a boy and a kestrel?
24 What is the first name of the girl who dies in *Love Story*?
25 In economics, who in the 90s was "Steady Eddie"?
26 What is the Royal Navy equivalent of the army rank of major general?
27 Which birthstone is linked to February?
28 Who is Welwyn Garden City's most famous golfer?
29 In which decade of the 20th century was Placido Domingo born?
30 What is the name of the Vatican's army?

Answers

Pot Luck 10 (see Quiz 23)
1 Busy Lizzy. 2 Xian. 3 Royal Canadian Mounted Police. 4 The Railway Children. 5 Coffee. 6 June Brown. 7 The decimal halfpenny. 8 Powys. 9 Richard I. 10 Snowdon. 11 19th. 12 Fyodor Dostoevsky. 13 Malcolm X. 14 Take That. 15 Coca-Cola. 16 29. 17 Kim Philby. 18 "The Paradise Club". 19 India. 20 Michael Aspel. 21 "Rain". 22 Slate. 23 Lulu. 24 Mohammed Sarwar. 25 50s. 26 Angling. 27 Napoleon. 28 Pandora's. 29 Peter. 30 Norwich City's.

Quiz 22 Technology & Industry

Answers - see page 263

LEVEL 2

1 Which country was the first to legalize trade unions?
2 In which decade was British Petroleum privatized?
3 Which revolutionary product did Proctor & Gamble launch in 1969?
4 Where did one of the worst industrial accidents take place in 1984?
5 Along with Corn Flakes which cereal did Kellogg's export to the UK in 1922?
6 What name is given to an alloy that joins surfaces together?
7 Which company's first computer, the 701, was produced in 1953?
8 Which company's red-triangle trademark was the first to be registered?
9 Which industrialist became first Lord Mayor of Dublin in 1851?
10 Who invented and marketed a vehicle powered by a washing-machine motor?
11 Which company did Israel Moses Sieff develop?
12 The jelly Vaseline was a bi-product from which industry?
13 Which convenience product was launched from its factory in St Andrews Road, Walthamstow, in 1945?
14 Which London retailer sold the first Heinz products in the UK 1895?
15 Who formed the Electric Suction Sweeper Co. in 1908?
16 How is a complex electronic circuit built on a small piece of silicon more commonly known?
17 Which two companies first developed the compact disc?
18 Who founded the British and North American Royal Mail Steam Packet Company which later bore his name?
19 Fred Dibnah was famous in which industry?
20 Which company introduced travellers' cheques?
21 Lord Nuffield was the first British mass producer of what?
22 Which of his names did Woolworth use as a brand name in stores?
23 Which business did Howard Hughes finance from his oil profits?
24 In which century was the first English patent granted?
25 Which Swiss company first developed waterproof watches?
26 How would polyvinyl chloride be relevant to a double-glazing salesman?
27 What was the first-ever household detergent?
28 What was founded as Fabbrica Italiana Automobili Torino in 1899?
29 Who gave his name to his invention the whirlpool bath?
30 Which company did Terence Conran found in 1971?

Movies: Superstars (see Quiz 24)

1 Jack Nicholson. 2 Harrison Ford. 3 Meg Ryan. 4 Clint Eastwood. 5 Sean Connery. 6 Clark Gable. 7 Katharine Hepburn. 8 Fletcher Christian. 9 Cary Grant. 10 Lawyer. 11 Tom Cruise. 12 Michael Douglas. 13 Michelle Pfeiffer. 14 Humphrey Bogart. 15 *Scent of a Woman*. 16 Spencer Tracy. 17 "Thanks For the Memory". 18 Fred Astaire and Ginger Rogers. 19 Joan Crawford. 20 Arnold Schwarzenegger. 21 *Waterworld*. 22 Anthony Hopkins. 23 Robert Redford. 24 Tony Curtis. 25 Demi Moore. 26 Dustin Hoffman. 27 Meryl Streep. 28 Bette Davis. 29 Sylvester Stallone. 30 Duke.

261

1 Which plant's scientific name is *Impatiens*?
2 Which Chinese city is home to the Terracotta Army?
3 What did the North West Mounted Police become in 1920?
4 Who were Roberta, Phyllis and Peter collectively known as?
5 Which drink is named after the Ethiopian city of Kaffa?
6 Who played Dot Cotton in "EastEnders"?
7 What coin was made compulsory in 1971 and illegal in 1985?
8 Which county is home to the Brecon Beacons?
9 Which King received the support of Robin Hood?
10 What is the highest UK peak south of the Scottish border?
11 In which century was Fred Astaire born?
12 Who wrote the novel *Crime and Punishment*?
13 How was Malcolm Little better known?
14 Who had a 90s No. 1 with "Pray"?
15 Which drink has "7X" as a secret formula?
16 How old was Brian Clough when he stopped playing soccer?
17 Who published *My Silent War* in the USSR in 1968?
18 In which series did Frank and Danny Kane appear?
19 Which country was the setting for *Carry On Up the Khyber*?
20 Who was the first presenter of "Give Us A Clue"?
21 What word can go after "rest" and before "hood"?
22 Which stone is used in snooker tables?
23 In song lyrics, you can bring Pearl or Rose but who can't you bring?
24 Who in 1997 became Britain's first Muslim MP?
25 In which decade did Minnie the Minx first appear in the *Beano*?
26 Alan Scotthorne was a 90s world champion in which sport?
27 Which well-known Frenchman designed Italy's flag?
28 Whose box was opened by Epimethius?
29 Which name derived from Greek means stone or rock?
30 Which team's football kit was designed by Bruce Oldfield in 1997?

Quiz 24 Movies: Superstars

Answers - see page 261

LEVEL 2

1   Who played Garrett Breedlove in *Terms of Endearment*?
2   Who was the male co-star with Sigourney Weaver and Melanie Griffith in *Working Girl*?
3   How is Margaret Mary Emily Anne Hyra better known?
4   Which superstar was mayor of his home town Carmel, California?
5   Who was contestant No. 24 in the 1950 Mr Universe contest?
6   Whose most famous line was "Frankly, my dear, I don't give a damn"?
7   Who used Eleanor Roosevelt as her inspiration for her role in *The African Queen*?
8   Clark Gable, Marlon Brando and Mel Gibson have all played which sailor on film?
9   On film who did Mae West invite to "come up some time an' see me"?
10 What was Tom Hanks's profession in *Philadelphia*?
11 Who co-starred with Paul Newman in *The Color of Money*?
12 Which actor had the line "Greed is good" in *Wall Street* in 1987?
13 Who sang "Makin' Whoopee" on Jeff Bridges' piano in *The Fabulous Baker Boys*?
14 Who won an Oscar as Charlie Allnut in *The African Queen*?
15 For which film did Al Pacino win his first Oscar?
16 Who received an Oscar nomination for his last film *Guess Who's Coming to Dinner*?
17 What is Bob Hope's signature tune?
18 Who were first paired on screen in *Flying Down to Rio*?
19 Which actress was the subject of the film *Mommie Dearest*?
20 Who married the journalist Maria Shriver, a niece of President Kennedy?
21 Which Kevin Costner film was one of the most expensive flops ever?
22 Who played the doctor in *The Elephant Man*?
23 Who founded the the Sundance Institute for new film-makers?
24 Who parodied his hero Cary Grant in *Some Like It Hot*?
25 How is Demetria Guynes better known?
26 Who played Carl Bernstein in *All the President's Men*?
27 Which actress sounded Polish in 1982, Danish in 1985 and Australian in 1988?
28 Who had six Best Actress Oscar nominations between 1938 and 1942?
29 Who wrote the script for *Rocky*?
30 What was John Wayne's nickname?

Technology & Industry   (see Quiz 22)
1 Britain. 2 1950s. 3 Ariel. 4 Bhopal, India. 5 All Bran. 6 Solder. 7 IBM.
8 Bass brewery. 9 Guinness. 10 Clive Sinclair. 11 Marks and Spencer.
12 Petroleum. 13 Andrex toilet roll. 14 Fortnum & Mason. 15 William
Hoover. 16 Microchip. 17 Philips and Sony. 18 Cunard. 19 Steeplejack.
20 American Express. 21 Cars - William Morris. 22 Winfield. 23 Film.
24 15th. 25 Rolex. 26 uPVC - used for window frames. 27 Persil. 28 Fiat.
29 Candido Jacuzzi. 30 Habitat.

Answers

Answers - see page 266

1 Which wartime hero had the same name as Hilda Ogden's cat?
2 What kind of plants is the name Harry Wheatcroft linked with?
3 Which ocean are the Seychelles in?
4 What expense became compulsory for cars in 1921?
5 Which university had Sir Robin Day as a former union president?
6 Which decade saw the first FA Cup Final at Wembley?
7 What kind of reference book was Bradshaw's?
8 What is a butterfly larva more commonly called?
9 Which actress appeared in Woody Allen's *The Purple Rose of Cairo*?
10 Which fictional doctor lived in Puddleby-on-Marsh?
11 In which decade of the 20th century was Mikhail Gorbachev born?
12 What was Bob Marley's middle name?
13 What is the only English anagram of TOENAIL?
14 If it's 12 noon GMT what time is it in Athens?
15 Who wrote *Journey To The Centre Of The Earth*?
16 Alan Hansen joined Liverpool from which club?
17 Who had a 90s No. 1 with "Rhythm Is A Dancer"?
18 Which is the only active volcano in mainland Europe?
19 In which century was Jane Austen born?
20 On which ranch was "Bonanza" set?
21 How many counters does backgammon have of each colour?
22 Who co-founded the Aldeburgh Festival in 1948?
23 What is the capital of Morocco?
24 Who authorized the authorized version of the Bible?
25 For how many years did David Coleman present "A Question of Sport"?
26 What is the next highest prime number above 23?
27 Who won the decathlon in the 1980 Olympics?
28 "The Lass That Loved A Sailor" is the subtitle of which light opera?
29 What is the name of Tony Blair's first-born son?
30 Careless and Invictor are types of which fruit?

Answers

Pot Luck 12 (see Quiz 27)
1 Noël Coward. 2 The discus. 3 Osborne House. 4 "No Woman No Cry".
5 Nicholas Nickleby. 6 Lungs. 7 Thomas. 8 A type of beetle. 9 Stephanie
Beecham. 10 The Cadburys. 11 Daniel Defoe. 12 William Joyce.
13 Mongooses. 14 Alvin Stardust. 15 19th. 16 Post meridiem. 17 Private
Charles Godfrey. 18 Latin. 19 Stagnation. 20 Nana. 21 Fire. 22 Quito.
23 One. 24 The MGs. 25 "The Refrigerator". 26 "Iron". 27 26p.
28 Nepal. 29 Pig. 30 Leicester.

1 Who fought Muhammad Ali in the Rumble in the Jungle?
2 Jennifer Susan Harvey is better known by what name?
3 Which Englishman scored the first 1997 Ashes century?
4 Which Italian said he could not "understand a word Dennis Wise is saying"?
5 Which Andy won rugby's Lance Todd Award in 1988 and 1990?
6 Who was skipper of Middlesbrough's 1997 FA Cup Final team?
7 Who was the female competitor excused a sex test at the 1976 Olympics?
8 Who was the first Swede to win Wimbledon's Men's Singles?
9 Who was Marvellous Marvin?
10 Who left Llanelli in 1989 to play rugby league for Widnes?
11 Who sponsored the 1997 one-day England v. Australia cricket?
12 Who won the 125th Open at Lytham?
13 Who was the first black athlete to captain Great Britain men's team?
14 Who retired in the 90s after 15 years as chairman of the FA?
15 Who is Michael Schumacher's younger racing driver brother?
16 Which Spanish player interrupted Graf's reign as women's singles champion at Wimbledon?
17 Who was the English captain of the 1980 British Lions tour?
18 Which boxer was born in Bellingham, London, on May 3 1934?
19 Which left-handed batsman has scored most test runs for England?
20 Who was Leeds's manager before George Graham?
21 Who is the first person to manage Everton three times?
22 Who was first to win the US Masters five times?
23 Who scored the last-minute play-off goal for Crystal Palace in 1997?
24 Who was first to ride seven Derby winners?
25 Who did Gazza flick the ball over for the Euro '96 goal against Scotland?
26 Who partnered Hingis to win Wimbledon's 1996 women's doubles?
27 Who won the US Tennis Open while her father was in a legal court?
28 Who had a set to with umpire Shakoor Rana at Faisalabad in 1987?
29 Who managed Frank Bruno?
30 Who scored Southampton's FA Cup Final winner in the 70s?

Answers

TV Times 1 (see Quiz 28)

1 James. **2** A bloodhound. **3** Xylophone. **4** Yorkshire. **5** Mary. **6** "Antiques Roadshow". **7** The Flintstones. **8** The Thrift. **9** Clarissa Dickson Wright. **10** Erica Matthews. **11** Aidensfield. **12** Lawyers. **13** Jack Davenport. **14** Dermot. **15** Napoleon. **16** Fireman Sam. **17** Tin Tin. **18** June Whitfield. **19** 1950s. **20** Harry Worth. **21** Gravesend. **22** Ulrika Jonsson. **23** CJ. **24** Gus Hedges. **25** Jane Seymour. **26** "The Thin Blue Line". **27** "Brookside". **28** "Due South". **29** "Paradise Gardens". **30** Diane-Louise Jordan.

Quiz 27 Pot Luck 12

Answers - see page 264

1. Who said, "There's always something fishy about the French"?
2. What is thrown in the Olympics weighing 4lb 6oz?
3. Which house on the Isle of Wight was home to Queen Victoria?
4. Which Bob Marley song got to 22 in 1975 then the top ten in 1981?
5. Which Dickens character had a friend called Smike?
6. What name is given to a whale's breathing organs?
7. Alphabetically, who was last of the Twelve Apostles?
8. What is a devil's coachhorse?
9. Which actress became Sable Colby after appearing as Connie?
10. Which family built the town called Bourneville?
11. Who wrote the novel *Moll Flanders*?
12. Whose nickname was "Lord Haw Haw"?
13. What is the plural of mongoose?
14. Who had a 70s No. 1 with "Jealous Mind"?
15. In which century was Al Capone born?
16. What does the time abbreviation p.m. stand for?
17. Which character did Arnold Ridley play in "Dad's Army"?
18. In which language did St Patrick write his autobiography?
19. What is the only English anagram of ANTAGONIST?
20. What is the name of the dog in Peter Pan?
21. Pyrophobia is a fear of what?
22. What is the capital of Ecuador?
23. In Scrabble, how many points is the letter S worth?
24. Who were Booker T's backing group?
25. What was American Footballer Wiliam Perry's nickname?
26. What word can follow "cast", "pig" and "steam"?
27. How much was the Dracula stamp worth when first issued?
28. Which country is Mount Everest in?
29. 1995 was the Chinese year of which creature?
30. Engelbert Humperdink is from which English city?

Answers

Pot Luck 11 (see Quiz 25)
1 Rommel. 2 Roses. 3 The Indian Ocean. 4 Tax discs. 5 Oxford.
6 1920s. 7 Railway timetable. 8 Caterpillar. 9 Mia Farrow. 10 Dr Doolittle.
11 30s. 12 Nesta. 13 Elation. 14 2 p.m. 15 Jules Verne.
16 Partick Thistle. 17 Snap. 18 Mount Vesuvius. 19 18th. 20 The Ponderosa. 21 15. 22 Benjamin Britten, Peter Pears. 23 Rabat. 24 James I.
25 18. 26 29. 27 Daley Thompson. 28 *HMS Pinafore*. 29 Euan.
30 Gooseberry.

1   What is the first name of Kavanagh QC?
2   What is the mascot for "The Great Antiques Hunt"?
3   Patrick Moore is famous for playing which musical instrument?
4   In which county was "Where the Heart Is" set?
5   What is Rab C. Nesbitt's wife called?
6   Henry Sandon became famous on which TV show?
7   Who did the Simpsons replace as TV's longest-running cartoon family in 1997?
8   What is the name of the infirmary in "Bramwell"?
9   Who is Jennifer Paterson's cooking partner?
10 Which female doctor succeeded Beth Glover in "Peak Practice"?
11 What is the fictional village where "Heartbeat" is set?
12 What is the profession of the chief characters in "This Life"?
13 Which actor is the son of Nigel Davenport and Maria Aitken?
14 Which role did Harry Enfield play in "Men Behaving Badly"?
15 What did the ARP warden call Mainwaring in "Dad's Army"?
16 Which children's TV character lives in Pontypandy?
17 Which detective has a dog called Snowy?
18 Who is the comedienne mother of the actress Suzy Aitchison?
19 In which decade was "Hi-De-Hi" first set?
20 Which comedian began his show with a shop-window illusion?
21 Where was Dot Cotton living before she returned to Walford in 1997?
22 Who was the blondest person on "Shooting Stars"?
23 Who was Reginald Perrin's boss?
24 Whose catchphrase in "Drop the Dead Donkey" was "I'm not here"?
25 Who plays the title role in "Dr Quinn: Medicine Woman"?
26 In which show would you find PC Goody?
27 Where would you find the Simpsons other than in "The Simpsons"?
28 In which series would you find Benton Fraser?
29 Which Geoff Hamilton series was first shown after his death?
30 Who left "Blue Peter" in 1996 and presented "Songs of Praise"?

Answers

Sport: Who's Who? (see Quiz 26)

1 George Foreman. 2 Jenny Pitman. 3 Graham Thorpe. 4 Gianfranco Zola. 5 Gregory. 6 Nigel Pearson. 7 Princess Anne. 8 Bjorn Borg. 9 Marvin Hagler. 10 Jonathan Davies. 11 Texaco. 12 Tom Lehman. 13 Kris Akabusi. 14 Sir Bert Millichip. 15 Ralf. 16 Conchita Martinez. 17 Bill Beaumont. 18 Henry Cooper. 19 David Gower. 20 Howard Wilkinson. 21 Howard Kendall. 22 Jack Nicklaus. 23 David Hopkin. 24 Lester Piggott. 25 Colin Hendry. 26 Helena Sukova. 27 Steffi Graf. 28 Mike Gatting. 29 Terry Lawless. 30 Bobby Stokes.

1 Which part of London is famous for its diamond trade?
2 What was first broadcast from Greenwich by the BBC in February 1924?
3 Who was the longest-reigning British king?
4 Which sport was the subject of the Popplewell Report in 1985?
5 Which building was Prime Minister Lloyd George the first to use?
6 Which group of islands includes Aran?
7 What is the Swiss author Johanna Spyri's best-known children's novel?
8 In sporting terms, what does the BBBC stand for?
9 On which river does New Orleans stand?
10 What was first published in *The Times* on February 1 1930?
11 In which century was Johan Sebastian Bach born?
12 Who wrote the novel *The Count of Monte Cristo*?
13 Who was the first presenter of "Grandstand"?
14 The "Cat And Mouse Act" was to counter activities of which movement?
15 Charles Ross and Epicure are types of which fruit?
16 What was Kojak's first name?
17 Which country has San Salvador as its capital?
18 Who had a 60s No. 1 with "I've Gotta Get A Message To You"?
19 Laurence Olivier took the title Baron Olivier of where?
20 In which drama series did Will Preston and Alice North appear?
21 How many laps are there in a single speedway race?
22 Which inflamed part of your body suffers from encephalitis?
23 In which decade of the 20th century was Che Guevara born?
24 What word can go after "race" and before "fly"?
25 How is the film director Sandor Kellner better known?
26 What is a Dorset Blue Vinney?
27 Where is the University of Strathclyde based?
28 Who is Melchester Rovers' most famous striker?
29 In April 1997 George Tenet became head of which US organization?
30 Which bird was on the old coin the farthing?

Answers

Pot Luck 14 (see Quiz 31)
1 Tower Bridge. 2 Idi Amin. 3 Personal best. 4 The ring. 5 Melbourne.
6 Cher. 7 Charlie Brown. 8 *Columbia*. 9 May Day. 10 London.
11 David Herbert. 12 David Soul. 13 Chronos. 14 Violin. 15 17th.
16 Bodies from graves. 17 E. 18 Sardonyx. 19 Skiing. 20 American
Independence. 21 Spain. 22 Piltdown Man. 23 The Goons. 24 Dublin.
25 Without an orchestra. 26 1970s. 27 Leskanich. 28 New York.
29 Daphne du Maurier. 30 Glasgow.

1   In which city is the largest Christian church in the world?
2   What is the official home of the French President?
3   On which island is Ajaccio?
4   What is the French town of Limoges famous for?
5   Which part of Paris is famous as the artists' quarter?
6   Where is the European Court of Justice?
7   Ibiza and Majorca are part of which island group?
8   The Oise and the Marne are tributaries of which river?
9   Where is the Abbey Theatre?
10 What is Germany's highest mountain?
11 On which river does Florence stand?
12 Which Mediterranean island was the HQ of the Knights of St John?
13 Which country has most European neighbours?
14 The RER is part of which city's underground system?
15 The Azores belong to which European country?
16 How many Benelux countries are there?
17 Andorra is among which mountains?
18 Piraeus is the port of which city?
19 In which country is Lake Garda?
20 Where does the river Loire flow into the Atlantic?
21 In which central European country is Lake Balaton?
22 Which country do the Faeroe Islands belong to?
23 The Skagerrak links the Kattegat with which Sea?
24 Which country's official name is Konungariket Sverige?
25 The parliament of which country is called the Cortes?
26 Ljubljana is the capital of which country of the former Yugoslavia?
27 Which Republic lies between Poland and Hungary?
28 Utrecht is in which European country?
29 Where is Monegasque spoken?
30 Which is the southernmost and largest of Greece's many islands?

Answers

Pop: No 1s (see Quiz 32)

1 Partners In Kryme. **2** The Aces. **3** Chrissie Hynde. **4** Levi's jeans. **5** "Tiger Feet". **6** Robson & Jerome. **7** Los Lobos. **8** "Cabaret". **9** "Free." **10** 90s. **11** "(Come Up And See Me)". **12** Blur. **13** "Dancing Queen". **14** David Soul. **15** "Saving All My Love For You". **16** Gary Brooker. **17** Eddie Calvert. **18** Jazzy Jeff. **19** "Day Tripper". **20** Reg Presley. **21** Kiki Dee. **22** Terry Jacks. **23** "Mr Blobby". **24** "The Legend Of Xanadu". **25** "Baby Come Back". **26** "Super Trouper". **27** Slim Whitman. **28** "Fairground". **29** "Let It Be". **30** "What's Another Year?".

1   Which bridge on the Thames is closest to the Tower of London?
2   Who seized power in Uganda in 1971??
3   What does "PB" against a runner's name indicate?
4   What was made by Sauron in a J.R.R. Tolkien book?
5   On TV, in which city is Ramsay Street?
6   Who was the female voice on "Deadringer For Love"?
7   Which character loves the little red-haired girl in "Peanuts"?
8   Which US space shuttle was the first to gain orbit into space?
9   Which annual holiday did the 1992 government want to move?
10   Which city provides the setting for *1984*?
11   What do the D and H stand for in D.H. Lawrence's name?
12   Who had a 70s No. 1 with "Don't Give Up On Us"?
13   Who was the Greek god of time?
14   What musical instrument was played by Sherlock Holmes?
15   In which century was Sir Isaac Newton born?
16   If you were a resurrectionist, what would you steal?
17   In Morse code what letter is represented by one dot?
18   Which birthstone is linked to August?
19   Albert Tomba has been a world champion in which sport?
20   In which war was the Battle of Bunker Hill?
21   In which country did the fandango originate?
22   Which Man was discovered in East Sussex in 1912?
23   Which comic team included a Welshman, an Indian-born Anglo-Irishman and an Anglo-Peruvian?
24   Handel's *Messiah* was first put on for the public in which city?
25   What does karaoke mean?
26   In which decade was "The Antiques Roadshow" first screened?
27   What is the surname of the Eurovision Song Contest winner Katrina?
28   In which city was "Fame" set?
29   Who wrote the novel *Jamaica Inn*?
30   Which Scottish city has Saint Mungo as its patron saint?

Quiz 32 Pop: No 1s

Answers - see page 269

1 Who had a 90s No. 1 with "Turtle Power"?
2 Who backed Desmond Dekker on "The Israelites"?
3 Who had a No. 1 with Cher, Neneh Cherry and Eric Clapton?
4 Stiltskin's "Inside" was used to advertise which product?
5 What was Mud's first No. 1?
6 Who kept Oasis and "Wonderwall" off the top?
7 Who had a 80s No. 1 with "La Bamba"?
8 What was on the other side of Louis Armstrong's "What A Wonderful World"?
9 What was the title of Deniece Williams's 1977 No. 1?
10 In which decade did Lulu first top the UK charts?
11 What in brackets is added to the title "Make Me Smile"?
12 Who had the first No. 1 on the Food label?
13 Which No1 contains the words "hear the beat of the tambourine"?
14 Who had a 70s No. 1 with "Silver Lady"?
15 What was Whitney Houston's first UK No. 1?
16 Who was Procol Harum's "Whiter Shade Of Pale" vocalist?
17 Which trumpeter had two No. 1s in the 50s?
18 Who had a No. 1 with the Fresh Prince?
19 What was on the other side of the Beatles' "We Can Work It Out"?
20 Who wrote "Love Is All Around"?
21 Who partnered Elton John on his first UK No. 1?
22 Who had a 70s No. 1 with "Seasons In the Sun"?
23 In the 90s, which single bounced back to No. 1 a week after losing the top spot?
24 What was the only No. 1 for Dave Dee, Dozy, Beaky, Mick and Tich?
25 Which song gave a No. 1 for both the Equals and Pato Branton?
26 What was Abba's last No. 1?
27 Who had a 50s No. 1 with "Rose Marie"?
28 What was Simply Red's first No. 1?
29 The Zebrugge ferry disaster led to which song topping the charts?
30 Which Eurovision Song Contest winner gave Johnny Logan a No. 1?

Answers

Euro Tour (see Quiz 30)

1 Rome. 2 Elysee Palace. 3 Corsica. 4 Porcelain. 5 Montmartre.
6 Luxembourg. 7 Balearics. 8 Seine. 9 Dublin. 10 Zugspitze. 11 Arno.
12 Malta. 13 Germany (Six). 14 Paris. 15 Portugal. 16 Three.
17 Pyrenees. 18 Athens. 19 Italy. 20 Nantes. 21 Hungary. 22 Denmark.
23 North Sea. 24 Sweden. 25 Spain. 26 Slovenia. 27 Czech Republic.
28 The Netherlands. 29 Monaco. 30 Crete.

Answers - see page 274

1 Which group of islands were the first discovery for Columbus in 1492?
2 Which actor from "The A-Team" appeared in *Rocky III*?
3 What is the inscription on the Victoria Cross?
4 Where is Frogmore?
5 What does an ice hockey match begin with?
6 Which family of birds includes the robin?
7 Who played Norman Bates in *Psycho*?
8 What did Steven Nice of Cockney Rebel change his name to?
9 What is Canada's largest port on the Pacific?
10 Which children's series featured the Soup Dragon?
11 Tony was the horse of which screen cowboy?
12 In which decade was Cadbury's Wispa bar launched?
13 Who had a 80s No. 1 with "The Edge Of Heaven"?
14 What is the capital of Latvia?
15 What colour was Moby Dick?
16 In which century was Walter Raleigh born?
17 What is another name for a natatorium?
18 Who wrote the novel *Silas Marner*?
19 Whose name is now used for a collaborator with the enemy?
20 In which country was Sir Alexander Fleming born?
21 Who introduced the "New Look" in 1947?
22 Tom Thumb, Tennis Ball and Winter Density are types of what?
23 What does "poly" mean as in "polygon" or "polyglot"?
24 In music, there must be at least how many flats if the D is played flat?
25 Which large bird is sacred in Peru?
26 In which decade of the 20th century was Prince Philip born?
27 Which type of course fishing uses a gag and gaff?
28 Which character did Catherine Zeta Jones play in "The Darling Buds of May"?
29 Euclid established the foundations of which branch of study?
30 How many were present at the Last Supper?

Quiz 34 Books

Answers - see page 275

LEVEL 2

1 What was the first book in English to be printed in England?

2 Which books do castaways automatically receive on "Desert Island Discs"?

3 Who was responsible for *The Complete Hip and Thigh Diet*?

4 In which century was the *Oxford English Dictionary* started in earnest?

5 Which book had to be owned compulsorily by every member of his country's adult population?

6 Which religious sect published *The Truth That Leads to Eternal Life*?

7 Who wrote *The Hitch Hiker's Guide to the Galaxy*?

8 Which British publisher launched Penguin titles in 1935?

9 In which decade did Guinness start to publish their *Book of Records* annually?

10 Who began publishing Beatrix Potter's books in 1902?

11 Who wrote *The Thorn Birds*?

12 What was Jeffrey Archer's first successful novel?

13 Which MP's first novel went straight to No. 1 in the *Sunday Times* bestsellers list in 1994?

14 What was Jeffrey Archer's sequel to *Kane and Abel*?

15 Who wrote *The Downing Street Years*?

16 Who created the character Emma Harte?

17 Which French novelist wrote *Gigi*?

18 What was the difference between Delia Smith's 1986 *Complete Cookery Course* and her 1989 *Complete Cookery Course*?

19 Who wrote *The Female Eunuch*?

20 Which book title links Jules Verne and Michael Palin?

21 Which Roddy Doyle bestseller won the Booker Prize in 1993?

22 What was Audrey Eyton's bestselling book of the 1980s?

23 In which county was Jane Austen born?

24 What is a bibliophile?

25 What colour are the French Michelin guides?

26 Who wrote *The Godfather*?

27 Who wrote *Possession*?

28 What was the name of *Poirot's Last Case*?

29 Who also writes as Barbara Vine?

30 In which county was Catherine Cookson born?

Answers

Movies: Who's Who? (see Quiz 36)

1 O.J. Simpson. 2 Glenn Close. 3 Dustin Hoffman. 4 Miriam Margolyes, Joanna Lumley. 5 Oliver Stone. 6 Val Kilmer. 7 Ralph Fiennes. 8 John Cleese. 9 John Hurt. 10 Ava Gardner. 11 20th Century Fox, Betty Grable. 12 Fay Wray. 13 Cher. 14 Sheriff of Nottingham. 15 Hugh Grant. 16 Mick Jagger. 17 George Clooney. 18 Grace Kelly. 19 Tina Turner. 20 Richard Gere. 21 Arthur Miller. 22 The Odd Couple (Walter Matthau and Jack Lemmon). 23 Sally Field. 24 Quentin Tarantino. 25 John Travolta. 26 Sean Connery. 27 Bruce Willis - he was the baby's voice in *Look Who's Talking*. 28 Barbra Streisand. 29 Sam. 30 Liz Hurley.

1 Which family of plants does garlic belong to?
2 Which is the largest country on the Iberian peninsula?
3 What was the value of a rugby union try prior to 1971?
4 Who is the eldest of the March girls in *Little Women*?
5 Which character was played by Doris Speed in "Coronation Street"?
6 Which gas was first used by the Germans in 1915 against Russia?
7 Which county formerly had Abingdon as its county town?
8 What shape is the trunk of a cottonwood tree?
9 Which doctor was in love with Lara Antipova?
10 Which country is the largest producer of meat in the world?
11 Who wrote the novel *Tom Jones*?
12 Who has also been known as Saloth Sar and Kompong Thom?
13 In which drama series did Marsham and Nurse Carr appear?
14 Who had a 90s No. 1 with "Killer"?
15 What is the only English anagram of CATALOGUE?
16 What nationality was Marie Curie?
17 What does "mono" mean as in the words "monocle" or "monorail"?
18 How many people are portrayed in da Vinci's *The Last Supper*?
19 Who was the first presenter of "Holiday" ?
20 In the Old Testament which book directly follows Psalms?
21 Which member of the Lords denounced privatization as "selling the family silver"?
22 Ichthyophobia is a fear of what?
23 Which country was the birthplace of the tennis player Ilie Nastase?
24 In which country was the composer Gustav Holst born?
25 In which century was Elizabeth I born?
26 What is the state capital of Indiana, USA?
27 What name was given to Sinclair's electric, three-wheeled car?
28 In which American state was Ray Charles born?
29 Who wrote a semi-autobiographical novel called *The Bell Jar*?
30 What is the RAF equivalent of the Royal Navy rank of vice-admiral?

Answers

Pot Luck 15 (see Quiz 33)
1 The Bahamas. **2** Mr T. **3** "For valour". **4** Windsor (Castle grounds).
5 A face-off. **6** Thrush. **7** Anthony Perkins. **8** Steve Harley. **9** Vancouver.
10 "The Clangers". **11** Tom Mix. **12** 1980s. **13** Wham! **14** Riga.
15 White. **16** 16th. **17** A swimming pool. **18** George Eliot. **19** Quisling.
20 Scotland. **21** Dior. **22** Lettuce. **23** Many. **24** Four. **25** Condor.
26 20s. **27** Pike Fishing. **28** Mariette. **29** Geometry. **30** 13.

Quiz 36 Movies: Who's Who?

Answers - see page 273

1   Who starred in *The Towering Inferno* and *Naked Gun 2½*?
2   Who played Cruella de Vil in the "real" version of *101 Dalmatians*?
3   Which movie star played Shylock in London's West End in 1989?
4   Who played the aunts in *James and the Giant Peach*?
5   Who directed *Born on the Fourth of July* and *Natural Born Killers*?
6   Who played the Saint in the 90s movie?
7   Who was chosen to play Heathcliff in the 90s *Wuthering Heights*?
8   Who was the British star of *Fierce Creatures*?
9   Who starred as the Elephant Man?
10 Who married Mickey Rooney and Frank Sinatra?
11 Who insured whose legs for a million dollars with Lloyd's of London?
12 Who was the heroine in the 30s version of *King Kong*?
13 Who played the mother in *Mermaids*?
14 Who did Alan Rickman play in *Robin Hood, Prince of Thieves*?
15 Who was once known in Los Angeles as BK 4454813 OG 2795?
16 Whose film production company is called Jagged Films?
17 Who played Batman in the 1997 *Batman and Robin*?
18 Which blonde screen legend made only 11 films, three for Hitchcock?
19 Which rock star did Angela Bassett play in a 1993 biopic?
20 Who was Jack Somersby in *Somersby*?
21 Who wrote the screenplay of *The Crucible*?
22 How are Felix Ungar and Oscar Madison better known?
23 Who played Robin Williams's estranged wife in *Mrs Doubtfire*?
24 Who directed *Pulp Fiction* and *Reservoir Dogs*?
25 Who played Vince Vega in *Pulp Fiction*?
26 Which ex-007 appeared for two minutes at the end of *Robin Hood: Prince of Thieves*?
27 Who was never seen in his most successful pre-'93 film performance?
28 Which actress directed *Prince of Tides* and *Yentl*?
29 Which role did Dooley Wilson play in *Casablanca*?
30 Who produced the Hugh Grant movie *Extreme Measures*?

Quiz 37 Pot Luck 17

Answers - see page 278

LEVEL 2

1   Who was Don Brennan's best man when he married Ivy Tilsley?
2   Which US president won a Nobel Prize in 1906?
3   Which national holiday was first celebrated in England in 1974?
4   What was Fletcher's first name in "Porridge"?
5   Which city is the capital of the Andalusia region of Spain?
6   What name is given to a coffin by Americans?
7   Who played Eddie in the musical movie *The Rocky Horror Picture Show*?
8   Which area of Spain did Don Quixote come from?
9   Which British birds are shot in braces and form a nye?
10 Who was England's 1980 rugby union Grand Slam winners captain?
11 Who wrote the novel *The Great Gatsby*?
12 In which decade of the 20th century was Paul Newman born?
13 What was the name of the chef in "Fawlty Towers"?
14 What was Margaret Thatcher's maiden name?
15 What word can go before "beans", "quartet" and "vest"?
16 Who succeeded Wordsworth as Poet Laureate?
17 What is the capital of Venezuela?
18 Who had a 70s No. 1 with "Don't Cry For Me, Argentina"?
19 Giles, Jak and Trog are all examples of what?
20 Which country has the football team Anderlecht?
21 What is dowsing?
22 Other than Austria, what other country do Tyroleans come from?
23 The artist Roy Lichtenstein comes from which country?
24 The song "Three Coins In A Fountain" came from which 50s film?
25 Who is the clown in Shakespeare's *Henry IV*?
26 Nitrous oxide is also known as what ?
27 What was Richard Nixon's middle name?
28 If it's 12 noon GMT what time is it in Jerusalem?
29 In which century was Charles Dickens born?
30 In which county is Ambridge?

Answers

Cricket (see Quiz 39)

1 Durham. **2** Australia. **3** Northamptonshire. **4** "Tich". **5** Glamorgan.
6 Warwickshire. **7** Dragon. **8** Phil Edmonds, John Emburey. **9** New
Zealand. **10** Yellow. **11** Derbyshire. **12** Ian Botham. **13** Surrey. **14** David
Lloyd. **15** Mike Denness. **16** Jim Laker. **17** Worcestershire. **18** Left-handed.
19 South Africa. **20** Bob Willis. **21** 25. **22** Dominic Cork. **23** Victoria.
24 Essex. **25** 1981. **26** Hampshire. **27** 1870s. **28** Graham Gooch.
29 Australia. **30** Yes.

Quiz 38 TV Game Shows

LEVEL 2

Answers - see page 279

1   Who presents "Fifteen To One"?
2   What was top prize on Anthea Turner's "Turner Round the World"?
3   Which Channel 4 show was devised and presented by Tim Vine?
4   What is the name of Channel 5's gardening quiz?
5   Who was host for the first series of "The Other Half"?
6   How many contestants were there on each show of "Blankety Blank"?
7   Which show handed out a bendy Bully?
8   Who was the first female presenter of "Busman's Holiday"?
9   Who hosted "Call My Bluff" in the late 90s?
10 Who was the first presenter of "Celebrity Squares"?
11 Which show has been hosted by Richard Madeley and Chris Tarrant?
12 Which show did Armand Jammot create?
13 Who did Ed Tudor-Pole replace in "The Crystal Maze"?
14 What was the top prize in "Double Your Money"?
15 Which quiz show had a dummy keyboard?
16 Which late afternoon quiz is hosted by Martyn Lewis?
17 Who was the second hostess on "The Generation Game"?
18 Who succeeded Bob Monkhouse as presenter of "Family Fortunes"?
19 Who originally recorded the theme song to "Whatever You Want"?
20 What shape are the letter blocks in "Blockbusters"?
21 Which mature team reached the finals of 1997's "University Challenge"?
22 Who succeeded Matthew Kelly as host of "You Bet!"?
23 Which show spawned the catchphrase "You get nothing for a pair - not in this show"?
24 Who first said, "Come on down" on "The Price is Right"?
25 Which word-puzzle show was hosted by Bradley Walsh and Jenny Powell?
26 Fred Housego was arguably the most famous winner on which show?
27 What are the two voting symbols in "Ready, Steady, Cook"?
28 Who introduced "Odd One Out" and "Wipeout"?
29 What was introduced as "The Quiz of the Week"?
30 What was the name of the game show on "Sunday Night at the London Palladium"?

1 Which county were admitted to the County Championship in 1992?
2 Which country batted first in the1997 Ashes First Test in England?
3 Which county did Allan Lamb play for?
4 What was Alfred Freeman's nickname?
5 Which county has its HQ at Sophia Gardens?
6 Which county did Dermot Reeve take to the championship?
7 What creature is on the Somerset badge?
8 Which pair of spinners - both with surnames beginning with an E - dominated the 80s at Middlesex?
9 Which country did Martin Crowe play for?
10 What is the colour of the *Wisden Cricketers' Almanac*?
11 Which county has its headquarters in Nottingham Road?
12 Which cricketer has advertised Nike boots, Dansk low-alcohol lager and Shredded Wheat?
13 Which county took to an all-chocolate strip in the 90s?
14 Which cricket personality is known as Bumble?
15 Who was the first Scotsman to captain England?
16 Who became the first Test bowler to take 19 wickets in a game?
17 Which county did Ian Botham join on leaving Somerset?
18 Is Brian Lara a right- or left-handed batsman?
19 Which country does umpire Cyril Mitchley come from?
20 Which England fast bowler took Dylan as a middle name in honour of Bob Dylan?
21 How old was Mike Atherton when he was made England captain?
22 In 1995, which Englishman took a Test hat-trick against the West Indies?
23 Shane Warne first captained which Australian state side?
24 Which county does Nasser Hussain play for?
25 In what year was the series that became known as Botham's Ashes?
26 Which county did Malcolm Marshall and Gordon Greenidge play for?
27 In which decade did the first Australia v England Test take place?
28 Who has played most Tests for England?
29 Which country did Ian Redpath play for?
30 Did Geoff Boycott ever captain England?

1 Which is the only star in our solar system?
2 What was Mr Jones's job other than a Corporal in "Dad's Army"?
3 Which river flows from the Cambrian Mountains to the Bristol Channel?
4 Which World Champion appeared on Isle of Man stamps in 1992?
5 Which organization replaced the League of Nations?
6 What was first produced listing 255 names in London in 1880?
7 What is the plural of gladiolus?
8 Who was the last person to hold both water- and land-speed records?
9 Which EastEnder had a screen affair with Michael Aspel's wife?
10 Which Welsh town gave its name to a style of sleeve?
11 Who wrote the novel *Howard's End*?
12 What was Eva Peron's maiden name?
13 In which century was Francis Drake born?
14 How many pedals does a grand piano have?
15 Who was Hiawatha's wife?
16 In Scrabble, how many points is the letter X worth?
17 How is Paul O'Grady better known?
18 Who was proved wrong when he said, "I believe it is peace for our time"?
19 Which sporting event did Bernard Hinault win three times in the 80s?
20 What is the diameter in inches of a basketball hoop?
21 Merton Glory and Napoleon Bigarreau are types of which fruit?
22 The Napier University is located in which city?
23 In American football which creatures come from Detroit?
24 Who wrote about the Mr Men?
25 Which of the Ten Commandments deals with adultery?
26 1996 was the Chinese year of which creature?
27 Which petals are used by the royal family as confetti?
28 Who had a 60s No. 1 with "Bad Moon Rising"?
29 What was the name of David Blunkett's dog at the 1997 election?
30 Which character did Tony Britton play in "Don't Wait Up"?

Answers

TV Game Shows (see Quiz 38)
1 William G. Stewart. 2 Two round-the-world air tickets. 3 "Fluke". 4 "The Great Garden Game". 5 Dale Winton. 6 Four. 7 "Bullseye". 8 Sarah Kennedy. 9 Bob Holness. 10 Bob Monkhouse. 11 "Cluedo".
12 "Countdown". 13 Richard O'Brien. 14 £1,000. 15 "Face the Music".
16 "Today's the Day". 17 Isla St Clair. 18 Max Bygraves. 19 Status Quo.
20 Hexagonal. 21 Open University. 22 Darren Day. 23 "Play Your Cards Right". 24 Leslie Crowther. 25 "Wheel of Fortune". 26 "Mastermind".
27 Green peppers, red tomatoes. 28 Paul Daniels. 29 "Sale of the Century".
30 "Beat the Clock".

LEVEL 2

1   What did widow Jackie K. become?
2   What was ITV's first live pop programme?
3   Where did the world-record-breaking runner Peter Snell come from?
4   Who was premier of Rhodesia when UDI was declared?
5   In what year was the death penalty abolished in Britain?
6   What did the L stand for in Mary Whitehouse's NVLA?
7   Who was best man at the wedding of David Bailey and Catherine Deneuve?
8   Which No. 1 started "The taxman's taken all my dough"?
9   Which group did away with the "magic circle" process of choosing a leader?
10 Which former boxing world champion was found shot dead in Soho?
11 Jan Palach set himself alight to protest against the Russian invasion of which country?
12 Who did Lulu marry on February 18 1969?
13 What was the nickname of the East End murder victim Jack McVitie?
14 What was the BBC's longest-running radio show which ended in 1969?
15 Which line on the Underground was opened in 1969?
16 In which city did John and Yoko hold their honeymoon bed-in?
17 Which senator was involved in the car crash at Chappaquiddick?
18 Who did Ann Jones beat in the 1969 Wimbledon women's singles?
19 Where did the Stones gave a free, open-air concert, after Brian Jones's death?
20 The Queen dedicated an acre of land in Runnymede to whom?
21 What did Dr Michael Ramsay become in June 1961?
22 Who phoned Neil Armstrong on his first moon walk?
23 Barbara Hulanicki founded which store?
24 How old was Prince Charles when he was invested as Prince of Wales?
25 On which course did Tony Jacklin win the British Open in 1969?
26 Where was the home town of round the world sailor Alec Rose?
27 Who designed the new cathedral at Coventry?
28 Who did Sharon Tate marry in 1968?
29 In which city did the first heart transplant operation take place?
30 Who was linked with the phrase "Turn on, tune in and drop out"?

Quiz 42 Pot Luck 19

Answers - see page 283

1   What is the capital of County Antrim in Ireland?
2   What was Roy Orbison's first UK No. 1 single?
3   What was banned by Napoleon which led to the development of sugar beet?
4   What was the fictional village in "All Creatures Great and Small"?
5   Which motorway goes across the Pennines west to east?
6   How many points win a game of badminton?
7   Who cut off Van Gogh's ear?
8   What musical invention was developed by David Rockola?
9   How many lines in a sonnet?
10 Which fruit is Spain's national symbol?
11 Who wrote stories about Kirrin Island?
12 What was the nickname of Milton Marx?
13 Who had a 90s No. 1 with "The One And Only"?
14 Which birthstone is linked to March?
15 In which series did Danny Wilde and Lord Brett Sinclair appear?
16 Which story was *West Side Story* based on?
17 In which century was John Constable born?
18 Who was the first presenter of "The Late Late Breakfast Show"?
19 What is special about the feet of a palmiped?
20 What was Lady Churchill's reaction to Graham Sutherland's portrait of her husband?
21 Which US general was nicknamed Old Blood and Guts?
22 What word can go after "leg" and before "ear"?
23 The Aldeburgh Festival is held in which county?
24 In which decade of the 20th century was Jack Nicklaus born?
25 Carnophobia is a fear of what?
26 What is the name of John Major's daughter?
27 Which "Dallas" actor also played the Man from Atlantis?
28 Bob Wyatt captained England in which sport?
29 Who was Ken Russell's film *A Song Of Summer* about?
30 What is the deepest land gorge in the world?

Answers

Pop: Superstars (see Quiz 44)
1 "Earth Song". 2 "Reason To Believe". 3 Barbra Streisand. 4 Pink Floyd.
5 Mississippi. 6 *Aladdin Sane*. 7 "Rocket Man". 8 Scotland. 9 Prince.
10 George Michael. 11 "Chain Reaction". 12 Breathless Mahoney. 13 Left.
14 Eric Clapton. 15 The Jordanaires. 16 Tina Turner. 17 Queen. 18 Bob
Marley. 19 *Off The Wall*. 20 Prince. 21 Jade. 22 Dolly Parton.
23 *Voulez-Vous*. 24 George Michael. 25 *Never A Dull Moment*.
26 Madonna. 27 Phil Collins. 28 Neil Diamond. 29 Elvis Presley.
30 Elton John.

LEVEL 2

1   Which planet appears brightest to the naked eye?
2   What creatures were Laska and Beny, who went into space in 1958?
3   Which space first was Vladimir Komarov in 1967?
4   Who first predicted correctly the intermittent return of a famous comet?
5   In which US state is the Keck Telescope?
6   Which planet's moons have names of Shakespearean characters?
7   How are Corona Australis and Corona Borealis also known?
8   How many Apollo missions resulted in successful moon landings?
9   When the Earth or the moon enters the other's shadow what is it called?
10 Which is the only sign of the zodiac named after two living things?
11 Jodrell Bank is the observatory of which university?
12 Which planet did Johann Galle discover in 1846?
13 What is the system of numbering asteroids?
14 Which "Star Trek" character is asteroid No. 2309 named after?
15 Whose spacecraft was called *Vostok VI*?
16 In moon exploration what was EVA?
17 Which planet lies between Venus and Mars?
18 How many orbits of the Earth did Gagarin make in *Vostok I*?
19 What are the Northern Lights also known as?
20 Ganymede and Io are moons of which planet?
21 How long does it take the moon to complete a revolution of Earth?
22 Which planet did Clyde Tombaugh discover in 1930?
23 Which planet's rings and moons were photographed by *Voyager 1* in 1980?
24 Which theory states that the universe came into being as a result of an explosion?
25 What does the abbreviation 'ly' stand for?
26 Which planet has two moons called Phobos and Demos?
27 In relation to the sun in which direction does a comet's tail point?
28 Which planet in our solar system is only slightly smaller than Earth?
29 What is the nearest star to our sun?
30 The sidereal period is the time it takes a planet to orbit what?

1 What was Michael Jackson's 1995 Christmas No. 1?
2 What was coupled with "Maggie May" on Rod Stewart's single?
3 Which singer co-wrote "Evergreen"?
4 Reclusive Syd Barrett was a founder of which supergroup?
5 In which state was Elvis Presley born?
6 Which album has Bowie with a red lightning flash design on his face?
7 Which Elton John song starts "She packed my bags last night pre-flight"?
8 In which country was Mark Knopfler born?
9 Whose albums include *Diamonds and Pearls* and *Symbol*?
10 In the 90s who got into legal battle with Sony over his contract?
11 Which Gibb brother's song gave Diana Ross a No. 1?
12 What role did Madonna portray in the film *Dick Tracy*?
13 On the cover of *Thriller* Jackson is leaning on which elbow?
14 Which guitarist was "Unplugged" in 1992?
15 Which vocal harmony group backed Elvis from the mid 50s?
16 Who appeared as the Acid Queen in the film *Tommy*?
17 Roger Taylor was a member of which supergroup?
18 Which reggae superstar was given a state funeral in Jamaica?
19 Which Michael Jackson album first included "Don't Stop 'Til You Get Enough"?
20 Which superstar produced music for the 1989 *Batman* film?
21 What is the name of Mick Jagger's daughter by Bianca?
22 Which female singer wrote "I Will Always Love You"?
23 Which Abba album had a French title?
24 Who was "In A Different Corner" in 1986?
25 Which album sleeve featured Rod Stewart sitting in an armchair?
26 A fly on the wall 90s documentary invited the public to be in bed with who?
27 Who recorded the album *Face Values*?
28 Who duetted with Streisand on "You Don't Bring Me Flowers"?
29 Who won a talent show, aged ten, singing "Old Shep"?
30 Who recorded the album *Sleeping With The Past*?

1   What is a compote?
2   Which of Boeing's jets were launched in 1958 seating 189?
3   Who sang the theme song to the Bond film *Octopussy*?
4   Which mining town is named Berneslai in the Domesday Book?
5   What is the main edible export of Argentina?
6   Who was assassinated by Satwant and Beant Singh?
7   What colour is a telephone kiosk which will take only phone cards?
8   Which family of fruit does the kumquat belong to?
9   Which Soviet football team was the first to make a European final?
10 Michael Henchard was the mayor of which fictional town?
11 Who had a 90s No. 1 with "Everything Changes"?
12 What is the only English anagram of FIENDISH?
13 Which desert spreads into South West Africa from Botswana?
14 "The King Of Barataria" is the subtitle of which light opera?
15 In which suburb was "The Good Life" set?
16 In which decade was "Baywatch" screened for the first time in the UK?
17 Which play by George Bernard Shaw inspired *My Fair Lady*?
18 Which letter and number follow Albert Square, Walford?
19 Which England soccer keeper had the first names Raymond Neal?
20 Who wrote the novel *The French Lieutenant's Woman*?
21 Who sits on the Woolsack?
22 Athene is the Greek goddess of wisdom. Who is the Roman?
23 Who wrote "Hark, the Herald Angels Sing"?
24 Which state became the 50th American state?
25 Who created Perry Mason?
26 Which former film star was US Ambassador to Ghana in the 70s?
27 Who got the sack from the Beatles before they hit the big time?
28 What do H and G stand for in H.G. Wells's name?
29 What was called the Pluto Platter when it was originally sold?
30 In which century was Captain James Cook born?

Answers

Pot Luck 21   (see Quiz 47)
1 A lake. 2 Suspenders. 3 Dotrice. 4 Matt Monro. 5 Windsor (St Georges Chapel). 6 The Great Gatsby. 7 Sand. 8 Margaret Thatcher. 9 Cloves. 10 Wednesday. 11 Graham Greene. 12 Erwin (Rommel). 13 Tennis. 14 Kinshasa. 15 Ten. 16 Teeth. 17 19th. 18 Enforcement. 19 Hockey. 20 Boy George. 21 North. 22 Lillie Langtry. 23 47. 24 Narcissus. 25 50s. 26 Rhubarb. 27 Red with a white flash. 28 Purple. 29 Robin Beck. 30 Electrician.

1   In which sensational case was wireless telegraphy first used to apprehend a murderer?
2   At what number in Rillington Place did John Christie live?
3   In the 60s who did James Earl Ray assassinate?
4   What treasure trove did Colonel Thomas Blood try to steal in the 17th century?
5   To two years, when was the last hanging in Britain?
6   In 1981, which leading figure was wounded by John Hinckley?
7   Which parts of the body went into a pillory?
8   Albert de Salvo was better known as what?
9   In which city did Burke and Hare operate?
10 In light opera who wanted "to let the punishment fit the crime"?
11 To ten years each way, when was Dick Turpin hanged?
12 In which month was President Kennedy assassinated?
13 Mary Ann Nicholas and Mary Kelly were victims of who?
14 In which Gloucester street was the West's House of Horrors?
15 The Old Bailey figure of justice holds a sword and what else?
16 What was the the profession of Mary Ann Cotton, hanged in 1873?
17 Who was Britain's last chief hangman?
18 Alphonse Bertillon and Sir Francis Galton were concerned with which aid to criminal detection?
19 George Cornell was shot in which East End pub?
20 In the 70s who was accused of stealing a fur coat and passport from Miss World?
21 In the 17th century which judge sat for the so-called Bloody Assizes?
22 Hawley Harvey were the first names of which murderer?
23 On August 6 1890, Auburn Prison, New York, had the first what?
24 In what decade was flogging finally abolished in Britain?
25 What weapon was used to murder the Bulgrian defector Georgi Markov in London in the 70s?
26 In the 90s which Kray brother was found guilty of drug trafficking?
27 Who shot the person believed to have shot President Kennedy?
28 Who was the first British PM murdered while in office?
29 In the 70s who became the first convict executed in the US for ten years?
30 Which doctor was at the centre of the Profumo affair?

Quiz 47 Pot Luck 21

Answers - see page 284

LEVEL 2

1   What is the Caspian Sea, as it is not a sea?
2   What do Americans call braces?
3   Which Michelle played Betty, Frank Spencer's wife?
4   Who sang the Bond theme "From Russia With Love"?
5   Where is the tomb of King Henry VIII?
6   Who was James Gatz better known as?
7   What accounts for only 28 per cent of the Sahara Desert ?
8   Who was the youngest female Conservative candidate in the1951 General Election?
9   Which spice is the most produced in Zanzibar?
10 If April Fools' Day is a Tuesday what day is St George's Day?
11 Who wrote the novel *The Power and The Glory*?
12 What was the first name of the man known as the Desert Fox?
13 Todd Woodbridge was conected with which sport?
14 What is the capital of the People's Republic of Congo?
15 In Scrabble, how many points is the letter Q worth?
16 What do frogs have that toads do not in their mouths?
17 In which century was T.S. Eliot born?
18 In "The Man from UNCLE", what did the E stand for?
19 In 1971 Pakistan won the first World Cup in which sport?
20 Kirt Brandon brought a court case against which rock star?
21 Which direction does the Nile River flow?
22 Which character did Francesca Annis play in "Edward VII" in the 70s?
23 What is the next-highest prime number above 43?
24 Who pined for the love of his reflection?
25 In which decade of the 20th century was Bjorn Borg born?
26 Hawk's Champagne and Prince Albert are types of which fruit?
27 What colour was Starsky and Hutch's car?
28 What is the most common colour of amethyst?
29 Who had a 80s No. 1 with "First Time"?
30 What was Lech Walesa's job in the Gdansk shipyards?

Answers

Pot Luck 20 (see Quiz 45)
1 Stewed fruit. **2** The 707. **3** Rita Coolidge. **4** Barnsley. **5** Beef. **6** Mrs Indira Gandhi. **7** Green. **8** Citrus. **9** Moscow Dynamo. **10** Casterbridge. **11** Take That. **12** Finished. **13** Kalahari. **14** *The Gondoliers*. **15** Surbiton. **16** 1990s. **17** *Pygmalion*. **18** E20. **19** Clemence. **20** John Fowles. **21** Lord Chancellor. **22** Minerva. **23** Charles Wesley. **24** Hawaii. **25** Erle Stanley Gardner. **26** Shirley Temple Black. **27** Pete Best. **28** Herbert George. **29** The Frisbee. **30** 18th.

1   In which sitcom did Bootsie and Snudge first appear?
2   Who played Bertie Wooster in the 60s Wodehouse adaptation?
3   What was Terry's sister called in "The Likely Lads"?
4   Who played the blustering headmaster in "Whack-O!"?
5   Who was the third of "Take Three Girls" with Kate and Avril?
6   How was the "Tomorrow's World" presenter Robert Alexander Baron Symes-Schutzmann von Schutzmannstorf better known?
7   Who was Jim London in "Up the Elephant and Round the Castle"?
8   What relation was Hattie Jacques to Eric in their "Sykes and ..." series?
9   What did Harold Steptoe always call his father?
10 Who played Sid Stone in the UK sitcom "Taxi"?
11 What was the Richard O'Sullivan spin-off from "Man About the House"?
12 Who lived in the Suffolk village of Stackton Tressel?
13 Daphne Manners and Hari Kumar were characters in which series?
14 Jimmy Jewel and Hylda Baker were Eli and Nellie Pledge in which show?
15 Which TV family were headed by Herman and Lily?
16 Which veteran actress played the wife in "Meet the Wife"?
17 In which classic did you find Blanco, Lukewarm and Gay Gordon?
18 What was Bernard Hedges' nickname in "Please Sir"?
19 Who were the two stars of "Marriage Lines"?
20 What was the surname of George and Mildred?
21 What does M*A*S*H* stand for?
22 Which flatmates originally lived in Huskisson Road, Liverpool?
23 Who or what was Mr Ed?
24 Which classic drama centred on the Marchmain family?
25 What make of car did Nurse Emmanuel drive in "Open All Hours"?
26 In which show did Reg Varney play Stan Butler?
27 Who was the fourth Doctor Who?
28 What was the name of the young blonde witch in "Bewitched"?
29 In which series were Figgis, Glover and Norman hospital patients?
30 Which sitcom was about Fenner Fashions and starred Miriam Karlin?

1   Which James Bond actor covered his tattoos when filming?
2   What name is given to a hill in the centre of any Greek city?
3   What canal was closed from 1967 to 1975?
4   Which comedy series saw Oliver Smallbridge with Simon Peel?
5   Which Olympic sport needs a planting box?
6   Which popular tourist area is Northern Africa's smallest country?
7   Who was the leader of Cuba's rebel July 26 faction?
8   In which American TV show would you find the Cunningham family?
9   What animal was the first sent into space by the Americans?
10 Which city did the Cowardly Lion want to get to?
11 In which century was Charles Darwin born?
12 Who was the first female presenter of "Magpie"?
13 What did the D stand for in Franklin D. Roosevelt's name?
14 In which series did Phyllida Erskine-Brown appear?
15 Which radio and TV star used the phrase "in the best possible taste"?
16 What colour was the Trotter's Independent Trading van?
17 What is the capital of Costa Rica?
18 Which store group's slogan is "Never Knowingly Undersold"?
19 Scott Hamilton was a world champion in which sport?
20 Who wrote "Honeysuckle Rose" and "Ain't Misbehavin'"?
21 What do we call the place known by the Romans as Camulodunum?
22 In which place does Desperate Dan live?
23 What was the original meaning of the name Sarah in Hebrew?
24 Karl Landsteiner's work centred of discovering which groups?
25 Which rock star named his son Zowie?
26 Who wrote the novel *She*?
27 Where did the rumba originate?
28 Who had a 60s No. 1 with "Do It Again"?
29 If it's 12 noon GMT what time is it in Cairo?
30 What was the first issued decimal coin in Britain?

Answers

Pot Luck 23 (see Quiz 51)
1 Grace Kelly. 2 Victoria. 3 Peter Gabriel. 4 Moll Flanders. 5 A tidal wave.
6 Ervin Johnson. 7 Salzburg. 8 Felix. 9 Cancer. 10 Liberia. 11 Ernest
Hemingway. 12 S. 13 Spoonerism. 14 Coffee/Chocolate. 15 19th.
16 Berlin. 17 "A Ruby Murray". 18 Green. 19 Bach. 20 Duke of
Wellington. 21 26. 22 Rembrandt. 23 Lancashire. 24 Niece. 25 Mad dogs
and Englishmen. 26 Ronald Reagan. 27 Rooster. 28 *David Copperfield*.
29 TV. 30 30s.

Quiz 50 Movies: Westerns

LEVEL 2

1 *The Magnificent Seven* was a remake of which 50s Japanese film?
2 In which film did John Wayne play his first leading role?
3 Which London-born actor played a boy adopted by Indians in *Last of the Mohicans*?
4 In which 1992 western with Gene Hackman did Clint Eastwood star and direct?
5 What was the sequel to *A Fistful of Dollars* called?
6 Who played the sheriff in *High Noon*?
7 Who was the female star of *Butch Cassidy and the Sundance Kid*?
8 Who played Bernardo in *The Magnificent Seven*?
9 Who co-starred with John Wayne in *The Man Who Shot Liberty Valance*?
10 Who played Wyatt Earp in the 1946 film *My Darling Clementine*?
11 Which musical western has the song "You Can't Get A Man with a Gun"?
12 Who was a singing "Calamity Jane"?
13 Which country singer starred in *True Grit*?
14 In which film did John Wayne play Davy Crockett?
15 Which then romantic partner of Clint Eastwood starred with him in *Bronco Billy* in 1980?
16 Who was the star of *Jeremiah Johnson* in 1972?
17 Which director was famous for his so-called "Cavalry Trilogy"?
18 Who was famous for playing the Man With No Name?
19 Which Indian tribe features in *Dances With Wolves*?
20 Who starred with Bob Hope in the comedy western *The Paleface*?
21 Which former child star starred in *Fort Apache* in 1948?
22 Which western star's theme song was "Back in the Saddle Again"?
23 Who starred in the musical western *Don't Fence Me In* in 1945?
24 Which 1994 western starred Mel Gibson and Jodie Foster?
25 In which 1969 musical western did Clint Eastwood sing?
26 Who was *Little Big Man*?
27 Who sang "Blaze of Glory" in *Young Guns II*?
28 Which director of westerns was born Sean Aloysius O'Fienne?
29 Which comedian did Roy Rogers star with in *Son of Paleface*?
30 Where was *A Fistful of Dollars* filmed?

Answers

Media 1 (see Quiz 52)
1 British Academy of Film and Television Arts. 2 Channel 4. 3 Director General. 4 *Independent on Sunday.* 5 Preston. 6 Autocue. 7 Parliament. 8 News. 9 The Discovery Channel. 10 A mounting for a camera. 11 Gaffer. 12 *Sunday Times.* 13 Sheepdog. 14 *Expression!.* 15 *Lloyd's List.* 16 Cardiff. 17 Japan. 18 Four. 19 Grip. 20 *Daily Herald.* 21 Sport Newspapers. 22 *Financial Times.* 23 *Exchange and Mart.* 24 *Liverpool Echo.* 25 Classic FM. 26 Independent Local Radio. 27 *Old Moore's Almanac.* 28 Oracle. 29 Harlech Television. 30 IBA.

Quiz 51 Pot Luck 23

LEVEL 2

1   Which actress had her wedding televised in April 1956?
2   What is Africa's largest lake and Australia's smallest mainland state?
3   Who was vocalist in Genesis before Phil Collins?
4   Which character was born in Newgate Prison in the Defoe novel?
5   What hit the ship in *The Poseidon Adventure* causing it to turn over?
6   What is Magic Johnson's real name?
7   Which Austrian city was Mozart's birthplace?
8   Which famous cat was created by Otto Mesmer?
9   Who or what killed Eva Peron?
10 Which country boasts the world's largest registered shipping fleet?
11 Who wrote the novel *The Old Man and The Sea*?
12 In Morse code what letter is represented by three dots?
13 What describes inverting the initial letters of two words?
14 Which two flavours combined make mocha?
15 In which century was Charlotte Brontë born?
16 Who had an 80s No. 1 with "Take My Breath Away"?
17 How would Del Boy have ordered a curry?
18 What colour is the inside of a pistachio nut?
19 Which classical composer's *Air* has been used by Hamlet cigar ads?
20 Who was nicknamed the Iron Duke?
21 What was the percentage rise that MPs voted for themselves in 1996?
22 Who painted *The Night Watch*?
23 In which county was "Juliet Bravo" set?
24 What relation was Queen Victoria to her predecessor on the throne?
25 According to Noël Coward, who go out in the midday sun?
26 Who married the American actress Nancy Davis?
27 1993 was the Chinese year of which creature?
28 In which Dickens novel does Dora Spenlove appear?
29 What went from 405 lines to 625 lines?
30 In which decade of the 20th century was Melvyn Bragg born?

1   What does BAFTA stand for?
2   Jeremy Isaacs was the first chief executive of which channel?
3   Which title is given to the chief executive of the BBC?
4   Which London-based Sunday paper was founded in 1990?
5   In which town is Red Rose radio based?
6   What is the more common name for a teleprompt?
7   Who sets the rate for the television licence?
8   *Izvestia* was a Soviet newspaper. What does Izvestia mean?
9   Which channel has the slogan "Make the voyage"?
10 In a TV studio what is a dolly?
11 What is a studio's chief electrician called?
12 Which was the first British newspaper to issue a colour supplement?
13 In comics what was Black Bob?
14 What is the American Express magazine called?
15 Which daily publication is Britain's oldest?
16 Where is the *Western Mail* based?
17 In which country is *Yomiuri Shimbun* a daily newspaper?
18 How many Sky channels were there originally in 1989?
19 Which TV technician is responsible for hardware such as props, cranes etc.?
20 Which newspaper did the *Sun* replace in 1964?
21 Which newspaper group is David Sullivan associated with?
22 Which UK broadsheet has issues published in Frankfurt and New York?
23 Which publication, founded in 1868, consists wholly of adverts?
24 What is Liverpool's own regional daily paper called?
25 In 1997 Michael Barry stepped down in his post at which independent radio station?
26 What does ILR stand for in the media?
27 What has been published anually since 1697?
28 Which telext system was replaced on ITV by Teletext UK?
29 What was HTV originally called?
30 What did the ITC replace in 1991?

Quiz 53 Famous Names

LEVEL 2

1 Who did the former model Victoria Lockwood marry?
2 How is the actress Estelle Skornik better known in the advertising world?
3 Who are Jane Fellowes and Sarah McCorquodale?
4 What is Lord Lloyd-Webber's wife's first name?
5 Which post was English-born Pamela Harriman given by President Clinton?
6 What are Steffi Graf's parents called?
7 Who is patron of the National Osteoporosis Society?
8 Helen O'Reilly is known on TV as who?
9 In which role is Marion Crawford best known?
10 Who was the first public-school-educated PM of the last third of the 20th century?
11 Who are the parents of Lady Gabriella Windsor?
12 Which TV personality is the wife of the editor Michael Wynn-Jones?
13 How is James Crossley better known?
14 How is the challenging former Mrs Nick Allott better known?
15 Who is sometimes known as TPT?
16 Whose file states she was Mrs Clyde Klotz?
17 Which two comedy actors have a daughter called Billie?
18 Whose name was Henriette Peace first linked with in 1997?
19 Who was Martin Bell's campaigning daughter in the 1997 General Election?
20 What is Earl Spencer's first name?
21 Who left "EastEnders" to have baby daughter Maia?
22 Which illness do cook Michael Barry and actress Mary Tyler Moore suffer from?
23 What is Carol Vorderman's university degree in?
24 Romantically, Dani Behr and Victoria Adams have been linked with which football club?
25 Charles Worthington is a famous name in which field?
26 Which actress was the first Mrs Mike Tyson?
27 Sue Barker and Penelope Keith's respective spouses have been members of which profession?
28 In whose garden was Alistair Coe found in 1997?
29 What would Claire Latimer provide for a society occasion?
30 Who did Renate Blauel marry in 1984?

Quiz 54 Pot Luck 24

LEVEL 2

Answers - see page 295

1　Which Sinatra sang the Bond theme "You Only Live Twice"?
2　Which part of France would you come from if you were a Breton?
3　Huey Lewis had a hit with "The Power of Love" from which film?
4　Which South American country's name translates to "Rich Coast"?
5　How many inches wide should a wicket be?
6　What make of car was Lesley Crowther driving in his 1992 accident?
7　Who was seriously injured at the Nurburgring circuit in August 1976?
8　In which county is the Duke of Norfolk's castle at Arundel?
9　Which Chicago rock band was formed by Terry Kath in 1967?
10　Name Switzerland's largest city?
11　Who wrote the novel *Eyeless In Gaza*?
12　Which character did Ruby Wax play in "Girls on Top"?
13　How is Lev Davidovich Bronstein better known?
14　Who played Prue Manson in "Bouquet of Barbed Wire"?
15　What was the name of Darwin's survey ship?
16　Who had a 80s No. 1 with "Ghost Town"?
17　How many finger holes are there in a tenpin bowling ball?
18　What was the name of Gene Autry's horse?
19　What is the capital of Liechtenstein?
20　The gemstone Sapphire is linked to which month?
21　Who has a friend called Pie-Face?
22　Who redesigned the Girl Guide and Brownie uniforms in 1990?
23　Who captained the MCC in the "Bodyline" series of the 30s?
24　Whose 1977 autobiography was called *Dear Me*?
25　What is produced by the lacrymal glands?
26　In which century was Beethoven born?
27　Which sea contains four ounces of salt to every pint of water?
28　Apiphobia is a fear of what?
29　Which piece of music was used as the Monty Python theme?
30　Which liner made her maiden voyage in 1946?

Answers

Pot Luck 25 (see Quiz 56)

1 Ghana. 2 Opossum. 3 Cave paintings. 4 *Lorna Doone*. 5 Echo Beach. 6 Boy Scouts. 7 Brands Hatch. 8 Smoking. 9 Henley. 10 Bank Manager. 11 James Joyce. 12 Foxtrot. 13 Speed of sound. 14 "Second Thoughts". 15 Malachi. 16 Australia. 17 Phil Drabble. 18 19th. 19 Alaska. 20 Wendy Craig. 21 Rievaulx. 22 "Butter". 23 Field Marshal. 24 Port-au-Prince. 25 Andres Segovia. 26 Frankie Fraser. 27 Adam and the Ants. 28 20s. 29 Christopher Columbus. 30 Gladstone.

Quiz 55 Sporting Records

Answers - see page 292

LEVEL 2

1 Who was Barcelona's boss for their record fourth European Cup Winner's Cup Final triumph in 1997?

2 In November '95 Jansher Khan won his seventh World Open title in which sport?

3 Which Derbyshire wicket-keeper set a career record number of dismissals from 1960 to 1988?

4 David Watkins scored 221 goals in a season for which rugby league club?

5 Which athlete Mary was BBC Sports Personality of 1964?

6 Who was the first overseas manager to win the FA Cup?

7 At which venue did Greg Norman set a lowest four-round Bittish Open total in 1993?

8 What record will Alf Common always hold?

9 Who was the first rugby union player to reach 50 international tries?

10 Who overtook Sunil Gavaskar's Test appearance record for India?

11 Sergei Bubka has broken a record over 30 times in which event?

12 Peter Shilton played his 1,000th league game with which club?

13 What was athlete Kathy Cook's maiden name?

14 Fred Perry was world champion in which sport before becoming a major tennis star?

15 Which soccer club is generally accepted to be the oldest in England?

16 Who is the youngest ever winner of the US Masters?

17 In which decade did Clive Lloyd first play Test cricket?

18 Who was the first player to hit 100 Premiership goals?

19 Bob Nudd had been a world champion in which sport?

20 Which British driver was first to have seven Grand Prix wins in a year?

21 Francis Chichester made his 60s solo round the world trip in which boat?

22 Which Billy set an appearance record for West Ham?

23 From the 40s to the 60s, who set a league record for tries in a career?

24 Who in the 80s and early 90s set a record for captaining Pakistan at cricket?

25 Who in 1972 became the youngest F1 Motor Racing world champ?

26 Which record beaker won the first major Marathon she entered?

27 George Lee has been three time world champ in which sport?

28 Which Australian holds the world record for most Test runs in cricket?

29 Gianlucca Vialli moved for a then record £12 million from Sampdoria to which club in 1992 ?

30 What is Seb Coe's middle name?

Famous Names (see Quiz 53)

Answers

1 Earl Spencer. 2 Nicole. 3 Princess Diana's sisters. 4 Madeleine. 5 US Ambassador to Paris. 6 Peter, Heidi. 7 Camilla Parker-Bowles. 8 Panther. 9 Governess to Princesses Elizabeth and Margaret. 10 Tony Blair. 11 Prince and Princess Michael of Kent. 12 Delia Smith. 13 Gladiator Hunter. 14 Anneka Rice. 15 Tara Palmer-Tomkinson. 16 Gillian Anderson. 17 Lenny Henry and Dawn French. 18 Prince Andrew. 19 Melissa. 20 Charles. 21 Michelle Collins. 22 Diabetes. 23 Engineering. 24 Manchester United. 25 Hairdressing. 26 Robin Givens. 27 Policemen. 28 The Queen's (Buckingham Palace). 29 The food. 30 Elton John.

1   What is the former colony of the Gold Coast now called?
2   Which marsupial's native home is North America?
3   What was discovered at Lascaux in 1940?
4   Which work by Blackmore has a hero called John Ridd?
5   Which place was a hit for Martha and the Muffins?
6   Which organization had its first troop formed in 1908 in Glasgow?
7   Which racing circuit has a bend called Paddock?
8   What became illegal in 1984 on the London Underground?
9   Where is the world's oldest rowing club, Leander, based?
10   What was Captain Mainwaring's occupation?
11   Who wrote the novel *Finnegans Wake*?
12   If A is alpha and B is bravo what is F?
13   What is exceeded to produce a sonic boom?
14   In which sitcom did Bill Macgregor and Faith Grayshot appear?
15   Which is the last book of the Old Testament ?
16   Which country is partly surrounded by the Coral and Tasman Seas?
17   Who was the first presenter of "One Man and his Dog"?
18   In which century was J.M. Barrie born?
19   What did America buy from Russia for a mere two cents an acre?
20   Who played Ria Parkinson in "Butterflies"?
21   Harold Wilson became Baron of where when he became a peer?
22   What word can go before "cup", "scotch" and "fly"?
23   What is the army equivalent of the Royal Navy rank of Admiral of the Fleet?
24   What is the capital of Haiti?
25   Which guitarist was the Marquis of Salobrena?
26   Which Kray twin enforcer gave East End gangland tours in the 90s?
27   Who had a 80s No. 1 with "Stand And Deliver"?
28   In which decade of the 20th century was Marlon Brando born?
29   Which famous Italian explorer is buried in the Dominican Republic?
30   Who was the first British prime minister to take office four times?

Answers

Pot Luck 24   (see Quiz 54)

1   Nancy Sinatra. **2**   Brittany. **3**   *Back to the Future.* **4**   Costa Rica. **5**   Nine.
6   Rolls-Royce. **7**   Niki Lauda. **8**   West Sussex. **9**   Chicago. **10**   Zurich.
11   Aldous Huxley. **12**   Shelley. **13**   Leon Trotsky. **14**   Susan Penhaligon.
15   The *Beagle*. **16**   The Specials. **17**   Three. **18**   Champion. **19**   Vaduz.
20   September. **21**   Dennis the Menace. **22**   Jeff Banks. **23**   Douglas Jardine.
24   Peter Ustinov. **25**   Tears. **26**   18th. **27**   The Dead Sea.
28   Bees. **29**   "Liberty Bell". **30**   *Queen Elizabeth.*

1 Which veteran feline star of the Kattomeat adverts died in 1976?
2 Which outstanding female runner died of cancer at the age of 22?
3 What free item to schools did Education Secretary Thatcher cancel?
4 Who was Arsenal's double winning captain?
5 Who led the Madison Square Garden concert for Bangladesh?
6 Which team bought Bob Latchford from Birmingham making him Britain's costliest player?
7 Who was Randolph Hearst's kidnapped daughter?
8 Who did Ruby Flipper replace?
9 What was Lord Louis Moutbatten doing when murdered by the IRA?
10 What was Gail's last name before her marriage to Brian Tilsley?
11 What did Brighton Council agree to on a section of the beach?
12 In which month did Princess Anne marry Captain Mark Phillips?
13 Singers Lyn Paul and Eve Graham went solo to break up which group?
14 What did Rolls-Royce declare in February 1971?
15 Which northern town was advertised for the vodka it produced?
16 Who was British prime minister during the Winter of Discontent?
17 Who did Virginia Wade beat in the ladies singles final at Wimbledon?
18 Who wrote *Roots*, adapted as a TV blockbuster?
19 In 1978 Pope John Paul I died after roughly how long in office?
20 Who were Jilly, Kelly and Sabrina?
21 What was Saigon renamed after the North Vietnamese take over?
22 Percy Shaw passed away, but what had he passed on to road users?
23 Where was cricket's first World Cup Final held?
24 In which country was vanishing Labour MP John Stonehouse arrested?
25 What was the name of Edward Heath's Admiral's Cup yacht?
26 Where in Ireland did the Bloody Sunday shootings take place?
27 Who was leader of the Khmer Rouge in the Killing Fields?
28 In 1976, it was goodnight all for which copper after 20 years on TV?
29 Pele went on the dollar trail in 1975 with which team?
30 Who was Live At Treorchy?

1   In which book would you find Magwitch?
2   Who opened the Manchester Ship Canal in 1894?
3   What did Anna Ford once throw over Jonathan Aitken?
4   Which paper was formerly called the *Daily Universal Register*?
5   Which brothers in the film industry were Jack, Sam, Harry & Albert?
6   Who sang the theme song for "Absolute Beginners"?
7   Which horse ran the 1973 Grand National in record time?
8   What was the nickname of the landscape gardener Lancelot Brown?
9   Which American-owned store opened in 1909 in Oxford Street?
10 Which country was formerly known as Southern Rhodesia?
11 Who wrote the novel *The Honourable Schoolboy*?
12 In which decade was "Birds of a Feather" screened for the first time?
13 What was Idi Amin's nickname?
14 In which decade was 80s TV series "The Charmer" set?
15 Who had a 90s No. 1 with "The Real Thing"?
16 In which century was Christopher Columbus born?
17 What runs every July in Pamplona?
18 What do the letters DPP stand for?
19 What is the only English anagram of GRAPHICALLY?
20 In Scrabble, how many points is the letter Z worth?
21 Who signs himself as Ebor?
22 Turnhouse Airport serves which city?
23 What letter goes before 100 to categorize Curcumin?
24 Which American actress was the first to appear on a postage stamp?
25 Who was the mother of John the Baptist?
26 How old was the boy named Sue when his daddy left home?
27 The 1997 London Proms featured "Yellow Shark" by which rock musician?
28 Blackburn's ground Ewood Park stands by which river?
29 What is the height, in feet, of a football goal?
30 In which city was "Albion Market" set?

LEVEL 2

1 Which duo were Solid?
2 Which track on Kate Bush's *The Kick Inside* was a No. 1 single?
3 What was Rod Stewart's first No. 1 album?
4 "The Weight" by the Band was on which album?
5 *Dead Ringer* was the first No. 1 album for who?
6 Who released a series of Singalonga songs?
7 Which composer gave Nigel Kennedy the chance to chart through the four seasons?
8 Who recorded *Graffiti Bridge*?
9 Mike Oldfield's *Tubular Bells* came out on which label?
10 What was the Spice Girls first album called?
11 In the 70s which singer/songwriter recorded *Back To Front*?
12 Which 60s group came back in the 90s producing a *Carnival Of Hits*?
13 Whose album was *Made In Heaven*?
14 Who were the voices behind Derek and Clive?
15 Who was on Neck and Neck with Mark Knopfler?
16 On *Sergeant Pepper*, how many holes were in Blackburn, Lancashire?
17 Which group's best-of album was called *Carry On Up The Charts*?
18 Which group had Jerry Hall as a siren on the rocks on an album cover?
19 What are the first names of the chart-topping Three Tenors?
20 Which David spent most weeks in the charts in 1973,1974 and 1983?
21 Who recorded *Captain Fantastic & The Brown Dirt Cowboy*?
22 Which group had eight No. 1 albums in a row from 1969 to 1979?
23 Which album did Paul Young record with an almost French title?
24 Who in 1987 became the first solo female to spend most weeks in the charts?
25 Which group produced their *Greatest Hits* before their *Arrival*?
26 Who had a mid-80s No. 1 with *Invisible Touch*?
27 Which heavy rock group recorded *Fireball* and *Machine Head*?
28 Which Phil spent most weeks in the charts in 1990?
29 "Money For Nothing" first appeared on which Dire Straits album?
30 Which Beatles album featured a zebra crossing on the cover?

1. Which range of hills has Cleeve Hill as its highest point?
2. Who painted a "Self Portrait with Bandaged Ear"?
3. Who co-wrote "We Are The World" with Michael Jackson?
4. Where, on the River Stort, was the birthplace of Cecil Rhodes?
5. Which year was the Hiroshima bombing?
6. Which lager is the name of Britain's second-most important men's tennis tournament?
7. Which toll bridge crosses the River Severn?
8. Which band joined Girlschool on the "St Valentine's Day Massacre"?
9. What is the first thing you should do if you have a motor accident?
10. What is Cape Kennedy now called?
11. What do P and G stand for in P.G. Wodehouse's name?
12. Who had a 90s No. 1 with "Everything Changes"?
13. What were the Harts first names in "Hart to Hart"?
14. Which character did Simon Cadell play in "Hi-De-Hi!"?
15. What word can go after "gall" and before "hem"?
16. What is the capital of Vietnam?
17. Which actor portrayed Rowdy Yates in "Rawhide"?
18. In which century was Chopin born?
19. Whose was the voice of Dangermouse in the cartoon series?
20. Which Sheffield theatre opened in 1972?
21. Where are British monarchs crowned?
22. Whose Organ Symphony was used for the theme of *Babe*?
23. Who made the first nonstop double flight across the English Channel?
24. In which Dickens novel does Alfred Jingle appear?
25. What colour caps do the Australians cricket team wear?
26. Which girl's name means grace and favour in Hebrew?
27. Who wrote *The Rainbow*?
28. In which decade of the 20th century was Ray Charles born?
29. Alfresco, Golden Boy and Shirley are types of what?
30. What is the capital of Sri Lanka?

Answers

Pot Luck 26 (see Quiz 58)

1 *Great Expectations*. 2 Queen Victoria. 3 A glass of red wine. 4 *The Times*. 5 The Warner Brothers. 6 David Bowie. 7 Red Rum. 8 Capability. 9 Selfridge's. 10 Zimbabwe. 11 John Le Carre. 12 1980s. 13 Dada. 14 1930s. 15 Tony Di Bart. 16 15th. 17 Bulls. 18 Director of Public Prosecutions. 19 Calligraphy. 20 Ten. 21 The Archbishop of York. 22 Edinburgh. 23 E. 24 Grace Kelly. 25 Elizabeth. 26 Three. 27 Frank Zappa. 28 River Darwen. 29 Eight feet. 30 Manchester.

Quiz 61 TV Sitcoms

Answers - see page 302

LEVEL 2

1 Who is Gary's wartime wife in "Goodnight Sweetheart"?
2 Which ministry did Jim Hacker run before he became PM?
3 What are the names of Father Ted's equally eccentric colleagues?
4 What is the name of the Vicar of Dibley?
5 Who had an incompetent personal assistant called Bubbles?
6 Which sitcom was set in the stately home of Lord Meldrum?
7 In which show did Brenda and Malcolm enjoy ornithology?
8 Who was the slave played by Frankie Howerd in "Up Pompeii"?
9 What are the Porter children called in "2 Point 4 Children"?
10 Which 80s series took its name from a 50s Little Richard song title?
11 Whose son-in-law was to him a "randy Scouse git"?
12 What was the name of the cab firm in the US sitcom "Taxi"?
13 In which show did Dr Sheila Sabatini appear?
14 What was Steptoe and Son's horse called?
15 Which character did Ronnie Corbett play in "Sorry!"?
16 Which US sitcom character was mother to Becky, Darlene and DJ?
17 David Jason won a BAFTA for the role of Skullion in which sitcom?
18 What were Fletcher's two first names in "Porridge"?
19 In "Birds of a Feather" what is Dorien's husband called?
20 What is the TV news company called in "Drop the Dead Donkey"?
21 Who, collectively, had a landlord called Jerzy Balowski?
22 Which show had Diana and Tom at the Bayview Retirement Home?
23 Who was the caretaker, played by Deryck Guyler, in "Please Sir"?
24 What was Henry Crabbe's restaurant called?
25 What type of shop was the setting for "Desmond's"?
26 Which spin-off about a couple followed "Man About the House"?
27 What was the occupation of Peter in "The Peter Principle"?
28 What was the profession of Victor Meldrew's neighbour Pippa?
29 In which sitcom did Charlie Burrows work for Caroline Wheatley?
30 Which sitcom had butler Brabinger and the Czech Mrs Polouvicka?

Answers

On The Map (see Quiz 63)
1 They are all new towns. 2 San Andreas Fault. 3 Andes. 4 California.
5 Iceland. 6 Romania. 7 Archipelago. 8 Brown. 9 Paris. 10 Hobart.
11 Mountain. 12 Edinburgh. 13 Winchester. 14 Belize. 15 Zambesi.
16 Channel Islands. 17 Venezuela. 18 Columbus. 19 Bury St Edmunds.
20 Romney. 21 Canada. 22 St Paul's. 23 Cemetery. 24 Sudan.
25 North. 26 Parliament Square. 27 Yorkshire Dales. 28 Scotland
(Highland Region). 29 Parishes. 30 Don.

Quiz 62 Pot Luck 28

Answers - see page 303

LEVEL 2

1   What name is given to dried and germinated barley?
2   Which TV rat had a hit with "Love Me Tender"?
3   Where was the original Capodimonte factory in Italy?
4   On which ship did Sir Francis Drake receive his knighthood?
5   Which chemical formula represents ice?
6   What day of the week did the 1984 Boat Race take place on?
7   Sutton Coldfield is a suburb of which city?
8   What fruit is grown by viticulturists?
9   On which day of the week are US elections always held?
10 Who joined the Pogues on "Fairytale of New York"?
11 Who wrote the novel *Coming Up For Air*?
12 What was the nickname of Herbert Marx?
13 In which police series did Captain Dobey and Huggy Bear appear?
14 What was the name of Labour's '97 General Election campaign bulldog?
15 Which actress played Sandra's mum in "The Liver Birds"?
16 With which sport do we associate the term "double axel"?
17 Who had a 50s No. 1 with "Dream Lover"?
18 To ten years, when was the storming of the Bastille?
19 Jonathan Edwards specialised in which athletics event?
20 Which birthstone is linked to April?
21 Bathophobia is a fear of what?
22 Corinthian, Doric and Ionian are all types of what?
23 In which century was Samuel Taylor Coleridge born?
24 How many points are there in a perfect hand of cribbage?
25 In which decade was the first Chelsea Flower Show?
26 What was Muhammad Ali's name when he was born?
27 In Morse code what letter is represented by two dots?
28 What is the name of Tony Blair's first-born daughter?
29 Who was the first presenter of "Points of View"?
30 Which is darker - muscovado or demerara sugar?

Answers

Movies: The Oscars (see Quiz 64)
1 *Casablanca*. 2 Clarice Starling. 3 *On Golden Pond*. 4 Forrest Gump.
5 *The Philadelphia Story*. 6 Muhammad Ali v. George Foreman in Zaire.
7 Chicago. 8 A roll of film. 9 *The Color Purple*. 10 *Gone With the Wind*.
11 Richard Burton. 12 Jessica Tandy. 13 Jeremy Irons. 14 Turned it down.
15 Kristin Scott Thomas. 16 *Cabaret*. 17 Fred Astaire and Ginger Rogers.
18 Best Director. 19 John Wayne. 20 *Schindler's List*. 21 Glenda Jackson.
22 Vanessa Redgrave. 23 Walt Disney. 24 Peter Finch. 25 Nun. 26 1920s.
27 Kathy Bates. 28 Three. 29 "Can You Feel the Love Tonight".
30 Anthony Minghella.

Quiz 63 On The Map

Answers - see page 300

LEVEL 2

1 What do Washington, Basildon and Cwmbran have in common?
2 What is the fault in San Francisco called?
3 What is the world's longest mountain range?
4 What is the third largest US state after Alaska and Texas?
5 Which country has IS as its international registration letters?
6 Where is Transylvania?
7 What is a sea containing many islands called?
8 What colour is the Bakerloo line on the London Underground map?
9 Orly airport is near which city?
10 What is the capital of Tasmania?
11 In Austria what is the Grossglockner?
12 Where are Waverley and Haymarket stations?
13 Where is the administrative HQ of Hampshire?
14 How was British Honduras subsequently known?
15 On which river is the Kariba Dam?
16 Herm is one of which group of islands?
17 Which South American country was named after Venice?
18 What is the capital of the US state of Ohio?
19 In which East Anglian town is the Greene King brewery based?
20 Which of the Cinque Ports has six letters in its name?
21 Which country has the longest coastline?
22 How is London Cathedral now known?
23 Which 77-acre site was founded at Kensal Green in London in 1832?
24 What is the largest country in Africa?
25 Which of the divisions of Yorkshire has the largest perimeter?
26 Which Square is in front of the Palace of Westminster?
27 After the Lake District which is England's largest National Park?
28 Which country of the British Isles has the largest county in terms of area?
29 What are the smallest units of local government in rural areas?
30 On which river does Sheffield stand?

Answers

TV Sitcoms (see Quiz 61)
1 Phoebe. 2 Administrative Affairs. 3 Dougal, Jack. 4 Geraldine Granger.
5 Edina Monsoon. 6 "You Rang, M'Lord". 7 "Watching". 8 Lurcio.
9 Jenny, David. 10 "Tutti Frutti". 11 Alf Garnett. 12 Sunshine Cab
Company. 13 "Surgical Spirit". 14 Hercules. 15 Timothy Lumsden.
16 "Roseanne". 17 "Porterhouse Blue". 18 Norman Stanley. 19 Marcus.
20 Globelink. 21 The Young Ones. 22 "Waiting For God". 23 Potter.
24 Pie in the Sky. 25 Barber's. 26 "George and Mildred". 27 Bank
manager. 28 Bus driver. 29 "The Upper Hand". 30 "To the Manor Born".

1 Which film ends, "Louis, I think this is the beginning of a beautiful friendship"?
2 Who did Jodie Foster play in *The Silence of the Lambs*?
3 What was Henry Fonda's last film, for which he won an Oscar?
4 Who said, "Life is like a box of chocolates, you never know what you're going to get"?
5 James Stewart won his only Best Actor Oscar for which classic?
6 The film documentary *When We Were Kings* told of which sports clash?
7 In which city is *The Sting* set?
8 What does the male figure stand on, on the Oscar statuette?
9 Which Whoopi Goldberg film had 14 nominations and no win at all?
10 Which film was the first all-colour winner of the Best Picture award?
11 From 1952 to 1977, which Brit had 10 nominations and never won?
12 Who was the oldest Best Actress award recipient when she won in 1989?
13 Which British star was the first Best Actor award winner of the 1990s?
14 What did Marlon Brando do with his 1972 Oscar?
15 Who played Katharine Clifton in *The English Patient*?
16 Best Director Bob Fosse was the only 70s winner whose film was not Best Picture that year. Which picture was it?
17 Who danced together for the last time at the 1966 Oscar ceremony?
18 Kevin Costner was nominated for Best Director and Best Actor for *Dances With Wolves*, which did he win?
19 Which cancer sufferer's last public appearance was at the 1979 Oscar ceremony?
20 Which was the first black-and-white film to win Best Picture after *The Apartment* in 1960?
21 Which British actress won two Oscars in the 70s?
22 Who criticised "militant Zionist hoodlums" in her '77 Oscar speech?
23 Who was given one large Oscar and seven small ones in 1938?
24 Who was the first posthumous recipient of the Best Actor award?
25 What is Susan Sarandon's occupation in *Dead Man Walking*?
26 In which decade were the first Academy Awards given?
27 Who won the Oscar for Best Actress for her role in *Misery*?
28 How many Oscars did Katharine Hepburn win after her 60th birthday?
29 Of the three *The Lion King* songs nominated, which won the Oscar?
30 Who directed *The English Patient*?

Quiz 65 Pot Luck 29

Answers - see page 306

LEVEL 2

1 How much did the wedding ring of the Owl and the Pussycat cost?
2 Which country was the first to retain the football World Cup?
3 Who sang about 99 red balloons?
4 What do the Mexicans make from the Agave cactus?
5 Which horse was kidnapped in February 1983?
6 What trade was abolished in 1807 in England?
7 Who did Maradona play for immediately before Napoli?
8 Who walked the length of the South Coast for charity in 1992?
9 Which doggy event was originally held in Newcastle?
10 Whose first UK top ten hit was "When Doves Cry"?
11 In which decade of the 20th century was Neil Armstrong born?
12 What was Al short for in Al Capone's name?
13 What is the only English anagram of GYRATED?
14 Where was soccer's Terry Butcher born?
15 Who wrote *Brideshead Revisited*?
16 Who was the narrator of "Paddington" on TV?
17 In World War II, what were Chindits?
18 Where was "Home and Away" set?
19 Which monarch reigned for only 325 days?
20 If A is alpha and B is bravo what is R?
21 Who first won the Embassy World Snooker Championship twice?
22 In which century was Geoffrey Chaucer born?
23 Are there more days in the first six months or the last six months of the year?
24 "The Merryman And His Maid" is the subtitle of which light opera?
25 How long in years is a French presidential term?
26 How many edges does a cube have?
27 What is the main colour of Biffo the Bea?
28 What is heraldic black called?
29 Clint Eastwood was born in which city?
30 Who had a 60s No. 1 with "I'm Alive"?

Answers

Pot Luck 30 (see Quiz 67)

1 Vanessa Paradis. 2 Black-and-white. 3 Books of stamps. 4 Someone's life.
5 The Turkey. 6 Batons. 7 "Hit" or "Miss". 8 Four. 9 Harry. 10 Green.
11 18th. 12 Jilly Cooper. 13 Manchester Airport new runway. 14 Barbie
Batchelor. 15 David Essex. 16 *The Tempest*. 17 37. 18 Chicago. 19 Radio
Luxembourg. 20 "Her". 21 El Greco. 22 Zagreb. 23 Maria. 24 2 pm.
25 Joseph Stalin. 26 One. 27 Johannesburg. 28 Greenland. 29 Hydrogen.
30 Dorothy Wordsworth.

Quiz 66 Hobbies & Leisure 2

Answers - see page 307

LEVEL 2

1   In which city is the National Railway Museum?
2   What is the maximum number of players in a game of poker?
3   Which game takes its name from the Chinese for sparrow?
4   How many pieces are on a chess board at the start of a game?
5   Which card game derives its name from the Spanish word for basket?
6   Which stately home is sometimes called the Palace of the Peak?
7   In which county would you visit Sissinghurst Gardens?
8   In which museum is the "Mona Lisa"?
9   How did Canterbury Cathedral announce it would emulate St Paul's in 1997?
10 In which city is Tropical World, Roundhay Park?
11 In which French château is there a Hall of Mirrors?
12 Which Suffolk Hall hosts days where Tudor life is re-created in great detail?
13 The Bluebell Railway straddles which two counties?
14 What does *son et lumiere* mean?
15 What do you use to play craps?
16 How many dominoes are there in a double-six set?
17 How many different topics are there in a game of Trivial Pursuits?
18 In which month would you go to watch Trooping the Colour?
19 Where in Paris would you go to see Napoleon's tomb?
20 In which county is Whipsnade Park Zoo?
21 *Chemin de fer* is a type of which game?
22 Which is England's most visited zoo after London?
23 What is Margarete Steiff famous for making?
24 Which phenomenon might you be interested in if you went to Drumnadrochit?
25 UK Legoland is near which town?
26 What sort of leisure attraction is Twycross?
27 In which country is the De Efteling theme park?
28 The National Trust adminsters properties in which three countries?
29 Which tourist attraction is next door to Madamme Tussaud's in London?
30 Which two Cluedo weapons begin with the same letter?

1   Who had her first UK hit with "Joe Le Taxi"?
2   What two colours were five pound notes before 1961?
3   Which necessity was first sold in Post Offices in 1904?
4   What do you save in order to win an Albert Medal?
5   Who conducted the Owl and the Pussycat's wedding ceremony?
6   What were first used by relay racers in 1893?
7   Which choice of verdict could the Juke Box Jury make?
8   How many sides does a tetrahedron have?
9   What is songwriter/singer Nilsson's first name?
10 Which colour is the Libyan flag?
11 In which century was Robbie Burns born?
12 Who wrote the novel *Appassionata*?
13 At which site were the Jimi Hendrix camp and Zion Tree camp?
14 Which character did Peggy Ashcroft play in "The Jewel in the Crown"?
15 Who had a 70s No. 1 with "Hold Me Close"?
16 Which Shakespeare play begins with a storm at sea?
17 What is the next highest prime number above 31?
18 Where did Frank Sinatra say was his "kind of town"?
19 On which radio station did "Opportunity Knocks" begin?
20 What word can go after "heat" and before "on"?
21 Which Greek artist painted the "View of Toledo"?
22 What is the capital of Croatia?
23 What is Jose Carreras' middle name?
24 If it's 12 noon GMT what time is it in Helsinki?
25 Which Russian succeeded Lenin?
26 In Scrabble, how many points is the letter E worth?
27 The rugby ground Ellis Park is in which city?
28 Which is the largest island in the world?
29 Which element has the atomic number 1?
30 Who wrote *Grasmere Journal*?

Pot Luck 29 (see Quiz 65)

Answers

Pot Luck 29 (see Quiz 65)
1 A shilling. 2 Italy. 3 Nena. 4 Tequila. 5 Shergar. 6 The Slave Trade.
7 Barcelona. 8 Ian Botham. 9 Cruft's. 10 Prince. 11 30s. 12 Alphonse.
13 Tragedy. 14 Singapore. 15 Evelyn Waugh. 16 Michael Horden.
17 Jungle troops in Burma. 18 Summer Bay. 19 Edward VIII. 20 Romeo.
21 Steve Davis. 22 14th. 23 Last six. 24 *The Yeomen Of the Guard*.
25 Seven. 26 12. 27 Black. 28 Sable. 29 San Francisco. 30 The Hollies.

1   Which British monarch succeeded Queen Victoria?
2   Richard III died at which battle?
3   Who was the last viceroy of India?
4   Which English monarch married Eleanor of Aquitaine?
5   Who was the last wife of Henry VIII?
6   Which country did Britain fight in the War of Jenkins' Ear?
7   Which King George did the Prince Regent become?
8   At the Siege of Mafeking who led the British forces?
9   The House of Lancaster kings were all called what?
10 Under what name is Gregor Efimovich better known?
11 Apart from Mad George which kinder nickname did George III have?
12 Which English queen married Prince George of Denmark?
13 Blucher commanded which country's troops at the Battle of Waterloo?
14 Who had a horse called Bucephalus?
15 Queen Elizabeth II's grandfather was which monarch?
16 Who was the Wisest Fool In Christendom?
17 Who was the first Prince of Wales?
18 Whose last words are reputed to be, "My neck is very slender"?
19 Which Spanish king sent his unsuccessful Armada?
20 Which monarch was murdered in Berkeley Castle?
21 In what year did Edward VIII abdicate?
22 In Britain, who first held the office that today is known as Prime Minister?
23 In the 15th century which Duke was drowned in Malmsey wine?
24 Who ruled England between Henry I and Henry II?
25 How did Lord Kitchener die?
26 Who with royal connections had the middle name Warfield?
27 In 1066 how many monarchs ruled England in the year?
28 Which ruler referred the English to a nation of shopkeepers?
29 Which monarch ordered the execution of Sir Walter Raleigh?
30 Which wife gave Henry VIII the male heir that he wanted?

1   What colour did the legendary keeper Lev Yashin play in?
2   Which striker was known as the Octopus in his own country?
3   Bobby Robson left which club to join Barcelona?
4   Oscar Ruggeri became the highest capped player for which country?
5   Who had the final kick of the 1994 World Cup Final?
6   In which decade did Bayern Munich first win the UEFA Cup?
7   Former Italian prime minister Silvio Berlusconi took over which club?
8   Thomas Ravelli became the most capped player for which country?
9   The stadium the Monumental is in which country?
10   Which Dutchman came with Arnold Muhren to Ipswich in the 80s?
11   Alfredo di Stefano played for Argentina, Spain and which other country?
12   Before 1994 when did Brazil last win the World Cup?
13   The club Feyenoord is based in which city?
14   Which club play at the Bernabeu Stadium?
15   Who scored England's last gasp winner against Belgium in Italia 90?
16   What colour are Germany's shorts?
17   How old was Maradona when he first played for Argentina?
18   Who captained Italy in the 1994 World Cup Final?
19   Gullit, Van Basten and Rijkaard lined up at which non-Dutch club?
20   Which country does Stefan Schwartz play for?
21   Who was first player from Ghana to play in the English league?
22   Which Arsenal manager signed Dennis Bergkamp?
23   Which French league club did Glenn Hoddle play for?
24   Who were the first African country to reach the World Cup quarter-finals?
25   Which Swede played for Arsenal, Everton and Birmingham?
26   Which club play at the Olympiastadion?
27   Ravanelli joined Middlesbrough from which club?
28   What colour are Portugal's shorts?
29   Which country did Mario Kempes play for?
30   Which Spanish side did John Aldridge play for?

1   What is the official currency of Liechtenstein?
2   Who was the longest reigning British monarch before Victoria?
3   Which ponies were originally used in coal mines?
4   Who was the first post war British winner of a British Grand Prix?
5   At which London tourist attraction would you find a Chinese pagoda?
6   What do Americans call the silencer on the car?
7   Which bird-shooting season runs from October 1 to February 1?
8   What is the name of Andy Capp's wife?
9   Who was the original owner of *Today* newspaper?
10 What name is given to America's most westerly time zone?
11 Who wrote the novel *Sharpe's Tiger*?
12 In which decade of the 20th century was George Harrison born?
13 What word can go before "beer", "bread" and "nut"?
14 Who lit the Eternal Flame on the grave of John F. Kennedy?
15 What is the capital of Colombia?
16 What do G and K stand for in G.K. Chesterton's name?
17 What specialist line of trade did Tom Keating follow?
18 What would a Mexican submerge into a beer to make a "Submarino"?
19 What night is Burns Night?
20 Abbas Gokal got the Old Bailey's longest fraud sentence for scams centred on which company?
21 Who was the first TV newsreader to be knighted?
22 Which monarch was murdered at Pontefract Castle?
23 Which actress's real surname is Anistonopoulos?
24 Who was the first presenter of "A Question of Sport"?
25 Which club has members called Barkers?
26 Who are the landlords of the Bull, Ambridge?
27 Glen Cova and Joy are types of which fruit?
28 Who had a 80s No. 1 with "Jealous Guy"?
29 In which century was Lewis Carroll born?
30 Which car company has the Corolla range?

Quiz 71 Animal World

Answers - see page 308

LEVEL 2

1   What does the aardvark feed on?
2   What colour is an ocelot?
3   What is the only member of the giraffe family other than the giraffe itself?
4   What sort of animal feeds on plants and other animals?
5   Which ape's natural habitat is restricted to Sumatra and Borneo?
6   What are ossicles?
7   Which group has more teeth - mammals or reptiles?
8   What is the North American equivalent of the reindeer?
9   What colour is a coyote's coat?
10 What name is given to a creature equally at home on land and in water?
11 What term describes an animal which cannot control its body temperature and has to rely on its environment?
12 What was the first animal to be domesticated?
13 Which special mouth parts inject poison into prey?
14 The llama is a relative of which African animal?
15 Which is the only vertebrate capable of sustained flight?
16 The wapiti is a member of which family of animals?
17 What protects a vertebrate's nerve cord?
18 Which extinct animal's name is the Portuguese for "stupid"?
19 What is another name for the Russian wolfhound?
20 What colour tongue does a chow chow have?
21 Other than the Australian mainland the platypus is native to where?
22 Where does a gopher make its home?
23 What is the most intelligent of land animals after man?
24 What type of apes were imported into Gibraltar in the 18th century?
25 What do mammary glands produce?
26 The brown bear is also known by what name?
27 What is the only true amphibious member of the weasel family?
28 Which American native has a black masked face and a distinctive ringed tail?
29 The anteater is native to which continent?
30 What is a marmoset?

Quiz 72 Pot Luck 32

Answers - see page 309

LEVEL 2

1 Which actor used the word "perfick" in "The Darling Buds of May"?
2 Which kingdom was the setting for "Yellow Submarine"?
3 What do most humans lose 15 million of every second?
4 Who was the second wife that Henry VIII divorced?
5 What colour, traditionally, is an Indian wedding sari?
6 Who was the first suffragette martyr?
7 In which country is the Spanish Riding School?
8 Who hosted "Every Second Counts"?
9 What is the subject of Renoir's painting "Les Parapluies"?
10 Which part of the body is known as the thorax?
11 To five years, when was Louis Armstrong born?
12 Who wrote the novel originally titled *Ten Little Niggers*?
13 What word can go after "brandy" and before "dragon"?
14 In Shakespeare, who kills Desdemona?
15 What is Snoopy's brother's name?
16 Who had a 90s No. 1 with "End Of The Road"?
17 How is Teodor Josef Korzeniowsky better known?
18 How many records is a castaway allowed on "Desert Island Discs"?
19 What flower is on the shirts of the English Rugby Union team?
20 In which part of New York was "Kojak" set?
21 Tim Holley and David Rigg found their pay rises in the news while at which company?
22 Which birthstone is linked to October?
23 In which decade was "Blankety Blank" first screened in the UK?
24 In which city did Phileas Fogg begin his trip around the world?
25 Which grandson of 50s Labour home secretary Herbert Morrison played a leading part in the 1997 election?
26 Bourbon, Gallica and Rugosa are types of what?
27 Which House in England may not be entered by the Queen?
28 Nephophobia is a fear of what?
29 Clare Short has represented which Birmingham constituency?
30 What was the first Australian city to have hosted the Olympics?

Answers

Pot Luck 31 (see Quiz 70)

1 The Swiss Franc. 2 George III. 3 Shetland. 4 Stirling Moss. 5 Kew Gardens. 6 A muffler. 7 Pheasant. 8 Flo or Florrie. 9 Eddy Shah. 10 Pacific. 11 Bernard Cornwell. 12 40s. 13 "Ginger". 14 Jacqueline Kennedy. 15 Bogota. 16 Gilbert Keith. 17 Art forger. 18 Tequila. 19 January 25th. 20 BCCI. 21 Alastair Burnet. 22 Richard II. 23 Jennifer Aniston. 24 David Vine. 25 Variety Club. 26 Sid and Kathy Perks. 27 Raspberry. 28 Roxy Music. 29 19th. 30 Toyota.

1   All Cilla Black's 60s hits were on which record label?
2   What was the Beach Boys' first British No. 1?
3   Which same-surname artists both charted with "Memphis Tennessee"?
4   Which No. 1 starts "I'm in heaven when I see you smile"?
5   The Byrds' first two British hits were written by who?
6   Which was the first No. 1 for the Shadows?
7   Who was backed by the Stingers?
8   Who had No. 1s that had the colours red and black in the titles?
9   Which group featured drummer Anne Lantree?
10 Which US group sang "Rhythm Of The Rain"?
11 What was the surname of Desmond and Molly in "Ob-La-Di-Ob-La-Da"?
12 Which Tom wrote and produced for the Seekers?
13 In the Ricky Valance song, who loves Laura?
14 "5-4-3-2-1" was the signature tune of which TV pop show?
15 Who sang "I'll Never Fall In Love Again"?
16 Which ex-Shadows hit No. 1 with "Diamonds"?
17 Who backed Tomy Bruce?
18 Jim Capaldi and Steve Winwood came together in which group?
19 Which animal did Cat Stevens first sing about in the charts?
20 Which husband-and-wife team wrote a string of Pet-Clark hits?
21 Who were the first to have a No. 1 - the Beatles or the Stones?
22 In "A Whiter Shade Of Pale" where were the vestal virgins leaving for?
23 On which label did Mary Hopkin record "Those Were The Days"?
24 Gladys Knight and Marvin Gaye had separate hits with which song?
25 "Yeh Yeh" was a No. 1 for who?
26 Which city did the Dave Clark Five come from?
27 Who became the first female singer to have three No. 1s?
28 Who wrote Chris Farlowe's "Out of Time"?
29 Which classic starts "Dirty old river"?
30 Whose last Top Ten hit of the 60s was "San Franciscan Nights"?

1　What would you measure on the cephalic index?
2　Which name links Gwent, Rhode Island, USA, and the Isle of Wight?
3　When was VAT introduced in Britain?
4　What are the surnames of the TV presenters Judy and Richard?
5　Which breakfast dish was originally a hangover cure?
6　Which girls' name gave the Damned their only UK Top 10 hit?
7　Where would you find the Doge's Palace?
8　What is the minimum number of points to win on a tennis tie-break?
9　What colour hair did Churchill have before he went bald?
10　What is the main range of hills in gloucestershire?
11　Who wrote the novel *The Children Of Men*?
12　What is the only English anagram of PIMENTOS?
13　What is studied by a heliologist?
14　In which century was Thomas à Becket born?
15　In Morse code what letter is represented by one dash?
16　Which golfer first won the US amateur title three years in a row?
17　Which London street is famous for men's tailoring?
18　Which was the frequency of Radio Luxembourg?
19　Which famous chair was kidnapped by students from the Cranfield Institute of Technology in 1978?
20　Which character did Bonnie Langford play in "Just William"?
21　What was Spain's General Franco's first name?
22　In the Chinese calendar which year follows the year of the dragon?
23　What is the RAF equivalent to the army rank of Major?
24　What was Jacques Cousteau's research ship called?
25　Which city does the Halle Orchestra come from?
26　The fox-hunting season covers which months in Britain?
27　What is the Archbishop of Canterbury's official residence?
28　Who had a 50s No. 1 with "Young Love"?
29　In which decade of the 20th century was Jack Nicholson born?
30　What is the main flavour of aioli?

Answers

Performing Arts　(see Quiz 76)
1　Theatre Royal Drury Lane. 2　Ballet. 3　*The Magic Flute*. 4　Puccini. 5　Six hours. 6　UK. 7　Paris. 8　The Old Vic. 9　Tchaikovsky. 10　Bix Beiderbecke. 11　Ellington. 12　The Savoy. 13　Artie Shaw. 14　Olivier. 15　Blackpool. 16　*Le Nozze di Figaro*. 17　*Hamlet*. 18　Norma (Major). 19　Spanish. 20　Sam Wanamaker. 21　Kirov Ballet. 22　*The Madness of George III*. 23　Alan Ayckbourn. 24　Tom Stoppard. 25　The Queen Mother when Queen consort. 26　*Evening Standard*. 27　Olivier. 28　Cameron Mackintosh. 29　The Strand. 30　New York.

1 Who was dubbed TV's Mr Sex?
2 Which drama/comedy was set in St Elgius Hospital?
3 What was Zoë's job in "May to December"?
4 In "Lovejoy" what was Tinker's surname?
5 Which ex-breakfast TV presenter has had a nightly show on Sky 1?
6 Where were the first three series of "Animal Hospital" based?
7 Who drew the animated titles sequence for "Yes Minister"?
8 What was the job of the heroes of "Common as Muck"?
9 Who was the most successful act on "The Big Time"?
10 Which city is "Casualty"'s Holby said to be?
11 What was the nickname of Sam Malone of "Cheers"?
12 In which month does the "Children in Need" appeal normally take place?
13 Who was the undertaker in "Dad's Army"?
14 Whose children included Primrose, Petunia, Zinnia and Montgomery?
15 Who was the sports commentator on "The Day Today"?
16 Who was Detective Sergeant Andy Crawford's father-in-law?
17 Which House was the surgery for Drs Finlay and Cameron?
18 Who was the third Doctor Who?
19 In the early 60s what was Radio 2 known as?
20 Which TV marriage began with "Happy Ever After" in 1969?
21 Which adolescent did Gian Sammarco play?
22 What was the sequel to "Are You Being Served"?
23 Where did Tom Good work before he began the Good Life?
24 In which series did Dawn French as Amanda work for *Spare Cheeks* magazine?
25 Which was the first UK TV listings magazine to join the Internet?
26 Who played Rocky in "Boon"?
27 Whose boss was Dr Gillespie?
28 Where does Marc Freden report from on GMTV?
29 Who played Frank Stubbs in "Frank Stubbs Promotes"?
30 How many episodes of "Fawlty Towers" were made?

1   Which is London's oldest theatre?
2   The Royal Opera House in London is home to which branch of the arts other than opera?
3   How is Mozart's *Die Zauberflöte* known in English?
4   Who wrote *Tosca*?
5   Including intervals, approximately how long does Wagner's *Götterdämmerung* last?
6   Where is the Ballet Rambert based?
7   In which city is Europe's largest opera house?
8   Which theatre was the National's temporary home from 1963?
9   Who wrote the ballet *The Nutcracker*?
10 Which cornetist/pianist was considered to be the first great white jazz musician?
11 Which Duke's first names were Edward Kennedy?
12 Which London theatre was gutted by fire in 1990?
13 Which US clarinettist's real name was Arthur Jacob Arshawsky?
14 In 1984 The Society of West End Theatre Awards were renamed in honour of whom?
15 In which town is the largest stage in the UK?
16 How is *The Marriage of Figaro* known in Italian?
17 What is Shakespeare's longest play?
18 Which former prime minister's wife shares her name with a Bellini opera?
19 What nationality are two of the Three Tenors?
20 Which US director was the impetus behind the new Globe Theatre in London?
21 How is the Ballets Russes of Sergei Diaghelev now known?
22 What was *The Madness of King George* called as a play?
23 Which British playwright wrote the trilogy *The Norman Conquests*?
24 Which Czech-born playwright wrote *Jumpers and Arcadia*?
25 Who laid the foundation stone for the National Theatre on the South Bank?
26 Which newspaper presents awards for excellence in the London theatre?
27 Which of the three theatres within the National was named after the theatre's first Lord?
28 Who first produced *Les Miserables* in London?
29 In which street is London's Savoy Theatre?
30 In which city is the world's largest opera house?

Answers

Pot Luck 33 (see Quiz 74)
1 Human head. 2 Newport. 3 1973. 4 Finnigan and Madeley. 5 Eggs Benedict. 6 Eloise. 7 Venice. 8 Seven. 9 Red. 10 The Cotswolds. 11 P.D. James. 12 Nepotism. 13 The sun. 14 12th. 15 T. 16 Tiger Woods. 17 Savile Row. 18 208. 19 Mastermind chair. 20 Violet Elizabeth Bott. 21 Francisco. 22 Snake. 23 Squadron Leader. 24 The Calypso. 25 Manchester. 26 November-April. 27 Lambeth Palace. 28 Tab Hunter. 29 30s. 30 Garlic.

1   Who had a hit with "The Oldest Swinger in Town"?
2   Which Danish statue is a memorial to Hans Christian Andersen?
3   Where are rods and cones found in your body?
4   Which classic golf course is referred to as the Old Lady of golf?
5   What were the Boston Tea Party protesters unhappy about?
6   Which well-known trench was devised by Ferdinand De Lesseps?
7   Which royal owns the Castle of Mey?
8   Which short-lived soap saw Polly Perkins as Trish?
9   Which state in America is the Gambling State?
10 Which band included Martin Fry and Mark White?
11 On which island did Nelson Mandela serve most of his sentence?
12 What is the only English anagram of HEDONIST?
13 Who won the Australian Open as a Yugoslavian in 1993 and as American citizen in 1996?
14 Who was found guilty of the Oklahoma City bombing?
15 Who wrote the novel *Rob Roy*?
16 Which musical instrument does Tasmin Little play?
17 Who had a 60s No. 1 with "Mighty Quinn"?
18 How was Domenikos Theotocopolous better known?
19 Who shared the 1993 Nobel Peace prize with F.W. de Klerk?
20 Cecil Parkinson's affair with whom caused a scandal in 1983?
21 If A is alpha and B is bravo what is V?
22 What was the sport of Emerson's brother Wilson Fittipaldi?
23 In which series did Marion Jefferson and Beatrice Mason appear?
24 What name is given to the positive electrode of a battery?
25 Who was the first presenter of "Question Time"?
26 Who wrote "Love Shine A Light"?
27 What ship was Sir Francis Drake in when he circled the world?
28 In Norse mythology, who was god of thunder and war?
29 Gennifer Flowers claimed to have had a 12-year affair with whom?
30 In the Old Testament which book directly follows Numbers?

LEVEL 2

1   What was Barbra Streisand character called in *Funny Girl*?
2   In which musical do Tracy Lord and CK Dexter Haven appear?
3   In which musical is *The Duelling Cavalier* a film in the making?
4   Who sings "As Long as He Needs Me" in *Oliver!*?
5   Who directed *A Chorus Line*?
6   Which singer - famous for dubbing other actresses' voices - played Sister Sophia in *The Sound of Music*?
7   What was the follow-up to *Saturday Night Fever* called?
8   Who did Betty Hutton replace as Annie in *Annie Get Your Gun*?
9   What was the job of Joel Grey's character in *Cabaret*?
10 Which musical was based on a Harold Gray comic strip?
11 What instrument does Robert de Niro play in in *New York New York*?
12 Which musical does "The Ugly Duckling" come from?
13 Who sang "Moon River" in *Breakfast at Tiffany's*?
14 Which song in *Evita* was composed specially for the film?
15 How many Von Trapp children are there in *The Sound of Music*?
16 "Hopelessly Devoted to You" is sung in which movie?
17 Who are the two gangs in *West Side Story*?
18 Which character did Liza Minnelli play in *Cabaret*?
19 Which movie musical has the song "Feed the Birds"?
20 Who played Mama Rose in the 1993 movie *Gypsy*?
21 Which two musical legends starred in *Easter Parade*?
22 "Shall We Dance" features in which movie?
23 What was Stanley Holloway's role in *My Fair Lady*?
24 In which film does Fat Sam fight it out with Dandy Dan?
25 "The Bare Necessities" comes from which film?
26 In which film did Gordon Macrae play Billy Bigelow after Frank Sinatra dropped out?
27 Which daughter of Judy Garland appeared in *Grease II*?
28 Which actress was I in *The King and I*?
29 In which musical would you see Lina Lamont?
30 Who directed *Everyone Says I Love You*?

Answers

Celebs (see Quiz 80)

1 Ireland. 2 Michael Jackson and Debbie Rowe. 3 Sulaiman. 4 Jackie Kennedy-Onassis. 5 Clothes design. 6 David Frost. 7 Madonna. 8 Scarlet. 9 Larry Fortensky. 10 Underwear. 11 Linley. 12 Hairdressing. 13 Chanel. 14 Raine. 15 Julia and Will Carling. 16 Costner. 17 Michael Heseltine. 18 Sylvester Stallone. 19 Joan Collins. 20 Fergie's Argentinian polo-playing step father. 21 Simpson's of Piccadilly. 22 Hawaii. 23 Barbara Hulanicki. 24 Marmaduke Hussey. 25 Frances Edmonds. 26 Britt Ekland. 27 Lady Diana Spencer. 28 Mark McCormack. 29 Norman Hartnell. 30 Sharon Maughan.

Quiz 79 Pot Luck 35

Answers - see page 316

LEVEL 2

1 Whose state visit was featured on the TV documentary "EIIR"?
2 Which hit for the Shadows is also a balsa raft?
3 In which county is Silbury Hill, Europe's biggest manmade mound?
4 Which film featuring David Bowie is also an organ of balance?
5 Which country does Martina Hingis represent in tennis?
6 Who founded the Communist newspaper *Pravda* in 1912?
7 What do we call the heating process which destroys enzymes in milk?
8 Who is the unproven author of the *Iliad*?
9 Which associate member of the EC is also a Commonwealth island?
10 In which century was Hans Christian Andersen born?
11 What word can follow "but", "car" and "bat"?
12 Who had a heart attack on his Never Ending Tour?
13 Which element has the atomic number 2?
14 In music, how many sharps in the key of A?
15 What are substitutes in cricket not normally allowed to do?
16 The College of Brasenose is part of which university?
17 Who had a 70s No. 1 with "Baby Jump"?
18 What was Captain Bligh's most famous ship?
19 What disaster did Kenny Morgan and Albert Scanlon survive?
20 In which county was HMP Slade from "Porridge"?
21 In Scrabble, how many points is the letter O worth?
22 In 1997 who stood for Tory leader but dropped out before the first ballot?
23 Which European city was the first home of the Statue of Liberty?
24 The composer Percy Grainger came from which country?
25 What is the profession of radio's Anthony Clare?
26 In which Dickens novel does Joe Gargery appear?
27 In the 60s who did hairdresser Maureen Cox marry?
28 Which John Wayne movie won him his only Oscar?
29 What is the capital of Chile?
30 In measuring a horse, how many inches in a hand?

Answers

Pot Luck 34 (see Quiz 77)

1 Fred Wedlock. 2 Little Mermaid. 3 Eyes. 4 St Andrew's. 5 Tea taxes.
6 The Suez Canal. 7 The Queen Mother. 8 "Eldorado". 9 Nevada.
10 ABC. 11 Robben Island. 12 Dishonest. 13 Monica Seles. 14 Timothy
McVeigh. 15 Sir Walter Scott. 16 Violin. 17 Manfred Mann. 18 El Greco.
19 Nelson Mandela. 20 Sara Keays. 21 Victor. 22 Motor racing.
23 "Tenko". 24 Anode. 25 Robin Day. 26 Kimberley Rew. 27 *The Golden
Hind*. 28 Thor. 29 Bill Clinton. 30 Deuteronomy.

1 Which country shares its name with Kim Basinger's daughter?

2 Who are the parents of Prince Michael Jr?

3 What is the son of Jemima and Imran Khan called?

4 Who was the famous sister of Lee Radziwill Ross?

5 In what field is Tommy Hilfiger a famous name?

6 Who is the son-in-law of the 17th Duke of Norfolk?

7 Carlos Leon has a famous daughter; who is the child's mother?

8 What colour dress did Paula Yates wear to marry Bob Geldof?

9 Who was Liz Taylor's eighth husband?

10 What type of clothes would you buy from Janet Reger?

11 Which Viscount attended Elton John's 50th birthday dressed as a lion?

12 In which field is Patrick Cameron famous?

13 Which fashion house does Stella Tennant model for?

14 What was Princess Diana's stepmother's first name?

15 Which couple advertised Quorn before their much-publicised split?

16 Which Cindy's divorce settlement from her actor/director husband was reputedly in the region of £50 million?

17 Which MP's children are called Annabel, Alexandra and Rupert?

18 Who married Jennifer Flavin as his third wife?

19 Who is Tara Newley's famous mother?

20 Who was the late Hector Barrantes?

21 Mrs Anthony Andrews' family own which London store?

22 On which island was model Marie Helvin brought up?

23 Which Polish-born designer founded Biba?

24 Which ex-BBC Chairman's wife was Lady-in-Waiting to the Queen?

25 Whose first book was *Another Bloody Tour* in 1986?

26 Who has been married to Peter Sellers and Jim McDonnell?

27 Who used the pseudonym Deborah Smithson Wells when arranging fittings for her wedding dress?

28 Which agent married tennis star Betsy Nagelson?

29 Who made the wedding dresses of Princesses Elizabeth and Margaret?

30 Which actress was known as the lady in the Gold Blend commercials?

Answers

Musical Movies (see Quiz 78)

1 Fanny Brice. 2 *High Society.* 3 *Singing in the Rain.* 4 Nancy. 5 Richard Attenborough. 6 Marni Nixon. 7 *Staying Alive.* 8 Judy Garland. 9 Master of Ceremonies. 10 *Annie.* 11 Saxophonist. 12 *Hans Christian Andersen.* 13 Audrey Hepburn. 14 "You Must Love Me". 15 Seven. 16 *Grease.* 17 Jets, Sharks. 18 Sally Bowles. 19 *Mary Poppins.* 20 Bette Midler. 21 Fred Astaire, Judy Garland. 22 *The King and I.* 23 Alfred P. Doolittle. 24 *Bugsy Malone.* 25 *Jungle Book.* 26 *Carousel.* 27 Lorna Luft. 28 Deborah Kerr. 29 *Singing in the Rain.* 30 Woody Allen.

LEVEL 2

1   Which organ in the body produces bile?
2   Which county first won cricket's Benson & Hedges Cup twice?
3   Who are the main characters in Milton's *Paradise Lost*?
4   Which continent is wider in the south than in the north?
5   Which game is played to the Harvard rules?
6   Which Pennsylvanian power station had a nuclear accident in 1979?
7   Who was Lord Vestey's dessert-loving, opera-singing, grandmother?
8   How many cards does each player start with in gin rummy?
9   If you have herpes labialis, what are you suffering from?
10 Where would you find the Dogger Bank?
11 In which century was Lord Byron born?
12 Who wrote the novel *East Of Eden*?
13 Which golfer declared that racially he was a "Cablinasian"?
14 What opened when Ali Baba said "Open sesame"?
15 Which character did Sean Blowers play in "London's Burning"?
16 Which birthstone is linked to May?
17 What word can go after "machine" and before "dog"?
18 Who was called the Serpent of the Nile?
19 In the New Testament which book directly follows Romans?
20 Who was head of Polly Peck International when it crashed in 1991?
21 Which sport includes sculls, strokes and slides?
22 Godfrey Evans played cricket for which county?
23 Which former prison chief wrote the book *Hidden Agendas*?
24 Cynophobia is a fear of what?
25 "The Slave Of Duty" is the subtitle of which light opera?
26 In which county do Bulls battle against Rhinos?
27 In Morse code what letter is represented by two dots?
28 Who had an 80s No. 1 with "Nothing's Gonna Change My Love For You"?
29 What was the nickname of Julius Marx?
30 In 1997 Jonathan Aitken dropped a court case against which TV company?

1. In 1990 Mr Frisk set a record time in which major race?
2. Which Earl of Derby gave his name to the race?
3. To a year each way, when was Red Rum's third Grand National win?
4. Where is the Lincoln Handicap held?
5. Which three races make up the English Triple Crown?
6. How did 19th century jockey Fred Archer die?
7. Which Irish rider won the Prix de L'Arc de Triomphe four times?
8. To two years each way, when did Lester Piggott first win the Derby?
9. Which classic race was sponsored by Gold Seal from 1984-92?
10. Who rode Devon Loch in the sensational 1956 Grand National?
11. What colour was Arkle?
12. How long is the Derby?
13. Sceptre managed to win how many classics outright in a season?
14. Shergar won the 1981 Derby by a record of how many lengths?
15. Which National Hunt jockey retired in 1993 with most ever wins?
16. What was the nickname of Corbiere?
17. Who rode Nijinsky to victory in the Derby?
18. In which decade was the Prix de L'Arc de Triomphe first run?
19. Who triumphed in the Oaks on Ballanchine and Moonshell?
20. Which horse was National Hunt Champion of the Year four times in a row from 1987 on?
21. Which horse stopped Red Rum getting three in a row Grand National wins?
22. How many times did the great Sir Gordon Richards win the Epsom Derby?
23. The Preakness Stakes, Belmont Stakes plus which other race make up the American Triple Crown?
24. Which Frank established a record nine victories in The Oaks?
25. Which jockey was the first ever winner of The Derby?
26. What actually is Frankie Detorri's first name?
27. Who holds the world record of riding 8,833 winners?
28. Riding Erhaab in 1994 which jockey won his fourth Epsom Derby?
29. What colour was Red Rum?
30. How old was Lester Piggott when he returned to racing in 1990?

1 Which war did Charles Bronson return from in *Mr Majestyk*?
2 What name is given to a student of the alphabet?
3 Which illness killed Oliver Cromwell?
4 Who commissioned Holbein's painting of Anne of Cleves?
5 What is the metric word for one million?
6 What was tennis star Ann Haydon's married name?
7 Which company developed the pottery called Jasper Ware?
8 What did Monkee Mike Nesmith's mother invent?
9 Which travellers met at the Tabard Inn, Southwar?
10 What colour blood cells do lymph glands produce?
11 Who had a 90s No. 1 with "Oh Carolina"?
12 What are the colours of Humphrey the Downing Street cat?
13 Who wrote the novel *The Silmarillion*?
14 On which Canadian island is the city of Victoria?
15 In which century was Isambard Kingdom Brunel born?
16 What is the only English anagram of IMPRESSIVE?
17 In which country was Joe Bugner born?
18 In Scrabble, how many points is the letter A worth?
19 Which creature lives in a formicary?
20 What make of car was Jim Clark driving when he died?
21 In which drama did Father Ralph de Bricassart and Meggie Cleary appear?
22 If A is alpha and B is bravo what is T?
23 Which monster hit the British headlines in 1933?
24 Who were "overpaid, oversexed and over here"?
25 Which name means bringer of joys in Latin?
26 What was the nickname of the giant sperm whale grounded in the Firth of Forth in 1997?
27 What drug is obtained from foxgloves?
28 Ben Lomond and Baldwin are types of which fruit?
29 Which element has the atomic number 50 and the symbol Sn?
30 In which decade of the 20th century was Alan Ayckbourn born?

1 Which controversial BBC Falklands film was broadcast in May 1988?
2 In which month was the marriage of Prince Charles and Lady Diana?
3 The SAS stormed which embassy in Knightsbridge?
4 Where did the 1980 Olympics take place?
5 Where did the Polish Solidarity movement start its strikes?
6 In August 1980 unemployment in Britain reached what figure?
7 Which US President ordered the aborted rescue of US hostages in Tehran?
8 Which Lord prepared a report following the Brixton riots?
9 Who did Pat Cash beat in the final when he won Wimbledon?
10 Who became the first Pope to visit Britain in 400 years?
11 Which charity record was the last to reach No.1 in the 80s?
12 Who were Liverpool's opponents in the FA Cup semi-final Hillsborough disaster?
13 Who "got on his bike and looked for work"?
14 What did Prince Edward resign?
15 How did Princess Grace of Monaco die?
16 Which Tory MP Keith was involved in dodgy applications for shares?
17 In which month of 1982 did Argentine forces invade the Falkland Islands?
18 Nuclear protests were based at Greenham Common in which county?
19 Which police officer was shot outside the Libyan embassy?
20 To a year, how old was Bjorn Borg when he retired from tennis?
21 What did Reagan's Strategic Defence Initative become known as?
22 What did Monday, October 19th, 1987 become known as?
23 Which North Sea oil rig exploded with the loss of over 150 lives?
24 Which former M15 man wrote *Spycatcher*?
25 Which American politician made the famous "watch my lips" speech?
26 In which books were golliwogs replaced by gnomes?
27 Which crazed gunman committed the Hungerford atrocities?
28 In which month was Michael Fish embarrassed by the gales of '87?
29 Where was the jumbo travelling to when it crashed at Lockerbie?
30 Who was Neil Kinnock's deputy when he became Labour leader?

Answers

Horse Racing (see Quiz 82)
1 Grand National. 2 12th. 3 1977. 4 Doncaster. 5 2,000 Guineas, Derby, St Leger. 6 Committed suicide. 7 Pat Eddery. 8 1954. 9 The Oaks. 10 Dick Francis. 11 Bay. 12 1 mile 4 furlongs. 13 Four. 14 Ten. 15 Peter Scudamore. 16 Corky. 17 Lester Piggott. 18 1920s. 19 Frankie Dettori. 20 Desert Orchid. 21 L'Escargot. 22 Once. 23 Kentucky Derby. 24 Buckle. 25 Sam Arnull. 26 Lanfranco. 27 Billie Lee Shoemaker. 28 Willie Carson. 29 Bay. 30 54.

Quiz 85 Easy Listening

Answers - see page 326

1 Who wrote "For The Good Times"?

2 Who charted in the 70s with "A Little Love And Understanding"?

3 Who made the Top Ten in 1952, had a 1968 No. 1 and was back in 1994?

4 Who had an album cryptically called *Last The Whole Night Long*?

5 After 60s success, which single charted for Mr Acker Bilk in the 70s?

6 Which close harmony Sisters were Connee, Martha and Helvetia?

7 Who had a No. 1 with the title in brackets of "Voler A Empezar"?

8 Which Nat King Cole song was re-issued and charted 30 years after the original?

9 In Sinatra's "High Hopes" what can't move a rubber-tree plant?

10 What was Lena Martell's only No. 1?

11 What was Perry Como's job before he became a singer?

12 Which 70s duo took the standard "Whispering Grass" to No. 1?

13 To two years, when did Johnny Mathis first have a Top Ten single?

14 Who did Gerry Dorsey become to sell thousands of 60s singles?

15 Who sang "I Just Want To Dance With You"?

16 Which Dickie had a 50s No. 1 with "Christmas Alphabet"?

17 Which singer/songwriter David fronted Bread?

18 What was Glenn Miller's main instrument?

19 Who wrote "Annie's Song"?

20 Where did Pat Boone write love letters?

21 Which city does James Galway come from?

22 How many were there in the Ink Spots?

23 Who had a British hit with "Guantanamera"?

24 Under what name did Brenda Gail Webb find fame?

25 Who wrote "This Guy's In Love With You"?

26 Whose singers invite radio listeners to "Sing Something Simple"?

27 Who had a 50s No. 1 with "Mary's Boy Child"?

28 What was Ken Dodd's huge 60s No. 1?

29 Which group used to accompany Herb Alpert?

30 In which decade of the 20th century was Mantovani born?

Quiz 86 Pot Luck 38

Answers - see page 327

LEVEL 2

1 Which river is nearest to Balmoral Castle?
2 Which country and western singer appeared in *Gunfight*?
3 Which US probe was sent to land on Mars in 1997?
4 Which London park would you be in to ride along Rotten Row?
5 Which Swiss resort awards the Golden Rose TV awards?
6 How did Jane Austen's character Mr Woodhouse like his boiled egg?
7 Who was the first non-Englishman to play James Bond?
8 Which British airport was the first with its own railway station?
9 What did the 17 people in the dock at the Mike Tyson trial all ask for?
10 How many wives are allowed at one time under Islamic Law?
11 In which century was religious reformer John Calvin born?
12 Who had a 50s No. 1 with "Who's Sorry Now"?
13 If it's 12 noon GMT what time is it in Oslo?
14 Who is Jemima Khan's father?
15 Who wrote the novel *Anna Karenina*?
16 Which bridge joins a palace and a prison in Venice?
17 What word can follow "band", "mass" and "pass"?
18 Which battle came first - Agincourt or Bosworth Field?
19 What is the next highest prime number above 53?
20 In which American state are the Everglades?
21 What position in the House of Commons did George Thomas hold?
22 How did cabinet maker David Ashcroft become a multi-millionaire?
23 Which banned insecticide was the first to be manmade?
24 Which Marx Brother played the piano?
25 What is the capital of Georgia of the former USSR?
26 Whose motto is *Ich Dien*?
27 Who was the first presenter of "Tomorrow's World"?
28 Where was the Bayview Retirement Home in "Waiting for God"?
29 In which decade was "Blue Peter" screened for the first time?
30 Which river was Jesus Christ baptized in?

Answers

Pot Luck 39 (see Quiz 88)
1 Sean Connery. 2 "Mastermind". 3 Blue. 4 12. 5 19th. 6 Eat it. 7 O.
8 *The Old Curiosity Shop*. 9 Edward Heath. 10 Jack and Annie Walker.
11 American football. 12 Johnny Preston. 13 Refraction. 14 Oxford.
15 Horses. 16 France. 17 His ear. 18 Women being members. 19 Bishop
of Salisbury. 20 30s. 21 Keir Hardie. 22 Mark Knopfler. 23 Tessa Piggott
(later Carver). 24 Sheena Easton. 25 Greece. 26 In the sea. 27 Queen
Victoria. 28 H.G. Wells. 29 Cabbage. 30 A pancake.

LEVEL 2

1 Which 1997 series featured detectives Slade and Holly?
2 Which TV detective is based in Shrewsbury?
3 Maddy Magellan assisted which offbeat TV detective?
4 In which show would you see Superintendent Hatcher and DC Hames?
5 Which series set in a northern town featured Sergeant Bonney?
6 Who had a business card which included a matchstick-man logo?
7 In which series did Detective Isbecki appear?
8 What was Callan's first name?
9 In which series did Louise Lombard star as Liz Shaw?
10 How was John Mannering better known?
11 Which horror actor played Sherlock Holmes in the 60s?
12 Chief Superintendent Charles Brownlow was in charge of which police station?
13 How many Angels did Charlie have?
14 Which drama featured Assistant Chief Constable Anne Stewart?
15 Who worked for the Bureau des Etrangers?
16 Where was "Columbo" set?
17 What is Cracker's job?
18 At what time of day was "Crown Court" first broadcast?
19 Who was the American half of "The Persuaders"?
20 How was 60s secret agent John Drake better known?
21 Which detective often embarrassed Inspector Slack?
22 Which writer created Superintendent Jane Tennison?
23 Who played the detective Bob Louis?
24 Which 60s series based on John Creasey's novels starred John Gregson?
25 How was Detective Sergeant Johnny Ho known?
26 Who had a secretary called Miss Lemon?
27 In which fictional town was "Hamish Macbeth" set?
28 In "Inspector Morse" what were the professions of Max and Dr Russell?
29 In "Dempsey and Makepeace" where was Dempsey from?
30 Who did Magersfontein Lugg assist?

1 Which actor was James Bond in the *Thunderball* movie?
2 Which TV show's format was based on the producer's experience at the hands of the Gestapo?
3 What colour is Scooby Doo's collar in the cartoons?
4 How many pairs of ribs does a human adult have normally?
5 In which century was Paul Cezanne born?
6 What do you do with a wonton?
7 In Morse code what letter is represented by three dashes?
8 In which Dickens novel does Kit Nubbles appear?
9 Which politician sailed the yacht *Morning Cloud*?
10 Who were the first married couple to be landlords of the Rovers in "Coronation Street"?
11 Which sport featured in the film *Semi Tough* starring Burt Reynolds?
12 Who had a 60s No. 1 with "Running Bear"?
13 What describes the bending of light as it passes from one medium to another?
14 Which university athletics team had Jeffrey Archer as a member?
15 What was the favourite subject of the artist George Stubbs?
16 Which European country is split by the Canal Du Midi?
17 What part of his anatomy did Carl Wells nail to a tree in the Manchester Runway protests?
18 In April 1997, Leander Rowing Club overturned a 179-year ban on what?
19 Who signs with the name Sarum?
20 In which decade of the 20th century was Brigitte Bardot born?
21 Who was the first Labour leader?
22 Which mega pop star formed the Notting Hillbillies?
23 Which character did Zoë Wanamaker play in "Love Hurts"?
24 Who performed the title song in the Bond film *For Your Eyes Only*?
25 Which country includes the Peloponnese?
26 Where were Olympic swimming events held prior to 1908?
27 Who laid the foundation stone at the Victoria and Albert Museum?
28 Who wrote the novel *The History Of Mr Polly*?
29 What variety of vegetable does kale belong to?
30 What is stuffed to make a blini or a blintz?

Answers

Pot Luck 38 (see Quiz 86)
1 The Dee. 2 Johnny Cash. 3 Pathfinder. 4 Hyde Park. 5 Montreux.
6 Very soft. 7 Sean Connery. 8 Gatwick. 9 His autograph. 10 Four.
11 16th. 12 Connie Francis. 13 1 p.m. 14 Sir James Goldsmith. 15 Leo Tolstoy. 16 The Bridge of Sighs. 17 "Age". 18 Agincourt. 19 59.
20 Florida. 21 Speaker. 22 He won the National Lottery. 23 DDT.
24 Chico. 25 Tbilisi. 26 The Prince Of Wales. 27 Raymond Baxter.
28 Bournemouth. 29 1950s. 30 The Jordan.

Quiz 89 Food & Drink 2

Answers - see page 330

LEVEL 2

1   What is ciabatta?
2   What is the predominant flavour of fennel?
3   What type of pulses are used in hummus?
4   What flavour is the drink Kahlua?
5   What is added to butter in a *beurre manié* ?
6   What type of wine is traditionally used in zabaglione?
7   What is radicchio?
8   What do the Spanish call a medium dry sherry?
9   What is panettone?
10 What are the three main ingredients of an Hollandaise sauce?
11 In the kitchen, what would a mandolin be used for?
12 What is harissa?
13 Which liqueur is used in a White Lady?
14 What sweet substance is added to whisky to make Drambuie?
15 From which continent does couscous originate?
16 What is the dish of stuffed vine leaves called?
17 In wine bottle sizes what is another name for a double magnum?
18 In the food world what is rocket?
19 From which country does balsamic vinegar originate?
20 Which spirit is used in a Daiquiri?
21 In which century was chocolate introduced into the UK?
22 Everards beers were originally based near which town?
23 What type of meat is used in moussaka?
24 What is the main ingredient of rosti?
25 Which traditional pudding ingredient comes from the cassava plant?
26 What is ghee?
27 Slivovitz is made from which fruit?
28 From what is angostura obtained?
29 What type of milk is a basic ingredient of Thai cookery?
30 What is a bruschetta?

1   Who was the first Tory leader to have gone to a grammar school?

2   In the 70s who was the Minister for Drought?

3   In 1997 David Blunket won which constituency?

4   What was the name of Harold Wilson's wife?

5   Who published the white paper "In Place Of Strife"?

6   Mrs Thatcher became Baroness Thatcher of where?

7   Which Tory Scottish Secretary lost his seat in 1997?

8   Who was deputy prime minister when Harold Macmillan resigned?

9   Who threw herself under the king's horse at the 1913 Derby?

10 What was the Tory slogan on posters of a queue of the unemployed?

11 Who first became prime minister - Gladstone or Disraeli?

12 To two years, when did John Major first win Huntingdon?

13 Who was beaten to the Labour leadership by Michael Foot in 1980?

14 What was the name of the male model in the Jeremy Thorpe affair?

15 Prime Minister Arthur James Balfour belonged to which party?

16 Dennis Skinner is known as the Beast of where?

17 Who followed Anthony Crossland as Labour's Foreign Secretary?

18 Who said that Gorbachev was "a man we can do business with"?

19 Who was Labour leader when the party adopted the red rose symbol?

20 Which politician was responsible for the creation of the police force?

21 How may rounds were there in the Tory leadership election of 1997?

22 Who was acting Labour leader on the sudden death of John Smith?

23 Who is Kingston-upon-Hull's most famous MP?

24 John Redwood and William Hague have held which cabinet post?

25 Who was Britain's first Socialist MP?

26 Who courted disaster with a weekend at the Paris Ritz in September 1993?

27 Roy Jenkins, David Owen, Shirley Williams and who else were the Gang Of Four?

28 Prime Minister Andrew Bonar Law belonged to which party?

29 How many general elections did Mrs Thatcher win for the Tories?

30 What constituency has Sir Edward Heath represented for many years?

Answers

Animation Movies (see Quiz 92)

1 Bashful. 2 Nick Park. 3 Mortimer. 4 *Snow White and the Seven Dwarfs.*
5 *Yellow Submarine.* 6 Tim Rice. 7 Jessica. 8 *Pinocchio.* 9 Scar.
10 Arthur. 11 *One Hundred and One Dalmatians.* 12 Mickey Mouse.
13 "Whole New World". 14 *Fantasia.* 15 Orang-utan. 16 Jasmine.
17 Pongo and Perdita. 18 Rabbit. 19 *Jungle Book.* 20 Basil. 21 15.
22 *Cinderella.* 23 Donald Duck. 24 *Pocahontas.* 25 *The Hunchback of Notre
Dame.* 26 *The Return of Jafar.* 27 *Space Jam.* 28 1930s. 29 Ostriches.
30 Spaniel.

1 Which country includes the Isle of Tiree ?
2 Which British songwriter/actor wrote the first *Tarzan* movie script?
3 In which year did John Major become Prime Minister?
4 What is the only English anagram of KITCHENS?
5 Brontophobia is a fear of what?
6 Who wrote the novel *The Prince And The Pauper*?
7 What is the gas nitrous oxide also called?
8 Which Welsh town became a city in 1969?
9 In which century was Venetian painter Canaletto born?
10 What name describes a crack in a glacier?
11 Which leader of the Apache tribe died in 1909?
12 Which element has the atomic number 18 and the symbol Ar?
13 Which cuddly Hollywood sex symbol was born in 1935 in Dagenham?
14 Which fruit provides the basis for Cumberland Sauce?
15 Which birthstone is linked to November?
16 Which boxer was allegedly in an affray with Ray Sullivan in Legends nightclub?
17 In which series did Suzie Kettles and Eddie Clockerty appear?
18 Which Arthur Miller play is about witchcraft?
19 What is Scully's first name in "The X Files"?
20 Which bird's cry is known as a boom?
21 Which fish are turned into rollmops?
22 Who opened the recreated Globe Theatre in 1997?
23 Which Briton has been F1 World Champion on the most occasions?
24 Which country was the nearest to where *The Titanic* was found?
25 Which counties does Thames Valley FM serve?
26 The 400th edition of which radio comedy went out in May 1997?
27 How many hours in April?
28 Who had a 60s No. 1 with "Blue Moon"?
29 Which Florida national park is split by a road called Alligator Alley?
30 What bird was banned from fighting in Britain after 1848?

Answers

Food & Drink 2   (see Quiz 89)
1 An Italian bread. 2 Aniseed. 3 Chick peas. 4 Coffee. 5 Flour.
6 Marsala. 7 Red-leaved lettuce. 8 Amontillado. 9 Fruit bread. 10 Butter,
egg yolk, wine vinegar. 11 Slicing. 12 Hot spicy paste. 13 Cointreau.
14 Heather honey. 15 Africa. 16 Dolmas. 17 Jeroboam. 18 Salad leaf.
19 Italy. 20 Dark rum. 21 17th. 22 Leicester. 23 Lamb. 24 Potatoes.
25 Tapioca. 26 Clarified butter. 27 Plums. 28 Tree bark. 29 Coconut milk.
30 Fried or toasted bread.

1   Which of the Seven Dwarfs had the longest name?
2   Who created Wallace and Gromit?
3   What was Mickey Mouse originally called?
4   What was Disney's first full-length cartoon called?
5   Which film takes place in Pepperland?
6   Who wrote the song lyrics for Aladdin?
7   Who is the *femme fatale* with Kathleen Turner's voice in *Who Framed Roger Rabbit*??
8   "When You Wish Upon A Star" is from which Disney film?
9   What is Simba's uncle called in *The Lion King*?
10 *The Sword in the Stone* centres on the legend of which King?
11 Which film has the signal of the "twilight bark"?
12 Which character was the star of Disney's *Steamboat Willie*?
13 Which song from *Aladdin* in 1992 won an Oscar?
14 In which Disney film are Leopold Stokowski and the Philadelphia Orchestra seen?
15 What sort of animal is King Louie in *The Jungle Book*?
16 What is the Princess called in *Aladdin*?
17 Who were the original two Dalmatians in the 1961 classic?
18 What sort of creature was Thumper in *Bambi*?
19 Which was the first major Disney cartoon film released after Walt Disney's death in 1966?
20 What was the name of Disney's Great Mouse Detective?
21 How many puppies does Perdita produce in her first Dalmatian litter?
22 In which film is magic summoned by "Bibbidi-Bobbidi-Boo"?
23 Who had nephews called Dewey, Huey and Louie?
24 In which 90s film did "Colors of the Wind" appear?
25 Which 90s Disney film was based on a Victor Hugo story?
26 Which Disney film was the sequel to *Aladdin*?
27 Which 90s film starred Bugs Bunny and Michael Jordan?
28 In which decade was *Snow White and the Seven Dwarfs* released?
29 Which birds take part in the ballet in *Fantasia*?
30 What breed of dog is Lady in Lady and the Tramp?

Answers

Politics (see Quiz 90)

1 Ted Heath. 2 Denis Howell. 3 Sheffield Brightside. 4 Mary. 5 Barbara Castle. 6 Kesteven. 7 Michael Forsyth. 8 Rab Butler. 9 Emily Davison. 10 Labour isn't working. 11 Disraeli. 12 1983. 13 Denis Healey. 14 Norman Scott. 15 Conservative. 16 Bolsover. 17 David Owen. 18 Margaret Thatcher. 19 Neil Kinnock. 20 Robert Peel. 21 Three. 22 Margaret Beckett. 23 John Prescott. 24 Secretary for Wales. 25 James Keir Hardie. 26 Jonathan Aitken. 27 William Rogers. 28 Conservative. 29 Three. 30 Old Sidcup & Bexley.

LEVEL 2

1 Who is the Queen's only nephew?

2 In cricket, which county were Ireland's first victims?

3 Which country do Hyundai cars originate from?

4 Which boxer trained at St Thomas's Boys and Girls Club, Sheffield?

5 Which future Tory MP was told he could not run in the Moscow Olympics?

6 In which century was Catherine the Great born?

7 Which famous guitarist played for Casey Jones & the Engineers?

8 Who had a 70s No. 1 with "Ring My Bell"?

9 Which area of London first installed parking meters?

10 Who wrote the novel *Busman's Honeymoon*?

11 Which cocktail was dedicated to Tom Harvey, the surfing star?

12 What is the naval equivalent of the army rank of General?

13 Which modern instrument was developed from the sackbut?

14 If A is alpha and B is bravo what is J?

15 What was Gandhi's profession before politics?

16 What is the capital of the Canadian province Alberta?

17 Which band produced an album called *London Calling*?

18 In which decade of the 20th century was Idi Amin born?

19 What is the largest bay in the world?

20 Who was the first male presenter of "Treasure Hunt"?

21 Which world-renowned writer lived at Bateman's in Sussex?

22 In which suburb was "2 Point 4 Children" set?

23 Which radio star/*Sun* columnist was sued by the Pet Shop Boys?

24 In the story, who fell asleep on the Catskill Mountains?

25 What is the American equivalent of the British bilberry?

26 Vivian Stanshall was in which band?

27 In music, if a piece is in three flats which notes will be flat?

28 Who had the 50s original hit with "This Ole House"?

29 What organisation was set up by Agnes, Baden-Powell's sister?

30 In the Chinese calendar which year follows the year of the goat?

Pot Luck 42 (see Quiz 95)

Answers

1 Martin Bell (at Tatton). 2 Bake them. 3 Ice hockey. 4 Band Aid. 5 "For".
6 Ten years. 7 Will Carling. 8 Leo Tolstoy. 9 "Ode To Joy". 10 Blue whale.
11 15th. 12 Elvis Presley. 13 Cube. 14 Basil. 15 Ruth Rendell.
16 Melvin. 17 Lamentations. 18 Imelda Marcos. 19 Aneka. 20 Ministry of
Defence. 21 Chrissy Plummer. 22 Zimbabwe. 23 Richard Nixon. 24 30.
25 Two. 26 Latin. 27 Bad breath. 28 Barbara Cartland. 29 Goebbels.
30 Asparagus.

LEVEL 2

1 What can follow "milk" and "rag" in the plant world?
2 What sort of fruit is a mirabelle?
3 Which Princess had a rose named after her at the 1997 Chelsea Flower Show?
4 Which grain is used to make semolina?
5 Which term is used for plants which store moisture in their thick fleshy leaves or stems?
6 Which part of a plant protects it as a bud?
7 What shape is a campanulate flower?
8 What is a morel?
9 What does lamina mean when referring to a leaf?
10 Which part of the tree is cinnamon obtained from?
11 Which parts of the potato are poisonous?
12 If a leaf is dentate what does it mean?
13 What colour are the flowers of a St John's Wort?
14 What is a prickly pear?
15 What is the main vegetation of the South African veld?
16 Why is the grapefruit so called?
17 What colour are borage flowers?
18 What is kelp?
19 Which plant's name means lion's tooth?
20 What is another name for the lime tree?
21 What is to be found in a plant's anther?
22 How long is the life cycle of a biennial plant?
23 The sycamore is native to which continent?
24 How many leaves does the twayblade orchid have?
25 What colour are the fruits on the deadly nightshade?
26 What type of plants are traditionally seen in a herbarium?
27 Which tree did archers need to cultivate to make bows?
28 Which King reputedly sought refuge in an oak tree?
29 The loganberry is a cross between which fruits?
30 What colour is the blossom of the blackthorn?

Answers

Media 2 (see Quiz 96)
1 Cable News Network. 2 Lord Reith. 3 Adverts. 4 Small satellite dish.
5 The Caravan Club. 6 *Manchester Evening News.* 7 Sky Television and BSB.
8 Michael Grade. 9 The National Anthem. 10 1930s. 11 *Birds.* 12 *Bunty.*
13 Norwich. 14 *Reader's Digest.* 15 Discovery Channel. 16 Arrival of colour TV. 17 S4C. 18 Columbia Broadcasting System. 19 London Weekend Television. 20 *Take A Break.* 21 *Majesty.* 22 GMTV. 23 Ipswich.
24 Border. 25 *Radio Times.* 26 *The Guardian.* 27 "Play School". 28 Five.
29 "Woman's Hour". 30 Truth.

Quiz 95 Pot Luck 42

Answers - see page 332

LEVEL 2

1 Who did David Soul campaign for in the 1997 General Election?
2 What do you do to mashed potatoes to make them Duchesse?
3 What sport do the Cardiff Devils play?
4 Which charity ceased in 1989 after 5 years and raising £90 million?
5 What word can go before "tress", "tune" and "ward"?
6 How often is a modern national census held in the UK?
7 Which England sports captain was born 12 December 1965, in Bradford-on-Avon?
8 Which famous Russian writer died on Astapova railway station?
9 What was the BBC theme for Euro 96?
10 Which creatures give birth to the world's biggest babies?
11 In which century was the astronomer Copernicus born?
12 Who earned $15 million on the tenth anniversary of his death in '88?
13 Height times breadth times 6 gives the surface area of which shape?
14 What is the main herb in pesto sauce?
15 Who wrote the novel *Simisola*?
16 In the BT TV commercials, what was the name of Beatie's son?
17 In the Old Testament which gloomy sounding book directly follows Jeremiah?
18 Which Philippino was accused of smuggling $225 million out of her country?
19 Who had a 80s No. 1 with "Japanese Boy"?
20 Which Government department is the second biggest UK landowner?
21 Which character did Paula Wilcox play in "Man About the House"?
22 Bruce Grobbelaar kept goal for which country?
23 Who was the first US president to visit China?
24 How old did women have to be to vote in 1918?
25 In music, how many sharps in the key of D?
26 What language is the Magna Carta written in?
27 What is halitosis?
28 Which royal-linked writer is renowned for her false eye lashes?
29 Who was Hitler's propaganda minister between 1933-45?
30 Which vegetable gives the flavour to a Bruxelloise sauce?

Answers

Pot Luck 41 (see Quiz 93)

1 Viscount Linley. 2 Middlesex. 3 Korea. 4 Naseem Hamed. 5 Sebastian Coe. 6 18th. 7 Eric Clapton. 8 Anita Ward. 9 Mayfair. 10 Dorothy L. Sayers. 11 Harvey Wallbanger. 12 Admiral. 13 Trombone. 14 Juliet. 15 Lawyer. 16 Edmonton. 17 The Clash. 18 20s. 19 Hudson Bay. 20 Kenneth Kendall. 21 Rudyard Kipling. 22 Chiswick. 23 Jonathan King. 24 Rip Van Winkle. 25 Blueberry. 26 The Bonzo Dog Doo Dah Band. 27 B,E,A. 28 Rosemary Clooney. 29 Girl Guides. 30 Monkey.

LEVEL 2

1 What does CNN stand for?
2 Who was the first director general of the BBC?
3 What must not be shown during religious broadcasts?
4 What is a squarial?
5 Which organisation's magazine is called *En Route*?
6 What is Manchester's own regional daily paper called?
7 BSkyB was an amalgam of which two companies?
8 Who was chief executive of Channel 4 from 1989 to 1997?
9 What was played at the end of daily transmission before the arrival of 24-hour TV?
10 In which decade was the *Beano* first issued?
11 What is the RSPB's own magazine called?
12 Which girls' magazine did *Mandy and Judy* amalgamate with in 1997?
13 Where is the *Eastern Daily* Press based?
14 Which subscription-bought periodical was founded in 1922 in the US?
15 Which channel had the slogan "From viewing to doing"?
16 What caused a change in licence fee funding in 1967?
17 What replaces Channel 4 in Wales?
18 What does CBS stand for?
19 How was the London Television Consortium better known?
20 Which women's weekly owned by H. Bauer was in the bestsellers list during the 90s?
21 Which magazine about the royals has had Ingrid Seward as Editor-in-Chief?
22 Which TV company launched its own magazine in May 1997?
23 In which town is Radio Orwell based?
24 Which TV company is based in Carlisle?
25 Sue Robinson became the first woman editor of which long-running magazine in 1996?
26 Which broadsheet newspaper has a tabloid-format Media section every Monday?
27 What was the first children's programme broadcast on BBC2?
28 How many colours were there in the original Channel 4 logo?
29 Which radio programme, begun in 1946 is still broadcast each weekday morning?
30 *Pravda* was a Soviet newspaper. What does Pravda mean?

Answers

Plant World (see Quiz 94)
1 "Wort". 2 Plum. 3 Princess of Wales. 4 Wheat. 5 Succulent. 6 Sepal. 7 Bell shaped. 8 Mushroom. 9 Blade. 10 Bark. 11 Green parts including leaves. 12 Toothed or notched. 13 Yellow. 14 Cactus. 15 Grass. 16 Grows in grape-like clusters. 17 Blue. 18 Seaweed. 19 Dandelion (*dent de lion*). 20 Linden. 21 Pollen. 22 More than one year, but less than two. 23 Europe. 24 Two. 25 Black. 26 Dried plants. 27 Yew. 28 Charles II. 29 Raspberry and blackberry. 30 White.

1   Which country did motor racing's Juan Manuel Fangio come from?
2   Who set a world record for the fastest ever maximum snooker break at the Crucible in April 1997?
3   Which England fast bowler received damages from *Wisden Cricket Monthly* over the article "Is It In The Blood?"?
4   What was the nost notable thing about Julio McCaw who raced against Jesse Owens?
5   In which event did Redgrave and Pinsent win Olympic gold?
6   Who was the first driver to register 50 Grand Prix victories?
7   Which horse won the 1996 Grand National?
8   In motor cycling, at what cc level was Barry Sheene world champ?
9   What was Mary Slaney's surname before her marriage?
10   Which Australian quick bowler is known as Pigeon?
11   To a year each way, when was James Hunt Formula 1 world champ?
12   Graeme Obree is connected with which sport?
13   Who holds the record for most Olympic swimming medals?
14   To a year each way, how old was Nigel Mansell when he was F1 world champion?
15   What famous first will Diomed always hold?
16   Where did the 93 Linford Christie v Carl Lewis challenge take place?
17   In April 1997 what did younger brother Florian give to Niki Lauda?
18   Colin Jackson's 60m hurdle record was set in Sindelfingen – in which country?
19   Who did Frank Williams recruit from IndyCar for the 1996 GP season?
20   Who succeeded Linford Christie as England's athletics team captain?
21   Which country does Donovan Bailey run for?
22   What nationality was Keke Rosberg?
23   Where in 1996 did Oliver Panis have his debut Grand Prix victory?
24   Who was the first man to swim 100 metres in less than a minute?
25   Who was Man Utd's left winger in the 60s European Cup triumph?
26   What are Daley Thompson's first two names?
27   Which Grand Prix did Damon Hill win first win when he became 1996 world champion?
28   Which England fast bowler was nicknamed George?
29   Which horse was Lester Piggott's first Derby winner?
30   Who in 1996 completed his hat-trick of titles as 500cc motor cycle world champ?

Answers

Soul & Motown (see Quiz 99)

1 Supremes. 2 James Brown. 3 Whitney Houston. 4 1980s. 5 Georgia. 6 Billie Holliday. 7 Aretha Franklin. 8 Berry Gordy. 9 Organ. 10 Shot (by his father). 11 Aretha Franklin. 12 Gladys Knight. 13 "I Want You Back". 14 Michael Bolton. 15 Stevie Wonder. 16 Jimmy Ruffin. 17 The Wicked Pickett. 18 Four Tops. 19 1966. 20 The Commodores. 21 The Four Tops. 22 Michael Jackson. 23 James Brown. 24 Rose. 25 Smokey Robinson. 26 1960s. 27 "I Was Made To Love Her". 28 Stax. 29 Lionel Richie. 30 Floyd.

LEVEL 2

1   Which film featured the single "Vogue" by Madonna?
2   In medical terms, what does an ECG stand for?
3   What was the occupation of Stephanie Slater who was kidnapped by Michael Sams?
4   With which two surnames did Aussie Evonne win Wimbledon?
5   Who had a 80s No. 1 with "Move Closer"?
6   Which canal linked Liverpool to London?
7   Which piece of attire took its name from a Pacific nuclear test site?
8   Who wrote the novel *Nostromo*?
9   Who was lost for six days in 1982's Paris-Dakar desert rally?
10   Which dessert is named after a ballerina?
11   Who invented the magnetic telegraph?
12   What word can go after "tea" and before "fast"?
13   Which word links a TV quiz show with space launches?
14   In which century was Boticelli born?
15   Who was Miss California in 1978?
16   What is the capital of Albania?
17   Which heroine was awarded Freedom of the City of London in 1908?
18   In Scrabble, how many points is the letter J worth?
19   In which country would you find the Great Sandy Desert?
20   In Morse code what letter is represented by four dots?
21   Alphabetically what is the last of the chemical elements?
22   What name is given to the larva of a fly?
23   Who became a Saint in 1909, nearly 500 years after she was killed?
24   In which Dickens novel does Jerry Cruncher appear?
25   What fruit can be made from the letters in TRANSCIENCE?
26   In which sitcom did Caroline Wheatley and Laura West appear?
27   In which decade of the 20th century was Warren Beatty born?
28   Which pop star ran for Mayor of Detroit in 1989?
29   What name describes the loose rocks on the side of a mountain?
30   Which hat took its name from a novel by George Du Maurier?

Answers

Pot Luck 44   (see Quiz 100)
1   Nicholas. 2   Sunderland. 3   Monopoly. 4   The Samaritans. 5   Agate.
6   Pink. 7   1970s. 8   Knesset. 9   Pennines. 10   Mrs Doubtfire. 11   A dotted line. 12   *Iolanthe*. 13   Ian Rush. 14   *Home Alone*. 15   Boeing.
16   Rosamunde Pilcher. 17   3 p.m.. 18   Housemartins. 19   Orange juice.
20   1958. 21   Clay. 22   16th. 23   Turkey. 24   Little Lord Fauntleroy.
25   Lynn Faulds Wood. 26   Marge & Homer. 27   Newcastle Upon Tyne.
28   India. 29   Michael Jackson. 30   St Mark.

LEVEL 2

1   "Nathan Jones" was a 70s hit for which group?

2   The Famous Flames backed which classic soul performer?

3   Which pop star did Bobby Brown marry in 1992?

4   In which decade did Stevie Wonder have his first British No. 1?

5   In "Dock Of The Bay" Otis Redding left his home in where when he headed for the Frisco Bay?

6   Who did Diana Ross play in *Lady Sings The Blues*?

7   Who duetted with George Michael on "I Knew You Were Waiting"?

8   Who founded Motown records?

9   What instrument did Booker T. play?

10 How did Marvin Gaye die?

11 Which female soul singer has recorded with the Eurythmics and George Benson?

12 In 1972, who recorded "Help Me Make It Through The Night"?

13 Which Jackson 5 hit of 1970 was remixed and back in 1988?

14 Who recorded the 90s album *Soul Provider*?

15 The song from the film *The Woman In Red* gave which star his first solo No. 1?

16 Who recorded the original "What Becomes Of The Broken Hearted"?

17 What nickname was applied to Wilson Pickett?

18 "Reach Out I'll Be There" was the first British No. 1 for which group?

19 To two years each way, when did Percy Sledge first chart with "When A Man Loves A Woman"?

20 Lionel Richie first charted with which group?

21 Levi Stubbs was lead singer with which group?

22 "One Day In Your Life" was a No. 1 for which superstar?

23 Who declared "Get Up I Feel Like Being A Sex Machine"?

24 What flower did Marv Johnson pick for his Rose?

25 Who wrote "Tracks Of My Tears" and "My Guy"?

26 In which decade did Sam Cooke die?

27 What was Stevie Wonder's first British top ten hit?

28 Otis Redding recorded on the Atlantic and which other label?

29 Who did Diana Ross duet with on "Endless Love"?

30 Which Eddie recorded the classic "Knock On Wood"?

1 What is the name of Tony Blair's second-born son?
2 Which English town became a city in 1992?
3 Which game features a top hat, a boot and a racing car?
4 "Love Shine A Light" was written for the 30th anniversary of which organisation?
5 What birthstone is linked to June?
6 What colour is the 39p postage stamp?
7 In which decade was "Emmerdale Farm" screened for the first time?
8 What is the Israeli parliament called?
9 Which range of Cumbrian hills has the highest point at Cross Fell?
10 How is the Robin Williams character Daniel Hillard better known?
11 How is a footpath indicated on a map?
12 "The Peer And The Peri" is the subtitle of which light opera?
13 Who returned to Liverpool in 1988 for £2.8 million from Juventus?
14 Which 1990 film featured a clip from the film *It's a Wonderful World*?
15 Who built the aircraft which dropped the bomb on Hiroshima?
16 Who wrote the novel *The Shell Seekers*?
17 If it's 12 noon GMT what time is it in Moscow?
18 Who had a 80s No. 1 with "Caravan Of Love"?
19 What is added to champagne to make a Bucks Fizz cocktail?
20 In what year was "Blue Peter" first broadcast?
21 What material is used to make a sumo wrestling ring?
22 In which century was Oliver Cromwell born?
23 What is the modern name for the country Asia Minor?
24 In literature, what title was inherited by Cedric Errol?
25 Who was the first female presenter of "Watchdog"?
26 Who are Bart Simpson's parents?
27 In which city was "Spender" set?
28 Which country has 845 languages with English and Hindu the main?
29 For Elton John's 50th birthday party who did Lenny Henry go dressed as?
30 Who is the patron saint of Venice?

1 How many programmes had "Blue Peter" notched up on their anniversary programme in May 1997?
2 Which pre-school characters live in Home Hill?
3 Who presented the first series of "Live and Kicking"?
4 What were the Teenage Mutant Hero Turtles called?
5 What was the name of the alien discovered, by Mike, in a wardrobe?
6 Who is the postmistress of Greendale?
7 What sort of creature is Children's BBC's Otis?
8 In which US state is "Sweet Valley High" set?
9 Which spacecraft was flown by Steve Zodiac?
10 Which character did Susan Tully play in "Grange Hill"?
11 Which comedian wrote the theme music for "Supergran"?
12 Where would you find Hugh, Pugh, Barney McGrew, Cuthbert, Dibble and Grubb?
13 Who numbered Barnabas, Willy and Master Bate in his crew?
14 Who did Captains White, Blue, Grey and Magenta deal with?
15 Which "historical" series included Barrington, Rabies and Little Ron?
16 What sort of creature is Dilly?
17 How many legs did the Famous Five have on TV?
18 Where is the teenage drama series "Sweat" set?
19 In which show would you find Dump-Pea?
20 In "Rag, Tag and Bobtail" what was Tag?
21 What is "Fablon" called on "Blue Peter"?
22 What did every contestant win on "Crackerjack"?
23 Who was the longest-lasting presenter of "Rainbow"?
24 The cartoon series about Willy Fogg was based on which book?
25 What sort of animal said, "I'm just a big silly old Hector"?
26 What day of the week was "The Woodentops" originally broadcast?
27 In "The Herbs" what were schoolteacher Mr Onion's pupils called?
28 Which characters live in Springfield?
29 Who has presented "How" and "How 2"?
30 What was Huckleberry Hound's favourite song?

Answers

The 90s (see Quiz 103)

1 43. 2 Tiger Woods. 3 Kuwait. 4 John Redwood. 5 "Unchained Melody" (Righteous Brothers). 6 Jefferson. 7 National Lottery. 8 President F.W. de Klerk. 9 Spurs. 10 John Bird and John Fortune. 11 Darren Gough. 12 *The Guardian*. 13 John Bryan. 14 Kenneth Clarke. 15 Barcelona. 16 George Carey. 17 Bowls. 18 Andrew Morton. 19 Robert Maxwell. 20 Tom Hanks. 21 Spongiform. 22 Baseball. 23 Whitney Houston. 24 Michael Heseltine. 25 Rod Stewart. 26 *Annus horribilis*. 27 22. 28 Road-rage attack. 29 George Bush. 30 Tony Adams.

1   Which harbour is the most famous on the island of Oahu?
2   What, in March 1988, ceased to be legal tender in England?
3   Who had the first-ever million-selling CD with *The Joshua Tree*?
4   What kind of vehicle was Charles Rolls of Rolls-Royce in when he died?
5   Which tree family is the basket-making osier a member of?
6   On which ground in England is the last cricket Test in a series held?
7   Which Italian ingredient helps to make a Harvey Wallbanger?
8   Who co-wrote with Bob Geldof the hit "Do They Know It's Christmas"?
9   Which sea did the Romans call *Mare Nostrum*?
10 Where is the largest gulf in the world?
11 Which royal resigned from the Royal Marines in January 1987?
12 What type of material was used by Rene Lalique for ornaments?
13 Who wrote the book *Aunts Aren't Gentlemen*?
14 Whose 100th single was called "The Best of Me"?
15 What do Australian's call a budgerigar?
16 What name is athlete Florence Griffith-Joyner better known as?
17 Which Liberal is known for the 1909 People's Budget?
18 Which No. 1 hit links Prince with Sinead O'Connor?
19 Which country had Queen Wilhelmina as Queen until she died in 1962?
20 What is the official language of Haiti?
21 Which actor co-starred with Sandra Bullock in the film *Speed*?
22 Which country has Jakarta as its capital?
23 What are the Southern Lights also called?
24 If June 1 is a Sunday what day is July 1?
25 Which US state has the largest share of Yellowstone National Park?
26 What is craved by phagomanicas?
27 Which Spanish region is so named because of its many castles?
28 Which comic-strip photographer used the alias Peter Parker?
29 Which character did Philip Michael Thomas play in "Miami Vice"?
30 Which country hosted Expo '88 and celebrated its bicentenary?

Answers

World Tour (see Quiz 104)
1 The Pentagon. **2** Sirocco. **3** Vancouver. **4** USA. **5** Indian. **6** Texas.
7 Ecuador. **8** Las Malvinas. **9** Harvard. **10** States with and without slavery.
11 China (16). **12** Florida. **13** Northern Territory. **14** The Zambesi.
15 Tanganyika, Zanzibar. **16** St Lawrence. **17** Fort Knox. **18** Vietnam.
19 Moscow. **20** Rio Grande. **21** New York. **22** Bechuanaland.
23 Venezuela. **24** Ellis Island. **25** K2. **26** Istanbul. **27** Texas.
28 Argentina. **29** Canaries. **30** McKinley.

1 How old was Tony Blair when he became Prime Minister?
2 Who first won the US Amateur Championship in 1994?
3 The invasion of which country sparked off the Gulf War?
4 Who was third in the 1997 Tory leadership election?
5 Which 25-year-old recording was 1990's best-selling single?
6 What is Bill Clinton's middle name?
7 Anthea Turner became the first female presenter of which live weekly event?
8 Who shared the 1993 Nobel Peace Prize with Nelson Mandela?
9 Paul Stewart scored an FA Cup Final goal for which team?
10 On TV, who were the Long Johns?
11 Which English fast bowler took the first wicket in the 1997 Ashes?
12 Jonathan Aitken withdrew from his court case against which paper?
13 Which royal financial advisor used toes for more than counting on?
14 In the 90s, who was Education Secretary, Home Secretary and Chancellor?
15 Which city hosted the 1992 Olympic Games?
16 Who succeeded Robert Runcie as Archbishop of Canterbury?
17 Andy Thomson became world indoor champion at what?
18 Which journalist helped write *Diana: Her True Story*?
19 Who made his last trip on the yacht *Lady Ghislaine*?
20 Who was the first man to win two Oscars in the 90s?
21 What does the S stand for in BSE?
22 Which sport's world series was cancelled due to the players' strike in 1994?
23 Who was No. 1 when Michael Jackson was No. 2 for five weeks with "Heal the World"?
24 Who stood against Margaret Thatcher for Tory leadership in 1990?
25 Who did 22-year-old model Rachel Hunter marry in 1990?
26 According to Queen Elizabeth what was 1992?
27 How many teams were in the Premier League's first season?
28 What tragic British first was the death of Stephen Cameron in 1996?
29 Who was US President at the time of the Gulf War?
30 In 1990 which England soccer player was jailed for drink driving?

Answers

Children's TV (see Quiz 101)
1 3000. **2** The Teletubbies. **3** Andi Peters, Emma Forbes. **4** Leonardo, Michaelangelo, Raphael, Donatello. **5** Angelo. **6** Mrs Goggins. **7** Aardvark. **8** California. **9** *Fireball XL5*. **10** Suzanne Ross. **11** Billy Connolly. **12** Trumpton. **13** Captain Pugwash. **14** The Mysterons. **15** Maid Marian and her Merry Men. **16** Dinosaur. **17** 12. **18** Australia. **19** "Poddington Peas". **20** Mouse. **21** Sticky back plastic. **22** Crackerjack pencil. **23** Geoffrey Hayes. **24** *Around the World in Eighty Days*. **25** Dog. **26** Friday. **27** The Chives. **28** The Simpsons. **29** Fred Dinenage. **30** Clementine.

1   What is the largest office building in the USA?
2   Which wind blows from the Sahara to southern Italy?
3   Which Canadian island has Victoria as its capital?
4   Which country has the time zones Eastern, Central, Mountain and Pacific?
5   In which ocean are the Maldives?
6   Which US state is known as the Lone Star State?
7   In which country is Cotopaxi, the world's highest volcano?
8   How do the Argentinians refer to the Falkland Islands?
9   What is the USA's oldest educational institution called?
10 What did the Mason Dixon Line divide in the USA?
11 Which country has most neighbouring countries?
12 The Keys are islands off which US state?
13 Darwin is the capital of which Australian state?
14 Which river flows over the Victoria Falls?
15 Which two territories joined together to form Tanzania?
16 On which river are Quebec and Montreal?
17 Where are the US gold reserves?
18 In which country is the Mekong Delta?
19 Which capital is on the Moskva river?
20 Which river divides the USA and Mexico?
21 Where is Madison Square Garden?
22 How was Botswana known immediately prior to independence?
23 In which country is the world's highest waterfall?
24 Which US island was a registration point for immigrants until 1954?
25 Which of the world's highest mountains between India and China is not in the Himalayas?
26 How is Byzantium and Constantinople now known?
27 What is the second largest state of the US?
28 Tierra del Fuego is off which country?
29 Fuerteventura is in which island group?
30 Which is the highest mountain in North America?

Quiz 105 Pot Luck 46

Answers - see page 346

LEVEL 2

1   Which leader of Bronski Beat also had solo hits?
2   Which British wild animal is quicker going uphill than downhill?
3   In which forest does the River Danube rise?
4   Who was the first person to score 100 runs and take 10 wickets in the same Test Match?
5   What was the nickname of Leonard Marx?
6   How many legs has a crane fly?
7   Which part of your body could suffer from astigmatism?
8   Which City is the capital of the US state of Nevada?
9   What nationality is Leonard Cohen?
10 Which star has Marilyn Monroe's signature tattooed on her bottom?
11 What was the first thing to leave the Ark when the rain stopped?
12 Which Irish singer was a schoolgirl in the *Hush A Bye Baby* film?
13 What is the opposite of aestivation?
14 Which tonic water flavour is taken from the cinchona tree?
15 What is the official language of Chile?
16 Who made the famous 70s album *Harvest*?
17 What is the longest river in France?
18 Who beat Kevin Curren in the '85 Wimbledon men's singles final?
19 Which Rochdale singer turned on the 1992 Blackpool Illuminations?
20 What comprises the diet of a pangolin?
21 Which country invented the duffel coat and bag?
22 Which British artist was greatly promoted by Delacroix in France?
23 Who beat President Marcos in the 1986 Philippines election?
24 What name are the Funchal Islands usually called?
25 Who wrote the book *Porterhouse Blue*?
26 What is the modern name for Hangman's Corner in London?
27 What are morels and chanterelles?
28 Who recorded the *Commoner's Crown* album featuring Peter Sellers?
29 Which channel separates Norway and Denmark?
30 In a title of a Bizet opera what were the people fishing for?

Answers

Pot Luck 47   (see Quiz 107)

1 Paisley Park. 2 Catalonia. 3 Townsend Thoresen. 4 Isle of Wight. 5 Holland. 6 Queen Nefertiti. 7 12. 8 Big Ben. 9 "Food Glorious Food". 10 M25. 11 Director General of the BBC. 12 Madrid. 13 Clowder. 14 India. 15 Solicitor. 16 I. 17 Liz McColgan. 18 Smell. 19 *Rainbow Warrior*. 20 Jason Donovan. 21 Jeremy Beadle. 22 Vanilla. 23 Great Maple. 24 Venice. 25 Hendersons. 26 Black, green, red. 27 "A Year in Provence". 28 Liza Goddard. 29 Fergal Sharkey. 30 Frederick Forsyth.

LEVEL 2

Answers - see page 347

1   What was the first Lassie film called?
2   What was the most successful "creature" film of the 1970s ?
3   What was Clint Eastwood's co-star in *Every Which Way But Loose*?
4   What breed of dog was Beethoven?
5   Which country is the setting for *Born Free*?
6   Which animal adopts the piglet in *Babe*?
7   How many movie versions of *Black Beauty* had been made up to 1997?
8   In which decade was the first Lassie film made?
9   White Fang is a cross between which two animals?
10 What is Dorothy's dog called in *The Wizard of Oz*?
11 What was the sequel to *The Incredible Journey* called?
12 Which animals starred with Sigourney Weaver in a biopic of Dian Fossey?
13 Which film about rats had a theme song with lyrics by Don Black?
14 Which horse eventually had co star billing with Gene Autry?
15 Which film was described as "Eight legs. Two fangs. And an attitude"?
16 What was the Lone Ranger's horse called?
17 What sort of creature is Flicka in *My Friend Flicka*?
18 Which two types of animal feature in *Oliver and Company*?
19 Which nation's army dog was Rin Tin Tin?
20 What is the principal lioness called in *Born Free*?
21 In which decade was one of the first successful animal films *Rescued By Rover* released?
22 Which studio made the seven official Lassie films?
23 Which fictional whale did Keiko play in a 1993 movie?
24 Who wrote the book on which *Babe* was based?
25 Which film was directed by Hitchcock from a Daphne Du Maurier novel, other than *Rebecca*?
26 What was the sequel to *Beethoven* called?
27 What breed of dog features in K-9?
28 Which 1971 film was the predecessor of Ben a year later?
29 Which creatures contributed to the most successful film of 1993?
30 "Bright Eyes" was used as the music for a film about which animals?

Quiz 107 Pot Luck 47

Answers - see page 344

LEVEL 2

1 What is the name of the artist formerly known as Prince's house and record label?
2 Barcelona is the capital of which region in Spain?
3 Who owned the capsized ferry *Herald of Free Enterprise*?
4 Which English county is completely surrounded by water?
5 The sport of speed skating originates from which country ?
6 Who was the wife of the Egyptian king, Ahkenaton?
7 How many yards is the penalty spot from a soccer goal line?
8 What stopped at 3.45 on 5 August 1975 in London?
9 Which musical song starts, "Is it worth the waiting for"?
10 Where did Chris Rea get held up which led to the hit "Road to Hell"?
11 Which job links Milne, Trethowan and Checkland?
12 What is the highest capital city in Europe?
13 Which term describes cats collecting together?
14 Which country invented snooker?
15 What was Bob Mortimer's job before joining up with Vic Reeves?
16 What is the chemical symbol for Iodine?
17 Which well-known athlete's maiden name was Elizabeth Lynch?
18 Which is the most sensitive of the human senses?
19 Which Greenpeace ship was sunk by the French in New Zealand?
20 Which Australian singer/soap star has a fear of boomerangs?
21 Who was the first presenter of "You've Been Framed"?
22 In music, which flavour ice was chosen by Bob van Winkle?
23 Which tree is the American version of the British Sycamore?
24 Which city is affectionately called the "Mistress of the Adriatic"?
25 Which TV family were friendly with Big Foot?
26 What three colours are on a roulette wheel?
27 Which 90s TV series was set in Luberon?
28 Which actress has been married to Alvin Stardust and Colin Baker?
29 Who had a 80s No. 1 with "A Good Heart"?
30 Who wrote the novel *The Devil's Alternative*?

Answers

Pot Luck 46 (see Quiz 105)
1 Jimmy Somerville. 2 Hare. 3 Black Forest. 4 Ian Botham. 5 Chico. 6 8.
7 Eyes. 8 Carson City. 9 Canadian. 10 Madonna. 11 A raven. 12 Sinead
O'Connor. 13 Hibernation. 14 Quinine. 15 Spanish. 16 Neil Young.
17 The Loire. 18 Boris Becker. 19 Lisa Stansfield. 20 Ants or termites.
21 Belgium. 22 John Constable. 23 Corazon Aquino. 24 Madeira.
25 Tom Sharpe. 26 Marble Arch. 27 Mushrooms. 28 Steeleye Span.
29 The Skagerrak. 30 Pearls.

1   What is the national game of Japan?
2   Which card game is based on dealing on the stock market?
3   Who is the only known unmarried person in Cluedo?
4   What is painted on to fabric in batik?
5   Carillon is a popular branch of what?
6   At which stately home would you see trees laid out in the form of troops at a famous battle?
7   In which month would you go to a Burns Night celebration?
8   Where is the National Museum of Geography?
9   The YOC is the junior branch of which society?
10 In bungee-jumping, what is a bungee?
11 Which type of wax is most commonly used in candle-making?
12 What is the traditional women's outfit in Scottish country dancing?
13 In which county would you visit St Michael's Mount?
14 What would you be making if you were following the bobbin or pillow method?
15 What order are trumps normally played at a whist drive?
16 How many counters does each player have at the start of a game of backgammon?
17 Which two Cluedo weapons are traditional weapons?
18 What are the two main activities in macrame?
19 Which manufacturer produces Sonic the Hedgehog computer games?
20 Which French theme park is named after a cartoon character?
21 Metroland is near which town?
22 In which city would you be if you went to the Ashmolean Museum?
23 In which resort is the golfing area of Birkdale?
24 How is the former Museum of Ornamental Art in London now known?
25 Which cathedral has ceiling decorations designed by "Blue Peter" viewers?
26 Which shopping centre in north-west London is near the foot of the M1?
27 Which world heritage site is near Amesbury in southern England?
28 Which is England's largest castle?
29 Which Safari Park is near Liverpool?
30 What is Edinburgh's main shopping street?

Answers

Movies: Animal Stars (see Quiz 106)

1 *Lassie Come Home*. 2 *Jaws*. 3 Orang-utan. 4 St Bernard. 5 Kenya.
6 Sheepdog. 7 Three. 8 1940s. 9 Dog and wolf. 10 Toto. 11 *Homeward Bound*. 12 Gorillas. 13 *Ben*. 14 Champion. 15 *Arachnophobia*. 16 Silver.
17 Horse. 18 Cats and dogs. 19 German. 20 Elsa. 21 1900s. 22 MGM.
23 Willy. 24 Dick King-Smith. 25 *The Birds*. 26 *Beethoven's 2nd*.
27 Alsatian. 28 *Willard*. 29 Dinosaurs (*Jurassic Park*). 30 Rabbits.

1 Who had a 80s No. 1 with "Eye Of The Tiger"?
2 Which officer gives the results of a by-election?
3 Which gas was discovered in 1774 by Joseph Priestley?
4 What is the official language of Chad?
5 Which fruit has a variety called Ellison's Orange?
6 Which Disney film is based on a book by Dodie Smith?
7 Which country borders the Dead Sea together with Israel?
8 Bogota is the capital of which country?
9 Which sister group comprised Patty, Maxine and Laverne?
10 What event took place at Sears Crossing, Bedfordshire in August '63?
11 In which film did Michael Caine say, "Not a lot of people know that"?
12 Which former F1 champion has played golf in the Australian Open?
13 Who refused to appear on Virgin Island stamps with Michael Jackson?
14 Which England football manager was given the sack in 1974?
15 In which country was the Battle of Arnhem?
16 Whose best friend in the Movies was a boy called Elliot?
17 Kimberley, South Africa is famous for producing which gem?
18 Which everyday steel was invented by Harry Brearley in 1913?
19 Which character did Bruce Willis play in "Moonlighting"?
20 What word can go before "pet", "ton" and "mine"?
21 At which major English tourist attraction are the Aubrey Holes?
22 Which TV programme included Lisa Stansfield as a presenter?
23 Who invented 0 and 100 as freezing and boiling points of water?
24 The Harvard University is in which US state?
25 Which radio DJ featured a social worker called Damien in his show?
26 Who wrote the novel *Wild Swans*?
27 Which swimmer hit gold for Britain in the 1980 Olympics?
28 Which European country owns the island of Elba?
29 Which artist painted his garden's water lillies and bridges?
30 What is an appaloosa?

LEVEL 2

1 How would you orally address an Archbishop?

2 Which seaside resort has Squires Gate airport?

3 Which charity can you phone on 0345 90 90 90 from anywhere in the country?

4 Which is a Freephone prefix other than 0800?

5 What is the emergency phone number in the US?

6 In Braille which letter consists of a single dot?

7 What does CompuServe provide access to?

8 What is a TAM ?

9 In telecommunications what is polling?

10 Which number can be used as an alternative to 999?

11 How often is *Reader's Digest* published?

12 What number do you dial for BT UK Directory Enquiries?

13 What do you dial if you do not want the person you are calling to know your phone number?

14 What would an Italian call a motorway?

15 What colour are telephone boxes in France?

16 What is the maximum weight you can send letters at the basic rate?

17 Which three cities are termini for the Eurostar service?

18 What is a local rate number other than 0345?

19 What colour is a 1p postage stamp?

20 What colour is an airmail sticker?

21 Which two cities are the termini for the Anglia rail region?

22 Which underground line goes to Heathrow Terminals?

23 In which US city is O'Hare airport?

24 Between which hours are BT's evening and night time phone rates?

25 What is the UK's oldest Sunday newspaper?

26 What do you dial for International Directory Enquiries?

27 Which newspaper cartoon strip is translated into Latin with characters Snupius and Carolius Niger?

28 Before 1991 which periodical had the highest circulation?

29 What colour is the logo for Virgin trains?

30 What is the most expensive denomination of UK postage stamp?

Answers

TV Times 3 (see Quiz 112)
1 Motorbike and sidecar. 2 Grand Prix racing. 3 Helen Mirren. 4 Eleanor, Robert. 5 "Have I Got News For You?". 6 Kenny Everett. 7 "Red Dwarf". 8 David Soul. 9 Kate. 10 Holland Park. 11 Anthony Jay. 12 "ER". 13 Joanna Lumley. 14 Alaska. 15 MP. 16 Alan B'Stard. 17 Cissie and Ada. 18 Ork. 19 "Minder". 20 "Happy Days". 21 Sport. 22 Pauline Quirke. 23 Compo and Clegg. 24 Elizabeth and Emmet. 25 Five. 26 "Solo". 27 Kenny Dalglish. 28 1940s. 29 Vince and Penny ("Just Good Friends"). 30 Alf Garnett .

LEVEL 2

1 Which meter was invented in 1935 by C.C. Magee?
2 In which country is the port of St. Malo?
3 Which territory was Britain's last in Latin America?
4 What is the USA's rugby union team called?
5 Who was the author of *Gunga Din*?
6 Which London police station, 230 years old, closed in 1992?
7 What was not included in a pack of cards until 1857?
8 Who recorded an album called *Hello, I Must Be Going*?
9 Which bridge links the mainland to Anglesey?
10 Which fatal gas does burning coke emit?
11 Which civilization invented the arch?
12 Which musical instrument is played by Bart Simpson's sister?
13 Which country has the most coastline in the world?
14 Who beat Michael Dukakis in the US Presidential election in 1988?
15 Where was tennis star Ivan Lendl born?
16 Which book had Peter Wright as a co-author?
17 In 1949, what did Eire leave?
18 Which Californian band was joined in 1965 by Glen Campbell?
19 Miles Coverdale's greatest work was in which field?
20 Who released an autobiography titled *I Wanna Tell You a Story*?
21 Which town in Illinois was Superman's childhood home?
22 What colour are wild budgerigars?
23 Whose feathers according to superstition should not be in a house?
24 The letter W is the chemical symbol for what?
25 Which ship has the ID number NCC 1701?
26 Who followed Peter May as chairman of the Test Selectors?
27 Who had a 80s No. 1 with "Only You"?
28 What does Volkswagen actually mean?
29 Where are the sweat glands of a cow?
30 What nationality was the composer Sibelius?

1   What is the favoured transport of the Two Fat Ladies TV cooks?
2   Jamiroquai's Jay Kay composed the theme music for coverage of which sport new to ITV in 1997?
3   In '97 who was voted sexiest woman on TV by *Radio Times* readers?
4   What are the first names of the Doctors Bramwell in the TV series?
5   Which show pits Merton v. Hislop with Deayton as referee?
6   Whose characters included Marcel Wave and Sid Snot?
7   In which sci-fi series did the red-suited Kochanski appear?
8   Which US actor accompanied Martin Bell on his election campaign?
9   What was the name of Nick's first wife in "Heartbeat"?
10 In which area of London was the "Ab Fab" Monsoon household?
11 Who co-wrote "Yes Minister" with Jonathan Lynn?
12 Which series featured the Carol Hathaway/Doug Ross saga?
13 Who was on a desert island as a "Girl Friday" in the mid-90s?
14 In which American state is "Northern Exposure" set?
15 What was the Job in "No Job For A Lady"?
16 Who was Conservative MP for Haltemprice?
17 What were Les Dawson and Roy Barraclough's old gossips called?
18 Which planet was Mork from?
19 In which series was business conducted at the Winchester?
20 "Laverne and Shirley" was a spin-off from which 70s US series?
21 What type of features would Eleanor Oldroyd present on TV?
22 Which Bird starred as 22-stone Olive in "The Sculptress"?
23 Who were Blamire's two companions in 1973?
24 Who are Hyacinth Bucket's most frequently seen neighbours?
25 How many children were there in the Partridge family?
26 In which series did Felicity Kendal play Gemma Palmer?
27 Which football star appeared as himself in Alan Bleasdale's "Scully"?
28 In which decade was "Shine On Harvey Moon" set?
29 Whose parents were Les and Rita, and Daphne and Norman?
30 Who was looked after by Mrs Hollingberry when his wife died?

1   In which country is the town of Waterloo?
2   If you perform a rim shot, what instrument are you playing?
3   In the Chinese calendar which year follows the year of the rat?
4   What are you in if you are caught in a Haboob?
5   What is wrestler Big Daddy's real name?
6   What trade did a webster follow?
7   Who wrote the book *The Prodigal Daughter*?
8   Where does the River Seine empty?
9   What is the fourth letter of the Greek alphabet?
10 What day of the week did Solomon Grundy get married?
11 Which bone is the hardest in the human body?
12 Who was the last Chancellor of West Germany prior to reunification?
13 What was the pen name of Eric Blair?
14 In which decade was "Jim'll Fix It" screened for the first time?
15 Who solved the crime in *Death on the Nile*?
16 Who was the first presenter of "Wheel of Fortune" in the UK?
17 Who was John Major's last Party Chairman?
18 Which breed of dog does not have a pink tongue?
19 Who portrayed Jesus in the TV adaptation "Jesus of Nazareth"?
20 Which novel by Louisa May Alcott sold millions of copies?
21 Which city in India has an airport called Dum Dum?
22 What links a group of whales to a group of peas?
23 If a Vietnamese was depositing a dong, where would he be?
24 Which hat originates from Ecuador?
25 What medical procedure was Iceland the first country to legalise?
26 What was crossed on a tightrope by Charles Blondin in 1855?
27 Who had a 80s No. 1 with "Start"?
28 What colour smoke announces the election of a new Pope?
29 Which birthstone is linked to December?
30 Which Canadian province has Halifax as its capital?

LEVEL 2

1   Which country won league's World Cup from 1975 to 1995?

2   Which Scot was British Lions captain for the '93 New Zealand tour?

3   How old was Will Carling when he first captained England?

4   Which superstar singer opened the 1995 World Cup?

5   The league Lions tour of 1996 visited Fiji and New Zealand and where else?

6   On his return to union which Jonathan said, "It's a challenge I don't particularly need"?

7   Which nation has won the Grand Slam most times?

8   Where was Jeremy Guscott born?

9   Which sponsor called last orders on its sponsorship of the Welsh League?

10   Which stadium hosted the League's 1995 World Cup Final?

11   The Ranfurly Shield is contested in which country?

12   Over half of the 1997 Lions squad came from which country?

13   In which decade was the John Player/Pilkington Cup begun?

14   Which English club did Franco Botica join when he left Wigan?

15   Which Michael has scored most points for Australia?

16   Which team ended Wigan's Challenge Cup record run in the 90s?

17   Which team won the first match in the Super League?

18   Which was the first team in the 90s other than Bath to win the Pilkington Cup?

19   Which two countries contest the Bledisloe Cup?

20   In the 1995 World Cup who were on the wrong end of an 89-0 score to Scotland?

21   Which ground staged the Wigan v Bath cross code game of 1996?

22   In which decade was Fran Cotton born?

23   Which country did Grant Fox play for?

24   Who did Bath beat 16-15 in the 95-96 Pilkington Cup?

25   What was Martin Offiah's first league side?

26   Which player – a Frenchman – became the first to win 100 caps?

27   Which Belfast born solicitor went on five British Lions tours?

28   Which Nick captained Australia from 1984 to 1992?

29   Who was director of rugby as Wasps won the 96-97 championship?

30   Where do St Helens play?

Quiz 115 General Knowledge

Answers - see page 352

LEVEL 2

1 Who was the first British astronaut on the space station *Mir*?
2 Who was the second wife Henry VIII beheaded?
3 How many Popes were there in 1978?
4 What game is being played on the back of a £10 note?
5 David Mellor's affair with whom caused a scandal in the 90s?
6 What is Jennifer Aniston's character's full name in "Friends"?
7 What colour are the seats in the House of Lords?
8 What numbers do Barclaycards begin with?
9 Which ex sports minister won a Court action to have the family title?
10 In which county did Britain's first lifeguard training centre open?
11 In which career is Jodie Kidd famous?
12 Who was the first Mrs Warren Beatty?
13 Who presented "Desert Island Discs" immediately before Sue Lawley?
14 Which TV programme moved to radio in 1997?
15 Which drink was Lucky Vanous famous for advertising?
16 In the early 60s what was Radio 4 known as?
17 Who was the GP in Ambridge who lived with Usha Gupta?
18 What is the regulator of the National Lottery called?
19 Who played Ripley in the *Alien* movies?
20 A frittata is an Italian version of what?
21 Who unexpectedly won the 1997 Men's French Open?
22 Which childhood disease has the same virus as shingles?
23 Who was England ladies athletics team captain at the '96 Olympics?
24 What is Mulder's first name in "The X Files"?
25 What is the official language of Morocco?
26 Who was the British producer of *The Killing Fields*?
27 How many hours were there in February 1997?
28 Who wrote *The Partner*?
29 What was Ronald Reagan's most senior political role before he became president?
30 If you buy pamplemousses in France what do you buy?

Answers

Pot Luck 50 (see Quiz 113)
1 Belgium. 2 Drums. 3 Ox. 4 A sandstorm. 5 Shirley Crabtree.
6 Weaving. 7 Jeffrey Archer. 8 The English Channel. 9 Delta.
10 Wednesday. 11 The jawbone. 12 Helmut Kohl. 13 George Orwell.
14 1970s. 15 Hercule Poirot. 16 Nicky Campbell. 17 Brian Mawhinney.
18 Chow. 19 Robert Powell. 20 *Little Women*. 21 Calcutta. 22 They both
collect in pods. 23 A Bank. 24 Panama. 25 Abortion. 26 Niagara Falls.
27 Jam. 28 White. 29 Turquoise. 30 Nova Scotia.

Quiz 116 Pot Luck 51

Answers - see page 356

LEVEL 2

1   Stamp duty is normally paid on the sale of what?
2   Where is the Ceremony of the Keys held every evening?
3   What does a BACS system transfer?
4   Who wears a chasuble?
5   Who or what is your doppelganger?
6   Emphysema affects which part of the body?
7   Which term for school or university is from the Latin meaning 'bounteous mother'?
8   Which salts are hydrated magnesium sulphate?
9   What is the UK equivalent of the US Bureau of Consumer Protection?
10   What did Plaid Cymru add to its name in 1998?
11   Which punctuation mark would an American call a period?
12   At what age does a student now take a GCE exam?
13   Where were the Elgin marbles from originally?
14   Which song starts, "Friday night and the lights are low"?
15   According to legend, what will happen to Gibraltar's ape population if the British leave?
16   Is BST before or behind GMT?
17   What is notable about the staff and patients of the Elizabeth Garrett Anderson Hospital?
18   How many valves does a bugle have?
19   What name is given to the compulsive eating disorder?
20   What is a Blenheim Orange?
21   Which childhood disease is also called varicella?
22   What do citronella candles smell of?
23   Which part of the anatomy shares its name with a punctuation mark?
24   Which tax did council tax immediately replace?
25   Which English archbishop signs his name Ebor?
26   Which saint was born in Lourdes?
27   Which proposal for a single currency shares its name with a bird?
28   Where is the auditory canal?
29   Where is a fresco painted?
30   How long must a person have had to be dead to qualify for a blue plaque?

Sport: Cricket (see Quiz 117)
Answers
1 Geoffrey Boycott. **2** Richie Benaud. **3** Tony Lewis. **4** Trevor McDonald.
5 Terrence. **6** Kapil Dev. **7** Somerset. **8** Denis Compton. **9** Shakoor Rana.
10 Dennis Lillee. **11** Michael Atherton. **12** The Oval. **13** Graham Alan Gooch.
14 Wasim Akram. **15** Headingley. **16** Muthiah Muralitharan. **17** William
Gilbert. **18** David Gower. **19** Leicestershire. **20** Lancashire. **21** Sunglasses.
22 Sunil Gavaskar. **23** Hansie Cronje. **24** Don Bradman. **25** Graeme Hick.
26 Imran Khan. **27** Antigua. **28** The Times. **29** Sri Lanka. **30** Left.

1 Who did David Gower overtake as England's most prolific run scorer in 1992?
2 Which Australian commentates on BBC TV each summer?
3 Which former test cricketer became President of the MCC in 1998?
4 Which newsreader has written biographies of Viv Richards and Clive Lloyd?
5 What is Ian Botham's middle name?
6 Which Indian was the second bowler to reach 400 Test wickets?
7 Which English county did Viv Richards play for?
8 Which cricketer was the first British sportsman to appear in a major advertising campaign?
9 Which umpire did Gatting publicly argue with in Faisalabad?
10 Which Australian was the first man to take 300 wickets in Test cricket?
11 Who stood in the most tests as England captain?
12 Which is the most southerly of the six regular English Test grounds?
13 Which cricketer's initials are GAG?
14 Who left Lancashire in 1998 to return to Pakistan to clear his name?
15 At which ground did England beat South Africa to clinch the 1998 series?
16 David Lloyd was reprimanded for criticising which Sri Lankan bowler in 1998?
17 What were W.G. Grace's first two names?
18 Whose record did Graham Gooch pass when he became England's leading run scorer?
19 Which county has two two championships in the last three years?
20 Who won the 1998 Nat West Trophy?
21 In 1996 Darren Gough became the first England bowler to bowl wearing what?
22 Which Indian cricketer scored 10,122 runs in 125 matches between 1971 and 1987?
23 Who captained the South Africans on their 1998 England tour?
24 Which cricketer's bat was auctioned for £23,000 in 1997?
25 Which Rhodesian became Zimbabwe's youngest professional at the age of 17 in 1985?
26 Who captained Pakistan in the 1992 World Cup victory?
27 On which island did Brian Lara make his record breaking 375?
28 In which newspaper was it announced that English cricket had died, leading to competition for the Ashes?
29 In which country is Khettarama Stadium?
30 Which hand does David Gower write with?

1 Which Dunfermline East MP has been in the Cabinet in the 90s?
2 Why does a glow worm glow?
3 Who wrote the Kirsty MacColl hit A New England?
4 Princess Margaret was advised against marrying Peter Townsend for what reason?
5 Cambodian leader Saloth Sar was better known by what name?
6 How many holes are most major golf tournaments played over?
7 In the song, what colour rose is linked with Texas?
8 Tokai wine comes from which country?
9 In which month did Samuel Pepys begin his famous diary?
10 Who was Lord Lucan said to have murdered?
11 Mont Blanc stands in France as well as which other country?
12 William Wilkins designed which London gallery?
13 Which city has an American football team called the Cowboys?
14 Which is the world's oldest surviving republic?
15 Which Latin words did H M the Queen use to describe the year 1992?
16 Which cave is the most famous on the Scottish Isle of Staffa?
17 Cars with the international vehicle registration SF come from where?
18 Number 22 in bingo is represented by a pair of little what?
19 What is the core of an ear of maize called?
20 What was the title of the Eurovision winner for Bucks Fizz?
21 In Porterhouse Blue which actor played Skullion?
22 Which country's stamps show the word "Hellas"?
23 Who were the subject of the Cat and Mouse Act of 1913?
24 How many points are scored for a motor racing Grand Prix win?
25 What is the largest structure ever made by living creatures?
26 Papworth Hospital is in which county?
27 Who said, "Float like a butterfly, sting like a bee"?
28 Which magazine was first published in the 1840s and last in the 1990s?
29 Which road is crossed by the horses during the Grand National?
30 Which religious ceremony comes from the Greek word for 'to dip'?

LEVEL 2

1　Which Bond film shares its name with Ian Fleming's Jamaican home?
2　What was the third of Oliver Stone's films about Vietnam?
3　Which English Oscar winner was the villain in Die Hard III?
4　Patriot Games was the sequel to which film with Alec Baldwin?
5　Who played Bernardo in The Magnificent Seven and Danny Velinski in The Great Escape?
6　Who was The Riddler in Batman Forever?
7　Which Oscar did Kevin Costner win for Dances With Wolves?
8　Who played the defrosted super-villain in Demolition Man?
9　What was Roger Moore's first Bond film in 1973?
10　Who had her first major starring role in Bonnie & Clyde?
11　Who plays the President in Escape From New York?
12　Which was the third Die Hard film?
13　Who played Indiana Jones?
14　Where was French Connection II set?
15　Astronaut Jim Lovell was portrayed by Tom Hanks in which film?
16　Who heads the crew which saves the world in Armageddon?
17　Who did Gene Hackman play in The French Connection?
18　Who played Sonny Corleone in The Godfather and its sequel?
19　What nationality cop did Sean Connery play in The Untouchables?
20　Who co starred with Morgan Freeman in Seven?
21　Which 1998 film of a 60s cult TV series starred Gary Oldman and William Hurt?
22　Who played the train robber of the title role in Buster?
23　What was Mel Gibson's job in the 1997 thriller Conspiracy Theory?
24　Which husband and wife were Oscar nominated for the song from Live And Let Die?
25　Which Oliver Stone movie with Kevin Costner was about events prior to Kennedy's assassination?
26　Which Yorkshireman played the IRA terrorist in Patriot Games?
27　In which '79 movie with Jack Lemmon was Jane Fonda urged to keep quiet about a nuclear accident?
28　Who was the construction worker who had flashbacks in Total Recall?
29　Where does the action of Godzilla take place?
30　Who played two roles in the 90s version of The Man in the Iron Mask?

1   Which U2 member was once the All-Ireland Junior Chess Champion?
2   Who won 100m gold at the 1988 Olympics and was then disqualified?
3   Spy-writer David J. Cornwell writes under which name?
4   What is the unit of measurement for the brightness of stars?
5   Which "-ology" is the study of birds' eggs?
6   Which Dire Straits album included Money for Nothing?
7   Who were Janet, Pam, Barbara, Jack, Peter, George and Colin?
8   In which country would you be to visit Agadir?
9   What name is given to a bell tower not attached to a church?
10 Van Pelt is the surname of which Peanuts character?
11 What is the best hand in a game of poker?
12 The Virgin record label was launched by which instrumental album?
13 Which crab lives in a whelk or winkle shell?
14 In the official conker rules, how many strikes per turn are allowed?
15 Which country celebrated its bicentenary in 1988?
16 What word commonly describes a spasm of the diaphragm?
17 Daniel Carroll found theatrical fame under which name?
18 In pop music, who looked into his father's eyes?
19 Who lit the funeral pyre of Mrs Indira Gandhi?
20 Which country has Jones as its most common name but no J in its alphabet?
21 What name was given to the first antibiotic?
22 According to the advert, which city is home to "probably the best lager in the world"?
23 Switzerland's Mont Cervin is better known by what name?
24 Who wrote the novel Where Eagles Dare?
25 Which England cricket captain had the middle name Dylan?
26 What do the initials CND stand for?
27 What is the collective name for a group of frogs?
28 Who was the first act to have seven consecutive US No 1 singles?
29 Eton school is in which county?
30 Which country was first to host Summer and Winter Olympics in the same year?

1   The illness pertussis is more commonly called what?
2   Why do woodpeckers peck at trees?
3   Which rock is the largest monolith in the world?
4   Which Spanish team were the first winners of the European Cup?
5   What type of animal can be Texel and Romney Marsh?
6   Where would you hurt if you were kicked on the tarsus?
7   The Bee Gees were born on which island?
8   What action does a dromophobic fear?
9   In which country is the world's second highest mountain, K2?
10 What nationality is Salman Rushdie?
11 Which Test cricketer played in an FA Cup Final for Arsenal?
12 Which tanker went down on the Seven Stones reef off Land's End?
13 Which large forest is the nearest to London's Liverpool Street Station?
14 Which hit by Judy Collins entered the UK charts on eight occasions?
15 In 1978 how many different Popes were there?
16 In which decade did Constantinople become Istanbul?
17 How many bridesmaids attended Princess Diana?
18 Which poet gave his name to a Cape to the south of Brisbane?
19 Which Russian town produced deformed sheep after a 90s disaster?
20 What is Paul McCartney's first name?
21 Which drug took its name from the Greek god of dreams?
22 Which is the largest borough in the city of New York?
23 Which doll's name gave Aqua a No 1 hit?
24 Which other brook is there on the Grand National course with Becher's?
25 What is examined using an otoscope?
26 What is measured on the Mercalli Scale?
27 Along with Doric and Ionic, what is the third Greek order of architecture?
28 What is lowered by a Beta Blocker?
29 How many pieces does each backgammon player use?
30 A Blue Orpington is a type of what?

1 What type of food is gravadlax?

2 Which type of brandy is made from cherries?

3 Which spirit is Pimm's No 1 based on?

4 Aspartame is an alternative to what when added to food?

5 In which month does Beaujolais Nouveau arrive?

6 Which powder includes turmeric, fenugreek, chillies and cumin?

7 Which country produces more than 70% of the world's olive oil?

8 What name is given to food prepared according to Muslim law?

9 How many standard wine bottles make up a Nebuchadnezzar?

10 Which fruit is also called the Chinese gooseberry?

11 Agar agar is a vegetarian alternative to what?

12 Which 50s pop star's name is cockney rhyming slang for mild?

13 How is cook Isabella Mary Mayson better known?

14 What sort of food is a macadamia?

15 Atlanta is the headquarters of which drinks company?

16 Which pioneering cookery writer wrote Mediterranean Food and French Country Cooking in the 50s?

17 What is ghee?

18 Caraway is related to which family of vegetables?

19 Which queen's nickname is the name of a cocktail?

20 Which football team does Gary Rhodes support?

21 Which term coined in the 70s describes food which does not have rich sauces?

22 What are most beer and soft drinks cans made from?

23 Which of the Two Fat Ladies rides the motorbike?

24 What was Gary Rhodes range of convenience foods called?

25 What colour are fully ripened olives?

26 The Fiery Fred pub was named after whom?

27 Why do cashew nuts have to be roasted to be eaten?

28 What is a morel?

29 What is a morello?

30 Which drink did Bob Geldof advertise?

1 How do the anaconda's victims die?
2 What is the badger's system of burrows called?
3 What is the skin on a deer's antlers called?
4 What colour face does a Suffolk sheep have?
5 Which small breed of dog has a German name meaning badger dog?
6 What is unusual about the sound of the dingo?
7 Aardvark means 'earth pig' in which African language?
8 On which island was the dodo formerly found?
9 What is an impala?
10 What type of leopard is another name for the ounce?
11 Pit bull terriers were bred to do what?
12 To which family does the prairie dog belong?
13 Does the Indian rhinoceros have one or two horns?
14 Bovine Spongiform Encephalitis is a fatal disease of which animals?
15 Tinnitus affects which of the senses?
16 How many teeth do human adults have?
17 What is the most common colour of a Great Dane?
18 What does an ungulate animal have?
19 What do vampire bats feed on?
20 Lanolin is a by product of which domestic animal?
21 If a mammal has albinism what colour are its eyes?
22 What colour are dalmatians when they are born?
23 The tosa is a dog native to which country?
24 What is the reindeer of North America called?
25 Which group of primates are found only on Madagascar?
26 What colour is the coat of a samoyed?
27 What shaped mark does an adder have on its head?
28 What is another name for the wapiti?
29 What do alligators lay their eggs in?
30 Which dog do shepherds now most commonly use for herding sheep?

Pot Luck 54 (see Quiz 122)

Answers

1 Whooping cough. 2 To catch insects. 3 Ayers Rock. 4 Real Madrid.
5 Sheep. 6 Ankle. 7 Isle of Man. 8 Crossing the road. 9 Pakistan.
10 British. 11 Denis Compton. 12 Torrey Canyon. 13 Epping Forest. 14
Amazing Grace. 15 Three. 16 1930s. 17 Five. 18 Byron. 19 Chernobyl.
20 James. 21 Morphine. 22 Queens. 23 Barbie. 24 Valentine's. 25 Ear.
26 Earthquakes. 27 Corinthian. 28 Blood pressure. 29 15. 30 Chicken.

1 In which US state is Death Valley?
2 Which Sea does the River Jordan flow into?
3 Who was Speaker of the House after Bernard Weatherill?
4 Who had Top Ten hits with All Night Long and I Surrender?
5 Which BBC magazine was launched in 1929?
6 What did Captain Cook call the Islands of Tonga?
7 Which celebrity was murdered in 1980 outside New York's Dakota Building?
8 Who played Lennie Godber in the TV series Porridge?
9 Which naval base is situated in Hampshire?
10 Which TV actress links EastEnders with The Hello Girls?
11 What is Marc Bolan's son's Christian name?
12 Which war is the first for which there are photographic records?
13 Writer Mary Westmacott is better known by what name?
14 Who or what was a ducat?
15 Which day is the last quarter day in a calendar year in England?
16 Which actor links The Charmer with Dangerfield?
17 In The Bible, who was Jacob's youngest son?
18 What was suffragette Mrs Pankhurst's Christian name?
19 In which sport is the Plunkett Shield competed for?
20 Which animal has breeds called Roscommon, Kerry Hill, Ryedale?
21 Which two countries was the Cod War of the 70s between?
22 What colour are Rupert Bear's trousers?
23 Who is Gary Lineker's sidekick on They Think It's All Over?
24 Which animal can be red, arctic, bat-eared and fennec?
25 Newman Noggs appears in which Charles Dickens novel?
26 What name is given to the base of your spine?
27 Who did Sandy Powell ask "Can You Hear Me, ..?"
28 Which actress links the films Ghostbusters and Alien?
29 Who had hits with Do You Feel My Love and Electric Avenue?
30 Which word describes both a blunt sword and a very thin sheet of metal?

Answers

Geography: The UK (see Quiz 125)
1 Brighton. 2 Melinda Messenger. 3 South Kensington. 4 Stoke Mandeville.
5 Suffolk. 6 Severn Tunnel. 7 Newgate. 8 Canary Wharf (Isle of Dogs).
9 Salopian. 10 Army exercises. 11 Essex & Suffolk. 12 Bristol. 13 M6.
14 Glastonbury. 15 Big Ben. 16 Fruit, vegetables & flowers. 17 Windscale.
18 Horses. 19 Clyde. 20 Nottingham. 21 Wiltshire. 22 Edinburgh.
23 Petticoat Lane. 24 Papworth. 25 Hyde Park. 26 Aberdeen. 27 Bath.
28 Straits of Dover. 29 Swansea. 30 Bristol.

1   Which seaside resort has Lanes and a nudist beach?
2   Which Page Three blonde is Swindon's most famous export?
3   In which part of London is the Natural History Museum?
4   Where is the National Spinal Injuries Unit?
5   In which county is Sizewell nuclear power station?
6   What is Britain's longest tunnel?
7   The Old Bailey is on the site of which former prison?
8   Where in London would a Canary sit on Dogs?
9   What is a native of Shropshire called?
10 What is Sailsbury Plain primarily used for?
11 In which two counties is Constable Country?
12 Where is the Clifton Suspension Bridge?
13 Spaghetti Junction is on which road?
14 Which Somerset town is said to be the burial place of King Arthur?
15 Which bell was named after Benjamin Hall?
16 What is sold at Spitalfields market?
17 What was the former name of Sellafield?
18 Which animals are kept in the Royal Mews near Buckingham Palace?
19 Holy Loch is an inlet of which river?
20 Which city has an annual Goose Fair?
21 In which English county is Europe's largest stone circle?
22 Which castle is at the west end of the Royal Mile?
23 How is the Sunday market in London's Middlesex Street better known?
24 Which Cambridgeshire hospital is famous for its transplant surgery?
25 Speaker's Corner is on the corner of what?
26 Where is the administrative headquarters of the Grampian region?
27 Which city has a famous Royal Crescent?
28 The Goodwin Sands are at the entrance to which straits?
29 Where is the DVLC?
30 Where is Temple Meads railway station?

1 Carol Vorderman was sacked from Tomorrow's World for advertising what?
2 Which credit card did Rowan Atkinson publicise by not having one?
3 Which opera singer has sung on Kenco Coffee and Renault car ads?
4 Who played the jilted lover in the 80s VW commercial?
5 Which 'pensioner' advertised British Gas with her 'son' Malcolm?
6 For which supermarket did Wood & Walters push their trolleys round country lanes?
7 Which Blankety Blank presenter did Polly Peck hire to advertise their tights?
8 Which soap powder did Shane Richie promote in his doorstep raids?
9 Who advertised Cinzano with Leonard Rossiter?
10 Which juice did Fergie advertise in the US?
11 Lynda Bellingham first found fame advertising what?
12 Which supermarket did John Cleese promote in a loud checked suit?
13 Which company had the slogan 'It's good to talk'?
14 Which cat put its paw in the tine of cat food?
15 Which soap star appeared in a BT ad digging his allotment?
16 Which star of Brushstrokes can be found cleaning bathrooms and kitchens in TV ads?
17 In the Renault ad did Nicole marry Reeves or Mortimer?
18 What type of coffee did Gareth Hunt and Diane Keen enjoy?
19 Which star of Friends uses L'Oreal "Because I'm worth it!"?
20 Which song accompanies Ian McCaskill's BT ad?
21 Emma Forbes' mother advertised which washing up liquid?
22 Which margarine did 'Victor Meldrew' encourage us to eat?
23 Who cried when his Walkers Crisps were taken from him?
24 Ironically Julie Peasgood advertised which product?
25 Which fast food chain did soccer stars Waddle, Pearce and Southgate promote?
26 Which breakfast cereal was Jackie Charlton seen eating with his grandson?
27 Messrs Venables, Robson and Taylor collectively promoted which book?
28 Geoffrey Palmer from As Time Goes By advised to "slam in" what ?
29 Bruce Forsyth dresses up as a judge to advertise what product?
30 Which supermarket did Michael Barrymore advertise in the autumn of 1998?

Quiz 127 Pot Luck 56

Answers - see page 365

LEVEL 2

1 In which US National Park is the Old Faithful geyser?
2 What do the initials IMF stand for?
3 What is emitted from a fumarole?
4 What is the main ingredient in dhal, the Indian dish?
5 In which city is Bramall Lane?
6 Which female had a UK top-three LP in 1982 called The Dreaming?
7 Mozambique is the world's largest producer of which nut?
8 How is Josephina Jacques known in Carry On films?
9 To what would a codicil be added?
10 Which American annual celebration was first marked during 1789?
11 The first Girl Guides had to wear what colour stockings?
12 Which band claimed fifty per cent of Bob Marley's estate?
13 Which film was the follow-up to National Velvet?
14 What does NEC stand for around Birmingham?
15 Who left Bow Wow Wow to form Culture Club?
16 What is the maximum score in blackjack?
17 Which building in France has a famous Hall of Mirrors?
18 What is the modern name of the country where the Hanging Gardens of Babylon were?
19 Which country did Arsenal keeper Bob Wilson play for?
20 In The Bible, which character saw the first writing on the wall?
21 A Daiquiri is made from fruit juice and which alcoholic drink?
22 Astraphobia is the fear of which meteorological event?
23 Which male pop superstar once played with the Frantic Elevators?
24 Machu Picchu is in which mountain range?
25 What is the English equivalent of the Melbourne Cup?
26 What is surrounded by amniotic fluid?
27 Who links Fawlty Towers and After Henry?
28 Which bird is India's national symbol?
29 Which sea is the least salty in the world?
30 Where was The Duke of Windsor buried in 1972?

Answers

TV: Adverts (see Quiz 126)
1 Ariel. 2 Barclaycard. 3 Lesley Garrett. 4 Paula Hamilton. 5 Mrs Merton.
6 Asda. 7 Lily Savage. 8 Daz. 9 Joan Collins. 10 Cranberry. 11 Oxo.
12 Sainsbury's. 13 BT. 14 Arthur. 15 Arthur Fowler. 16 Karl Howman.
17 Mortimer. 18 Nescafe. 19 Jennifer Aniston. 20 Bring Me Sunshine.
21 Fairy. 22 Flora. 23 Paul Gascoigne. 24 Frozen peas. 25 Pizza Hut.
26 Shredded Wheat. 27 Yellow Pages. 28 The lamb. 29 Furniture.
30 Kwik Save.

LEVEL 2

1 Which No 1 hit for the Archies was in the charts for twenty six weeks?
2 Which Park was a hit for the Small Faces in 1967?
3 Who was singing about Sheila in 1962 and Dizzy in 1969?
4 Which 60s hit for Kitty Lester was an 80s hit for Alison Moyet?
5 When did the Shirelles want to know Will You Still Love Me...?
6 Which crime busting organisation gave the Shadows a 1961 hit?
7 What was Petula Clark's first No 1 UK hit in 1961?
8 Which three numbers gave Len Barry his No 3 hit in 1965?
9 Who had consecutive hits with Daydream and Summer In The City?
10 What was over for the Seekers in their 1965 UK No 1 hit?
11 Which 1965 Shirley Ellis hit was a 1982 hit for the Belle Stars?
12 What were Emile Ford and the Checkmates Counting in 1960?
13 What was the Searchers first No 1 ?
14 What was on the other side of Shirley Bassey's Reach for the Stars?
15 Whose first Top Ten hit was 5-4-3-2-1 in 1964?
16 Which country was in the title of a '63 hit by Matt Monro?
17 Who recorded the original of the song used in Four Weddings and a Funeral?
18 What Girl was Neil Sedaka singing about in 1961?
19 The song Starry Eyed was a No 1 on 1st January 1960 for which Michael?
20 Which words of exclamation were a 1960 No 4 hit for Peter Sellers?
21 Which Opportunity Knocks star had a hit with Those Were The Days?
22 What did The Move say they could hear grow in a 1967 hit title?
23 Which 60s hit for Kenny Lynch was a No 1 for Robson and Jerome in 1995?
24 Who were Glad All Over in their No 1 hit from 1963?
25 What was 'skipped' in the lyrics of Whiter Shade Of Pale?
26 What type of Feelings did Tom Jones have in his 1967 hit?
27 Which Group had consecutive No1s with Keep On Running and Somebody Help Me?
28 To which religious building were the Dixie Cups going in 1964?
29 Which weather sounding group had hits with Robot and Globetrotter?
30 Which 1960s star appeared with Zoe Wanamaker in Love Hurts?

1   In which decade did Lester Piggott first win the Derby?
2   Who had hits with My Perfect Cousin and Jimmy Jimmy?
3   Which folklore fantasy tale is subtitled There and Back Again?
4   Who was Nelson Eddy's singing partner in many musical films?
5   Which famous sword is sometimes called Caliburn?
6   Which famous film director has a son called Satchel?
7   Which is further north, Chelmsford or Colchester?
8   Children's broadcaster Derek McCulloch was known on the radio as whom?
9   What is your mode of transport if you go by Walker's Bus?
10 What is former MP Bernadette Devlin's married name?
11 Which Wizzard star formed ELO in 1971?
12 In which TV soap was Trevor Jordache buried under the patio?
13 Who played Old Mother Riley in films and on stage?
14 Which member of the Monty Python team was born on the same day as John Major?
15 What does the word piliferous mean?
16 Who won the Toyota world matchplay championship at his first attempt in 1994?
17 Which King George bought Buckingham Palace?
18 What kind of animal is a Schnauzer?
19 Which Oscar winning film gave Vangelis a No 12 hit in 1981?
20 In which famous Square is St Basil's cathedral?
21 In the series Dad's Army which soldier's daytime job was an undertaker?
22 Who had hits with All Stood Still and Visions in Blue?
23 Which animals are attacked by a disease called Scrapie?
24 Which childhood disease affects the parotid salivary gland?
25 Which female MP was one of the founder members of the SDP?
26 What can be fired by a crossbow?
27 In which city was Anne Frank when she wrote her diary?
28 Which actress played lead in the films Dimples and Curly Top?
29 Lard is mainly produced from which animal?
30 Which king was the last Emperor of India?

LEVEL 2

1 Who succeeded Ossie Ardiles as Spurs manager?
2 Which football team was involved in an aircrash in March 1998?
3 Which English international played for three Italian clubs before moving to Arsenal?
4 Who was fined £20,000 for making a video on how to foul players?
5 Whose 1996 penalty miss prompted Des Lynam to say "You can come out from behind your sofas now."?
6 Who was PFA Young Player of the year in '95 and '96?
7 Who left Tottenham immediately before George Graham took over?
8 Which football manager is singer Louise's father in law?
9 Which club side was Alan Ball playing for during the 1966 World Cup?
10 What is Glenn Hoddle in the cockney rhyming slang dictionary?
11 Which was the first Lancashire side Kenny Dalglish managed?
12 How is Mrs Paul Peschilsolido better known?
13 Which striker has been player of the year at Everton and at Spurs?
14 Who was Man Utd manager immediately prior to Alex Ferguson?
15 Ian McShane's father was on the books of which football club?
16 Who was the first UK manager to walk out on a contract and work abroad?
17 Who has managed Internazionale of Milan and Blackburn Rovers?
18 Which 80s FA Cup winners came nearest the start of the alphabet?
19 Who was Gullit's first signing when he took over at Newcastle?
20 How does the resolving of the 1999 FA CUP Final differ from those 127 years before?
21 Who did Bruce Rioch replace at Norwich for the start of the 1998-99 season?
22 Who was made Northern Ireland manager in February 1998?
23 Which England player was seen on the town wearing a sarong prior to France 98?
24 Who should Scotland have been playing when they arrived for a World Cup qualifier with no opposition?
25 Which ex international managed Burnley in the 1997-98 season?
26 Who did Jack Charlton play all his League football with?
27 George Graham was accused of taking a 'bung' in the transfer of which player?
28 Who sponsored the Scottish Premier Division in the 1995-96 season?
29 What did Man Utd have advertised on their shirts in the 1998 Charity Shield game?
30 Which Yorkshire side does actor Sean Bean support?

Quiz 131 Pot Luck 58

Answers - see page 369

LEVEL 2

1   Canary Wharf is in which London development?
2   Who wrote twelve volumes on Casanova?
3   Which superstar was a former member of the group the King Bees?
4   Which Florida national park has a highway called Alligator Alley?
5   What do Australians mean when they talk about a billabong?
6   How old was Billy The Kid when he died?
7   What was the former name of Turkey?
8   Julia Smith became the wife of which famous sportsman?
9   What on a mountainside is scree?
10 Which city is James Callaghan the Baron of?
11 What killed Sir Francis Drake?
12 What type of hat took its name from a novel by George DuMaurier?
13 The Aegean Sea is linked to the Ionian Sea by which canal?
14 Florence Nightingale was given the Freedom of which city in 1908?
15 Who is the heroine in Jane Austen's Pride and Prejudice?
16 What game started the 1969 war between El Salvador and Honduras?
17 In the 80s two thousand people were killed by a gas leak in which Indian town?
18 Which Bay is the largest in the world?
19 What is the highest break in snooker with the advantage of a free black ball?
20 Which blind music star ran for Mayor of Detroit in 1989?
21 In which country was Ted Dexter born?
22 Who was responsible for setting up the Girl Guides movement?
23 In what year was Nelson Mandela released from prison?
24 Which charity was in business from 1984-89 and raised £90 million?
25 Rhodes is the largest of which group of islands?
26 What is a sumo wrestling ring made from?
27 The film Dick Tracy was promoted by which Madonna single?
28 The Battle of Britain is remembered on which date?
29 Which year did John Lennon perform his final live concert?
30 The 1959 Royal Variety Performance was cancelled for what reason?

Sport: Football UK (see Quiz 130)
1 Gerry Francis. 2 Leeds Utd. 3 David Platt. 4 Vinnie Jones. 5 Gareth Southgate. 6 Robbie Fowler. 7 Christian Gross. 8 Harry Redknapp. 9 Blackpool. 10 Doddle. 11 Blackburn Rovers. 12 Karren Brady. 13 Gary Lineker. 14 Ron Atkinson. 15 Manchester United. 16 Graeme Souness. 17 Roy Hodgson. 18 Coventry. 19 Rui Costa. 20 No replay. 21 Mike Walker. 22 Lawrie McMenemy. 23 David Beckham. 24 Estonia. 25 Chris Waddle. 26 Leeds Utd. 27 John Jensen. 28 Bell's. 29 SHARP. 30 Sheffield United.

Answers

1 Which Ponchielli piece features in Fantasia?
2 Which US born Australian was the voice of John Smith in Pocahontas?
3 In which film did we first meet Timon and Pumbaa?
4 What was the sequel to Aladdin called?
5 What colour are Mickey Mouse's gloves?
6 Perdita and Pongo are what type of animals?
7 How many Oscars in total, was Disney given for Snow White and the Seven Dwarfs?
8 Which 1991 animated film was later a musical in London and the US?
9 Who is the best known rabbit in Bambi?
10 Which king is 'the King of the Swingers' in Jungle Book?
11 Which of the Gabor sisters was a voice in The Aristocats?
12 Who created Tom and Jerry at MGM in the 40s?
13 What did Dumbo do immediately before his ears grew so big?
14 Which film of a fairy tale features the song Bibbidy Bobbidy Boo?
15 Which part did Kathleen Turner voice in Who Framed Roger Rabbit??
16 Which Disney film was the first with a synchronised soundtrack?
17 Colours of the Wind was a hit song from which movie?
18 Which film with an animated sequence featured Angela Lansbury using her magic powers against the Nazis?
19 Who sings 'he's a tramp' in Lady and the Tramp?
20 Where did Kim Basinger star as a sexy animated doodle, Holly, brought over to the real world?
21 Who sang in Aladdin after making her name in Miss Saigon?
22 Which 1990 film was about pizza loving, sewer dwelling reptiles?
23 Which was the first film to feature, appropriately enough, computer-animated sequences?
24 What type of orphaned creature featured in The Land Before Time?
25 Which was the first animated film in the 90s which Tim Rice won an Oscar for?
26 Which dancer commissioned Hanna and Barbera to do an animation sequence in Anchors Aweigh in 1945?
27 Which Tchaikovsky ballet piece features in Fantasia?
28 In which film does Shere Khan appear?
29 Which characters made their debut in Puss Gets the Boot in 1940?
30 Which animals feature in Oliver and Company?

1   Cars with the international vehicle registration C come from where?
2   The Paul Getty Museum is in which American state?
3   What is the American equivalent of an English bilberry?
4   What is added to Galliano to make a Harvey Wallbanger?
5   Which country is nearest to where the Titanic was found?
6   An average man has twenty square feet of what about his person?
7   In which country were the last summer Olympics of the 20th century in Europe?
8   In which decade was Cassius Clay - later Muhammad Ali - born?
9   From which tree family is the basket making osier a member?
10 Which sport other than rugby is played for the Currie Cup?
11 In which country is the Great Sandy Desert?
12 Who had Sticky Moments On Tour?
13 The Cheviot hills run along the boundary between which countries?
14 Which seeds are in the sweet, Halva?
15 What note does an orchestra tune to?
16 In which county is Damon Hill's mansion called Hydon End?
17 Which Shakespeare play was banned during George III's time of madness?
18 Before being used as a name for US soldiers, what did 'GI' stand for?
19 Who played Pauli in the TV series Liverpool One?
20 Which gas is produced by adding water to calcium carbide?
21 Which berries are used in a Cumberland sauce?
22 What is a wadi?
23 In which country is the Potomac River?
24 Which element has the highest melting point?
25 Which University did Jeffrey Archer attend?
26 Which part of a tree gives Angostura Bitters its taste?
27 What is the metric word for a million?
28 What is the southern American stew of rice and okra called?
29 Which famous pop guitarist performed with the Notting Hillbillies?
30 Whose catchphrase was "Hello my darlings"?

Quiz 134   Leisure: Books 1

LEVEL 2

Answers - see page 374

1　Where according to The Bible is the site of the final battle between nations which will end the world?

2　In which Dickens novel did Uriah Heep appear?

3　Old Possum's Book of Practical Cats is composed of what?

4　To £5,000 how much do you receive for winning the Booker Prize?

5　In which book did John Braine introduce Joe Lampton?

6　What type of book is the OED?

7　What is the subject of Desmond Morris's The Naked Ape?

8　What type of books did Patricia Highsmith write?

9　Which detective first appeared in A Study in Scarlet in 1887?

10　In which Holy Book other than The Bible is there the Garden of Eden?

11　Which Gothic horror story has the alternative title The Modern Prometheus?

12　For what types of book is Samuel Pepys famous for?

13　Who wrote The Female Eunuch in 1970?

14　In which county were Jane Austen and Charles Dickens born?

15　Which former politician narrated the diaries of his dog Buster?

16　In Charlie and the Chocolate Factory, what is Charlie's surname?

17　Which ex jockey wrote a book of short stories called Field of Thirteen?

18　Whose horror stories include Carrie and The Shining?

19　According to the 1998 Guiness Book of Records, who is the most mentioned man on the Internet?

20　Who wrote Das Kapital?

21　How many lines are there in a limerick?

22　Which writer and politician bought poet Rupert Brooke's house?

23　Which fictional barrister was created by John Mortimer?

24　Whose first novel, A Woman of Substance became a best seller?

25　Which nonagenarian has written nearly 700 romantic novels?

26　The Day of the Jackal is about an assassination plot on whom?

27　For which Salman Rushdie book did the Ayatollah impose a fatwa?

28　Who wrote It's All Over Now after her brief marriage to Bill Wyman?

29　To five years, how old was Mary Wesley when her first bestseller was published?

30　Award winning novelist Ben Okri hails from which country?

Quiz 135 Pot Luck 60

Answers - see page 373

LEVEL 2

1 What is the highest point of the Pennines?
2 What F1 team was James Hunt in when he won the World Championship?
3 How many years was Nelson Mandela held in prison?
4 Which British boxer was the first to win three Lonsdale belts outright?
5 Who, according to a NOP survey in 1998, do young men call most on their mobile phones?
6 In which London park is Rotten Row?
7 Who said, "Scared of Tyson? I'm more scared of your hair-do"?
8 What will a green phone kiosk only take for payment?
9 Which snooker star was nicknamed 'Interesting' by Spitting Image?
10 In 1988 who scored 405 not out at Taunton?
11 Who died first Gilbert or Sullivan?
12 Which was the first London football club to win a European title?
13 In which century did Joan of Arc become a saint?
14 Which American state is called the 'Gambling State'?
15 Did John Glenn's first spaceflight last five, ten or 24 hours?
16 Which dessert is named after a famous ballerina?
17 Which river flows from northern Moscow to the Caspian Sea?
18 A Bruxelloise sauce is flavoured with which vegetable?
19 Who was the leading actor in Play Misty for Me with Jessica Walker?
20 Who created the Keystone Cops?
21 Who was the Mayor of Casterbridge in the Thomas Hardy novel?
22 What does an alphabetarian study?
23 What occasioned the replacement of the Royal Variety Performance in 1990 with a concert?
24 In which Swiss resort are the Golden Rose TV accolades awarded?
25 Which island is the largest of the Dodecanese group?
26 In which Papers would you find Count Smorltork?
27 Which F1 team scored a 1-2 at Monza during the 1998 Italian GP?
28 To which flower family does garlic belong?
29 Which drink can be green, black and oolong?
30 In which decade was the first American Superbowl?

Answers

Leisure: Books 1 (see Quiz 134)
1 Armageddon. 2 David Copperfield. 3 Poems. 4 £20,000. 5 Room at the Top. 6 Dictionary. 7 Man. 8 Crime fiction. 9 Sherlock Holmes. 10 Al Koran. 11 Frankenstein. 12 Diary. 13 Germaine Greer. 14 Hampshire. 15 Roy Hattersley. 16 Buckett. 17 Dick Francis. 18 Stephen King. 19 Bill Clinton. 20 Karl Marx. 21 Five. 22 Jeffrey Archer. 23 Rumpole. 24 Barbara Taylor Bradford. 25 Barbara Cartland. 26 Charles de Gaulle. 27 The Satanic Verses. 28 Mandy Smith. 29 70. 30 Nigeria.

LEVEL 2

Answers - see page 376

1   What colour is the flesh of a cantaloupe melon?
2   Simnel cake was traditionally eaten on which Sunday?
3   What is the fishy ingredient in Scotch woodcock?
4   What is a champignon?
5   Which spirit is Russia famous for producing?
6   Which drink did Paul Hogan advertise?
7   What is added to pasta to make it green?
8   Which drink is grown in the Douro basin and exported from Oporto?
9   Which cooking pot boils food at a higher temperature than boiling point?
10 What is another name for dietary fibre?
11 Which sauce/salad shares its name with Latin big band music?
12 Where did satsumas originate?
13 What are cornichons?
14 Puerto Rico and Jamaica are the main producers of which spirit?
15 What colour is cayenne pepper?
16 What type of pastry is used to make a steak and kidney pudding?
17 Which drink is served in a schooner?
18 What is a Laxton's Superb?
19 Which seafood, usually fried in breadcrumbs, is the Italian name for shrimps?
20 Tofu and TVP come from which bean?
21 Tartrazine colours food which colour?
22 What is added to whisky to make a whisky mac?
23 Where would you buy a pint of Shires?
24 What colour is Double Gloucester cheese?
25 Which Mexican drink is distilled from the agave plant?
26 Which black, gourmet fungus is a native of France's Perigord region?
27 Which expensive vinegar is aged in wooden barrels?
28 Which grain is whisky made from?
29 What is red wine made with that white wine is not?
30 Vermouth is wine flavoured with what?

1 On which show did The Muppets first regularly appear?
2 Which star of Swop Shop and Saturday Superstore went to the same university as Bill Clinton?
3 In which show was Humpty a regular feature?
4 Who presented Live and Kicking with Zoe Ball?
5 What was the name of elephant who disgraced herself on Blue Peter?
6 What is the profession of Newsround's David Bull?
7 Rugrats appears within which other programme?
8 Which former Play School presenter has a famous DJ daughter?
9 Tucker's Luck was a spin off from which drama series?
10 Who was executive director of 'yoof TV's' Def II?
11 Which sci fi series hit the screens at teatime the day after Kennedy was assassinated?
12 Which best selling book by Russell Ash was turned into a TV show?
13 What colour was Andy Pandy's suit?
14 Which puppet fox had the catchphrase "Boom boom"?
15 Which Good Life star narrated Roobarb and Custard?
16 Other than a TV show what is a Blue Peter?
17 Where do The Teletubbies live?
18 Which ex Crackerjack presenter now has a daily show on Radio 2?
19 Whose catchphrase is "Yabba dabba doo!"?
20 Which Neil has presented Art Attack?
21 Which TV artist designed the Blue Peter logo?
22 Who has presented How and How 2?
23 Which show has a Poppy Stop?
24 Which hero did Prince Adam turn into with the aid of power from Greyskull castle?
25 What colour are Smurfs?
26 In which show would you see Zip-Pea?
27 Where is the Rev Timms' parish in Postman Pat?
28 What sort of creature is Sooty's friend Ramsbottom?
29 Rod, Jane and Freddy was a spin off from which children's series?
30 Who was the voice of Dangermouse?

1 Who supposedly brought about the downfall of Barings Bank?
2 Which country was the first to legalise abortion?
3 Which Eurovision winning group formed the Polar Music Company?
4 In 1954, which Chris won the first BBC Sports Personality of the Year?
5 Mount Elbert is the highest peak in which American mountain range?
6 Adam and Eve were the main characters in which work by John Milton?
7 In 1992, London and which other English city were home to over a million people?
8 Whose murder conviction was overturned after 45 years in 1998?
9 Which famous riding school is in Austria?
10 What colour traditionally is an Indian wedding sari?
11 Which county first won the Benson and Hedges Cricket Cup twice?
12 Which Copenhagen statue is a memorial to Hans Christian Andersen?
13 Which Derbyshire town is famous for the church with a crooked spire?
14 The Parthenon in Athens was built as a temple to whom?
15 Martin Fry and Mark White were members of which 1980s band?
16 Which glands produce white blood cells?
17 What sort of creature is a guillemot?
18 What was the first film Bogart and Bacall starred in together?
19 Which Norfolk model advertises L'Oreal Elvive hair products?
20 Which girl's name gave the Damned their only top ten hit?
21 Which chess piece can only move diagonally?
22 Which gentle water creature gives its name to a Florida river?
23 William 'Fatty' Foulkes played which sport?
24 Which oil company was founded by John D Rockefeller?
25 At which Southwark inn did Chaucer's Canterbury Pilgrims meet?
26 Joseph Marie Jacquard is most remembered for which invention?
27 Before Winston Churchill went bald, what colour was his hair?
28 The word micro is what fraction in the metric system?
29 Which county included W. G. Grace as a team member?
30 Which musical instrument was first developed by Bartolomeo Cristofori?

Past Law & Order (see Quiz 139)

Answers
1 Haiti. 2 Bluebeard. 3 20th (1941). 4 Ruth Ellis. 5 Dr Crippen. 6 Philip Lawrence. 7 Official Secrets Act. 8 Lester Piggott. 9 Slavery. 10 Director of Public Prosecutions. 11 Cape Town. 12 St Valentine's Day. 13 Nick Leeson. 14 Michael Howard. 15 Iceland. 16 Back To Basics. 17 Treason. 18 Colditz. 19 Ethiopia didn't have electricity. 20 Cromwell Street. 21 Richard I. 22 Jack Straw. 23 Louise Woodward. 24 Road rage attack. 25 Robert Maxwell. 26 Peter Sutcliffe. 27 The Butcher of Lyon. 28 The Ritz. 29 Saudi Arabia. 30 The Clintons.

LEVEL 2

Answers - see page 377

1 Which country had the private security force the Tontons Macoutes?
2 What was the nickname of mass murderer Gilles de Rais who killed six of his seven wives?
3 In which century was the last execution at the Tower of London?
4 Which woman was hanged in 1955 for murdering David Blakely?
5 Cora was the wife of which doctor who murdered her?
6 In the 90s which London head teacher was killed outside his school?
7 Which Act bans the disclosure of confidential items from government sources by its employees?
8 Which world famous jockey was jailed in 1987 for tax evasion?
9 What did abolitionism seek to abolish?
10 What is the DPP, a post created in 1985?
11 Robben Island was a prison near which city?
12 Which Day saw seven of Bugs Moran's gang murdered by members of Al Capone's, disguised as policemen?
13 Whose crime was recounted in the film Rogue Trader?
14 Which ex Home Secretary spent a night behind bars in October '98?
15 The Althing is the parliament of which country?
16 Which phrase used by John Major in 1993 was used as a slogan to return to traditional British values?
17 In 1965 capital punishment was abolished except for which crime?
18 How was the prison camp Oflag IVC near Leipzig better known?
19 In what way was Ethiopian Emperor Menelik III thwarted in bringing the electric chair to his country?
20 What was the Gloucester street where Rose & Frederick West lived?
21 Robin Hood is said to have lived in Sherwood Forest during the reign of which king?
22 Which Home Secretary took his son to the police after allegations of drug selling?
23 Which British nanny's US trial was televised after a baby died in her care?
24 Why was the death of Stephen Cameron in 1996 a tragic first?
25 Who fell from the Lady Ghislaine leaving debts behind him?
26 What is the real name of the criminal dubbed The Yorkshire Ripper?
27 What was the nickname of Nazi war criminal Klaus Barbie?
28 Jonathan Aitken's court case centred on a stay in which Paris hotel?
29 Where had Deborah Parry been imprisoned before her return in '98?
30 In the US whose involvement in the Whitewater affair had lengthy repercussions?

Pot Luck 61 (see Quiz 138)

1 Nick Leeson. 2 Iceland. 3 Abba. 4 Chris Chataway. 5 The Rockies. 6 Paradise Lost. 7 Birmingham. 8 Derek Bentley. 9 The Spanish Riding School. 10 Scarlet. 11 Leicestershire. 12 The Little Mermaid. 13 Chesterfield. 14 Athena. 15 ABC. 16 Lymph glands. 17 Bird. 18 To Have and Have Not. 19 Kate Moss. 20 Eloise. 21 The Bishop. 22 The Manatee. 23 Football. 24 Standard Oil. 25 The Tabard Inn. 26 The Jacquard loom. 27 Red. 28 A millionth. 29 Gloucestershire. 30 The piano.

Quiz 140 Pot Luck 62

LEVEL 2

1   What nationality was the spy Mata Hari?
2   The Dickens' work Edwin Drood is different for what reason?
3   Which Australian soap star had the biggest selling UK single in 1988?
4   What were the Boston Tea Party protesters against?
5   What is a Wessex Saddleback?
6   Which former Olympian advertised Ribena?
7   Lyncanthropy involves men changing into what?
8   Which city's American football team is known as the Vikings?
9   Queen Wilhelmina who died in 1962 was Queen of which country?
10   The pop band America were formed in which country?
11   In curling how many shots at the target is each player allowed?
12   What was Janet Street-Porter's beastly last name before marriage?
13   Which Band Aid No 1 hit was written by Midge Ure and Bob Geldof?
14   What was the capital of West Germany?
15   Which American symbol was famously painted by Jasper Johns?
16   In fencing how many hits must a male fencer score for a win?
17   In gin rummy how many cards are dealt per player?
18   What nationality was the inventor of the Geiger counter?
19   Before it moved to Wales on which London hill was the Royal Mint?
20   In which century was the first circumnavigation of the earth?
21   Which is further south, Cardiff or Oxford?
22   Which river rises in the Black Forest?
23   Which road vehicle takes its name from the Hindu God Jagganath?
24   In which South American country is the condor sacred?
25   The first modern Olympics were held in which city?
26   Which East Anglian Cathedral spire is second highest in the country?
27   What have you on your mouth if you suffer from herpes labialis?
28   Prince Edward resigned from which part of the military in 1987?
29   Mike Burden is the sidekick to which TV detective?
30   What was Fred Wedlock according to the title of his one off hit?

Answers

Communications (see Quiz 141)
1 Stansted. 2 Leeds. 3 Philips. 4 Decibel. 5 British Airways. 6 Telephone handset. 7 Trans Siberian. 8 Paris. 9 999 service. 10 Nothing. 11 £500. 12 Acoustics. 13 The Speaking Clock. 14 Swiftair. 15 Video Cassette Recorder. 16 USA. 17 FBI's. 18 Derbyshire. 19 A12. 20 ADA. 21 Dundee. 22 Grand Canal. 23 Alaska. 24 A. 25 M62. 26 Some insects. 27 8. 28 Moscow. 29 Madam Mayor. 30 Channel Tunnel.

Quiz 141 Communications

Answers - see page 379

1   What is Britain's third largest airport?
2   Which northern city has the dialling code 0113?
3   Which company launched the CD-i in 1992?
4   dB is the symbol for what?
5   Which major company owns the budget airline Go?
6   An acoustic coupler allows computer data to be transmitted through what?
7   Which railway links European Russia with the Pacific?
8   Which city linked up with London by phone in 1891?
9   Which vital communications linked began in July 1937?
10 How much is the maximum charge for postage in Andorra?
11 What is the maximum compensation offered by Royal Mail on their Registered service?
12 What is the science of sound and its transmission called?
13 What is another name for Timeline?
14 What is the Royal Mail's express airmail service called?
15 What is a VCR?
16 Which country has the most telephone subscribers?
17 On whose website did Leslie Ibsen Rogge appear, leading to his arrest?
18 In which county is East Midlands airport?
19 Which A road links London with East Anglia?
20 Which computer language was named after Ada Augusta Byron?
21 Which is the nearest city to the Tay road bridge?
22 Which waterway does Venice's Rialto bridge span?
23 Which state is the northern terminus of the Pan American highway?
24 In France all motorways begin with which letter?
25 Which motorway links Hull and Leeds?
26 Which living creatures can you send through the post?
27 How many bits are there in a byte?
28 In which city is the TASS news agency based?
29 How would you verbally address a Mayor who is a woman?
30 Which tunnel goes from Cheriton to Sargette?

LEVEL 2

Answers - see page 382

1 Who had a No 1 UK hit with The Reflex?
2 In English what is the only anagram of the word ENGLISH?
3 Which rules are American football played to?
4 In which South African city was the 1995 Rugby Union World Cup Final?
5 Which musical was based on the play Pygmalion?
6 If you suffer from bulimia, what do you have a compulsive urge to do?
7 Who is Boo-Boo's best friend?
8 Which triangular shaped Indian pastry contains meat or vegetables?
9 Which part of Spain is named after its many castles?
10 The range of the pH scale is zero to what?
11 Which everyday objects can be decorated with the King's Pattern?
12 Stage performer Boy Bruce the Mighty Atom became known as who?
13 Which Russian word means "speaking aloud"?
14 Which Top Ten "ride" was taken by the group Roxette?
15 What is the name of the world's largest Gulf?
16 Which actor played Selwyn Froggatt on TV?
17 Ouzo is what flavour?
18 What does a trishaw driver do with his legs?
19 Which hospital did TV Doctor Kildare work at?
20 Which is the slowest swimming stroke?
21 What is the best selling single of all time?
22 What does E stand for in "E-numbers"?
23 In Peter Pan which part of Peter was kept in a drawer?
24 What word links an ice cream holder and a brass instrument?
25 The thistle is the heraldic emblem of which country?
26 What is the middle name of Princess Margaret?
27 What is the epicarp of an orange?
28 Which character was played by Ken Kercheval in Dallas?
29 Which three Time Travel films were directed by Robert Zemeckis?
30 Which European country has the only active volcanoes in Europe?

LEVEL 2

1 Which 70s hit by the Osmonds gave Boyzone a hit in '94?
2 Which Lieutenant's only UK No 1 hit was Mouldy Old Dough ?
3 Who sang that she was 'born in the wagon of a travelling show'?
4 (Hey There) Lonely Girl was the only UK hit for which vocalist?
5 Tony Orlando sang in which group that had a girl's name?
6 Rupert Holmes' 1980 No 23 hit Escape is also known as what?
7 Which part of the body was mentioned in the title of a Blondie hit?
8 Who were Up The Junction in 1979?
9 Which month links Pilot and part of a song title for Barbara Dickson?
10 Whose hits from 1970 include Victoria and Apeman?
11 What was the number of ELO's Overture in their first hit?
12 The No 1 UK hit Woodstock was a one hit wonder for which group?
13 What Talk gave Dave Edmunds his 1979 No 4 UK hit?
14 What in 1979 was the only Top Ten hit by the group Selector?
15 What links Terry Wogan and the Brighouse and Rastrick Brass Band?
16 Loving You was a high pitched No 2 UK hit for which female singer?
17 Which group had a No 1 UK hit with Sad Sweet Dreamer?
18 Who wanted to be taken to the Mardi Gras?
19 Which 1971 Supremes hit was later a hit for Bananarama?
20 Who had hits with Bang Bang and Knocked It Off in 1979?
21 The 1979 No 6 hit Since You've Been Gone was a hit for who?
22 Which US city was named twice in a Gerard Kenny hit from 1978?
23 Who did Cliff Richard say Hello to when he said Goodbye to Sam?
24 In which song do the chorus beg, "Tell me more, tell me more!"?
25 Which group had hits in the 70s with Easy, Still and Sail On?
26 What was on the other side of Boney M's Brown Girl In The Ring?
27 What time was Gladys Knight's train leaving for Georgia?
28 Which Mungo Jerry hit was used in an anti drink-drive campaign?
29 Which disco style singer had the word Love in the title of four of her first five Top Ten hits?
30 Which No1 from 1972 was the theme for the Van Der Valk series?

1　If a bridge player has a Yarborough, what is the top scoring card?
2　In the film Batman Forever, which actor played Batman?
3　In the Grand National, how many times did Red Rum run?
4　Which was the first railway terminus in London?
5　Which term is used when a mortgage is more than the value of a house?
6　Whose hits include Slave to Love and This is Tomorrow?
7　What is a Clouded Yellow?
8　How was Agatha Miller better known?
9　El Paso is in which American state?
10　Which road leads from Westminster to Blackfriars along the north bank of the Thames?
11　The first player to score 100 Premier League goals played for which club?
12　In which board game is FIDE the governing body?
13　Which colour links an imperial butterfly and a medal?
14　In which year did TV soap EastEnders first appear?
15　What is the Mirror of Diana, located in Northern Italy?
16　Beta Vulgaris is the Latin name for which crop?
17　Which film featured the Joe Cocker hit Up Where We Belong?
18　Who wrote the opera from which Here Comes the Bride is taken?
19　Lime Street Station is in which English city?
20　Cars with the international vehicle registration IS come from where?
21　Which magazine, established in 1922, claims to be the most widely read in the world?
22　What happened to Ken Barlow's second wife in Coronation Street?
23　What type of fruit is a Laxton Superb?
24　Which airport is near to the English city of Carlisle?
25　A sericulturist breeds which creatures?
26　Who played the young Emma Harte in A Woman of Substance?
27　What term describes the fineness of yarns?
28　Where do mice live who are proverbially poor?
29　Joseph Grimaldi achieved everlasting fame as what?
30　Who made history in 1982 by going to an Anglican service in Canterbury Cathedral?

1 In which country is the club Grampus Eight?
2 Which Italian team did Gazza play for?
3 Who was Dutch captain when they won the European Championship in 1988?
4 Who was leading scorer in the 1986 World Cup finals?
5 Which international side did Venables manage after England?
6 Who won the third place final in the 1998 World Cup?
7 Which side did Cruyff move to from Ajax in 1973?
8 Dukla and Sparta are from which European city?
9 Where did Emerson go when he left Middlesborough?
10 Which Brazilian football coach was sacked after France '98?
11 Which Portuguese side did Graeme Souness manage?
12 Which country ran a full page 'thank you' ad in The Times after Euro 96?
13 Who won the Golden Boot in the 1998 world cup?
14 Cesar Menotti managed which victorious World Cup side?
15 Who is the oldest player ever to score in the world cup finals?
16 Penarol is a club side in which country?
17 Which Frenchman moved to Liverpool when Ronnie Moran retired?
18 What is Pele's full name?
19 Who, with England and Holland, was eliminated from France 98 on penalties?
20 In which country is the world's largest football stadium?
21 Who scored the last goal in France 98?
22 Whose much seen girlfriend in France 98 was Suzana Werner?
23 Which Yugoslavian international midfielder played for Luton Town?
24 Which overseas star won most Premiership player of the month awards in 1997-98?
25 Which German won European Player of the Year in 1996?
26 In which stadium was the opening match of France 98?
27 Who captained Brazil in the 98 World Cup Finals?
28 Who was the first European Footballer of the Year?
29 Which club did Brian Laudrup transfer to in November 1998?
30 Which US star of the 94 World Cup became the first American player to take part in Italy's Serie A?

LEVEL 2

1   In which UK city was the de Lorean sports car factory set up in '78?

2   The TV show It'll Be Alright on the Night is presented by whom?

3   Which group had a No 1 UK hit in 1992 with Ebenezer Goode?

4   In which sport were Jack Broughton and James Figg champions?

5   Which Aldous Huxley novel is set in the seventh century AF?

6   Which instrument was Jose Feliciano famous for playing?

7   Which Queen was played in films by Jean Simmons and Bette Davis?

8   Which actor links Chancer, Chariots of Fire and The Whistle Blower?

9   Which musical instruments represent Peter in Peter and the Wolf?

10   Which WPC was shot and murdered at the Libyan Embassy?

11   A glaive was what kind of weapon?

12   In which century was the first Indianapolis 500 first held?

13   In which country do soldiers wear skirts called fustanella?

14   What can be done if an object is scissile?

15   Which film studios were founded by Harry, Sam, Albert and Jack?

16   Which word can describe a listening device, an illness and an insect?

17   Which famous actress starred in Courage of Lassie and Lassie Come Home?

18   Who was older when they died, Benny Hill or Richard Burton?

19   Who did Mark Hughes join when he left Man Utd for a second time?

20   What type of fruit is a jargonelle?

21   Which part of the head is studied by a phrenologist?

22   Whose ancestral home is Woburn Abbey?

23   Who wrote the poem Four Quartets?

24   Which children's game is played on the fingers with looped string?

25   Jane Harris and Nel Mangel appeared in which soap?

26   Brassica Rapa is the Latin name for which vegetable?

27   Which band's hits include Infinite Dreams and Holy Smoke?

28   Which Generation Game assistant was born on the same day as Julian Lloyd Webber?

29   Excess bile pigment in the bloodstream causes which illness?

30   Who was Dennis Bergkamp named after?

Blockbusters (see Quiz 147)

Answers

1 Five. 2 Chocolate. 3 The Robe 4 Francis Ford Coppola. 5 Normandy.
6 M*A*S*H. 7 Hearst. 8 Crocodile Dundee. 9 Gary Oldman. 10 Midnight
Cowboy. 11 Dan Aykroyd. 12 The English Patient. 13 Vito Corleone.
14 Pierce Brosnan. 15 Ron Kovic. 16 Gone With the Wind. 17 Wall Street.
18 Braveheart. 19 Dune. 20 John Huston. 21 Terminator II. 22 Austrian.
23 All About Eve. 24 1930s. 25 Goldblum. 26 Jim Carrey. 27 Carrie Fisher.
28 Celine Dion. 29 Judi Dench. 30 Cop.

1   How many crew members were there in the Nostromo in Alien?
2   What type of sauce was used in the shower scene in Psycho?
3   Which 1953 film was the first made in Cinemascope?
4   Who directed The Godfather and all its sequels?
5   Saving Private Ryan dealt with events in which part of France?
6   Which antiwar comedy did Robert Altman direct?
7   Which newspaper magnate was said to be the model for Orson Welles' Citizen Kane?
8   Which 80s film was the most profitable in Australian history?
9   Who played The Count in Bram Stoker's Dracula?
10 What was John Schlesinger's first US film, made in 1969 with Dustin Hoffman and Jon Voight?
11 Who starred in, and co wrote Ghostbusters?
12 Which film starred Juliette Binoche and Kristin Scott Thomas?
13 What was the name of Marlon Brando's character in The Godfather?
14 Which James Bond actor starred in Dante's Peak?
15 What was the name of Tom Cruise's character in Born on the Fourth of July?
16 In which classic did Olivia de Havilland play Melanie Wilkes?
17 In which film did Michael Douglas say "Greed is good"?
18 What was Mel Gibson's first film as actor, director and producer?
19 Which David Lynch space epic was based on the work of Frank Herbert?
20 Who was directing The African Queen when his daughter Anjelica was born?
21 Which sequel had the subtitle Judgement Day?
22 What is Schindler's nationality in Schindler's List?
23 What was the last film before Titanic to win 14 Oscar nominations?
24 In which decade was Gone With the Wind made?
25 Which Jeff was the mathematician in Jurassic Park?
26 Who became a human cartoon in The Mask?
27 Who played Princess Leia in the Star Wars Trilogy?
28 Who sang the theme song for Titanic?
29 Who was M in Tomorrow Never Dies?
30 What was Michael Douglas' profession in Basic Instinct?

Quiz 148 Cops & Robbers

Answers - see page 388

1 Which TV cop was christened Ilynea Lydia Mironoff?
2 In the title of the program, what shows Life on the Streets?
3 Which show features DCI Michael Jardine?
4 What was Paul Nicholls' first major series after leaving EastEnders?
5 Who was Don Johnson's character in Miami Vice?
6 What was the name of law enforcer Michael Knight's computer buddy?
7 Which show consists of films of dangerous driving shot by traffic police?
8 Which series featured the Wentworth Detention Centre?
9 Who played the TV Avengers role played by Uma Thurman on the big screen?
10 Which member of the Ruth Rendell Mysteries cast also scripted some of the shows?
11 In which series did the character Charlie Barlow first find fame?
12 Which Blue Peter presenter played Dangerfield's son in the police surgeon series?
13 In which 90s series did Neil Pearson star as Det Sup Tony Clark?
14 In which police station was Frank Farillo the chief?
15 What was Fitz's full name in Cracker?
16 Peter Falk played which offbeat TV cop?
17 Which real crime series was based on the German File XY Unsolved?
18 In which series did Rowan Atkinson appear as a police officer?
19 Who was the British half of Dempsey and Makepeace?
20 Which long-running show increased the length of episodes in 1998 to one hour in a bid to improve ratings?
21 Stacey Keach played which detective from Mickey Spillane's novels?
22 The Body in the Library was the first in an 80s series about which sleuth?
23 Which series began with an Armchair Theatre production Regan?
24 Loretta Swit from M*A*S*H was replaced by Sharon Gless in which US series?
25 Who played barrister Kavanagh in the TV series?
26 Which detective was based at Denton police station?
27 How long did the Morse episodes usually last?
28 In which series did Samantha Janus star as Isobel de Pauli?
29 In which series did Charlie Hungerford appear?
30 Which series was based on the Constable novels by Nicholas Rea?

Pot Luck 66 (see Quiz 149)
1 Hamlet. 2 Liverpool. 3 Take That. 4 Surrey. 5 Elizabeth I.
6 Argentinean. 7 Tutti Frutti. 8 A boat. 9 Rockall. 10 Portillo. 11 Fox.
12 Rudyard Kipling. 13 Van Gogh. 14 Trams. 15 George I. 16 Johnny
Dankworth. 17 Chaka Khan. 18 Martyn Lewis. 19 Stirling Moss. 20 Michel
Platini. 21 Scurvy. 22 Household linen. 23 Glucose. 24 Sheridan.
25 Cinzano. 26 Best Supporting Actress. 27 July, August. 28 Fairy tales.
29 Epiglottis. 30 Much.

1 In which Shakespeare play does a ghost walk on the battlements?
2 Which city did comedian Tommy Handley come from?
3 Which group had No 1 hits with Babe and Pray in 1993?
4 Charterhouse Public School is found in which county?
5 Miranda Richardson played who in the second Blackadder series?
6 What nationality is Javier Frana, the tennis player?
7 Which 1987 TV series featured the ageing rock band The Majestics?
8 What is a gallivat?
9 Which British island is 230 miles west of the Hebrides in the Atlantic?
10 Which Michael lost his Enfield seat in the 1997 general election?
11 A skulk is the collective name for a group of which animal?
12 Who wrote How the Leopard Got His Spots?
13 Who painted the picture called Irises?
14 On which forms of transport would you find knifeboards?
15 Handel's Water Music was composed for which English King?
16 Who is Cleo Laine's bandleader husband?
17 Who had UK hits with Ain't Nobody and I'm Every Woman?
18 Which BBC newsreader advertised Cow & Gate baby food as a child?
19 Which racing driver appeared in the film Casino Royale?
20 From 1983-85 which Frenchman was European Footballer of the Year?
21 What disease are you suffering if you are scorbutic?
22 If you bought something in a white sale, what would you be buying?
23 What is the other name for grape-sugar?
24 Who wrote the play The School for Scandal?
25 Which drink was advertised by Joan Collins and Leonard Rossiter?
26 The film The Piano received Oscars for Best Actress and Best what?
27 In a single calendar year which two consecutive months total most days?
28 What did Charles Perrault collect?
29 Which flap of cartilage prevents food from entering your windpipe?
30 Which member of Robin Hood's gang was the son of a miller?

Quiz 150 Euro Tour

LEVEL 2

1 What are the three Baltic states?
2 In which country does the Douro reach the Atlantic?
3 What is the capital of Catalonia?
4 What is Northern Ireland's chief non edible agricultural product?
5 What do the Germans call Bavaria?
6 Which European capital stands on the river Liffey?
7 What is the Eiffel Tower made from?
8 How is the Danish region of Jylland known in English?
9 In which forest does the Danube rise?
10 Which was the first country to legalise voluntary euthanasia?
11 What covers most of Finland?
12 In which country is the world's highest dam?
13 What is the capital of the Ukraine?
14 What is a remarkable feature of the caves at Lascaux in SW France?
15 What is Europe's highest capital city?
16 Where is France's Tomb of the Unknown Soldier?
17 Which area of the Rhone delta is famous for its nature reserve?
18 In which country would you find Kerkyra?
19 What are the two official European languages of Luxembourg?
20 The Magyars are the largest ethnic group of which country?
21 Where is Castilian an official language?
22 Abruzzi is a mountainous region of which country?
23 Which is the largest of the Balearic Islands?
24 On which island was the Mafia founded?
25 What is the UK's chief Atlantic port?
26 Tallinn is the capital of which Baltic state?
27 What is the main religion of Albania?
28 In which country would you meet Walloons?
29 What is the official residence of the French President?
30 Where in Britain is Europe's second tallest building?

Pot Luck 67 (see Quiz 151)
Answers
1 Matt Frewer. 2 Culture Club. 3 Keith. 4 High Chapparal. 5 Midsummer Day. 6 Ronnie Biggs. 7 Elvis Presley. 8 Mary Quant. 9 Ice skating. 10 Henry Crabbe. 11 Hedges and shrubs. 12 Michael Caine. 13 Saint Swithin. 14 C & F. 15 A vaulting horse. 16 Cricket. 17 A fox. 18 A tub of lard. 19 Isle of Man. 20 Correct English. 21 1,440. 22 Dr Hook. 23 A duck. 24 Hurdles. 25 Idaho. 26 The Winchester. 27 Brunel. 28 Griffith. 29 Spiders. 30 Paul Young.

Quiz 151 Pot Luck 67

Answers - see page 389

LEVEL 2

1 Which actor played the TV android Max Headroom?
2 Whose hits include Victims and Church of the Poison Mind?
3 What is Rupert Murdoch's first name?
4 Which ranch was owned by John Cannon?
5 In a calendar year what is the second quarter day in England?
6 Which robber on the run was in the film The Great Rock and Roll Swindle?
7 Who was older when they died John Lennon or Elvis Presley?
8 Which fashion designer opened a shop in 1957 called Bazaar?
9 In which sport would you find a movement called a Salchow?
10 What is the name of the detective in Pie In The Sky?
11 What material does a topiarist work with?
12 Which actor was Rita's tutor in the film Educating Rita?
13 Which Saint has 15th July as his Feast Day?
14 Which two musical notes do not have flats on black keys?
15 In The Wooden Horse what was used to disguise the digging of an escape tunnel?
16 Sabina Park is most famous for which sport?
17 Which animal can be described as vulpine?
18 In Have I Got News for You what stood in for Roy Hattersley ?
19 Where are Union Mills and Onchan Head in the British Isles?
20 Author H.W. Fowler produced a book in 1926 as a guide to what?
21 How many minutes are there in a day?
22 Who had a hit on the telephone in 1972 with Sylvia's Mother?
23 What was Howard in the film Howard - A New Kind of Hero?
24 What can be 84cm, 91cm or 106cm in height in sport ?
25 The towns of Anaconda and Moscow are in which US State?
26 In the TV series Minder which club was owned by Dave?
27 The university sited in Uxbridge is named after which engineer?
28 Which Melanie has been the partner of Antonio Banderas?
29 Which creatures mainly belong to the arachnidae family?
30 Who had hits with Senza Una Donna and Come Back and Stay?

Answers

Euro Tour (see Quiz 150)
1 Estonia, Latvia and Lithuania. 2 Portugal. 3 Barcelona. 4 Flax. 5 Bayern.
6 Dublin. 7 Iron. 8 Jutland. 9 Black Forest. 10 Netherlands. 11 Trees.
12 Switzerland. 13 Kiev. 14 Cave paintings. 15 Madrid. 16 Under L'Arc
de Triomphe. 17 Camargue. 18 Green. 19 French & German. 20 Hungary.
21 Spain. 22 Italy. 23 Majorca. 24 Sicily. 25 Liverpool. 26 Estonia. 27
Muslim. 28 Belgium. 29 Elysee Palace. 30 Canary Wharf.

Answers - see page 392

LEVEL 2

1 The Sealed Knot Society re-enacts what?
2 Which racecourse has a famous Royal Enclosure?
3 What is the Quorn in Leicestershire?
4 What colour are hotels in Monopoly?
5 Where is the National Motor Museum?
6 What is the maximum number of pieces on a chessboard at any one time?
7 What was the yachting trophy the America's Cup named after?
8 In which month do the French celebrate Bastille Day?
9 If you played outdoor hockey in the US what would it be called?
10 In which musical is the song Summertime?
11 Where in London did Laura Ashley open her first shop?
12 What is the world's biggest selling copyrighted game?
13 Which organisation is the largest private landowner in Britain?
14 How high is a netball post?
15 If you have a credit card what is an APR?
16 Where did karaoke singing originate?
17 Who opened a bistro called Le Petit Blanc in 1984?
18 Who replaced Melvyn Bragg on Radio 4's Start the Week?
19 Where was the first Virgin record shop?
20 During which months was the museum to Diana, Princess of Wales open at Althorp in 1998?
21 What might a numismatist collect along with coins?
22 Which day at Royal Ascot is Ladies' Day?
23 Who founded a theme park called Dollywood?
24 Bronco busting and steer wrestling take place at what type of event?
25 Which form of tennis is played on a smaller court usually by children?
26 In which US state did skateboarding begin as an alternative to surfing?
27 How many pins must be knocked down in skittles?
28 Which game is played at Hurlingham?
29 In slalom skiing what must you turn between?
30 What would be your hobby if you used slip?

1 Which animal can be described as ursine?

2 Who was older when they died Graham Hill or James Hunt?

3 Which prize for fiction was instigated in 1969?

4 Which Jackie Wilson hit was No 1 nearly thirty years after it was made?

5 A tarpon is a type of what?

6 Who played Frasier Crane in Frasier and Cheers?

7 If something is vernal, what is it connected with?

8 Where do Southend United football club play their home games?

9 How did both James I's mother and son die?

10 The sidewinder belongs to which group of snakes?

11 Who in 1987 presented the TV show Sweethearts?

12 Which was the first commercial jet aircraft in the world?

13 Jazz musician John Coltrane played which instrument?

14 Who had UK hits with Run to the Hills and The Evil That Men Do?

15 Which part was played by Audrey Hepburn in the film My Fair Lady?

16 Wapentakes, hundreds and hides were all areas of what?

17 What is the collective name for a litter of piglets?

18 Who gave Pip his wealth in Great Expectations?

19 Who wrote the novel Jurassic Park?

20 How many squares have pieces on them at the start of a chess game?

21 In which London park are The Holme, The Broad Walk and Winfield House?

22 What does the differential on a car allow the driving wheels to do?

23 The abbreviation GDP stands for what?

24 The Gulf of Sidra is located off the coast of which continent?

25 Which day of the week is named after the Norse Goddess Freya?

26 Winnipeg is the capital of which Canadian province?

27 What type of creature is a flying fox?

28 Whose hits include I Wish, Lately and Do I Do?

29 Where in Belgium were the 1920 Olympics held?

30 In a calendar year what is the first quarter day in England?

Answers

Leisure 1 (see Quiz 152)

1 Battles of the English Civil War. **2** Ascot. **3** Hunt. **4** Red. **5** Beaulieu.
6 32. **7** Schooner America. **8** July. **9** Field hockey. **10** Porgy & Bess.
11 Kensington. **12** Monopoly. **13** National Trust. **14** 10 feet (3.05m).
15 Annual Percentage Rate. **16** Japan. **17** Raymond Blanc. **18** Jeremy
Paxman. **19** Oxford Street. **20** July and August. **21** Medals. **22** Second day.
23 Dolly Parton. **24** Rodeo. **25** Short tennis. **26** California. **27** Nine.
28 Polo. **29** Flags. **30** Pottery.

1 Which US President's father was a former Ambassador in the UK?

2 Edith Cresson was which country's PM from 1991-1992?

3 The Downing Street Declaration in 1993 involved the Prime Ministers of which two countries?

4 Which family died at Ekaterinburg in 1918?

5 Which school provided the UK with 19 Prime Ministers before 2000?

6 In which war did British soldiers first wear balaclava helmets?

7 Which mountaineer was the first person since Scott to reach the South Pole overland, in 1958?

8 The 'Bomb Plot' of 1944 failed to assassinate whom?

9 What was the minimum age for joining the UK Home Guard in WWII?

10 Which former US President was a distant relative of Princess Diana?

11 Who was the first woman President of Ireland?

12 In which US state did Martin Luther King lead the 1955 bus boycott?

13 Who lost power in Germany in 1998 after 16 years?

14 Who became Secretary General of the UN in 1997?

15 Who was Bonnie Prince Charlie disguised as when he escaped to France with Flora MacDonald?

16 Who defected to the USSR with Guy Burgess in 1951?

17 Carlos Menem became President of which country in 1989?

18 Who was the first Governor General of India, until 1948?

19 What was the alliance between the Germans and the Italians in World War II called?

20 Where in the East End of London did Jack the Ripper operate?

21 As a double agent, Mata Hari was executed by whom?

22 Mrs Meir was the first woman PM in which country?

23 Who was the USA's first Roman Catholic President?

24 Aung San Suu Kyi is an opposition leader in which country?

25 Which Panamanian leader was nicknamed Pineapple Face?

26 Which Pass did Hannibal use to cross the Alps?

27 Who became President of Ireland in 1997?

28 In which Vietnamese village were 109 civilians massacred by US troops in 1968?

29 Who was the first woman US Secretary of State?

30 Where did Tung Chee-Hwa become chief executive in July 1997?

Pot Luck 69 (see Quiz 155)

Answers
1 One square mile. 2 Slaves. 3 Stocks & share prices. 4 Fleet Air Arm. 5 Father of the House. 6 70. 7 Park Lane. 8 Moses. 9 Cunard. 10 Corgi. 11 Kent and Sussex. 12 Red. 13 RAF. 14 Director of Public Prosecutions. 15 48. 16 Ageism. 17 Antarctica. 18 Railway carriage. 19 High blood pressure. 20 Wheel clamp. 21 Vice Squad. 22 When ill. 23 The soul. 24 Smith Square. 25 A cough. 26 Westminster Cathedral. 27 Orange. 28 Siouxsie and the Banshees. 29 Single parent families. 30 A Stateless Person.

Quiz 155 Pot Luck 69

Answers - see page 393

LEVEL 2

1 What is the area of the City of London?
2 What is the last word of Rule Britannia?
3 What does the Footsie show?
4 Which branch of the Royal Navy is concerned with aviation?
5 What name is given to the MP who has served in the House of Commons the longest?
6 A driving licence is issued until the driver reaches what age?
7 In which Lane is London's Dorchester Hotel?
8 In The Old Testament Aaron was the elder brother of which prophet?
9 Which shipping company operated the Queen Mary and the Queen Elizabeth?
10 Which dog's name comes from the Welsh for dwarf dog?
11 In which two English counties are the Cinque Ports?
12 What colour coats do Chelsea Pensioners wear in the summer?
13 Cranwell trains cadets for which of the armed forces?
14 Who is the DPP?
15 How many kilometres per hour is 30 miles an hour?
16 What is discrimination against the elderly called?
17 In 1991 a 50 year mining ban was agreed for which area of the world?
18 In what type of vehicle was the 1918 World War armistice signed?
19 What is another name for hypertension?
20 What is another name for a Denver boot?
21 Which police department deals with illegal gambling and pornography?
22 When might an employee receive SSP?
23 In religious terms what does absolution purify?
24 In which London square is the HQ of the Tory party?
25 Which condition will an antitussive help alleviate?
26 What is the principal Roman Catholic church in England?
27 What colour is a disabled driver's badge?
28 Who had hits with Dear Prudence and Hong Kong Gardens?
29 Which families does Gingerbread help?
30 In law, what is a citizen of no particular nation called?

Answers

People & Places (see Quiz 154)
1 Kennedy. 2 France. 3 UK & Ireland. 4 The Romanovs. 5 Eton.
6 Crimean War. 7 Edmund Hillary. 8 Hitler. 9 17. 10 Ronald Reagan.
11 Mary Robinson. 12 Alabama. 13 Helmut Kohl. 14 Kofi Annan.
15 Flora's maid. 16 Donald Maclean. 17 Argentina. 18 Lord Mountbatten.
19 Axis. 20 Whitechapel. 21 The French. 22 Israel. 23 John F Kennedy.
24 Myanmar. 25 Noriega. 26 Little St Bernard. 27 Mary McAleese.
28 My Lai. 29 Madeleine Albright. 30 Hong Kong.

Answers - see page 396

LEVEL 2

1 Which hit was No 2 for Rick Astley and No 4 for Nat King Cole in '87?
2 What was the first Top Ten hit for Tanita Tikaram?
3 What were 'shattered' in the 1987 No 5 hit for Johnny Hates Jazz?
4 Who joined Kenny Rogers on We've Got Tonight?
5 Which Jimmy Nail hit was a cover of a Rose Royce hit?
6 New Edition got to No 1 in '83 with which Girl?
7 Who were spun around by their No 1 You Spin Me Round (like a record)?
8 Which group had top ten hits with Breakout and Surrender?
9 Whose first UK No 1 hit West End Girls?
10 What was KC and the Sunshine Band's only UK No 1 in the 80s?
11 Which twins had hits with Love On Your Side and Doctor Doctor?
12 Which town got The Specials to No 1 in 1981?
13 What followed Ooh La La La in the 1982 hit for Kool and the Gang?
14 The name of which Asian country gave Kim Wilde an 80s hit?
15 What followed the title of Soul II Soul's first UK No 1 Back To Life?
16 Where did Lipps Inc. take us to in their No 2 from 1980?
17 Which antipodean title was a No 1 for Men at Work in 1983?
18 The song Intuition was the only UK Top Ten single for which duo?
19 Mental As Anything had a No 3 with Live It Up from which film?
20 Who joined Julio Inglesias on his No 5 success My Love ?
21 Which animal was sleeping on the No 1 hit by Tight Fit?
22 Which '87 Billy Idol hit was a cover of an earlier Tommy James hit?
23 What was Simply Red's first Top Ten UK hit?
24 Which Del Shannon hit became an 80s hit for Icehouse?
25 Which Dutch female group had hits with History and Body and Soul?
26 What in 1986 was Spandau Ballet's last UK Top Ten hit?
27 Who joined Fun Boy Three on It Ain't What You Do in 1982?
28 Which day links a No 2 by the Bangles with a No 3 by New Order?
29 Who gave Karel Fialka his only Top Ten success in 1987?
30 Whose first Top Ten hit was Harvest For The World in 1988?

Quiz 157 Pot Luck 70

Answers - see page 395

LEVEL 2

1   Which drink did American Indians call Firewater in the Wild West ?
2   In which city are the Ferens Art Gallery and Town Docks Museum?
3   Who sends encyclical letters?
4   The White Death was a name for which former common disease?
5   According to the song, where does everyone dance in Avignon?
6   Who wrote, "To err is human, to forgive, divine"?
7   In which TV series were the agents given orders by Mr Waverly?
8   Which leaves taste of aniseed?
9   Which group had a top ten hit with Black Knight?
10 What is the fruit of a baobab tree called?
11 What was a bridewell?
12 Which model's childhood nickname was 'Mosschops'?
13 Which actor Ian played the leading role in the film Private's Progress?
14 "A week is a long time in politics," was said by which politician?
15 Which animal movie star was nicknamed Greer Garson in furs?
16 What is the official language of the Ivory Coast?
17 What are pruned in coppicing?
18 Which group featured in The Great Rock 'n Roll Swindle?
19 Which Ava was one of Frank Sinatra's wives?
20 If a plant is a hydrophyte where does it live?
21 A papillon is a type of what?
22 What was Bing Crosby's first name?
23 Which two countries are separated by the Skagerrak?
24 Which royal film star appeared in Dial M for Murder?
25 What does the Blue Cross Charity, founded in 1897, provide aid to?
26 In which Scottish city are Salisbury Crags?
27 Which South American country has the sucre as the unit of currency?
28 Who composed the music for the musical Strike Up The Band?
29 What does the C stand for in ACAS?
30 Which song was sung in three different films by Doris Day?

Answers

Pop Music: The 80s (see Quiz 156)
1 When I Fall In Love. 2 Good Tradition. 3 Dreams. 4 Sheena Easton.
5 Love Don't Live Here Anymore. 6 Candy Girl. 7 Dead Or Alive. 8 Swing Out Sister. 9 Pet Shop Boys. 10 Give It Up. 11 Thompson Twins. 12 Ghost Town. 13 Let's Go Dancin'. 14 Cambodia. 15 However Do You Want Me. 16 Funky Town. 17 Down Under. 18 Linx. 19 Crocodile Dundee. 20 Stevie Wonder. 21 Lion. 22 Mony Mony. 23 Holding Back the Years. 24 Hey Little Girl. 25 Mai Tai. 26 Through the Barricades. 27 Bananarama. 28 Monday. 29 Matthew. 30 Christians.

1 Which American was UK champion jockey in 1984, 1985 and 1987?
2 In which month does the Cheltenham Festival take place?
3 Which two races make up the autumn double?
4 How long is the Derby?
5 How many times did Willie Carson win the Derby?
6 Which Cabinet Minister has been the Glasgow Herald's racing tipster?
7 Who had nine Derby wins and was champion jockey 11 times?
8 Which British racehorse owner sold Vernons Pools in 1988?
9 Who was Champion Jockey a record 26 times between 1925 and 1953?
10 Which John and Peter were joint Champion Jockeys in 1982?
11 Which Classic was the first to be run on a Sunday in England?
12 In 1995 which horse won the Derby, the King George VI and the Prix de l'Arc de Triomphe?
13 Alex Greaves was the first female jockey in which race?
14 Where is Valentine's Brook?
15 At which racecourse is the Steward's Cup competed for annually?
16 Who was riding Devon Loch when it so nearly won the National?
17 What is Frankie Dettori's real first name?
18 Which Monkee was an apprentice jockey?
19 Which horse won the Cheltenham Gold Cup in 1964, '65 and '66?
20 Who was the UK's first overseas champion jockey after Steve Cauthen?
21 Where is Tattenham Corner?
22 What is the highest jump in the Grand National?
23 Where did Walter Swinburn sustain severe injuries in February 1997?
24 Who won the Grand National in 1993?
25 Which auctioneers were founded in London in 1766 but now have annual sales in Newmarket?
26 Which racecourse is near Bognor Regis?
27 What was unusual about the status of Mr Frisk's winning rider in the 1990 National?
28 How old are horses who run in nursery stakes?
29 In which month is Royal Ascot?
30 Whose total of 1,374 winners was a world record after the 1990-91 season?

1   What was the name of Harry Enfield's character in Men Behaving Badly?
2   What was the name of the Chef in Chef!?
3   What was the most successful sitcom of the 80s?
4   Which series took place at the Globelink News Office?
5   Which sit com star worked in a hospital laboratory before becoming an actor?
6   Which former soap star plays Auntie Wainwright in Last of the Summer Wine?
7   Which US sitcom, which had 180 episodes, finished in May 1998?
8   Who was the 40s publican's daughter in Goodnight Sweetheart?
9   All in the Family was a US spin off from which UK sitcom?
10   Where would you find guests Major Gowen, Miss Tibbs and Miss Gatsby?
11   Going Straight was the sequel to what?
12   What was the name of Jim Hacker's wife in Yes Minister?
13   In The Good Life, who or what was Lenin?
14   In The Likely Lads, who did Bob marry?
15   In Dad's Army what did the air raid warden always call Mainwaring?
16   Who was Edina's PA in Absolutely Fabulous?
17   Which series with Prunella Scales as Sarah France had three years on radio before transferring to TV?
18   Grace and Favour was a sequel to which sitcom?
19   What is the name of the time traveller in Goodnight Sweetheart?
20   Which show's theme song begins, "You must remember this..."?
21   Which Ronnie's famous roles have included Arkwright and Fletcher?
22   Which obnoxious character did Chris Barrie play in Red Dwarf?
23   What was strange about Samantha Stephens and her mother Endora?
24   Who was Blackadder's servant?
25   Which sitcom was a send up of Secret Army?
26   What was Dorien's surname in Birds of a Feather?
27   Who was the effeminate Lukewarm in Porridge?
28   What was the Vicar of Dibley's name?
29   In which series did Richie and Eddie first appear?
30   What was Brittas's first name in The Brittas Empire?

Sport: Horse Racing (see Quiz 158)
Answers

1   Steve Cauthen. **2**   March. **3**   Cesarewitch and the Cambridgeshire. **4**   A mile and a half. **5**   Four. **6**   Robin Cook. **7**   Lester Piggott. **8**   Robert Sangster. **9**   Gordon Richards. **10**   Scudamore & Francome. **11**   1,000 Guineas. **12**   Lammtarra. **13**   The Derby. **14**   Aintree. **15**   Goodwood. **16**   Dick Francis. **17**   Lanfranco. **18**   Davy Jones. **19**   Arkle. **20**   Frankie Dettori. **21**   Epsom. **22**   The Chair. **23**   Hong Kong. **24**   No one, it was abandoned. **25**   Tattersall's. **26**   Fontwell Park. **27**   Amateur. **28**   Two. **29**   June. **30**   Peter Scudamore.

Quiz 160 Pot Luck 71

LEVEL 2

1   If you nictitate at someone, what do you do?
2   Who offered Demi Moore a million dollars in Indecent Proposal?
3   Monument Valley is in which American state?
4   Which island off the north Devon coast is named after the Norse for puffin?
5   Who had a Top Ten hit in the 80s with Sledgehammer?
6   On 14th April 1912, what occurred off Newfoundland?
7   Who was Des Lynam's co-presenter on the first series of How Do They Do That?
8   Which instrument was played by David in The Bible?
9   Who is taller Madonna or Dawn French?
10 Which organisation was founded in 1953 by Reverend Chad Varah?
11 In corned beef what are the corns?
12 Which people used knotted cords called quipu for calculation?
13 Which character was played by Maggie Smith in Sister Act?
14 Who wrote the novel Journey to the Centre of the Earth?
15 At which school was Thomas Arnold a famous headmaster?
16 What was a Mae West to an airman?
17 How many squadrons make up a wing in the Royal Air Force?
18 Who followed U Thant as Secretary General of the United Nations?
19 Which high street chain was founded in 1961 by Selim Zilkha?
20 What does the book Glass's Guide contain?
21 Who had a big hit with Sowing the Seeds of Love?
22 Actor Bruce Willis played which character in Moonlighting?
23 What is an aspen?
24 The Battle of Pinkie of 1547 was fought in which country?
25 What nationality was Amy Johnson?
26 Which animal has the longest pregnancy?
27 Anything above scale 12 on the Beaufort Scale would describe what?
28 Which group were made up of Cass, Michelle, John and Denny?
29 Cars with the international vehicle registration PA come from where?
30 Who did Shylock want to take his pound of flesh from?

1 What was the name of the smash movie about 70s superband Abba?

2 Which Bond girl starred with Elvis Presley in Fun in Acapulco?

3 Who danced with Gene Kelly in the Broadway Ballet section Of Singin' In the rain?

4 Who sang Thank Heaven for Little Girls in Gigi?

5 High Society was a musical version of which classic?

6 Which controversial figure directed the musical New York, New York?

7 In which film did Bill Haley sing Rock Around the Clock?

8 Who sang most of the soundtrack of The Bodyguard?

9 Who had a managerial role in Spiceworld?

10 Joel Grey won an Oscar for which role in the 70s classic Cabaret?

11 Who played Che in the film version of Evita?

12 Which Tim Burton film featured a hostile takeover of present delivery at Christmas?

13 Who played the Doctor in the musical film version of Doctor Doolittle?

14 Where is Gigi set?

15 Which tough guy actor played Sky Masterson in Guys and Dolls?

16 Which star of The King and I was born in Russia?

17 Who does Julie Andrews marry in The Sound of Music?

18 Which character sings On the Street Where You Live in My Fair Lady?

19 Which 70s film became a stage musical in London in 1998?

20 Which Gene was the singing cowboy?

21 In which decade does the action of Grease take place?

22 Which English actor played the millionaire benefactor in Annie?

23 In which musical does Nurse Nellie Forbush appear?

24 Which of the many songs in Mary Poppins won the Oscar?

25 What was The Beatles' second film?

26 Which musical is the tale of a Jewish milkman in pre revolutionary Russia?

27 Who played Eva's husband in Evita?

28 Who led 'The Rhythm of Life' sequence in Sweet Charity?

29 Which 70s musical film was set in pre war Berlin?

30 Which Marylin sung Diamonds are a Girl's Best Friend?

1 What is a pickled gherkin made from?
2 Which cricketer is a team captain on TV's They Think It's All Over?
3 Who had hits with Ben and Take That Look Off Your Face?
4 Pooh Bah appears in which Gilbert and Sullivan operetta?
5 Which Classic race is run over the longest distance?
6 Who was the brother of Flopsy, Mopsy and Cottontail?
7 What form did the head of the Sphinx take?
8 Which voice in singing is pitched between a tenor and a soprano?
9 Which birds collect in a covey?
10 Who wrote The Phoenix and the Carpet?
11 Titian is what colour?
12 What part did Madonna play in the film Shanghai Surprise?
13 Which former England manager was born on the same day as Yoko Ono?
14 Which almost eradicated disease was called Phthisis?
15 The Moonstone by Wilkie Collins is about a jewel from which country?
16 In which country is Lake Bala the largest natural lake?
17 In which town were the Marsh Farm riots in July 1995?
18 The US state of Maryland was named after the wife of which King?
19 Who had hits with Be Bop A Lula and Pistol Packin' Mama?
20 Which tennis star was sued by Judy Nelson for palimony?
21 Who played Mark Antony opposite Liz Taylor in the film Cleopatra?
22 Who was Gloria Hunniford named after?
23 Which football manager once played in a band called Revelation Time?
24 What is the first name of P.D. James' detective Dalgleish?
25 Which part did Dustin Hoffman play in the film Hook?
26 What was the title of the 1994 East 17 Christmas No 1 UK hit?
27 Who was British PM directly before Edward Heath?
28 Which Open win was Nick Faldo's first?
29 What can be solo boxing, a lush mineral or a round timber?
30 Which part did Gene Hackman play in the Superman films?

Answers

Living World (see Quiz 163)
1 Tidal wave. 2 On the skin. 3 CJD. 4 Worm. 5 Haematology.
6 Hermaphrodite. 7 Falcon. 8 Ear. 9 Marine snail. 10 Knee. 11 Pigeons.
12 Anaemia. 13 Orange. 14 Fungus. 15 Skin. 16 Abdomen.
17 Shoulder blade. 18 Fish. 19 Short sighted. 20 12. 21 Lungs.
22 Acne. 23 The kiss of life. 24 Tuberculosis. 25 Base of the brain.
26 Achilles tendon. 27 Liver. 28 Green. 29 Kidney. 30 Herring.

1 Tsunami is another name for what type of wave?
2 Where would a melanoma appear?
3 Which disease in humans has been linked to the cattle disease BSE?
4 What sort of creature is a fluke?
5 Which branch of medicine is concerned with disorders of the blood?
6 What name is given to an organism which is both male and female?
7 What sort of bird is a Merlin?
8 Which part of the body might suffer from labyrinthitis?
9 What sort of creature is an abalone?
10 Where is a bird's patella?
11 Which racing creatures live in lofts?
12 What condition is caused by a shortage of haemoglobin?
13 What colour are the spots on a plaice?
14 What is a puffball?
15 Which part of the body does scabies affect?
16 Which digestive organ lies below the thorax in invertebrates?
17 Where is a human's scapula?
18 What do most sharks live on?
19 If a person has myopia what problem does he or she have?
20 How many pairs of ribs does a human have?
21 Pulmonary refers to which part of the body?
22 Which skin disorder is caused by inflammation of the sebaceous glands?
23 What is the popular name for mouth to mouth recussitation?
24 A BCG is a vaccination against which disease?
25 Where is the pituitary gland?
26 Which tendon pins the calf muscle to the heel bone?
27 Hepatic refers to which organ of the body?
28 What colour head does a male mallard usually have?
29 The adrenal gland is above which organ?
30 The pilchard is a member of which fish family?

Quiz 164 Pot Luck 73

LEVEL 2

Answers - see page 404

1 Which Diane has been Sean Connery's partner?
2 The city of Philadelphia was founded by which religious group?
3 Where would you normally play shovel-board?
4 Which is further north Blackburn or Blackpool?
5 Whose hits include Gangsters and Too Much Too Young?
6 Which motor racing team is named after the sacred flower in India?
7 Donald McGill was particularly associated with what seaside art form?
8 Who wrote Willie Wonka and the Chocolate Factory?
9 Who narrates Treasure Island other than Jim Hawkins?
10 What is the New Zealand National Day called?
11 Paul Merson made his league debut with which club?
12 Which ship sent the first S.O.S?
13 What did the craft in the film Fantastic Voyage enter into?
14 In the Bond movie Goldeneye which Dame played M?
15 Which flower is on the badge of the Boy Scouts?
16 Which former Lebanese hostage wrote a book with Jill Morrell?
17 Maddy Magellan is the partner of which fictional detective?
18 Which Marlon Brando film is based on Conrad's Heart of Darkness?
19 In which group of islands is Panay?
20 HMS Ark Royal featured in which TV series?
21 The Sierra Nevada mountains are in which American state?
22 Who played Edward in TV's Edward and Mrs Simpson?
23 STASHING is an anagram of which famous battle?
24 Which pop star Linda took the lead in the film of Pirates of Penzance?
25 Whose hits include Kayleigh and Lavender?
26 Was the Sopwith Camel designed by Sopwith or Camel?
27 Which county did Godfrey Evans play cricket for?
28 Who wrote The Singing Detective?
29 Which word links a pastime, a small horse and a small falcon?
30 Which daily food includes the protein casein?

Quiz 165 Famous Celebs

LEVEL 2

1 Who owns The Ritz in Paris?

2 Which stately home and safari park belongs to the Marquis of Bath?

3 What were two out of Andrew Lloyd-Webber's three wives called?

4 Who has Tommy Lee's name tattooed on her wedding finger?

5 Which Tory MP philanderer said "Only domestic servants apologise" after his Diaries were published?

6 The story of whose affair with David Mellor broke in 1992?

7 Which outspoken ex MP shares her birthday with Margaret Thatcher?

8 What was the previous title of Raine, Comtesse de Chambrun?

9 Where did Geri Halliwell have a meeting behind closed doors to launch 1998 Breast Cancer Awareness Week?

10 For what offence was Stephen Fry jailed, aged 17?

11 Jerry Hall is from which US state?

12 Whose heart attack in Venice prevented him from pursuing the Tory leadership?

13 Theatre impresario Bill Kenwright is a director of which soccer club?

14 Which late billionaire's daughter has a son called Sulaiman?

15 Which PR man acted for Mandy Allwood and Bienvenida Buck?

16 Lady Lucinda Lambton is an expert on which convenient necessity?

17 Which knighted impresario had a record six West End musicals running in 1996?

18 Which estranged wife made a spoof film clip of Diana watching open heart surgery?

19 Which photographer discovered Jean Shrimpton in the Sixties?

20 Who became the face of Estee Lauder in the mid 90s?

21 Who was Mrs Frances Shand Kydd's youngest daughter?

22 How was Anthony Armstrong-Jones known after his royal marriage?

23 Which future Earl did model Victoria Lockwood marry in 1990?

24 Which Sheffield born nightclub owner's most famous club is named after him?

25 What is the nationality of designer Catherine Walker?

26 Which outrageous designer was once the partner of Sex Pistols' manager Malcolm McLaren?

27 In which profession did Marco Pierre White find fame?

28 Whose name was linked with researcher Henrietta Peace's in '97?

29 Dame Shirley Porter is heiress to which supermarket chain?

30 Model Rachel Hunter married which rock star in 1990?

Answers

Pot Luck 73 (see Quiz 164)
1 Cilento. 2 The Quakers. 3 On a ship's deck. 4 Blackpool. 5 The Specials. 6 Lotus. 7 Postcards. 8 Roald Dahl. 9 Dr Livesey. 10 Waitangi Day. 11 Arsenal. 12 Titanic. 13 A Man's body. 14 Judi Dench. 15 Fleur de Lis. 16 John McCarthy. 17 Jonathan Creek. 18 Apocalypse Now. 19 Philippines. 20 Sailing. 21 California. 22 Edward Fox. 23 Hastings. 24 Ronstadt. 25 Marillion. 26 Sopwith. 27 Kent. 28 Dennis Potter. 29 A hobby. 30 Milk.

LEVEL 2

1 Which England player was likened to Mary Poppins by a director of his own club?
2 What would you do with a saxhorn?
3 Who was singer Lorna Luft's famous actress mother?
4 Who had hits with Living on the Ceiling and Blind Vision?
5 Who built the second block of nine cells at Wormwood Scrubs?
6 In Moonlighting which actress played Maddie Hayes?
7 Which is the largest and oldest Australian city?
8 Which sport says "Go out there and win one for the Gipper"?
9 How is the wife of a Knight addressed?
10 Light, Home and Third used to be what?
11 What name is given to a person who eats no food of animal origin?
12 Who wrote the song Moon River?
13 Who led the Scottish troops at Bannockburn?
14 Which Palace is the official home of the French president?
15 What is a water moccasin?
16 In which group of islands are St Martin's, St Mary's and Tresco?
17 Which people made an idol in the form of a Golden Calf in The Bible?
18 Which actor starred in the film North By Northwest?
19 Which city is called the City of Brotherly Love?
20 In which sport were John Louis and Barry Briggs associated?
21 Whose biography was called Neither Shaken Nor Stirred?
22 Which famous Falls are on the Zambezi river?
23 What kind of flower can be a goldilocks?
24 Which state was TV's Knots Landing set in?
25 If you are member of the Q Guild, what is your profession?
26 Which creature's name can go in front of crab, plant, wasp and monkey?
27 How many cards are in a tarot pack?
28 In Trading Places who traded places with Dan Aykroyd?
29 Diluted acetic acid is the correct name for which foodstuff?
30 Whose hits include The Bitch is Back and Kiss the Bride?

LEVEL 2

1 What imaginative type of Game is known by the initials RPG?
2 Which French game's name is the French word for balls?
3 In which month is Spring Bank Holiday?
4 In World Cup Monopoly which team was the equivalent of Old Kent Road?
5 How many balls are needed to play a game of snooker?
6 What is the national sport of Japan?
7 What is lawn tennis called when played on shale or clay?
8 In volleyball what do players hit the ball with?
9 What is the Chinese for 'dark' and 'light' believed to maintain equilibrium?
10 Where is the Jorvik Viking Museum?
11 In which sport would you snatch and jerk?
12 The name of which type of tree cultivation comes from the Japanese for 'bowl cultivation'?
13 Which major change was introduced in badminton in 1949?
14 In which country is the oldest angling club in the world?
15 What is another name for boardsailing?
16 Which toy was invented by Danes Ole and Godtfred Christiansen?
17 If you were at or playing Newmarket which leisure pursuits would you be following?
18 Which cockney actor was a part owner of Langan's Brasserie?
19 Who played Dr Doolittle when it first appeared on the London stage?
20 Approximately how long does the journey from London to Paris take via Eurostar?
21 What are canoes made from?
22 If you received cotton, how many wedding anniversaries would you be celebrating?
23 Which UK motoring association describes itself as the fourth emergency service?
24 Which is the largest country where membership of the Scouts is not allowed?
25 Which club founded in 1787 voted to allow women members in 1998?
26 Where is the world's oldest toyshop?
27 Where does a Steiff teddy bear have its tag of authenticity?
28 What was the 1998 movie based on Cinderella, and starring Drew Barrymore called?
29 If you joined the Wasps in Wigan what sport would you compete in?
30 How many tournaments make up the Grand Slam in golf?

Quiz 168 Pot Luck 75

Answers - see page 408

LEVEL 2

1   Dame Anna Neagle played which part in the 1950 film Odette?
2   Dove Cottage was home of which poet?
3   Which Pole was first reached in 1909?
4   Which Day replaced Empire Day in 1958?
5   Alfred the Great ruled which Kingdom?
6   Estoril is a resort north east of which major city?
7   The Duke of Windsor was Governor of which island group in 1939?
8   Who was the founder lead singer with Led Zeppelin in 1968?
9   Freddie Powell found fame as which crazy comic?
10 Which British surgeon was a pioneer in improving surgery hygiene?
11 Who was the female lead in Singing in the Rain?
12 Which common garden flower has the name Dianthus barbatus?
13 Where were the Spode pottery works established in the 1760s?
14 Cars with the international vehicle registration BG come from where?
15 Which Club included Mr Winkle and Mr Tupman as members?
16 Never Say Die was the first Derby winner for which famous jockey?
17 Which steam locomotive record is held by The Mallard?
18 Which castle is the largest in Britain?
19 Edwin Hubble was concerned with which branch of science?
20 Which part did Albert Finney play in the 1974 film Murder on the Orient Express?
21 Sir Alfred Munnings is famous for painting which animals?
22 Comic character Dan Dare was known as the pilot of what?
23 Colonel Thomas Blood tried to steal what in 1671?
24 Which country is the major exporter of teak in the world?
25 What sort of creature was a brawn?
26 If you suffered a myocardial infraction, what would have happened?
27 Who partnered Annie Lennox in the Eurythmics?
28 The Peace River is in which country?
29 In 1957, in which US state were there race riots at Little Rock?
30 Which racing driver once played in a band called Sex Hitler and the Hormones?

Pop Music: 90s (see Quiz 169)

Answers

1 I Believe. 2 Clannad. 3 Sting & Bryan Adams. 4 Saturday. 5 Gabrielle.
6 Boombastic. 7 Colchester. 8 Dunblane. 9 Without You. 10 Would I Lie To
You. 11 Gina G. 12 The Bodyguard. 13 Shanice. 14 Fairground. 15 Boyz
II Men. 16 Looking Up. 17 I Wonder Why. 18 Spice Girls. 19 Cecilia.
20 Peter Andre. 21 Too Young to Die. 22 Ebeneezer Goode. 23 The
Simpsons. 24 Kylie Minogue. 25 Think Twice. 26 Shiny Happy People.
27 Doop. 28 Beverley Craven. 29 The Real Thing. 30 Lady Marmalade.

1   What was the other side of Robson and Jerome's Up On The Roof?
2   Which Irish band did a TV concert as a tribute to Brian Keenan in '91?
3   Which two singers joined Rod Stewart on the 1994 hit All For Love?
4   What night links Whigfield, Alexander O'Neal and Omar?
5   Who featured on East 17's No. 2 If You Ever in 1996?
6   Which 1995 hit gave Shaggy his second No 1?
7   Blur were formed in which East Anglian town?
8   Knockin' On Heaven's Door was covered following which tragedy?
9   Which song title links No 1s for Mariah Carey and Nilsson?
10 Which title links the Eurythmics to a 1992 No 1 for Charles and Eddy?
11 Which female sang the British Eurovision entry the year before Katrina and the Waves?
12 Which film featured the song that was Whitney Houston's fourth UK No 1?
13 I Love Your Smile was a hit in '92 for which US female artist?
14 What was Simply Red's first UK No 1 in 1995?
15 Who partnered Mariah Carey on One Sweet Day?
16 What was EastEnders' Michelle Gayle's first hit?
17 What was Curtis Stigers' first UK Top Ten success?
18 Which group held the Christmas single and album top spots in 1996?
19 Which female name was a No. 4 hit for Suggs in 1996?
20 Whose first two UK No 1s were Flava and I Feel You?
21 What was Jamiroquai's first UK Top Ten hit?
22 Which song title gave The Shamen their only No 1 in 1992?
23 Who were No.1 in 1991 with Do the Bartman?
24 Better the Devil You Know was a hit for Sonia and which soap star?
25 What was the first UK No 1 for Celine Dion?
26 What kind of people did R.E.M. take to No 6 in 1991?
27 What was the one hit wonder of the Dutch duo Doop?
28 Whose highest chart position was No 3 in 1991 with Promise Me?
29 Which Tony Di Bart No 1 hit from 1994 is the name of a group?
30 Which All Saints No 1 was a cover of a 70s hit for Labelle?

1   Who in EastEnders had an affair with his mother in law?
2   What was Coronation Street originally going to be called?
3   What was the name of Joan Collins' character in Dynasty?
4   The Hart family appeared in which daily soap?
5   Which ex husband of Joan Collins appeared on EastEnders?
6   Who played mechanic Chris in Coronation Street and left to pursue a pop career?
7   Which Corrie star produced a fitness video called Rapid Results?
8   In Coronation Street, what is Spider's real name?
9   In which soap were Shane and Angel an item?
10 How did Kathy Glover's husband die in Emmerdale?
11 In Coronation Street what was Fiona's baby called?
12 Where did Kathy Mitchell go when she left Albert Square?
13 What form of transport did Cindy use to leave for France in EastEnders?
14 Who did Dannii Minogue play in Home & Away?
15 Which Kemp joined Ross Kemp on the EastEnders cast?
16 In Corrie which of the Battersby girls is Janice's daughter?
17 Which Kim disappeared from Emmerdale and was thought to have been murdered?
18 Which soap did Silent Witness star Amanda Burton appear in?
19 Which TV company first produced Emmerdale Farm?
20 Which role did Norman Bowler play in Emmerdale?
21 Who left Albert Square for America but returned as a director of the soap?
22 Which member of Emmerdale's Dingle family went on to present You've Been Framed?
23 Who was buried under the patio in Brookside?
24 Which TV comedian's daughter is in the radio soap The Archers?
25 Whose son in Corrie was once played by his real son Linus?
26 Where did Mavis go when she left The Street?
27 Which country group is made up of members of the Emmerdale cast?
28 Damon & Debbie was a short lived spin off from which soap?
29 Which star of The Good Sex Guide shared a cell with Deirdre in Coronation Street?
30 Which soap had a bar called the Waterhole?

1 In which TV series did Scott Bakula leap in time?
2 Which Kenny Rogers' hit starts, "On a bar in Toledo..."
3 In which sport is there a piste other than skiing?
4 Who wrote The French Lieutenant's Woman?
5 Which Chancellor of the Exchequer introduced TESSA?
6 Which character was played by Dooley Wilson in Casablanca?
7 Who wrote the play Private Lives?
8 Which politician once played in a band called Ugly Rumours?
9 Whose hits include Waterfront and Alive and Kicking?
10 Voords, Krotons and Autons have all appeared on which TV series?
11 Which children's writer's real name was Mrs Heelis?
12 How many seconds are there in three hours?
13 What was the dog called in the Famous Five books?
14 If you were using Dutch or Diaper Bonds what would you be doing?
15 What was Herman's Hermits only No 1 UK hit?
16 In which country was Salman Rushdie born?
17 What are you doing if you are mendicanting?
18 Who wrote the novel Murder in Mesopotamia in 1936?
19 Which team from outside Glasgow won the Scottish FA Cup three times from 1982-84?
20 In Monopoly, what is the next property after the Old Kent Road?
21 Whose mountain retreat was at Berchtesgaden?
22 Dorothea Brooke is the central character in which novel?
23 Which was the first British National Park?
24 Fred Perry was World Champion in 1929 in which sport?
25 Which licence was abolished in 1988 after 192 years?
26 The condor belongs to which family of birds?
27 In which country is Arnhem Land?
28 Whose hits include Promise Me and Woman to Woman?
29 Which actor was Gandhi in the 1982 film?
30 Who was first to win four World Snooker Championships in a row?

1   What does TT stand for in the Isle of Man races?
2   Who first had a record breaking car and a boat called Bluebird?
3   Which is the nearest motor racing track to Towcester?
4   Which team did Jim Clark spend all his racing career with?
5   How many people are in the car in drag racing?
6   Which Belgian cyclist was known as 'The Cannibal'?
7   How many times did Stirling Moss win the world championship?
8   In which country was the first organised car race?
9   Which Labour Party supporter is the head of Formula 1?
10 By 1993 which French driver had won 51 Grand Prix from 199 starts?
11 Which ex world champion was killed at the San Marino Grand Prix in 1993?
12 Which motor racing Park is east of Chester?
13 What type of racing is known in the US as Demolition Derbies?
14 How frequently does the Tour de France take place?
15 Who was the first man to be world champion on two and four wheels?
16 What relation was Emerson to Christian Fittipaldi?
17 Which Japanese team won its first F1 Grand prix in 1967?
18 Who was the first man to win a Grand Prix in a car he designed?
19 Who was Williams' highest placed driver in 1995?
20 In 1994 who was the first Austrian to win the German Grand Prix since Niki Lauda?
21 Which Briton was the first world driver's champion to win Le Mans, in 1972?
22 In which country did the first mountain bike world championship take place?
23 Which Briton did Alain Prost overtake for a record number of Grand Prix wins?
24 Which was the first manufacturer to have over 100 Grand Prix wins?
25 Which famous British car won the Monte Carlo rally in 1967?
26 Who was the first Briton to wear the Tour de France yellow jersey after Tommy Simpson?
27 Who was the first British F1 Champion after James Hunt?
28 Who was the first driver to be sacked by Benetton twice?
29 Who was the first Frenchman to win the World Grand Prix title in '85?
30 Where is the home of the French Grand Prix?

1 Which tennis player died on the same day as Donald Pleasence?
2 Whose hits include Ball Park Incident and Rock'n Roll Winter?
3 Who produced the Communist Manifesto with Friedrich Engels?
4 What is a firebrat?
5 Where are your fontanelles?
6 Which American protest singer is linked to the 'dustbowl ballads'?
7 Who wrote the stories subsequently televised as Poldark?
8 In which time device would you find an escapement?
9 The port of Archangel is in which country?
10 The Titanic was launched in which city?
11 Film star Lee Yuen Kam achieved fame as which kung fu expert?
12 Which famous woman who worked with African wildlife was murdered in 1985?
13 Which dirty insects are members of the Diptera family?
14 John Hancock was first to do what at the American Declaration of Independence?
15 In a calendar year what is the third quarter day in England?
16 What is a dirndl?
17 What, in 1902, destroyed the Martinique village of St Pierre?
18 Cork is produced mainly from which species of tree?
19 In which Bond film does the character 'Oddjob' appear?
20 What does the word 'Bedouin' mean?
21 Which family made typewriters and invented the breech-loading rifle?
22 Who was the first Roman Emperor?
23 Which word can be a unit of measure, a stick or a fishing implement?
24 Which actor played a black prostitute's minder in the film Mona Lisa?
25 What did Robert Burns call "great chieftain o' the puddin' race"?
26 Welcome To My World was the first Top Ten hit for whom?
27 Is St Gabriel the patron saint of messengers, millers or musicians?
28 Which actress played the daughter of Alf Garnett?
29 A love apple is an archaic term for what?
30 Whose hits include Manchild and Buffalo Stance?

Answers

Sport: Hot Wheels (see Quiz 172)
1 Tourist Trophy. 2 Malcolm Campbell. 3 Silverstone. 4 Lotus. 5 One.
6 Eddie Merckx. 7 Never. 8 France. 9 Bernie Ecclestone. 10 Alain Prost.
11 Ayrton Senna. 12 Oulton Park. 13 Stock car racing. 14 Annually.
15 John Surtees. 16 Uncle. 17 Honda. 18 Jack Brabham. 19 Damon Hill.
20 Gerhard Berger. 21 Graham Hill. 22 France. 23 Jackie Stewart.
24 Ferrari. 25 Mini. 26 Chris Boardman. 27 Nigel Mansell. 28 Johnny
Herbert. 29 Alain Prost. 30 Magny Cours.

1 Which actor/director started the trend for spaghetti westerns?

2 What was the nationality of Meryl Streep's character in A Cry in the Dark?

3 Who was shunned by Hollywood in the 40s when she left her husband for Roberto Rossellini?

4 Which poet's name was the middle name of James Dean?

5 Who was Hollywood's first black superstar?

6 Which famous dancer played a straight role in On the Beach?

7 Which Burt appeared in Bean-The Ultimate Disaster Movie?

8 On the set of which film did the Richard Burton/Elizabeth Taylor affair begin?

9 Who, famous as a gangster roles, was a founder of the Screen Actors Guild?

10 Who received her first Oscar nomination for Silkwood?

11 Whose roles vary from Cruella de Vil on film to Norma Desmond on stage?

12 How old was Macaulay Culkin when he was first married?

13 Which married superstars starred in The Big Sleep in 1946?

14 Which comedian co founded United Artists in 1919?

15 Dietrich appeared in the German The Blue Angel, who appeared in the US version?

16 Which actor's last film was The Misfits in 1960?

17 Who was voted No 1 pin up by US soldiers in WWII?

18 How many parts did Alec Guinness play in Kind Hearts and Coronets?

19 What is the profession of Nicole Kidman's father?

20 In which country did Charlie Chaplin spend the final years of his life?

21 Who was Truman in The Truman Show?

22 Which superstar did Tony Curtis parody in Some Like It Hot?

23 Who played the title role in the 1990 Cyrano de Bergerac?

24 Who is the physician in the 90s remake of Doctor Doolittle?

25 How many Road films did Crosby, Hop and Lamour make?

26 Who was the psychotic cabbie in Scorsese's Taxi Driver?

27 Who announced her retirement when she married Ted Turner in '91?

28 Who was Jodie Foster's character in The Silence of the Lambs?

29 Who directed The Horse Whisperer?

30 Who played Margo Channing in All About Eve?

Pot Luck 78 (see Quiz 175)

Answers

1 Three. 2 A Helicopter. 3 Maria Callas. 4 M People. 5 Labrador. 6 Gabrielle. 7 The Old Curiosity Shop. 8 Greece. 9 On the seabed. 10 Kent. 11 Shoes. 12 Melvyn Hayes. 13 Sistine. 14 Sonny Bono. 15 Bismarck. 16 Le Mans. 17 Sap. 18 Peru. 19 The World War. 20 Pregnant. 21 Jackie Rae. 22 Aphrodite. 23 Bits and pieces. 24 Guildford. 25 Isle of Wight. 26 The Lion King. 27 Nkima. 28 Whitesnake. 29 Commissioner Dreyfus. 30 A supermarket.

1 How many times did Joe Frasier fight Muhammad Ali?
2 What was designed and made in a viable form by Sikorsky in 1941?
3 Which opera singer died on the same day as Marc Bolan?
4 Who had hits with One Night in Heaven and Moving On Up?
5 Which 'dog like' peninsula formed Canada's tenth province in 1949?
6 What was Coco Chanel's Christian name?
7 Quilp appears in a book about what kind of Shop?
8 In which European country are the Pindus Mountains?
9 If a creature is demersal, where does it live?
10 In which county was the first Youth Custody Centre set up in 1908?
11 Espadrilles are a type of what?
12 Who played the part of 'Gloria' in It Ain't Half Hot, Mum?
13 Michaelangelo painted the ceiling of which famous Chapel?
14 Which rock musician died on the same day as cricketer David Bairstow?
15 Who was called the 'Iron Chancellor'?
16 Where is motor racing's Grand Prix d'Endurance staged?
17 If a creature is succivorous what does it feed on?
18 The source of the Amazon is in which South American country?
19 Al Capone said he was accused of every death except the casualty list of what?
20 If something or someone is gravid what does it mean?
21 Who was the first presenter of the TV series The Golden Shot?
22 In Greek mythology, who was the mother of Eros?
23 What does 'Chop Suey' literally mean?
24 In which city is the University of Surrey?
25 Carisbrooke Castle is on which Isle?
26 In which Disney film is a young lion called Simba?
27 What was the name of Tarzan's monkey friend in the Tarzan stories?
28 Which heavy band's hits include Here I Go Again and Is This Love?
29 Which part was played by Herbert Lom in the Pink Panther films?
30 The 1984 TV series Tripper's Day was set in what type of shop?

1   Which South American city has a famous Copacabana beach?
2   The Bass Strait divides which two islands?
3   Which Middle East capital is known locally as El Qahira?
4   Where is the official country home of US Presidents?
5   Whose Vineyard is an island off Cape Cod?
6   Where was Checkpoint Charlie?
7   Which US state has a 'pan handle' separating the Atlantic from the Gulf of Mexico?
8   In which two countries is the Dead Sea?
9   The site of ancient Babylon is now in which country?
10   On which river is the Aswan Dam?
11   Which continent produces almost 50% of the world's cars?
12   The Fens were formerly a bay of which Sea?
13   What is Japan's highest peak?
14   To which country do the Galapagos Islands belong?
15   Aconcagua is an extinct volcano in which mountain range?
16   Where in California is the lowest point of the western hemisphere?
17   In which London Square is the US Embassy?
18   Ellis Island is in which harbour?
19   Which city is known to Afrikaaners as Kaapstad?
20   On which Sea is the Gaza Strip?
21   What are the three divisions of Glamorgan?
22   Which river cuts through the Grand Canyon?
23   In which Ethiopian city is the HQ of the Organisation of African Unity?
24   Which continents are separated by the Dardanelles?
25   Which US state capital means 'sheltered bay' in Hawaiian?
26   Hampstead is part of which London borough?
27   Which country owns the southernmost part of South America?
28   Where is the seat of the UN International Court of Justice?
29   The Golan Heights are on the border of which two countries?
30   Which is the saltiest of the main oceans?

Answers

Pot Luck 79 (see Quiz 177)
1 West Side Story. 2 Tom and Jerry. 3 Love. 4 John Hunt. 5 Solomon.
6 The Real Thing. 7 Rugby League. 8 Potato famine. 9 Language sounds.
10 Joe Louis. 11 Tom Cruise. 12 Robert Mugabe. 13 Calcium. 14 40.
15 Honeysuckle. 16 Basil Brush. 17 Mike McGear. 18 Nine. 19 Rock
Hudson. 20 Fred Astaire. 21 Trampolining. 22 Niagara Falls.
23 Bournemouth. 24 Pele. 25 Mariah Carey. 26 A Nelson. 27 Britain.
28 Freddie Laker. 29 Holland. 30 15th.

1   The song America comes from which musical?
2   Which cartoon duo starred in the Oscar winning film Quiet Please?
3   Kate Bush had an album called The Hounds Of ...what?
4   In 1953 who was leader of the British expedition which conquered Everest?
5   In The Bible who did the Queen of Sheba visit according to Kings I?
6   Who had a UK Top Ten hit with Can You Feel the Force?
7   Which sport was founded in Britain on 28th August 1895?
8   Black Forty Seven in Ireland in the 19th century related to what?
9   What is phonetics the study of?
10 Who was World Heavyweight boxing champion in WWII?
11 Which actor links Risky Business, Cocktail and Top Gun?
12 Who was the first president of Zimbabwe?
13 Which element is found in shells, bones and teeth?
14 How old are you if you are a quadragenarian?
15 Which flower is also called the Woodbine?
16 Which children's TV puppet was operated by Ivan Owen?
17 Paul McCartney's brother Mike is known as whom?
18 What is the most times a day of the week can occur in two months?
19 Who was older when they died Humphrey Bogart or Rock Hudson?
20 Who starred opposite Judy Garland in the film Easter Parade?
21 In which sport are there moves called Triffus, Rudolf and Miller?
22 The Horseshoe and American combine to form which famous falls?
23 Which is further west, Bognor or Bournemouth?
24 Which Brazilian footballer appeared in a film called Hotshot?
25 Who has had hits with Hero and Anytime You Need A Friend?
26 What name is given to a score of 111 in cricket?
27 In Orwell's 1984 what is called Airstrip One?
28 Whose cheap transatlantic air service in 1977 was called 'Skytrain'?
29 Which team did Argentina beat in the 1978 Football World Cup Final?
30 In which century was the Battle of Agincourt?

Answers

On the Map (see Quiz 176)
1 Rio de Janeiro. 2 Australia & Tasmania. 3 Cairo. 4 Camp David.
5 Martha's Vineyard. 6 Between East and West Berlin. 7 Florida. 8 Israel &
Jordan. 9 Iraq. 10 Nile. 11 Europe. 12 North Sea. 13 Mount Fujiyama.
14 Ecuador. 15 Andes. 16 Death Valley. 17 Grosvenor. 18 New York.
19 Cape Town. 20 Mediterranean. 21 Mid, South, West. 22 Colorado.
23 Addis Ababa. 24 Europe & Asia. 25 Honolulu. 26 Camden. 27 Chile.
28 The Hague. 29 Israel & Syria. 30 Atlantic.

1   Which cereal can survive in the widest range of climatic conditions?
2   The hellebore is known as what type of rose?
3   What colour are edelweiss flowers?
4   Which plant is St Patrick said to have used to illustrate the Holy Trinity?
5   Succulents live in areas lacking in what?
6   How many points does a sycamore leaf have?
7   What is the ornamental shaping of trees and shrubs called?
8   What is an alternative name for the narcotic and analgesic aconite?
9   What colour are laburnum flowers?
10   What is another name for a yam?
11   What shape are flowers which include the name campanula?
12   What is a frond on a plant?
13   Which climbing plant is also called hedera helix?
14   Agronomy is the study of what?
15   What is a Sturmer?
16   Which fruit is called 'earth berry' in German from where the plant grows?
17   What is another name for belladonna?
18   What is the effect on the nervous system of taking hemlock?
19   Are the male, female or either hop plants used to make beer?
20   What is the most common plant grown in Assam in India?
21   Aspen is what type of tree?
22   Which ingredient in tonic water is found in cinchona bark?
23   The ground powder form turmeric dyes food which colour?
24   The pineapple plant is native to which continent?
25   What is the purpose of a plant's petals?
26   Which type of pesticide is used to kill weeds?
27   What colour are the leaves of a poinsettia?
28   What name is given to the wild yellow iris?
29   Which plant is famous for having a 'clock'?
30   What colour are borage flowers?

1 Which former First Lady was nicknamed 'The Smiling Mamba'?
2 Who had hits with Joanna and Celebration?
3 Where would you see a facula?
4 DJ Alan Freeman was born in which country?
5 Which country has a unit of currency called the Leone?
6 The seaside town of Westward Ho is in which county?
7 Oloroso is a type of which drink?
8 Which car manufacturer designed the winning bike for Chris Boardman?
9 Which Wonder of the World statue was at Olympia?
10 In which century did William Caxton establish the first English printing press?
11 Cocoa is prepared from the seeds of which tree?
12 Who wrote Androcles and the Lion?
13 What is driven by a mahout?
14 What does the cooking expression al dente mean?
15 Which Oliver was Lord Protector of Britain?
16 Which label is distinguished as fashion designed by Armani?
17 Which celeb's childhood nickname was Liver Lips?
18 Who would use a jacquard?
19 In The Wizard of Oz, which animal was seeking courage?
20 Who captained the US Ryder Cup team in 1997?
21 In which city is the HQ of Amnesty International?
22 Pumpkin Pie is the traditional dessert on which special American day?
23 Who played Eleanor Bramwell in the TV series of the same name?
24 Who painted The Starry Night?
25 Which word can be a swan, a horse, a bread roll and a basket?
26 What was Diana Ross's first solo Number 1 in the UK?
27 What are progeny?
28 Who had hits with I Can't Dance and Invisible Touch?
29 Who preceded Ed Tudor-Pole as host of the Crystal Maze?
30 If you heard a John Gabel Entertainer, what would be playing?

LEVEL 2

1 Germany's Red Army Faction was popularly called what after its two founders?
2 The Equal Opportunities Commission was set up to implement which act?
3 Who became US Vice President after Spiro Agnew resigned?
4 Where did the Gang of Four seize power in 1976?
5 Which natural disaster did Guatemala city suffer in 1976?
6 In the Vietnam War who or what was Agent Orange?
7 Who was Nixon's White House Chief of Staff at the height of the Watergate scandal?
8 On which Pennsylvania Island was there a nuclear leak in 1979?
9 In 1978 Mujaheddin resistance began in which country?
10 Who made a precocious speech aged 16 at the 1977 Tory Party conference?
11 Who opened her first Body Shop in 1976?
12 Where was Obote replaced by Amin in 1971?
13 The Pahlavi Dynasty was overthrown by the Islamic revolution in which country?
14 Which Argentine leader died in 1974 and was succeeded by his third wife?
15 Which woman MP did Jack Straw replace as MP for Blackburn?
16 How were Patrick Armstrong, Gerard Conlon, Paul Hill and Carole Richardson known collectively?
17 Which dictator was deposed in Cambodia in 1979?
18 Which 'King' died in 1977 aged 42?
19 What was Harare called until the end of the 1970s?
20 What was inside US incendiary bombs during the Vietnam War?
21 Which title did Quintin Hogg take when made Lord Chancellor in '70?
22 SALT negotiations took place between which two countries?
23 Which future Labour leader became Trade & Industry Secretary in '78?
24 Mario Soares was exiled from which country in 1970?
25 In which country was a monarchy restored in 1975?
26 The Sandinistas overthrew which government in 1979?
27 Who succeeded Heath as Tory leader?
28 Sapporo was the centre of the 1972 winter Olympics in which country?
29 Which country did the USSR invade in 1979?
30 In which department was Thatcher a Minister before leading the Party?

Quiz 181 TV Times 4

Answers - see page 419

LEVEL 2

1 What is the name of the singing group in The Hello Girls?
2 What relation is ER's George Clooney to US singer Rosemary?
3 Which Gladiator was jailed in 1998 for corruption?
4 Superwoman Lynda Carter held which beauty queen title?
5 On which TV show was Jim Davidson 'discovered'?
6 Outside TV what type of transport business does Noel Edmonds run?
7 Where was This Morning first broadcast from?
8 Which They Think It's All Over panellist wears most make up?
9 The TV profile Tantrums and Tiaras was about which pop superstar?
10 Which TV presenter's relationship with Stan Collymore ended violently in Paris during the 1998 World Cup?
11 Who was the first landlady of Fitzgerald's in Ballykissangel?
12 Which TV playwright founded Animal Line with Linda McCartney?
13 What was Richard Madeley arrested for in 1990?
14 Which veteran sports commentator won the Manchester Mile in 1949?
15 What colour does TV critic Nina Myskow usually wear?
16 Which News At Ten presenter had the first British TV interview with Nelson Mandela after his release?
17 Which game was Bob's Full House based on?
18 Which TV cook wears a diamond studded crash helmet?
19 Who presented the C5 medical quiz show Tibs and Fibs?
20 Who were the first couple to be BBC Sports Personality of the Year?
21 Which cook founded Sainsbury's The Magazine with her husband?
22 In the US Jim Bakker and Jimmy Swaggart are famous for what type of show?
23 Which star of Brideshead Revisited shares a birthday with sports commentator Brendan Foster?
24 Which weather girl went to the same university as Glenys Kinnock?
25 Which character did Ted Danson play in Cheers?
26 Which pop group walked out on Clive Anderson on his All Talk show?
27 Which London soccer side does June Whitfield support?
28 Which talk show hostess appeared in the film Hairspray with Divine?
29 Who is the resident snooker player on Big Break?
30 Where did Paula Yates conduct her Big Breakfast interviews?

Answers

Past Times: 70s (see Quiz 180)
1 Baader-Meinhof Gang. 2 Sex Discrimination Act. 3 Gerald Ford. 4 China. 5 Earthquake. 6 Weedkiller. 7 Alexander Haig. 8 Three Mile Island. 9 Afghanistan. 10 William Hague. 11 Anita Roddick. 12 Uganda. 13 Iran. 14 Peron. 15 Barbara Castle. 16 The Guildford Four. 17 Pol Pot. 18 Elvis Presley. 19 Salisbury. 20 Napalm. 21 Lord Hailsham. 22 USA & USSR. 23 John Smith. 24 Portugal. 25 Spain. 26 Nicaragua. 27 Thatcher. 28 Japan. 29 Afghanistan. 30 Education.

1   What was Annie Oakley's first name?
2   Which famous survey started in 1086?
3   What was Roger's wife called in the film Who Framed Roger Rabbit?
4   Ronald Reagan was in which political party?
5   Who is taller – Claire Rayner or Pauline Quirke?
6   In The Bible, what was the prophet Elijah carried up to heaven in?
7   What nationality was Casanova?
8   What was Al Jolson's most famous line?
9   If a substance is oleaginous what does it mainly contain?
10 Which General led the junta in the 1982 seizure of the Falklands?
11 Which famous Castle is on the River Dee?
12 What did the Owl and the Pussycat dine on?
13 Vera Welch sang under what name?
14 Which Christopher was a policeman before he became a champion skater?
15 Which outlandish musician's real name was Simon Ritchie?
16 Which handicapped physicist has appeared in adverts for 'BT'?
17 Who is buried at the Arc de Triomphe?
18 During exercise which acid builds up in the muscles?
19 Who is spiritual leader to the Ismaili sect of Muslims?
20 Which singer had a backing group called the Checkmates?
21 What is added to egg yolks and vanilla to make advocaat?
22 Who played 'Blanco' in the TV series Porridge?
23 What nationality was Rachmaninov the composer?
24 What is xerography?
25 Which 1956 hit links The Platters with a 1987 Freddie Mercury hit?
26 Which Dutch town is particularly famous for its blue pottery?
27 Where would you find an apse?
28 What was abolished on 18th December 1969 in Britain?
29 Which tycoon started the newspaper called Today?
30 Who was the first golfer to lose play-offs in all four majors?

Pop Music: Albums (see Quiz 183)
Answers
1 Chris Rea. 2 Chicago XIII. 3 Eternal. 4 George Michael. 5 News of the World. 6 The Revolution. 7 Pet Shop Boys. 8 Frank Sinatra. 9 Wet Wet Wet. 10 Sting. 11 No Parlez. 12 River Deep - Mountain High. 13 Wannabe. 14 Definitely/Maybe. 15 Pulp. 16 Just Good Friends. 17 Emmerdance. 18 Blue. 19 Physical. 20 Slippery When Wet. 21 The Rolling Stones. 22 Sex. 23 Nigel Kennedy. 24 Gasoline Alley. 25 Goat. 26 The Wall. 27 Enya. 28 Waterloo. 29 Ten. 30 Diva.

1 Who released the album Auberge?
2 What was the thirteenth album released by Chicago?
3 Which group's debut album, Always & Forever, shadowed their name?
4 Whose debut solo album was called Faith?
5 Which Queen album shares its name with a newspaper?
6 On the 80s album Purple Rain who backed Prince?
7 Which duo released albums called Introspective and Very?
8 Which US superstar has had over 70 chart albums in his career?
9 High On the Happy Side was a No 1 album for which band in '92?
10 Who guested with Dire Straits on the Money For Nothing track?
11 Which phrase with a French flavour was the title of Paul Young's debut album?
12 What was the title of Ike and Tina Turner's only album?
13 What is the first track on Spice?
14 A picture of Burt Bacharach appeared on the cover of which best selling 90s album?
15 Whose debut album was called Different Class?
16 Which Paul Nicholas album was named after a sitcom in which he starred?
17 What was the title of the album by the Woolpackers?
18 On the Beautiful South's 1996 album what is the Colour?
19 Which Olivia Newton-John '81 album could describe some exercise?
20 Which Bon Jovi album was best kept dry?
21 What was the title of the first album released by The Rolling Stones?
22 What were Madonna's book and 1992 album called?
23 Which musician took Vivaldi's The Four Seasons into the charts?
24 Rod Stewart's first album was called after which alley?
25 What animal is on the cover of the Beach Boy's album Pet Sounds?
26 Which construction has given its name to a Pink Floyd album?
27 Which Irish singer got to No 1 with Shepherd Moons?
28 Which battle was the title of the first Abba album?
29 How many Good Reasons had Jason Donovan on his first No 1?
30 Which Annie Lennox album topped the charts in 1993?

1   Who formed the famous dance troupe the Bluebell Girls?

2   Whose CDs include Seven Year Itch and Stickin' to my Guns?

3   What would you do with a futon?

4   Which play is performed every ten years at Oberammagau?

5   Which wood was mainly used by Thomas Chippendale?

6   In which London area is The Royal Hospital?

7   Which Lynne is Duggie Brown's sister?

8   Bruce Willis destroyed a plane with his cigarette lighter in which film?

9   What does a blue flag at a beach mean?

10 Which carbohydrate causes jam to gel?

11 If a dog is suffering from 'hard pad' what form of disease has it got?

12 What is a hawser?

13 What was Roy Schneider's profession in the film Jaws?

14 Theophobia is a fear of what?

15 In which French town was Joan of Arc burnt at the stake?

16 What was the name of cowboy Tom Mix's horse ?

17 The quail is the smallest member of which bird species?

18 What is the singular of axes in mathematics?

19 Which actress's real name was Maria Magdalena von Losch?

20 Which port is the most easterly in Britain?

21 What is the common weather in a pluvial region?

22 Which Polynesian word means prohibited or forbidden?

23 What colour is the egg of a kingfisher?

24 The Dodecanese Islands are in which sea?

25 What nationality was Secretary General of the UN Boutros Boutros Ghali?

26 What part was played by Irene Handl in For the Love of Ada?

27 Whose hits include Sunny Afternoon and Tired of Waiting For You?

28 What is on top of the Mona Lisa's left hand?

29 What do Americans call Perspex?

30 In fishing what is another name for a pike-perch?

Answers

Leisure 6 (see Quiz 185)
1 Deep sea diving. 2 Stamps. 3 Green. 4 Circular. 5 Yoga. 6 Cribbage.
7 Admiral's Cup. 8 Lacrosse. 9 Gare Du Nord. 10 RSPB. 11 Pottery.
12 Star Wars. 13 13 tricks by one team. 14 Harrods. 15 Synchronised
swimming. 16 Cadbury, Fry, Rowntree. 17 The Netherlands. 18 Tennis.
19 Pizza Express. 20 Golf Club. 21 Women's Institute. 22 World Wildlife
Fund. 23 Whipsnade. 24 Tintin. 25 Dark green. 26 Hammer.
27 Wrestling. 28 Isle of Wight. 29 York. 30 Leicester.

Quiz 185 Leisure 6

Answers - see page 423

LEVEL 2

1 After what sort of activity might you suffer from the bends?
2 What would you buy from Stanley Gibbons?
3 What colour are houses in Monopoly?
4 What shape is a sumo wrestling ring?
5 Which Hindu system of philosophy is used as a means of exercise and meditation in the west?
6 In which game do you score 'one for his knob'?
7 The Fastnet race is part of the contest for which Cup?
8 Which game's name comes from a piece of its equipment looking like a bishop's crosier?
9 At which station do you arrive in Paris if you have travelled from the UK by Eurostar?
10 The YOC is the junior branch of which organisation?
11 If you were a collector of Clarice Cliff what would you collect?
12 A Monopoly game based on which Sci-fi film was released in 1997?
13 What is a grand slam in Bridge?
14 House of Fraser owns which major London store?
15 What sort of swimming takes place with musical accompaniment?
16 Which three Quaker families made most of Britain's chocolate?
17 In which country is De Efteling Theme Park?
18 Which sport is played at London's Queen's Club?
19 Which pizza restaurant was the first of a chain founded in London?
20 What sort of club is the Royal and Ancient?
21 Which organisation's anthem is Jerusalem?
22 What was the Worldwide Fund for Nature formerly called?
23 Which open air zoo is near Dunstable in Bedfordshire?
24 Which boy reporter was created by Belgian artist Herge?
25 What colour carrier bag do you get when you shop at Laura Ashley?
26 In athletics, what is attached to a chain and a handle and thrown?
27 Which sport has Greco-Roman and Freestyle, as two distinct styles?
28 The annual Round the Isle race goes round which Isle?
29 Where is the National Railway Museum?
30 Where were Walker's Crisps first made?

Answers

Pot Luck 82 (see Quiz 184)

1 Margaret Kelly. 2 Etta James. 3 Sleep on it. 4 The Passion Play. 5 Mahogany.
6 Chelsea. 7 Lynne Perrie. 8 Die Hard 2. 9 Clean & pollution free. 10 Pectin.
11 Distemper. 12 A rope. 13 Police Chief. 14 God. 15 Rouen. 16 Tony.
17 Partridge. 18 Axis. 19 Marlene Dietrich. 20 Lowestoft. 21 Rain.
22 Taboo. 23 White. 24 Aegean Sea. 25 Egyptian. 26 Ada. 27 The Kinks.
28 Her right hand. 29 Plexiglass. 30 Zander.

Quiz 186 Pot Luck 83

Answers - see page 426

LEVEL 2

1 What describes descending a sheer face by sliding down a rope?
2 Donna Reed replaced Barbara Bel Geddes in which TV series?
3 Who is Princess Alexandra's son?
4 Which animal is feared by a hippophobe?
5 Whose hits include Wide Boy and Wouldn't It Be Good?
6 The novel Shirley was written by which of the Bronte sisters?
7 In which London building does the Lutine Bell hang?
8 Which is further south, Folkestone or Southampton?
9 Which American sportsman was said to be earning more than the US president in 1925?
10 Which famous bear came from Peru?
11 What did the S stand for in Charlie Chaplin's middle name?
12 Who was Shirley Maclaine named after?
13 What is a passepied?
14 Which species can be Fairy, Black-footed and Crested?
15 Which game uses flattened iron rings thrown at a hob?
16 What was the title of Captain Sensible's No 1 UK hit in 1982?
17 Which European Commissioner once played in a band called The Rebels?
18 Which country won the 1992 World Cup cricket final?
19 What is tansy?
20 Which island is in the Bay of Naples?
21 Whose hits include Something About You and Lessons In Love?
22 Cyril Mead became known as which comic?
23 In the order of accession to the British throne who is the first female?
24 In which London Square is the American Embassy?
25 What is a taipan?
26 Is Coventry north or south of Leicester?
27 Which English King was the last to die in battle?
28 Who was older when they died Peter Sellers or Tony Hancock?
29 What is the smallest administrative unit in the Church of England?
30 In Pride and Prejudice who does Elizabeth Bennet finally marry?

1 Which American was the first to win the Men's Singles Grand Slam?
2 Who in 1979 became the youngest player to complete the double of 1,000 runs and 100 wickets?
3 Which Swede, in 1987 was the first man for 40 years to win a match at Wimbledon without losing a game?
4 Who was the first woman tennis player to win $1 million?
5 Who was the first Briton after 1950 to win the British Open golf three years in succession?
6 Who was the first woman athlete to win the athletics Grand Slam?
7 Which woman won 20 Wimbledon titles between 1961 and 1979?
8 Franz Klammer was a record breaker in which sport?
9 Which woman became the youngest Wimbledon semi finalist for 99 years in 1986?
10 Who broke the world record for an individual innings of 501 in 1994?
11 How many world records did Mark Spitz break when he won his seven gold medals?
12 Who, in 1987, was the first British golfer to win the World Match-Play Championship?
13 Whose 1500m world record did Steve Cram break in 1985?
14 Who was the first British woman swimmer to win a world title?
15 Who made the first televised 147 break in snooker in 1982?
16 Which Namibian was the first to break the indoor 20 second barrier?
17 Who was the first British winner of the US Masters in 1988?
18 In 1988 who became the first boxer to win world titles at five official weights?
19 Who in 1991 was the youngest woman ever to have the No 1 tennis ranking?
20 Who was the first Thai snooker player to win a major tournament?
21 In 1972 Mark Spitz broke Olympic records doing which two strokes?
22 Who holds the record for most goals scored in FA Cup Finals?
23 Who broke Bob Beaman's long jump record set at the 1968 Olympics?
24 Who was the then youngest ever winner of the US Masters in 1980?
25 Who was the first British soccer player to earn £100 per week?
26 Which US hurdler was undefeated in 122 races?
27 Which British shot putter was world No 1 in 1975?
28 Which Liz won the fastest ever debut marathon when she won in New York in 1991?
29 Which Town did Man Utd beat by a record nine goals in 1995?
30 Who in 1968 became the oldest Briton to win a Grand Prix?

1 Where is fibrin found in your body?
2 Which two countries are on the Iberian peninsula?
3 Which group had hits including Homely Girl and Kingston Town?
4 The word 'ketchup' comes which language?
5 Who played the priest in the TV series The Paradise Club?
6 Which species of bird does the wapacat belong to?
7 Which Marx brother died on the same day as Joyce Grenfell?
8 Woburn Abbey is the home of which family?
9 What is a durian?
10 Which film starred John Cleese as an under pressure headmaster?
11 The composer Bela Bartok came from which country?
12 What can be an animal enclosure or a unit of weight?
13 What does the abbreviation BHP stand for?
14 Which poetic names lend themselves to an expression for a devoted, elderly couple?
15 How does a judge hear a case when it is heard In Camera?
16 From 1968 to 1970 which actor was Mr Universe?
17 What does the word 'biscuit' literally mean?
18 The Lent Lily is sometimes used as another name for which flower?
19 What is a Tree Ear?
20 What was Little Lord Fauntleroy's name?
21 Toad of Toad Hall was a dramatised version of which Kenneth Grahame tale?
22 Which sport is Clare Francis famous for?
23 In the film Look Who's Talking whose voice was the baby's thoughts?
24 Which tree usually provides the wood for the Highland Games caber?
25 Whose hits include Wishing Well and All Right Now?
26 What colour is the tongue of a giraffe?
27 Which actor played the title role in Judge Dredd?
28 Californian, Yellow Horned and Opium are all types of which flower?
29 Where is the Sea of Vapours?
30 What is the wading bird the bittern's cry called?

Quiz 189 The Oscars

LEVEL 2

1 Which singing Oscar winner said, "women get all excited about nothing - then marry him"?

2 Which World War II film would have been called Dar el-Beida had it been titled in the local language?

3 Which Michael Cimino film about Vietnam won five Oscars in the 70s?

4 Who did Daniel-Day Lewis portray in My Left Foot?

5 Which veteran won an Oscar in 1981 two years after his daughter?

6 For which movie did Helen Hunt win in 1997?

7 For which film did Tom Hanks win playing a lawyer dying from AIDS?

8 Who overcame deafness to win for Children of a Lesser God?

9 Who won the Best Director award for Titanic?

10 For which films did Tom Hanks win in successive years?

11 Who won the Best Actor Oscar for High Noon?

12 What type of worker did John Gielgud play when he won his Oscar for Arthur?

13 In which decade did Katharine Hepburn win her first Oscar?

14 Who won three Oscars for Annie Hall?

15 For which film did Brando win his second Oscar?

16 Who won his first best actor Oscar for Kramer vs. Kramer?

17 Which singer won an Oscar for From Here to Eternity?

18 For which film did Steven Spielberg win his first award?

19 What was unusual about Holly Hunter's performance in The Piano?

20 Which father and son actor and director won for The Treasure of the Sierra Madre?

21 In the year Gandhi won almost everything who was Best Actress for Sophie's Choice?

22 Who won Oscars for Dangerous, Jezebel and All About Eve?

23 Who won as Dan Aykroyd's mother in Driving Miss Daisy?

24 How many times between 1990 and 1997 did Best Picture and Best Director Oscars go to the same film?

25 Who played the psychotic nurse in Misery and won Best Actress?

26 What did Anthony Hopkins win first, a knighthood or an Oscar?

27 Who won for her role as Blanch in A Streetcar Named Desire?

28 Who won Best Director for The English Patient?

29 Who won for her first film Paper Moon?

30 Which actress was nominated for The Wings of the Dove?

Quiz 190 Pot Luck 85

Answers - see page 431

1. What are Spode, Bow and Chelsea all types of?
2. A covey is the collective name for a group of which birds?
3. Which Italian area produces Chianti?
4. Which scale measures the level of alkalinity and acidity?
5. Who did Jackie Kennedy marry in 1968?
6. Where will you return to if you throw a coin into the Trevi Fountain?
7. What in your body are affected by phlebitis?
8. In which Open did Ballestero's win his first pro tournament, in 1974?
9. Whose hits include Again and That's the Way Love Goes ?
10. Which TV character lived on Scatterbrook Farm?
11. Which High Street travel agent's devised the holiday package tour?
12. In finance what is a PEP?
13. Which store chain claims they are "never knowingly undersold"?
14. What does the Greek odeon mean?
15. If you were using a tambour, what needlecraft would you be doing?
16. What is the currency of Greece?
17. Which TV detective was played by George Peppard?
18. In which century was cockfighting banned?
19. Which supermarket chain paid for the new National Gallery wing opened in 1991?
20. Cars with the international vehicle registration ET come from where?
21. Who started the Habitat chain of shops in 1964?
22. Who is smaller Janet Street Porter or Naomi Campbell?
23. Edmonton is the capital of which Canadian province?
24. Who played Shirley Valentine in the film?
25. What is the white of an egg called as an alternative to albumen?
26. Which 007 actor was also TV's Remington Steele?
27. The Ashanti tribe live in which African country?
28. Whose hits include Finally and We Got a Love Thing?
29. What is held annually in London in Ranelagh Gardens?
30. Where was tennis star Monica Seles playing when she was stabbed?

Quiz 192 TV Times 5

Answers - see page 432

LEVEL 2

1   Which show provided BBC sales with a third of their 1997 profits?
2   Which woman writer created the character Jane Tennison?
3   Which ex Home Secretary was born the same day as ex Goodie Bill Oddie?
4   What is Dr Ross's first name in ER?
5   In which decade was Parliament first televised?
6   Which daughter of a famous footballer presented On The Ball with Barry Venison?
7   Which rugby player joined Ulrika Jonsson as a Gladiators presenter?
8   Who played Owen Springer in Reckless?
9   Which priest replaced Father Peter in Ballykissangel?
10 Who presents the rural life show Countryfile?
11 On GMTV where did Mark Freden regularly report from?
12 Which superstar did Matthew Corbett abandon finally in 1998?
13 Which role did Denise Robertson have on This Morning?
14 Who is the male wine expert on Food and Drink?
15 Who was the blonde captain on Shooting Stars?
16 How is TV presenter Leslie Heseltine better known?
17 How many letter make up the conundrum in Countdown?
18 What is Channel 5's daily quiz for older contestants called?
19 Who contracted amoebic dysentery while making a Holiday show with her daughter?
20 Frasier was a spin off from which series?
21 Who plays Ally McBeal?
22 How many points do you get for a starter in University Challenge?
23 To whom did The Duchess of York dedicate the first of her Sky chat shows in October 1998?
24 On which show did Tommy Walsh and Charlie Dimmock find fame?
25 For which sport did Frank Bough win an Oxbridge blue?
26 Who did David Dimbleby replace on Question Time?
27 Who wrote the acclaimed series of monologues Talking Heads?
28 Who played Darcy in Pride and Prejudice?
29 Which fivesome helped launch Channel 5?
30 Jimmy Savile received an honorary doctorate from which university?

Answers

Pot Luck 86 (see Quiz 193)

1 Michael Praed. 2 Leprosy. 3 Sugar Candy. 4 Mustard. 5 Tam O'Shanter. 6 On the Moon. 7 Peach & plum. 8 Chromium. 9 The bones. 10 An oak tree. 11 Aspirin. 12 Your Eminence. 13 1983. 14 Vicky MacDonald. 15 Blackcurrant. 16 Belisha Beacon. 17 Arizona. 18 Daphne du Maurier. 19 Leo Sayer. 20 The Netherlands. 21 1/10th. 22 Aestivation. 23 88. 24 Niamh Kavanagh. 25 A flower. 26 Oxo. 27 The brain. 28 Cannon. 29 Bathsheba. 30 J. B. Priestley.

1 Whose funeral in Milan in 1997 was attended by Elton John and Naomi Campbell?
2 Which Frenchman was the first to launch menswear and ready to wear collections?
3 How is the former Lady Elizabeth Bowes-Lyon better known?
4 What is the first name of Mrs William Hague?
5 Which oil billionaire founded the world's highest funded art gallery?
6 Which famous American enrolled her baby daughter for Cheltenham Ladies College in September 1998?
7 What is John and Norma Major's daughter called?
8 Where did Diana make a fund raising trip to with Jemima Khan?
9 Chiang Ching was the third wife of which political leader?
10 Linda Tripp was the confidante of which famous name?
11 Which singer has a son called Otis after Otis Redding?
12 Which fashion designer launched a perfume called Boudoir?
13 According to the Guiness Book of Records who is the most mentioned woman on the Internet?
14 Who is Nanette Newman's famous TV presenter daughter?
15 What did David Frost's and Virginia Wade's father have in common?
16 Whose first names are Anthony Charles Lynton?
17 Which playwright is Maureen Lipman's husband?
18 Which Rolling Stone bought, and died at A.A. Milne's house?
19 Who was described in Blackwell's Worst Dressed list as 'the bare toed terror of London town'?
20 What is Margaret Thatcher's journalist daughter called?
21 At which sport did Pope John Paul II excel in his youth?
22 What is the nationality of ex UN secretary Boutros Boutros-Ghali?
23 Which name is shared by the Duchess of York's sister and one of Princess Diana's sisters?
24 Who married millionaire hairdresser Stephen Way in 1998?
25 Who was the wife of Ferdinand Marcos at the time of his death?
26 What relation was Cherie Blair to Pat Phoenix, who played Elsie Tanner in Coronation Street?
27 What was the first name of Marks of Marks & Spencer?
28 What links Nataraja in Hinduism and performer Michael Flatley?
29 Who was the first basketball player to declare he was HIV positive?
30 What is Red or Dead?

Answers

Pot Luck 85 (see Quiz 190)
1 Porcelain. 2 Partridges. 3 Tuscany. 4 pH scale. 5 Aristotle Onassis. 6 Rome. 7 Veins. 8 Dutch. 9 Janet Jackson. 10 Worzel Gummidge. 11 Thomas Cook. 12 Personal Equity Plan. 13 John Lewis Partnership. 14 Theatre. 15 Embroidery. 16 Drachma. 17 Banacek. 18 19th century. 19 Sainsbury's. 20 Egypt. 21 Terence Conran. 22 Naomi Campbell. 23 Alberta. 24 Pauline Collins. 25 Glair. 26 Pierce Brosnan. 27 Ghana. 28 Ce Ce Peniston. 29 Chelsea Flower Show. 30 Hamburg.

LEVEL 2

1 Which actor played both Prince of Moldavia and Robin Hood on TV?
2 What did Robert the Bruce die of?
3 What type of kisses did Mac and Katie Kissoon sing about?
4 Dijon is famous for which condiment?
5 Which Robbie Burns hero gave his name to a flat cap?
6 Where is the Bay of Rainbows?
7 A nectarine is a cross between which two fruits?
8 What makes stainless steel stainless?
9 What is affected by osteomyelitis?
10 What is Charles II said to have hidden in after the Battle of Worcester?
11 What is the common name for the medication acetylsalicylic acid?
12 How is a Cardinal addressed?
13 When was the wearing of seat belts in the front of a car made compulsory?
14 In Coronation Street who was Alec Gilroy's grand daughter?
15 Which fruit is in creme de cassis?
16 Which beacon was named after a 1930s Minister of Transport?
17 The Painted Desert is in which American state?
18 Who wrote My Cousin Rachel and Frenchman's Creek?
19 Whose hits include Moonlighting and More Than I Can Say?
20 Queen Juliana abdicated from which country's throne in 1980?
21 What fraction is a cable of a nautical mile?
22 What is the opposite of hibernation?
23 How many keys does a normal piano have?
24 Which female Irish singer won the Eurovision Song Contest with In Your Eyes?
25 What is a corn-cockle?
26 What did Mary Holland advertise on TV for eighteen years?
27 Which part of the body uses forty per cent of the oxygen in blood?
28 Which corpulent TV detective was played by William Conrad?
29 Who was the mother of King Solomon?
30 Who wrote The Good Companions?

LEVEL 2

1 Where are the headquarters of the European Space Agency?
2 Which word describes a body in free fall in space?
3 Which planet has the satellite Europa?
4 Which space station is named after the Russian word for 'peace'?
5 Ranger and Surveyor probes preceded exploration of where?
6 What name is given to a site for watching astronomical phenomena?
7 In which decade was Sputnik 1 launched?
8 Saturn rockets were developed for which moon programme?
9 Who was Soyuz TM-12's British passenger in 1991?
10 The first non-stop transatlantic flight was between which two countries?
11 What does a space shuttle land on when it returns to Earth?
12 What is the Oort cloud made out of?
13 Which Space Agency built Ariane?
14 Which communications satellite was the first to relay live TV transmissions?
15 Which rockets shared their name with the giant children of Uranus and Gaia in Greek myth ?
16 Which part of the moon did Armstrong first walk on?
17 Which of our planets is nearest the end of the alphabet?
18 Claudie Andre-Deshays was the first woman in space from which country?
19 Whose spacecraft was Vostok 1?
20 After retiring as an astronaut John Glenn followed a career in what?
21 Which clouds are formed highest above the ground?
22 How was Michael Collins a pioneer of lunar flight?
23 What is the largest planet in the solar system?
24 Phobos is a moon of which planet?
25 What was Skylab?
26 Which pioneering spacecraft was first launched in April 1981?
27 What is Jupiter's red spot made from?
28 Which country launched the first space probe in 1959?
29 Which constellation is known as The Hunter?
30 Which is larger, Mars or Earth?

1   In what capacity did Boy George work for the RSC?
2   Which king unveiled the Victoria memorial?
3   What is made by a testator?
4   Who telephoned Neil Armstrong during his first moon walk?
5   Which novelist had three novels adapted by Alfred Hitchcock to films?
6   Which wine growing region is divided into Baja, Alta and Alavesa?
7   What does fibrin cause to happen to blood?
8   Did Buddy Holly die in 1956, 1959 or 1961?
9   Which Florida city was the setting for Burt Reynolds' Bandits?
10 Which director appeared in The Blues Brothers?
11 In which century was the Taj Mahal constructed?
12 A Bordelaise sauce is flavoured by which vegetable?
13 Ben Nevis is in which mountain range?
14 Where would you probably be looking at a Snellen Chart?
15 In Bingo, what are numbers ending in zero called?
16 What do Sunderland and Benfica soccer clubs share?
17 Who is the Patron Saint of Venice?
18 What are Mycerinus and Cheprun the second two greatest of?
19 What would you be eating if you ate a Spanish chorizo?
20 Which scientist first discovered the composition of air?
21 Which ex Yorkshire cricketer was born on the same day as Manfred Mann?
22 Which letter and number represent the vitamin riboflavin?
23 Derby, Pelham and Russell have all been what?
24 Who was John the Baptist's father?
25 In 1909 what were imprisoned suffragettes forced to do?
26 Euston became Britain's first railway station to have what in 1848?
27 In 1921 which political party burnt down Dublin's Custom House?
28 Which part of your body is protected by puttees?
29 Which river flows through six different European countries?
30 What is the main ingredient in an Indian raita?

Answers

Science: Space (see Quiz 194)

1 Paris. 2 Weightless. 3 Jupiter. 4 Mir. 5 The Moon. 6 Observatory.
7 50s. 8 Apollo. 9 Helen Sharman. 10 Canada & Ireland. 11 Runway.
12 Comets. 13 European. 14 Telstar. 15 Titan. 16 Sea of Tranquillity.
17 Venus. 18 France. 19 Yuri Gagarin. 20 Politics. 21 Cirrus. 22 He didn't
walk on the moon on the first lunar flight. 23 Jupiter. 24 Mars. 25 Space
station. 26 Space shuttle. 27 Gases.. 28 USSR. 29 Orion. 30 Earth.

LEVEL 2

1 Which opera venue is near Lewes?
2 Sir John Barbirolli was conductor of which orchestra at the time of his death?
3 If a sonata is for instruments what is a cantata written for?
4 Which London theatre was the home of Gilbert & Sullivan operas?
5 Sadler's Wells theatre is famous for which performing arts?
6 Equity in the USA deals only with performers where?
7 Wayne Sleep was principal dancer with which ballet company?
8 What do you press with the right hand on an accordion?
9 Which of the Three Tenors played the title role in the film version of Otello in 1986?
10 How many strings are there on a double bass?
11 Richard Eyre replaced Peter Hall as artistic director at which London theatre?
12 What were all Joseph Grimaldi's clowns called?
13 What shape is the sound box on a balalaika?
14 Which male voice is between bass and tenor?
15 Where is an annual Fringe Festival held?
16 In which US city was the Actors Studio founded?
17 What is the official name of London's Drury Lane theatre?
18 Miles Davis is famous for playing which musical instrument?
19 Which king did Handel write The Water Music for?
20 Whose 1986 recording of Vivaldi's The Four Seasons sold over a million copies?
21 What was Paul McCartney's first classical oratorio?
22 An anthem is usually accompanied by which musical instrument?
23 Which mime artist created the clown-harlequin Bip?
24 Who is The Violinist?
25 Which theatre near Blackfriars was London's first new theatre in 300 years when opened in 1959?
26 What was the slogan of London's Windmill Theatre?
27 Which musical instruments did Leo Fender create?
28 What was the first black-owned record company in the USA?
29 Who has written more plays, Shakespeare or Ayckbourn?
30 Alan Bleasdale hails from which city?

1 Hemel Hempstead and St Albans are in which county?
2 Who would use a quern?
3 Who played the title role in the film The Wizard of Oz?
4 What does the acronym TESSA stand for?
5 The Spanish Steps are in which European city?
6 Cars with the international vehicle registration CDN come from where?
7 Which zany comedian devised the TV show It's A Square World?
8 Which Russian sounding horse won the 2000 Guineas, St Leger and the Derby in 1970?
9 What kind of a plant is fescue?
10 Who had hits with Swords of a Thousand Men and Who Killed Bambi?
11 What type of sea creature is a brittle star?
12 Musically which note is half the value of a crotchet?
13 Murder At The... where was Miss Marple's first appearance?
14 Who was Glenn Hoddle named after?
15 Which writer Anthony created the county of Barsetshire?
16 What is the largest island in Asia?
17 Which part of an elephant has 40,000 muscles?
18 Who played the lead role in the film The Prime Of Miss Jean Brodie?
19 Which type of sugar is found in milk?
20 What word can describe a lucky chance and the hook of an anchor?
21 Which female vocalist was known as 'The Forces Sweetheart'?
22 Which novel preceded Good Wives?
23 Which pop star married Bianca de Macias in May 1971?
24 Which breed of dog were originally bred to hunt badgers?
25 Herod the Great ruled which kingdom?
26 Which Prince's childhood nickname was JAWS?
27 In Coronation Street who was Reg Holdsworth's mother-in-law?
28 Who had hits with Whodunnit and More Than A Woman?
29 What is the English equivalent of a Scottish Advocate?
30 What shape is a dish called a coquille?

Answers

Performing Arts (see Quiz 196)
1 Glyndebourne. 2 Halle. 3 Voices. 4 Savoy. 5 Opera and ballet.
6 Theatre. 7 Royal Ballet. 8 Piano-style keyboard. 9 Placido Domingo.
10 Four. 11 National. 12 Joey. 13 Triangular. 14 Baritone.
15 Edinburgh. 16 New York. 17 Theatre Royal. 18 Trumpet. 19 George I.
20 Nigel Kennedy. 21 Liverpool Oratorio. 22 Organ. 23 Marcel Marceau.
24 Vanessa Mae. 25 Mermaid. 26 We never closed. 27 Electric guitars.
28 Tamla Motown. 29 Ayckbourn. 30 Liverpool.

LEVEL 2

1   Who had a hit in 1972 with A Thing Called Love?
2   Which hit in letters followed Stand by Your Man for Tammy Wynette?
3   Which group had a No 1 hit in 1976 with Mississippi?
4   Which famous country singer was kidnapped in 1979?
5   Whose song was a No. 1 for John Denver in 1974?
6   Which Patsy Cline hit was covered by Julio Iglesias in 1994?
7   In which year was Achey Breaky Heart a hit for Billy Ray Cyrus?
8   Who had a No 11 UK hit with Talking In Your Sleep in 1978?
9   Hiram Williams is the real name of which singer?
10 Which opera singer joined John Denver to record Perhaps Love?
11 What surname links 70s star Daniel and 50s star Pat?
12 Which Kris wrote Help Me Make It Through the Night?
13 Who had a hit in the summer of 1998 with How Do I?
14 Who wrote the autobiography Coal Miner's Daughter?
15 Who joined Kenny Rogers on the No 7 hit Islands In The Stream?
16 What is Reba McEntire's real name?
17 Which specialist type of singing links Frank Ifield and Slim Whitman?
18 Who duetted with Mark Knopfler on the album Neck and Neck?
19 In the No 1, which drums were heard by Jim Reeves?
20 Who sang All I Have To Do Is Dream with Bobbie Gentry in 1969?
21 Who had a backing band called the Waylors?
22 What is the name of the theme park owned by Dolly Parton?
23 George Jones' 1975 hit The Battle told of the split from his wife. Who was she?
24 Which Banks were a hit in 1971 for Olivia Newton-John?
25 Which song was a No 2 UK hit for Tammy Wynette and KLF in 1991?
26 Who wrote the classic song Crazy?
27 Who formed the Trio with Dolly Parton and Linda Ronstadt?
28 Who took Cotton Eye Joe to No 1 in 1994?
29 Which No 9 for Elvis was a No 10 for Carl Perkins in 1956?
30 Which 'modern girl' joined Kenny Rogers on We've Got Tonight ?

1 What was the name of Kate Winslet's character in Titanic?
2 What is the relationship between Prince Edward and Lord Lindley?
3 Which Caribbean country won the 1992 Olympic Gold Medal for baseball?
4 What is kelp?
5 Who had hits with Fox On The Run and Wig-Wam Bam?
6 What name is an African lake, a station and a former Queen?
7 What type of vessel was the Torrey Canyon?
8 What is the name of the most famous theatre in London's Drury Lane?
9 What is the more common name for toxaemia?
10 Which members of the big cat family collect in a leap?
11 Who preceded Harold Macmillan as Prime Minister?
12 In the Shakespeare play who killed Macbeth?
13 The Christian name George lends itself to which part of a plane?
14 Newmarket and Ipswich are both in which county?
15 Reflexology treats your body through what?
16 What can be a short jacket and a dance?
17 What are auctioned at Tattersalls?
18 Who was Phileas Fogg's companion in Around the World in 80 Days?
19 Which French-Canadian became Canadian Prime Minister in 1968?
20 Archibald Leach born in Bristol became which Hollywood star?
21 In which decade did John Wayne die?
22 Which novel was set in the magical kingdom of Narnia?
23 Which part of your body would interest a rhinologist?
24 In 1926 what was held for the first time at Brooklands?
25 Mesopotamia was the ancient name for which modern day country?
26 Who had hits with Alright and Going Out in '95 and '96?
27 Whose report in the 1940s was vital in setting up the welfare state?
28 Which Stevie Wonder No 1 was in the film The Woman In Red?
29 What type of animal is a Lippizaner?
30 Which digit is your pollex?

1 Which Australian was the first to score 60 tries in international rugby?

2 Who will play the opening match at the new Millennium Stadium for the 1999 World Cup?

3 Who was the first English player to play in 50 internationals?

4 Which country in 1995 asked to increase the number of teams in the Five Nations Cup?

5 Which colours do Bath play in?

6 Which Welsh Union player was a regular captain on A Question of Sport?

7 In which part of London did the London Bronco's start out?

8 Which TV channel sponsored a Floodlit Rugby League Trophy?

9 For which side did Brian Bevan score 740 tries in 620 matches?

10 What were Bradford before they were Bulls?

11 Who retired as Scottish captain after the 1995 World Cup?

12 Who was Wigan's leading try scorer in the 1994/5 season?

13 Where would you watch Rhinos playing rugby?

14 Which Harlequins hooker was nicknamed 'Pitbull'?

15 Which international side has the shortest name?

16 Who are the two sides in the Varsity Match?

17 Which rugby team plays its home games at Welford Road?

18 Who was leading try scorer in the 1995 rugby union World Cup?

19 In 1998 what colour cards were substituted for yellow ones?

20 Who joined Leeds in 1991 after playing on the other side of the Pennines since 1984?

21 What did Bath Football Club change its name to in the mid 90s?

22 Who was the first non-white Springbok, before the end of apartheid?

23 Which rugby side added Warriors to its name?

24 In which decade was Rugby Union last played in the Olympics?

25 How old was Will Carling when he was first made England Captain?

26 Who played a record breaking 69 times at fly half for England between 1985 and 1995?

27 In 1980 who led England to their first Grand Slam in 23 years?

28 Where is the annual Varsity match played?

29 How many years had Wigan's unbeaten run in the FA Challenge Cup lasted when it ended in 1996?

30 Who did Martin Offiah play for in his first years as a League player?

Quiz 201 Pot Luck 90

LEVEL 2

1 Where in your body is your scapula?
2 Canterbury stands on which river?
3 Who had hits with God Save The Queen and C'Mon Everybody?
4 Sebastian Coe became MP for which constituency in 1992?
5 Which former colony was called the jewel in Queen Victoria's crown?
6 What was the sport of Karen Briggs and Nicola Fairbrother?
7 Which Henry became King of England in 1100?
8 In the film Mary Poppins, Mary said she would stay until what changed?
9 Which Treaty on European Union was signed in December 1991?
10 Which character is played by Derek Fowlds in Heartbeat?
11 What was the former name of Belize?
12 Which actor married Melanie Griffith twice?
13 What was Ffion Hague's maiden name?
14 Which River does Leicester stand on?
15 What is decathlon champion Daley Thompson's first name?
16 Which Vera Lynn song was a No 1 UK hit in 1954?
17 In finance what is an ISA?
18 Who was given Blenheim Palace as a reward for his military service?
19 In The Bible, who denied Jesus three times before the cock crowed twice?
20 A Turk's Head is a type of what?
21 Alphabetically which chemical element is the last?
22 Which European capital was considered cleanest in a 1995 survey?
23 What is a frigatoon?
24 'The Garden of the Gods' is in which American state?
25 Who had hits with Lay Your Love On Me and Some Girls?
26 Which castle was bought by the Queen Mother in 1952?
27 Which TV series has characters called Gracie, Sicknote and George?
28 What was King Charles II's nickname?
29 Kings Lynn and Norwich are both in which county?
30 Which actor links Bobby Ewing to The Man From Atlantis?

1   What was the first film in which Clint Eastwood starred as 'The man with no name'?
2   Who played the sadistic sheriff in Eastwood's Unforgiven?
3   Which actor's films include Big Jim McLain, McLintock and McQ?
4   Which star of Maverick played Brett Maverick in the TV series?
5   Which Oscar did Kevin Costner win for Dances With Wolves?
6   What is the name of the original tale that the Magificent Seven is based on?
7   What weather feature was in the title of the song from Butch Cassidy won an Oscar?
8   Who was the star of Jeremiah Johnson?
9   Which comedy actor starred in the comedy western The Paleface?
10 Who starred with brother Charlie Sheen in Young Guns?
11 Who was the title character in the surreal western The Seven Faces of Dr. Lao?
12 Who played the woman poker player in Maverick?
13 Which actor was The Bad?
14 Which Back to the Future film returns to the Wild West?
15 In which musical western does the song Wandrin' Star appear?
16 Which Hollywood legend was the narrator in How The West Was Won?
17 Which film was originally called Per un Pugno di Dollari?
18 Which country singer was in True Grit?
19 Which son of a M*A*S*H star appeared in Young Guns II?
20 Who did John Wayne play in The Alamo?
21 Clint Eastwood became mayor of which town?
22 Which 1985 film was a revised remake of the classic Shane?
23 Where is the village where the action of The Magnificent Seven centres?
24 Where was The Good, the Bad and the Ugly made?
25 What was the name of Mel Brooks' spoof western?
26 Which English comic appeared in Desperado?
27 Which 80s teenage western starred actors known as the Brat Pack?
28 What was Tonto's horse called?
29 Who was Gene Autry's most famous horse?
30 Traditionally, what colour is the western hero's hat?

Quiz 203 TV Times 6

LEVEL 2

1 Men Behaving Badly's Leslie Ash was born the same day as which Prince?
2 Who presents Channel 4's Fifteen To One?
3 Alice Beer first found fame on which show?
4 Which show was first broadcast on Friday 9th December 1960?
5 Which Cardiac Arrest star also starred in Friends?
6 What was the lawyer played by Daniela Nardini in This Life called?
7 Which series featured celebs returning to a previous vacation destination?
8 Which children's show has the theme music Barnacle Bill?
9 Whose last series was Paradise Gardens?
10 In which city did the docu soap Hotel take place?
11 Which comedy duo are famous for their head-to-head discussions?
12 In which city did lifeguard Mitch Buchanan work?
13 Who was the female team captain in the 90s Call My Bluff?
14 What did the BBC's Breakfast Time change its name to?
15 Fully Booked was first on which channel?
16 Who moved to GMTV after his The Time The Place was axed?
17 Which voice of motor racing moved to ITV to cover the sport?
18 In which show might a contestant ask "Could I have a P please, Bob?"
19 Who is Robbie Coltrane's son Spencer named after?
20 Which redhead assists Rolf Harris at the Animal Hospital?
21 What was the name of the spotty teenager played by Harry Enfield?
22 Presenter Suzanne Dando represented Great Britain at which sport?
23 Which series centred on Skeldale House?
24 Who has hosted Antiques Roadshow through most of the 90s?
25 Who tried to emulate Phileas Fogg in a 1989 documentary?
26 Who did Roseanne offer a million dollars to appear on her talk show in October 1998?
27 Which Lancashire soccer side does Jim Bowen support?
28 Which store was the subject of The Shop?
29 How much are the ingredients worth on Ready Steady Cook?
30 What did Susan Brookes do on This Morning?

LEVEL 2

1 Which Queen wrote the Casket Letters?
2 Which former Take That star had Child at No 3 in 1996?
3 What can be metric royal, metric demy and metric crown?
4 In which TV series was the character 'Boss Hogg'?
5 Which film star married Prince Aly Khan?
6 Which almond cake is traditionally made for Mothering Sunday?
7 Who had hits with We Are Glass and Cars ?
8 What would an Australian call trousers?
9 Which actress had lead roles in the films Out of Africa and Silkwood?
10 Which two European languages are spoken in Madagascar?
11 Which country has the shortest coastline in the world?
12 What were the giant insects in the science fiction film Them?
13 Which famous TV cook took his show Around Britain?
14 During which war does Norman Mailer's The Naked and the Dead take place?
15 Aylesbury and Milton Keynes are both in which county?
16 Which actress is Jack Davenport's mother?
17 Which animal was used by Jenner to develop the vaccine against smallpox?
18 What is a davenport?
19 Which singer starred alongside Kyle McLachlan in Dune?
20 Who composed the music for The Good, the Bad and the Ugly?
21 Who had hits with Blue Monday and World In Motion?
22 What kind of musical instrument was a kit?
23 Which former tennis player bought Hull FC?
24 Which John Carpenter film set in the antarctic starred Kurt Russell?
25 Name the first yacht to win the America's Cup?
26 Which singing sisters were called Patti, Laverne and Maxine?
27 In which country are the guerrilla group the Tamil Tigers?
28 What name is given to the principal female singer in an opera?
29 The dish Eggs Florentine contains which vegetable?
30 Which town was Barbara Castle's parliamentary constituency?

Answers

World Tour (see Quiz 205)
1 Atlantic. 2 Las Vegas. 3 Broadway. 4 Inuit (Eskimos). 5 Cape of Good Hope. 6 Wind. 7 Honshu. 8 Australia. 9 Washington. 10 K2.
11 Okovango. 12 Indian. 13 Hawaii. 14 China. 15 Namibia. 16 Gobi.
17 Dow Jones. 18 Eskimo. 19 Michigan. 20 Zambia and Zimbabwe.
21 Trinidad. 22 French. 23 Canaries. 24 North coast of Africa.
25 Manhattan. 26 Tip of South America. 27 Greenland. 28 Kilimanjaro.
29 Israel. 30 Pakistan & Afghanistan.

1 The Sargasso Sea is part of which ocean?
2 Which US city's name means 'The Fields'?
3 How is New York's 'Great White Way' also known?
4 Which Canadians speak Inuktitut?
5 Which Cape was originally called the Cape of Storms?
6 In America what type of natural phenomenon is a Chinook?
7 What is the principal island of Japan?
8 Where is the town of Kurri Kurri?
9 Where is the HQ of the International Monetary Fund?
10 By which abbreviation is the mountain Chogori known?
11 What is the only permanent river in the Kalahari desert?
12 Which Ocean's deepest point is the Java Trench?
13 Where would you be if someone put a lei round your neck?
14 Where is the world's longest canal?
15 Afrikaans is the official language of which country in addition to South Africa?
16 In which desert is the Bactrian camel found?
17 What is the name of the index on the New York Stock Exchange?
18 Which group of people have a name meaning 'eater of raw meat'?
19 Which is the only Great Lake wholly in the USA?
20 The Kariba Dam is on the border of which two countries?
21 Calypso is the traditional song form of which Caribbean island?
22 Which European language is spoken in Chad?
23 Las Palmas is in which island group?
24 Approximately where was Carthage to be found?
25 Wall Street and Broadway lie on which island?
26 Where is the Magellan Strait?
27 What is the largest island between the North Atlantic and the Arctic?
28 What is Africa's highest volcano?
29 Where is there a Parliament called the Knesset?
30 Which two countries does the Khyber Pass separate?

Quiz 205 Pot Luck 92

Answers - see page 446

LEVEL 2

1 What is saxifrage?
2 Family wise what do Henry Cooper and Carol Thatcher have in common?
3 Who hoisted himself onto Sinbad the Sailor's shoulders?
4 How much are you paid if you hold an honorary post?
5 Which actor played the leading role in the film Brothers In Law?
6 What can be a five card game, a smooth, woolly surface or a sleep?
7 Which club did Will Carling play for?
8 Which sport is Britain's Yvonne MacGregor associated with?
9 Whose music albums have included An Innocent Man?
10 'Englander' is an anagram of which country?
11 Which actress played Michael Douglas's wife in Fatal Attraction?
12 What is a melodeon?
13 Which animal family are impala, eland and dik-dik all from?
14 Who would have been granted a Ticket of Leave?
15 In TV's Upstairs Downstairs what was the name of the cook?
16 Whose hits include Dancin' On the Ceiling and Do It To Me?
17 Which stone is inscribed "Cormac McCarthy fortis me fieri fecit AD 1446"?
18 Which actor played the leading role in the TV drama Shogun?
19 What name is given to withered apples used to make rough cider?
20 Who composed the music for the musical Lady Be Good?
21 What is a grackle?
22 Which building was erected in 1851 for the Great Exhibition?
23 Which children's TV series has included Tucker Jenkins and Zammo?
24 Which Corrie character died with Gilbert and Sullivan playing in his car?
25 Which branch would you hold out to seek peace?
26 Arthur Hastings was the sidekick of which fictional sleuth?
27 Whose hits include Detroit City and Love Me Tonight?
28 The leader of an orchestra plays which instrument?
29 What was Mab's job in fairy folklore?
30 Which actress was left on a desert island in TV's Girl Friday?

1   The Hillsborough Agreement was between which two countries?
2   Where was there a major nuclear leak in the USSR in 1986?
3   Who was the last white President of South Africa, elected in 1989?
4   Which former liberal leader was made speaker of the national assembly of Czechoslovakia in 1989?
5   A fatwa calling for the death of which writer was made by Iran in '89?
6   Who succeeded Callaghan as Labour leader?
7   Who became France's first socialist president in 1981?
8   Who was Argentine President during the Falklands Conflict?
9   Which ex deputy leader of Liverpool Council was expelled form the Labour Party in 1987?
10 Michael Manley became leader of where in 1989?
11 Who owned Rainbow Warrior, sunk by the French in 1985?
12 Vigdis Finnbogadottir became head of state in which country?
13 How many times was Margaret Thatcher elected PM in the 80s?
14 Who was the only woman founder of the SDP?
15 Who was leader of the GLC from 1981-86?
16 What was the Black day of the week of the 1987 stockmarket crash?
17 Who moved from Transport House to Walworth Road in 1980?
18 In which hotel was the Brighton bomb in 1984?
19 Who became President of Serbia in 1986?
20 Most of which Caribbean island's buildings were destroyed by hurricane Hugo in 1989?
21 Who became Egyptian President after Sadat's assassination?
22 What was the name of the scandal over arms for hostages in which Oliver North was implicated?
23 Which Cabinet Minister was leader of Sheffield City Council for most of the 80s?
24 Who did Ronald Reagan defeat to become US President in 1980?
25 Which spin doctor did Neil Kinnock engage to run the 1987 election campaign?
26 In 1989 state schools were allowed to opt out of whose control?
27 Which woman became PM of Pakistan after the death of Zia in a plane crash?
28 Where did the parties of ZANU and ZAPU merge in 1987?
29 In 1986 the pass laws, concerning the carrying of identity documents, were repealed in which country?
30 Which Russian leader introduced the policy of perestroika?

LEVEL 2

1 What type of animal is a Sooty Mangabey?
2 Which drink was advertised as 'drunk for a penny; dead drunk for tuppence'?
3 Who did William III defeat in 1690 at the Battle of the Boyne?
4 Rupert Bear is linked with which newspaper?
5 In Old English which word meant a field?
6 What were the eldest sons of French kings called from the 14th century?
7 Ely stands on which river?
8 Which 60s singer married the designer Jeff Banks?
9 In 1945, who became British Prime Minister?
10 Which plant has a flower called the 'poor man's weather-glass'?
11 Who had hits with The Streak and Misty in the 70s?
12 Who was President of the Philippines from 1965 to 1986?
13 Which Gate is a memorial for British Soldiers who fell at Ypres?
14 Who played Fred Kite in the film I'm Alright, Jack?
15 Which entertainer was married to his manager Cheryl St Clair?
16 Which complaint was the Jacuzzi originally developed to help?
17 What did Anna Karenina throw herself under in the Tolstoy novel?
18 Who wrote Dr Zhivago?
19 In which soap does the Cat & Fiddle rival The Bull?
20 Which comedian was Connie Booth married to?
21 What did people find in the book Lost Horizon?
22 Who preceded Edward VI as Monarch?
23 In the film The Tommy Steele Story who played Tommy Steele?
24 Who finished his radio show with "B.F.N. Bye for now"?
25 Who had hits with The Logical Song and Dreamer?
26 In which year was Lord Mountbatten murdered?
27 What is the start of Psalm 23?
28 Which shaggy horned wild cattle live in the Tibetan mountains?
29 What was a gulag in Russia?
30 In the 1953 film Houdini who played the title role?

Answers

Leisure: Books 2 (see Quiz 209)
1 Oxford. 2 Lake District. 3 Slavery. 4 Dictionary. 5 Jeeves. 6 The Greatest. 7 Lord Peter Wimsey. 8 Black Beauty. 9 Spycatcher. 10 Childcare. 11 Joan Collins. 12 Nigel Lawson. 13 Maeve Binchy. 14 Oranges. 15 Ruth Rendell. 16 Bill Bryson. 17 Agatha Christie. 18 The Godfather. 19 The English Patient. 20 John Le Carre. 21 Schindler's Ark. 22 Marie Stopes. 23 The Odessa File. 24 Edwina Currie. 25 Detective novel. 26 Jeffrey Archer. 27 Wales. 28 A Tale of Two Cities. 29 Exodus. 30 Simenon.

Quiz 209　Leisure: Books 2

LEVEL 2

1　In which university city is the Bodleian Library?
2　In which District did Beatrix Potter live?
3　Uncle Tom's Cabin was a novel which argued against what?
4　In the US what type of book is Webster famous for?
5　Who is the most famous manservant created by P.G.Wodehouse?
6　What was Muhammad Ali's autobiography called?
7　Which Dorothy L Sayers' creation was Harriet Vane's husband?
8　Which children's classic was written to encourage adults to be kinder to horses?
9　Which book by ex intelligence agent Peter Wright, did the British government try to have banned?
10　What was the subject of Benjamin Spock's most famous books?
11　Which soap star wrote Prime Time?
12　Which ex Chancellor of the Exchequer wrote a diet book?
13　Whose first successful novel was Light A Penny Candle?
14　What 'Are Not the Only Fruit' according to Jeanette Winterson?
15　Who wrote the detective novel Road Rage?
16　Who wrote A Walk in the Woods?
17　The Murder of Roger Ackroyd was an early novel by whom?
18　Which is Mario Puzo's most famous novel, first published in 1969?
19　Which Michael Ondaatje book was made into an Oscar winning film with Ralph Fiennes?
20　Who created George Smiley?
21　Which was the first Thomas Keneally book to win the Booker Prize?
22　Which birth control campaigner wrote the book Married Love?
23　What was Frederick Forsyth's follow up to The Day of the Jackal?
24　Which ex MP's first novel was A Parliamentary Affair?
25　The Woman in White is the first novel of what type in English?
26　Whose Not a Penny More, Not a Penny Less was written to clear bankruptcy debts?
27　In Colin Dexter's books where does Lewis come from?
28　Which Dickens' novel is about the French Revolution?
29　What is the second book of the Old Testament?
30　Which Georges wrote over a hundred novels featuring Jules Maigret?

LEVEL 2

1 What did MGM stand for?

2 What colour is puce?

3 What is the French equivalent of the Italian race Giro D'Italia?

4 Who was the first presenter of the TV series Tomorrow's World?

5 Which cartoon character was the 'fastest mouse in Mexico'?

6 Who had 90s No 1 hits with The Power and Rhythm Is A Dancer?

7 Which US state is the second smallest?

8 According to the saying, who rush in where angels fear to tread?

9 What is Blue Vinney?

10 Who wrote Five Children and It and Wet Magic?

11 Which terrier is the largest of the breed?

12 Who was the head of the German SS?

13 What is studied by a haematologist?

14 Which county is Morganwg Ganol in Welsh?

15 What type of creature is a turnstone?

16 Which country from 1867-1914 had a governor called The Khedive?

17 In the film The Great Escape which actor played the Forger?

18 Which Egyptian President was assassinated in 1981?

19 In the TV series To The Manor Born what was the name of the butler?

20 What is Paddy Ashdown's first Christian name?

21 Who had hits with Kiss from a Rose and Crazy?

22 The town of Newcastle is in which Australian state?

23 What was Marc Bolan's real name?

24 What type of food is a bullace?

25 What is a snake's cast off skin called?

26 The holiday camp Maplins featured in which TV series?

27 Which TV Arts presenter was Director General of the BBC from 1968-75?

28 What is mineral water mixed with quinine called?

29 Cars with the international vehicle registration CDN come from where?

30 What was sought by Jason and the Argonauts?

Answers

Pop Music: Groups (see Quiz 211)
1 The Blue Flames. 2 Swedish. 3 Two. 4 Summer Love. 5 The News.
6 Chairmen of the Board. 7 Our eyes. 8 In Perfect Harmony. 9 Vic Reeves.
10 Def Leppard. 11 Live Forever. 12 Good Vibrations. 13 New York.
14 Three Lions. 15 Cream. 16 Rainbow. 17 California. 18 All Day and All
of the Night. 19 Computer Love/The Model. 20 To Trancentral. 21 Bread.
22 Jake. 23 The Bangles. 24 Clannad. 25 Moving On Up. 26 My Perfect
Cousin. 27 Elkie Brooks. 28 Heaven 17. 29 Cosmic Girl. 30 Las Vegas.

1   What was the name of Georgie Fame's backing group?
2   What nationality were All That She Wants group Ace of Base?
3   How many Princes were in the Spin Doctors UK No 3 hit?
4   What Sensation were the Bay City Rollers singing about in 1974?
5   Huey Lewis was vocalist for which group?
6   Which Company band had a hit with Give Me Just A Little More Time?
7   What did Go West close in their No 5 from 1985?
8   What followed in brackets on I'd Like To Teach the World to Sing?
9   Who did the Wonder Stuff serve as backing group for?
10 Which heavy band took When Love and Hate Collide to No 2?
11 What was Oasis' first UK Top Ten single?
12 What was The Beach Boys' first UK No 1?
13 In Which American city was the Pogues Fairytale?
14 Which Lightning Seeds No 1 was the official song of the England Football
    Team in 1996?
15 Ginger, Jack and Eric formed which trio?
16 Which British group had a No 3 hit with I Surrender in 1981?
17 Which Hotel was visited by the Eagles in 1977?
18 What part of the day took the Stranglers to No 7 in 1988?
19 In 1982, what was the name of the first UK No 1 by a German group?
20 Which Last Train did KLF catch in their No 2 UK hit in 1991?
21 Singer/ songwriter David Gates led which group?
22 Who was the brother in the title of a track by Free from 1970?
23 Which girl band had hits with Manic Monday and Walk Like An Egyptian?
24 Which Irish group had a No 5 hit with the Theme from Harry's Game?
25 What action were M People doing in their No 2 UK hit from 1993?
26 What relative was Perfect according to the hit by the Undertones?
27 Who was the female artist in Vinegar Joe?
28 Which group had hits in '83 with Temptation and Come Live With Me?
29 What sort of girl took Jamiroquai to No 6 in 1996?
30 Where was ZZ Top on the No 10 hit Viva?

Quiz 212 Pot Luck 95

Answers - see page 452

LEVEL 2

1   Who was the first Briton to hold a world javelin record?
2   Who performed and wrote the theme for Ghostbusters?
3   How many players are there in a Canadian football team?
4   Chester Whites, Durocs and Hampshire are all types of what animal?
5   What is killed by an analgesic?
6   The Dufourspitze is the highest mountain where?
7   When do ducks always lay their eggs?
8   Which Laura had a hit with Gloria?
9   Who preceded Corazon Aquino as President of the Philippines?
10   Which test would you be taking if you underwent a polygraph test?
11   Which American city's football team is called the Bears?
12   Which vitamin deficiency causes rickets?
13   Which suspension bridge crosses the River Avon?
14   Which volcano erupted in 1883 and lies between Java and Sumatra?
15   What is the vocal tinkling sound made by a deer called?
16   Which sea surrounds Heligoland?
17   How many inches above grass should the top of a croquet hoop be?
18   The pituitary gland controls the production of what in the body?
19   Which prefix is a tenth in the metric system?
20   How many pounds does the Olympic hammer weigh?
21   What was the name of the Boswell's daughter in Bread?
22   What was a Minster originally attached to?
23   What is the popular name for the wood-hyacinth?
24   Where is Britain's National Horseracing Museum?
25   Who did James Earl Ray assassinate?
26   Who was the only female in Edward Heath's first cabinet?
27   Which fault line is San Francisco on?
28   Who won 100m gold at the 1988 Olympics after Ben Johnson's disqualification?
29   Where was the terrorist group ETA mainly active?
30   Who was called the Father of Medicine?

Answers

Sport: Who's Who? (see Quiz 213)
1 Sonny Liston. 2 Natalie Tauziat. 3 Rocky Marciano. 4 Al Joyner. 5 Joe DiMaggio. 6 Jake La Motta. 7 Silver. 8 Ray Reardon. 9 Boris Becker. 10 Mary Decker Slaney. 11 Italy. 12 Ernie Els. 13 Nick Faldo. 14 Steve Davis. 15 Goran Ivanisevic. 16 Paul Ince. 17 Chris Evert. 18 Davis. 19 Squash. 20 Denise Lewis. 21 Damon Hill. 22 Rocket. 23 John Conteh. 24 Judo. 25 Mike Tyson. 26 Conchita Martinez. 27 Bernard Gallacher. 28 Snooker. 29 Peter Fleming. 30 Nigel Benn.

1   Who did Muhammad Ali beat when he first became World Champion?

2   Who was runner up to Jana Novotna in the Wimbledon final in 1998?

3   Who was the first heavyweight boxing champion to retire undefeated?

4   Who was the late Flo Jo's husband?

5   Which husband of Marilyn Monroe was elected to the Baseball Hall of Fame?

6   Whose life was recorded on film in Raging Bull?

7   What colour individual medal did Sharron Davies win at the Moscow Olympics?

8   Which snooker champion was unkindly nicknamed Dracula?

9   Which German tennis player was born on Billie Jean King's 23rd birthday?

10   Who did Zola Budd trip up at the Los Angeles Olympics in 1984?

11   British born long jumper Fiona May represents which country in international athletics?

12   Which South African golfer's real first name is Theodore?

13   Which golfer split with his coach and his girlfriend in September '98?

14   Who did Stephen Hendry replace as world No 1 in the 1989-90 season?

15   Who is Croatia's No 1 tennis player?

16   Which sometime England captain is a cousin of boxer Nigel Benn?

17   Who lost most Ladies Singles finals at Wimbledon in the 80s?

18   Which surname has been shared by three world snooker champions?

19   Peter Nicol won Commonwealth gold for Scotland in which sport?

20   Who successfully defended her heptathlon title at the 1998 Commonwealth Games?

21   Who won his first Grand Prix since 1996 in Belgium in 1998?

22   Which Gladiator competed in the heptathlon in the 1998 Commonwealth Games?

23   Which Liverpudlian won the WBC Light Heavyweight Title in 1974?

24   Sharron Davies' one time fiancé Neil Adams was an international in which sport?

25   Who replaced Leon Spinks as Heavyweight Champion in 1987?

26   Who defeated Navratilova in the final at her last Wimbledon?

27   Who captained Europe to Ryder Cup success in 1995?

28   Allison Fisher is a former world champion in which sport?

29   Who did John McEnroe win five Wimbledon Doubles titles with?

30   Which boxer is nicknamed 'The Dark Destroyer'?

1 Which Game For a Laugh presenters had the same surname?
2 Who was the subject of The Naked Civil Servant with John Hurt?
3 Which sitcom told of Tooting revolutionary Wolfie?
4 Who found fame as The Saint?
5 Who played Louie de Palma in Taxi?
6 Which spaghetti western star played in Rawhide for six years?
7 Who conducted Eric Morecambe playing Grieg's Piano Concerto?
8 Which reporter found fame during her reporting of the Iranian Embassy siege in 1980?
9 In which weekly drama slot was Cathy Come Home first shown?
10 Before WWII which was the single most watched event on TV?
11 Who was the main character on The Phil Silvers Show?
12 Who became Mrs Clayton Farlow in Dallas?
13 Which series looked back at film clips 25 years old?
14 How were Bruce Wayne and Dick Grayson better known?
15 Which Carry On regular was the star of Bless This House?
16 Who was 'lower class' on The Frost Report after John Cleese and Ronnie Barker?
17 Which soap was originally called The Midland Road?
18 Which famous singer/actor's daughter shot JR?
19 Which Corrie star joined the cast in 1961 as Miss Nugent?
20 What was the surname of Morticia and Gomez?
21 Which area of the country received TV after the area London in 1949?
22 In which sitcom did Richard Beckinsale play Alan Moore?
23 Which series told of the bizarre life of the Clampett family?
24 Which comedian played Colin in Colin's Sandwich?
25 Which show has numbered David Jacobs, Noel Edmonds and Rosemarie Ford among its presenters?
26 What was the BBC's first soap of the 60s?
27 Who was the Scottish undertaker in Dad's Army?
28 The controversial Death of a Princess caused a rift with which country in 1980?
29 Who had a long running TV show before starring in Mary Poppins?
30 Who is the only Corrie star remaining from the original cast?

Quiz 215 Pot Luck 96

Answers - see page 453

LEVEL 2

1   In Cuba what is a habanera?

2   Which black powder is the oldest known explosive?

3   Who condemned Shadrach, Meshach and Abednego to the Fiery Furnace?

4   Which tribe did Sitting Bull belong to?

5   Sam Snead found fame in which sport?

6   Who was king at the time of the Gunpowder Plot?

7   Which musical instrument did Jack Benny play?

8   Which Latin phrase means 'in place of a parent'?

9   Dun Laoghaire is a port and suburb of where?

10   Gerald Durrell was a director of which zoo?

11   Michael Balcon was head of which influential studios?

12   Who wrote A Shropshire Lad?

13   What is the oldest university in the USA?

14   Who was the volt named after?

15   What is the lower house of the US Congress called?

16   Genocide is the destruction of what?

17   In Scandinavian myth what is Gotterdammerung?

18   Which animals' legs did the Griffin have?

19   Which magazine was famous for its nude centrefold?

20   Which director made Blackmail, Britain's first successful talkie?

21   How many tournaments make up tennis's Grand Slam?

22   With which woman aviator did Frederick Noonan perish?

23   In which country was Hitler born?

24   What is a puck made from in ice hockey?

25   On which three metals would you see a hallmark?

26   In modern currency how much is a guinea?

27   What is the Great Australian Bight?

28   Where in London was the Great Exhibition of 1851?

29   What is HRT?

30   Which canal is also called the gut?

1   Which actor is the son of a Poet Laureate?
2   Which 'Chinese Western' actor's real name was Lee Yuen Kam?
3   Which singer and actress was in Dick Tracy?
4   Kenneth Branagh cast which toothy comedian as Yorick in Hamlet?
5   Who played the adult Damien in The Omen films?
6   Which pop wife appeared with Robert Redford, aged four, in The Great Gatsby?
7   Which early screen comedian's real name was Louis Cristillo?
8   Who played Cruella de Vil's sidekick Jasper in 101 Dalmatians?
9   Who beat Meryl Streep for the lead role in The Horse Whisperer?
10 Which Glaswegian played a gangster in Goldeneye?
11 Which serious actress played comedy opposite Schwarzenegger in Junior?
12 Who directed, scripted, composed and starred in Yentl?
13 Which ex child star was US Ambassador to Czechoslovakia in 1989?
14 How were producers Harry, Albert, Sam and Jack known collectively?
15 What was Groucho Marx's real first name?
16 Which Cockney actor married the former Miss Guyana in 1973?
17 Which horror writer directed the film Maximum Overdrive?
18 Who had larger feet, Marilyn Monroe or Daryl Hannah?
19 Which star of Look Who's Talking Too was a regular on TV's Cheers?
20 Which Fonda starred in the remake of Nikita?
21 Who is Joely Richardson's famous mother?
22 Which comedies was Michael Balcon responsible for?
23 Which actress wrote Postcards From the Edge?
24 Who was the first Bond girl?
25 Which conductor is Woody Allen's father in law?
26 Which surname was shared by John, Lionel, Ethel and Drew?
27 Who played Batman in Batman Forever?
28 What was Ex-python Terry Gilliam's futuristic nightmare film, surreally named for a South American country?
29 Who bought the screen rights to Dick Tracy and made a film from it?
30 Which blonde actress is Mrs Alec Baldwin?

Pot Luck 97 (see Quiz 217)
Answers
1 The Pope. 2 Estate car. 3 The deaf. 4 Relate. 5 Ofwat. 6 Tibet. 7 Tax. 8 Munich. 9 Two. 10 SAS. 11 France (de Nimes). 12 Operation Desert Storm. 13 Franz Beckenbauer. 14 Leek. 15 Kite shaped. 16 Election. 17 Teeth or bone. 18 Variety Club. 19 Thames. 20 Houses of Parliament. 21 Special Branch. 22 Hospital. 23 American Revolution. 24 Sleeping policeman. 25 Nurse. 26 Merchant Navy. 27 Third degree. 28 Young children. 29 Lutine Bell. 30 Red.

1 Who would deliver an edict called a bull?
2 What is a shooting brake?
3 Who does the RNID provide help for?
4 What is the Marriage Guidance Council now called?
5 How is the Office of Water Services also known?
6 The Dalai Lama is the spiritual leader of where?
7 In English history what was danegeld?
8 What is the capital of Bavaria?
9 How many days does a decathlon event last?
10 The US Delta Force is based on which British anti terrorist force?
11 In which country did denim originate?
12 What was the codename for the operation to eject the Iraqis from Kuwait in 1991?
13 Who was the first person to manage and captain a World Cup winning soccer side?
14 David was responsible for the adoption of what as a Welsh emblem?
15 What shape is the approved mark of the British Standards Institution?
16 At what occasion do you see a returning officer?
17 Caries is the decay and deterioration of what?
18 Which Club's President is the Chief Barker?
19 On which river does swan-upping take place?
20 Where in London is the Strangers' Gallery?
21 Which police department deals with political security in the UK?
22 What sort of institution is UCH?
23 The Battle of Bunker Hill was the first major engagement of what?
24 What name is given to a bump in the road to slow down traffic?
25 What is the profession of an RGN?
26 Whose flag is the red ensign?
27 Which degree of burns is life threatening?
28 Who does a Norland nurse work with?
29 Which bell is found in the building of Lloyd's of London?
30 What colour is the ceremonial dress of a Yeoman of the Guard?

1   What is Portland Place's most famous House?
2   What does CNN stand for?
3   Which listings magazine celebrated its 75th birthday in 1998?
4   What is Britain's principal world news agency?
5   Which magazine is supposedly edited by Lord Gnome?
6   Where is Grampian TV based?
7   What does the ASA control?
8   What is the magazine of the Consumer's Association?
9   Who is the Daily Mail's most famous cartoon dog?
10 Where is The People's Daily a top selling papers?
11 Which long-running futuristic comic featured Judge Dredd and Rogue Trooper?
12 Country Life was once edited by which royal photographer?
13 Red and yellow were the colours of which comic strip Rovers?
14 What is the full official title of GQ?
15 Which organisation had a magazine called "Expression!"?
16 Which daily paper founded in 1859 is devoted to horse racing?
17 In which part of the Commonwealth might you tune in to Penguin Radio?
18 Which Times Supplement is aimed at teachers?
19 How is the New Musical Express better known?
20 How does Dennis the Menace's mother always address her husband?
21 Which US based magazine was the world's best seller until the 80s?
22 How is the journalists' trade union commonly known?
23 Which famous magazine was founded by Hugh Hefner?
24 Where is Yorkshire TV based?
25 In which part of London are Richard Murdoch's newspapers based?
26 Which was the ill-fated satellite TV company that competed with Sky?
27 Which major UK daily newspaper, still in circulation, did Robert Maxwell own?
28 Which left wing faction had a newspaper called Militant?
29 Which major Murdoch UK paper has the longest name?
30 Which women's magazine did Cherie Blair guest edit?

Quiz 219 Pot Luck 98

Answers - see page 457

LEVEL 2

1 In the music world what did NKOTB stand for?

2 Hartley was the fictional town setting for which TV police serial?

3 Variola is the proper name for which killer disease?

4 Who competed against Messala in a literary chariot race?

5 Where did Laika, the first dog in space, die?

6 Which British stadium saw the worst soccer tragedy in 1985?

7 Which sheriff killed Billy the Kid?

8 Who had a well publicised conversation with Michael Fagan in 1982?

9 In a 1991 survey which country's inhabitants used the most soap per capita?

10 Is a piri-piri sauce sweet, or hot and spicy?

11 Which Swiss resident won a Grammie for singing Downtown?

12 Which Richard died at the Battle of Bosworth Field?

13 Which is largest, the Isle of Wight or Anglesey?

14 Buster Bloodvessel was a member of which Ska-revival band?

15 Which holiday island saw the worst ever air crash with 582 deaths?

16 Which former world boxing champion has the Christian name Finbar?

17 What does the "C" stand for in the musical initials "CBS"?

18 Which motorway joins with the M25 at Heathrow Airport?

19 What is controlled by an Emir?

20 In World War II which German city suffered the most civilian deaths?

21 Which living motor racing driver had been given the last rites before becoming World Champion?

22 What name is given to the most westerly time zone in America?

23 What is an American football pitch also called?

24 Thomas Hardy wrote what type of material for the last twelve years of his life?

25 Which is further east, Cambridge or Peterborough?

26 Which male pop superstar wrote the Bangles Manic Monday hit?

27 Which is the slowest moving fish?

28 What did the "M" stand for in the name of the band OMD?

29 Cordwainers mainly worked with which material?

30 Which Elton John hit was the first name of Russian leader Kruschev?

Leisure: Media (see Quiz 218)
1 Broadcasting House. 2 Cable News Network. 3 Radio Times. 4 Reuters. 5 Private Eye. 6 Aberdeen. 7 Advertising. 8 Which?. 9 Fred Basset. 10 China. 11 2001AD. 12 Lord Snowdon. 13 Melchester. 14 Gentlemen's Quarterly. 15 American Express. 16 The Sporting Life. 17 Falkland Islands. 18 Educational. 19 NME. 20 Dad. 21 Reader's Digest. 22 NUJ. 23 Playboy. 24 Leeds. 25 Wapping. 26 BSB. 27 Daily Mirror. 28 Militant Tendency. 29 The News of the World. 30 Prima.

Answers

1   What is Computer Assisted in the acronym CAD?
2   In which US state is the so called Silicon Glen?
3   Which bank does the CWS own?
4   In the oil industry what is the tower called which hoists the drill pipes?
5   What does the T stand for in DTP?
6   Which early adding device comes from the Latin meaning 'a flat surface'?
7   What does DERV stand for?
8   Exxon is the US's largest concern in which industry?
9   What does ICI stand for?
10 Which industry's members belong to Unison?
11 Who founded Habitat?
12 What is antiknock added to to reduce knocking?
13 What type of institution was BCCI?
14 Who founded Amstrad?
15 What does a Geiger counter measure?
16 What is the full name of CFCs?
17 For which industry is London's Wardour Street famous?
18 Where is Britain's largest North Sea oil terminal?
19 Which copying machine did Chester Carlson invent?
20 Who is the US's largest vehicle manufacturer?
21 What was the world's longest bridge when it was opened in 1980?
22 What is a country's GNP?
23 What does W stand for in the AWACS surveillance system?
24 What is the study of motion and impact of projectiles?
25 Which country has the world's largest electricity grid system?
26 Where is the BASF group based?
27 What is the world's largest packaged food company?
28 What is a computer's smallest unit of information?
29 Where did Lord Nuffield, aka William Morris, build up his car business?
30 What does the 'M' in IBM stand for?

1   What are the metal discs in the rim of a tambourine called?
2   Which word can be a pole with a foot rest or a wading bird?
3   What annual event is the Cumbrian town of Appleby noted for?
4   On what date does the pheasant shooting season legally start?
5   Who or what is Cader Idris?
6   Mr Birdseye – of frozen food fame – came from which country?
7   Richard Baker was a regular panellist on which musical TV quiz?
8   Which 1950s pop star had the first names Charles Hardin?
9   Which animals can be affected by a disease called vives?
10 Which Brigadier appeared in Dr Who?
11 Who played Mr Brown in the film Mrs Brown?
12 What is the official language of Haiti?
13 What was the name of Geoff Hamilton's garden?
14 Jane Fonda won a Best Actress Oscar for her role in which 1978 film?
15 Barajas airport is in which city?
16 Jack Rolfe and Charles Frere were characters in which TV series?
17 What is the oldest daily newspaper in England?
18 Demetria Guynes is better known as which actress?
19 Which country surrounds San Marino?
20 Which Order is the highest in the Order of Chivalry in Britain?
21 Who played the leading role in the TV series Sorry?
22 What was the name of A.A. Milne's son?
23 How many hours are there in a dog watch at sea?
24 In a calendar year what is the name given to the final quarter day?
25 Fox and Dana are the first names of which pair?
26 What did Saint Patrick rid Ireland of according to legend?
27 What are osselets and ossicles?
28 Alton Towers Leisure Park is in which county?
29 Steve Backley held the world record in which sports event?
30 In The Merchant of Venice the suitors pick one of three what?

Quiz 222 The Royals

Answers - see page 462

LEVEL 2

1 What was Diana's official title at the time of her death?
2 Who is the oldest in line to the throne after Prince Charles?
3 Which Prince was a guest on the Des O'Connor Show in 1998?
4 On which island was Princess Margaret when she suffered a stroke?
5 Who was older, Princess Diana's mother or her stepmother?
6 In which country did the former Edward VIII marry Mrs Simpson?
7 Albert succeeded Baudouin in which country?
8 In which country did Fergie's mother spend the latter part of her life?
9 What does the Queen's only nephew do for a living?
10 At which sport did Harry excel in his first few weeks at Eton?
11 Who is the only child of the Queen not to have been divorced?
12 Who is third in line to the throne?
13 Who survived the crash in which Princess Diana died?
14 Which cavalryman co wrote A Princess In Love with Anna Pasternak?
15 Seven kings of which country have been called Haakon?
16 Which Princess is the mother of Viscount Linley?
17 Which Princess is known by her husband's name?
18 Which former Royal residence was damaged by fire in 1986?
19 'Tiggy' Legge-Bourke was PA to which Prince for three years?
20 Which Princess is the mother of Marina Mowatt?
21 Who was Princess Diana's chauffeur on her final fatal car journey?
22 Which Royal companion is the great granddaughter of Edward VII's mistress Alice Keppel?
23 Which grand child of the Queen had her tongue pierced?
24 Which Royal in law was dubbed 'Fog' because he was thick and wet?
25 Who took the official engagement photos of Charles and Diana?
26 Who is Lady Sarah Chatto's aunt on her mother's side?
27 Which Princess married the son of a director of Walls sausages?
28 In which royal castle is St George's Chapel?
29 Which musical instrument does Princess Margaret play?
30 In 1994 Diana took an advisory role for which organisation?

Answers

Pot Luck 100 (see Quiz 223)
1 Chester. 2 Sixpence. 3 Steal. 4 Laughing gas. 5 Florence Nightingale.
6 Liverpool. 7 1977. 8 A pack of tarot cards. 9 December 25th. 10 Arnold
Palmer. 11 Loyd Grossman. 12 Lou Reed. 13 Bailey. 14 Wigan Pier.
15 You have a bite. 16 Manchester. 17 Avalon. 18 Kingston Upon Hull.
19 MCC. 20 Steve Davis. 21 Andrew. 22 Beethoven. 23 X rays.
24 Three. 25 Rudolf Nureyev. 26 Barbara Cartland. 27 Saddle. 28
Zambia. 29 17th. 30 Four.

1 Deva was a Roman city now known as what?

2 What was the top price for goods in the first British Woolworth's?

3 What does a kleptomaniac do?

4 What is the popular name for the anaesthetic nitrous oxide?

5 Who was the first woman to be awarded the Order of Merit?

6 The doomed ship Titanic was registered in which English city?

7 In which year did Marc Bolan die?

8 What is made up of the minor arcana and the major arcana?

9 The Romanian dictator Ceausescu was executed on which day in 1989?

10 Who was the last playing Ryder Cup captain, in the 60s?

11 Which food show presenter once played in a band called Jet Bronx and the Forbidden?

12 Which Lou was vocalist with the Velvet Underground?

13 Which shipping forecast area is due north of Rockall?

14 Which pier featured in a George Orwell book title?

15 If you are an angler why are you pleased if your monkey starts to climb?

16 In which city was painter LS Lowry born?

17 Where was King Arthur taken after his last battle?

18 What is Hull's full name?

19 Which all male bastion allowed women members for the first time in September 1998?

20 Who made the first televised 147 in snooker, in 1982?

21 Which Prince's childhood nickname was 'The Sniggerer'?

22 Who wrote the Emperor Concerto?

23 For which medical breakthrough did Roentgen win the Nobel Prize in 1901?

24 How many Inns of Court are there in London?

25 Which ballet dancer died on the same day as Dizzy Gillespie?

26 Whose codename was 'Pink' before she was surprised on This Is Your Life?

27 What is a pommel a part of?

28 Cars with the international vehicle registration Z come from where?

29 In which century was the Battle of Naseby?

30 How many pecks are there in a bushel?

Answers

The Royals (see Quiz 222)
1 Diana, Princess of Wales. 2 Prince Andrew. 3 Edward. 4 Mustique.
5 Stepmother. 6 France. 7 Belgium. 8 Argentina. 9 Make furniture.
10 Football. 11 Prince Edward. 12 Prince Harry. 13 Trevor Reece Jones.
14 James Hewitt. 15 Norway. 16 Margaret. 17 Michael of Kent. 18
Hampton Court. 19 Charles. 20 Alexandra. 21 Henri Paul. 22 Camilla
Parker Bowles. 23 Zara Phillips. 24 Mark Phillips. 25 Lord Snowdon. 26
The Queen. 27 Anne. 28 Windsor. 29 Piano. 30 International Red Cross.

Quiz 224   Who Was Who?

Answers - see page 464

LEVEL 2

1   Who was Chancellor, Foreign Secretary and PM between 1964 and 1979?
2   Which nation introduced chocolate to Europe?
3   Which American was known as Ike?
4   Which future President organised the Free French Forces in WWII?
5   What was Indira Gandhi's maiden name?
6   Who became US Vice President in 1993?
7   Which title did Hitler take as Nazi leader?
8   Who was the last Tsarina of Russia?
9   Who was Soviet Foreign Minister from 1957 to 1985?
10   Whose resignation on 1st November 1990 began Thatcher's downfall?
11   Whose 1963 Report led to the closure of many railway stations?
12   Who was famous for his pictures of Campbell's Soup cans?
13   Who was British Prime Minister during the abdication crisis?
14   For how long were Hitler and Eva Braun married?
15   In 1996 who had served longer continuously as a Minister, John Major or Kenneth Clarke?
16   Which athlete became MP for Falmouth and Cambourne in 1992?
17   Which world leader celebrated his 80th birthday in July 1998?
18   Who was the first Archbishop of Canterbury?
19   Which US President publicly pardoned ex President Nixon?
20   Who had the title Il Duce?
21   Which US evangelist asked his flock to make a "decision for Christ"?
22   In 1990 which ex PM went to Iraq to try to secure the release of British hostages?
23   Who was the youngest queen of Henry VIII to be beheaded?
24   Which Prime Minister introduced the Citizen's Charter?
25   Who became Defence Secretary in May 1997?
26   What was the name of Horatio Nelson's daughter by Emma Hamilton?
27   Who said her boss Michael Howard had "something of the night about him"?
28   What was the religion of a French Huguenot?
29   Whose Report formed the basis for the British welfare state?
30   In which category did Einstein win his Nobel prize in 1921?

Answers - see page 465

1 The Longmuir brothers were in which 70s teeny bop group?
2 Who partnered Don Johnson on the Goya theme Till I Loved You?
3 Which Coronation Street star had a hit in '94 with Wind Beneath My Wings?
4 Which UK male vocalist's real name is Michael Barratt?
5 Who duetted with Peter Gabriel on Don't Give Up?
6 Christopher John Davidson is the real name of which Irish vocalist?
7 How many members are there in D:Ream?
8 Who launched the British Legion Poppy Appeal with Dame Vera Lynn in 1997?
9 Who featured on the 1986 Clannad hit In a Lifetime?
10 Which pianist and instrumentalist's real name is Philippe Pages?
11 Who was the younger of the two Wham! members?
12 Keith, Greg and Carl were the Christian names of which 70s trio?
13 Who was lead female singer with 60s group The Seekers?
14 Marvin Lee Aday is better known as which dead ringer vocalist?
15 Who had a No 5 UK hit with the theme song Because You Loved Me?
16 Which actor shares his name with a 1984 hit by Madness?
17 Who sang the theme tune to Dirty Dancing with Jennifer Warnes?
18 Which TV detective had a No 1 hit with Don't Give Up On Us in 1976?
19 Which group share their name with a Bernard Cribbins 1962 hit?
20 Who joined with Queen in the 1981 No 1 hit Under Pressure?
21 Who invented Medicinal Compound according to the 1968 No 1?
22 Which superstar has an autobiography called Bare?
23 Which pop legend said, "I really wanted to be a soccer star"?
24 Who partnered Chris Rea on the 1996 hit 'Disco' La Passione?
25 Complete the A-ha trio - Pal, Mags and ....?
26 Which character was played by Irene Cara in Fame?
27 Who interrupted Michael Jackson's Earth Song at the 1996 Brit Awards?
28 Which brothers were members of Spandau Ballet?
29 Who was the first Spice Girl to get engaged?
30 Who links the '86 hit Every Loser Wins and the '92 hit Heartbeat?

1   Which comedian wrote Blackadder with Richard Curtis?
2   Who hosted the talent spotting show My Kind of People?
3   Who replaced Anneka Rice on Carlton TV's Capital Woman?
4   David Dimbleby's first wife wrote what type of books?
5   Which comedian created the character Stavros?
6   Who has the car number plate COM 1C?
7   Which star of The Grand is President of the Dyslexia Institute?
8   Which first name is shared by subsequent stars of Dangerfield?
9   Who told Noel Edmonds live that co presenter Anthea Turner's interviews sent him to sleep?
10 Which radio name replaced Richard Baker presenting The Proms?
11 Which blonde first presented Big Breakfast with Chris Evans?
12 Julie Walters hails from which city?
13 Who replaced Carol Drinkwater as Helen in All Creatures Great and Small?
14 Which Doctor is a regular on Newsnight?
15 In which docu soap did Jeremy Spake find fame?
16 Who is actor Michael Williams' wife?
17 How is Derrick Evans better known?
18 Who became Jim Davidson's regular assistant on The Generation Game?
19 Which ex Radio 2 presenter moved to Open House on Channel 5?
20 Who could you regularly have Breakfast With... on Sunday mornings?
21 Who replaced Vanessa on ITV's morning talk show?
22 What did Trude Mostue train to be on TV?
23 Who first presented Changing Rooms?
24 In which drama series did the character Dr Beth Glover appear?
25 Who was the first woman tennis player to be BBC Sports Personality of the Year?
26 Who was the interviewer on C4's The Last Resort?
27 Who presented the National Lottery's fourth birthday show in 1998?
28 Who did Fergie play in Friends?
29 Who was the woman driver from hell in BBC's docu soap?
30 Who moved from Newsnight to Tomorrow's World?

Hard Questions

Are you bristling with intelligence? Do your pores seep clever stuff? Does knowledge flow through you like the mighty Nile, silting up your mind with facts? If not then get your head down because here's the HARD section. As difficult as plaiting fog, as tricky as puppy-juggling and yes, as taxing as a very hard question posed by the Inland Revenue in order to determine the amount of your income they can take away from you.

The Hard section; a quick scan through the pages will illustrate the point exactly your forehead will crease, your memory will strain and your patience will stretch. Just two of the questions rejected by quiz setters were: 'Who?' and the immensely complex 'Why?'

Use these questions like heavy artillery. Revel in the percussive resonance as you go about pounding down the teams' defences, leaving their minds racked and their knowledge plundered. Wield them wisely, though, for a quiz set entirely with the Hard questions would make you as welcome as a polecat at a foxes's Ball.

Quiz 1 Pot luck 1

Answers - see page 471

1 What were the names of the three tunnels dug by POWs in *The Great Escape*?
2 Who had an 80s No. 1 with "Star Trekkin'"?
3 In which country is the city of Abu Dhabi?
4 Which shipping forecast area is due north of Shannon?
5 What is the only English anagram of GRANDIOSE?
6 In which country are the Shakta Pantjukhina caves?
7 What was William Atheling's real name?
8 In Monopoly how much does it cost to buy the Angel Islington?
9 If it's noon at GMT, what time is it in Addis Ababa?
10 Who was the first player to be disqualified from Wimbledon?
11 Who wrote the novel *The Sea, The Sea*?
12 Which English county provided the setting for "The Farming Week"?
13 Who founded the Newman Haas Racing Indy Car Team?
14 In which decade were postal orders first issued in Britain?
15 Mick Harford scored in a League Cup Final for which team?
16 What is Mystic Meg's surname?
17 In which fictitious town was "'Allo 'Allo" set?
18 Which ex-champ did Doug Flach beat in round 1 of Wimbledon '96?
19 What was Frederick John Robinson's title when he was UK prime minister?
20 In which round did Tyson lose in his '96 clash with Evander Holyfield?
21 Who is the patron saint of wine merchants?
22 What was the first British Top Ten hit for Argent?
23 Lipari and Salina are in which island group?
24 On which river does St Petersburg stand?
25 Which magazine did Cherie Booth (Blair) guest-edit in 1996?
26 What was the computer called in the TV series "The Tomorrow People"?
27 From which language does the word "limousine" originate?
28 Who did Norma Major write her first book about?
29 The airline Sansa is based in which country?
30 Which character was played by Prunella Scales in "After Henry"?

Answers

Pot Luck 2 (see Quiz 3)
1 1940s. 2 Ghana. 3 Kingsley Amis. 4 Jack Ruskin. 5 Chord. 6 Spanish.
7 The moon. 8 Algeria. 9 Free Parking. 10 Truffle. 11 T'Pau.
12 A meteorite. 13 J.C. Morton. 14 Smiles. 15 Kriss Akabusi. 16 Simian
Films. 17 Abdel Benazzi. 18 1500. 19 Rock Hudson. 20 Shot. 21 Over
300. 22 1440. 23 *Patience*. 24 Clement Ader. 25 Alan Mills. 26 Bolton
Wanderers. 27 Playboy. 28 Moonee Ponds. 29 A lighthouse. 30 Dog Eat
Dog.

1 Which girlfriend of Ken Barlow was played by Joanna Lumley?
2 What was Maureen Holdsworth's name before she married Reg?
3 Other than the Duckworths, who are Tommy's grandparents?
4 In the 80s which soap character was voted Britiain's most popular person after the Queen, Queen Mother and Princess Diana?
5 What was Susan Tully's first documentary series called after she left "EastEnders"?
6 Which future Oscar winner played Irma Ogden's boyfriend Ron Jenkins?
7 Who was killed in the first episode of "EastEnders"?
8 Which number Albert Square did Pauline and Arthur Fowler live at?
9 What was the name of Len Fairclough's son, played by Peter Noone?
10 What was the name of the programme that looked back at the Albert Square of 1942?
11 What had the original working title of "Meadowcroft"?
12 What were Deirdre's first two surnames in "Coronation Street"?
13 Brookside Close was a real estate but what was its first fake addition?
14 On which days of the week was "Albion Market" first broadcast?
15 Which husband-and-wife team produced "The Colbys"?
16 In "Dallas" what was the name of the baby Kristin had by JR?
17 In "Dynasty" which character was Rock Hudson's final role?
18 At what times of day was "Neighbours" first screened in the UK?
19 Which character did ex-EastEnder Letitia Dean play in "The Hello Girls"?
20 What did *Private Eye* ridicule "Brookside" as when it first started?
21 Which "Dynasty" character wrote *Sister Dearest* about Alexis?
22 Who sang the "Neighbours" theme song?
23 In "Emmerdale" what was Annie Sugden's first husband called?
24 Which soap star was Charlie's voice in "Charlie's Angels"?
25 In "Dallas" how did Jock die?
26 Who were Madge Mitchell's children in "Neighbours"?
27 Which beers did the Woolpack first sell in "Emmerdale"?
28 What is the link between Ian McShane's role in "Dallas" and Gene Kelly's in "Singin' in the Rain"?
29 Who played Peggy Mitchell before Barbara Windsor?
30 Who was the first owner of the Albert Square launderette?

Quiz 3 Pot Luck 2

Answers - see page 469

1   In which decade was Gerard Depardieu born?
2   In which country is the city of Accra?
3   Who wrote *Jake's Thing*?
4   Which character was played by Roy Marsden in "Airline"?
5   What name is given to a straight line that joins any two points on the circumference of a circle?
6   From which language does the word "bravado" originate?
7   Louis Daguerre took the first photograph of what?
8   The international car registration DZ applies to which country?
9   On a Monopoly board what is between Vine Street and the Strand?
10 What is the only English anagram of FRETFUL?
11 Who had an 80s No. 1 with "China In Your Hand"?
12 What is known to the Eskimos as Abnighito and is in Cape York Greenland?
13 What was Beachcomber's real name?
14 Which series of stamps featured Dennis the Menace and Mona Lisa?
15 Whose middle names are Kezie Uche Chukwu?
16 Which film company was founded by Liz Hurley and Hugh Grant?
17 Who captained France v. the Springboks in rugby in 1996?
18 What is the approximate distance of Athens airport from London in miles?
19 Which famous actor played Sammy Jo's father in "Dynasty"?
20 In which sport did Suzanne Allday achieve fame?
21 How many islands are in the Andaman group?
22 What is the sum total of the internal angles in a decagon in degrees?
23 How is Gilbert and Sullivan's *Bunthorne's Bride* better known?
24 Who invented the steam-powered aeroplane?
25 Who became Wimbledon referee in 1982?
26 Which football team does the Dewsbury MP Ann Taylor support?
27 Which organization financed Roman Polanski's Macbeth?
28 In which Melbourne suburb was Dame Edna Everage brought up?
29 What type of building did Mary live in, in "The Life and Loves of a She-Devil"?
30 What was the first British Top Ten hit for Adam and the Ants?

Answers

Pot Luck 1 (see Quiz 1)
1 Tom, Dick & Harry. **2** Firm. **3** United Arab Emirates. **4** Rockall.
5 Organized. **6** Russia. **7** Ezra Pound. **8** £100. **9** 3 p.m. **10** Tim Henman.
11 Iris Murdoch. **12** Northamptonshire. **13** Carl Haas. **14** 1880s.
15 Luton. **16** Lake. **17** Nouvion. **18** Andre Agassi. **19** Viscount Goderich
of Nocton. **20** 11th. **21** St Nicholas. **22** Hold Your Head Up. **23** Aeolian.
24 Neva. **25** *Prima*. **26** Tim. **27** French. **28** Dame Joan Sutherland.
29 Costa Rica. **30** Sarah France.

1 Whose first solo single had the catalogue reference Virgin BOY 100?
2 Which 60s singer was backed by the Cruisers on his first recordings?
3 What is the middle name of Kenny Rogers?
4 What was Clarence Carter's one and only hit?
5 On what label did Buddy Holly record?
6 Where in America was Diana Ross born?
7 Rod Stewart's "Sailing" was used for a BBC series about which ship?
8 Which unlikely singer had a 50s hit with "Shifting Whispering Sands"?
9 Who was Marc of Marc and the Mambas?
10 Which country did Morris Albert come from?
11 "We Don't Talk Anymore" was Cliff's first No. 1 for how many years?
12 Which former singer became Leo Sayer's manager?
13 Who did Van Morrison record the *Irish Heartbeat* album with?
14 Under what name did David Spencer record?
15 What was Jennifer Rush's follow up to "The Power Of Love"?
16 What are Madonna's two middle names?
17 In the 50s who was accompanying Dion on his first single?
18 Peter Cunnah sang his way to No. 1 with who?
19 Which singer was backed by the Drells?
20 Both Carole King and Don McLean made an album called what?
21 Who was the most famous vocalist to sing with the Tourists?
22 Who is lead singer with UB40?
23 Who had a No. 1 with "Mambo Italiano"?
24 What was the first posthumous hit single for Jim Reeves?
25 Which Everly Brother sang the higher notes?
26 Who is the most successful singer to come from Douglas, Isle of Man?
27 Who played a character called Rachel Marron on film?
28 What was Joe Cocker's job before he became a singer?
29 What was Dionne Warwick's first Top Five hit in Britain?
30 What was Johnnie Ray's nickname?

Quiz 5 Pot luck 3

Answers - see page 475

LEVEL 3

1 Who wrote the novel *A Bend in the River*?

2 What was the first British Top Ten hit for Kenny Ball?

3 Who was the first host of "Wogan" other than Terry Wogan?

4 The airline Augusta Airways is based in which country?

5 Who led the British forces at the Battle of Princeton in 1777?

6 What number in Old Drum Lane was home to "Steptoe and Son"?

7 In which decade was Albert Finney born?

8 What was Acton Bell's real name?

9 What is the only English anagram of TRAGEDY?

10 On which river does Rangoon stand?

11 Who invented the swing-wing aeroplane?

12 If it's noon at GMT, what time is it in Casablanca?

13 From which language does the word "verandah" originate?

14 In Monopoly, what is the prize for winning a crossword competition?

15 Moluccas and Irian Jaya are in which island group?

16 Which character was played by Helen Shapiro in "Albion Market"?

17 Where was Nelson Piquet's last Formula 1 Grand Prix race in 1991?

18 In which country was J.R.R. Tolkien born?

19 If something is "fluviatile" what is it?

20 Alaska became what number state of America?

21 Bonny Lad and White Windsor are types of what?

22 In which country is the city of Dakar?

23 Who did Sharon Gless marry in 1991?

24 In which Dickens novel does Susan Nipper appear?

25 Which Frenchman became Armenia's representative at UNESCO?

26 If A is Alpha and B is Bravo what is H?

27 Who wrote the novel *The English Patient*?

28 When is Lammas Day?

29 What was the name of Elsie Tanner's nephew in "Coronation Street" played by Gorden Kaye?

30 Who had an 80s No. 1 with "Don't Turn Around"?

Answers

Pot Luck 4 (see Quiz 7)

1 Adverts. 2 Ken Boothe. 3 Svetlana Savitskaya. 4 Avenue Foch. 5 Italian. 6 Thames estuary. 7 167. 8 Erik Rotheim. 9 Rev Mervyn Noote. 10 Alessandro Filipepi. 11 6000. 12 Michael Moorcroft. 13 Stamford Brook. 14 Alex Stepney. 15 5-1. 16 1920s. 17 Tara Palmer-Tomkinson. 18 Golding. 19 Second cousin. 20 Between left thumb and forefinger. 21 "Manic Monday". 22 Marty McFly. 23 Edward Heath (1973). 24 Month of the grape harvest. 25 Nigel Mansell. 26. Dolly Parton economics. 27 Diana Rigg. 28 John Leslie. 29 Cobbold. 30 USA.

LEVEL 3

1   In which two films did Paul Newman play "Fast Eddie" Felson?
2   Who did Tom Cruise play in *Born on the Fourth of July*?
3   Whose first film, for Disney, was called *Napoleon and Samantha*?
4   Who played Sherman McCoy in *Bonfire of the Vanities*?
5   Which two superstars collaborated on the massive flop *Ishtar*?
6   Which film gave Michelle Pfeiffer her first Oscar nomination?
7   Who has been married to Judy Carne and Loni Anderson?
8   For which film did Meryl Streep win her second Oscar?
9   Which role did Kim Basinger play in *Batman* in 1989?
10 Who co-wrote the screenplay for *Yentl* with Barbra Streisand?
11 Which role did Elizabeth Taylor play in *The Flintstones*?
12 What was Disney's first PG movie, which starred Michael J. Fox?
13 Who was the star and executive director of the remake of *The Return of Martin Guerre*?
14 Who won the Best Supporting Actress award for *Cactus Flower*?
15 Who starred with Natalie Wood in *Splendor* in the Grass in 1961?
16 In which film did Jack Lemmon first direct Walter Matthau?
17 Who was Jimmy Bond in *Casino Royale*?
18 Aged 21, who wrote his autobiography *Absolutely Mahvelous*?
19 Who has played the Boston Strangler and Houdini on screen?
20 Who won an Oscar for playing an Irish cop in *The Untouchables*?
21 Who won an Oscar nomination for her first feature-film role as Robin Williams's mother?
22 Who played Sean Connery's son and Matthew Broderick's father in the same film?
23 Who posed nude covered in paint which looked like a man's suit?
24 Who was the attorney played by Kevin Costner in JFK?
25 Who did Jack Nicholson play in *One Flew Over The Cuckoo's Nest*?
26 Whose 1991 autobiography was called *Me*?
27 Which actor won Australia's equivalent of an Oscar for *Tim*?
28 Who played Horace Vandergelder in *Hello Dolly!*?
29 Who was the Penguin in *Batman Returns*?
30 Who did Cher play in Robert Altman's *The Player*?

Answers

Living World (see Quiz 8)

1 Use of feathers for the fashion trade. 2 Neotropical. 3 Demospongia.
4 Corals. 5 Red. 6 Harpy eagle. 7 Smell. 8 Three. 9 Starfish.
10 Bushman's clock. 11 Its diet. 12 On the sea bed. 13 Flightless bird.
14 Secretary bird. 15 Shellfish (not oysters!), worms, insects. 16 Cormorant.
17 South America. 18 Andean condor. 19 Mongoose. 20 Sprat.
21 Mexico. 22 Dome of the shell. 23 Red mullet. 24 Cassowary.
25 Lizard. 26 Wishbone. 27 Plains wanderer. 28 Madagascar.
29 Dogfish. 30 Whole.

1 What is the only English anagram of STARVED?
2 Who had a 70s No. 1 with "Everything I Own"?
3 Who was the first woman to walk in space?
4 On a French Monopoly board, what is the equivalent to Oxford Street?
5 From which language does the word "piano" originate?
6 Where did the world-travelling aviator Amy Johnson vanish in flight?
7 To ten, how many islands are in the Zemlya Frantsa-Iosifa group?
8 Who invented the aerosol?
9 Who did Derek Nimmo play in *All Gas and Gaiters*?
10 What was Botticelli's real name?
11 What is the approximate distance of Bangkok airport from London in miles?
12 Who wrote the book *A Cure for Cancer*?
13 Which was the first London Underground station to have an automatic ticket barrier?
14 Which Manchester United keeper was a mid-season joint top-scorer in the 70s?
15 What are the odds of rolling any combination totalling seven in dice-throwing?
16 In which decade was Dirk Bogarde born?
17 Which *Sunday Times* columnist has a sister called Santa?
18 Which William won the Nobel Prize for Literature in 1983?
19 What relation is the actor Ralph Fiennes to the explorer Ranulph Fiennes?
20 Where does the actress Helen Mirren have a tattoo?
21 What was the first British Top Ten hit for the Bangles?
22 What was Michael J. Fox's character in the *Back to the Future* films?
23 Which prime minister introduced a 10.30 p.m. TV curfew?
24 In the French Republican calendar what did Vendemiare mean?
25 Who celebrated a Formula 1 win a lap too soon at Montreal in '91, losing to Nelson Piquet?
26 What did Kenneth Clarke call Gordon Brown's policy of "an unbelievable figure, blown out of all proportion with no visible means of support"?
27 Who played Vincent Price's daughter in *Theatre of Blood*?
28 Who did Tim Vincent replace on "Blue Peter"?
29 Knebworth has been the home of which family for over 500 years?
30 In which country is the city of El Paso?

Answers

Pot Luck 3 (see Quiz 5)
1 V.S. Naipaul. 2 "Midnight in Moscow". 3 Selina Scott. 4 Australia.
5 Lord Cornwallis. 6 24. 7 1930s. 8 Anne Brontë. 9 Gyrated.
10 Irrawaddy. 11 Grumman Co. 12 12 noon. 13 Portuguese. 14 £100.
15 Indonesia. 16 Viv Harker. 17 Montreal. 18 South Africa. 19 Belonging to or formed by rivers. 20 49th. 21 Broad Bean. 22 Senegal. 23 Barney Rosenzweig. 24 *Dombey and Son*. 25 Charles Aznavour. 26 Hotel.
27 Michael Ondaatje. 28 August 1st. 29 Bernard Butler. 30 Aswad.

Quiz 8 Living World

Answers - see page 474

LEVEL 3

1 RSPB founders campaigned specifically against the slaughter of birds for what purpose?
2 Which faunal region covers South/Central America and the Caribbean?
3 What is the largest class of sponges called?
4 Sea fans and sea whips are types of what?
5 What colour is the underside of the pipesnake's tail?
6 What is the world's largest eagle?
7 Which sense does the New World vulture have which the Old World vulture doesn't?
8 How many eyes does a tuatara have?
9 A sunstar is a type of what?
10 How is the early bird from Australasia, the butcherbird also known?
11 How does the flamingo get its colour?
12 Where does a blenny live?
13 What is a ratite?
14 Which bird can walk up to 20 miles a day?
15 What do oystercatchers eat?
16 Which seabird is also called the shag?
17 Which continent is the home of the electric eel?
18 What has the largest wingspan of any living bird?
19 The Puerto Rican boa is endangered due to which predator?
20 What does a white bait grow into?
21 Where does the axolotl come from?
22 Which part of a turtle is its carapace?
23 How is the goat fish also known?
24 Which flightless bird in addition to the emu is native to Australia?
25 What is a skink?
26 Which bone of birds is also called the furcula?
27 Which Australian male bird incubates the eggs and raises the young?
28 Where is the mesite native to?
29 Which fish is known as rock salmon when sold for food?
30 How does the monitor lizard consume its prey?

Quiz 9 Pot Luck 5

Answers - see page 479

LEVEL 3

1 Which shipping forecast area is south of Sole?
2 Which fictional village was the TV series "Dear Ladies" set in?
3 Who was David Coulthard's teammate with the '97 Formula 1 McLaren team?
4 What was the lowest value on a Charles and Diana Royal Wedding stamp?
5 Who joined Michael Jackson on the 80s No. 1 "I Just Can't Stop Loving You"?
6 What is the northern boundary of South America?
7 To whom did Clive Anderson say, "Is there no beginning to your talents?"?
8 Whose autobiography was called *Crying With Laughter*?
9 Who wrote the novel *Nightmare Abbey*?
10 In which country is the city of Caracas?
11 What was Charlie Chaplin's first film?
12 How many islands are in the Azores group?
13 Who was President of the British Olympic Association from 1983?
14 Who won a Tony for his Broadway debut as Che in *Evita*?
15 Which soap had the characters Spanner and Craven and a drug dealer called Gibson?
16 Which character was played by Tim Healy in "Auf Wiedersehen Pet"?
17 If it's noon at GMT, what time is it in Mexico City?
18 What was the first British Top Ten hit for Shirley Bassey?
19 In which decade was Geoff Boycott born?
20 What is the only English anagram of GRIEVED?
21 What was Boz's real name?
22 The airline Tower Air is based in which country?
23 Who invented the non-rigid airship?
24 In Monopoly, what dividend does the Bank pay you in Chance?
25 Who followed Arthur Balfour as prime minister of the UK?
26 Which ex-Miss Black Tennessee was Oscar-nominated for *The Color Purple*?
27 In which sport did Chris Baillieu achieve fame?
28 What is the capital of the Canadian province New Brunswick?
29 From which language does the word "steppe" originate?
30 Which performer undertook the Serious Moonlight Tour?

Answers

Pot Luck 6 (see Quiz 11)
1 James Baldwin. **2** Electric Company. **3** Elizabeth II. **4** Brussels Sprout.
5 Switzerland. **6** Bangladesh. **7** Battersea. **8** Diana Ross, Ryan O'Neal.
9 Reims. **10** 1260. **11** Debbie Moore. **12** Jean Dominique Larrey.
13 Dutch. **14** New Edition. **15** Cranberry juice. **16** Mel Martin, John Bowe.
17 CQD. **18** Philippa Vale. **19** Hawaiian. **20** Cricket. **21** 1920s.
22 Ferns. **23** Friday. **24** Giovanni Antonio Canale. **25** Liz Hobbs.
26 Annika Reeder. **27** Kimbolton. **28** "Keep On Dancing". **29** 7000.
30 Gifted.

LEVEL 3

1　How many different French clubs did Eric Cantona play for before joining Leeds?
2　Which club has its ground in Bumpers Lane?
3　To three each way, how many England caps did Alan Ball win?
4　What was the last English league club that George Best played for?
5　The world's first artificial pitch was built in which stadium in Texas?
6　How old was John Aldridge when he first played international soccer?
7　Which city does the striker Chris Armstrong come from?
8　Who was the first manager to record six FA Cup Final wins?
9　Cec Podd created an appearance record for which club?
10　Which England player was born in Southampton on March 3 1972?
11　Which ground was featured in L.S. Lowry's painting *Going To the Match*?
12　Andy Cole scored his first League goal for which club?
13　Which team used to be called Shaddongate United?
14　Who scored for Manchester United in Cantona's "Kung-Fu" game v. Palace?
15　Which City play at home at Glebe Park?
16　To three, how many England clean sheets did Gordon Banks keep?
17　Colombia's Rene Higuita made an amazing scorpion kick save from which England player at Wembley in 1995?
18　Ray Graydon scored in a League Cup Final for which club?
19　Which two teams were involved in Scotland's first ground share?
20　Steve D'Eath set an English clean sheet record while at which club?
21　At which club did Brian Horton follow Mark Lawrenson as manager?
22　Who scored the winning goal in the 1953 Matthews Final?
23　Which future international failed to impress Ipswich in trials in 1982?
24　Which teams played in the first international on an artificial pitch?
25　What were Barnet FC previously known as?
26　Which sponsors name was on '94-'95 Premiership winners' Blackburn shirts?
27　Who did Hereford replace in the Football League in the 70s?
28　Who scored England's Italia '90 goal against Egypt?
29　Which team was the first to retain the FA Cup in the 20th century?
30　Who was the boss for Alan Shearer's league debut?

Quiz 11 Pot Luck 6

Answers - see page 477

1   Which woman was world water-skiing champion from 1981-5?
2   In Monopoly, where would you land with a double six from Go ?
3   Who was the first reigning sovereign to visit a television studio?
4   Widgen and Welland are types of what?
5   In which country did the Scottish writer A.J. Cronin die?
6   In which country is the city of Dhaka?
7   In which London suburb was the hospital drama "Angels" set?
8   Who were originally suggested for the two main roles in *The Bodyguard* back in the 70s?
9   Where was the first French Formula 1 Grand Prix held which counted toward the World Championship?
10 What is the sum total of the internal angles in a nonagon in degrees?
11 Who founded the Pineapple Dance Studios in London?
12 Who developed the ambulance?
13 From which language does the word "yacht" originate?
14 Who had an 80s No. 1 with "Candy Girl"?
15 In early '97, which drink did the Duchess of York advertise in the US?
16 Who played Demelza and Ross in the 90s "Poldark"?
17 What distress call did SOS replace?
18 Which character was played by Liza Goddard in "Bergerac"?
19 Niihau and Kahoolawe are in which island group?
20 In which sport did Enid Bakewell excel?
21 In which decade was Yassar Arafat born?
22 What does a pteridologist breed?
23 If Epiphany is on a Monday what day is Valentine's Day?
24 What was Canaletto's real name?
25 Which hit song refers to Guitar George?
26 Who was England's youngest Commonwealth Games gold medallist in 1994?
27 At which palace did Catherine of Aragon die?
28 What was the first British Top Ten hit for the Bay City Rollers?
29 What is the approximate distance of Buenos Aires airport from London in miles?
30 What is the only English anagram of FIDGET?

Answers

Pot Luck 5 (see Quiz 9)

1 Finisterre. 2 Stackton Tressle. 3 Mika Hakkinen. 4 14p. 5 Siedah Garrett. 6 The Panama Columbia boundary. 7 Jeffrey Archer. 8 Bob Monkhouse. 9 Thomas Love Peacock. 10 Venezuela. 11 *Making A Living*. 12 Nine. 13 Princess Anne. 14 Mandy Patinkin. 15 "The Archers". 16 Dennis Patterson. 17 6 a.m. 18 Banana Boat Song. 19 1940s. 20 Diverge. 21 Charles Dickens. 22 USA. 23 Henri Giffard. 24 £50. 25 Henry Campbell-Bannerman. 26 Oprah Winfrey. 27 Rowing. 28 Fredericton. 29 Russian. 30 Dave Bowie.

1   What is the highest peak in Scotland after Ben Nevis?
2   Where is the Whitworth Art Gallery?
3   On which river does Dumfries stand?
4   Where is the James Clerk Maxwell Telescope?
5   Which town has the car index mark AA?
6   Where is Dyce Airport?
7   Which Lough is in the centre of the Sperrin, Antrim and Mourne ranges?
8   Where is the National Library of Wales?
9   Which town's football ground is farthest away from any other?
10 Which UK town has its own telephone system?
11 Where is Warwick University?
12 What is Cambridge's county-class cricket ground called?
13 Which Milton Keynes theatre is named after a politician who was also a famous politician's wife?
14 Where is the East of England Orchestra based?
15 What was Scotland's capital in the 11th-15th centuries?
16 Where is Pontefract racecourse?
17 What is the longest river in Wales?
18 On which river does Winchester stand?
19 On which tube line is London's longest tunnel?
20 Which is farther north, Leeds or Halifax?
21 Where is Jurby Ronaldsway airport?
22 Where is the University College of North Wales?
23 Which town has a Theatre Royal and a Gardner Centre?
24 What is Bolton's theatre called?
25 Where is Queen of the South Football Club?
26 What are Edinburgh's two oldest universities called?
27 Which is farther east, Middlesbrough or York?
28 What is Oxford's county-class cricket ground called?
29 Where is the Royal and Ancient Golf Club?
30 On which river does Colchester stand?

UK Football (see Quiz 10)

1 Five. 2 Chester. 3 72. 4 Bournemouth. 5 Houston Astrodrome. 6 28.
7 Newcastle. 8 George Ramsay (all with Aston Villa). 9 Bradford City.
10 Darren Anderton. 11 Burnden Park. 12 Fulham (on loan). 13 Carlisle.
14 David May. 15 Brechin. 16 35. 17 Jamie Redknapp. 18 Aston Villa.
19 Clyde, Partick Thistle. 20 Reading. 21 Oxford. 22 Bill Perry. 23 Paul
Gascoigne. 24 Canada v USA. 25 Barnet Alston. 26 McEwan's Lager.
27 Barrow. 28 Mark Wright. 29 Newcastle Utd. 30 Chris Nicholl
(Southampton).

LEVEL 3

1 If it's noon at GMT, what time is it in Wellington?

2 Which soap was originally going to be called "One Way Street"?

3 Who wrote *The Pit and the Pendulum*?

4 What is the only English anagram of ORGANIST?

5 Since Christianity began when was the first visit by a Pope to the Holy Land?

6 The Bahamas is made up of approximately how many islands?

7 Which character was played by Luke Perry in "Beverley Hills 90210"?

8 Who invented the balloon?

9 Charles Eric are the middle names of which England soccer keeper?

10 What was the colour of the first decimal British 1/2p stamp?

11 Who had an 80s No. 1 with "Don't Leave Me This Way"?

12 In which decade was David Attenborough born?

13 Who became Mrs Jon Bigg in 1992?

14 In which country are the Sistema del Trave caves?

15 Which secretary to Oliver North admitted shredding certain documents?

16 Which actor's wife owns a horse called Hobb's Choice?

17 Caroline and Donald own which company in "Executive Stress"?

18 What was the first British Top Ten hit for the Beach Boys?

19 Where is the Circuit de Nevers, host of the French Formula 1 Grand Prix?

20 Who did George Thomas succeed as Speaker in the Commons?

21 What was Lewis Carroll's real middle name?

22 Who was Jennifer Aniston's most famous godfather?

23 Which was the first film to be released simultaneously in cinemas and on video?

24 Which Olympic finalist won the Nobel Peace Prize in 1959?

25 On which river does Tauton stand?

26 Which cars won Le Mans consecutively from 1928 to 1930?

27 What was the name of the character killed in the shower in Psycho?

28 From which language does the word "plunder" originate?

29 The airline Gronlandsfly is based in which country?

30 In Monopoly, what do you receive when your Building Loan matures?

1 Who was the housekeeper in "All Creatures Great and Small"?
2 Who narrated "Roobarb and Custard"?
3 Who replaced Anneka Rice on "Treasure Hunt"?
4 Which pseudonym did Ronnie Barker use when writing for "The Two Ronnies"?
5 Who sang the theme song for "Absolutely Fabulous"?
6 Which doctors presented "Where There's Life"?
7 Who was "concert chairman" at the "Wheeltappers and Shunters"?
8 Who played Princess Vicky in the drama "Edward VII"?
9 Who created the characters Mikki the Martian and Tich and Quackers?
10 Who was the first presenter of ITV's "World of Sport"?
11 Who played Shane O'Neill in TV's adaptation of "A Woman of Substance"?
12 Which job did Terry Wogan have before going into broadcasting?
13 Which TV presenter managed Dewsbury and Leeds rugby clubs?
14 Who played Mrs Bridges in "Upstairs Downstairs"?
15 Which MD of BBC Radio sacked Kenny Everett for insulting a politician's wife?
16 Which character did Timothy Spall play in "Outside Edge"?
17 Who created "Soldier Soldier"?
18 Who was the first female presenter of "New Faces"?
19 Who is the mother of the actress Gaynor Faye aka Judy Mallett in "Coronation Street"?
20 What relation, if any, are the TV news journalists Jon and Peter Snow?
21 Who was known as the "godmother of soap"?
22 Who starred with Cilla Black in the first series of "Surprise Surprise"?
23 In which country was the actress Carmen Silvera born?
24 Who wrote the first series of "Black Adder"?
25 Who succeeded Robin Day as regular presenter of "Question Time"?
26 Which sitcom star sang the theme music for the fly-on-the-wall documentary series "Starting Together"?
27 Who wrote "The Phantom Raspberry Blower of Old London Town" for "The Two Ronnies?
28 Which two MPs, unseated in 1997, were contestants on "University Challenge"?
29 Who achieved notoriety as the first person to use the F-word on British TV?
30 Which role did Robbie Coltrane play in "Tutti Frutti"?

Quiz 15 Pot Luck 8

Answers - see page 481

LEVEL 3

1   What was Cassandra's real name?
2   What was the first British Top Ten hit for George Benson?
3   In which decade was David Bailey born?
4   In Monopoly how much does it cost to buy Vine Street?
5   In which sport did Tim Birkin excel early in the 20th century?
6   From which language does the word "kiwi" originate?
7   How was the East End boxer Judah Bergman better known?
8   Vardo and Lemland are in which island group?
9   Why did Edward III ban bowls?
10 Who wrote the novel *The Razor's Edge*?
11 What is the only English anagram of ALIGNMENT?
12 In which country is the city of Jaboatoa?
13 Betty Shabazz was whose widow?
14 Who wrote Food For Free about edible wild plants?
15 What is the capital of Bhutan?
16 Who had an 50s No. 1 with "Here Comes Summer"?
17 Which two counties did Dickie Bird play for?
18 Who were the two Cherryble Brothers in *Nicholas Nickleby*?
19 What is Godfrey Baseley's most durable creation?
20 Who first patented barbed wire?
21 In what month did Mrs Thatcher first become prime minister?
22 What is the approximate distance of Chicago airport from London in miles?
23 Where did the Formula 1 racing driver Alain Prost obtain his maiden triumph?
24 How many successive years did Britain win the Davis Cup in the 30s?
25 What was Augustus Henry Fitzroy's title when he was UK prime minister?
26 In which sport did Nigel Boocock excel?
27 Who was elected Labour MP for North Bucks in 1964?
28 How is Salvatore Lombino better known?
29 The international car registration RA applies to which country?
30 Which character was played by Lindsay Wagner in "The Bionic Woman"?

Answers

Pot Luck 7 (see Quiz 13)

1 12 midnight. **2** "Neighbours". **3** Edgar Allan Poe. **4** Roasting. **5** 1960s. **6** 700. **7** Dylan McKay. **8** Jacques and Joseph Montgolfier. **9** Chris Woods 80. **10** Blue. **11** Communards. **12** 1920s. **13** Sally Gunnell. **14** Spain. **15** Fawn Hall. **16** Frazer Hines. **17** Oasis Publishing. **18** "I Get Around". **19** Magny Cours. **20** Selwyn Lloyd. **21** Lutwidge. **22** Telly Savalas. **23** *The Bitch*, starring Joan Collins. **24** Philip Noel Baker. **25** Tone. **26** Bentleys. **27** Marion Crane. **28** German. **29** Greenland. **30** £150.

Quiz 16 Books

LEVEL 3

1   What were the first US equivalent of Penguin paperbacks?
2   What is the title of Dr Benjamin Spock's top bestseller?
3   In which shorthand system did Samuel Pepys write his diary?
4   How many pages did a book have to have to be termed a book according to UNESCO in 1950?
5   Who marries Estella in *Great Expectations*?
6   To ten years, when was the *Oxford English Dictionary* first published?
7   Who wrote *Jonathan Livingstone Seagull*?
8   Which John won the Nobel Prize for Literature in 1932?
9   Who wrote the Asterix books?
10   Which British author has written over 700 books and has sold over 60 million copies about one particular character?
11   What was the first Agatha Christie book in Penguin paperback?
12   Who won the Booker Prize for Remains of the Day?
13   In whose novels are Myfleet, Stowerton and Cheriton Forest found?
14   In *Busman's Honeymoon*, who is on honeymoon?
15   Whose autobiography was called *Clinging to the Wreckage*?
16   To five years when did Rudyard Kipling win the Nobel Prize for Literature?
17   In which book would you find Captain Grimes, Mr Prendergast and Egdon Heath Prison?
18   In Leon Uris's *QBVII* what is QBVII?
19   Whose diaries tell of events at Saltwood and in government?
20   Who wrote the novel on which the Barbra Streisand film *Yentl* was based?
21   Which three pseudonyms did Eleanor Alice Burford Hibbert use?
22   Who wrote *Heat and Dust* later filmed by Merchant Ivory?
23   What did Colin Dexter eventually reveal to be Morse's first name?
24   Who followed up her first success with *Testament of Experience*?
25   Who are the two sisters in *Sense and Sensibility*?
26   Which novel was the film *Kes* based on?
27   How are the novels *The Great Fortune, The Spoilt City* and *Friends and Heroes* known collectively?
28   To five, how many novels did Georgette Heyer write?
29   Which Patrick won the Nobel Prize for Literature in 1973?
30   Who wrote *The Women's Room* in 1977?

Answers

TV Who's Who (see Quiz 14)
1 Mrs Hall. 2 Richard Briers. 3 Annabel Croft. 4 Gerald Wiley. 5 Adrian Edmondson, Julie Driscoll. 6 Miriam Stoppard, Rob Buckman. 7 Colin Crompton. 8 Felicity Kendal. 9 Ray Alan. 10 Eamonn Andrews. 11 Liam Neeson. 12 Bank clerk. 13 Eddie Waring. 14 Angela Baddeley. 15 Ian Trethowan. 16 Kevin Costello. 17 Lucy Gannon. 18 Marti Caine. 19 Kay Mellor. 20 Cousins. 21 Julia Smith. 22 Christopher Biggins. 23 Canada. 24 Rowan Atkinson, Richard Curtis. 25 Peter Sissons. 26 Su Pollard. 27 Spike Milligan. 28 Malcolm Rifkind, David Mellor. 29 Kenneth Tynan. 30 Danny McGlone.

1   What were the names of Harold Wilson's two sons?
2   Which character was played by Julie Walters in "The Boys from the Black Stuff"?
3   The airline Air Littoral is based in which country?
4   Who had a 70s No. 1 with "Yes Sir, I Can Boogie"?
5   From which language does the word "paddy" originate?
6   Who invented artificial blood?
7   Utila in the Caribbean is part of which island group?
8   In 1968 who became the first Briton to win Olympic Gold at shooting for 44 years?
9   Whose wives include Dorothy Squires and Luisa Mattioli?
10 Who wrote *One-Upmanship*?
11 Which shipping forecast area is east of Finisterre?
12 Who played Bob Champion in "Champions"?
13 Hispy and Quickstep are types of what?
14 Which Formula 1 racing circuit has bends called Estoril, Lycée and Adelaide?
15 How old was Mae West when she died?
16 Who was the first host of "Crackerjack"?
17 What is the only English anagram of ALSATIANS?
18 What was Leslie Charteris's real name?
19 What are the odds of rolling any combination totalling nine in dice-throwing?
20 How many islands are in the Virgin group?
21 Which John won the Nobel Prize for Literature in 1962?
22 In Monopoly, what is the amount of the speeding fine?
23 Which racehorse trainer was the first to win over £1 million?
24 Which hospital ward was "The Singing Detective" in?
25 Who guided Oxford to ten successive boat race victories from 1976?
26 What was the first British Top Ten hit for the Beverley Sisters?
27 If it's noon at GMT, what time is it in Yokohama?
28 Helen Liddell entered Parliament after winning the by-election caused by which MP's death?
29 Which two jockeys' injuries brought about the setting up of the Injured Jockeys Fund in 1964?
30 Which Nazi was played by Ian Holm in *Holocaust*?

Answers

Pot Luck 10 (see Quiz 19)
1 L.S. Lowry. 2 Ancestral. 3 Ross Davidson. 4 Brooklands. 5 "Love Shack". 6 VisiCalc. 7 Pentonville. 8 Alfred Hitchcock. 9 Ian Stark. 10 Saul Bellow. 11 Chinese. 12 Mohammed Al Fayed. 13 Chance. 14 Lord Sebastian Flyte. 15 Gilbert. 16 Windmill. 17 White sari with a blue border. 18 900. 19 Cullinan II. 20 Yvon Petra. 21 Tower of London. 22 Evanglelista Torricelli. 23 The Tremoles. 24 Michael and Margaret. 25 David Steele. 26 Dining car on a train. 27 Badminton. 28 1080. 29 Ohio. 30 Willie Carson.

1 What took the Les Baxter Orchestra, Al Hibbler and Liberace into the charts?
2 Frank Infante and Chris Stein first made No. 1 in which group?
3 Which record gave the 70s hearthrob David Cassidy a mid-80s hit?
4 Who wrote the Rolling Stones' first No. 1?
5 Which Beatle made it first to No. 1 with a solo single?
6 What was Peter Sarstedt's follow up to "Where Do You Go To My Lovely?"?
7 What finally knocked Wet Wet Wet's "Love Is All Around" off No. 1?
8 Who charted with "Britannia Rag" and "Coronation Rag"?
9 What was A-Ha's first British Top Ten hit?
10 "Don't Cry For Me Argentina" was a big flop for whom after a previous No. 1 single?
11 What word links a door and a tambourine in No. 1 titles?
12 Who had a 70s hit with "Oh Babe What Would You Say"?
13 Who first charted with "Cowpuncher's Cantata"?
14 Camp Grenada provided the setting for whose hit?
15 Kevin Parrot and Michael Coleman made No. 1 under what name?
16 What was Tracey Ullman's first UK Top Ten hit?
17 Which magazine produced the first record chart?
18 On which label did George Michael have his first solo No. 1s?
19 How many hits did Russ Conway have in 1959 and 1960?
20 Eddie Reader had her first No. 1 with which group?
21 Which hit's title had the words "And That's The Truth" in brackets?
22 Who had his first UK hit in the 50s with "Young At Heart"?
23 First charting in 1971, when did Elton John have a solo No. 1?
24 How many Top Ten singles did New Kids On the Block have in 1990?
25 On what label did Oasis first make the charts?
26 Which artist has spent most weeks at No1 in a calendar year?
27 What was New Order's first UK Top Ten single?
28 What was Elvis's folow up to "It's Now Or Never"?
29 Who did Annie Lennox duet with on "Why"?
30 Who had their only UK hit with "Let Me Try Again"?

Answers

Movie Tough Guys (see Quiz 20)
1 Ringo Kid. 2 Lee Van Cleef. 3 Edward G. Robinson. 4 Gert Frobe. 5 Medicine. 6 Steve Guttenberg. 7 Harvey Keitel. 8 Richard Gere. 9 *The Blob*. 10 Max Cady. 11 Gene Hackman. 12 *Sands of Iwo Jima*. 13 Charles Bronson. 14 James Cagney. 15 Clint Eastwood. 16 *Patriot Games, Clear and Present Danger*. 17 Ronald Reagan. 18 The Austrian Oak. 19 Duke Mantee. 20 *Mean Streets*. 21 James Cameron. 22 *In the Heat of the Night*. 23 *Bananas*. 24 *Drum Beat*. 25 Britt. 26 *The Public Enemy*. 27 A pregnant man. 28 Terry Molloy. 29 Kirk Douglas. 30 *First Blood*.

Quiz 19 Pot Luck 10

Answers - see page 485

1   Which artist said, "I draw like a child ... entirely out of my head"?
2   What is the only English anagram of LANCASTER?
3   Which actor went from "EastEnders" to present "Daytime Live"?
4   Where was Britain's first motor-racing course, opening in 1909?
5   What was the first British Top Ten hit for the B-52s?
6   What was the name of the first spreadsheet program developed by Apple in 1979?
7   In which prison was Dr Crippen executed?
8   Who featured on the 34p - the highest-priced - of the 1985 British Film Year stamps?
9   Who won double gold for three-day eventing at the European Championships in 1991?
10 Who wrote the novel *Herzog*?
11 From which language does the word "tea" originate?
12 Who bought Fulham FC in May 1997?
13 On a Monopoly board what is between Park Lane and Liverpool Street Station?
14 Who did Anthony Andrews play in "Brideshead Revisited"?
15 Beru and Nonouti are in which island group?
16 What do the Americans mean by a pinwheel?
17 What is the dress of the order of the Missionaries of Charity founded by Mother Teresa?
18 What is the approximate distance of Rome airport from London in miles?
19 What is the diamond the Second Star of Africa also called?
20 Before Cedric Pioline who was the last Frenchman to contest a Wimbledon singles final?
21 Josef Jakobs was the last man to be hanged where?
22 Who invented the barometer?
23 Who had an 60s No. 1 with "Silence Is Golden"?
24 What were the names of James Callaghan's two children?
25 Which BBC Sports Personality of the Year shares his name with a one-time political party leader?
26 In Germany what is a *speisewagen*?
27 In which sport did Ray Stevens excel?
28 What is the sum total of the internal angles in an octagon in degrees?
29 On which river does Cincinnati stand?
30 Who was the first Scot to be champion jockey?

1　Which character did John Wayne play in *Stagecoach*?

2　Who was lead villain to Clint Eastwood in *For a Few Dollars More*?

3　Who played the boxing manager in *Kid Galahad* in 1937?

4　Who played Goldfinger in 1964?

5　What did Humphrey Bogart study before entering the navy in the World War One?

6　Who was the star of the first four *Police Academy* films?

7　Which tough guy was Judas in Martin Scorsese's *The Last Temptation of Christ*?

8　Who was the violent hustler in *Looking For Mr Goodbar*?

9　Which film gave the real-life tough guy Steve McQueen his first lead role?

10　What was Robert De Niro's role in Scorsese's *Cape Fear* in 1991?

11　Who played Buck Barrow in *Bonnie and Clyde*?

12　Which film gave John Wayne his first Oscar nomination?

13　Who once said, "I look like a quarry that someone has dynamited"?

14　Which movie tough guy started out as a female impersonator?

15　Whose production company was called Malpaso?

16　What were Harrison Ford's first two films as the ex-CIA agent Jack Ryan?

17　Who played the crime boss to Lee Marvin's contract killer in *The Killers*?

18　What was Schwarzenegger's nickname after he won a record seven Mr Olympia titles?

19　Who did Bogart play in one of his first movies *The Petrified Forest*?

20　What was the first Martin Scorsese film Robert De Niro appeared in?

21　Who directed Schwarzenegger in the *Terminator* films?

22　For which movie did Rod Steiger win his first Oscar?

23　In which film was Sylvester Stallone a thug threatening Woody Allen?

24　In which 1954 film was Charles Bronson first credited as Charles Bronson?

25　Who was the tough knife-thrower James Coburn played in *The Magnificent Seven*?

26　In which 30s movie did James Cagney push half a grapefruit into Mae West's face?

27　What unusual character did Schwarzenegger play in *Junior*?

28　What was the name of Brando's character in *On The Waterfront*?

29　Whose autobiography was called *The Ragman's Son*?

30　In which film did Stallone first play Rambo?

Answers

Pop: Charts (see Quiz 18)

1 "Unchained Melody". 2 Blondie. 3 "The Last Kiss". 4 Bobby & Shirley Womack. 5 George Harrison. 6 "Frozen Orange Juice". 7 "Saturday Night". 8 Winifred Atwell. 9 "Take On Me". 10 Lena Martell. 11 Green. 12 Hurricane Smith. 13 Max Bygraves. 14 Allan Sherman. 15 Brian and Michael. 16 "Breakaway". 17 *New Musical Express*. 18 Epic. 19 11. 20 Fairground Attraction. 21 "I'd Lie For You" (by Meat Loaf). 22 Frank Sinatra. 23 1990. 24 Seven. 25 Creation. 26 Frankie Laine. 27 "Blue Monday". 28 "Are You Lonesome Tonight". 29 Al Green. 30 Tammy Jones.

LEVEL 3

1   Which character was played by Nicholas Lyndhurst in "Butterflies"?
2   What was Joseph Conrad's real name?
3   What did Dr Henry Durant first carry out in Britain in the 30s?
4   Which country has a top-selling newspaper called *Esto*?
5   What is another name for the scaly anteater?
6   To a hundred, how many names were in the first British telephone directory, published 1880?
7   Which shipping forecast area is north of Lundy?
8   Who was WBA's FA Cup Final keeper of the 60s?
9   What is the only English anagram of ANTIDOTES?
10 Who had an 50s No. 1 with "I See The Moon"?
11 What was Colonel Thomas Blood disguised as when trying to steal the Crown Jewels?
12 The Caroline Islands belong to which country?
13 What did Bill Clinton call "the most powerful song I have ever heard"?
14 How many islands are in the Tristan da Cunha group?
15 Which TV series featured the Western Stagecoach Service?
16 If it's noon at GMT, what time is it in Vancouver?
17 In Monopoly, what is the fine for being drunk in charge?
18 Who invented the bicycle?
19 What is Michael Crawford's real name?
20 Which MP died a week after the 1997 General Election?
21 From which language does the word "tycoon" originate?
22 The Lugano Cup is awarded in which sport?
23 In which city was Cary Grant born?
24 What was the first British Top Ten hit for Big Country?
25 What was William Lamb's title when he was UK prime minister?
26 Which boxing champ shares his birth day and year with Glenda Jackson?
27 The airline Dragonair is based in which country?
28 Where was Britain's first road-race circuit, opening in 1933?
29 Who was the main figure in a Michael Browne painting unveiled in April 1997?
30 Which writer produced the work *Gargantua*?

Answers

Pot Luck 12   (see Quiz 23)
1 Authoress. 2 Voltaire. 3 Hugo Montenegro. 4 Blue. 5 Bristol. 6 Charles Edouard Jeanneret. 7 Sir Joseph Whitworth. 8 London. 9 The King's Singers (1997). 10 Putney. 11 4800. 12 *La Cage Aux Folles*. 13 Avenue Matignon. 14 Silverstone. 15 Poland. 16 Frederica "Fred" Smith. 17 Sixth. 18 D.H. Lawrence. 19 Sri Lanka. 20 Two points. 21 Benjamin Franklin. 22 Dateline. 23 Captain Marryat. 24 Fiddler's Dram. 25 Alexander. 26 Punch Tavern. 27 Carrot. 28 Magyar (Hungarian). 29 Nautilus. 30 "Summer Set".

LEVEL 3

1   In which city was Spain's King Juan Carlos born?
2   Who followed Lloyd George as prime minister of the UK?
3   Who did Sanni Abacha overthrow in Nigeria in 1994?
4   How is Emperor Akihito known in Japan?
5   Who became president of Georgia in 1992?
6   What was the name of Mrs Ceausescu who was executed with her husband?
7   Who became King of Sweden in 1973?
8   What was the nationality of the former UN Secretary General, Boutros Boutros Ghali?
9   Who won the 1990 elections in Burma while under house arrest?
10   Who went from vice-president to president of Ghana in 1967?
11   Archibald Philip Primrose was prime minister of where?
12   Who established Bloc Quebecois in 1990 in Canada ?
13   Other than politics, what is the profession of Jean-Bertrand Aristide of Haiti?
14   Who was the first science graduate to become British prime minister?
15   What post was Chief Buthelezi given in Mandela's cabinet in 1994?
16   Which faction did Robert Mugabe head before becoming prime minister of Zimbabwe?
17   Who was Bill Clinton's first Secretary of State?
18   In 1997 who was the only monarch who had been reigning longer than Elizabeth II?
19   Which Spanish prime minister took Spain into the EC?
20   Who became leader of Italy's Forza Italia Party in 1993?
21   Al Gore was senator of which state before becoming vice-president?
22   Who became the German president in 1994?
23   Who was the next non-Italian Pope after Adrian VI in 1522?
24   Who did Lionel Jospin succeed as French prime minister in 1997?
25   Who did T.N.I. Suharto overthrow to become president in 1967?
26   Who became Helmut Kohl's deputy in 1993?
27   Who is heir to the throne of Monaco?
28   Flight Lieutenant Jerry Rawlings first took power where in 1979?
29   What is the nationality of Jacques Santer?
30   Who became Portugal's first civilian president for 60 years in 1986?

The Royals (see Quiz 24)

Answers

1 Lady Diana Spencer. 2 Princess Margaret. 3 Balmoral. 4 University Labour Club. 5 Prince and Princess Michael of Kent. 6 Fabergé. 7 Les Jolies Eaux. 8 British Lung Foundation. 9 Four. 10 George Cross. 11 The Hon. Lady Ogilvy. 12 Bryan Organ's. 13 Before her father's coffin at his funeral. 14 Princess Diana. 15 Shand. 16 Princess Diana's flatmates before her marriage. 17 17 Bruton St, London W1. 18 George VI. 19 Architect. 20 Kanga. 21 The Duchess of Kent. 22 Prince Philip. 23 *The Heart Has Its Reasons*. 24 Wednesday. 25 Queen Sonja. 26 Prince Philip. 27 Queen Victoria. 28 Dan Maskell. 29 *War and Peace*. 30 Duchess of Kent.

1   What is the only English anagram (minus its hyphen) of SHARE-OUTS?
2   How is François Marie Arouet better known?
3   Who had a 60s No. 1 with "The Good, The Bad and The Ugly"?
4   What colour was *Monty Python's Big Red Book* cover?
5   At which city did Concorde make its first supersonic test flight?
6   What was Le Corbusier's real name?
7   Which mechanical engineer standardized screw threads?
8   Where were the first Olympics after the World War Two held?
9   Who first brought Lennon and McCartney music to the Proms?
10 In which London suburb was the TV series "Bless This House" set?
11 What is the approximate distance of Vancouver airport from London in miles?
12 Which musical contains "A Little More Mascara" and "Masculinity"?
13 On a French Monopoly board, what is the equivalent to the Strand?
14 Which Formula 1 circuit includes Maggotts Curve, Abbey Curve and Priory?
15 In which country is the city of Katowice?
16 Which character was played by Leslie Ash in "C.A.T.S. Eyes"?
17 In the Bible which commandment says, "Thou shalt not kill"?
18 Which writer was born at 8a Victoria Street, Eastwood?
19 The international car registration CL applies to which country?
20 In Scrabble, how much is a letter D worth?
21 Who invented the bifocal lens?
22 Which agency was launched by John Patterson in 1966?
23 Who wrote *Mr Midshipman Easy*?
24 Which group went on a Day Trip To Bangor?
25 Baranof and Prince of Wales are in which island group?
26 What is the 20th-century name of Fleet Street's pub, the Crown and Sugarloaf?
27 Favourite and Figaro are types of what?
28 From which language does the word "goulash" originate?
29 What was the name of the first US nuclear submarine?
30 What was the first British Top Ten hit for Mr Acker Bilk?

Answers

Pot Luck 11 (see Quiz 21)

1 Adam Parkinson. 2 Jozef Korzeniowski. 3 Gallup opinion poll. 4 Mexico.
5 Pangolin. 6 255. 7 Irish Sea. 8 John Osborne. 9 Stationed. 10
Stargazers. 11 Clergyman. 12 USA. 13 "Eleanor Rigby". 14 Five.
15 Wells Fargo. 16 4 a.m. 17 £20. 18 Kirkpatrick MacMillan. 19 Michael
Dumble-Smith. 20 Sir Michael Shersby. 21 Japanese. 22 Walking.
23 Bristol. 24 "Fields Of Fire". 25 Viscount Melbourne. 26 Terry Downes.
27 Hong Kong. 28 Donington Park. 29 Eric Cantona. 30 François Rabelais.

Quiz 24 The Royals

Answers - see page 490

LEVEL 3

1 Who was the first new royal to include her family's motto on her marital coat of arms?
2 Who said, "I have as much privacy as a goldfish in a bowl"?
3 Which royal residence did George V not visit during World War One?
4 Which club was Prince Charles not allowed to join by the master of his Cambridge college?
5 Which royals were not allowed to marry where they wished in 1978?
6 In 1907 who was commissioned to make models of Sandringham farm animals?
7 What is the name of Princess Margaret's house on Mustique?
8 Thirty per cent of the proceeds of Princess of Wales roses went to which charity at the Chelsea Flower Show?
9 How many British kings were emperors of India?
10 Which medal did Inspector Beaton receive after Princess Anne was attacked in the Mall in 1974?
11 Which title does Princess Alexander now have through her husband?
12 Whose portrait of Diana was damaged in the National Portrait Gallery in 1981?
13 When did Queen Elizabeth II last curtsey officially?
14 Who switched on the Christmas lights in Regent Street in November '81?
15 What was Camilla's surname before marrying Andrew Parker-Bowles?
16 Who were Virginia Pitman and Carolyn Pride?
17 Where was Queen Elizabeth II born?
18 Which 20th-century monarch is or was left-handed?
19 What was the Duke of Gloucester's profession before he became a duke?
20 What is the Prince of Wales's nickname for his friend Lady Tryon?
21 Sir William Worsley was the father of which royal?
22 Who said, "Constitutionally, I don't exist"?
23 What was the autobiography of the Duchess of Windsor called?
24 On what day of the week was Queen Elizabeth II born?
25 Who is the wife of King Harald of Norway?
26 Who is taller, Prince Philip or Prince Charles?
27 Which royal wrote *Our Life in the Highlands*?
28 Who taught Princess Anne to play tennis?
29 Which book did Princess Margaret choose for her desert island on "Desert Island Discs"?
30 Which royal performed with the Bach Choir at the Albert Hall?

Answers

World Leaders (see Quiz 22)

1 Rome. 2 Andrew Bonar Law. 3 General Babangida. 4 The Heisei Emperor. 5 Edvard Shevardnadze. 6 Elena. 7 Carl Gustaf XVI. 8 Egyptian. 9 Aung San Suu Kyi. 10 Omar Bongo. 11 UK. He was the Earl of Rosebery. 12 Lucien Bouchard. 13 Clergyman. 14 Margaret Thatcher. 15 Minister of the Interior. 16 ZANU - Zimbabwe African National Union. 17 Warren Christopher. 18 King Bhumipol of Thailand. 19 Felipe Gonzalez. 20 Silvio Berlusconi. 21 Tennessee. 22 Roman Herzog. 23 John Paul II. 24 Alain Juppé. 25 Achmed Sukarno. 26 Klaus Klinkel. 27 Prince Albert. 28 Ghana. 29 Luxembourgeois. 30 Mario Soares.

1   Where did Jacques Villeneuve take his first Formula 1 victory?
2   In Monopoly, how much is payed for school fees? ·
3   Which character was played by Cheryl Ladd in "Charlie's Angels"?
4   Which shipping forecast area is north of Rockall?
5   From which language does the word "bungalow" originate?
6   How many cricket caps did Alan Butcher - Mark's dad - win?
7   What cabinet post did Michael Heseltine resign from over the Westland affair?
8   Transavia Airlines is based in which country?
9   In which Dickens novel does Thomas Traddles appear?
10   Who had an 60s No. 1 with "Do You Mind"?
11   How old was King George III when he died?
12   Who wrote *All Quiet on the Western Front*?
13   The first Boy Scouts to be registered were based in which city?
14   If A is Alpha and B is Bravo what is N?
15   What is the American equivalent to "University Challenge"?
16   How was novelist Henri Beyle better known?
17   If it's noon at GMT, what time is it in Tehran?
18   How many islands are in the Bismarck Archipelago group?
19   What was Robin Leigh-Pemberton's job between 1983 and 1993?
20   Who invented the burglar alarm?
21   What is the only English anagram of BARGAINED?
22   What was the first British Top Ten hit for Black Sabbath?
23   Who was George Oldfield determined to catch?
24   Who created Dan Dare?
25   What does ALGOL stand for?
26   Who did Martina Navratilova beat to win her ninth Wimbledon?
27   In which churchyard was Sir Winston Churchill buried?
28   Which Mel became the Manchester City soccer boss in 1987?
29   When did Britain first occupy Hong Kong?
30   What was Colin Cowdrey born?

Answers

Pot Luck 14   (see Quiz 27)
1   W. Ritter. 2   "The Yeomen Of the Guard". 3   Versatile. 4   Boris Yeltsin.
5   "Living On The Ceiling". 6   John Stalker. 7   British Racing Drivers' Club.
8   Richmal Lambourn. 9   Sudan. 10   John McEnroe. 11   Sow. 12   Flight
Lieutenant Simon Carter. 13   Arabic. 14   Robert Louis Stevenson.
15   Thunderclap Newman. 16   Newcastle. 17   Marengo. 18   Marlborough St.
19   900. 20   1910s. 21   Jim Dale. 22   August. 23   *Gloriana*. 24   Halifax
Building Society turning into a bank. 25   Willie Whitelaw. 26   Arnold Ridley.
27   8-1. 28   4000. 29   John Braine. 30   Galapagos.

1 Who scored 11 goals for QPR in their first season in Europe?

2 Who delighted in the nickname Ambling Alp?

3 The first university boat race was contested from where to where?

4 Which brothers asked to wear England shirts while playing at Wimbledon during Euro '96?

5 Which great soccer manager was boss at Grimsby and Workington?

6 Who died during a bout with Drew Docherty in October 1995?

7 Who was Rob Andrew's first signing at Newcastle RFC?

8 Who were the only team not to score in soccer's Euro '96?

9 Who won cricket's Gillette Cup in 1970, '71 and '72?

10 Who took 5-67 on his first class debut, for Hants, in August 1996?

11 Which horse was Carson riding when he sustained serious injuries arguably hastening his retirement?

12 Who scored twice for Villa in the 50s FA Cup Final win over Manchester United?

13 Who did Steven Redgrave win Olympic Gold with in 1988?

14 Who was the first woman to be elected to the Wimbledon Championships Committee?

15 Who did Monica Seles beat to win her first Grand Slam after her attack?

16 Which soccer keeper was known as the Flying Pig?

17 What did Robbie Paul win for scoring a hat trick in the 1996 Challenge Cup Final?

18 In the 1990s who first won the World ProSnooker Championship after Stephen Hendry?

19 Mike Tyson pulled out of a fight with Buster Mathis Jnr in 1995 due to an injured what?

20 Who followed Geoff Hurst as manager of Chelsea?

21 Who coached Torvill and Dean to Olympic success?

22 Who rode Red Rum for the third Grand National triumph?

23 Who was the first footballer to marry a managing director of football?

24 Who was the manager who brought Dwight Yorke to Aston Villa?

25 Who in 1995 became the first favourite to win the Grand National for 14 years?

26 Which breaking of the law was revealed about Jack Charlton in '95?

27 Who kept goal for Spurs in the 1981 FA Cup Final?

28 Who was the first woman to ride in the Derby?

29 What were the odds on Dettori's seven-race card win in 1996?

30 Who was Manchester United manager when they were last relegated?

TV Game Shows (see Quiz 28)

1 Robert Robinson. 2 A certificate. 3 Geoffrey Wheeler. 4 1970s.
5 Arlington Grange. 6 "Whodunnit?". 7 "3-2-1". 8. Brian Aldridge (Charles Collingwood). 9 Bob Danvers-Walker. 10 Hot Spot. 11 £1, £3, £5.
12 Monica Rose. 13 Stuart Hall. 14 Princess Anne. 15 William G. Stewart.
16 Two minutes. 17 "Love Me Do". 18 Sandi Toksvig. 19 Newlyweds.
20 Gloria Hunniford. 21 Terry Wogan. 22 20 minutes. 23 Jackie Rae.
24 "The Generation Game" ("One From Eight"). 25 "Family Fortunes".
26 TV set. 27 "The Sky's The Limit". 28 Anne Aston. 29 Dictionaries.
30 "Going For A Song".

1 Who invented the cable car?
2 The 18p stamp - the cheapest in the 1992 set - showed which Gilbert and Sullivan opera?
3 What is the only English anagram of RELATIVES?
4 Which Russian wrote *Against the Grain*?
5 What was the first British Top Ten hit for Blancmange?
6 Which former policeman presented "Beat the Cheat"?
7 Who owns Silverstone Motor Racing Circuit?
8 What was Richmal Crompton's real name?
9 In which country is the city of Khartoum North?
10 Which Wimbledon winner was born the day Castro took over in Cuba?
11 On which river does Stafford stand?
12 Which character was played by David McCallum in "Colditz"?
13 From which language does the word "algebra" originate?
14 Whose nickname was Tusitala the Samoan for *The Storyteller*?
15 Who had a 60s No. 1 with "Something In The Air"?
16 Chris Waddle first played for England while with which club?
17 What was the name of Napoleon Bonaparte's favourite horse?
18 In Monopoly, where would a throw of seven from Pall Mall land you?
19 What is the sum total of the internal angles in a heptagon in degrees?
20 In which decade were photographs first required on British passports?
21 Which *Carry On* film actor had a hit with "Be My Girl"?
22 In which month does the oyster season open?
23 Which Benjamin Britten opera was commisioned for the Coronation of Queen Elizabeth II?
24 What made Mike Blackburn send out millions of letters in 1997?
25 Which Home Secretary talked about a "short, sharp shock"?
26 Who wrote the classic play *The Ghost Train*?
27 With two dice, what are the odds of rolling any combination totalling five?
28 What is the approximate distance of Karachi airport from London in miles?
29 Who wrote the novel *Room at the Top*?
30 Fernandina and Floreana are in which island group?

1 Who asked the questions in "Ask the Family"?
2 What was the prize in the early series of "What's My Line?"?
3 Who created "Winner Takes All" and co-presented it unseen?
4 In which decade did "A Question of Sport" begin?
5 In TV's "Cluedo" where does the mystery take place?
6 Which show was a 70s forerunner of "Cluedo"?
7 Which show was based on the Spanish programme "Uno, Dos Tres"?
8 Which "Archers" character read out the scores in "Telly Addicts"?
9 Who announced the prizes in the original "Take Your Pick"?
10 What indicated you were doing well in "Blockbusters" but cancelled success in "Strike It Lucky"?
11 In 70s/80s "Sale of the Century" how much were the questions worth?
12 Which contestant on "Double Your Money" became a permanent hostess on the show?
13 Who succeeded Barry Davies as presenter of "Quiz Ball"?
14 Which sportswoman was on Emlyn Hughes's team when "A Question of Sport" celebrated its 200th edition?
15 Which quizmaster first produced "The Price Is Right" in the UK?
16 How long did you have to answer the questions in "Mastermind"?
17 Which quiz shared its name with a Beatles hit?
18 Who was the first regular female captain on "Call My Bluff"?
19 What was special about the contestants in "Bob's Your Uncle"?
20 Who was the female team captain opposing Kenny Everett in "That's Showbusiness"?
21 Which radio DJ was on the very first "Celebrity Squares"?
22 How long do the chefs have to cook a meal in "Ready Steady Cook"?
23 Who first presented "The Golden Shot"?
24 Which show was originally called "Een Van De Aacht"?
25 Which show featured Mr Babbage?
26 What was the top prize when "Double Your Money" came from Communist Moscow in 1966?
27 Under what title was "Double Your Money" revived in the 70s?
28 Who was the regular innumerate blonde on "The Golden Shot"?
29 What is the prize for the ultimate champion of the series on "Countdown"?
30 Which programme had a mechanical caged bird over the opening and closing credits?

Quiz 29 Pot Luck 15

Answers - see page 499

1 In which country are the San Agustin caves?
2 What was Sir Robin Day's profession before he turned to TV?
3 From which language does the word "divan" originate?
4 Who had an 60s No. 1 with "Michael"?
5 How was the Birmingham Royal Ballet previously known?
6 What is the capital of the Canadian province Saskatchewan?
7 How many islands are in the Shetland group?
8 When did Swansea become a city?
9 In which city was Felix Mendelssohn born?
10 If it's noon at GMT, what time is it in Sydney?
11 What is the only English anagram of LACRYMOSE?
12 Alpha and Snow Cap are types of what?
13 In which city did Harold MacMillan deliver his "Wind of Change" speech?
14 John Arlott was a fan of which soccer club?
15 How is Tiziano Vecelli better known?
16 Where did Gina G finish in the 1996 Eurovision Song Contest?
17 Which Robert discovered the law of elasticity that is now known by his name?
18 On television, in which fictitious road was Shelley's flat set?
19 In which country is the city of Kigali?
20 Which character was played by Lewis Collins in "The Cuckoo Waltz"?
21 What was Daniel Defoe's real name?
22 Where was the first German Formula 1 Grand Prix staged in 1926?
23 Which England soccer captain was born in Ironbridge, Shropshire?
24 Who wrote *The Raj Quartet*?
25 How long after Jock Stein's death in 1985 was there another Wales v. Scotland game?
26 What was the first British Top Ten hit for Blondie?
27 In Monopoly, how much do you receive on 7% preference shares?
28 Who did Ramsay MacDonald follow when he first became prime minister of the UK?
29 How old was Buddy Holly when he died?
30 The airline Kyrnair is based in which country?

1   Who was the first young man to win the Junior Grand Slam?
2   Before Henman and Rusedski who were the last two Brits to be in the men's last eight together at Wimbledon?
3   Whose match had been interrupted by rain when Cliff Richard did an impromptu concert on Centre Court?
4   Where was Martina Hingis born?
5   How many times did Navratilova win the Wimbledon singles as a Czech?
6   Who holds the record for the most Wimbledon titles?
7   What was Chris Evert's second married name?
8   Who is Vera Puzejova's daughter?
9   Who won the women's singles at the 1992 Olympics?
10 Who took over sponsorship of the Virginia Slims Tournament in '79?
11 Where was the US Open played before Flushing Meadow?
12 What is Boris Becker's eldest son called?
13 What did Major Wingfield call lawn tennis when he first showed off his new game?
14 Who were known as the Three Musketeers?
15 Who was the first European to win the women's singles at Roland Garros in the 70s?
16 Who did Billie Jean Moffitt win her first women's doubles with?
17 With whom did Ann Jones win the Wimbledon mixed doubles in '69?
18 Who was the first male Brit to win a Wimbledon title after Fred Perry?
19 Where did Fred Perry die?
20 Who did Chris Evert beat to win her first Wimbledon title?
21 Who was known as the Rockhampton Rocket?
22 Who was the first Swede to win the Australian men's singles?
23 Who contested Wimbledon's longest-ever match?
24 Which tennis trophy did Hazel Hotchkiss donate?
25 Who was the first man to hold all four Grand Slam titles at once?
26 Which two countries has Hana Mandlikova played for?
27 Where were the very first US Championships held?
28 Who was the last men's singles champion at Wimbledon before it became open?
29 Who was the first person to lose in the opening round in the defence of his championship?
30 Where were the Australian Championships held in 1906 and 1912?

Pop: No. 1s (see Quiz 32)

Answers

1 Pussycat. 2 Scott McKenzie. 3 Celine Dion. 4 Seal. 5 Jane Morgan.
6 "Two Little Boys" (Rolf Harris). 7 "The Fly" (U2). 8 Tony Visconti.
9 Rotherham. 10 October. 11 Joe Dolce Music Theatre. 12 Victoria Wood.
13 "His Latest Flame". 14 1957. 15 None. 16 "Sailor". 17 The Buggles.
18 Kriss Kristofferson. 19 "Temptation". 20 David Gates. 21 Johnny Kidd.
22 St Winifred's School Choir. 23 "Goody Two Shoes". 24 San Pedro.
25 "Vincent". 26 Aneka. 27 Mitch Miller. 28 "Oh Boy". 29 Shirley
Bassey. 30 "You Spin Me Round (Like A Record)".

Quiz 31 Pot Luck 16

LEVEL 3

Answers - see page 497

1   Who had an 70s No. 1 with "Hey Girl Don't Bother Me"?
2   Which title is the Irish prime minister also known by?
3   Who wrote *The Sea-Wolf*?
4   Waitangi Day, the national day of New Zealand, is in which month?
5   Brian McClair made his soccer league debut with which club?
6   Haiti and Puerto Rico are in which island group?
7   Which character was played by Lee Majors in *The Fall Guy*?
8   In the 1990s Richard Roberts discovered what to win a Nobel prize?
9   From which language does the word "kiosk" originate?
10 What was the Hockenheimring circuit originally built to test?
11 Which cast from a TV series had a hit with "Hi-Fidelity"?
12 What do the initials JRR stand for in J.R.R. Tolkien's name?
13 In the 70s, where did Mick Burke, a cameraman, lose his life?
14 Canada was ceded to Britain by which treaty in 1763?
15 What is the approximate distance of Lima airport from London in miles?
16 What was the first British Top Ten hit for the Boomtown Rats?
17 In which country is the city of Kitchener?
18 In Monopoly how much does it cost to buy Coventry Street?
19 In ITV's "The Dustbinmen", which soccer team did Winston support?
20 Who invented canning?
21 "Um" appears how many times in the title of a Major Lance hit?
22 Who did Bolton Wanderers play in their last league game at Burnden Park?
23 Anne Hyde was the mother of which British monarch?
24 At which university did Steve Heighway get his BA degree?
25 Who was the first Russian to win the Nobel Peace Prize?
26 Who played Sergeant Major Bullimore in "The Army Game"?
27 Gerald Carr, Edward Gibson and William Pogue returned from what in 1974?
28 What is the only English anagram of SECTIONAL?
29 What was the trade of Abraham Lincoln's father?
30 What was an MP's basic pay in 1975?

Answers

Pot Luck 15   (see Quiz 29)

1 Mexico. 2 Barrister. 3 Persian. 4 Highwaymen. 5 Sadlers Wells.
6 Regina. 7 100. 8 1969. 9 Hamburg. 10 10 p.m. 11 Claymores.
12 Cauliflower. 13 Cape Town. 14 Reading. 15 Titian. 16 Seventh.
17 Hooke. 18 Pangloss. 19 Rwanda. 20 Gavin Rumsey. 21 Daniel Foe.
22 Avus Street Circuit, Berlin. 23 Billy Wright. 24 Paul Scott. 25 12 years
(May 1997). 26 "Denis". 27 £25. 28 Stanley Baldwin. 29 22. 30 Corsica.

1 Who were the first Dutch group to top the British charts?
2 Philip Blondheim had a 60s No. 1 under what name?
3 Which female spent 13 weeks on the chart before making No. 1 in February 1995?
4 Who was the uncredited vocalist of Adamski's "Killer"?
5 Who had a 50s No. 1 with "The Day The Rains Came"?
6 What was the final No. 1 of the hippy decade the 60s?
7 Which record ended Bryan Adams's 16-week record run at No. 1?
8 Who produced all the T. Rex No. 1s?
9 Where in England was the Music Factory Studios that mixed the Jive Bunny discs?
10 In which month did "Here Comes Summer" top the charts in 1959?
11 Who had a No. 1 with "Shaddap Your Face"?
12 Who was on the other side of Hale and Pace and the Stonkers' No. 1?
13 Which song was coupled with Elvis's "Little Sister"?
14 Jackie Wilson's "Reet Petite" made No. 1 in 1986, but in what year did it first chart?
15 How many instrumentals topped the charts in the 80s?
16 What was Petula Clark's first No. 1?
17 Under what name did Trevor Horn and Geoff Downes make No. 1?
18 Who wrote Lena Martell's chart-topper "One Day At A Time"?
19 What was the fourth and last No. 1 for the Everly Brothers?
20 Who wrote "Everything I Own"?
21 Who was the first artist at No. 1 to wear an eye patch?
22 Who were the last all-girl group to reach No. 1 before Eternal in 1989?
23 Which was the first No. 1 for Adam Ant as opposed to Adam and the Ants?
24 Which island is lamented in "La Isla Bonita"?
25 Which No. 1 begins, "Starry, starry night"?
26 Under what name did Mary Sandeman reach No. 1?
27 Who produced No. 1s for Guy Mitchell, Frankie Lane and Johnnie Ray?
28 What was Mud's last No. 1?
29 Who had a 50s No. 1 with "As I Love You"?
30 What was the first Stock, Aitken and Waterman-produced No. 1?

1   What was the first solo British Top Ten hit for Cher?
2   If it's noon at GMT, what time is it in Tangier?
3   In which school was "Whack-O" set?
4   What was George Eliot's real name?
5   Which shipping forecast area is west of forecast area Plymouth?
6   What plants were featured on a set of 1993 British stamps?
7   On which river does Calcutta stand?
8   How many islands are in the Bissagos group?
9   Who was widowed by the death of Stefano Casiraghi in 1990?
10 Who had a 70s No. 1 with "You To Me Are Everything"?
11 The airline Flitestar is based in which country?
12 In the 1850s what did the discovery by Edward Hargreaves lead to?
13 Who won the Formula 1 German Grand Prix in three successive years, 1988/89/90?
14 In Monopoly, how much do you collect following a bank error?
15 What is the only English anagram of CONTINUED?
16 Matilda Alice Victoria Wood was known for what type of entertainment?
17 Which Road in Drumcree was the centre of unrest in July 1997?
18 Who did Danniella Westbrook play in "Frank Stubbs Promotes"?
19 Who was the youngest MP after the 1997 general election?
20 In Bob Dylan's view what "don't work 'cos the vandals took the handles"?
21 Where did the 1997 Tour de France start?
22 Autumn Jackson claimed to be whose illegitimate daughter?
23 Which valley gives the setting for the TV soap "A Country Practice"?
24 In which month was John Lennon murdered?
25 Which beaten finalist said, "Pete [Sampras] doesn't let you breathe"?
26 Who invented the cannon?
27 The writer John Buchan became Governor General of where?
28 From which language does the word "floe" originate?
29 How was the actress Beatrice Stella Tanner better known?
30 Mary Shelley's novel was called *Frankenstein; or the...* what?

LEVEL 3

1   The Croatian currency kuna is divided into 100 what?
2   On which river does Berlin stand?
3   Which three major Spanish international airports begin with "V"?
4   In which city is Interpol's HQ?
5   Where was the World Council of Churches established in 1948?
6   Which country's official name is Republika e Shqipërisë?
7   What is Europe's lowest point below sea level?
8   Where is the UN's Food and Agriculture agency - FAO - based?
9   Who are the two heads of state of Andorra?
10   What is the capital of Saxony?
11   Which country has Letzeburgish as its most widely used language?
12   What is Europe's highest waterfall called?
13   Where is the European Investment Bank?
14   Where is the petroleum company ENI based?
15   What are the only armed forces in Monaco?
16   The Aland Islands belong to which country?
17   Where is the HQ of the World Meteorological Organization?
18   The Glomma is one of the principal rivers of which country?
19   Which three French regions begin with A?
20   Which country's highest point is Rysys?
21   Which has the greater area, Iceland or Ireland?
22   What is San Marino's second-largest town?
23   Where is Ulemiste Airport?
24   Which is farther north, Moscow or Copenhagen?
25   Where was the UN peacekeeping mission UNPROFOR in force?
26   What is Belgium's highest point?
27   On which river does Amsterdam stand?
28   Other than Denmark where is Danish currency used?
29   Where is Italy's principal stock exchange?
30   Gozo and Comino are to the north west of which island?

Answers

Movies: Who's Who? (see Quiz 36)
1 Louis Malle. 2 Simone Signoret. 3 Anne Fine. 4 Kiefer Sutherland.
5 Tilda Swinton. 6 Patrick Swayze, Lisa Niemi. 7 Catherine Deneuve.
8 Gerard Depardieu. 9 Bo Derek's. 10 Divine. 11 Whoopi Goldberg.
12 Michael Gough. 13 Richard E. Grant. 14 Melanie Griffith. 15 Bernard
Herrmann. 16 Charlton Heston. 17 Glenn Close. 18 John Malkovitch.
19 Steve Martin. 20 Melina Mercouri. 21 Liza Minnelli. 22 Carmen
Miranda. 23 Val Kilmer. 24 Joanne Woodward. 25 Michael Douglas.
26 Pee-Wee Herman. 27 Henry Mancini. 28 Joanne Whalley-Kilmer.
29 Natalie Wood. 30 Dr Kellogg.

Quiz 35 Pot Luck 18

LEVEL 3

1. Which character was played by Julie Walters in "GBH"?
2. Which literary figure was born at Somersby rectory in Lincolnshire?
3. On a Monopoly board what is between Marylebone Station and Community Chest?
4. At which circuit did Damon Hill achieve his first GP victory in 1993?
5. Who was massacred on Valentine's Day in 1779 at Kealakekua Bay?
6. Which Dickens novel was set in Cloisterham?
7. What is John Cleese's middle name?
8. Who had a 70s No. 1 with "Son Of My Father"?
9. Who said William Hague had "no ideas, no experience and no hope"?
10. In the1984 charts, who felt like Buddy Holly?
11. What is the only English anagram of MADDENING?
12. Amrum and Nordstrand are in which island group?
13. What was William Henry Cavendish's title when he was UK prime minister?
14. What is the sum total of the internal angles in a hexagon in degrees?
15. In which county was Southfork Ranch in "Dallas"?
16. Which writer used the assumed name Peter Goldsmith?
17. Who protected her nursery school class from a machete wielding attacker in 1996?
18. Philippa Roberts was a world champion in which sport?
19. From which language does the word "gauntlet" originate?
20. Who wrote the book *Greenmantle*?
21. What was the first British Top Ten hit for Chicago?
22. Who designed Queen Elizabeth II's coronation gown?
23. The international car registration ET applies to which country?
24. Tokyo Slicer and Pepita are types of what?
25. Who founded the Creation record label?
26. In what decade did Malta become independent after British rule?
27. Who did the US *Entertainment Weekly* magazine's Jim Mullen say was "the only known antidote to 'Baywatch'"?
28. Which soccer club did the ex-PM Harold Wilson support?
29. Who was the first black person on "The Black and White Minstrel Show"?
30. What is the approximate distance of Manila airport from London in miles?

---

1   Who directed Brooke Shields in *Pretty Baby*?

2   Who was born in Germany as Simone Kaminker?

3   Who wrote the book that *Interview with the Vampire* was based on?

4   Whose first screen role was in *Max Dugan Returns* with his father?

5   Who played Queen Isabella in Derek Jarman's *Edward II*?

6   Which husband-and-wife team starred in *Steel Dawn* in 1987?

7   Who earned her first Oscar nomination in 1992 for *Indochine*?

8   Whose film US debut was opposite Andie MacDowell in *Green Card*?

9   David Letterman once introduced a plank of wood as whose acting coach?

10   How was Harris Glenn Milstead better known?

11   Who was the voice of Shenzi in *The Lion King*?

12   Who played Alfred in the 1989, 1992 and 1995 *Batman* films?

13   Who played the harrassed executive in *How to Get Ahead in Advertising*?

14   Which 18-year-old divorcee made her screen debut in *Night Moves*?

15   Who died the night after conducting his score for *Taxi Driver* in '75?

16   Whose diary, *The Actor's Life* was published in 1978?

17   Andie MacDowell starred in the Tarzan film *Greystoke*, but who was later asked to dub her voice?

18   Who played the Vicomte de Valmont in *Dangerous Liaisons*?

19   Whose first film role saw him enacting "Maxwell's Silver Hammer" in the *Sgt Pepper* movie?

20   Which actress and political activist was married to the director Jules Dassin?

21   Whose movie debut was in a film starring her mother, *In the Good Old Summertime*, in 1949?

22   Who died of a heart attack after a dance routine on Jimmy Durante's TV show?

23   Who played Elvis's spirit in *True Romance*?

24   Who narrated Martin Scorsese's *The Age of Innocence*?

25   Who appeared in and co-produced *The China Syndrome*?

26   Who played the Penguin's father in *Batman Returns*?

27   Who published his life story, *Did They Mention the Music?* in 1989?

28   Who has played Christine Keeler on film and Vivien Leigh on TV?

29   Who was the little girl who did not believe in Santa Claus in the 1947 film *Miracle on 34th Street*?

30   Who was the hero of *The Road to Welville*, played by Anthony Hopkins?

Answers

Euro Tour (see Quiz 34)

1 Para. 2 Spree. 3 Valencia, Vigo, Vitoria. 4 Lyon. 5 Amsterdam. 6 Albania. 7 Caspian Sea. 8 Rome. 9 President of France, Spanish Bishop of Urgel. 10 Dresden. 11 Luxembourg. 12 Ormeli. 13 Luxembourg City. 14 Italy. 15 Palace guard. 16 Finland. 17 Geneva. 18 Norway. 19 Alsace, Aquitaine, Auvergne. 20 Poland. 21 Iceland. 22 Serraville. 23 Tallinn, Estonia. 24 Moscow. 25 Bosnia-Herzegovina and Macedonia. 26 Mount Botrange. 27 Amstel. 28 Greenland and the Faeroe Islands. 29 Milan. 30 Malta.

1   What was the first British Top Ten Hit for Clannad?
2   What was Richard Gordon's real name?
3   What are the odds of rolling double six in dice-throwing?
4   How many islands are in the Seychelles group?
5   Who invented air conditioning for cars?
6   Which Radio 2 presenter's first novel was called *Charlotte's Friends*?
7   What is the only English anagram of DIAMETRIC?
8   What was the title of the "Coronation Street" creator Tony Warren's autobiography?
9   Which rock star had been a grave digger and a Brentford footballer?
10 In which country is the city of La Paz?
11 Who wrote the novel *Saturday Night and Sunday Morning*?
12 Liverpool signed Ian St John from which club?
13 Which Kirsty MacColl record did Gordon Brown choose on "Desert Island Discs"?
14 Which 19th-century trainer won the St Leger 16 times?
15 Who had the first British No. 1 with a song titled "Tears On My Pillow"?
16 Which song did Aled Jones forget the words of during a Royal Variety Show?
17 Which character was played by Tony Adams in "General Hospital"?
18 From which language does the word "tattoo" originate?
19 Who won the 1989 Hungaroring Formula 1 Grand Prix, giving Ferrari their only success at the track?
20 If it's noon at GMT, what time is it in Cape Town?
21 How much is the doctor's fee in Monopoly?
22 Which British newspaper was founded in 1843?
23 The Rowe sisters were world champions in which sport?
24 What was co-founded by Denise O'Donoghue in 1985?
25 What was Sir Allan Green, then Director of Public Prosecutions, cautioned for in 1992 ?
26 What do the initials AJ stand for in A.J. Cronin's name?
27 In which century was Nostradamus born?
28 What was the codename for the 1941 German plan to invade the Soviet Union?
29 The airline NFD is based in which country?
30 Who was given a mess of pottage in return for his birthright in the Book of Genesis?

Answers

Pot Luck 20   (see Quiz 39)
1 Byron. 2 Hedonists. 3 Spa-Francorchamps. 4 "Manimal". 5 Carrickfergus Castle. 6 December. 7 Psephologist. 8 Mexico. 9 Franz Kafka. 10 Snap. 11 George Best. 12 *The Times*. 13 Andrew. 14 Guy Lofthouse. 15 Rumen. 16 25th October. 17 Frankie Laine. 18 St. Ogg's. 19 Latin. 20 Lesser Antilles. 21 Rosie Barnes. 22 Frederick W Lanchester. 23 Chesterfield. 24 Sir Adrian Boult. 25 6,000. 26 "The Little Shoemaker". 27 Freddie Starr. 28 Delaware. 29 Pineapple Face. 30 Boulevard de La Villette.

1 What was Billy Cotton's theme tune?
2 In the Street what were Ken Barlow's parents called?
3 Who was the leader of the Daleks?
4 Who had his own series "Do It Yourself" in 1957?
5 Which adventurer battled against "The Face"?
6 Which future TV prime minister was one of Robin Hood's Merry Men?
7 Who first presented "Sunday Night at the London Palladium"?
8 Which programme replaced "Tonight"?
9 "Watchdog" was originally part of which programme?
10 Who succeeded Robert Wilson as host of "The White Heather Club"?
11 Who owned the corner shop in "Coronation Street" until 1974?
12 Which role did Gabrielle Drake play in "The Brothers"?
13 Who played Governor Faye Bowell in "Within These Walls"?
14 What was the name of the pub in "Albion Market"?
15 Who succeeded Keith Fordyce as presenter of "Thank Your Lucky Stars"?
16 Which star of "Jason King" was born Cyril Louis Goldbert?
17 Which role did Jane Wyman play in "Falcon Crest"?
18 Who were the first two teams on "University Challenge"?
19 Which three ports featured in "Triangle"?
20 Who was the host on "Stars and Garters"?
21 Who was the first Sports Personality of the Year in 1954?
22 In "Coronation Street" who was Linda Cheveski's mother?
23 Who were the first presenters of "Top Gear"?
24 Who played Dr Richard Moone in "Emergency Ward 10"?
25 Which arts programme did "The South Bank Show" replace?
26 Who played Emma Callon in "The Onedin Line"?
27 What was the first series to feature John Wilder and Scott Furlong?
28 Which bandleader introduced "Television Dancing Club"?
29 Who created "Come Dancing"?
30 Who was the original choreographer of Pan's People?

Answers

Sporting Speed Stars (see Quiz 40)
1 Jean-Pierre Jabouille. 2 Gay Lord. 3 Jesse Owens. 4 1926. 5 100 metre sprint. 6 Bruce McLaren. 7 Joyce Smith. 8 Nelson Piquet. 9 Ron Hutchinson (one win). 10 Lammtarra. 11 Roller skating. 12 Hungary. 13 Drum Taps. 14 Stephen Roche. 15 Heinz-Harald Frentzen. 16 Scobie Breasley. 17 Alan Morton. 18 Nelson Piquet. 19 Cecil Sandford. 20 Rallying. 21 Johnny Herbert. 22 Paul Seaton. 23 Sherry's Prince. 24 9 for 57 (v. SA, Oval 1994). 25 Mill Reef. 26 Carlos Pace. 27 John Surtees. 28 Leroy Burrell. 29 1,000 Guineas. 30 Eddie Irvine.

1 What was James Dean's middle name?
2 What is the only English anagram of DISHONEST?
3 Where is the Formula 1 motor racing circuit in Belgium?
4 What series saw Simon MacCorkindale changing into animals?
5 The 80s British castle stamps showed Caernarfon, Edinburgh, Windsor and where?
6 In which month in 1960 was "Coronation Street" first screened?
7 What word is given to someone who studies elections and voting?
8 In which country is the city of Leon?
9 Who wrote the book *The Castle*?
10 Who had a 90s No. 1 with "The Power"?
11 Who owned the nightclubs Blinkers and Slack Alice?
12 Which was the first paper to publish a daily weather chart?
13 Which name comes from the Greek and means manly?
14 Which character was played by Keith Barron in "The Good Guys"?
15 What is the first stomach of a cow called?
16 When is St Crispin's Day
17 Under what name did Frank Paul Lo Vecchio become a singing star?
18 What was the name of the Cathedral in "All Gas and Gaiters"?
19 From which language does the word "premium" originate?
20 Leeward and Windward are in which island group?
21 Who was the only female Social Democrat MP when the party was wound up?
22 Who invented car disc brakes?
23 Morris, Dyche and Hewitt were FA Cup semi-final scorers for whom?
24 Who founded the BBC Symphony Orchestra in 1930?
25 What is the approximate distance of Hong Kong airport from London in miles?
26 What was the first British Top Ten hit for Petula Clark?
27 What is Freddie Starr's real name?
28 On which river does Philadelphia stand?
29 What nickname was given to the dictator President Noriega?
30 On a French Monopoly board, what is the equivalent to Pall Mall?

1   Which Formula 1 racing driver secured Renault their first victory at Dijon in 1979?
2   What was the name of Gordon Richards's first winning horse?
3   Which great athlete died at Tuscon, Arizona, in 1980?
4   In which year did Brooklands stage its first Formula1 Grand Prix?
5   Armin Harry and Harry Jerome set world records in what?
6   Who was driving for McLaren when they won their first Fomula 1 race?
7   Which UK woman won the first two London Marathons?
8   Who won the first Formula 1 Grand Prix at Hungaroring in 1986, 38 seconds in front of Senna?
9   Who won the St Leger from 1967 to 1972 appart from Lester Piggott?
10 In 1995 on which horse did Walter Swinburn set a Derby record time?
11 Chloe Ronaldson was a speed star of the 60s, 70s and 80s at what?
12 At which 1992 race did Nigel Mansell secure enough points to win the Formula 1 World Championship?
13 Frankie Dettori won the Ascot Gold Cup in 1992 and 1993 on which horse?
14 Who was the first Irishmam to win the Tour de France?
15 Who partnered Jacques Villeneuve at the Williams team in 1997?
16 Who won the Derby on the unseasonably named Santa Claus?
17 Which Rangers speedy left winger made goals for Gallagher and James in the 1920s?
18 Who won the first Formula 1 world championship San Marino Grand Prix in 1981?
19 Who was the first British motorcycle rider to be world 125cc champ?
20 What was the sport of Stirling Moss's sister Pat?
21 Who, surprisingly, won the 1995 Formula 1 British Grand Prix at Silverstone?
22 Who was the first UK man to be European water sking champ?
23 Which greyhound first won a hat trick of Grand National races?
24 What is Devon Malcolm's best return in a Test innings?
25 In the 70s, which horse gave Geoff Lewis his only Derby triumph?
26 Who gave his name to the Brazilian Formula 1 Grand Prix circuit?
27 Who was the first man to have been world champ on two wheels as well as four?
28 Who was the first person to officially run 100 metres in 9.9 seconds?
29 Which of the five Classics has Lester Piggott won least times?
30 Who partnered Michael Schumacher at Ferrari in 1997?

LEVEL 3

1 Which character was played by Susan Tully in "Grange Hill"?
2 Remus and Sprite are types of what?
3 What is a paronomasia?
4 Who had an 70s No. 1 with "So You Win Again"?
5 If it's noon at GMT, what time is it in Ho Chi Minh City?
6 In whose fictitious fashion workshop was "The Rag Trade" set?
7 How much is received in Monopoly from the sale of stock?
8 Who invented the carpet sweeper?
9 Which UK paper size is 52 x 74 mm?
10 Which shipping forecast area is north of Malin?
11 What was O. Henry's real name?
12 What did John Mason Neale write?
13 Roger Palmer is all-time top league scorer for which soccer club?
14 What was founded in 1844 by George Williams?
15 Achluophobia is the fear of what?
16 Who was the first woman to win the tennis French Open two years running on more than one occassion?
17 What is the only English anagram of FOUNDLING?
18 What was the name of the first custom-built oil tanker?
19 What was the first British Top Ten hit for Russ Conway?
20 From which US state would a Nutmegger come from?
21 The airline Norontair is based in which country?
22 Who wrote *The Adventures of Peregrine Pickle*?
23 Which South African played in Ireland's first-ever victory over a county cricket side?
24 The Indy car racer Bobby Unser was born on the same day as which fashion designer?
25 What was Edward George Stanley's title when he was UK prime minister?
26 What is Joan Collins's middle name?
27 In which country is the city of Medellin?
28 Which soap had a building with three white feathers as its logo?
29 From which language does the word "robot" originate?
30 How many islands are in the Cape Verde group?

Answers

Pot Luck 22 (see Quiz 43)
1 Coventry Street. 2 540. 3 "Chain Gang". 4 "Pot Black". 5 James Wight.
6 Eskimo. 7 Cycling. 8 Citroën. 9 Finland. 10 Anthony Burgess.
11 Surtees. 12 The Delrons. 13 Alabama. 14 Cartoonist Vicky (Victor Weisz). 15 Metal strips were added. 16 Names used by crossword compilers.
17 Wonder Woman. 18 Argentina. 19 Cyborg. 20 Fiji. 21 John W. Hyatt.
22 15th. 23 3,200. 24 Mountaineer (died on Everest). 25 Robin Beck.
26 Gradients. 27 Jim Clark. 28 Piltdown Man. 29 Perón. 30 Austria.

1   Which one-hit wonders sang "Gimme Gimme Good Lovin'"?
2   What was the first No. 1 single on the Apple label?
3   Which hit came from James Garner's film *A Man Could Get Killed*?
4   Which group backed Mike Berry?
5   Who had a hit with "Gin House Blues"?
6   Which label did the Bee Gees record on in the 60s?
7   What's the only 60s No. 1 to mention a soft fruit in the title?
8   Denny Doherty and Michelle Gillam were part of which group?
9   Who co-wrote "Sugar Sugar" with Jeff Barry?
10 Who sang about "Ramona", "Marie" and "Marta"?
11 Under what name did John Henry Deighton have his only No. 1?
12 Tony Hatch was an in-house producer for which company?
13 "A Whiter Shade of Pale" was released on which label?
14 Which No. 1 had the backing vocals "ook-a-chunka, ook-a-chunka"?
15 What was on the other side of Roy Orbison's "Blue Bayou"?
16 Freddie Heath and the Nutters became who for a 1960 No. 1?
17 What was the Stones' last No. 1 of the 60s (and 70s, 80s and 90s!)?
18 What was the Beatles' next album after *A Hard Day's Night*?
19 What was the number of the flight on which Ebony Eyes was killed?
20 What were the real surnames of the one-hit wonders Zager and Evans?
21 What was Billy J. Kramer's last chart success of the 60s?
22 What was Sinatra's follow-up to "Strangers in the Night"?
23 Clem Curtis was lead vocalist with which chart-topping group?
24 Who produced the Kinks' No. 1 hits?
25 Which group were first to get a cover of a Beatles album track to No. 1?
26 Who wrote the hippy anthem "San Francisco"?
27 Which No. 1 mentioned "a friend of Sacha Distel"?
28 What was Elvis's last hit of the 60s?
29 Who wrote "MacArthur Park"?
30 Who produced Cilla's No. 1 hits?

Answers

Food & Drink (see Quiz 44)

1   Lettuce. 2   Calves' stomachs. 3   Auvergne. 4   Buffalo milk. 5   Thiamin. 6   Ram's horn. 7   Chicken Marengo. 8   Pine nuts. 9   Parmigiano-Reggiano. 10   Wormwood. 11   Tomato purée. 12   In foil or paper. 13   USA. 14   A type of cider. 15   Angel hair. 16   Still water. 17   Japan. 18   President Thomas Jefferson. 19   Preservative. 20   Moulin Rouge. 21   Eggs. 22   Perrier water. 23   Wimpy. 24   Chopsticks. 25   Whey. 26   Haagen-Dazs ice cream. 27   Two legs and saddle. 28   Hass. 29   Bows - means butterflies. 30   Cake.

LEVEL 3

1 In Monopoly, where would a double four from Vine Street land you?
2 What is the sum total of the internal angles in a pentagon in degrees?
3 What was the first British Top Ten hit for Sam Cooke?
4 Which sports programme had a theme tune called "Ivory Rag"?
5 What was James Herriot's real name?
6 From which language does the word "kayak" originate?
7 Eileen Sheridan was a record-breaker at which sport?
8 Which car manufacturer made the first front-wheel-drive vehicle?
9 The international car registration SF applies to which country?
10 Who wrote the novel *Time for a Tiger*?
11 Which John was BBC Sports Personality of the Year in 1959?
12 Who sang with Reparata on "Captain Of Your Ship"?
13 Which US state is known as the Camellia State?
14 Who first dubbed Harold Macmillan "Supermac"?
15 What happened to Bank of England £1 notes in 1940?
16 Who or what are Chifonie, Orlando and Paul?
17 What was the other name for Princess Diana of Paradise Island?
18 In which country is the city of Mendoza?
19 The TV series "Six Million Dollar Man" was based on which book?
20 Viti Levu and Vanua Levu are in which island group?
21 Who invented celluloid?
22 In which century was Martin Luther born?
23 What is the approximate distance of Montreal airport from London in miles?
24 What was the profession of Malcolm Duff, who died in April 1997?
25 Who had an 80s No. 1 with "First Time"?
26 What is the only English anagram of ASTRINGED?
27 Who won the Belgian Formula 1 Grand Prix each year from 1962 to 1965?
28 Charles Dawson was involved in which discovery?
29 Which president gave backing to the Argentine Formula 1 Grand Prix circuit which opened in 1952?
30 In which country are the Schwersystem caves?

1 A batavia is a variety of what?
2 From where is rennet normally obtained?
3 Which part of France does Cantal cheese come from?
4 What was mozzarella cheese originally made from?
5 What is the chemical name of vitamin B1?
6 A rhyton was a drinking vessel in the shape of what?
7 Which chicken dish was named after a Napoleonic battle of June 1800?
8 What sort of nuts are used to make a pesto sauce?
9 What does authentic Parmesan cheese have stamped on its rind?
10 The leaves of which plant are the main ingredient of absinthe?
11 What do you add to a white sauce to make an aurore sauce?
12 How do you cook food *en papillote*?
13 Where is the home of the Anheuser-Busch Inc. brewery?
14 What is Ameleon?
15 What does the name of the pasta *capelli d'angelo* mean?
16 What sort of drink is Volvic?
17 Where is the Kirin Brewery based?
18 Who had signed the wine bottle sold for £105,000 at Christie's in 1985?
19 What are the ingredients with E numbers 200-29 used for in foods?
20 In which restaurant did Escoffier begin his career?
21 What is the main ingredient of a piperade?
22 Which drink is Les Bouillens famous for?
23 Which fast-food chain opened its first UK outlet in London in 1954?
24 What do the Chinese call "lively fellows"?
25 What is ricotta cheese made from?
26 What was Reuben Mattus's most famous creation of 1961?
27 What does a baron of lamb consist of?
28 Which type of avocado has a knobbly skin?
29 What shape is farfalle pasta?
30 What is a *kugelhopf*?

1 Under what name did William White open the door to stardom?
2 In Monopoly, how much do you inherit in Community Chest?
3 Which British TV personality was Australia's first female newsreader?
4 Who was Damon Hill's teammate with the 1997 Formula 1 Arrows Team?
5 Who played Chingachgook in the old TV series "Hawkeye and the Last of the Mohicans"?
6 Who had an 80s No. 1 with "Seven Tears"?
7 How did Ivan Owen's voice become widely heard on TV?
8 Who invented Portland cement?
9 Where in England was Mystic Meg born?
10 Androphobia is the fear of what?
11 In which country is the city of Mogadishu?
12 What is the only English anagram of SIGNATORY?
13 Which character was played by David McCallum in "The Invisible Man"?
14 If A is Alpha and B is Bravo what is P?
15 How was Mikhail Khristodoulou Mouskos better known?
16 Who wrote *Corridors of Power*?
17 Who was the voice of Buzby in the BT adverts?
18 Who was Nigel Mansell's teammate in the year he won the Formula 1 World Championship?
19 How many islands are in the Scilly group?
20 On which river does Kilmarnock stand?
21 The adjective hircine refers to which creatures?
22 Who replaced Aldershot in the Football League?
23 What is the capital of the US State of Kansas?
24 What was the name of the dog in the TV series "Hart to Hart"?
25 Who was painted by both Antony Williams and Susan Ryder?
26 If it's noon at GMT, what time is it in Panama City?
27 What was the first British Top Ten hit for Rita Coolidge?
28 In which Dickens novel does Dolly Varden appear?
29 What was Harry Lauder's real name?
30 From which language does the word "lemming" originate?

1   Which Italian king was assassinated in 1900?
2   In 1903 Panama was seceded from which country?
3   What was nationalized first in Britain, the railway or coal industry?
4   Where did the 1929 Hunger March to London begin?
5   The Chaco War broke out in 1928 between which two countries?
6   Which US Acts of the 1930s prevented involvement in non-American wars?
7   Who annexed Bosnia and Herzegovina in 1908?
8   Who first reached the North Pole in 1909?
9   Who was emperor of Japan during World War One?
10 What did the 1948 Marshall Plan provide?
11 In World War One who made up the Triple Entente?
12 What did the British Citizenship Act of 1948 guarantee?
13 Where in Europe did women gain the vote in 1971?
14 What did the Balfour Declaration of 1917 support?
15 How many independent republics was the USSR divided into in 1991?
16 Who clashed at the Battle of Midway Island in 1942?
17 Which dynasty was overthrown in China in 1912?
18 Who established a Nationalist Chinese Government in 1923?
19 Who left the Commonwealth in 1949?
20 Who was deposed from the Spanish throne in 1931?
21 In World War One how was the third battle of Ypres also known?
22 Where did a military coup bring about the first Marxist state in Africa?
23 Who seized power in Iran in 1921?
24 Where was there a war against Portuguese rulers from 1962-74?
25 In which country was the Mau Mau uprising?
26 In which war was the Battle of Ebro River?
27 Who was head of the Turkish republic formed in 1923?
28 Immediately after which war was the PLO formed?
29 Whose murder took place at Birla House?
30 Contrary to tradition, whose presence was not required at the birth of Prince Charles?

Quiz 47 Pot Luck 24

LEVEL 3

Answers - see page 513

1 What is the approximate distance of Nairobi airport from London in miles?
2 What is the only English anagram of FIREIRONS?
3 Under what name did Jean Garvelet ply his high-risk trade?
4 What are the odds of rolling any combination totalling four in dice-throwing?
5 Who had a 50s No. 1 with "Butterfly"?
6 What is Nelson Mandela's middle name?
7 George Lee was three times world champion in which sport?
8 Concord is the capital of which US state?
9 Which city was the TV series "The Champions" set in?
10 Musselburgh and Early Market are types of what?
11 Who wrote the poems "Mental Cases" and "Futility"?
12 Who appeared on stamps for the Penny Black's 150th anniversary?
13 Formigar and Terceira are in which island group?
14 What handicap did Sydney Smith overcome to win Wimbledon doubles?
15 Who was the first Englishman to win the British Grand Prix?
16 Who worked at an undertaker's with the motto "Taste, Tact, Economy"?
17 From which language does the word "assassin" originate?
18 George I was born at which castle?
19 In Monopoly how much does it cost to buy Bond Street?
20 Who co-wrote "Fawlty Towers" with John Cleese?
21 What links Hampstead Heathens, Reigate Priory and Maidenhead?
22 Whose first DIY programme was broadcast in 1957?
23 What plagued Mark Twain, Groucho Marx and Franz Kafka?
24 In which country is the city of Monrovia?
25 What was the first British Top Ten hit for Randy Crawford?
26 Who designed the 1992 Barcelona Olympics team outfit for Lithuania?
27 Who rode Troy and Henbit to Derby triumphs?
28 What is the Norwegian parliament called?
29 In which teaching hospital was "Doctor in the House" set?
30 What is formed by the metamorphosis of limestone?

Pot Luck 23 (see Quiz 45)

1 Larry Grayson. 2 £100. 3 Jan Leeming. 4 Pedro Diniz. 5 Lon Chaney Jnr.
6 Goombay Dance Band. 7 Voice of Basil Brush 8 Joseph Aspdin.
9 Accrington. 10 Men. 11 Somalia. 12 Gyrations. 13 Dr Daniel Westin.
14 Papa. 15 Archbishop Makarios. 16 C.P. Snow. 17 Bernard Cribbins.
18 Riccardo Patrese. 19 About 150. 20 Irvine. 21 Goats. 22 Barnet.
23 Topeka. 24 Freeway. 25 Queen Elizabeth II. 26 7 a.m. 27 "We're All
Alone". 28 *Barnaby Rudge*. 29 Hugh MacLennan. 30 Norwegian.

1   What was the name of Gomez Addams's pet octopus?
2   Which character did Kevin Whatley play in "Auf Wiedersehen Pet"?
3   What was the name of the club in the 80s sitcom "Dear John"?
4   What was Captain Mainwaring's first name in "Dad's Army"?
5   Who sang the theme to "You Rang M'Lord" with its star Paul Shane?
6   Which former secretary was consultant on the first two series of "Yes Minister"?
7   Who starred in his own sitcom as Rob Petrie?
8   Who was the older secretary in "May to December"?
9   In "Up Pompeii" who was the daughter of Ludicrus and Ammonia?
10 In "2 Point 4 Children" what was Bill's mum called?
11 Who was assistant manager at Eddie Brown's turf accountant?
12 What was the surname of Terry and June in the sitcom?
13 Who were Timothy Lumsden's parents in "Sorry"?
14 Who was the Spencers' neighbour in the last series of "Some Mothers Do 'Ave 'Em"?
15 What was the goat called in "The Good Life"?
16 In "The Upper Hand" what did Charlie do before he was a housekeeper?
17 What was the name of the ghost in "So Haunt Me"?
18 Which 90s sitcom featured the "Jackie Onassis of Bethnal Green"?
19 Who was Shelley's landlady in Pangloss Road?
20 What was the name of Adrian Mole's parents?
21 What and where was "Robin's Nest"?
22 Which sitcom resulted from a one-off play called "The Banana Box"?
23 In "Agony", of which magazine was Jane Lucas problems-page editor?
24 What was Miriam Karlin's militant character in "The Rag Trade"?
25 In "Blackadder" who played Richard III?
26 What were Rab C. Nesbitt's children called?
27 What was the fictitious setting for "The River" with David Essex?
28 Which company did Sarah first work for in "After Henry"?
29 By which film star's name did Alf Garnett refer to his son-in-law?
30 What is the "day job" of ARP Warden Hodges in "Dad's Army"?

1 Which celebrity fell over on the first of his own UK television chat shows?
2 Charlottetown is the capital of which Canadian province?
3 Who invented the chronometer?
4 Gilles Villeneuve was killed during testing at which 1982 Formula 1 Grand Prix race?
5 What is the only English anagram of INTRODUCE?
6 Who wrote *The Gulag Archipelago*?
7 Who had an 80s No. 1 with "The Model"?
8 How was Ferdinand Joseph Lemott better known?
9 If it's noon at GMT, what time is it in Brasilia?
10 Who is the villain in the Wilkie Collins novel *The Woman In White*?
11 Who followed Lord North as prime minister of the UK?
12 In Monopoly, how much do you receive when your annuity matures?
13 In which country is the city of Monterrey?
14 Which shipping forecast area is east of Shannon?
15 The author Tom Wolfe was born on the same day as which Soviet leader?
16 Against which team did Alan Shearer hit his first Newcastle hat-trick?
17 How many islands are in the Caroline group?
18 What do the letters WG stand for in W.G. Grace's name?
19 What was the first British Top Ten hit for Bing Crosby?
20 Which TV play was based on the football-pools winner Viv Nicholson?
21 Anthophobia is the fear of what?
22 Who made the album *Bad Penny Blues*?
23 From which language does the word "census" originate?
24 Parson Lot was an assumed name of which writer?
25 Who was Foreign Secretary before John Major replaced him in 1989?
26 Which US state is known as the Badger State?
27 The picosecond is the smallest unit of what?
28 Whose three-volume autobiography was called *Diary of a Genius*?
29 The airline Malev is based in which country?
30 Which character was played by Charles Dance in "The Jewel in the Crown"?

1 For what did *Four Weddings and a Funeral* win Oscar nominations?
2 Who was Juliet to Gielgud's Romeo in 1935?
3 How many roles did Alec Guinness play in *Kind Hearts and Coronets*?
4 Who was Jane Seymour's first father-in-law?
5 What was Anthony Hopkins's role in *Bram Stoker's Dracula*?
6 Who played Stephen Ward in *Scandal*?
7 In which film did Emma Thompson play a 1940s European and a present-day Californian?
8 Which actor won a BAFTA for *Chariots of Fire*?
9 Which was Julie Andrews's first film with her husband Blake Edwards?
10 Who appeared with Robert Redford, when just six, in *The Great Gatsby*?
11 Who played Schindler's Jewish accountant in *Schindler's List*?
12 What was Roger Moore's second movie as James Bond?
13 Who starred in and composed the score for *Bedazzled*?
14 Which actor has been co-owner of London's Langan's Brasserie?
15 Who played General Allenby in *Lawrence of Arabia*?
16 The reciting of whose poem in *Four Weddings and a Funeral* resulted in a book of his poetry becoming a bestseller?
17 Who won an Oscar for Best Picture in 1968, which his nephew also starred in?
18 Who played Anne Boleyn in *A Man For All Seasons*?
19 What was Glenda Jackson's film debut?
20 What was Cilla Black's first feature film?
21 Who wrote an autobiography *Beginning* in 1989, aged 28?
22 What was Robert Donat's final film?
23 Who said she was "the only sex symbol England produced since Lady Godiva"?
24 Who played opposite Hayley Mills in *The Family Way*?
25 Who played Poirot in *Murder on the Orient Express*?
26 Which character did Alec Guinness play in *Dr Zhivago*?
27 Which *Carry On* film was called *Carry On Venus* in the US?
28 Who directed *Whistle Down the Wind* in 1961?
29 Who wrote of his relationship with his actress wife in *Meeting Mrs Jenkins*?
30 Who played Noël Coward in *Star!*?

Quiz 51 Pot Luck 26

LEVEL 3

Answers - see page 517

1   What does S stand for in Ulysses S. Grant's name?
2   Who wrote the book *The Napoleon of Notting Hill*?
3   What is the approximate distance of Paris airport from London in miles?
4   What was the first British Top Ten hit for the Cure?
5   How many degrees are there in each internal angle of a dodecagon?
6   Which character was played by Bonnie Langford in "Just William"?
7   From which language does the word "horde" originate?
8   The 50s tennis player Joy Gannon became mother of which tennis player?
9   Nanumea and Nukulailai are in which island group?
10 Who was the most famous comedian to be born in Ulverston, north-west England?
11 Where is the HQ of the CIA?
12 Who had a 70s No. 1 with "Yellow River"?
13 What is buried under Cleopatra's Needle with a razor and cigars?
14 Who inflicted Chris Eubank's first defeat as a professional fighter?
15 What is the capital of the US State of New Jersey?
16 What was the name of Perry Mason's secretary?
17 On a Monopoly board what is between Water Works and Go To Jail?
18 Which UK paper size is 74 x 105 mm?
19 Raoul Grimoin-Sanson devloped what for the entertainment world?
20 Who did Keith Richards work for before becoming a Rolling Stone?
21 Which Irish poet wrote detective novels under the pseudonym Nicholas Blake?
22 Where was the Spanish Formula 1 Grand Prix held prior to 1991?
23 What did the physicist and chemist Michael Faraday train to work with?
24 What is the only English anagram of LIONESSES?
25 Who was US president when racial discrimination was made illegal?
26 Before the 20th century how many moons of Jupiter had been discovered?
27 Lestor Piggott overtook whose record for English classic wins?
28 In light opera, who "led his regiment from behind"?
29 When Elsie Tanner left the Street, which country did she move to?
30 Who were the first UK pairing of world champion and runner-up in Formula 1 Grand Prix racing?

Quiz 52 Plant World

Answers - see page 518

1　Who bred the first Peace rose?

2　What sort of tree is a gean?

3　How are Boston or pinto beans also known?

4　Where did liquorice originate?

5　Which part of asafoetida is used as a spice?

6　What is a clouded agaric?

7　What is the practice of growing plants in liquid nutrients instead of soil called?

8　What colour is the pigment leghaemoglobin found in legumes?

9　The breakdown of what produces malic acid?

10　What is the milky juice of the dandelion called?

11　What colour is a cloudberry?

12　What term applies to a plant which is lime-hating?

13　What does the bladderwort live on?

14　Which shrubs are also known as bush honeysuckles?

15　What does a batologist study?

16　What is litmus obtained from?

17　A halophyte tolerates soil or water containing what?

18　What is the ring of fine down on a dandelion called?

19　What would you grow if you grew Peruvian apples?

20　What fruit is produced on a banyan tree?

21　Which common vegetable family does chervil belong to?

22　What is a toadstool's pileus?

23　Cauliflowers are vegetables but technically what are caulis?

24　Where would you normally find a bracket fungus?

25　What is phytopathology?

26　What is *Camellia sinensis* more commonly called?

27　From what is the oil copra obtained?

28　What does edaphic mean?

29　What is a saguaro?

30　Which part of the plants are the cloves you buy as a spice?

Movies: The Brits　(see Quiz 50)

1 Best Film, Writer (Richard Curtis). **2** Peggy Ashcroft. **3** Eight. **4** Richard Attenborough. **5** Dr Van Helsing. **6** John Hurt. **7** *Dead Again*. **8** Ian Holm. **9** *Darling Lilli*. **10** Patsy Kensit. **11** Ben Kingsley. **12** *The Man With the Golden Gun*. **13** Dudley Moore. **14** Michael Caine. **15** Jack Hawkins. **16** W.H. Auden. **17** Carol Reed (*Oliver!* – Oliver Reed). **18** Vanessa Redgrave. **19** *This Sporting Life*. **20** *Work is a Four Letter Word*. **21** Kenneth Branagh. **22** *The Inn of the Sixth Happiness*. **23** Diana Dors. **24** Hywel Bennett. **25** Albert Finney. **26** Zhivago's half-brother Yeugraf. **27** *Carry On Jack*. **28** Bryan Forbes. **29** Richard Burton. **30** Daniel Massey.

1 What was Alicia Markova's real name?
2 Who did Stacy Dorning play in "Keep It In The Family"?
3 What was the number of the London bus involved in the bomb explosion of February '96?
4 Who invented the mechanical clock?
5 Astraphobia is the fear of what?
6 What is the only English anagram of MEANS TEST?
7 Who played McHeath in the TV adaptation of *The Beggar's Opera*?
8 Springfield is the capital of which US state?
9 How many sets of tyres can an Indy Car use in a race weekend?
10 Who had an 80s No. 1 with "Give It Up"?
11 If it's noon at GMT, what time is it in Halifax, Nova Scotia?
12 When was the first race meeting at Royal Ascot?
13 Whose recording of which piece was the first classical record to sell over a million copies?
14 How many islands are in the Queen Charlotte group?
15 In which century was John Bunyan born?
16 Which instrument brought fame to Shirley Abicair?
17 From which language does the word "ombudsman" originate?
18 In Scrabble what is the letter T worth?
19 What was the number of the Trotter's flat in Nelson Mandela House?
20 A set of British stamps was issued in 1990 for which charity's 150th anniversary?
21 On which river does Milan stand?
22 What word is given to the fear of bees?
23 Whose autobiography was called *Child of Change*?
24 In how many test matches did Ian Botham captain England?
25 What was the first British solo Top Ten hit for Roger Daltrey?
26 In which country is the city of Murcia?
27 In Monopoly, how much do you receive for your birthday if there are four players?
28 Longleat is the stately home of whom?
29 The airline Crossair is based in which country?
30 Sabine and Saladin are types of what?

Answers

Pot Luck 28 (see Quiz 55)
1 Richard Thorpe. 2 Boulevard de Belleville. 3 The Simon Park Orchestra. 4 Henry James. 5 Italian. 6 Bahamas. 7 Fred Noonan. 8 Keith Chegwin. 9 Wrestling. 10 Leslie Poles. 11 Samuel de Champlain. 12 *The Pickwick Papers*. 13 Leicester. 14 The name Winston. 15 "Eloise". 16 Oscar Wilde. 17 1954. 18 Christiaan Huygens. 19 Olivier Panis. 20 No place (Greek). 21 5800. 22 Violet Robinson. 23 Carnation. 24 On the moon. 25 Lord Grenville. 26 Monte Marmolada. 27 Derby-winning horses. 28 Delaware. 29 Mobilises. 30 Royal Opera House.

1   Who was Tiger Woods's caddie for his first Masters win?
2   When did Great Britain first win the Walker Cup?
3   Where did Nick Faldo win his first British Open?
4   What was Jack Nicklaus's nickname in his first Walker Cup in the 50s?
5   What is the name of Hole 8 at Troon?
6   In the 1996 US Masters, how many strokes did Norman lead Faldo before the final round?
7   Who won the British Open the year after Lee Trevino's first triumph?
8   Henry Cotton won the British Open at Sandwich, Muirfield and where?
9   Who was the first South African to win the British Open?
10 Which champion's father was a pro at Hawkstone Park golf course?
11 Where in England was Tony Jacklin born?
12 Where in America did Great Britain and Ireland first win the Walker Cup?
13 Who got the nickname the Walrus?
14 Who is Jack Nicklaus's personal clubmaker?
15 After World War Two, who got the first three-in-a-row hat-trick of British Opens?
16 Who set the course record of 64 at Troon in the Open of 1989?
17 Horton Smith was the first winner of which major event?
18 Which management group did Tiger Woods sign up to on turning pro?
19 What was the original prize for winning the British Open?
20 In what year did Nick Faldo turn professional?
21 Who was the first New Zealander to win the British Open?
22 In which decade was the Walker Cup staged at an English course?
23 Who got the nickname Dough Boy?
24 In what capacity did Devereux Emmet leave his mark on golf?
25 Who was the last golfer before Faldo to be BBC Sports Personality of the Year?
26 What first did Peter Butler manage in the 1973 Ryder Cup?
27 Which golfer's first tour victory was the 1982 Swiss Open?
28 Which course contains the Rabbit and the Seal?
29 Tom Lehman became the first American since who to win an Open at Royal Lytham?
30 Where was the great Harry Vardon born?

Pop: Who's Who (see Quiz 56)

Answers

1 Culture Beat. **2** Paul Anka. **3** Mickie Most. **4** Beats International.
5 Graham Gouldman. **6** Marco Pirroni. **7** John Barry Orchestra.
8 Boomtown Rats. **9** Renée of Renée and Renato. **10** Dave Ball. **11** Craig
Logan. **12** Kenny Ball and his Jazzmen. **13** Belinda Carlisle. **14** Procul
Harum. **15** Hungary. **16** Geno Washington. **17** New Edition. **18** Boy
George. **19** John Gorman. **20** Helen Shapiro. **21** Jeff Lynne. **22** The
Jordanaires. **23** Mr Blobby. **24** Dusty Springfield's ("You Don't Have to Say
You Love Me"). **25** Earth Wind and Fire. **26** Eddie Cochran. **27** 2 Unlimited.
28 Shaggy. 29 Brook Benton and Dinah Washington. **30** Godley & Creme.

1   Which "Emmerdale" actor was Dr Rennie on "Emergency Ward 10"?
2   On a French Monopoly board, what is the equivalent to Old Kent Road?
3   Who had an 80s No. 1 with "Eye Level"?
4   Who wrote *The Turn of the Screw*?
5   From which language does the word "parasol" originate?
6   Cat Crooked and Acklins are in which island group?
7   Who died with Amelia Earhart on her round-the-world attempt?
8   Who is the brother of the former Radio 1 DJ Janice Long?
9   Which sport was dropped from our screens by ITV in 1988?
10 What do the letters LP stand for in L.P. Hartley's name?
11 Which explorer founded Quebec?
12 In which Dickens novel does Job Trotter appear?
13 Where in Britain did the first women traffic wardens go on duty?
14 What did John Lennon share with Gary Lineker?
15 What was the first British Top Ten hit for the Damned?
16 What was Sebastian Melmoth's real name?
17 In which year did food rationing end in Britain?
18 Who invented the pendulum clock?
19 Who broke both legs in a Montreal 1997 Formula 1 Grand Prix crash ?
20 What does the word "Utopia" mean?
21 What is the approximate distance of Rio de Janeiro airport from London in miles?
22 Who did Pat Coombs play in *Lollipop Loves Mr Mole*?
23 What is the national flower of Spain?
24 Where is the Marsh of Sleep located?
25 What was William Wyndham's title when he was UK prime minister?
26 What is the highest peak of the Dolomites called?
27 What's the link between Blue Peter, Pearl Diver and Sir Peter Teazle?
28 Which US state is known as the Diamond State?
29 What is the only English anagram of OMNISSIBLE?
30 Genista McIntosh resigned as chief executive of what in May 1997?

Quiz 56 Pop: Who's Who

Answers - see page 522

LEVEL 3

1 Tania Evans and Jay Supreme are part of which group?

2 Who was the first person to write a British No. 1 both for himself and for someone else?

3 Who produced "House Of The Rising Sun" for the Animals?

4 With what did the ex-Housemartin Norman Cook next hit No. 1?

5 Who sang lead on "Sausalito (Is the Place to Go)" as Ohio Express?

6 Which ex-Siouxsie and the Banshees guitarist penned the Adam Ant No. 1s?

7 Whose first Top Ten hit was "Hit and Miss"?

8 Who were the next Irish group to top the British charts after the Bachelors?

9 Who was Hilary Lefter when she hit the top of the charts in 1982?

10 Who was the synthesizer player in Soft Cell?

11 Who wasn't one of the brothers in Bros?

12 Acapulco, Casablanca and Moscow feature in whose record titles?

13 Who left the Go Gos in '85 and had her first UK No. 1 in 1988?

14 Whose last single, in 1975, was called "Pandora's Box"?

15 The fifties "Pickin' A Chicken" singer, Eve Boswell, came from which country?

16 Who led the Ram Jam Band in the 60s?

17 In which band did Bobby Brown make No. 1 in 1983?

18 In Praise of Lemmings wisely changed their name but kept which name-change singer?

19 Who made up Scaffold with Roger McGough and Mike McGear?

20 Who was the first British female to have two consecutive No. 1s?

21 Who wrote the hits for ELO?

22 Who provided backing vocals on Elvis's "It's Now or Never"?

23 Whose first hit song started out with the title "Mr Jellybun"?

24 Whose first No. 1 was originally called "Io Che No Vivo Senza Te"?

25 The percussionist of which band duetted with Phil Collins on "Easy Lover" in 1985?

26 Who had the second posthumous No. 1 in the British charts?

27 Who were Anita Dels and Ray Slijngaard?

28 Who was born Orville Richard Burrell in Jamaica in 1968?

29 Who had the original hit with "A Rockin' Good Way" in 1960?

30 Who directed Duran Duran's video of "Girls on Film"?

Quiz 57 Pot Luck 29

LEVEL 3

1   What did George Shillibeer introduce in London in 1829?
2   Who won the first Australian Formula 1 Grand Prix in Adelaide in 1985?
3   Who is credited with having conceived the first automatic digital computer.
4   Who had a 70s No. 1 with "Up Town Top Ranking"?
5   What is the only English anagram of SCHEMATIC?
6   What did Lovejoy affectionately call his Morris Minor?
7   Which Samuel won the Nobel Prize for Literature in 1969?
8   The comic actor Eric Idle was born on the same day as which British prime minister?
9   What is Denis Healey's middle name?
10   How many islands are in the Cyclades group?
11   Which shipping forecast area is east of Fastnet?
12   Which poet referred to himself as Merlin in a summing-up of his poetical career?
13   What is the capital of the US State of Florida?
14   Who replaced Darlington when they dropped out of the Football League?
15   In 1973 Mrs Susan Shaw became the first woman to set foot where?
16   Batrachophobia is the fear of what?
17   In which country are the Abisso Olivifer caves?
18   What was the first ventriloquist's dummy to have a TV series?
19   Who wrote "Keep the Home Fires Burning"?
20   What was the first British solo Top Ten hit for Doris Day?
21   In the Monopoly Community Chest, how much is the insurance premium?
22   The airline Linjeflyg is based in which country?
23   Which character was played by Tom Baker in "Medics"?
24   Which Royal has Albert Christian Edward as his three other names?
25   What are the odds of rolling any combination totalling eleven in dice-throwing?
26   What is the opposite of occidental?
27   From which language does the word "bazaar" originate?
28   What was the title of the theme tune from the TV series "Top Secret"?
29   Which country's secret police is called Savak?
30   If it's noon at GMT, what time is it in Managua?

Answers

Pot Luck 30 (see Quiz 59)
1 Blair General Hospital. 2 Enigma. 3 David Coleman. 4 Morocco.
5 144. 6 Italian. 7 Onion. 8 Peritonitis. 9 Arthur C. Clarke. 10 Surfers
Paradise, Australia. 11 Peter Sellers. 12 Claire Bloom (Blume). 13 Maine.
14 Spottable. 15 Hockey. 16 Dodecanese. 17 14th February. 18 Phyllis
Dorothy. 19 Damon Hill. 20 "Candida". 21 François Hennebique. 22 Go
To Jail. 23 Leeches. 24 6,800. 25 Caitlin Davies. 26 Milkman. 27 *Sunday
Post*. 28 Poker World Series. 29 Neckar. 30 Fort Sill (Oklahoma).

1　Which company marketed the first diesel-engined private car?

2　Which north-west town has Central and Bank Quay stations?

3　What was the first vehicle-registration plate in Britain?

4　How many London Underground lines begin with letters in the second half of the alphabet?

5　Where, near Calais, is the French terminus of the Channel Tunnel?

6　Who was with Jean Pierre Blanchard in the first balloon crossing of the English Channel?

7　Which two Great Lakes does the Welland Canal link?

8　Who was the first person to walk in space without a safety line?

9　What did TML stand for in Channel Tunnel construction?

10　In which American state was the first railway station opened?

11　Which airline did British Airways acquire in 1988?

12　Where is Baltasound Airport?

13　What did Enrico Forlanini develop in 1898?

14　The first section of the London Underground ran from Paddington to where?

15　Which was Thor Heyerdahl's third raft after *Kontiki* and *Ra*?

16　Lord King, ex-chairman of British Airways, was Lord King of where?

17　Where was the flight from London going to when Concorde entered supersonic service in 1976?

18　Which aircraft from which company crashed on the motorway near Kegworth in 1989?

19　What was the first turbine-driven steamship called?

20　Where were the *Apollo 1* astronauts when they perished in the 60s?

21　Who were the first two countries to offer flags of convenience?

22　Which two rivers does the Albert Canal link?

23　How many major private rail companies were nationalized in 1947?

24　What does the Seikan Tunnel link?

25　Which international airport company was the first to be floated on the Stock Exchange?

26　What was the *Queen Elizabeth* called when it was destroyed by fire in Hong Kong?

27　Who was the first person to fly over both Poles and the Atlantic?

28　Which report recommended changes after the 1987 King's Cross fire?

29　Where is the deepwater port of Tuticorin?

30　What did the Soviets call their first nuclear-powered ship?

Quiz 59 Pot Luck 30

Answers - see page 525

LEVEL 3

1   In which hospital was "Dr Kildare" set?
2   Who had a 90s No. 1 with "Sadness Part 1"?
3   Which sports commentator was a champion mile runner for Cheshire?
4   In which country is the city of Oujda?
5   How many degrees are there in each internal angle of a decagon?
6   From which language does the word "scenario" originate?
7   Turbo and Stuttgarter Giant are types of what?
8   What was Rudolph Valentino's cause of death?
9   Who wrote *The City and the Stars*?
10 Where did Nigel Mansell achieve his first pole position and win in an Indy car race?
11 Who featured on the 17p - the cheapest - of the 1985 British Film Year stamps?
12 Which 30s-born actress Claire changed two vowels for her stage name?
13 Augusta is the capital of which US state?
14 What is the only English anagram of TABLETOPS?
15 In which sport was Mary Russell-Vick famous?
16 Tilos and Astipalaia are in which island group?
17 What special birthday links Kevin Keegan and P.G. Wodehouse?
18 What do the letters PD stand for in P.D. James's name?
19 Who won the inaugural Melbourne Formula 1 Grand Prix in 1996?
20 What was the first British Top Ten hit for Dawn?
21 Who invented reinforced concrete?
22 In Monopoly, where would double one from Water Works land you?
23 The adjective hirudinal refers to which creatures?
24 What is the approximate distance of Singapore airport from London in miles?
25 Which character was played by Sheena Easton in "Miami Vice"?
26 What was Benny Hill's trade before he became a comic?
27 Which Dundee-based paper first appeared in 1920?
28 Huckleberry Seed won which World Series in 1996?
29 On which river does Stuttgart stand?
30 Geronimo died at which US Fort?

Answers

Pot Luck 29   (see Quiz 57)

1 First regular bus service. 2 Keke Rosberg. 3 Charles Babbage. 4 Althia and Donna. 5 Catechism. 6 Miriam. 7 Beckett. 8 John Major. 9 Winston. 10 About 220. 11 Lundy. 12 Alfred, Lord Tennyson. 13 Tallahassee. 14 Maidstone. 15 Floor of the London Stock Exchange. 16 Reptiles. 17 Italy. 18 Archie Andrews. 19 Ivor Novello. 20 "My Love and Devotion". 21 £50. 22 Sweden. 23 Professor Geoffrey Hoyt. 24 Prince Andrew. 25 17.5-1. 26 Oriental. 27 Persian. 28 "Sucu Sucu". 29 Iran. 30 6 a.m.

1 Who were the private investigators played by the Two Ronnies?
2 Which folk song was the "Z Cars" theme based on?
3 Which Edgar Allen Poe detective did Edward Woodward play in the "Detective" series?
4 What was Van de Valk's first name?
5 Which medal had Detective Inspector Frost won?
6 Which TV drama featured Detective Steve Hackett?
7 Which character did David Suchet play in "Reilly - Ace of Spies"?
8 Where was "Strangers" first set?
9 Who had a street contact called Huggy Bear?
10 Who was assisted by Detective Sergeant Peter Livingstone?
11 Which future "Coronation Street" actress played Jimmy Nail's wife in "Spender"?
12 Craven and Haggerty starred in which series?
13 Where did the action of "Softly Softly" take place?
14 Which agent was played by Jaclyn Smith in "Charlie's Angels"?
15 Who did Eddie Shoestring work for?
16 Who played Inspector Lestrade in the 60s Sherlock Holmes series?
17 Which detective on children's TV had a bloodhound called Pedro and a Rolls-Royce called the Grey Panther?
18 Which 70s/80s series was based on the books of Dick Francis?
19 Where did Quincy work?
20 Which role did Angie Dickinson play in "Police Woman"?
21 In the TV series what was Hercule Poirot's London address?
22 Which police force was Henry Crabbe retired from?
23 What year and model were Morse's most famous red Jaguar?
24 What was the secret entrance to the headquarters of U.N.C.L.E.?
25 Which police officer was a regular adversary of Simon Templar?
26 Who did Inspector Mike Burden assist?
27 How many Babies did Rockliffe have in the 80s series?
28 What did each episode of "The Rockford Files" begin with?
29 Who owned Remington Steele Investigations?
30 Which TV company made the "Prime Suspect" series in the UK?

Quiz 61 Pot Luck 31

1   In which month is Venezuela's national day?
2   How was Angelo Giuseppe Roncalli better known?
3   What was the nickname of the Locomotives and Highway Act of 1865?
4   Who wrote *Tortilla Flat*?
5   Which mountain range gave the setting for most of TV's "William Tell" series?
6   Where was the first Formula 1 World Championship race held outside Europe in 1953?
7   Which newspaper first introduced box numbers in the UK?
8   What was Moliere's real name?
9   If it's noon at GMT, what time is it in Montevideo?
10 Which character was played by Hattie Jacques in "Miss Adventure"?
11 In Scrabble what is the letter L worth?
12 Which film was based on Sir Laurence Van Der Post's novel *The Seed and the Sower*?
13 In Monopoly, how much is paid to the Hospital in Community Chest?
14 How many islands are in the Philippines group?
15 Where was the news presenter Pamela Armstrong born?
16 What is the name of Scotland's largest cave?
17 In which university was "A Very Peculiar Practice" set?
18 What are the Sudanese Dunka tribe recognized to be?
19 Who led the French Protestants known as the Huguenots?
20 Which UK paper size is 105 x 148 mm?
21 What is the only English anagram of SUBLINEAR?
22 Which bridge was opened by Lady Thatcher in Hong Kong giving access to the airport of Lantau Island?
23 Which star sign links the sportsman Bill Beaumont and the presenter/singer Cheryl Baker?
24 In which US state would a Hoosier be a native inhabitant?
25 From which language does the word "parallax" originate?
26 What was George Hamilton-Gordon's title when he was UK prime minister?
27 Who invented contact lenses?
28 Belonophobia is the fear of what?
29 What was the first British Top Ten hit for Depeche Mode?
30 The airline Bell-Air is based in which country?

1 Other than being his wife what relation was Eleanor Roosevelt to Franklin D.?
2 What was the profession of Roger Moore's father?
3 What is the real name of the author Nigel West?
4 Which celebrity photographer wrote *My Royal Past*?
5 Who captained the first all-female crew to sail round the world?
6 Who was Mia Farrow's second husband?
7 What relation is Jonathan Aitken to Lord Beaverbrook?
8 What is David Bailey's middle name?
9 Which contest was Kiki Haakonson the first winner of?
10 Which MP competed at the Tokyo Olympics and was UK 100m record holder from 1967-74?
11 Which son of the late US Ambassador to Paris, Pamela Harriman, has been a British MP?
12 Who wrote a book of comic verse called *I Have No Gun But I Can Spit*?
13 Which 13-year-old gained a First in maths at Oxford in 1985?
14 Which Earl of Lichfield is the photographer Patrick?
15 Which Guinness heiress died of a drink/drugs overdose at Oxford University in the 80s?
16 Who is Wath-on-Dearne Comprehensive School's most famous old boy?
17 What was US President Nixon's wife called?
18 How was the designer Miss Mountney of Merthyr Tydfil better known?
19 Who said she was famous first as someone's daughter, then someone's wife, and probably finally as someone's mother?
20 Which ex-Tory Party chairman is the son of the actress Dinah Sheridan?
21 What relation, if any, is Vanessa Redgrave to Jemma Redgrave?
22 What is the first name of Martin Luther King's widow?
23 Who was Britain's youngest-ever city councillor at 21, and youngest - then - MP aged 28?
24 What are Prince Edward's four given names?
25 Where was Pierre Cardin born?
26 How was Vera Jane Palmer better known?
27 Who tried to assassinate Pope John Paul II in 1981?
28 Who was the first woman general of the Salvation Army?
29 Which prime minister was a former football referee and coach?
30 Whose second shop was called Nostalgia of Mud?

Answers

Screen Greats (see Quiz 64)

1 *Grand Hotel*. 2 Clark Gable, Jean Harlow. 3 James Stewart. 4 Claudette Colbert. 5 Robert Mitchum. 6 *Thoroughbreds Don't Cry*. 7 *Blue Skies*. 8 Rita Hayworth. 9 Orson Welles. 10 Olivia de Havilland. 11 *Stromboli*. 12 Spencer Tracy & Katharine Hepburn. 13 *Flying Down to Rio*. 14 Claude Rains. 15 Susan Hayward. 16 Paramount. 17 Deborah Kerr. 18 Lola-Lola. 19 Donald O'Connor. 20 Debbie Reynolds. 21 Joan Crawford. 22 Humphrey Bogart. 23 Gene Kelly. 24 Neath, Wales. 25 W.C. Fields. 26 *Safety Last*. 27 Lita Grey. 28 Mack Sennett. 29 Ginger Rogers. 30 Rita Hayworth.

1 What was the first British Top Ten hit for Booker T. and the MGs?
2 What is the only English anagram of ALARMING?
3 In which part of London were parking meters first introduced?
4 In Monopoly how much does it cost to buy Whitehall?
5 Who invented the contraceptive pill?
6 Which US state is known as the Apache State?
7 Which star sign links the TV presenter Michael Aspel and the botanist David Bellamy?
8 Who was the first Briton to win the World Show Jumping Championships?
9 From which language does the word "fuselage" originate?
10 Which singer moved to the USA for an acting role in "McKenzie"?
11 Cabrera and Formentera are in which island group?
12 Who wrote the poem "After Apple Picking"?
13 Sir John Houblon was the first governor of what?
14 Who had his jaw broken in 1973 by Ken Norton?
15 What was the work of Fulgence Bienvenue in Paris?
16 What is the approximate distance of Tokyo airport from London in miles?
17 Who designed the Sydney Opera House?
18 Who was the first person to swim the Channel underwater?
19 What was Jacques Offenbach's real name?
20 In which century was Alexander the Great born?
21 How many chromosomes are there in a normal human body cell?
22 Who had an 80s No. 1 with "Nothing's Going To Stop Us Now"?
23 At the scene of which of his pictures did Van Gogh shoot himself?
24 In which country was the actress Lynda Bellingham born?
25 The international car registration WAN applies to which country?
26 Who officially opened the Panama Canal?
27 Who was the first Englishman to climb the Matterhorn?
28 What law did Margaret Thatcher specialize in when she studied for the Bar?
29 Which two Formula One Drivers lost their lives at Imola in 1994?
30 Who did Sheila Hancock play in *Mr Digby, Darling*?

LEVEL 3

1 In which movie did Greta Garbo say, "I want to be alone"?
2 Which two Hollywood greats were the stars of *Red Dust* in 1932?
3 Which Oscar-winner in 1940 received the DFC and the Croix de Guerre?
4 How was Lily Cauchoin better known?
5 Who did Ernest Borgnine say was "the best two-fisted drinker I've ever known"?
6 In which film did Judy Garland first team with Mickey Rooney?
7 What was the second film in which Bing Crosby co-starred with Fred Astaire?
8 Who starred opposite Fred Astaire in *You'll Never Get Rich*?
9 About whom did Marlene Dietrich say, "People should cross themselves when they say his name"?
10 Who played Maid Marian to Errol Flynn's Robin Hood in 1938?
11 What was the first Ingrid Bergman film directed by Roberto Rossellini?
12 Who were first teamed in *Woman of the Year* in 1942?
13 In which film were Fred Astaire and Ginger Rogers first together?
14 Who played Ingrid Bergman's husband in *Notorious*?
15 Who was born Edythe Marrener?
16 Which studio signed Gary Cooper in the late 20s?
17 Whose promotion for her first Hollywood film advised Americans that her name rhymed with "star"?
18 Who was Marlene Dietrich in *The Blue Angel*?
19 Who played the title role in *The Buster Keaton Story*?
20 Who had a career in films after being crowned Miss Burbank 1948?
21 Who married the chairman of Pepsi-Cola in 1955 and remained on the board of directors after his death?
22 Who played Captain Queeg in *The Caine Mutiny* in 1954?
23 Which film star first found fame playing the lead role in *Pal Joey* on Broadway in 1940?
24 Where was Ray Milland born?
25 Who replaced Charles Laughton as Mr Micawber in the 1935 film *David Copperfield*?
26 In which 1923 film did Harold Lloyd hang from the hands of a skyscraper clock?
27 Which wife was not mentioned by name in Chaplin's autobiography?
28 Whose life story was told in the 1939 movie *Hollywood Cavalcade*?
29 Who played "Anytime Annie" in *42nd Street*?
30 Whose pin-up photo was on the atomic bomb that was dropped on Bikini?

LEVEL 3

1 At which Formula 1 Grand Prix circuit are the Tamburello and Acque Minerale?
2 Which fictitious bus company was featured in "On The Buses"?
3 What was Willie Carson's last ride to win the Derby?
4 In Monopoly, how much is won for second prize in a beauty contest?
5 Which shipping forecast area is east of Fair Isle?
6 If A is Alpha and B is Bravo what is U?
7 Dromophobia is the fear of what?
8 Who had a 50s No. 1 with "Hernando's Hideaway"?
9 Where did Shirley Williams become a professor when she left politics?
10 How many countries competed in the first soccer World Cup?
11 What is the capital of the US State of Kentucky?
12 In Scrabble what is the letter M worth?
13 What was Dorothy Parker's real name?
14 John Solomon represented England at which sport?
15 From which language does the word "cherub" originate?
16 In fiction, who was David Copperfield's first wife?
17 When did the Bank of England move to Threadneedle Street?
18 What was the first British Top Ten hit for Bow Wow Wow?
19 Which character was played by Jane Asher in *The Mistress*?
20 Who invented corrugated iron?
21 Ailsa Craig and Dobies Allrounder are types of what?
22 On which river does Lisbon stand?
23 Marlon Brando was born on the same day as which US actress/singer?
24 If it's noon at GMT, what time is it in Karachi?
25 How many islands are in the Dodecanese group?
26 Who replaced Accrington Stanley in the Football League?
27 What is the only English anagram of ANIMATED?
28 Which city on the signpost in "M*A*S*H*" is 6,133 miles away?
29 In which country is Dalaman Airport?
30 Who wrote *A Tale of a Tub*?

Quiz 66 The Media

Answers - see page 536

LEVEL 3

1 Which TV company was formed when ABC merged with Associated Rediffusion in the late 60s?

2 What was the BBC's first broadcast on June 7 1946 after the station had been closed down for seven years?

3 What is Rupert Murdoch's first name?

4 Which country has a national newspaper *B.T.*, founded in 1916?

5 Which company bought out NBC in 1985?

6 What is the Journal of the Society of Antiquities called?

7 Which BBC channel was launched in 1991?

8 Which newspaper is older - the *Daily Express* or the *Daily Mirror*?

9 What is ENG?

10 Who set up Britain's oldest daily trade newspaper?

11 In the US what does Nielsens show?

12 Which production company was founded by Lee Rich and Merv Adelson in 1968?

13 Where was the SECAM TV transmission system developed?

14 What is Britain's oldest national newspaper?

15 Which SES broadcast satellite was launched in December 1978?

16 In the 60s, what was an oater?

17 Which radio company set up NBC?

18 Which US cable channel was launched in 1980 specializing in foreign films?

19 What is the oldest weekly publication in the UK?

20 Which independent radio station began in the UK in March 1990?

21 Which town did Sky use as its UK satellite/cable testing ground?

22 Who was the first chairman of the Broadcasting Standards Authority?

23 What is the major daily paper of Denver Colorado called?

24 Which Sunday paper was founded in 1989?

25 In which three cities are Scotland's three major evening newspapers?

26 What is the full name of the Welsh fourth channel S4C?

27 Where was the Agenzia Internazionale Fides agency set up in 1926?

28 Which British city has produced a *News Letter* daily since 1855?

29 Which US TV network did Rupert Murdoch establish in the mid-80s?

30 What is Britain's oldest surviving provincial newspaper?

1   What is the only English anagram of ARROGANT?
2   Who read the "Picture Book" stories on Monday afternoons?
3   Who wrote *An Outcast of the Islands*?
4   Who had a 50s No. 1 with "Poor People Of Paris"?
5   Which star sign links Eric Bristow and Joe Brown?
6   Tinos and Siros are in which island group?
7   Who invented the credit card?
8   What links the roses Silver Jubilee, *Rosa moyesii* and Harvest Fayre?
9   Who did Cheri Lunghi play in *The Monocled Mutineer*?
10 What is the approximate distance of Bejing Airport from London in miles?
11 Who was the first-ever world sidecar champion?
12 In what year did the sixpence cease to be legal tender?
13 Who had a female slave called Morgiana?
14 On which island was the children's presenter Floella Benjamin born?
15 Which lucky Formula 1 driver, who crashed heavily at Imola in 1994, escaped without injury?
16 Who appeared on the first two US adhesive stamps?
17 From which language does the word "cafeteria" originate?
18 At which house was Diana, Princess of Wales, born?
19 Which famous nursery rhyme was written by Sarah Josepha Hall?
20 What was the title of the 1994 book by the model Naomi Campbell?
21 Where in London was the first Salvation Army Revival Meeting?
22 What was the first British Top Ten hit for Bread?
23 What are the odds of rolling any combination totalling four in dice-throwing?
24 Bismarck is the capital of which US state?
25 Who won the first ten UK Closed Pro Squash Championships?
26 In Scrabble what is the letter B worth?
27 Who said, "Rock journalism is people who can't write interviewing people who can't talk for people who can't read"?
28 Which quiz show's questions were guarded by Detective Fabian?
29 On a Monopoly board what is between Angel Islington and Euston Rd?
30 What was Phiz's real name?

1   Which English monarch had a horse called White Surrey?
2   When was Paul Revere's ride to warn of the British advance?
3   What was the family name of Prince Albert of Saxe-Coburg-Gotha?
4   In which city did the Old Pretender die?
5   Which monarch communicated with his ministers in French?
6   Why did George V say *La Bohème* was his favourite opera?
7   Who was Napoleon Bonaparte's eldest brother?
8   Who was George V's elder brother?
9   Who was the first prime minister to occupy Chequers?
10 Who was George II's mother?
11 Who were the last two British monarchs to have two children who became British monarchs?
12 Who followed Sir Robert Walpole as prime minister of the UK?
13 Who was the first Hanoverian monarch to visit Ireland and Scotland ?
14 Which English king had the nickname Curtmantle?
15 Who was the father of the last Tsar of Russia?
16 Who attempted to assassinate Queen Victoria in 1849?
17 Which French painter was known as "Le Douanier"?
18 Who was the founder of the Standard Oil Company?
19 Who died in Britain's last public execution?
20 Who gave birth to Emile, Yvonne, Cecile, Marie and Annette in 1934?
21 Who was the first reigning pope to visit Britain?
22 Who was the first unmarried president of the USA?
23 Who opened Regent's Park Children's Zoo in 1938?
24 Who died at his Castle of Dux in Bohemia in 1798?
25 Which king was buried in Gloucester Cathedral in the 14th century?
26 Which British monarch had mistresses nicknamed the Elephant and the Maypole?
27 Who was the father of Edward VII's consort Alexandra?
28 Who founded Britain's first museum in 1683?
29 Who followed Herbert Henry Asquith as prime minister of the UK?
30 Where was Edward VIII born?

Answers

The Media (see Quiz 66)

1 Thames Television. 2 "Mickey Mouse". 3 Keith. 4 Denmark. 5 General Electric. 6 *Archaeologia*. 7 World Service Television. 8 *Daily Express*. 9 Electronic News Gathering. 10 Licensed Victuallers' Association. 11 TV audience ratings. 12 Lorimar Productions. 13 France. 14 Glasgow's *Herald*. 15 Astra. 16 TV western. 17 RCA. 18 Bravo. 19 The *Lancet*. 20 Jazz FM. 21 Swindon. 22 Lord Rees Mogg. 23 *Denver Rocky Mountain News*. 24 *Sunday Correspondent*. 25 Edinburgh, Glasgow, Dundee. 26 Sianel Pedwar Cymru. 27 Vatican City. 28 Belfast. 29 Fox. 30 Berrow's *Worcester Journal*.

1 From which language does the word "bantam" originate?
2 In which country are the Anou Ifflis caves?
3 Who won the first "Pot Black" Trophy?
4 Who wrote *A Connecticut Yankee in King Arthur's Court*?
5 Which US state is known as the Panhandle State?
6 Who was prime minister of the UK in between William Pitt's two terms in office?
7 In Monopoly, how much is the income tax refund?
8 Which Scottish writer and statesman was the first Baron Tweedsmuir?
9 Who had a 50s No. 1 with "Whole Lotta Woman"?
10 What do the letters CS stand for in C.S. Lewis's name?
11 What is the capital of the Canadian province Yukon Territory?
12 In which country was the TV and radio presenter Katie Boyle born?
13 What did Hippolyte Mega Mouries patent in Paris in 1869?
14 Where in California is Disneyland?
15 Which character was played by Allyce Beasley in "Moonlighting"?
16 Eisoptrophobia is the fear of what?
17 Which star sign links Richard Baker and Thelma Barlow?
18 Who invented the automatic dishwasher?
19 What was Q's real name?
20 If it's noon at GMT, what time is it in Quebec?
21 Which Formula 1 driver has won the Monaco Grand Prix a record six times?
22 Who founded the Sûreté?
23 Where did the TV detective Jessica Fletcher live?
24 What is the only English anagram of PARTISAN?
25 What was the first British Top Ten hit for Tony Brent?
26 In which country is Findel Airport?
27 How did the Channel swimmer Matthew Webb perish?
28 How many islands are in the Pelagian group?
29 In Scrabble what is the letter G worth?
30 Whose 1987 autobiography was called *Little Wilson* and *Big God*?

Answers

Pot Luck 36 (see Quiz 71)

1 Five. 2 "Pearl's A Singer". 3 Peter Lorre. 4 Parsnip. 5 Uzbekistan.
6 Cilla Black. 7 A5. 8 Helena. 9 Robert Burns. 10 Herman Hesse.
11 Crimpton On Sea. 12 Rue La Fayette. 13 Wasps. 14 Aston Villa.
15 Dave Lee Travis. 16 Frederic Dannay and Manfred Lee.
17 Dreamweavers. 18 George Bush. 19 Earliest. 20 Tobogganing.
21 Nero. 22 Bay. 23 Rowed solo across the Atlantic. 24 Deimos. 25 2,800.
26 Germain Sommelier. 27 German. 28 McConnell. 29 Aries. 30 Vault and asymmetric bars.

1 What were Roobarb and Custard?
2 Who narrated "Tales of the Riverbank"?
3 In the 50s, what name was given to the one-hour gap after children's and before adults' television programmes?
4 In which decade did "Watch With Mother" finish?
5 Which part did Letitia Dean play in "Grange Hill"?
6 Which female presented "Lift Off" in the 70s?
7 On which Farm did Worzel Gummidge live?
8 Who were the twins in "The Woodentops"?
9 Where did Torchy the Battery Boy live?
10 Who narrated "The Wombles"?
11 In "TISWAS" what was Bob Carolgees's punk dog called?
12 Who designed the Italian sunken garden on "Blue Peter"?
13 Who took over from Ringo Starr narrating "Thomas the Tank Engine"?
14 Where did Supergran's adventures take place?
15 Which two inventors invented Supercar?
16 Who was the Storyteller in the Channel 4 series?
17 In "Stingray" what did WASP stand for?
18 Who ran the sweetshop in the early days of "Sesame Street"?
19 What was the first weekend programme which Phillip Schofield presented regularly?
20 In "Rainbow" what colour were Moony and Sunshine?
21 Which humans appeared with Pussy Cat Willum?
22 What is the parish of the Reverend Timms?
23 Who were the first presenters of "Television Top of the Form"?
24 Who was the voice of Penfold in the "Dangermouse" series?
25 Which Tracy piloted *Thunderbird 2*?
26 Which clay model accompanied Tony Hart's programmes and who created him?
27 Who has presented "Screen Test" and "Blue Peter"?
28 What was the name of the Pogles' pet squirrel?
29 What were Bit and Bot on "Playschool"?
30 In "Vision On" what were Phil O'Pat and Pat O'Phil made from?

1 How many times did Graham Hill win the Formula 1 Monaco Grand Prix?
2 What was the first British Top Ten hit for Elkie Brooks?
3 How is Laszlo Lowenstein better known?
4 Tender and True and White Gem are types of what?
5 In which country is the city of Tashkent?
6 Which TV celebrity dressed as a waitress to promote Typhoo tea?
7 Which UK paper size is 148 x 210 mm?
8 What is the capital of the US State of Montana?
9 Who was said to have "loved mankind in general and women in particular"?
10 Who wrote *Der Steppenwolf*?
11 In which fictitious resort was "Hi-De-Hi" set?
12 On a French Monopoly board, what is the equivalent to Piccadilly?
13 The adjective vespine refers to which creatures?
14 Who were runners-up when Man. United first won a 90s championship?
15 Who joined the DJ Paul Burnett to become Laurie Lingo & the Dipsticks?
16 What was Ellery Queen's real name?
17 Who had an 50s No. 1 with "It's Almost Tomorrow"?
18 Who was the US Navy's youngest pilot in World War Two?
19 What is the only English anagram of ATELIER?
20 St Moritz is home to the world's oldest sporting club in what?
21 Whose second wife was Poppaea?
22 Roatan and Guanja are in which island group?
23 How had Tom McClean arrived in Blacksod Bay, Co Mayo, in 1969?
24 What is the partner of Phobos, the moon of Mars?
25 What is the approximate distance of Teheran airport from London in miles?
26 Who invented the pneumatic drill?
27 From which language does the word "poltergeist" originate?
28 What was Mindy's surname in the TV series "Mork and Mindy"?
29 Which star sign links the broadcasters Sue Cook and Jeremy Beadle?
30 Aside from floor and beam, what are the two other events for women gymnasts in the Olympics?

1 Who had a 1981 album *Hedgehog Sandwich*?
2 Which girl's name provides a track on *Bridge Over Troubled Water*?
3 On which album did Phil Collins make his vocal debut for Genesis?
4 "Can't Buy Me Love" first appeared on which Beatles album?
5 *Dark Side Of The Moon* was first released on which label?
6 Which album's sleeve featured David Bowie wearing boxing gloves?
7 Who recorded the soundtrack for the Oscar-winning film *The Piano*?
8 What type of surgery did Emerson, Lake and Palmer come up with?
9 Which Beatle holds a trumpet on the *Sgt. Pepper* album sleeve?
10 What are Gallagher and Lyle doing on the back cover of *Breakaway*?
11 What was Stevie Wonder's follow-up album to *Innervisions*?
12 Who is credited on the Worzels' first album?
13 Who recorded the album *Graceland*?
14 Which albums did Sarah Brightman and Andrea Bocelli release separately, each containing "Time To Say Goodbye"?
15 What was Sheryl Crow's debut album?
16 What colour stripe along with red and blue is on Police's *Synchronicity* sleeve?
17 What was the first original-cast recording of a show to top the charts?
18 "The Winner Takes It All" comes from which Abba album?
19 Whose first album was *No Secrets*?
20 Which album sleeve has the boxer John Conteh among the faces?
21 Who was the second British female artist to top the album charts?
22 Who was the narrator on Jeff Wayne's *War Of The Worlds*?
23 In 1994 whose CD won the Album of the Year Grammy in the US?
24 Which 60s character made a comeback in 1979 with *Broken English*?
25 Where was *Canto Gregoriano* recorded?
26 Who was the first solo artist to be a year's top-seller with a debut disc?
27 How many albums were in the first *Melody Maker* chart in 1958?
28 Pearl was a posthumously released album from which singer?
29 What was subtitled "The Best of the Boomtown Rats and Bob Geldof"?
30 What part of the body was on the sleeve of Pink Floyd's *Meddle*?

Quiz 73 Pot Luck 37

LEVEL 3

1   What was Raphael's real name?
2   Who did Richard Wilson play in "My Good Woman"?
3   What is the only English anagram of ALLEGORIST?
4   Who had a 60s No. 1 with "You're Driving Me Crazy"?
5   In which country is General Manuel Marquez de Leon Airport?
6   In which century was Sir Humphrey Davy born?
7   In Scrabble what is the letter F worth?
8   Which shipping forecast area is south of Humber?
9   Which TV character's wives were played by Peggy Bates and Marion Mathie?
10 Which TV teddy was 40 in 1992?
11 In 1980 who described Ronald Reagan's monetarist policy as "voodoo economics"?
12 Actress Debra Winger was born on the same day as which Soviet gymnast?
13 How did the boxer Rinty Monaghan like to celebrate victory?
14 Who invented the electric oven?
15 From which language does the word "ketchup" originate?
16 How many islands are in the Falklands group?
17 Which team was Alain Prost with for his 80s hat-trick of Monaco wins?
18 Who wrote the novel *A Handful of Dust*?
19 In which country is the city of Tbilisi?
20 What do the letters LS stand for in Lowry's name?
21 What was the first British Top Ten hit for Bronski Beat?
22 In which sport were Wilfred and Herbert Baddeley famous?
23 In which country was the TV journalist Sandy Gall born?
24 Which star sign links Floella Benjamin and Judith Chalmers?
25 If it's noon at GMT, what time is it in Delhi?
26 Des Moines is the capital of which US state?
27 Ergasiophobia is the fear of what?
28 What is James Callaghan's first name?
29 Who was the only real-life comic to feature on the British "Smiles" stamps of the 1990s?
30 On which river does Munich stand?

Answers

Pot Luck 38 (see Quiz 75)

1 William Sturgeon. 2 A giant hedgehog. 3 The Overlanders. 4 David Niven. 5 Dutch. 6 Aquarius. 7 140. 8 Robert Gould Shaw. 9 Albania. 10 Athletics. 11 Georgia. 12 Richard Austen. 13 *The Old Curiosity Shop*. 14 Hayley Mills. 15 Cook. 16 Stagnation. 17 He had only one arm. 18 A Flower. 19 3,200. 20 "United We Stand". 21 Danielle Steele. 22 Colorado. 23 Pinza. 24 Joel Chandler Harris. 25 Marriage. 26 British India, now Pakistan. 27 Benjamin Disraeli. 28 Lord Byron. 29 Olivier Panis. 30 Northumberland Avenue.

1 Which 90s England player had the middle names Edward Riche?
2 Who was the first player to score over 200 in an English Sunday league game?
3 In what year did Graham Gooch make his county debut?
4 Who was the first England cricketer to be fined for conduct during a Test?
5 What sport - other than cricket - did Graeme Hick play for Zimbabwe?
6 Who scored the first fifty in a one-day international?
7 Who is the only player to represent both Australia and South Africa?
8 What is Ben Hollioake's middle name?
9 In 1996's NatWest Final Glen Chapple took six for how many?
10 Which England spinner shared his debut with Shane Warne's test arrival in England?
11 When did Essex first win the county championship?
12 Which one cap Neil took 2 for 148 and hit 38 runs in his one innings?
13 Where was the England bowler Andy Caddick born?
14 The Oval and Lord's were the first English test grounds - which was the third?
15 Who was the first keeper to make 10 test dismissals?
16 Which England cricketer was named after the Australian Neil Harvey?
17 Who in 1966, aged 16 years, 180 days, became Northants' youngest-ever player?
18 Bob Willis's eight for 43 ended the Ashes third test of 1981, but how many wickets did he take in the first innings?
19 Which team were the first after Lancashire to win the John Player League?
20 Which England player had the middle name Cleophas?
21 Who scored the first century in a one day international?
22 In which decade did Derby first win the county championship?
23 How many wickets did Neil Mallender take in his two test matches?
24 Which was the one county in 1997 not to have a player whose surname began with a W?
25 At which ground did Jim Laker take 19 test wickets in 1956?
26 And how many runs did Laker score in that fourth test against Australia?
27 How many times did Ian Botham skipper England in tests?
28 What is David Gower's middle name?
29 Who were the opposition when Mike Atherton played his first test?
30 Who took the catch that gave Fred Trueman his 300th test wicket

1 Who invented the electromagnet?
2 What was Dinsdale in "Monty Python's Flying Circus"?
3 Who had a 60s No. 1 with "Michelle"?
4 Who was classed as "Anglo Saxon Type 2008" when he first went to Hollywood?
5 From which language does the word "schooner" originate?
6 Which star sign links Michael Bentine and Bamber Gascoigne?
7 How many degrees are there in each internal angle of a nonagon?
8 Which character was played by Pierce Brosnan in *Nancy Astor*?
9 In which country is the city of Tirana?
10 In which sport was Emmanuel McDonald Bailey famous?
11 Which US state is known as the Empire State of the South?
12 What were R.A. (RAB) Butler's first two names?
13 In which Dickens novel does Sampson Brass appear?
14 Which actress's first film was *Tiger Bay*?
15 Mangaia and Palmerstone are in which island group?
16 What is the only English anagram of ANTAGONIST?
17 In "Robin's Nest" what disablement was suffered by the dishwasher?
18 What is a Rafflesia the largest of in the world?
19 What is the approximate distance of Bahrain airport from London in miles?
20 What was the first British Top Ten hit for the Brotherhood of Man?
21 Who wrote *Thurston House" Palamino* and *Fine Things*?
22 Which US state is directly north of New Mexico?
23 On which horse did Gordon Richards have his only Derby success?
24 What was Uncle Remus's real name?
25 Juno was the Roman goddess of what?
26 In which country was the TV presenter Gordon Honeycombe born?
27 Who wrote *Vivian Grey*?
28 Who in 1812 said, "I awoke one morning and found myself famous"?
29 Who gave Ligier their first Formula 1 Grand Prix win since 1981 when he won at Monaco in 1996?
30 In Monopoly, if you were on Income Tax and got double five, where would you land?

1   What was Vivaldi's only oratorio called?
2   Where was the composer William Walton born?
3   What was Shakespeare's first tragedy?
4   For how many instruments is Xenakis's *Pithoprakta* for?
5   Who wrote the text for Benjamin Britten's *On this Island*?
6   Who is the subject of Jean Anouilh's play *L'Alouette*?
7   Which major European orchestra is the oldest?
8   Who wrote *Where the Wild Things Are* in 1980?
9   Who first used the organ in a symphony?
10 Who wrote the earliest concerto for flute?
11 What is the nickname of Mahler's Symphony No. 1 in D?
12 Who founded the Australian Ballet?
13 Who wrote the controversial opera *Lulu*?
14 Which Austrian wrote around 250 operas before his death in 1835?
15 Who wrote the earliest concerto for piccolo?
16 Which company for black dancers did Arthur Mitchell form in 1969?
17 Who gives Tony Awards?
18 Who wrote *Marlene* about Dietrich?
19 What was Shakespeare's first comedy?
20 How many symphonies did Bruckner write?
21 Who won the Leading Actor Tony in 1991 for *Shadowlands*?
22 How was the classical dancer Sydney Healey-Kay better known?
23 Where is the Santa Cecelia Academy Orchestra based?
24 Which instrument was invented in 1821 and had the first concerto written for it in 1951?
25 What is the nickname of Shostakovich's Symphony No. 7 in C written during World War Two?
26 What did the Festival Ballet change its name to?
27 Who wrote *The Duchess of Malfi*?
28 For which play did Margaret Tyzack win the Feature Actress Tony in 1990?
29 Who wrote the opera *Punch and Judy*?
30 Who was the founding choreographer of the New York City Ballet?

Quiz 77 Pot Luck 39

Answers - see page 547

LEVEL 3

1 Which character was played by Jimmy Jewel in "Nearest and Dearest"?
2 What was Frank Richard's real name?
3 Who had a 70s No. 1 with "Double Barrel"?
4 The Spanish Formula 1 Grand Prix is held on the outskirts of which city?
5 How many main islands are in the Novaya Zemlya group?
6 Gatophobia is the fear of what?
7 In which town in Texas was Roy Orbison born?
8 On which Isle was the entertainer Rod Hull born?
9 Which parliamentary constituency did William Hague first contest?
10 If it's noon at GMT, what time is it in Honolulu?
11 From which language does the word "khaki" originate?
12 Who wrote *Love and Mr Lewisham*?
13 Who replaced Barrow in the Football League?
14 Which US state is north of Wyoming?
15 Shaft, Meteor and Onward are types of what?
16 In which country is Varna International Airport?
17 Who invented the endoscope?
18 What are the odds of rolling any combination totalling ten in dice-throwing?
19 Who in 1952 wrote *Water Music*, in which the pianist blows whistles under water?
20 In which fictitious village was "Oh No! It's Selwyn Froggitt" set?
21 In which sport was William James Bailey famous?
22 Which star sign links the entertainer Max Bygraves and the journalist Sandy Gall?
23 What is the only English anagram of CANE CHAIRS?
24 Niels Henrik Abek pioneered several branches of modern what?
25 Who won Emmy awards as an actor, writer and director of "M*A*S*H"?
26 The adjective aquiline refers to which creatures?
27 What is the capital of the US state of Idaho?
28 What is Shari Lewis's best-known puppet called?
29 Who was Mohammed Reza Pahlavi?
30 What was the first British solo Top Ten hit for Bobby Brown?

Answers

Pot Luck 40 (see Quiz 79)
1 £180. 2 Anita Dobson. 3 Libya. 4 Greek. 5 1986. 6 Bowls. 7 Pope Paul VI. 8 J.J. Barrie. 9 Peter Chamberlen. 10 Gilles Villeneuve. 11 Harmonicas. 12 White. 13 Virgo. 14 Nelson. 15 New Mexico. 16 Seth's donkey. 17 C.P. Scott. 18 Ernest Hemingway. 19 5,300. 20 John Boynton. 21 Alcohol. 22 *The Black Pig*. 23 India. 24 Maryland. 25 Veronica Barton. 26 Greenalnd. 27 "Living In America". 28 Lefkosa or Leukosia. 29 Pichincha. 30 Bismarck Archipelago.

1   What was the second *Road* film?
2   Which comedy included the song "Somewhere in My Memory"?
3   In which city does *Sister Act 2* take place?
4   Who was turned down for the Spencer Tracy role in *Father of the Bride*?
5   Which two performers won BAFTAs for *A Fish Called Wanda*?
6   What is the name of the jewel thief in *The Pink Panther*?
7   Who starred opposite Michell Pfeiffer in *One Fine Day*?
8   What was the Doris Day remake of *My Favorite Wife* called?
9   In which film was Chaplin's Little Tramp seen for the last time?
10   Who wrote the books on which the *St Trinians* films were based?
11   What was Morecambe and Wise's first film called?
12   What is Nicole Kidman's job in *To Die For*?
13   Which classic comedy won BAFTA best film in 1951?
14   What was the first film the Marx Brothers made in Hollywood?
15   After which 1923 film did Harold Lloyd marry his leading lady Mildred Davis?
16   What was the follow-up to *A Fish Called Wanda* called?
17   In which 1936 film did Laurel and Hardy each play their own twins?
18   In which 1983 movie did Dan Aykroyd team with Eddie Murphy?
19   What was Woody Allen's first film as screenwriter and actor?
20   Who was the bungling Sherlock Holmes in *Without A Clue* in 1988?
21   Who wrote and starred in *L.A. Story*?
22   How was the screen comedian Louis Francis Cristillo better known?
23   What was the second *Carry On* film?
24   Which *Pink Panther* sequel mentions neither the Pink Panther nor Inspector Clouseau in the title?
25   Which comedy team first appeared in *One Night in the Tropics*?
26   Who played opposite Debbie Reynolds in *Tammy and the Bachelor*?
27   Who was the witch in *Spellbinder*?
28   Which 1982 film told of a concert party in Singapore in 1948?
29   Who wrote *Ghostbusters* with Harold Ramis?
30   Which was the first of the Rock Hudson/Doris Day comedies?

Celebs (see Quiz 80)

1 Mohammed Al Fayed. **2** Graca Machel. **3** Mia Farrow. **4** Kennedy. **5** Fibreglass elephant. **6** Countess de Chambrun. **7** Julio Iglesias. **8** Christian Dior. **9** Mrs Steven Spielberg. **10** Camilla Parker-Bowles. **11** Tara Newley. **12** John Paul Getty. **13** Joaquin Cortes. **14** *Hello, She Lied*. **15** "Tantrums and Tiaras". **16** Socks. **17** Audrey Hepburn. **18** Jane Seymour. **19** Princess Di's mum. **20** Marisa Berenson. **21** Fergie's sister. **22** Duke of Gloucester. **23** Lisa Potts. **24** David Hicks. **25** Darius Guppy. **26** The Bushes' cat Millie. **27** Ivana Trump. **28** Grimaldi. **29** Mick Jagger. **30** Lord Snowdon.

Answers

1 In Monopoly how much does it cost to buy Bow Street?
2 Which "EastEnders" actress appeared in the comedy "Split Ends"?
3 In which country is the city of Tripoli?
4 From which language does the word "elastic" originate?
5 In what year were the British Halley's Comet stamps issued?
6 In which sport was Edwin Percy Baker famous?
7 How was Giovanni Battista Montini better known?
8 Who had an 70s No. 1 with "No Charge"?
9 Who invented obstetric forceps?
10 Which Formula 1 racing driver gave his name to the Grand Prix circuit in Montreal?
11 What is the only English anagram of MARASCHINO?
12 On which river does Indianapolis stand?
13 Which star sign links Carol Barnes and Johnny Briggs?
14 In cricket, what name is given to 111 runs?
15 Which US State is directly east of Arizona?
16 Which "Emmerdale" animal was called either Jenny or Amos?
17 Which newspaper editor said, "Comment is free, facts are sacred"?
18 Who wrote the novel *Death in the Afternoon*?
19 What is the approximate distance of San Francisco airport from London in miles?
20 What do the letters JB stand for in J.B. Priestley's name?
21 If you are crapulous, what are you full of?
22 What is the name of the ship sailed by Captain Pugwash?
23 In which country was the presenter Kenneth Kendall born?
24 Annapolis is the capital of which US state?
25 Who did Honor Blackman play in *Never The Twain*?
26 In which country is the mineral cryolite found?
27 What was the first British Top Ten hit for James Brown?
28 What would a Cypriot call his capital of Nicosia?
29 Which volcano has the capital Quito, Ecuador, on its edge?
30 New Britain and Admiralty are in which island group?

Quiz 80 Celebs

Answers - see page 546

LEVEL 3

1   Who bought the Windsors' house in Paris in 1986?
2   Who was Nelson Mandela's companion on his July 1997 trip to London?
3   Who wrote her memoirs in "What Falls Away"?
4   Whose family estate is at Hyannis Port?
5   What did Goldie Hawn ride to open Harrods sale in January 1997?
6   After being Countess Spencer which title did Raine have?
7   Which singer was the celeb Isabel Preysler married to?
8   Which fashion house did John Galliano first design for in 1997?
9   What is Kate Capshaw's married name?
10 Who lives at Ray Mill House?
11 Which daughter of Joan Collins married in 1997?
12 Who owns a motor yacht called *Talitha G*?
13 Who was Naomi Campbell staying with in the Canaries when she was rushed to hospital in 1997?
14 Pamela Anderson won a court case over her withdrawal from which film?
15 What was the name of the Elton John documentary made by David Furnish?
16 What is the name of the Clintons' cat?
17 Who did the supermodel Vendela replace as UNICEF international spokesperson?
18 Who is Mrs James Keach?
19 How did Frances Roche become widely known?
20 Which actress is the granddaughter of the designer Elsa Schiaparelli?
21 In which capacity did Jane Makim attend Prince Andrew's wedding?
22 Whose family home is at Barnwell Manor?
23 Who was awarded the second-highest civilian medal for bravery in 1997?
24 Which interior designer was the son-in-law of Lord Mountbatten?
25 Who was Earl Spencer's best man who was jailed for fraud?
26 Who produced six offspring in the Lincoln Bedroom at the White House?
27 Which rich divorcee did Riccardo Mazzucchelli marry?
28 Which royal family name was Princess Stephanie born with?
29 Which rock star has granddaughters called Assisi and Amba?
30 Which ex-royal's family home was at Nymans in Sussex?

Answers

Movie Comedies (see Quiz 78)
1 *Road to Zanzibar.* 2 *Home Alone.* 3 Las Vegas. 4 Jack Benny. 5 John Cleese, Michael Palin. 6 The Phantom. 7 George Clooney. 8 *Move Over Darling.* 9 *The Great Dictator.* 10 Ronald Searle. 11 *The Intelligence Men.* 12 Weather girl. 13 *The Lavender Hill Mob.* 14 *Monkey Business.* 15 *Why Worry?* 16 *Fierce Creatures.* 17 *Our Relations.* 18 *Trading Places.* 19 *What's New Pussycat?* 20 Michael Caine. 21 Steve Martin. 22 Lou Costello. 23 *Carry On Nurse.* 24 *A Shot in the Dark.* 25 Abbott and Costello. 26 Leslie Nielsen. 27 Kelly Preston. 28 *Privates on Parade.* 29 Dan Aykroyd. 30 *Pillow Talk.*

Quiz 81 Pot Luck 41

Answers - see page 551

LEVEL 3

1   Which shipping forecast area is south of Forties?
2   In which sport did Charles Smith make a fourth Olympic appearance aged 45?
3   How many islands are in the Faroe group?
4   In motor racing, what is the ECU?
5   Which character was played by Johnny Briggs in "No Hiding Place"?
6   If it's noon at GMT, what time is it in Bombay?
7   From which language does the word "cigar" originate?
8   In which US state would a Downeaster be a native inhabitant?
9   In which country is Trivandrum Airport?
10 Who had an 80s No. 1 with "99 Red Balloons"?
11 What is a dasyure?
12 The botanist Gregor Mendel belonged to which order of monks?
13 What did Howard Keel sell before he won a singing scholarship?
14 In which country, as well as Spain, is the city of Valencia ?
15 What name is given to a plant that doesn't have leaves?
16 In Scrabble what is the letter K worth?
17 What did Wonder Woman's lasso always make people do?
18 Helminthophobia is the fear of what?
19 How many main islands are in the Hawaiian group?
20 Who had *The Battle of the Books* published in 1704?
21 What did Shevardnadze call the idea that "each country should construct its foreign policy on a 'My Way' basis"?
22 What was the first British Top Ten hit for Joe Brown and the Bruvvers?
23 Which star sign links Henry Cooper and Bob Carolgees?
24 What was Henry John Temple's title when he was UK prime minister?
25 Which US state is directly south of Georgia?
26 In which sport was Gerald Matthews Balding famous?
27 Gene Wilder was born on the same day as which racing driver?
28 Which UK paper size is 420 x 594 mm?
29 Whose first book was called *Jigsaw*?
30 What is the only English anagram of INTERLACED?

Answers

Pot Luck 42 (see Quiz 83)

1 135. 2 The Four Pennies. 3 Reinvented. 4 Electric Company. 5 Nero. 6 Casablanca. 7 Pisces. 8 Philippines. 9 The *Daily Mail*. 10 "Word Up". 11 Venezuela. 12 Owens Illinois. 13 T.E. Lawrence. 14 Jezebel. 15 Clara Danby. 16 Golf. 17 Minnesota. 18 Arthur Conan Doyle. 19 200. 20 Con Brio. 21 Tuscany Valley. 22 Babar the Elephant. 23 Mintonette. 24 1,600. 25 17th. 26 Malay. 27 Arkansas. 28 Comoros. 29 Potato. 30 1989.

LEVEL 3

1 Allegheny and Blue Ridge are in which mountain range?
2 Where is the N'Gorongoro Crater?
3 The Commonwealth of Australia set up in 1901 comprised two territories and how many states?
4 Flores, Corvo and Pico belong to which group of islands?
5 Which city had a street called The Bowery?
6 Who links the Cenotaph in London and New Delhi?
7 What do the straits of Magellan separate?
8 On which river does Adelaide stand?
9 What is the capital of the Canadian province Manitoba?
10 Fagatogo is the capital of what?
11 What are the three volcanic islands of the British Virgin Islands?
12 Avarua is on which of the Cook Islands?
13 What are the Monte Titano peaks made from?
14 Who owns Bouvet Island?
15 How many official languages does South Africa have?
16 In which country is the largest expanse of sand in the world?
17 The Fouta Djallon mountains are to the south of which country?
18 On which river does Nashville stand?
19 Lake Kivu forms much of the western boundary of which country?
20 What is the former name of Nizhny Novgorod?
21 Where is the Kara-Kum Desert?
22 Doi Inthanon is the highest point of which country?
23 What is the capital of Anguilla?
24 Where is the largest phosphate deposit in the world?
25 Flying Fish Cove is on which island?
26 Which country lies between Guyana and French Guiana?
27 What does the Nile split into at Khartoum?
28 Aruba is off which country's coast?
29 Which islands were annexed to the Clunies-Ross family until 1978?
30 In the US which state is immediately west of Colorado?

Answers

Musicals (see Quiz 84)
1 *Hair*. 2 *South Pacific*. 3 *Sweet Charity*. 4 Frank Loesser. 5 *Smokey Joe's Cafe*.
6 *Always*. 7 "Oh What A Beautiful Morning". 8 *Blood Brothers*.
9 The Shadows. 10 *Cats*. 11 "With One Look". 12 Steve Harley. 13
Buddy. 14 *Memories*. 15 *Martin Guerre*. 16 *Chess*. 17 *Grease*. 18 Judi
Dench. 19 *Phantom of the Opera*. 20 *Funny Girl*. 21 Marti Webb, Wayne Sleep.
22 Charles Hart & Richard Stilgoe. 23 Stephen Fry 24 Patti LuPone. 25
Cameron Mackintosh. 26 Dr Barnardo. 27 Anita Dobson. 28 Marvin
Hamlisch. 29 *Joseph and the Amazing Technicolor Dreamcoat*. 30 Fagin.

1   How many degrees are there in each internal angle of an octagon?
2   Who had an 60s No. 1 with "Juliet"?
3   What is the only English anagram of INTERVENED?
4   On a Monopoly board what is between Pall Mall and Whitehall?
5   What was the name of the caterpillar in "Dangermouse"?
6   Which port is known in Arabic as Dar el-Beida?
7   Which star sign links the author Jilly Cooper and the presenter Andy Crane?
8   In which country was the actress Susan Penhaligon born?
9   What was launched by Alfred Harmsworth and Viscount Northcliffe in 1896?
10 What was the first British Top Ten hit for Cameo?
11 The international car registration YV applies to which country?
12 Who invented industrial glass fibre?
13 What was T.E. Ross's real name?
14 In the Bible, who was King Ahab married to?
15 Which character was played by Pauline Collins in "No, Honestly"?
16 In which sport was John Ball famous?
17 Which US state is north of Iowa?
18 Who wrote *The White Company*?
19 How many 2.5 mile laps are completed in the car race, the Indy 500?
20 What term is given to a piece of music played vigorously?
21 In which valley was "Falcon Crest" set?
22 Which animated animal was married to his cousin, Celeste?
23 What was the original name of volleyball?
24 What is the approximate distance of Moscow airport from London in miles?
25 In which century was Daniel Defoe born?
26 From which language does the word "caddy" originate?
27 Which US state is known as the Bear State?
28 Moheli and Mayotte are in which island group?
29 Vanessa and Wilja are types of what?
30 Which year first saw red noses on cars in support of Comic Relief?

Answers

Pot Luck 41   (see Quiz 81)

1 Dogger. 2 Water polo. 3 22. 4 Electronic Control Unit. 5 Det Sgt Russell.
6 5.30 p.m. 7 Spanish. 8 Maine. 9 India. 10 Nena. 11 A marsupial.
12 Augustinian. 13 Aircraft. 14 Venezuela. 15 Aphyllous. 16 Five.
17 Tell the truth. 18 Worms. 19 Eight. 20 Jonathan Swift. 21 Sinatra
Doctrine. 22 "A Picture of You". 23 Taurus. 24 Viscount Palmerston.
25 Florida. 26 Polo. 27 Jackie Stewart. 28 A2. 29 Barbara Cartland.
30 Credential.

1 Which Broadway musical was the first to include nudes on stage?
2 Which musical opens on Emile de Becque's plantation?
3 "Big Spender" comes from which show?
4 Who wrote the lyrics for *Guys and Dolls*?
5 Which musical is based on the songs of Leiber and Stoller?
6 Which new 90s musical starred Sheila Ferguson, formerly of the Three Degrees'?
7 Which song opens the music for *Oklahoma*?
8 Which musical has the songs "Light Romance" and "My Child"?
9 Who next charted with "Don't Cry For Me, Argentina" after Julie Covington?
10 Elaine Paige's first Top Ten hit was from which musical?
11 What was Barbra Streisand's first hit from *Sunset Boulevard*?
12 Who duetted with Sarah Brightman on the chart single, "Phantom of the Opera" ?
13 Paul Hipp first played the title role in which musical?
14 Which album was subtitled "The Best of Elaine Paige"?
15 Which musical has the same theme as the Richard Gere film *Sommersby*?
16 Frederick Trumper was one of the heroes in which show?
17 Ian Kelsey of "Emmerdale" went on to star in which musical?
18 Whose withdrawal from "Cats" meant Elaine Paige starred in it?
19 Which Lloyd Webber show gave Cliff Richard a hit single?
20 Which musical does the song "People" come from?
21 Who were the first "Song" and "Dance" of *Song and Dance*?
22 Who wrote the lyrics of "Love Changes Everything"?
23 Which English comedian and novelist was said to have been made a millionaire in his 20s with his work on the West End hit *Me and My Girl*?
24 Who was the first Norma Desmond in *Sunset Boulevard* in London?
25 Who sponsored Oxford University's first professorship in drama and musical theatre?
26 Who was the subject of Rice and Lloyd Webber in *The Likes of Us*?
27 Who played opposite Adam Faith in the doomed *Budgie*?
28 Which musical writer wrote "Sunshine Lollipops And Rainbows" for Lesley Gore?
29 What was the longest-running show ever at the London Palladium when it finished in 1994?
30 Which role has been played by Barry Humphries, Jonathan Pryce and Russ Abbot?

Answers

World Tour (see Quiz 82)
1 Appalachian Mountains. 2 Serengeti National Park, Tanzania. 3 Six.
4 Azores. 5 New York. 6 Sir Edward Lutyens (designed the first, planned the second). 7 Tierra de Fuego and South American mainland. 8 Torrens.
9 Winnipeg. 10 American Samoa. 11 Tortola, Virgin Gorda, Jost van Dyke.
12 Rarotonga. 13 Limestone. 14 Norway. 15 11. 16 Saudi Arabia.
17 Senegal. 18 Cumberland. 19 Rwanda. 20 Gorky. 21 Turkmenistan.
22 Thailand. 23 The Valley. 24 Bu Craa, Western Sahara. 25 Christmas Island. 26 Suriname. 27 Blue Nile, White Nile. 28 Venezuela.
29 Cocos Islands. 30 Utah.

1 On which river does Melbourne stand?

2 How did Barbara Betts become known in public life?

3 Who had an 80s No. 1 with "Save Your Love"?

4 Which character was played by Jane Seymour in "The Onedin Line"?

5 What was Saki's real name?

6 Lyon, Nord and Saint-Lazare are three stations on a French Monopoly board - what's the fourth?

7 What is the capital of the US state of Mississippi?

8 In which sport is Paul Jason Barber famous?

9 Who was the first indy car rookie to start from pole and win in 84 years?

10 In which country is the city of Windhoek?

11 What is the only English anagram of INTOXICATE?

12 The drunken midwife Sarah Gamp appeared in which Dickens novel?

13 What was the first British Top Ten hit for Canned Heat?

14 How many islands are in the Marquesas group?

15 If A is Alpha and B is Bravo what is K?

16 St Boniface is the patron saint of which country?

17 Who replaced Workington in the Football League?

18 In which country is Turku Airport?

19 Who wrote *The Once and Future King*?

20 Which US state is south of Kansas?

21 Who is the actress Catherine Oxenberg's mother?

22 In Scrabble what is the letter W worth?

23 Linonophobia is the fear of what?

24 In which country are the Siebenhengste System caves?

25 Which Swede did Frank Bruno beat in 1985 to become European heavyweight champ?

26 Which star sign links Steve Davis and Jim Bowen?

27 Who invented heat-resistant glass?

28 If it's noon at GMT, what time is it in La Paz?

29 Why was the 1961 world figure skating championships cancelled?

30 The adjective murine refers to which creatures?

Quiz 86 TV: Stateside

LEVEL 3

1   Which role did Mr T play in "The A Team"?
2   Who was the local sheriff in "Twin Peaks"?
3   "All in the Family" was the US version of which UK sitcom?
4   In which state was "Thirtysomething" set?
5   Which actress has played Chris Cagney and Margaret Hoolihan?
6   "The Toast of the Town" was renamed what after its presenter?
7   Who were the two families in the US spoof "Soap"?
8   Which show's catchphrases included "You bet your sweet bippy"?
9   Which US TV network was founded in 1943 by Edward J. Noble?
10 Which blockbuster series, watched by over half of the US, had O.J. Simpson as Kadi Toura?
11 In which street did the Addams Family live?
12 Who was Executive Producer of "Star Trek: The Next Generation"?
13 Which non-profitmaking organization originally funded "Sesame Street"?
14 In "The Rockford Files" how much did Jim charge for a day's work?
15 To two years, when did "The Price Is Right" begin in the US?
16 Who owns the channel TNT?
17 Which sitcom was originally called "You'll Never Get Rich"?
18 What was the first US soap sold to Britain?
19 Who guest-starred as the judge in the final Perry Mason's case of the 60s series?
20 Who played the lead role in the US version of "Agony"?
21 On which US series was "University Challenge" based?
22 Which US network was the first to broadcast in colour?
23 Who transferred her radio role in "My Favourite Husband" to long-running TV success?
24 Which TV station was home to Ed Murrow and Walter Kronkite?
25 Which company did Lucille Ball create with her then real-life husband?
26 What was the name of "Play Your Cards Right" in the US?
27 Alan Alda hosted the US version of which UK satirical show?
28 What were the real names of the two known as Smith and Jones?
29 Which company bought the rights to "Prime Suspect" and didn't want Helen Mirren as the lead?
30 In the series where did Roseanne and Dan Conner live?

Answers

Olympics (see Quiz 88)
1 200m Individual Medley. 2 Marie-Jose Perec. 3 Cuba, Japan. 4 Lanier.
5 Belarus. 6 Renata Mauer. 7 Garmisch-Partenkirchen. 8 Tim Henman & Neil Broad. 9 Christa Luding, née Rothenburger. 10 Liechtenstein. 11 St Moritz. 12 Twice (1908, 1948). 13 Head garland of wild olive leaves.
14 Three. 15 Equestrian dressage. 16 Armenia, Azerbaijan. 17 Kenny Harrison. 18 Penny Heyns. 19 1994. 20 Carl Lewis. 21 Ian Walker, John Merricks. 22 Seppo Raty. 23 Mark Phillips. 24 Paul Palmer. 25 Steve Redgrave. 26 Mountain biking. 27 Over transport problems. 28 One.
29 Krisztina Egerzegi. 30 Eric Heiden (speed skating).

1 Which character was played by Peter Bowles in "Only When I Laugh"?
2 Who wrote "La Marseillaise"?
3 The world's second TV service was beamed from which landmark?
4 What are the odds of rolling any combination totalling three in dice-throwing?
5 What was pioneered by the physicist Dennis Gabor?
6 What creature appeared on the most expensive of the British 1991 dinosaur stamps?
7 Cheyenne is the capital of which US state?
8 Which star sign links Sir Robin Day and John Cleese?
9 What was George Sand's real name?
10 Who had an 70s No. 1 with "January"?
11 Which *Carry On* actor was in "The Army Game" and "Secret Army"?
12 From which language does the word "jungle" originate?
13 Which US state is south of the State of Washington?
14 What term describes peacocks congregating together?
15 Which castle is the Scottish home of the Duke of Roxburgh?
16 Roxa and Caravela are in which island group?
17 Which Formula 1 driver won the Monaco Grand Prix each year from 1989-93?
18 What is the approximate distance of Lagos airport from London in miles?
19 Who wrote *The Thin Man*?
20 What was the first British Top Ten hit for Vikki Carr?
21 Banks and Baffin are in which island group?
22 In Scrabble what is the letter H worth?
23 The Mason-Dixon line is the boundary between which two states?
24 Patty Berg was the first winner of which major sporting event?
25 Alphabetically, what is the first station on the London Underground?
26 On a French Monopoly board, what is the equivalent to Euston Road?
27 In which country was the actress Victoria Principal born?
28 What is the only English anagram of MAIN STREET?
29 Which Ernest won the Nobel Prize for Literature in 1954?
30 In which sport was Edward Barrett famous?

Quiz 88 Olympics

Answers - see page 554

1 Which race gave Michelle Smith her third gold medal in Atlanta?
2 Who was the first Olympic athlete to win the 200m/400m double gold?
3 Who were the finalists in basketball in the 1996 Games?
4 On which Olympic lake did Steve Redgrave win a fourth gold?
5 With whom did Britain tie for 35th place in the medals table in Atlanta?
6 Who was the first gold medallist of the Atlanta Games?
7 Where were the 1936 Winter Olympics held?
8 Who were beaten by the Woodies in the 1996 men's doubles final?
9 Who was the first woman to win gold at winter and summer Games?
10 Which is the only country to have won winter but not summer gold?
11 Between 1928 and 1948 where were the winter Olympics held twice?
12 How many times have the Olympics been held in Britain?
13 What were victors given in the ancient Olympics?
14 How many of Mark Spitz's seven golds in 1972 were for team events?
15 In which event did Hilda Johnstone compete in the 1972 Games aged 70?
16 Which two countries beginning with A won first time medals in 1996?
17 Who beat Jonathan Edwards in the Triple Jump final in Atlanta?
18 In Atlanta who became South Africa's first gold medallist since 1952?
19 In which year were the Winter Olympics first held in the middle of the four-year cycle of the summer games?
20 Who was the second track and field athlete in Olympic history to win four successive titles in the same event?
21 Who won silver medals for Britain for yachting in Atlanta?
22 Who did Steve Backley beat into third place in 1996?
23 Whose horse Cartier forced him to withdraw from the Three-Day Event competition in 1988?
24 Who won Britain's first medal of the Atlanta Games?
25 Who carried the Olympic flag for the UK in Barcelona?
26 In which event, new in Atlanta, did Paolo Pezzo win gold?
27 Why did the Modern Pentathletes stage a sit-down protest at Atlanta?
28 How many people died because of the Centennial Park bomb?
29 Which woman won a record fifth individual swimming gold in 1996?
30 Who held the record from 1980 for most individual golds in one Games?

Answers

TV: Stateside (see Quiz 86)
1 Sgt Bosco "BA" Baracus. 2 Harry S. Truman. 3 "Till Death Us Do Part".
4 Philadelphia. 5 Loretta Swit. 6 "The Ed Sullivan Show". 7 Campbells and
Tates. 8 "Rowan and Martin's Laugh-In". 9 ABC. 10 "Roots". 11 Cemetery
Ridge. 12 Gene Roddenberry. 13 Children's Television Workshop. 14 $200
plus expenses. 15 1956. 16 Ted Turner. 17 "The Phil Silvers Show".
18 "Peyton Place". 19 His creator, Erle Stanley Gardner. 20 Lucy Arnaz.
21 "College Bowl". 22 NBC. 23 Lucille Ball. 24 CBS. 25 Desilu.
26 "Card Sharks". 27 "That Was The Week That Was". 28 Hannibal Heyes,
Jed"'Kid" Curry. 29 Universal. 30 Lanford, Illinois.

1   In which fictitious Manor House was "Mulberry" set?
2   Who gave Bill Wyman a walking frame when he married Mandy Smith?
3   Which country did Surya Bonaly represent at skating?
4   Who had an 80s No. 1 with "A Little Peace"?
5   Who invented the glider?
6   Mysophobia is the fear of what?
7   Which shipping forecast area is west of Dogger?
8   Who wrote *To the Lighthouse*?
9   In which country is the city of Aleppo?
10 What was Sapper's real name?
11 Mergoles and Kelvedon Marvel are types of what?
12 Where in Melbourne, is the Australian Formula 1 Grand Prix held?
13 Which US state is directly south of New Mexico?
14 Ernest Barry was a world champion which sport?
15 In Scrabble what is the letter P worth?
16 If it's noon at GMT, what time is it in Guatemala City?
17 Who was the last personality to be recorded on "This Is Your Life" before the death of Eamonn Andrews?
18 The athlete Carl Lewis was born on the same day as which royal?
19 What is the capital of the Canadian province Northwest Territories?
20 Which character was played by Patricia Hodge in "The Other 'Arf"?
21 What was the first British top Ten Hit for Ronnie Carroll?
22 How many islands and islets are in the Indonesia group?
23 Which star sign links actors Christopher Biggins and Lionel Blair?
24 Which US state is known as the Sooner State?
25 What is the only English anagram of MODERATORS?
26 In which country is Townsville Airport?
27 In which century was Franz Schubert born?
28 Who did Neville Chamberlain follow as prime minister of the UK?
29 On a French Monopoly board, how much is the fine on Impôts sur le Revenu?
30 In the TV series, what was Grizzly Adams's first name?

1   How is Caryn Johnson better known?
2   Who was Woody Allen's date right at the end of *Annie Hall*?
3   Which actress's novels include *Delusions of Grandma*?
4   Which actress sang under the pseudonym Rainbo?
5   Who was the chain-smoking scientist in *Brainstorm*?
6   Who played the actress born Lucille Le Sueur in 1981?
7   Whose first Oscar nomination was in *The Sterile Cuckoo* in 1969?
8   Who won an Oscar without speaking in 1993?
9   Who was known as Anna Marno when she first went to Hollywood?
10 Who replaced Jean Harlow in the 1953 remake of *Red Dust*?
11 A film of whose wedding was released by MGM in Technicolor?
12 Who made her film debut in Hitchcock's *The Trouble With Harry*?
13 Who at 19 was Charlie Chaplin's oldest bride when he was 44?
14 Who married a French editor and wrote a book *Every Frenchman has One*?
15 Who was created Miss New Orleans 1931?
16 Which two films did Marilyn Monroe make after playing Sugar Kane?
17 In which TV soap did Demi Moore find fame?
18 Who was the daughter of Lana Turner who stabbed Lana's boyfriend to death?
19 Who played the investigator V.I. Warshawski on film and on Radio 4?
20 Who was the only female founder of United Artists?
21 Which film gave Elizabeth Taylor her third successive Oscar nomination in the 50s?
22 Which actress was called the Look on arriving in Hollywood?
23 Who was Honey Hornee in *Wayne's World II*?
24 Who was Warren Beatty's first wife?
25 Which actress had a son called Satchel?
26 Who was directed by her husband in *Rachel Rachel*?
27 Who played her sister as a child in *The Searchers* in 1956?
28 Whose autobiography was called *Goodness Had Nothing to Do With It*?
29 Who was born in 1932 as Edna Rae Gillooly?
30 Who played Jerry Lewis's child bride cousin in *Great Balls of Fire!*?

Animal World (see Quiz 92)

Answers

1 Vegetation above ground. 2 Capybara. 3 Barn Owl. 4 In its ear.
5 Insects. 6 Three. 7 Oxen. 8 Guanaco. 9 Live young. 10 Antelope.
11 30. 12 Red blood cell. 13 Highland collie. 14 London Zoo.
15 Bandicoot. 16 Colugo. 17 The Cat Fanciers Association of the US.
18 Strictly monogamous. 19 Madagascar. 20 Fisher. 21 Spiral. 22 When
they stand up on hind legs and tail. 23 Squid. 24 Squamata. 25 Cold-
blooded animal. 26 Snake. 27 Fox, badger or otter hunting. 28 Scaled
waterproof skins, shelled yolk-bearing eggs. 29 Venomous snake. 30 Great
Dane.

1   What was the first British Top Ten hit for the Cars?
2   What is the approximate distance of Bombay airport from London in miles?
3   In Monopoly, where would a double six from Piccadilly land you?
4   Who wrote *The African Queen*?
5   Which Sao Paolo suburb hosts the Brazilian Formula 1 Grand Prix circuit?
6   Who shot Kate Hughes's dog in the soap "Emmerdale"?
7   The adjective cerine refers to which creatures?
8   Which US state is directly south of South Dakota?
9   The Palais Royal Saloon, San Francisco, had the first what installed?
10 Who had an 70s No. 1 with "Sad Sweet Dreamer"?
11 How many degrees are there in each internal angle of a hexagon?
12 Who was the first Labour prime minister to meet a pope?
13 The dachshund was originally bred for what purpose?
14 What is the only English anagram of NECTARINES?
15 What is the latest date for Ash Wednesday in the 1990s?
16 Which UK paper size is 594 x 841 mm?
17 Which US state is the setting for "The Little House on the Prairie"?
18 Which star sign links Michael Barrymore and Dickie Davies?
19 What distinguished the first day of the first Old Trafford cricket test?
20 What was T.E. Shaw's real name?
21 Melchior and James are in which island group?
22 In which country was the actor Andrew Sachs born?
23 Puskas and who chaired Stanley Matthews off after his last game?
24 In what decade was Pluto's moon Charon discovered?
25 From which language does the word "minaret" originate?
26 Which character was played by Bernard Bresslaw in "Our House"?
27 What happened to British eggs for the first time in June 1957?
28 Who wrote the scores for the films *Easter Parade* and *Blue Skies*?
29 In which sport was Pamela Barton famous?
30 What is the capital of the US state of Minnesota?

LEVEL 3

1   What does a browser forage for?
2   What is the largest living rodent?
3   What type of owl featured on the British Nature Conservation stamps of the 80s?
4   Where would a mammal have a malleus?
5   Echidna feed chiefly on what?
6   How many chambers does a camel have in its stomach?
7   What sort of creatures were the now extinct aurochs?
8   Which camelid is the ancestor of the llama and the alpaca?
9   What does a therian mammal produce?
10 In the animal world what is a bongo?
11 How many bones are there in the human arm?
12 What is an erythrocyte?
13 What is another name for the bearded collie?
14 Where is the world's largest zoological library?
15 Which marsupial has the highest reproductive rate?
16 What is another name for the flying lemur?
17 What is the world's largest pedigree cat registry?
18 Which unusual sexual characteristic does the Patagonian hare have?
19 The lemur is native to where?
20 Which species of marten can penetrate a porcupine's defences?
21 What shape are a bushbuck's horns?
22 In mongooses what is the tripod position?
23 What is the principal food of the sperm whale?
24 Which order of reptiles do snakes and lizards belong to?
25 What is a poikilotherm?
26 What is a taipan?
27 What were Dandie Dinmonts originally bred for?
28 Which two main features do reptiles have which amphibians don't?
29 What is a krait?
30 How is the German mastiff also known?

Quiz 93 Pot Luck 47

LEVEL 3

Answers – see page 563

1   Which character was played by Jeremy Irons in "The Pallisers"?
2   On which river does Perth, Australia, stand?
3   What was the lowest value of a British Andrew-and-Fergie wedding stamp?
4   Which biscuit TV ad featured a Mexican singing "I can't stand it"?
5   Who had an 80s No. 1 with "Feels Like I'm In Love"?
6   In Scrabble what is the letter C worth?
7   Which star sign links the TV personalities Katie Boyle and Gordon Burns?
8   St Jude's Institute formed the soccer club now known as what?
9   In which country is the city of Constantine?
10 From which language does the word "hammock" originate?
11 In which century was Cyrano de Bergerac born?
12 Which city was home to the TV puppet owl, Ollie Beak?
13 Nosophobia is the fear of what?
14 Which US state is directly east of Minnesota?
15 Fresh breeze equals which number on the Beaufort Scale?
16 What was the first British Top Ten hit for CCS?
17 On a French Monopoly board, how much does it cost to buy a utility?
18 Pele was born on the same day as which English test cricketer?
19 In which country is Yundam Airport?
20 Selene is the Greek goddess of what?
21 Sammy Duvall was an 80s world champion in which sport?
22 What is the only English anagram of PERCUSSION?
23 If it's noon at GMT, what time is it in Rio de Janeiro?
24 What was Stendahl's real name?
25 How many islands are in the Mariana group?
26 Who did Steve Davis beat in the final when he first became world champion?
27 In which country was the actress Carmen Silvera born?
28 Dave Bickers was a British 60s champion in which sport?
29 What is the approximate distance of Johannesburg airport from London in miles?
30 Juneau is the capital of which US state?

Pot Luck 48   (see Quiz 95)

1 1981. 2 Graham Greene. 3 Tomato. 4 Canada. 5 Prettiness. 6 Canaries.
7 Earl of Liverpool. 8 Tennis. 9 Gary Davies. 10 Typically Tropical.
11 Frederick Walton. 12 Vietnam. 13 Isabel De Gines. 14 Scotland. 15 St
Bridget and St Eric. 16 Hutton and Washbrook. 17 £120. 18 "Hit The Road,
Jack". 19 French. 20 Idaho. 21 Capricorn. 22 Oxbridge. 23 Table tennis.
24 10,600. 25 A. 26 *Our Mutual Friend*. 27 Michigan. 28 "The Good Life".
29 New Zealand. 30 Thomas Straussler.

1 In which show did Yogi Bear first appear?
2 Whose partners included Crazylegs Crane and the Aardvark?
3 Who was the most famous voice of Bugs Bunny?
4 What was Ding-A-Ling?
5 In "The Flintstones" what was Baby Rubble called?
6 Where did the Jetsons live?
7 What was Scooby-Doo's nephew called?
8 What was Bedrock's newspaper called?
9 In which series did Rock and Gravel Slag first appear?
10 What was the first name of Mr Magoo?
11 Who narrated Mr Benn?
12 What was the name of the four Banana Splits?
13 Whose gang included Brain, Spook and Benny the Ball?
14 Which vegetarian vampire was voiced by David Jason?
15 What was the racoon called in "Deputy Dawg"?
16 Who first produced the "Tom and Jerry" cartoons?
17 Whose catchphrase was "Drat and triple drat"?
18 Where did George Jetson work?
19 What were the first names of Hanna and Barbera?
20 What was Nero in "Dangermouse"?
21 Who created Frankenstein Jr in the 60s series?
22 Which cartoon character was first seen in "Le Petit Vingtieme"?
23 Hong Kong Phooey was the guise of whom?
24 For which railway company did Ivor the Engine work for?
25 Where was the series "Marine Boy" made?
26 In "The Flintstones" what was Wilma's vacuum cleaner?
27 What did Paddington's friend Mr Gruber do for a living?
28 In the Tin Tin stories what was Captain Haddock's ship called?
29 Who had purple hair and a dog called Alistair?
30 What was Yogi Bear's girlfriend called?

Answers

Communication (see Quiz 96)
1 Sound navigation and ranging. 2 Transistor. 3 Electronic funds transfer. 4 1,000. 5 Coordinate geometry. 6 Router. 7 New York City West Delaware water supply tunnel. 8 Anthony Trollope. 9 Electrically erasable read-only memory. 10 NW Alaska Brasilia. 11 ANIK-B. 12 American Standard Code for Information Interchange. 13 Andorra - it was free. 14 Dorset. 15 Telegraphones. 16 Pentagon (over 34,500 lines). 17 Gramophone. 18 UK and Japan. 19 Crude oil. 20 Seafloor/Bahamas. 21 KDKA. 22 Bellsouth network. 23 Sea crossing. 24 Cornwall to Newfoundland. 25 Monaco. 26 Arecibo, Puerto Rico. 27 EMI. 28 Sky Pod. 29 Merlin network. 30 Master Antenna Television.

1   When did Italy adopt a double race format for Formula 1 at Imola and Monza?
2   Who wrote *The Third Man*?
3   Sioux and Sleaford Abundance are types of what?
4   In the TV series which country did Shelley's daughter emigrate to?
5   What is the only English anagram of PERSISTENT?
6   Hierro and Gomera are in which island group?
7   What was Robert Banks Jenkinson's title when he was UK prime minister?
8   In which sport was Blanche Bingley famous?
9   Which Radio 1 DJ was given the nickname Medallion Man?
10 Who had a 70s No. 1 with "Barbados"?
11 Who invented linoleum?
12 In which country is the city of Da Nang?
13 Which character was played by Sylvia Sims in "Peak Practice"?
14 Who were the opponents for Bobby Charlton's first international?
15 Who are the patron saints of Sweden?
16 In the 40s who were England's regular test openers?
17 In Monopoly how much does it cost to buy Pentonville Road?
18 What was the first British Top Ten hit for Ray Charles?
19 From which language does the word "chassis" originate?
20 Which US state is known as the Gem State?
21 Which star sign links Richard Briers and Keith Chegwin?
22 In which General Hospital was "Emergency Ward 10" set?
23 The Corbillon Cup is awarded in which sport?
24 What is the approximate distance of Sydney airport from London in miles?
25 On a six-string guitar, what note is played fifth fret, top string?
26 In which Dickens novel does Bradley Headstone appear?
27 Which US state is directly north of Indiana?
28 What was filmed in Kewferry Road, Northwood, Middlesex in the 70s?
29 In which country was the comedienne Pamela Stephenson born?
30 What was Tom Stoppard's original surname name?

Quiz 96 Communication

Answers – see page 562

LEVEL 3

1   In communications what does SONAR stand for?
2   What did Bardeen, Shockley and Brattain invent in 1948?
3   What is EFT?
4   How many megabits are there in a gigabit?
5   What is the full name of the computer language COGO?
6   What is a computer that links one network to another called?
7   What was the longest tunnel of any kind when it was finished in 1944?
8   Which Post Office clerk suggested roadside postboxes be erected in Guernsey?
9   What does EEROM mean?
10 What are the two extremities of the Pan-American Highway?
11 What was the first regular direct broadcasting system called?
12 What does ASCII stand for?
13 In 1997 which country had the cheapest postal service?
14 In which UK mainland county is the oldest postbox in daily use?
15 What were early tape recorders, pioneered by Poulsen called?
16 Where is the largest switchboard in the world?
17 What did Emile Berliner first demonstrate in 1888?
18 Which countries does the submarine telephone cable FLAG link?
19 What does the Interprovincial Pipe Line Inc. carry?
20 What postmark did the first undersea post office have?
21 What was the name of the first radio station in the USA?
22 What was the name of the huge telecommunications exchange at the Atlanta Olympics?
23 On the international E-road network what do three dots mean?
24 The first transatlantic radio message was sent from where to where?
25 Which country in 1997 had the greatest number of telephone subscribers per head of population?
26 Where in 1997 was the world's largest dish radio telescope?
27 Which British company pioneered stereophonic sound?
28 What is the name of the restaurant on Canada's CN Tower?
29 On which network is the Lovell telescope at Jodrell Bank?
30 What is MATV?

Answers

TV: Cartoons (see Quiz 94)
1 "Huckleberry Hound Show". 2 Pink Panther. 3 Mel Blanc. 4 Fox.
5 Bamm Bamm. 6 Orbit City. 7 Scrappy-Doo. 8 The *Daily Slate*. 9 "Wacky Races". 10 Quincy. 11 Ray Brooks. 12 Fleegle, Bingo, Drooper and Snorky.
13 Top Cat (in "The Boss Cat"). 14 Count Duckula. 15 Ty Coon. 16 Fred Quimby. 17 Dastardly. 18 Spacely Space Sprockets. 19 William, Joseph.
20 Caterpillar. 21 Buzz Conroy. 22 Tin Tin. 23 Penrod "Penry" Pooch.
24 Llantissily Rail Traction Co. Ltd. 25 Japan. 26 Baby elephant on roller skates. 27 Antiques dealer. 28 *Karaboudjan*. 29 Crystal Tipps. 30 Cindy.

1 Ochlophobia is the fear of what?
2 If it's noon at GMT, what time is it in Lima?
3 Who had a 50s No. 1 with "Hoots Mon"?
4 The actor Danny Glover was born on the same day as which member of the Eagles?
5 Which character was played by Christopher Biggins in "Poldark"?
6 In which country is the city of Chittagong?
7 From which language does the word "iceberg" originate?
8 What is the capital of the US state of Louisiana?
9 Which country lost their Formula 1 Grand Prix after 1981 but re-entered the staging in 1995?
10 What was Tintoretto's real name?
11 On a French Monopoly board, how much is the Taxe De Luxe?
12 Which shipping forecast area is east of Dogger and Humber?
13 Who replaced Gateshead in the Football League?
14 Which pop singer appeared in "Happy Days" as Leather Tuscadero?
15 In which country was the actress Angela Thorne born?
16 The adjective "leporine" refers to which creatures?
17 Teddy Bourne competed in three Olympics at which event?
18 How many islands are in the Kuril group?
19 What was the first British Top Ten hit for Glen Campbell?
20 Which actor was Adrian Mole's grandfather and in "The Army Game"?
21 Alice Perrers was the mistress of which monarch?
22 Which US state is North of Arkansas?
23 What is the only English anagram of SHATTERING?
24 Where was the first by-election held after the 1997 general election?
25 Who invented margarine?
26 In Scrabble what is the letter Y worth?
27 Which ape was played by Roddy McDowall in "Planet of the Apes"?
28 Which US state is known as the Wolverine State?
29 Which star sign links Danny Baker and Roy Barraclough?
30 In which country is Yoff Airport?

Answers

Pot Luck 50 (see Quiz 99)
1 "I Hear You Now". 2 108. 3 Morgan Beaudine. 4 Tiziano Vecellio.
5 Chagos. 6 Misconstrue. 7 Germany. 8 Sagittarius. 9 A bird.
10 M/A/R/R/S. 11 John Fowles. 12 Monaco. 13 Leon Brittan. 14 800.
15 Detective Inspector. 16 Super Tax. 17 Equestrianism. 18 November.
19 Percy Le Baron Spencer. 20 Michigan. 21 Blue and white. 22 John Le
Carré. 23 Friday. 24 Ted Ray. 25 Mazanares. 26 Scott Welch. 27 Ohio.
28 Italian. 29 Duane Eddy. 30 Four.

Quiz 98 War Zones

Answers – see page 568

LEVEL 3

1   What was the last battle between Britain and America?
2   Who fought whom in the late 19th-century War of the Pacific?
3   In which war were Britain the victors in 1842?
4   What was the first battle in the American War of Independence?
5   Which British Army general was born at Westerham vicarage in 1788?
6   What was the largest carrier battle of World War Two?
7   Who was defeated at the battle of Pharsalus in 48 BC?
8   During which war was the battle of the Alamo?
9   In which battle were tanks first used?
10 Who was the German commander at Verdun in 1916?
11 What was the last major naval battle of World War Two?
12 Where did the Russians have their final conflict in Germany in World War One?
13 In which war did the Battle of Solferino take place in 1859?
14 In World War Two, the battle of Coral Sea stopped a Japanese attack on where?
15 The site of the battle of Koniggratz in 1866 is now in which country?
16 Canada fell under British control after which battle of the Seven-Years War?
17 Which treaty led to the withdrawal of US troops from Vietnam?
18 In which war was the battle of Tsushima?
19 Conflict between which two tribes brought about the Biafran war?
20 After which major battle did the French leave Vietnam?
21 At which World War One battle did the Germans use poison gas for the first time?
22 Which ships were involved in the first battle of the Atlantic in 1939?
23 Which British territory was captured on Christmas Day 1941?
24 Who was defeated at the battle of Lepanto in 1571?
25 Who fought the Romans in the Battle of Mons Grapius in AD 84?
26 Who was in charge of the Russian army when the Germans were defeated at Stalingrad?
27 Which war was precipitated by the rejection of the Nineteen Propositions?
28 Which treaty ensured the Boers lost their independence in 1902?
29 Which three countries along with Germany invaded Russia in 1941?
30 Which World War One campaign began with the arrival of Indian troops at Abadan?

Answers

Folk & Blues (see Quiz 100)
1 Judy Dyble. 2 Phil Ochs. 3 Paris. 4 Rolling Thunder Review. 5 "The Times They Are A-Changin'". 6 Blind Willie McTell (Ralph McTell). 7 The Humblebums. 8 Conor. 9 Travers (Peter, Paul and Mary). 10 Blind Lemon Jefferson. 11 *Rhymes and Reasons*. 12 Riley. 13 Troubador. 14 Elektra. 15 Martin Carthy. 16 John Lee Hooker. 17 Sandy Denny. 18 Alexis Korner. 19 Al Stewart. 20 *Basket Of Light*. 21 Wilson. 22 Chicago. 23 Cecil Sharp. 24 Macclesfield. 25 Al Kooper. 26 T-Bone Walker. 27 West Virginia. 28 Brain haemorrhage. 29 Bob Dylan. 30 Sam Hopkins.

1   What was the first British Top Ten hit for Jon and Vangelis?
2   How many degrees are there in each internal angle of a pentagon?
3   Which character was played by Kurt Russell in "The Quest"?
4   What was Titian's real name?
5   Banhos and Salomon are in which island group?
6   What is the only English anagram of CONSUMERIST?
7   In which country is the city of Duisburg?
8   Which star sign links Janet Brown and Christopher Cazenove?
9   One of the 1988 Edward Lear stamps depicted Lear as what?
10   Who had an 80s No. 1 with "Pump Up The Volume"?
11   Who wrote the book *The Collector*?
12   Where is the Autodromo Enzo e Dino Ferrari circuit?
13   Who was MP for Richmond, North Yorks, before William Hague?
14   What is the approximate distance of Madrid airport from London in miles?
15   What was Regan's rank in the last episode of "The Sweeney"?
16   On a Monopoly board what is between Park Lane and Mayfair?
17   In which sport was George Bowman famous?
18   What month did Channel 4 go on the air in 1982?
19   Who invented the microwave oven?
20   Lansing is the capital of which US state?
21   At half-time in 1995 Man. Utd changed shirts at the Dell from grey to what colour?
22   Who said, "Spies, like prostitutes, are always going to be with us"?
23   If March 1 is on a Monday in a leap year, what day was January 1?
24   The comic Charlie Olden was known by what name?
25   On which river does Madrid stand?
26   Who ended Joe Bugner's 1995 boxing comeback?
27   Which US state is West of Pennsylvania?
28   From which language does the word "manifesto" originate?
29   The theme tune for *Peter Gunn* was played by which lead guitarist?
30   In Scrabble what is the letter V worth?

Pot Luck 49   (see Quiz 97)
1 Crowds. 2 7 a.m. 3 Lord Rockingham's XI. 4 Don Henley. 5 Rev Ossie Whitworth. 6 Bangladesh. 7 German. 8 Baton Rouge. 9 Argentina. 10 Jacopo Robusti. 11 Formula 10,000. 12 German Bight. 13 Peterborough. 14 Suzi Quatro. 15 Pakistan. 16 Hares. 17 Fencing. 18 56. 19 "Wichita Lineman". 20 Bill Fraser. 21 Edward III. 22 Missouri. 23 Straighten. 24 Uxbridge. 25 Hippolyte Merge-Mouries. 26 Four. 27 Galen. 28 Michigan. 29 Cancer. 30 Senegal.

Answers

1   Who was the original female vocalist in Fairport Convention?
2   Who wrote "There But For Fortune"?
3   In which city was Alexis Korner born?
4   What was Bob Dylan's 1976 tour called?
5   Which cover version sneaked in the charts for Ian Campbell in 1965?
6   Who did Ralph May take his stage name from?
7   What name did Billy Connolly and Gerry Rafferty sing under?
8   What was the name of Eric Clapton's son whose death inspired "Tears In Heaven"?
9   Who made up the trio with Yarrow and Stookey?
10 In the 1920s, who recorded "Match Box Blues" and "That Black Snake Moan"?
11 What was John Denver's first album called?
12 What is B.B. King's actual first name?
13 What was the name of London's leading folk club in the 60s?
14 Tom Paxton's *Ramblin' Boy* album came out on which label?
15 Simon and Garfunkel took the song "Scarborough Fair" from whom?
16 Who used the pseudonyms Birmingham Sam and Delta John?
17 Who wrote "Who Knows Where the Time Goes"?
18 Which blues man had a speaking part on Hot Chocolate's hit "Brother Louis"?
19 Who recorded the album *Bedsitter Images*?
20 Pentangle's "Night Flight" came from which album?
21 What was Woody Guthrie's middle name?
22 Smitty's Corner and Pepper's Lounge were blues clubs in which city?
23 Who published in 1907 *English Folk Songs: Some Conclusions*?
24 John Mayall comes from which untraditional birthplace of bluesmen?
25 Who played organ on Dylan's "Like A Rolling Stone"?
26 Who made the album *Stormy Monday Blues*?
27 According to John Denver which state is "almost heaven"?
28 How did Sandy Denny die?
29 Which folk hero played piano in Bobby Vee's band the Shadows?
30 What was Lightnin' Hopkins's real name?

1 What was the first British Top Ten hit for Eartha Kitt?
2 On a French Monopoly board, how much does it cost to buy a station?
3 Who was the first British conductor to have his life dramatized on TV?
4 From which language does the word "typhoon" originate?
5 In which country is the city of La Plata?
6 Whose last Formula 1 Grand Prix race of his career was at Adelaide in 1985?
7 What was Robert Gascoyne-Cecil's title when he was UK prime minister?
8 Bert Turner got an FA Cup Final goal and an own goal playing for whom?
9 Which UK paper size is 841 x 1189 mm?
10 Who invented the parking meter?
11 In which country are the world's deepest caves?
12 Which star sign links the presenter Gavin Campbell and the comedian Jasper Carrott?
13 In which country was Alan Whicker born?
14 Mike Avory and Pete Quaife were members of which pop group?
15 What is the approximate distance of Frankfurt airport from London in miles?
16 What was Michael Angelo Titmarsh's real name?
17 How many clusters of islands are in the Maldives group?
18 In which US state would a Bay Stater be a native inhabitant?
19 Odynophobia is the fear of what?
20 Who had a hit in 1975 with "Loving You"?
21 If it's noon at GMT, what time is it in Riyadh?
22 Model White and Green Globe are types of what?
23 Which soccer club left the Scottish League in the 1960s?
24 Which US state is directly east of New Hampshire?
25 Which character was played by Julie Covington in "Rock Follies"?
26 What are Phoebe, Mimas and Rhea?
27 In which country is Spokane Airport?
28 What is the only English anagram of INTERSPERSE?
29 Who wrote books about the Wombles?
30 In which sport was Beryl Burton famous?

Quiz 102 Rugby

Answers – see page 572

Answers – see page 572

LEVEL 3

1 Which country were the first to play in two union World Cup Finals?
2 As a player Willie John McBride went on how many Lions tours?
3 To five years, when did France first win the Five Nations outright?
4 Who won league's first Man Of Steel award?
5 What was the half-time score when Wigan beat Bath 82-6 in the cross code challenge?
6 Who is Argentina's leading all-time point-scorer?
7 Who didn't go and collect his loser's medal after the 1996 Pilkington Cup Final?
8 Keith Elwell played in 239 consecutive games for which league side?
9 Who scored 45 individual points for New Zealand against Japan in 1995?
10 Which university did Will Carling go to?
11 Who is the only person to captain the Lions and the English cricket team?
12 Who said at the wedding of the All-Black Glen Osborne, "I'm not the best man: I'm one of the security guards"?
13 Who scored most tries in the first Super League season?
14 Which country first completed the Grand Slam in 1968?
15 How old was Barry John when he retired from playing rugby?
16 Who said, "I'd rather play for Gloucester for 10p than go to Newcastle for £85,000"?
17 Rory Underwood began his senior career with which club?
18 What is Martin Offiah's middle name?
19 Gavin Hastings scored how many points in the 1995 World Cup game against Ivory Coast?
20 Ellery Hanley first won the Man Of Steel award while with which club?
21 In which decade were Orrell founded?
22 Which club did Gareth Edwards play for?
23 Who was Warrington's first player to win the Man Of Steel award?
24 In the 1995 World Cup which two players scored seven tries?
25 Who captained Wasps to the 1990 Courage League championship?
26 Which team won league's Challenge Cup before Wigan's eight-in-a-row run?
27 the full-back J.P.R. Williams played once in a 1978 international in which position?
28 Who was the first person to play in and later coach an England Grand Slam team?
29 Where was Tony Underwood born?
30 Who said, "There is no place for racial prejudice in the teachings of the Lord"?

Movies: Oscars (see Quiz 104)
1 Diane Ladd, Laura Dern. 2 Frank Borzage. 3 Sessue Hayakawa. 4 Costume design. 5 *Kitty Foyle*. 6 Sophia Loren. 7 Sally Field. 8 *Broadway Melody*. 9 Marlee Matlin (*Children of a Lesser God*). 10 Geraldine Page. 11 Spencer Tracy. 12 Ingrid Bergman. 13 *It Happened One Night*. 14 *Cimarron, Cavalcade*. 15 Greer Garson. 16 Glenda Jackson. 17 11 nominations, no winners. 18 *Mr Skeffington*. 19 "Somewhere in My Memory". 20 Deborah Kerr. 21 Joan Fontaine, Olivia de Havilland. 22 Charlie Allnut (*The African Queen*). 23 *Giant*. 24 *The Man Who Knew Too Much*. 25 Hollywood Roosevelt Hotel. 26 Margaret Rutherford. 27 Louise Fletcher (*One Flew Over the Cuckoo's Nest*). 28 *Going My Way*. 29 Hayley Mills. 30 *All About Eve* (14)

Answers

Quiz 103 Pot Luck 52

Answers – see page 569

LEVEL 3

1 From which language does the word "balcony" originate?
2 In which century was the US novelist James Fenimore Cooper born?
3 In which country is the city of Nagpur?
4 What was the first British Top Ten hit for the Korgis?
5 Which character was played by O.J. Simpson in "Roots"?
6 On a French Monopoly board, what is the equivalent to Community Chest?
7 What is Malcolm's surname in the TV series "Watching"?
8 Which star sign links Stanley Baxter and Joan Collins?
9 Which US state is known as the Centennial State?
10 Who wrote the novel *King Solomon's Mines*?
11 What was the last major conflict between native North Americans and US troops?
12 Don Butcher was a champion in which sport?
13 Which finalist has won the fewest frames since snooker's world championship became first to 18 frames?
14 Whole gale equals which number on the Beaufort Scale?
15 Who did Fitzurse, de Tracy, de Merville and le Breton murder?
16 In which country was Bruce Willis born?
17 Boa Vista and Sao Nicolau are in which island group?
18 In which fictitious terrace did Eric Sykes and his sister Hat live?
19 What is the approximate distance of New York airport from London in miles?
20 Who had a hit in 1977 with "2-4-6-8 Motorway"?
21 What is the only English anagram of PATERNALISM?
22 How many minutes did Brian Little's England-playing career last for?
23 What name was given to the second of Neptune's moons to be discovered?
24 In which city was André Previn born?
25 When did Denmark join the European Union?
26 The international car registration V applies to vehicles from where?
27 Which US state is directly west of Vermont?
28 Who was the first Formula 1 driver to win at Monaco in three successive years in 1963-5?
29 In Greek mythology, Attis is the god of what?
30 Where did Frank and Pat go for their honeymoon in "EastEnders"?

Answers

Pot Luck 51 (see Quiz 101)

1 "Under the Bridges of Paris". **2** F20,000. **3** Sir Thomas Beecham.
4 Chinese. **5** Argentina. **6** Niki Lauder. **7** Marquess of Salisbury.
8 Charlton (1946). **9** A0. **10** Carlton C. Magee. **11** France. **12** Pisces.
13 Egypt. **14** The Kinks. **15** 400. **16** William Makepeace Thackeray.
17 19. **18** Massachusetts. **19** Pain. **20** Minnie Riperton. **21** 3 p.m.
22 Turnip. **23** Third Lanark. **24** Maine. **25** Devonia Dee Rhoades.
26 Satellites of Saturn. **27** USA. **28** Enterprises. **29** Elizabeth Beresford.
30 Cycling.

Quiz 104 Movies: Oscars

LEVEL 3

1 Who were the first mother and daughter to receive simultaneous Oscar nominations?
2 Who won the first Best Director Oscar?
3 Who was nominated for his role as the prison camp commander in *The Bridge on the River Kwai*?
4 Milera Canonero won an Oscar for *Chariots of Fire* for what?
5 For which film did Ginger Rogers win her only Oscar?
6 Who was the first person to receive an Oscar for a role played entirely in a foreign language?
7 Whose second Oscar prompted her "You like me" speech?
8 What was the first talkie to win an Oscar?
9 Who won an award in her first film, based on a Mark Medoff play?
10 Which actress won her first Oscar after her eighth nomination?
11 Who was the first Best Actor in successive years?
12 Of all the star cameos, who won the only Oscar for *Murder on the Orient Express*?
13 What was the first movie to win Best Actor, Actress, Director and Film?
14 Which two 30s Best Films had one-word titles?
15 Which Irish actress had one win in seven nominations by 1960?
16 Who was the first Best Actress to win the award twice in the 70s?
17 In Oscar terms what links *The Color Purple* and *The Turning Point*?
18 For which 1944 film did Bette Davis win her fifth successive nomination?
19 Which song from Home Alone as Oscar nominated?
20 Who received an honorary Oscar in 1994 after six unsuccessful nominations in 12 years?
21 Which sisters were nominated for Best Actress in 1941?
22 Which character won Humphrey Bogart an Oscar in 1951?
23 For which film did Rock Hudson receive his only nomination?
24 In which film was "Que Sera Sera" an Oscar-winner?
25 Where were the first Oscars presented?
26 Who was Best Supporting Actress winner in 1963 for *The VIPs*"?
27 Who won an Oscar playing Nurse Ratched?
28 In which film did "Swinging on a Star" win an Oscar?
29 In 1960 who received a miniature statuette for her "outstanding juvenile performance"?
30 Which 50s film had most Oscar nominations?

1   Who had a hit in 1985 with "My Toot Toot"?
2   What were the names of Timothy Lumsden's parents in "Sorry"?
3   Which shipping forecast area is south of Shannon and Fastnet?
4   What is the only English anagram of PROCREATION?
5   Which city introduced Britain's first trolley-bus service?
6   Who was Nigel Mansell's teammate at the Newman Haas Indy Team?
7   Who invented the slide rule?
8   In which country is the city of Nanning?
9   In which hospital is the TV comedy series "Surgical Spirit" set?
10   Joan Rivers was born on the same day as which opera singer?
11   If it's noon at GMT, what time is it in Rangoon?
12   In Scrabble what is the letter N worth?
13   In which Dickens novel does Jeremiah Flintwinch appear?
14   How many islands are in the Laccadive group?
15   What blood group did the Vulcan Mr Spock have?
16   What was the first British Top Ten hit for the Trammps?
17   From which language does the word "skippe" originate?
18   On which river does Pittsburgh stand?
19   Which star sign links the comics Stan Boardman and Ronnie Corbett?
20   Who replaced Bradford Park Avenue in the Football League?
21   What is the approximate distance of Mexico City airport from London in miles?
22   Which county gave the setting to the TV series "Rich Tea and Sympathy"?
23   In which sport was Philip Mario Caira famous?
24   What is the capital of the US state of Pennsylvania?
25   Phagophobia is the fear of what?
26   If A is Alpha and B is Bravo what is U?
27   Who invented the car speedometer?
28   Which character was played by Sean Maguire in "Grange Hill"?
29   How much was the weekly family allowance when first introduced?
30   In which country is Pago Pago Airport?

LEVEL 3

1 Who said, "Take it easy driving - the life you save might be mine"?
2 What was suggested that you "Buy some for Lulu"?
3 How much did "1001" clean your carpet for?
4 What did Patsy Kensit advertise in her first TV ad?
5 Pook's "Blow the Wind" was used to advertise what?
6 Which programme was interrupted with the first ever commercial on UK TV?
7 Who wrote "O Sole Mio", which advertised Wall's Cornetto?
8 Which brand of what featured in the first UK TV ad?
9 Who wrote "The Flight of the Bumble Bee", which urged us to buy Black & Decker paint-stripper?
10 Whose watches were advertised to the music of Ramirez?
11 Which Bobby Hodgens and Siobhan Fahey song hit No. 1 after being used in a VW ad?
12 Which Muddy Waters hit was reissued after it was used to advertise Levi's?
13 Which Mozart opera helped to sell the Citroën ZX?
14 Verdi's "Dies Irae" was used to advertise which newspaper?
15 Who were the original jingle artists for the song that became "I'd Like to Teach the World to Sing"?
16 Georgie Fame's "Get Away" started out as a jingle for what?
17 In 1960 the ad music for Strand cigarettes gave a hit to whom?
18 In the BT "EastEnders" ad what was the late Arthur Fowler doing?
19 Whose music was the theme from *Raging Bull* and used to advertise Heineken Export?
20 Whose wines were trumpeted to the sound of Pachelbel's *Canon in D Major*?
21 Which upmarket scent was advertised to Vivaldi's *Four Seasons*?
22 Which music by whom advertised Hamlet cigars?
23 Who wrote *The Force of Destiny* (*La forza del destino*), used for Stella Artois lager?
24 The Clash's only No. 1 was used to advertise what?
25 What was being advertised in the jingle which began "You'll wonder where the yellow went"?
26 Where did the spring water come from which was advertised by Elgar's Cello Concerto?
27 Which model ditched everything but her ex's VW keys?
28 What was Lorraine Chase advertising when she said "Nah, from Luton Airport"?
29 According to the ad, what did PAL stand for?
30 Which drink was advertised to the music of Offenbach's *Barcarolle*?

1 Asuncion is the capital of which country?
2 In the 1980s the town of Spitak was destroyed in which disaster?
3 Who had hits with Take Your Time and Got To Have Your Love?
4 What is a paravane used for?
5 Dr James Naismith devised which game?
6 In which decade was Jeremy Paxman born?
7 Which world wide magazine was conceived by DeWitt Wallace?
8 To within two years, when were postcodes introduced to the UK?
9 Waterways Airways operates from which country?
10 Who is the elder – Rowan Atkinson or Clive Anderson?
11 What is prase?
12 Who, in 1890, composed the music for the opera Ivanhoe ?
13 A poniard is a type of what?
14 Who led the Expedition of the Thousand in 1860?
15 Which 60s No 1 was written by Madden and Morse in 1903?
16 Which part of the body is affected by thlipsis?
17 Who was found dead in the first episode of EastEnders?
18 Which Mel Brooks' film was a spoof of Hitchcock movies?
19 Which road was part of the title of the TV series based on the true story of the Cavendish Hotel?
20 What did Princess Diana once describe as "hard work and no pay"?
21 Antonio Salazar was dictator for many years in which country?
22 Which US anti-terrorist force is based at Fort Bragg?
23 William Benting was an English pioneer of what?
24 By volume, what makes up about 21% of our atmosphere?
25 Who starred with his wife in the film Mr and Mrs Bridge?
26 Whose one and only hit was I've Never Been To Me in 1982?
27 Whose codename was Pink for This Is Your Life?
28 To which Court are US Ambassadors to Britain officially credited?
29 Which US poet had the middle names Weston Loomir?
30 Which was the first African team to compete in the Cricket World Cup?

1   Which playwright created the character Jane Tennison?
2   Which TV detective was played by Pauline Quirke?
3   In which series was Samantha Janus transferred from the Met to Merseyside?
4   Who was Morse's sidekick in The Wench is Dead?
5   Which novelist created the characters of Dalziel and Pascoe?
6   Which detective worked for Radio West?
7   Which series centred on Townsend Investigations?
8   Which novelist created Jack Frost?
9   Which acronymic part of the Met did Tony Clark work for in Between The Lines?
10 Which writer created off beat sleuth Jonathan Creek?
11 Who introduced the very first series of Detective?
12 In which series did Inspector Tsientsin appear?
13 Which famous series was introduced with a message on an answering machine?
14 In which series was Slade assisted by Holly?
15 Who played Frances Spender in the Jimmy Nail series?
16 Whose investigations are based in Shrewsbury but often filmed in central Europe?
17 Who played mini skirted detective Anna Lee?
18 Whose real-life daughter plays a nanny in The Archers?
19 Which long running series began with a pilot called Killer in 1983?
20 Where did The Cops take place?
21 What was the full name of TV's most famous Dutch detective?
22 Who had a Rolls Royce called The Grey Panther?
23 Which 60s series had Chief Inspector Keen aiding his Commander?
24 Who is the detective in An Unsuitable Job for a Woman?
25 Who was Regan's boss in The Sweeney?
26 Which detective lived at Whitehaven Mansions?
27 Which was the first Miss Marple adaptation to star Joan Hickson on TV?
28 Which actor linked Brookside with Liverpool One?
29 Who had retired from Barstock CID?
30 Claude Eustace Teal was invariably beaten in his dealings with whom?

LEVEL 3

1 Phil Read won several World Championships in which sport?
2 What did an alchemist use an alembic for?
3 What was Eternal's first UK Top Ten hit?
4 In Hindu mythology who was goddess of destruction and death?
5 In which country is the Mackenzie River?
6 Which instrument did Lionel Hampton play?
7 Which character was played by June Allyson in the film The Glenn Miller Story?
8 What was President Carter's wife's first name?
9 Who won the first squash World Open Championship?
10 Where is England's national hockey stadium?
11 Who is the elder – Dame Judi Dench or Barbara Taylor Bradford?
12 Who wrote the novel Rodney Stone?
13 How many times is Annie mentioned in the lyrics of Annie's Song?
14 In Swift's novel what was Gulliver's first name?
15 To which part of the body does the adjective 'cutaneous' refer?
16 In which sport were Hildon and Black Bears British Champions?
17 Whose first Top Ten hit was What A Waste in 1978?
18 Who was James I of England's father?
19 Which record label did Geri Halliwell sign up with when she left the Spice Girls?
20 What was the old name for stamp collecting?
21 In which decade was the Earl of Lichfield born?
22 Alfredo di Stefano of Real Madrid fame was born in which country?
23 What is the name of the police officer in West Side Story?
24 Which language's name means 'one who hopes'?
25 Which public figure resigned over dealings concerning prostitute Monica Coghlan?
26 In The Old Testament which two books are named after women?
27 The Prix Goncourt is awarded for what?
28 Who joined Patrick Macnee on the 1990 No 5 UK hit Kinky Boots?
29 Who or what is a dourousouli?
30 Which broadcaster died in June, 1988, at a Leeds hospital from hepatitis?

LEVEL 3

1   Which comedian wrote Families and How to Survive Them with psychiatrist Robin Skynner?
2   What was Andrew Neil's autobiography called?
3   Who wrote an anthology of critics' anecdotes called No Turn Unstoned?
4   Whose first novel was The Rachel Papers in 1974?
5   Which novelist recorded an Album of Love Songs in 1978?
6   Which pop celebrity wrote Be My Baby?
7   How many Barchester Chronicles are there?
8   Who wrote the novel on which the movie Prince of Tides was based?
9   Who went from Deceit and Betrayal to A Dark Devotion?
10 Whose book Sex, coincided with a dance album Erotica?
11 Which science fiction writer wrote the Foundation Trilogy?
12 In the title of the largely autobiographical 1957 Evelyn Waugh novel, what does the main character experience?
13 Who or what was PG Wodehouse's Empress of Blandings?
14 The founder of Wisden played for which English county?
15 Whose quest for speed is recorded in his book Thrust?
16 Which sports stars' autobiography was called Facing the Music?
17 Rider Haggard's colonial service where influenced his books?
18 Who publishes Hansard?
19 Whose 1998 best seller argued that our universe is a part of a super universe?
20 Which novelist's great great grandfather founded The Yorkshire Post?
21 What did Compton Mackenzie refer to each individual volume of his autobiography as?
22 Whose 19th century dictionary standardised US English?
23 Where was the Mysterious Affair in the first Agatha Christie in Penguin paperback?
24 Which colourful DH Lawrence book was banned because of its sexual content along with Lady Chatterley and Women in Love?
25 First appearing in 1931, what sold out of its new edition in three months in 1996?
26 In the Oxford English Dictionary which word has the longest entry?
27 Whose biography already has 22 volumes and is still being written?
28 What is the best-selling copyright book of all time?
29 Whose Diary was written by Helen Fielding?
30 Who wrote romantic novels as Mary Westmacott?

Quiz 111 Pot Luck 56

LEVEL 3

1 Who designed the tapestry behind the altar in Coventry Cathedral?
2 An odalisque is a female what?
3 Who founded the record label Maverick Records?
4 Who won the southern junior and senior cross country titles on the same day?
5 Which English poet had the middle name Chawner?
6 The Russian Revolution began in which year?
7 Which King of Hollywood died on the same day as broadcaster Gilbert Harding?
8 Who is the elder – Zoe Ball or Gary Barlow?
9 In the 1980s Greg Lemond became the first American to do what?
10 Whose one and only hit was Little Things Mean A Lot?
11 Who created the Statue of Zeus about 430 BC?
12 What did Lee Marvin throw in Gloria Grahame's face in The Big Heat?
13 What was film star Edward G Robinson's real name?
14 Who was the husband of cellist Jacqueline du Pre?
15 What is the drink kumiss made from?
16 Who came up with The Book of Heroic Failures?
17 What was discovered in 1930 by Clyde Tombaugh?
18 In The Bible, who was King David's father?
19 In 1865, where did the Confederates surrender?
20 Wellesley is the family name of which Dukes?
21 What is a dhole?
22 Norman Parkinson made his name in which field of art?
23 How many times did Steve Donoghue win the Derby?
24 What was Paula Abdul's first UK Top Ten hit from 1989?
25 Lynn Ripley shone under which name as a pop singer?
26 Which theory was formulated by the German physicist Max Planck?
27 Which poet wrote, "She was a phantom of delight"?
28 Which England soccer manager was born in Burnley, Lancashire?
29 The Haber Process manufactures which gas?
30 Who was Banquo's son in Macbeth?

Quiz 112 Albums

Answers - see page 579

1 Who released the biggest-selling album in Britain in the 70s?
2 What was the final track on Spice?
3 Which 1988 album confirmed a comeback by Roy Orbison?
4 Dire Straits first albums came out on which label?
5 Which 6.5 minute hit was the title track of Queen's 7th No 1 album?
6 Who charted with an album named after an English county?
7 Don McLean's Vincent came from which album?
8 Which superstar first charted with Come Fly With Me?
9 What was George Harrison's first solo album after the Beatles?
10 What was the first album to make its debut into the UK chart at No 1?
11 Which album contains the line, "My kingdom for a horse"?
12 Who is not on the front cover of Urban Hymns, but features on an inside cover shot?
13 What was Phil Collins' first solo No 1 album?
14 Whose debut album was Ancient Heart?
15 What was the main colour on the cover of Enya's Shepherd Moons?
16 Who along with Oasis gets production credits on Definitely Maybe?
17 Which group had five consecutive No 1 albums from 1979 to 1986?
18 Which original film soundtrack was on the charts for a staggering 382 weeks?
19 Which album first featured Candle In the Wind?
20 Paul Weller has topped the charts in which three guises?
21 Who was the first artist to enter the Swiss album charts at No 1?
22 What was the last Fleetwood Mac album released before the world smash Rumours?
23 Which double-album film soundtrack was a 30 million seller in 1978?
24 Why weren't the album charts published in 1971 for eight weeks?
25 What was the name of Mary Hopkin's debut album?
26 What was Pink Floyd's first album to top the UK charts?
27 Tubular Bells launched the Virgin label, but which label put out Tubular Bells II?
28 Which album originally featured Perfect Day?
29 Which Kate Bush album featured a song about Delius?
30 Which film soundtrack topped the first UK chart in November 1958?

Quiz 113 Pot Luck 57

LEVEL 3

Answers - see page 582

1   Who was 'The Radio Doctor' in the 1940s and 50s?
2   What was Golden Earring's first UK Top Ten hit?
3   Started in 1850, what were Children's Temperance Societies called?
4   Which motorcyclist appeared in the film Space Riders?
5   Gravure is a term connected with which industry?
6   Who played the leading role in the film The Stone Killer?
7   To the nearest hundred how many islands make up the Maldives?
8   Who was Prime Minister during the General Strike?
9   What does a mendicant do?
10   Mycology is the study of what?
11   What was the Carla Rosa, existing from 1875 to 1958?
12   Who was the last King of Troy according to legend?
13   What was George Burns real name?
14   The word Ombudsman comes from which language?
15   In which decade was Lord Rothschild born?
16   Who wrote the play The Homecoming?
17   Who was writer and producer for New Kids On the Block?
18   In which American state were Bonnie and Clyde killed in an ambush?
19   The Statue of Liberty's 100th birthday was celebrated in which year?
20   Who is the elder – Jeremy Beadle or Christopher Biggins?
21   What is studied by a pedologist?
22   Spencer Gore was the first winner of what?
23   George Galvin performed in music-hall under what name?
24   Placido Domingo studied music at which National Conservatory?
25   Who was the last Prime Minister during the reign of Queen Victoria?
26   The star Betelgeuse is in which constellation?
27   What does the Thomas Hardy novel The Dynasts deal with?
28   Who was the first woman to be Canadian Prime Minister?
29   What do a tinchel of men do?
30   Ahmed Sukarno was President of which country from 1945-62?

Answers

Cricket (See Quiz 114)
1 Vengsarkar. **2** Mark Taylor. **3** Leeward Islands. **4** Swansea, Glamorgan.
5 Old Trafford. **6** West Indies. **7** Geoff Boycott. **8** Old Trafford. **9** Cigarettes
& Alcohol by Oasis. **10** Warren Hegg. **11** Imperial. **12** Australia. **13** Shell
Shield. **14** Sunday Express. **15** New Zealand & India. **16** Charlton Athletic.
17 Steve Bucknor. **18** Ivon. **19** India v New Zealand. **20** India & Pakistan.
21 Bob Taylor. **22** No one. **23** Mike Gatting. **24** Wayne Larkins. **25** Mike
Atherton. **26** Six. **27** Alec Stewart. **28** Victoria. **29** Craig McDermott.
30 Surrey.

Quiz 114 Cricket

Answers - see page 581

LEVEL 3

1   Who was the first overseas batsman to score three Test centuries at Lord's?
2   Which Aussie equalled Don Bradman's batting record in October 1998 but declared rather than beat it?
3   Which West Indian islands did Viv Richards play for?
4   Where did Sobers hit his 36 runs in one over and against whom?
5   Where did Dennis Amiss score the first century in a one day international?
6   Against whom did Mike Atherton make his first international one-day century?
7   Who deputised for Mike Brearley as England skipper four times in 1977-8?
8   Where did Lance Gibbs take most of his wickets in England?
9   Which song did Phil Tufnell choose to escort him on to the field in the New Zealand test tour?
10 Who scored a maiden first class century in his fourth match in 1987?
11 Until 1965 what did 'I' stand for in ICC?
12 Which was the first women's side to win the World Cup in successive occasions?
13 Which competition in the West Indies was replaced by the Red Stripe Cup?
14 David Gower became which newspaper's cricket correspondent when he retired?
15 Graham Gooch became the first player to score 1000 Test runs in an English summer against which sides?
16 Which football team did Alec Stewart's father play for?
17 Who was the first overseas umpire to umpire a Test Match in England?
18 What is David Gower's middle name?
19 Who was playing when the first hat trick by a bowler was scored in a World Cup?
20 Where was the first World Cup outside England played?
21 In '95 Jack Russell broke whose record for dismissals in a Test match?
22 Who sponsored what became the AXA Equity & Law League in '92?
23 Whose autobiography was called Leading From the Front?
24 Who was the first batsman to score centuries against all the counties?
25 Who was the youngest Lancastrian to score a Test century, in 1990?
26 How old was Graeme Hick when he scored a century for his school?
27 Who was the first Englishman to score a century in each innings against the West Indies in 1994?
28 Which Australian state did Ben Hollioake's father play for?
29 Who was Australia's leading wicket taker on the 1994-5 Ashes tour?
30 Who won the first ever county championship?

Answers

Pot Luck 57 (See Quiz 113)
1 Charles Hill. 2 Radar Love. 3 Bands of Hope. 4 Barry Sheene. 5 Printing (platemaking). 6 Charles Bronson. 7 1200 (1196). 8 Stanley Baldwin. 9 Begs. 10 Fungi. 11 An Opera Company. 12 Priam. 13 Nathan Birnbaum. 14 Swedish. 15 1930s. 16 Harold Pinter. 17 Maurice Starr. 18 Louisiana. 19 1986. 20 Jeremy Beadle. 21 Soils. 22 Men's singles, Wimbledon. 23 Dan Leno. 24 Mexico. 25 Marquis of Salisbury. 26 Orion. 27 The war with Napoleon. 28 Kim Campbell. 29 Hunt. 30 Indonesia.

1   Who was the letter which revealed the Gunpowder Plot addressed to?
2   Which lecturer in philosophy wrote The Second Sex?
3   Which non-metallic element has the atomic number 6?
4   What was Marc Almond's first solo UK Top Ten hit?
5   Made in 1975 with George Segal The Black Bird was a spoof of which screen classic?
6   In surveying, how long is a Gunter's Chain in feet?
7   Susan Godfrey was the first victim of which atrocity?
8   In which city was the infamous Gatting and Rana Test Match flare up?
9   Who was older when they died Jimi Hendrix or Marc Bolan?
10 In which film did Chaplin first tackle dialogue?
11 How did Bruce Lee die?
12 What was a lamia in ancient mythology?
13 What date was the Stock Market's Black Monday of the 1980s?
14 Which saint was shot dead in 288 AD by arrows?
15 In TV's The Six Wives of Henry VIII who played wife number one?
16 The European Economic Community was established in which year?
17 In poetry what was hung around the neck of the Ancient Mariner?
18 In which decade was Greta Scacchi born?
19 Who was the first man to win a Grand Prix in a car he designed himself?
20 Whose one and only hit was Turtle Power in 1990?
21 The sword is the symbol of which of the twelve apostles?
22 Which artist painted Bubbles used by Pears to advertise their soap?
23 What can be a unit of length or a small island in Scotland?
24 Who is the elder – Kenneth Branagh or Rory Bremner?
25 What is the name of America's National Cemetery?
26 Where would you have found Zoroastrianism?
27 Robert, Grattan and Emmett were which famous Wild West outlaw gang?
28 Who wrote the play Old Times?
29 In 1941 which American defined the Four Freedoms?
30 What does Zymurgy magazine deal with?

1   Who led the British forces in the First Battle of El Alamein?
2   Where was the peace treaty signed after the Korean War?
3   What was the only place in India attacked by foreign forces in WWI?
4   Which dams were destroyed by bouncing bombs in 1943?
5   Which Norwegian leader aided the 1940 invasion of his country through non resistance?
6   Which part of his body did Lord Raglan lose at Waterloo?
7   Who was commander of the US forces in the Pacific from March '42?
8   In which city did the German High Command formally surrender to General Eisenhower?
9   What was the German 11th Chasing Squadron known as in WWI?
10 Who assassinated Archduke Franz Ferdinand in 1914 thus precipitating WWI?
11 What was the last of the treaties which ended WWI?
12 Which countries were on either end of the Maginot Line?
13 Which birthplace of Nero was the site of an Allied beachhead invasion in WWII?
14 How is the battle at St Quentin in 1918 also known?
15 Who led the military coup in Sierra Leone's Civil War in 1997?
16 How many countries made up the coalition v Iraq in the Gulf War?
17 In the Nicaraguan Civil War which faction had US support?
18 Where was France's defeat which brought about the division of Vietnam along the 17th parallel?
19 Hitler's plan 'Watch on the Rhine' was aimed at which troops?
20 In which area of Belgium/Luxembourg was the Battle of the Bulge?
21 Which navy was defeated at the Battle of Midway Island in 1942?
22 The retreat by the British from which port brought about the replacement of Auchinleck by Montgomery?
23 Where is Babi Yar, where 100,000 people were slaughtered in 1941?
24 In which war did the Battle of Ebro take place?
25 Which General declared a 'war of liberation' against Syrian occupation of Lebanon in 1989?
26 Which war was ended with the Peace of Vereeniging?
27 Who were the two opposing factions in the Ruandan Civil War in the mid 90s?
28 How is the third battle of Ypres in WWI also known?
29 Who was in charge of the German troops in the First Battle of the Marne?
30 What name was given to that part of France not occupied by the Germans until 1942?

1   What was the original family business of Shell Oil developer Marcus Samuel?
2   What was the middle name of Wallis Simpson, later Duchess of Windsor?
3   Which greedy giant was created by Rabelais?
4   Who is the elder – Tony Blair or Pierce Brosnan?
5   What is sorghum?
6   From what is the writing material true vellum made?
7   What is separated by the oval window and the round window?
8   Whose presidential hopes were ended by model Donna Rice?
9   What fraction of a gold object is a carat as a proportional measure?
10   What is a killick?
11   Which country hosted the first women's world angling championship?
12   What was the name of the cat which retired from 10 Downing Street in 1987?
13   What name is given to an animal that may be slaughtered to provide. food under Moslem law?
14   In which county did the Tolpuddle Martyrs form a trade union?
15   What is a bowyang ?
16   Which politician said that northerners die of "ignorance and crisps"?
17   In which decade was actress Kristin Scott Thomas born?
18   Which American duo had a Top Ten 8 hit in 1977 with Oh Lori?
19   Where did Alexander the Great die?
20   What relation was Queen Victoria to George IV?
21   Who won the first WBC cruiserweight title in boxing?
22   Why were the Piccard brothers famous in the 1930s?
23   Which Roman god was the god of beginnings and doors?
24   What is gneiss?
25   What was Florence Nightingale the first woman to receive in 1907?
26   What was a 'quod' in old slang?
27   Who preceded David II as King of the Scots?
28   What was Rainbow's first UK Top Ten hit?
29   The Purple Rose of Cairo was written and directed by which actor?
30   Nim was a type of what?

Answers **Quiz and Games** (See Quiz 118)
1   Chris Tarrant. **2** The Moment of Truth. **3** Patrick Kielty. **4** Alan Coren.
5 Kenny Everett. **6** Fern Britton. **7** Carry on Campus. **8** Vincent Price. **9**
Countdown (OED). **10** Ally McCoist. **11** Richard Wilson. **12** Blockbusters.
13 Magnus Magnusson kept it. **14** Pass the Buck. **15** Max Robertson. **16**
John Leslie. **17** Gaby Roslin. **18** Newspaper – day of birth. **19** Matthew Kelly.
20 Princess Diana. **21** Blind Date. **22** Max Bygraves. **23** Armand Jammot.
24 Ed Tudor-Pole. **25** Double Your Money. **26** Paul Daniels. **27** Round the
World. **28** Leslie Crowther. **29** The Great Garden Game. **30** Anthea Redfern.

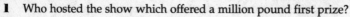

1 Who hosted the show which offered a million pound first prize?

2 Which show has a Dream Directory?

3 Who joined Anthea Turner on The National Lottery's Big Ticket?

4 Who opposed Sandi Toksvig in the 90s Call My Bluff?

5 Who was the first male team captain in That's Showbusiness?

6 Who hosts Ready Steady Cook?

7 Which student quiz was produced by Ginger Productions?

8 Which horror movie actor was on the first Celebrity Squares?

9 In which show might Mark Nyman adjudicate?

10 Who was the footballing A Question of Sport team captain when Sue Barker took over on a regular basis?

11 Who was the Reverend Green in the second series of Cluedo?

12 In which show were you pleased to be on the Hot Spot?

13 What happened to the black chair after the final Mastermind?

14 Which weekday elimination quiz is hosted by Fred Dinenage?

15 Who presented the original Going For a Song?

16 Which Blue Peter presenter took over Wheel of Fortune?

17 Who presented the show which had a Status Quo hit as its theme tune?

18 What do contestants receive at the end of Today's The Day?

19 Who hosted You Bet before Darren Day?

20 Who was the subject of an entire show of 100% in August 1998?

21 Sue Middleton and Alex Tatham famously followed a TV win on which show with marriage?

22 Who presented Family Fortunes immediately prior to Les Dennis?

23 Who created Countdown?

24 Who replaced Richard O'Brien on The Crystal Maze?

25 The Sky's The Limit was a variation of which show?

26 Who did Bob Monkhouse replace on Wipeout?

27 Where were contestants figuratively taken on the quiz show Anthea Turner presented after leaving GMTV?

28 Who first asked contestants to "Come on down"?

29 What was Channel 5's first gardening quiz called?

30 Who was the female half of the first husband and wife team to present The Generation Game?

1 Who led the British force in 1898 at Omdurman?
2 What was Adam Ant's first UK Top Ten hit?
3 How many cubic centimetres in a cubic metre?
4 In which decade was Selina Scott born?
5 Which real island, famed in fiction, is some 25 miles south of Elba?
6 Who would use a fyke?
7 Who was the first Irish cyclist to win the Tour de France?
8 What first did Bernard Harris achieve when he did his space walk?
9 Who or what is Katherine Gorge?
10 Which two countries are separated by the Kattegat?
11 In which decade did Picasso die?
12 Houses in Sherwood Crescent were destroyed in which disaster?
13 Which classic film was billed as "The Eighth Wonder of the World"?
14 Which Royal House ruled from 1461 to 1485 in England?
15 What is a gribble?
16 How many books are there in The New Testament?
17 Who narrated the TV series The World at War?
18 Which city is the capital of Tibet?
19 In No Way to Treat a Lady what did the killer leave on the brow?
20 What is bohea?
21 The Greek goddess Nyx was the personification of what?
22 What was Telly Savalas' Christian name?
23 What form did the Yahoos have in Gulliver's Travels ?
24 Who is the elder – Tamara Beckwith or Naomi Campbell?
25 Which Rumanian tennis star appeared in the film Players?
26 Whose one and only hit was First Time in 1988?
27 Which place is in Berkshire in England and Pennsylvania in America?
28 Where did the Great Britain rugby league team tour for the first time in 1984?
29 When George Bush was elected president who was his Democrat opponent?
30 Which rock star has children called Rufus Tiger and Tiger Lily?

Answers

50s Films (See Quiz 120)
1 Giant. 2 St Swithin's. 3 Robert Morley. 4 Kim Novak. 5 Darby O'Gill and the Little People. 6 Richard Burton. 7 George Cole. 8 Danny Kaye. 9 Mount Rushmore. 10 Carry On Nurse. 11 Operation Petticoat. 12 Dorothy Dandridge. 13 George Sanders. 14 High Noon. 15 Mike Todd. 16 Viva Zapata!. 17 Jack Lemmon. 18 Anastasia. 19 The Trouble With Harry. 20 The Swan. 21 Yul Brynner. 22 No Way Out. 23 1915. 24 The Long Hot Summer. 25 Bewitched Bothered and Bewildered. 26 Green Grow the Rushes. 27 William Wyler. 28 Yves Montand. 29 Larry Adler. 30 Judy Garland.

1 James Dean died during the filming of which film in 1955?
2 In which hospital would you find Sir Lancelot Spratt?
3 Who played George III in Beau Brummell ?
4 Who played the blonde that James Stewart was hired to follow in Vertigo?
5 In which 50s film did Sean Connery sing?
6 Which actor wins Christ's robe in a dice game in The Robe?
7 Who played the younger Scrooge in the classic with Alistair Sim?
8 Who replaced Astaire for the Holiday Inn remake White Christmas?
9 Where does the climax of North By Northwest take place?
10 What was the second Carry On film?
11 What was the only film where Tony Curtis and Cary Grant starred together?
12 Whose voice was dubbed by Marilyn Horne in Carmen Jones?
13 Who won Best Supporting Actor for All About Eve?
14 Which film was based on The Tin Star by John W Cunningham?
15 Which one time husband of Elizabeth Taylor produced Around the World in 80 Days?
16 What was the second of Brando's four consecutive Oscar nominations for. between 1951 and 1954?
17 Who contributed a song for his 1957 film Fire Down Below?
18 Ingrid Bergman won a second Oscar for which film, marking her return from Hollywood exile?
19 What was Shirley Maclaine's debut film in 1955?
20 What was the last film Grace Kelly made before becoming a princess?
21 Who played the Pharaoh in The Ten Commandments?
22 What was Sidney Poitier's first film, in 1950?
23 The African Queen, made in 1951, is about events in which year?
24 What was the first film in which Paul Newman and Joanne Woodward appeared together?
25 Which song did Rita Hayworth famously sing in Pal Joey?
26 What was Richard Burton's last UK film before turning to Hollywood?
27 Who won his third Best Director for his third Best Picture in 1959?
28 Which French superstar was the husband of the 1959 Oscar-winning Best Supporting Actress?
29 Who composed and played the music for Genevieve?
30 Who was replaced by Betty Hutton in Annie Get Your Gun?

1   The Euroroute E24 is from Birmingham to which county town?
2   Which Scottish university was named after a jeweller and an inventor?
3   Which polo ground is in the park of a burnt down former country house?
4   What is the smallest theatre at the Barbican in London called?
5   Where is Grimsetter Airport?
6   Which inlet of the Clyde was used as a US submarine base from the early 60s?
7   In which part of London is Kenwood?
8   Which shipping area is due north of Trafalgar?
9   In which county was the Open University founded?
10 Where in Berkshire is the Atomic Weapons Research Establishment?
11 How many national parks does the Pennine Way pass through?
12 Which wall runs from the river Forth in the east to Clyde in the west?
13 What is the real name of 'Petticoat Lane'?
14 Which county is due north of Buckinghamshire?
15 Where is the Post Office's main sorting office?
16 What name is given to someone born east of the Medway?
17 Which county is due South of Tyne and Wear?
18 Which colloquial name of the main church in Boston serves as a landmark for ships?
19 Who or what was London's Liverpool Street station named after?
20 Where is the official London residence of the Foreign Secretary?
21 What is the administration centre of Wiltshire?
22 How is London's Collegiate Church of St Peter better known?
23 Which House has an Egyptian Hall for banqueting?
24 Which important collection was given to the city of Glasgow in 1944?
25 Which World Heritage Site was built for the Duke of Marlborough?
26 Which house is headquarters and home to the BBC World Service?
27 What is MOMI on London's South Bank?
28 Which famous House is the only surviving part of Whitehall Palace?
29 Where is Scatsa Airport?
30 Which county is due south of Shropshire?

Quiz 122 Pot Luck 61

LEVEL 3

1   Where on your body is your philtrum?

2   In which decade was Delia Smith born?

3   Inigo Jones was famous in which profession?

4   Who discovered carbon dioxide in 1754 and called it "fixed air"?

5   Who was the first musician to be made a life peer?

6   What was the Iron Mistress in the film of the same name?

7   Who defeated Sweden's forces at Poltava in 1709?

8   What was the last film directed by Alfred Hitchcock?

9   Where does Russia launch their space missions from?

10 Where is the Louis Armstrong Stadium?

11 Who wrote Gary Barlow's second solo No 1?

12 What is a peri?

13 What was John Lennon's middle name?

14 The opera Billy Budd is set on what?

15 Whose only UK Top Ten hit from 1971 was called Rose Garden?

16 What is the more common name for the flower called the Kingcup?

17 What odds is a horse if it is "Burlington Bertie" in rhyming slang?

18 Who wrote Tropic of Cancer and Tropic of Capricorn?

19 Which ballet dancer died on the same day as Dizzy Gillespie?

20 What was Chris Rea's first UK Top Ten hit?

21 Who is the elder – Julia Carling or Helena Bonham-Carter?

22 What was Sir John Gielgud's first name?

23 Which poet wrote, "I have measured out my life with coffee spoons"?

24 Who was the first woman golfer to head the money lists in Europe and the US, in 1995?

25 Plasma in blood consists of platelets and red and white what?

26 Who was the drummer in the group Police?

27 Who invented the Polaroid camera in 1947?

28 Barefoot in the Park was written by which US playwright?

29 What is opposed by the John Birch Society in the USA?

30 Which famous inventor had the middle name Alva?

Answers

Around the UK (See Quiz 121)
1 Ipswich. 2 Heriot-Watt. 3 Cowdray Park. 4 The Pit. 5 Orkney. 6 Holy Loch. 7 Hampstead. 8 Finisterre. 9 Buckinghamshire. 10 Aldermaston. 11 Three. 12 Antonine Wall. 13 Middlesex Street. 14 Northamptonshire. 15 Mount Pleasant. 16 Man of Kent. 17 Durham. 18 The Boston Stump. 19 PM Earl of Liverpool. 20 Carlton House Terrace. 21 Trowbridge. 22 Westminster Abbey. 23 Mansion House. 24 The Burrell Collection. 25 Blenheim Palace. 26 Bush House. 27 Museum of the Moving Image. 28 Banqueting House. 29 Shetlands. 30 Hereford and Worcester.

1   Which TV presenter published his Unreliable Memoirs in 1980?
2   Whose novel A Time to Dance was adapted into a controversial TV drama?
3   In From One Charlie to Another, who did Charlie Watts write about?
4   Which singer wrote the book Tarantula?
5   What was the colour of the first Penguin paperback?
6   Which blonde wrote The Constant Sinner?
7   Which John Grisham book had a record initial print run of 2.8 million?
8   To be considered for the Booker Prize a book has to be published where first?
9   What according to Dickens was "the best of times, the worst of times"?
10 Whose only novel won the Pullitzer Prize in 1937?
11 Which PM wrote Sybil?
12 For which novel did Tom Clancy receive an advance of $14 million?
13 Which joint 1992 Booker Prize winner had his book made into an Oscar winning film?
14 Which Ian Fleming novel has the shortest title?
15 What was Hercule Poirot's last case called?
16 What did J.M. Barrie give the royalties from Peter Pan to?
17 Who received a record breaking advance of £17 million for three novels in 1992?
18 What was the sequel to D.H. Lawrence's The Rainbow?
19 Who created Pomeroy's wine bar for his hero?
20 Whose early thriller include The Eye of the Needle?
21 Who wrote The House of Stairs under a pseudonym?
22 Which detective novelist wrote the screenplay for Strangers on a Train?
23 What was Charles Dickens second novel, after Pickwick Papers?
24 Who wrote The Exorcist which was made into a successful film?
25 How are Patrick Dannay and Manfred B Lee better known?
26 Who produced The Truth That Leads to Eternal Life?
27 Who wrote the historical romance Micah Clarke?
28 Which novelist once owned a Rolls registration number ANY 1?
29 Whose early novels were Bella, Harriet and Prudence?
30 How is the wife of author Eric Siepmann better known?

Pot Luck 62 (See Quiz 124)
Answers
1 The Zulus. 2 Phyllis Nelson. 3 Jose Maria Olazabal. 4 Aldeburgh. 5 Jess Yates. 6 Varicella. 7 Baseball. 8 Robbie Coltrane. 9 National Theatre. 10 Georgie Fame. 11 Soot. 12 The tennis Grand Slam. 13 Lloyd Grossman. 14 Toulouse Lautrec. 15 A hangman. 16 Paul Gauguin. 17 Hero. 18 Wear it. 19 Picture Post. 20 Turner. 21 1970s. 22 Battle of Naseby. 23 1860 . 24 New Zealand. 25 A hoofed mammal. 26 Ipswich. 27 Love In Bloom. 28 Kim Appleby. 29 Margaret Atwood. 30 Land's End.

1 Cetewayo, Dingaan and Chaka have all led which people?
2 Whose one and only hit was Move Closer in 1985?
3 Which injured player did Ian Woosnam replace in the 1995 European Ryder Cup team?
4 Which Suffolk town was the first in Britain to have a woman mayor?
5 Which 1970s presenter of Stars on Sunday was nicknamed 'The Bishop'?
6 What is the correct name for chickenpox?
7 The film The Stratton Story featured which sport?
8 Who is the elder – Phil Collins or Robbie Coltrane?
9 In the 80s which building did Prince Charles compare to a "nuclear power station"?
10 Under what name did musician Clive Powell find fame and fortune?
11 The brown pigment bistre is prepared from what?
12 Maureen Connolly was the first female to perform what?
13 Which food show presenter once played in a band called Jet Bronx and the Forbidden?
14 Which character was played by Jose Ferrer in the film Moulin Rouge?
15 What did Jack Ketch do for a living?
16 Van Gogh's Sunflowers used to hang in the bedroom of which other famous artist?
17 In mythology, who did Leander swim the Hellespont nightly to see?
18 What would you do with a filibeg?
19 Bert Hardy was a staff photojournalist for which periodical?
20 Who painted Snow Storm – Steamboat off a Harbour's Mouth?
21 In which decade was Mandy Smith born?
22 Which battle was the decisive one in the English Civil War?
23 To ten years, when was the National Rifle Association of Great Britain formed?
24 In which country are the Sutherland Falls?
25 What is an alpaca?
26 At which Crown Court was Lester Piggot's tax evasion case?
27 What was American comedian Jack Benny's signature tune?
28 Who had UK Top Ten hits in the 90s with Don't Worry and G.L.A.D.?
29 Who wrote The Handmaid's Tale?
30 What did businessman Peter de Savray buy for £6.7 million in 1987?

Answers

Books 2 (See Quiz 123)
1 Clive James. 2 Melvyn Bragg. 3 Charlie Parker. 4 Bob Dylan. 5 Blue. 6 Mae West. 7 The Rainmaker. 8 Britain. 9 French Revolution (Tale of Two Cities). 10 Margaret Mitchell. 11 Disraeli. 12 Without Remorse. 13 Michael Ondaatje. 14 Dr No. 15 Curtain. 16 Children's Hospital. 17 Barbara Taylor Bradford. 18 Women in Love. 19 John Mortimer (Rumpole). 20 Ken Follett. 21 Ruth Rendell as Barbara Vine. 22 Raymond Chandler. 23 Oliver Twist. 24 William Blatty. 25 Ellery Queen. 26 Jehovah's Witnesses. 27 Conan Doyle. 28 Jeffrey Archer. 29 Jilly Cooper. 30 Mary Wesley.

1 Which Pete Ham and Tom Evans song has been at No 1 with two different artists?
2 The Isley Brothers and which other Motown act recorded Grapevine before Marvin Gaye?
3 To the nearest year, how long was there between Sinatra's first and second UK No 1s?
4 Where is the singer's home in the lyrics of On The Dock Of The Bay?
5 What was the first song to be Christmas No 1 in two different versions?
6 Which hit for Sweet was the longest running No 1 of 1973?
7 Which 1970 seven week No 1 was best selling UK single of the year?
8 Who did Billy Joel dedicate his 1983 version of Uptown Girl to?
9 What was Elvis Presley's closing number in his Las Vegas stage act?
10 What was Cliff Richard's first self-produced No 1?
11 What was the chief of the Diddymen's only UK No 1?
12 Which standard has the line, "I see friends shaking hands saying how do you do"?
13 Which Beatles hit stayed in the UK Top 50 for 33 weeks in 1963?
14 Who had the first UK No 1 with Unchained Melody?
15 Which film theme was the biggest selling single of 1979?
16 Who took Led Zeppelin's Stairway To Heaven into the singles charts?
17 Who wrote You'll Never Walk Alone?
18 Which heavenly body is mentioned in the title of the song that gave George Michael his 4th solo and Elton John his 3rd No 1?
19 Who played Buddy Holly in the 1978 movie The Buddy Holly Story?
20 Who wrote Aretha Franklin's first UK hit Respect?
21 Which classic was the Walker Brothers second No 1 hit from 1966?
22 Which 1967 No 1 recorded the longest-ever stay in the UK Top 50?
23 Who is the only French solo male singer to reach No 1?
24 How many weeks in total did Whitney Houston top the US and UK charts with I Will Always Love You?
25 Which hit is the only No 1 for writers Gerry Goffin and Carole King?
26 Which song includes the line, "nothing to kill or die for"?
27 What was the colour mentioned in the title of Tom Jones' final No 1 in the 1960s?
28 What is the biggest international hit from Eurovision Song Contest?
29 What was Sam Cooke's real name?
30 What was the Beatles first No 1 in America?

Quiz 126 Pot Luck 63

1 Which christian name derives from the Germanic for 'strong ruler'?

2 What did the Italian Amedeo Avogadro study?

3 The novel Robinson Crusoe was based on whose experiences?

4 What important post did Millard Fillmore hold?

5 Which magazine serialised The Adventures Of Sherlock Holmes in the 1890s?

6 Which group features Peter Salisbury on drums and Simon Jones on bass?

7 Where were the first Winter Olympics held in 1924?

8 Who preceded John Bruton as Prime Minister of Ireland?

9 What can be a type of musket or a type of rhomboid?

10 Walter, the robot with a lisp, featured in which comic strip?

11 Which long running radio quiz show was hosted by Wilfred Pickles?

12 In which John Braine book is Joe Lampton the central character ?

13 What does a manometer measure the pressure of?

14 What was R.E.M's first UK Top Ten hit?

15 Otto Lilienthal was associated with what form of transport?

16 Who is the elder – Sean Connery or Sir Terence Conran?

17 What amalgamated in 1918 with the Royal Naval Air Service to form the RAF?

18 What did the M stand for in E M Forster's middle name?

19 Where is the poet Wordsworth buried?

20 What is your columella?

21 Which Anna claimed to be Anastasia?

22 Who was the first UK golfer to win the World Match-Play Championship?

23 In folktales a silkie was half man and half what?

24 Who was Prince Philip's father?

25 Which British golf course has a hole called the 'Postage Stamp'?

26 Who composed Clair De Lune?

27 In which decade was the Earl of Snowdon born?

28 Who was Transport Secretary at the time of the King's Cross tube fire disaster?

29 Whose only UK Top Ten hit was Pick Up The Pieces in 1975?

30 Black Friars are members of the religious order established by whom?

LEVEL 3

1   Who preceded Frank O'Farrell as Man Utd manager?
2   How did Joan Bazely make history in 1976?
3   Who were the opponents in Peter Shilton's last game for England?
4   Who coached Cameroon to the latter stages of the 1990 World Cup?
5   Who offered the England and Scotland squads a week on his Caribbean island if they won the World Cup in 1998?
6   Which Mexican player in France 98 ran a chain of sandwich shops?
7   Which club's motto is 'Nil Satis Nisi Optimum'?
8   What was the name of the horse jointly owned by Liverpool's Fowler & McManaman?
9   Apart from Preson, which other team did Alan Ball's father play for?
10 Ray Wilkins was sent off while playing for England against which country?
11 Who did Denis Law play for immediately before Man Utd?
12 Who was the only side to beat England over 90 minutes when Venables was manager?
13 Who appeared in a TV ad for bacon before the 1998 World Cup?
14 Who is Sweden's most capped player of all time?
15 Who led Naples to their first ever Italian championship?
16 Which of the Italian sides David Platt played for had the shortest name?
17 Angus Deayton had a trial with which soccer club?
18 Who was fourth in the 1994 World Cup?
19 Roy Hodgson joined Blackburn Rovers from which club?
20 What was Arsenal tube station called before it was called Arsenal?
21 Who was the first Dutchman to play in an FA Cup Final?
22 Who were Man Utd playing when George Best made his debut?
23 Which sides competed in the first all British UEFA Cup Final?
24 Who were the first winners of the Inter Toto Cup?
25 How many times did Bobby Moore captain England in 108 internationals?
26 Which soccer side does Bank of England Governor Eddie George support?
27 Where did Paul Ince captain England for the first time?
28 Which club side were the first to win the South American Cup?
29 Which two members of the '98 Nigerian squad released rap albums?
30 Who won Olympic gold in Barcelona?

LEVEL 3

1 Who wrote the novel The Red Rover ?
2 Which creature is represented in the year the Chinese call hou?
3 A fear of cats is known as what?
4 Which country ruled Greece until 1830?
5 Who wrote the line: 'The female of the species is more deadly than the male'?
6 How many species of ostrich are there?
7 Dakar is the capital of which country?
8 Which theme gave Clannad their first UK Top Ten hit?
9 Who is the elder – John Prescott or Trevor McDonald?
10 The spice allspice is made from which part of a plant?
11 Which 'E' number is used to represent Tartrazine in products?
12 What is the main language of Andorra?
13 Which elderly couple were immortalised in a poem by Henry Woodfall?
14 Where on Dartmoor is Dartmoor prison?
15 Which jazz festival is held annually in Rhode Island?
16 What does the Latin ab initio mean?
17 Which Prime Minister was offered a dukedom when he retired in '55?
18 The constellation Aquila has which name in English?
19 In which country is the city of Baku?
20 What does the musical term 'con fuoco' mean?
21 Which bird appears with two heads on the Albanian flag?
22 Which letter in Braille comprises a single raised dot?
23 Who was Vice President when George Bush was President of the USA?
24 What is the administrative centre for the Scottish Borders region?
25 What are separated by the Cook Straits?
26 In which year did the UK become a member of the UN?
27 Whose one and only UK hit was Substitute in 1978?
28 Which country has the Ekuele and centimos as units of currency?
29 Prime Minister Wilfried Martens was leader of which country?
30 How would the letter E be formed in Morse Code?

Answers

Football (See Quiz 127)
1 Wilf McGuinness. 2 First woman ref of men's soccer. 3 Italy (1990). 4 Valeri Nepomaniachi. 5 Richard Branson. 6 Jorge Campos. 7 Everton. 8 Some Horse. 9 Halifax Town. 10 Morocco. 11 Torino. 12 Brazil. 13 Peter Schmeichel. 14 Thomas Ravelli. 15 Diego Maradona. 16 Bari. 17 Crystal Palace. 18 Bulgaria. 19 Inter Milan. 20 Gillespie Road. 21 Arnold Muhren. 22 West Brom. 23 Spurs v Wolves. 24 Ajax. 25 90. 26 Aston Villa. 27 Boston, USA. 28 Santos. 29 Amokachi & Okocha. 30 Australia.

Quiz 129 TV Sitcoms

Answers - see page 598

LEVEL 3

1 Who of the elderly trio in the first episode of Last of the Summer Wine is no longer in the cast?
2 Thirtysomething was set in which US state?
3 Who did Casualty's George play in May to December?
4 What were Private Godfrey's sisters called in Dad's Army?
5 Which bookie did Vince Pinner work for?
6 Who had a wife, daughter and mother in law who were witches?
7 Which sit com star made the album What Is Going To Become of Us All in 1976?
8 Who sang the theme music for You Rang M'Lord with Bob Monkhouse?
9 What was Richard's mother called in To The Manor Born?
10 Which lead character had the nickname Privet?
11 In which series did George, Kramer and Elaine appear?
12 Which TV husband and wife lived in Lanford Illinois?
13 Who was the first manager of the Bayview Retirement Home?
14 Who in his later years had a black home help called Winston?
15 What was the US series on which The Upper Hand was based?
16 Which property was left to Jim Davidson in Up The Elephant and Round the Castle?
17 In which hospital did Sheila Sabatini work?
18 Which sitcom was first called You'll Never get Rich in the US?
19 What was Reg Varney's character called in On the Buses?
20 What was Thelma's surname before she married Likely Lad Bob?
21 Elaine Nardo was the only female cabbie in which company?
22 In which advertising agency did Caroline work in The Upper Hand?
23 What was Harold Steptoe's middle names?
24 Which character in Soap was later given his own series?
25 Who wrote the original series of Shine on Harvey Moon?
26 Which sit com star played Vera Hopkins in Coronation Street?
27 Who was Roger's wife in Outside Edge?
28 Who was the barman of the Nag's Head as frequented by the Trotters?
29 Who created the theme music for One Foot in the Grave?
30 Which show centred round the 1-2-1 Club?

1 Who crossed Niagara Falls in 1859 on a tightrope?
2 What did the Romans call the Isle of Wight?
3 Mike Swain was the first male American World title winner in which sport?
4 What are gar, wrasse, alewife and blenny?
5 What was Jim Reeves' first UK Top Ten hit?
6 Who is the actress daughter of actress Phillida Law?
7 Who composed the music for Jaws and Star Wars?
8 What was the capital of the ancient empire of Assyria?
9 On what date in 1986 did Prince Andrew marry Fergie?
10 Which part did Prunella Scales play in A Question of Attribution?
11 Who wrote the series about the Whiteoak family?
12 Which presenter of That's Life was famous for his odd odes?
13 What is a futtock?
14 Which film star married Robyn Smith in 1980?
15 Which alloy contains 2% antimony, 8% copper and 90% tin?
16 In which decade was Tomasz Starzewski born?
17 How many No 1 singles did Take That have?
18 Which son of Henry VII married Catherine of Aragon in 1501?
19 In what year did Classic FM begin?
20 What are Lambda, Omicron and Tau all found in?
21 Charing, as in Charing Cross comes from an Old English word meaning what?
22 What can be a trump at cards or a type of sandpiper?
23 Who is the elder – Jilly Cooper or Shirley Bassey?
24 Where is English actor David Garrick buried?
25 Who followed up a No 1 with Find My Love?
26 Walter Gropius was famous in what field?
27 What is the natural water form which the Chinese call Huang Ho?
28 Which American speculator and philanthropist had the nickname Diamond Jim?
29 What is the practical purpose of a gargoyle?
30 Who directed the film You Can't Take It With You?

Quiz 131 Animal World

LEVEL 3

1 What is the only mammal to live as a parasite?
2 How is a Sibbald's rorqual also known?
3 For how many hours in a period of 24 does a giraffe sleep?
4 What is the world's largest rodent?
5 What gives the sloth its greenish appearance?
6 Which mammal lives at the highest altitude?
7 Which animals are famously sold at Bampton Fair?
8 The mammal which can live at the greatest depth is a species of what?
9 From which part of a sperm whale is ambergris obtained?
10 Where does a cane toad squirt poison from?
11 What is the longest type of worm?
12 Where would you find a shark's denticles?
13 What does the male mouse deer have that no other deer has?
14 Where does a browser find food?
15 What is the only bird which can fly backwards?
16 A Clydesdale was originally a cross between a Scottish draught horse and a what?
17 What colour is a mandrill's beard?
18 The wisent is native to where?
19 Lemurs are only found in their natural habitat where?
20 What is the oldest indigenous breed of cat in the US?
21 What is a koikoi?
22 What is the average life expectancy of the mayfly?
23 Which protein is cartilage made up of?
24 The term monkey refers to all primates except apes, humans and what?
25 Why were Samoyeds originally bred?
26 Falabellas are native to where?
27 What is another name for the aye-aye?
28 Which animal has the longest tail?
29 What name is given to the smaller of a rhino's horns?
30 What does it mean if an animal is homoiothermic?

Quiz 132 Pot Luck 66

LEVEL 3

1   What was Arthur Askey's middle name?
2   What was the trade of John Galliano's dad?
3   In the Beckett play which characters were Waiting for Godot?
4   Which disease is diagnosed by the Wasserman Test?
5   The King of Alba ruled in which country?
6   In which decade was Sting born?
7   Whose one and only hit was No Charge in 1976?
8   What does a petrologist study?
9   Which African country lies between the sea and Zimbabwe?
10 What are Temple-Tuttle and Kohoutek both types of?
11 In which London hall was England's first official showjumping event held in 1869?
12 Rod Stewart donated the royalties from which single to the Dunblane fund?
13 The ship Petit Pierre was the first to be driven by what in 1902?
14 Which island is in the middle of Niagara Falls?
15 Who was the first Blue Peter presenter to be sacked?
16 For what did John Singer Sargent achieve fame?
17 In which country is the majority of the Yucatan Peninsula?
18 The statue of Albert opposite the Albert Hall is made from what?
19 Which admiral was thrown ashore from his flagship Association in 1707?
20 Why was the Roman consul Incitatus unusual?
21 Who composed God Bless America?
22 Violinist Arthur Grumiaux came from which country?
23 When can a woman suffer puerperal fever?
24 Which George Crabbe poem was made into an opera?
25 The Dambusters film was based on which book?
26 Who is the elder – Michael Crawford or Eric Clapton?
27 Which of Jesus' disciples were sons of Zebedee?
28 What was the Baron Knights' first UK Top Ten hit?
29 Who won the first cycling World Cup?
30 By tonnage, which country is the world's top fishing nation?

Quiz 133 60s Films

LEVEL 3

1   In which 60s film did Richard Attenborough sing?
2   Who became head of production at EMI in 1969?
3   Between which two cities is The Great Race set?
4   Who directed the Civil War sequences of How the West Was Won?
5   Who was Camembert in Carry On – Don't Lose Your Head?
6   Who inspired the David Hemmings role in Antonioni's Blow Up?
7   What is unusual about Christopher Lee's terrifying role in Dracula – Prince of Darkness?
8   What was the sequel to A Million Years BC?
9   Who devised the dance routines in Half A Sixpence?
10 Who is the only American in King Rat?
11 Who was the Doctor in the big screen Doctor Who and the Daleks?
12 Which film classic inspired Billy Wilder to make The Apartment?
13 In which film did Peter Sellers first head the cast as Clouseau?
14 Who took over directing Cleopatra mid way through production?
15 Who was the singing voice of Tony in West Side Story?
16 Who wrote the music for Lawrence of Arabia?
17 In which film of her father's did Anjelica Huston make her screen debut?
18 Which golf course featured in Goldfinger?
19 What was Tracy and Hepburn's final movie together?
20 Which pop star starred in Rag Doll in 1960?
21 Which '62 Best Actor studied medicine at the University of California?
22 Who was Oscar nominated for Pasha in Doctor Zhivago?
23 Which 60s Oscar winner was narrated by Michael MacLiammoir?
24 Who killed Ronald Reagan in his last film The Killers?
25 Who did John Wayne play in North to Alaska?
26 For which film did Elizabeth Taylor win her second Oscar?
27 For which role was Dustin Hoffman nominated in 1969?
28 Which of the Redgrave clan appeared in A Man For All Seasons?
29 Who played opposite then wife Claire Bloom in The Illustrated Man?
30 Who was the older winner of the shared Best Actress Oscar in 1968?

Answers

Food & Drink 1 (See Quiz 134)
1 Liebfraumilch. 2 Warm. 3 Salsa. 4 Stomach remedy. 5 Ice cream.
6 Tomatoes. 7 Crescent shaped (roll). 8 Steen. 9 Stum. 10 Browned at the edges due to age. 11 Sicily. 12 Semi sparkling, fully sparkling. 13 Calzone. 14 Maize. 15 Grapes are partly sun dried before use. 16 San Lorenzo. 17 Portugal. 18 Barsac, Bommes, Fargues, Preignac. 19 Britain. 20 Jennifer Paterson. 21 Canary Islands. 22 Wine and methylated spirits. 23 Salsify. 24 Remuage. 25 Pomerol. 26 Wine award in Germany. 27 Bechamel. 28 Oenology. 29 Escoffier. 30 Mirin.

1 Which wine comes from Worms?
2 How is sake usually drunk?
3 Which food shares its name with Latin American big band music?
4 What were angostura bitters originally used for?
5 In the US if a dessert is served 'a la mode' what is served with it?
6 Which vegetable is a passata made from?
7 What shape is a rugelach?
8 What is chenin blanc wine known as in South Africa?
9 Which term describes the fermented grape juice added to wine that has lost its strength to perk it up?
10 If a wine is madeirized what has happened to it?
11 Where is Marsala, famed for its fortified wine?
12 In wine terms what is the difference between frizzante and spumante?
13 Which folded pizza dough dish takes its name from the Italian for trouser leg?
14 Which cereal is polenta made from?
15 How does Malaga wine achieve its dark colour?
16 Which Kensington restaurant was co founded by Mara Berni in 1963?
17 Where does Dao wine come from?
18 In addition to Sauternes itself which four communes can call their wine Sauternes?
19 Where did balti cooking originate?
20 Who has cooked lunches for The Spectator magazine and written for The Oldie?
21 Other than Spain and Portugal where does sack come from?
22 What is a red biddy?
23 Which food is also called the vegetable oyster?
24 In wine making which term describes turning the bottles so the sediment collects at the cork end?
25 In which district of Bordeaux is Chateau Petrus produced?
26 What is pradikat?
27 Which classic French sauce was named after a courtier of Louis XIV?
28 What is the study of wine called?
29 Which chef created the Bombe Nero and the peche melba?
30 Which sweet rice wine is used in Japanese cookery?

Answers

60s Films (See Quiz 133)
1 Doctor Dolittle. 2 Bryan Forbes. 3 New York & Paris. 4 John Ford.
5 Kenneth Williams. 6 David Bailey. 7 He has no dialogue. 8 When Dinosaurs Ruled the Earth. 9 Gillian Lynne. 10 George Segal. 11 Peter Cushing. 12 Brief Encounter. 13 A Shot in the Dark. 14 Joseph Mankiewicz. 15 Jimmy Bryant. 16 Maurice Jarre. 17 A Walk With Love and Death. 18 Stoke Poges. 19 Guess Who's Coming to Dinner. 20 Jess Conrad. 21 Gregory Peck. 22 Tom Courtenay. 23 Tom Jones. 24 Lee Marvin. 25 Big Sam. 26 Who's Afraid of Virginia Woolf?. 27 Ratso Rizzo. 28 Corin. 29 Rod Steiger. 30 Katherine Hepburn.

Quiz 135 Pot Luck 67

Answers - see page 604

LEVEL 3

1 A zinfandel is used for making what?
2 What separates Alaska from the other 48 US states?
3 How many times is 'Um' sung in the chorus of 60s hit Um Um Um Um Um Um?
4 Which TV personality launched the 1998 poppy appeal?
5 On which island which is also a country is Adam's Peak?
6 In which year did London Underground's Bakerloo Line open?
7 Who won Best Actor Oscar for his part in the musical film Amadeus?
8 If you have comedos, what are you suffering from?
9 What is the third largest city in Britain?
10 Who is the elder – David Bowie or Edwina Currie?
11 What is Warwickshire's county motif?
12 What was Cat Stevens' first UK Top Ten hit?
13 What kind of weapon was an arbalest?
14 Which Austrian physicist gave his name to perceived frequency variations under certain conditions?
15 Imran Khan played cricket for which two English counties?
16 From 1957 to 1985, who was the Russian Foreign Minister?
17 Which optical aid was invented by Benjamin Franklin?
18 What was the Bay City Rollers' first UK Top Ten hit?
19 Where are the ethmoid, vomer and zygomatic bones in your body?
20 In which decade was Peter Stringfellow born?
21 The capital of Japan is an anagram of which former capital?
22 Who rode both Toulon and Moonax to St Leger triumphs?
23 Who wrote All Quiet on the Western Front?
24 Where did John McGregor found the first Canoe Club in 1866?
25 What is the main colour on the cover of Celine Dion's album Let's Talk About Love?
26 Who wrote The Sea Wolf?
27 Which European country lost the battle of Ulm in 1805?
28 Who had hits in the 70s with Love Me and If I Can't Have You?
29 Which country has Guyana to the east and Colombia to the west?
30 How did Emiliano Zapata, the Mexican revolutionary, die in 1919?

Answers

Kings and Queens (See Quiz 136)
1 17 Bruton St, London. 2 The Delhi Durbar. 3 Edward VII. 4 Adelaide.
5 George I. 6 Hit with a cricket ball. 7 George V. 8 Henry II's wife Eleanor of Aquitaine. 9 Edward I (19). 10 It was his second. 11 The Pope.
12 Dunfermline. 13 Square, she was so obese. 14 Richard II. 15 River Soar.
16 Tax collectors. 17 Charles II. 18 St Stephen's Abbey Caen. 19 Henry I.
20 Edward VIII. 21 George I. 22 William IV. 23 Edward VII. 24 Christian IX of Denmark. 25 William II. 26 Opening Blackfriars Bridge. 27 Norfolk.
28 Two. 29 Jane Seymour & Catherine Parr. 30 Gloucester Cathedral.

Quiz 136 Kings & Queens

Answers - see page 603

1   At which address was Elizabeth II born?
2   Where were George V and Queen Mary crowned Emperor and Empress of India?
3   Who was the only British monarch from the House of Wettin?
4   Who was William IV's queen?
5   Which monarch's mother was Sophia of Bohemia?
6   How did George II's eldest son die?
7   Who was the first British monarch to make a Christmas Day broadcast?
8   Which English king's wife was a former wife of Louis VII of France?
9   Which British monarch produced the most legitimate children?
10 What was notable about Henry VI's coronation in 1470?
11 Who made Henry VIII Fidei Defensor?
12 Where was Charles I born?
13 What shape was Queen Anne's coffin and why?
14 Which English king is reputed to have invented the handkerchief?
15 Where were Richard III's bones thrown when his grave was desecrated?
16 Why was Henry VIII's execution of Richard Empson and Edmund Dudley a popular move?
17 Who was threatened by the Rye House Plot?
18 Where is William the Conqueror buried?
19 Which king founded the first English zoo?
20 Who was the penultimate Emperor of India?
21 The Duchess of Kendal was mistress of which king?
22 Who was the first monarch born in Buckingham Palace?
23 Who was the first Emperor of India?
24 Who was Edward VII's father in law?
25 Which English king was killed by Walter Tyrel?
26 What was Victoria's only public ceremony in 1870?
27 In which county did George V die?
28 How many shirts did Charles I wear for his execution?
29 Who were Henry VIII's two oldest wives?
30 Where was Henry III crowned?

Pot Luck 67 (See Quiz 135)
1 Wine. 2 British Columbia. 3 24. 4 Des Lynam. 5 Sri Lanka. 6 1906. 7 F. Murray Abraham. 8 Blackheads. 9 Glasgow. 10 Edwina Currie. 11 A standing bear next to a ragged staff. 12 Matthew and Son. 13 A giant crossbow. 14 Christian Doppler. 15 Worcestershire and Sussex. 16 Gromyko. 17 Bifocal lenses. 18 Keep On Dancing. 19 Skull. 20 1940s. 21 Kyoto. 22 Pat Eddery. 23 Erich Remarque. 24 Richmond, Surrey. 25 Black. 26 Jack London. 27 Austria. 28 Yvonne Elliman. 29 Venezuela. 30 Assassinated.

604

Quiz 137 Pot Luck 68

Answers - see page 606

LEVEL 3

1　Who directed the1930s film Mr Deeds Goes To Town?

2　Which disease did Prince Albert die from?

3　Shogi is a Japanese form of which game?

4　Who wrote The Seven Pillars of Wisdom?

5　Which bird would you find in a squab pie?

6　Who played the lead character in the film The Loneliness of the Long Distance Runner?

7　In which decade was the Marquis of Tavistock born?

8　What was Rolf Harris' first UK Top Ten hit?

9　Which famous actor played Philo Beddoe in two films?

10　Who did Australia beat when they first won cricket's World Cup?

11　What is the legendary ship The Flying Dutchman doomed to do?

12　Which queen of England had most fingers?

13　Who wrote the novel Fair Stood the Wind for France?

14　Who is the elder – Joan Collins or Michael Caine?

15　Whose one and only hit was Eye Level in 1973?

16　To three years, when did the M1 motorway open?

17　What was found in 1939 at Sutton Hoo, in Suffolk?

18　What is of interest to a thanatologist?

19　Where would you find calderas?

20　Who wrote The Lost World?

21　If something is napiform which vegetable shape is it?

22　What part of the body is studied by a myologist?

23　Which song features the words, "Here am I floating round my tin can"?

24　What was the Triangular Trade mainly concerned with?

25　What, in America, is a cayuse?

26　How many strokes underwater may a competitive breast-sroke swimmer make at the start and turn?

27　The town of Carrara in Italy is famous for what?

28　Who wrote humour books naming Mussolini and Hitler in the titles?

29　Who is thought to be the author of the Acts of the Apostles?

30　The Battle of Antietam was in which war?

Answers

Classic No 1s (See Quiz 138)

1 Wet Wet Wet. 2 Unchained. 3 My Sweet Lord. 4 Wooden Heart. 5 Maggie May. 6 Frankie Laine. 7 Love. 8 Ticket To Ride. 9 Peter Cetera. 10 Herbert Kretzmer. 11 Girls' School. 12 Elton John. 13 The Fly (U2). 14 The Fleet's In. 15 Slade. 16 I Know Him So Well. 17 Whatever Will Be Will Be. 18 Do They Know It's Christmas? 19 Hello Goodbye. 20 Careless Whisper. 21 Bridge over Troubled Water. 22 Who's Sorry Now? 23 Three Times A Lady. 24 John Travolta. 25 You Wear It Well. 26 Claudette. 27 Mike Read. 28 I'm Not In Love. 29 Bohemian Rhapsody. 30 Living Doll.

1 Who were the first Scottish group to have three No 1s?

2 Which 1955 American movie had Unchained Melody as theme tune?

3 Which No 1 was the first solo single by George Harrison?

4 Which Elvis hit made him the first artist with three consecutive British No 1s?

5 Which Rod Stewart hit was originally the B-side of Reason to Believe?

6 Who was on top of the charts the week Everest was first climbed?

7 What word appears three times in the title of the Gary Glitter No 1 that was covered by Joan Jett in America?

8 What was the first No 1 from the Beatles' second film Help!?

9 Who wrote Chicago's No 1 classic If You Leave Me Now?

10 Which lyricist of Aznavour's She was a writer on Les Mis?

11 What was on the other side of the double A No 1 Mull of Kintyre?

12 Who co-wrote a No 1 duet song under the pseudonym Ann Orson?

13 What finally knocked (Everything I Do) I Do It For You off the No 1 spot?

14 Which film did Frank Ifield's I Remember You originally come from?

15 Which group holds the record for the most consecutive years in which a songhas charted?

16 What became the all time best UK selling single by a female duo?

17 Which Doris Day Oscar-winning song was from The Man Who Knew Too Much in 1956?

18 What was the first debut single to enter straight at No 1?

19 Which No 1 hit by the Beatles equalled 7 weeks at the top with From Me To You?

20 What is the only George Michael song for which Andrew Ridgeley takes equal writing credit?

21 Which album title track gave Simon and Garfunkel their biggest hit?

22 Which 1920s standard gave Concetta Franconero a 6 week No 1 hit?

23 Which Commodores classic became Motown's best UK seller?

24 Who is the male half of the duo that have spent most weeks at No 1?

25 Which No 1 mentions Jackie Onassis?

26 Apart from Cathy's Clown, which other No 1 for the Everly Brothers had a girl's name in the title?

27 Which Radio 1 DJ banned Frankie Goes to Hollywood's Relax?

28 Which 10cc hit was covered by Johnny Logan in 1987?

29 Which 1975 megahit remained at No 1 for 9 weeks?

30 Which No 1 hit was Cliff Richard's first million seller?

Quiz 139 Pot Luck 69

LEVEL 3

Answers - see page 608

1   What is Kyzyl Kum in Russia?
2   Neville Cardus was associated with which sport?
3   Who played Paul Henreid's wife in the film Casablanca?
4   What was the first woman's magazine to be published in 1693?
5   Where did the Dryad nymphs live in Greek mythology?
6   What sort of creature is a killdeer?
7   What type of music is Ira D Sankey particularly noted for composing?
8   How old was Louis Braille when he invented his reading system for the blind?
9   Which actor starred in the silent films Robin Hood, The Three Musketeers and The Black Pirate?
10 What was Five Star's first UK Top Ten hit?
11 Ficus Elastica is the Latin name for which plant?
12 In which sport is there a bonspiel?
13 Arch, loop and whorl are all parts of what?
14 What is pishogue a form of?
15 Permission was given to whom in 1988 to rebuild London's Globe Theatre?
16 In which decade was Emma Thompson born?
17 A fylfot is better known as a what?
18 Alton Byrd was famous in which sport?
19 Who played the magical Supergran in the 1985 TV series?
20 Whose one and only UK Top Ten hit was called Tarzan Boy?
21 Which actor was The Virginian on TV?
22 Who is the elder – Timothy Dalton or Charles Dance?
23 Richard Meade won Olympic gold in which sport?
24 What is the main difference between squash and rackets?
25 In which year was the CBI set up?
26 Whose first Top Ten hit was House of Love?
27 Where is the Caledonian market held?
28 Which battle in 1813 was the last battle of the Peninsular War?
29 Who would use a trochee?
30 Who wrote the play called A Taste of Honey?

1　How is David Sutton better known?
2　Sue Nicholls alias Audrey in Coronation Street made which record?
3　Which soap did Demi Moore appear in?
4　Who played Graham Lodsworth in Emmerdale?
5　What is the post code of the London Borough of Walford?
6　Which former soap star played Christine Keeler's mother in Scandal?
7　Which role did impresario Bill Kenwright play in Coronation Street?
8　Jo Warne played which Albert Square character?
9　Which soap featured the 'Free George Jackson' campaign?
10　On which Australian network was Neighbours first shown?
11　In Dallas what three surnames did Miss Ellie have?
12　Who ran the cafe when EastEnders started?
13　Sharon and Kelvin in EastEnders made a record under what name?
14　What were Ken Barlow's parents called?
15　In which village was the BBC's ill fated Eldorado set?
16　Which role did Ryan O'Neal play in Peyton Place?
17　In Dallas who were the parents of baby Christopher?
18　When Emmerdale was filmed at Esholt which pub was used as The Woolpack?
19　Which Radio 2 regular played Chris Anderson in Emergency Ward 10?
20　Who played Blake Carrington in the pilot for Dynasty?
21　In which county was Southfork ranch?
22　Jambo from Hollyoaks recorded which song as Will Mellor?
23　In Dynasty what name did Blake's supposed son Adam use when he first arrived on the scene?
24　Whose funeral was seen in the first episode of Emmerdale Farm?
25　Where was there a pub called The Waterman's Arms?
26　Who lived at 45 Albert Square?
27　Which soap star directed Son of Blob in 1972?
28　A one off 'prequel' about Albert Square was set in which year?
29　Which BBC 1 controller was responsible for moving Neighbours to a prime time viewing slot?
30　In Dallas, how and where did Jock Ewing die?

Answers

Pot Luck 69 (See Quiz 139)
1 A desert. 2 Cricket. 3 Ingrid Bergman. 4 The Ladies' Mercury. 5 In trees. 6 A bird (Type of plover). 7 Hymns. 8 15. 9 Douglas Fairbanks. 10 System Addict. 11 Rubber plant. 12 Curling. 13 Fingerprints. 14 Sorcery. 15 Sam Wanamaker. 16 1950s. 17 Swastika. 18 Basketball. 19 Gudrun Ure. 20 Baltimora. 21 James Drury. 22 Timothy Dalton. 23 3 Day Eventing. 24 Squash uses a softer ball. 25 1965. 26 East 17. 27 East end of London. 28 Battle of Vittoria. 29 A poet . 30 Shelagh Delaney.

1 With which police identification system is Francis Galton associated?
2 Which trees mainly produced the fossilised resin which becomes amber?
3 Who is the elder – Sarah Brightman or Jill Dando?
4 If a ship is careened, what has happened to it?
5 What did Henry Segrave break at Daytona in 1927 and 1929?
6 What was the Beautiful South's first UK Top Ten hit?
7 Which event is the first in a Decathlon?
8 Which US President died on the same day as Aldous Huxley?
9 When is Haley's Comet predicted to make its next visit in Earth's vicinity?
10 Who wrote the Gormenghast Trilogy?
11 In which county is Chequers?
12 The King of which country was the Prisoner of Zenda?
13 Who was the first jockey to record three consecutive Derby wins?
14 What relation to King Arthur was Mordred?
15 Who designed the first lightning conductor?
16 In which decade was Vivienne Westwood born?
17 What is matzo?
18 Which actor played Captain Bligh, Quasimodo and Henry VIII in films?
19 Which Archbishop of Canterbury was burnt at the stake in 1556?
20 Who is the most capped English hockey player?
21 Which country did Frenchman Patrick Juvet love in his 70s UK hit?
22 Who played King Arthur in First Knight?
23 Whose one and only hit was Michelle in 1966?
24 What can be grapnel, sheet and bower?
25 A trudgen is used in which sport?
26 Which river was first explored by Mungo Park, a Scottish surgeon?
27 To five years, when were Nobel Prizes first awarded?
28 In the poem Beowulf, what kills Beowulf?
29 What would you do with a gigot?
30 The sitcom in which Warren Mitchell made his name took its title from which book?

LEVEL 3

1 Who retained golf's Dunhill Cup in 1998?
2 Who was the first man to with the US PGA and the US Open in the same year?
3 What was the world's first golf club called?
4 Which golfer was born on Bernard Gallacher's ninth birthday?
5 What was Payne Stewart's first. victory in a major?
6 In 1986 Greg Norman equalled whose record low score of 63 in the US Masters?
7 Who did Tony Jacklin replace as Ryder Cup captain?
8 Who was only the second person after Jack Nicklaus to win two successive US Opens?
9 Who did Nick Faldo sensationally beat to win his third US Masters?
10 In August 1996 who made his debut as a pro in the Czech Open?
11 In 1968 what became the longest course ever used for the British Open?
12 Where did Tom Lehman win his first major?
13 When Steve Jones first won the US Open he was the first qualifier to win a Major since who?
14 Where did the very first Ryder Cup take place?
15 Who won the first ever British Open?
16 Who is the President of Augusta National Golf Club?
17 Who did Nick Faldo sack as his coach at the same time as divorcing wife number two?
18 Who was the last American to win the British Open before John Daly in 1995?
19 Who was the first European to win the US Masters in the 90s?
20 Who was the first US born winner of the British Open?
21 How old was Nick Faldo when he was first in a Ryder Cup team?
22 Which golf course boasts a Postage Stamp?
23 What was Craig Stadler's nickname?
24 By how many strokes did Tony Jacklin win his first US Open?
25 Gary Player won all the Majors but which did he win first?
26 Who were the USA's opponents in the Ryder Cup from '73 to '77?
27 How many times did Jack Nicklaus win the US Amateur title before turning pro?
28 Who was the first American to win the US Masters in the 90s?
29 Who admitted losing half a million gambling in 1996?
30 What is the only Irish course to have staged the British Open?

1   What was discovered by Garcia Lopez de Cardenas in 1540?
2   Whose first Top Ten hit was titled September?
3   In the Seven Years War who were Britain's two allies?
4   In which decade was Paula Yates born?
5   Who was the first player to score 100 points in a NBA basketball game?
6   Rose Louise Hovick achieved fame under what name?
7   Who is the father of Marsha Hunt's daughter Karis?
8   What is the final line in the film Gone With the Wind?
9   Which newspaper was featured in the TV series Hot Metal?
10 The gemstone ruby is associated with which month?
11 What is the name of Phil and Jill Archer's farm?
12 Who directed the film It Happened One Night?
13 What was the Tote originally known as?
14 Where on your body are the Mounts of the Sun, Mercury and Venus?
15 Which fungal disease has the name Ceratostomella Ulmi?
16 Who created the cartoon character Colonel Blimp?
17 Where is the village of Skara Brae?
18 Who won the 1989 Best Actor Oscar for the film My Left Foot?
19 Who is the elder – Ian Botham or Jim Davidson?
20 Which actor played the title role in the TV series Dear John?
21 Whose theme was a No 4 UK hit in 1959 for Elmer Bernstein?
22 If you are an encratic person, what do you possess?
23 Who said, "There never was a good war, nor a bad peace"?
24 David Beckham made his league debut on loan at which club?
25 Who wrote The White Company?
26 Which general was the youngest in the American Civil War?
27 What was the Fine Young Cannibals first UK Top Ten hit?
28 With which profession is the organisation RIBA associated?
29 Who founded the record label Respond?
30 Who in 1632 painted The Anatomy Lesson of Dr Tulip?

1 Whose first husband was John Dunbar when she was 18?

2 Which photographer married Faye Dunaway in 1981?

3 Who announced her engagement to Riccardo Mazzucchelli in 1995?

4 What did Tara Palmer Tomkinson use to hide her modesty when posing nude with three friends?

5 What relation is Camilla Parker Bowles to Edward VII's mistress Mrs Keppel?

6 Who was Mandy Smith's second husband?

7 Who owns the private zoos, Howletts and Port Lympne?

8 Which Tory MP did Maria-Bienvenida Perez Blanco marry?

9 Former deb Henrietta Tiarks became which Marchioness?

10 Who designed the deep blue, lingerie style dress Diana wore in New York in 1996?

11 Who was Duchess of York before Fergie?

12 Who designed Diana's dress when she danced with John Travolta at the White House?

13 Heller Toren is the mother of which blonde celeb?

14 Which title did Raine have before she married the late Earl Spencer?

15 Whose Regency home is Ray Mill House in Wiltshire?

16 What were Regan Gascoigne's step siblings called?

17 Who is famous for his 'wifelets'?

18 Who is Watford Grammar School's most famous old girl?

19 Who was Mick Jagger's best man when he married Bianca?

20 What is Tiggy Legge-Bourke's real first name?

21 Fergie was appointed Chancellor of which University?

22 Who founded the Pineapple Dance Studios in 1979?

23 Who discovered Jean Shrimpton in the 60s?

24 Queen Noor of Jordan studied for what profession before her marriage?

25 Who was the first wife of the ninth Earl Spencer?

26 Whose husbands were Alexander McCorquodale then his cousin Hugh?

27 Who was the most famous daughter of Major Bruce Shand?

28 Who replaced Claudia Schiffer as the face of Chanel?

29 Who became Dior's chief designer in 1996?

30 Which model Hamilton co founded the elephant charity Tusk Force?

Quiz 145 Pot Luck 72

Answers - see page 614

1 Who died in the avalanche in Klosters in 1988 involving Prince Charles' party?
2 Who was chairman of the Joint Chiefs of Staff during the Gulf War?
3 How many hours are there in a fortnight?
4 Which modern day explorer has Twisleton-Wykeham as part of his name?
5 In whose reign was the Chelsea Hospital founded?
6 Who was Elizabeth I's State Secretary from 1573 to 1590?
7 Edward Whymper is associated with which leisure activity?
8 What did alchemists call the imaginary object that would turn base metals to gold?
9 What was the surname of the Lord in the TV series The Buccaneers?
10 Who designed and built the world's first iron bridge?
11 Who took her Toot Toot into the pop charts in the 80s?
12 Who is the elder – Sean Bean or Daniel Day-Lewis?
13 What was Michel Platini's club when he was three times European Footballer of The Year?
14 On the Chinese calendar, what is the only bird?
15 Where are the Padang Highlands?
16 What are you if you are described as being an ectomorph?
17 Where did Indian ink originally come from?
18 In which town is Channel TV based?
19 In which decade was Catherine Zeta Jones born?
20 What bird was the symbol of Persia's monarchy from 1739 to 1979?
21 What is the metal zinc extracted from?
22 Which game uses the expression 'J'adoube'?
23 In London what was the Tyburn?
24 Who attempted the programme of social reform called Fair Deal?
25 Where in England might you do a Furry Dance?
26 What are measured in hadal, abyssal and bathyl zones?
27 The Australian Aborigines' creation legend is told in what stories?
28 The word Eskimo means the eaters of what?
29 If you were banting, what would you be doing?
30 What was the Michael Bolton's first UK Top Ten hit?

Communications (See Quiz 146)
Answers
1 Atlanta, Georgia. **2** Stephen Wozniak & Steven Jobs. **3** Olympic Games in Atlanta. **4** Fibre-optic Link Around the Globe. **5** Puerto Rico. **6** The Branch Mall. **7** Hand held fax machine. **8** Grote Reber. **9** MERLIN. **10** Analogue Digital Converter. **11** 13. **12** So drivers will concentrate. **13** Siding Spring Mountain. **14** 1866. **15** British Library. **16** Tim Berners-Lee. **17** The Confederation Bridge. **18** The Times. **19** Japan. **20** 1940. **21** BBC & ITV. **22** Betamax. **23** Deep Blue. **24** Leslie Ibsen Rogge. **25** Isaac Newton. **26** Nuffield. **27** The Met Office. **28** Water. 29 Catadioptric. **30** Decca.

Quiz 146 Communication

Answers - see page 613

1   Where is the HQ of CNN?
2   Who founded the Apple Computer Company?
3   Why was the Bellsouth telephone exchange the world's busiest in 1996?
4   What is FLAG?
5   In which country is the world's largest single dish radio telescope?
6   What was the first shopping mall on the Internet called?
7   What sort of communications device is "Pagentry"?
8   Who built the only purpose built radio telescope before WWII?
9   The Lovell Telescope is part of which network?
10 What is an ADC?
11 On household goods how many lines are there on a bar code?
12 Why was the Confederation Bridge built with so many curves?
13 Which mountain is the site of the Anglo Australian telescope in New South Wales?
14 In which decade of which century was the first transatlantic telegraph cable sent?
15 Where is BLAISE used?
16 Who was the World Wide Web originally created by?
17 Which bridge links Prince Edward Island with New Brunswick?
18 Marconi began a regular news service between the UK and US for which newspaper?
19 Where did the world's first major ISDN centre begin operating in '88?
20 When were the first experimental transmissions of colour TV in the US?
21 Who introduced the world's first teletext systems?
22 What was Sony's video cassette system for domestic viewers called?
23 What was the name of the first computer to beat a world chess champion?
24 Who was the first man to be arrested after having his picture on the Internet?
25 The telescope on La Palma in the Canary Islands is named after which scientist?
26 As which Radio Astronomy Laboratory is Jodrell Bank also known?
27 Who owns the Cray Supercomputer?
28 The New York City West Delaware tunnel is used to supply what?
29 What name is given to a telescope which uses lenses and mirrors?
30 Which company in Britain pioneered the videodisc?

Pot Luck 72 (See Quiz 145)
1 Major Hugh Lindsay. 2 Colin Powell. 3 336. 4 Sir Ranulph Fiennes. 5 Charles II. 6 Sir Francis Walsingham. 7 Mountaineering. 8 Philosopher's Stone. 9 Brightlingsea. 10 Abraham Darby. 11 Denise La Salle. 12 Daniel Day-Lewis. 13 Juventus. 14 Cockerel. 15 Sumatra. 16 Thin. 17 China. 18 St Helier. 19 1960s. 20 Peacock. 21 Sphalerite. 22 Chess. 23 A stream. 24 President Truman. 25 Helston, Cornwall. 26 Ocean depths. 27 Dreamtime Stories. 28 Raw Meat. 29 Dieting. 30 How Am I Supposed To Live Without You.

1 What is a line joining any two points on a curve called in geometry?
2 What was Suzi Quatro's first UK Top Ten hit?
3 Which battle is remembered in the USA in April on Patriots' Day?
4 Who directed the films Marathon Man and Billy Liar?
5 Who was the eldest son of Henry III?
6 Who preceded Douglas Hurd as Foreign Secretary?
7 Which part of the body is affected by chorea?
8 Who was William Shakespeare's mother?
9 Which pop singing duo had the real first names of Reg and Pauline?
10 Who founded the Outward Bound Trust?
11 In which decade was Gary Rhodes born?
12 How old was Klaus Barbie when he was sentenced to life for wartime atrocities?
13 What would you do with a kaki?
14 What are Purple Laver and Devil's Apron types of?
15 Where would ichor supposedly have flowed?
16 Which singing twins were Hal and Herbert?
17 In The Bible, what did Job suffer with?
18 Which straits separate India from Sri Lanka?
19 Who referred to international financiers as "gnomes of Zurich"?
20 Who was the second oldest Goon?
21 What was author John Buchan's real title?
22 Which country do the Hausa people live in?
23 What was the name of Don Quixote's horse?
24 Who wrote the opera The Love for Three Oranges?
25 Christopher Nolan was a Whitbread Book of the Year winner with what?
26 Which fur comes from the coypu?
27 Whose only UK Top ten hit was called Shake You Down. in 1986?
28 Who became Minister of Defence when Churchill became PM in 1940?
29 In which Asian country is there an edition of the FT printed?
30 Who is the elder – Paddy Ashdown or Lord Archer?

1 What is hanepoot?
2 Who or what was Buck's Fizz named after?
3 Which snack's name comes from the Turkish for rotating?
4 Where is the yeastless beer faro made?
5 Where was Anton Mosimann's first position as chef in the UK?
6 Kummel is a Russian liqueur extracted from what?
7 The macadamia is native to where?
8 What is the main ingredient of a brandade?
9 Who opened the Miller Howe restaurant in 1971?
10 In his diary what did Pepys call 'jucalette'?
11 Where in a dish would you put gremolata?
12 Which country has a wine growing area called O'Higgins?
13 Which term indicates the amount of wine by which a container falls short of being full?
14 Who is credited with creating camembert cheese in about 1790?
15 What is the base of a florentine biscuit made from?
16 Where did malmsey wine originate?
17 Balti is the Indian word for what?
18 Which abbreviation indicates wine between the qualities of vin de pays and appellation controle?
19 What are the ingredients of a Mr Callaghan?
20 What is cocose?
21 What did TV cook Sophie Grigson study at university?
22 In Swiss cooking what is a leckerli?
23 What is added to an omelette to make an omelette Argenteuil?
24 Which herbs are put in a béarnaise sauce?
25 Which fruit is used to make slivovitz?
26 Foie gras is the liver of which creatures?
27 In ceviche raw fish is marinated in what?
28 What is a mesclun?
29 A brochette is another name for what?
30 In Mexican cookery what is a quesadilla?

1 What was Sting's debut movie?

2 What was Justin Henry's surname in a 70s Oscar winner?

3 In which film does railwayman Cleavon Little become sheriff?

4 That's Entertainment was a compilation of clips from which studio?

5 Who played Siegfried to Simon Ward's James in All Creatures Great and Small?

6 Which music plays in the background in 10?

7 What was Alan Parker's first feature film?

8 Who starred in and produced The China Syndrome?

9 What was Tom Selleck's first film, in 1970?

10 Who played Winston's father in Young Winston?

11 Whose was the disembodied voice narrating Agatha Christie's And Then There Were None?

12 Who wrote the music for Shaft?

13 Who was the landlord of 10 Rillington Place?

14 Who sang the title song in The Aristocats?

15 For the trailer of which Hitchcock film was the director seen floating in then Thames?

16 Stacy Keach starred in Fat City after who turned it down?

17 Who directed Death Wish?

18 Who was the first director to cast Goldie Hawn in a non comedy film?

19 Who did Jane Fonda play in Julia?

20 Why did Peter Finch not collect his Oscar for Network?

21 Whose music did Malcolm McDowell like in A Clockwork Orange?

22 Who was the only female Oscar winner for One Flew Over the Cuckoo's Nest?

23 Who played the editor of the Washington Post in All the President's Men?

24 Which club features in Cabaret?

25 Who played the brother in The Railway Children?

26 Who was Maid Marian opposite Sean Connery in Robin and Marian?

27 What was the first film in which Julie Christie and Warren Beatty starred together?

28 What was Peter Ustinov's first film as Hercule Poirot?

29 What was the sequel to Love Story?

30 Which film of a Frederick Forsyth novel starred Jon Voight?

1　What is eaten by a pantophagist?
2　Who were the Fuggers?
3　What do isohyet lines indicate on a map?
4　What are the dark, lowland plains on the moon known as?
5　Where, in 1855, is ice hockey thought to have originated?
6　What was the only UK Top Ten hit for the group Black Sabbath?
7　In which country was musician Leopold Stokowski born?
8　Which Scottish order has the motto 'Nemo me impune lacessit'?
9　What was the name of Fingal's dog in Gaelic legend?
10　The Schich Test can be used to test for which disease?
11　In the Oliver Stone film Natural Born Killers, who played Mickey?
12　What do you do with a maduro?
13　Who was Hector's mother in mythology?
14　Which novel starts "The past is a foreign country: they do things differently there"?
15　Which metals is a 50p piece made from?
16　What is the main colour on the cover of the album Spice?
17　In which decade was Betty Boothroyd born?
18　Coptic Christians are found in Egypt and which one other country?
19　Which 1996 tennis tournament saw the debut of a fluorescent ball?
20　What was Errol Flynn's last film in 1959?
21　In which decade was playwright Sir Alan Ayckbourn born?
22　The Festival Garden in Battersea Park are based on which continental gardens?
23　Which part did Brian Wilde play in the TV series Porridge?
24　Which phobia describes a fear of marriage?
25　What was Bjork's first UK Top Ten hit from 1995?
26　Which female media personality has been President of the Ramblers Association?
27　What was a carrack?
28　What term describes using a gentler expression to soften a hard one?
29　Who is the elder – Lynsey de Paul or Noel Edmonds?
30　What was the profession of Jane Asher's father?

1   Who played Emperor Nero in I, Claudius?

2   Who was the female presenter of Tiswas?

3   Which presenter once played Sir Julius Berlin in Corrie?

4   Which future Oscar nominee played Samantha Briggs in Dr Who?

5   Who was the only female on the first Top of the Pops?

6   In which TV pub did Vince Hill find fame?

7   On The Golden Shot who famously always got her sums wrong?

8   Who was the housekeeper in All Creatures Great and Small?

9   Who was the first presenter of World of Sport on ITV?

10   What was the booby prize on Crackerjack?

11   Who were the trio in Take Three Girls?

12   Who had the role of George Starling written for him in 1963?

13   Who originally shared a flat with Sandra in The Liver Birds?

14   Which comedian starred as himself in the Northern town of Woodbridge?

15   Who played the shop treasurer in The Rag Trade?

16   The lead singer of Herman's Hermits played whose son on TV?

17   Who was the first Teenage Mutant Hero Turtle alphabetically?

18   Who played Yosser in Boys From the Blackstuff?

19   Who was doing the asking in Ask the Family?

20   Who frequently appeared as Nymphia in Up Pompeii?

21   Who starred as Charley Farley, partner of Piggy Malone?

22   Who was the author played by Elaine Stritch in Two's Company?

23   Which sitcom began with a one off play called The Offer?

24   Who played Nancy Astor's husband in the 80s series Nancy Astor?

25   As which character did David Cassidy shoot to fame in the 70s?

26   In My Wife Next Door which sitcom doyenne played George's mother?

27   Who was the only person the horse Mr Ed would talk to?

28   Which character shot Alan Rickman to fame in The Barchester Chronicles?

29   Who played Tom the tap dancing pimp in Pennies From Heaven?

30   Which corporal in M*A*S*H took to wearing women's clothes in order to be
discharged?

Pot Luck 75 (See Quiz 152)
Answers
1 A group hired to applaud. 2 1982. 3 A torture device. 4 Fabrics.
5 Margaret Atwood. 6 Japan. 7 A crash. 8 A.J. Cronin. 9 His wife
Clytemnestra. 10 Kenya. 11 Daddy Cool. 12 Conscription. 13 Ernest
Hemingway. 14 Dawn French. 15 Blucher. 16 Trial of the Pyx. 17 Jennie
Lee. 18 Newcastle-upon-Tyne. 19 Goldsbrough Orchestra (after its founder).
20 1868. 21 Princess Yashara. 22 Tiger. 23 1970s. 24 Veterinary Surgeon.
25 Big Ben. 26 Blow Monkeys. 27 Lord Nolan. 28 Groucho Marx. 29
Massaging you. 30 The farthing.

LEVEL 3

1   What is a claque?
2   In which year did Channel 4 start to broadcast?
3   What was the Scavenger's Daughter used for in the 16th century?
4   What can be sornick, nainsook and samite?
5   Who wrote Life Before Men and The Edible Woman?
6   Which country launched a strike against Russia's fleet in 1904 at Port Arthur?
7   What is the collective name for a group of rhinoceroses?
8   Who created the character Doctor Finlay?
9   In mythology, who murdered the Greek king Agamemnon?
10 The Flame Trees of Thika was set in which country?
11 What was Boney M's first UK Top Ten hit from 1976?
12 What was the Derby Scheme of 1915?
13 Who wrote A Farewell to Arms?
14 Who is the elder – Dawn French or Jennifer Saunders?
15 What name was given to George Stephenson's first locomotive?
16 At which ceremony are coins of the realm tested?
17 Who was Britain's first Minister for the Arts in 1967?
18 Which Northern city was given the Latin name Pons Aelius?
19 What was the English Chamber Orchestra originally called?
20 When was Exchange & Mart first published?
21 Who did Buddha marry before searching for enlightenment?
22 Alphabetically what is the last of the Chinese Zodiac signs?
23 In which decade was actress Dervla Kirwan born?
24 What was the profession of the pneumatic tyre patentee John Dunlop?
25 What, on 31st December 1923, gave its first broadcast?
26 Whose only UK Top Ten hit was It Doesn't Have To Be This Way?
27 Which Lord headed the investigating committee into 'sleaze' in public life in 1995?
28 Who said, "Don't point that beard at me: it might go off"?
29 If someone was Rolfing you, what would they be doing?
30 What ceased to be legal at midnight, December 31st, 1960?

1 What are Celine Dion's first two words on My Heart Will Go On?
2 What is Tina Turner's highest ever UK solo singles chart position?
3 What did Geri write by her signature on the cover notes of Spice?
4 Which sisters gave Stock/Aitken/Waterman their first No1 hit?
5 In which year was Diana Ross's first UK solo Top Ten hit?
6 Which hit made Helen Shapiro the youngest British artist to reach No 1?
7 Who sang female vocals on the Beautiful South's first No 1?
8 Belinda Carlisle and Bonnie Tyler both covered which 1970 No 1?
9 Who partnered Janet Jackson on her UK No 3 hit Scream ?
10 Who was the first British female soloist to have three chart No 1 hits?
11 Whose first UK Top Ten hit as a solo artist was Light of My Life?
12 Which character was played by Kylie Minogue in The Delinquents?
13 What is Enya's full name?
14 Which Bananarama star went on to join Shakespear's Sister?
15 What was Madonna's first UK No 1?
16 Whose first UK Top Ten hit was Love Resurrection ?
17 When did Shirley Bassey first reach the UK Top Ten?
18 Formed in 1981, girl band The Colours charted under which name?
19 What was Dina Carroll's first solo Top Ten hit?
20 Which UK vocalist released an album in 1974 called Ma?
21 Which film featured the Eternal hit Someday in 1996?
22 Whose first UK Top Ten hit was My One Temptation?
23 Which UK No 3 for Stacy Lattisaw was a No 8 for Dannii Minogue?
24 Which lady recorded the original Midnight Train To Georgia?
25 Which lady was Rockin' Around The Christmas Tree in 1987?
26 What did Belinda Carlisle want in her UK No 6 hit from 1990?
27 Which female star first reached No 1 29 years after her first hit?
28 What was the No 3 hit by Youssou N'Dour featuring Neneh Cherry?
29 What type of girl gave Tori Amos her first UK Top Ten hit in 1994?
30 Who was the first solo female to enter the UK charts at No 1?

1   How did Marie Curie's husband Pierre die?

2   Which group of people were once known as Millennial Dawnists?

3   In which decade was musician Mark Knopfler born?

4   What are you like if you are described as being saurian?

5   Who was the father of Enoch in The Bible?

6   Who created the character Tristram Shandy?

7   What was the title of Oran 'Juice' Jones only UK hit from 1986?

8   In which country is there a political party called Likud?

9   What was Tammy Wynette's real first name?

10 Which part did Carl Weathers play in the Rocky movies?

11 Where is a howdah normally found?

12 Which Spaniard painted the picture The Rokeby Venus?

13 Which River mouth was discovered by Amerigo Vespucci in 1499?

14 Who joined Boyz II Men in their 1995 No 6 UK hit One Sweet Day?

15 What did P.T. Barnum allegedly say is born every minute?

16 Richard Kuhn, Jutus Liebig and Harold Urey were famous in which scientific field?

17 Who was the first undisputed heavyweight world champion boxer to be European?

18 Who is the elder – Ben Elton or Harry Enfield?

19 Who played the lead male role in the 1995 film Loch Ness ?

20 Horace Saussure made the first ascent of where in 1787?

21 Which title is traditionally given to the second son of the monarch?

22 What sort of food is Dunlop?

23 What is a cow's first milk after calving called?

24 Which country celebrates the National holiday, the 'Day of the Dead'?

25 Who wrote A Handful of Dust?

26 What's Geri Halliwell's middle name?

27 The train the Cornish Riviera ran from where to where?

28 In the Second World War what did the Germans send out in 'wolf packs'?

29 What was Bow Wow Wow's first UK Top Ten hit?

30 Who wrote the poems Maud and Locksley Hall?

Answers

Girl Power (See Quiz 153)
1 Every Night. 2 Three. 3 Girl Power. 4 Mel and Kim Appleby. 5 1970.
6 You Don't Know. 7 Briana Corrigan. 8 Freda Payne's Band of Gold.
9 Michael Jackson. 10 Sandie Shaw. 11 Louise. 12 Lola Lovell. 13 Eithne
Ni Bhraonain. 14 Siobhan Fahey. 15 Into The Groove. 16 Alison Moyet.
17 1957. 18 The Bangles. 19 Don't Be A Stranger. 20 Lena Zavaroni.
21 Hunchback of Notre Dame. 22 Mica Paris. 23 Jump To The Beat.
24 Cissy Houston. 25 Kim Wilde. 26 (We want) The Same Thing. 27 Lulu.
28 7 Seconds. 29 Cornflake Girl. 30 Mariah Carey.

Quiz 155 Sport Moments

LEVEL 3

Answers - see page 624

1 Which Grand National winner was the first to be trained by a woman?
2 David Broome was the first British showjumping champion on which horse?
3 Who was the only player to kick the ball when the crowd sang "There's only one team in Tallinn"?
4 Who broke the world 5,000m by 11 seconds in 1995?
5 Jesse Owens was part of which university team when he set his three world records?
6 Who was the second player to hit a maximum 36 runs off one over?
7 In which road in Oxford did Roger Bannister run his four minute mile?
8 How many people witnessed Brazil's defeat by Uruguay in the 1950 World Cup Final?
9 Who was the first athlete to break 13 minutes for the 5,000m?
10 Who made Chris Boardman's winning bicycle in Barcelona?
11 Which famous pacemaker founded the London Marathon?
12 Which Grand National horse was the first to cross the line the year the race was abandoned?
13 By what score did Steve Davis lose the World Professional Championship Final in 1985?
14 Who was the first man to break one minute for 100m breaststroke in a 25m pool?
15 With whom did Steve Redgrave take the second of his four Olympic golds?
16 Which British man ran the fastest mile in the 80s?
17 Why did Susan Brown make history in 1981?
18 Which was the last horse before Lammtarra in 1995 to win the classic triple?
19 How many times did Nadia Comaneci score a perfect 10 at Montreal in 1976?
20 To the nearest 10 minutes, how long did it take Brian Lara to score his record 501 against Durham in 1994?
21 Who caddied for Tiger Woods on his first US Masters victory?
22 How many races out of the 16 did Nigel Mansell win to become World Champion?
23 Who was the first player since WWII to score more than 30 goals in three consecutive seasons?
24 Where was Harvey Smith when he made his infamous V sign?
25 Who did Virginia Wade beat to win her Wimbledon Singles title?
26 How many League games had Stanley Matthews played before his final match aged 50?
27 Seb Coe simultaneously held three world records, at which distances?
28 To the nearest 100 what were the odds against Frankie Dettori's seven Ascot wins?
29 Who broke the 1500, 3000 and 5000m records in 1994?
30 Who did Mike Tyson beat to become the youngest WBC champion?

1 How many chapters are in the book of Genesis in The Bible?
2 The Salk vaccine was developed against which disease?
3 What is a Venus's Looking Glass?
4 Who wrote White Fang?
5 What were constructed in the Highlands by General Wade in 1724?
6 What was the name of the John Gielgud character in the film Arthur?
7 What is a dossal?
8 What happened in Northern Ireland to Bananarama's road manager?
9 What was the Royal name of the band formed by Jimmy Nail?
10 Who is the elder – Chris Evans or Paul Gascoigne?
11 In the film Isadora who played the role of Isadora Duncan?
12 What is a barrico?
13 How many American colleges and universities are in the Ivy League?
14 Who played the lead role in the film Take Me High?
15 Cicada are types of what?
16 Who are in charge in a theocracy?
17 How many lines has a clerihew?
18 What was Patty Sheehan the first woman to do in the same year?
19 Breathe Again was the first UK Top Ten hit for which female vocalist?
20 Who had been Britain's youngest cabinet member before William Hague?
21 Frederick is born on which day in The Pirates Of Penzance?
22 Who was Archbishop of Canterbury from 1974 to 1980?
23 What was Bifrost in Norse mythology?
24 Which Labour leader was accused by The Sunday Times of being a Russian agent?
25 Which unit of measurement is equal to 3.2616 light years?
26 Which Man Utd manager appeared in a film called Cup Fever?
27 What was sendal?
28 What is a firearm called if it has a calibre over 20mm?
29 Which British liner was the first to be sunk by a U-boat on the first day of the Second World War?
30 In which decade was actor David Jason born?

Quiz 157 20th Century

1   What was the last ruling dynasty of China?

2   Which oil field blow-out caused an 8.2 million gallon spill in April 1977?

3   Who became Europe's youngest head of state at 28 in 1993?

4   Where was Archbishop Makarios exiled by the British in the mid 50s?

5   Which Deputy Ministerial post did Winnie Mandela hold in Nelson Mandela's first government?

6   Which German Chancellor achieved post war reconciliation with France in the 50s and early 60s?

7   Who became the youngest ever member of the GLC in 1969?

8   Which political parties linked in the UK in the 80s to form the Alliance?

9   Which Middle East leaders were awarded the Nobel Peace Prize in 1994?

10 Which film studio released the first talking film?

11 In the Watergate scandal, who or what was CREEP?

12 What was the occupation of Jean Bertrand Aristide of Haiti?

13 Wembley Stadium was completed for which event?

14 Harold Wilson became Baron of where on his elevation to the peerage?

15 Which quotation from Richard III was used to describe the end of 1978 and beginning of 1979?

16 What was nicknamed 'The Flapper Vote' in 1928?

17 Who succeeded the Ayatollah Khomeini as political leader of Iran?

18 Who was the first president of an independent Mozambique?

19 J Arthur Rank entered films in the 30s to promote which cause?

20 In 1987, what did the Tower Commission investigate in the US?

21 Where was the Recruit Scandal of 1988?

22 Which minister in Thatcher's government shared his name with Henry VIII's chaplain?

23 What did the initials of film company RKO stand for?

24 Whose gang did Al Capone's men massacre on Valentine's Day 1929?

25 A shortage of which commodity was a major issue in the 1998 Indian election?

26 At what number Cromwell Street did Rose and Fred West live?

27 King Michael abdicated which throne in 1947?

28 Who did Jacques Santer replace as President of the European Commission?

29 The 1964 Rivonia Trial involved those opposed to what?

30 What was the name of Franco's fascist party in Spain?

Quiz 158 Pot Luck 78

Answers - see page 625

LEVEL 3

1 Who is the elder – Paul McKenna or Vanessa Feltz?
2 In which city in 1882 were the Phoenix Park murders?
3 What is Roxburghe a style of?
4 Actor Thomas Doggett is remembered by an award in which sport?
5 Which writer died in Zurich after an operation for an ulcer in 1941?
6 Which city's underground has more stations than any other?
7 Which weaving invention was invented by John Kay?
8 Who was first to take Everything I Own to No 1 ?
9 What is hydroponics?
10 The Rye House Plot of 1683 was aiming to assassinate which king?
11 What is a quirt?
12 Who wrote A Connecticut Yankee in King Arthur's Court?
13 The Christian name Kenneth derives from the Gaelic for what?
14 Which Soviet dictator died on the same day as composer Prokofiev?
15 What is the unit of currency in The People's Republic of Congo?
16 How many No 1 albums did Take That have?
17 Which animals can suffer the disease strangles?
18 Who went with Ranulph Fiennes on his trek across Antarctica in '95?
19 In which decade was Gloria Hunniford born?
20 What were discovered by David Livingstone in 1855?
21 What is a strobilus another name for?
22 The name Commandos comes from an Afrikaans word for what?
23 Where did Nick Faldo win his first British Open?
24 Which European King died in 1993?
25 Which Biblical woman is the Jewish festival Purim a celebration to?
26 In which month is Prince Harry's birthday?
27 In America what is the 2nd February called?
28 What was Boyz II Men's first UK Top Ten hit?
29 Bragi was the Norse god of what?
30 Grilse, Alevins and Kelts are all forms of what?

Quiz 159 Hobbies 1

Answers - see page 628

LEVEL 3

1   Who owns the Sydney Harbour Casino?

2   Which eating house did Ruthie Rogers found?

3   What was the name of the board game launched by Terry Venables?

4   1949 saw what innovation in the game of badminton?

5   Who founded the Harlem Globetrotters?

6   How many tiles are there in a game of mah-jong?

7   Who designs clothes for younger people under the Emporio label?

8   What type of art was known as Jugenstil in Germany?

9   How long is the rope in water skiing?

10   In the early days of cinema how long would a 'two reeler' last?

11   Serigraphy is also known as what?

12   What name is given to the style of skiing on a single broad ski?

13   Which type of outdoor spectacular was created by Paul Houdin and first shown at the Chateau de Chambord in 1952?

14   Which craft takes its name from the Arabic for 'striped cloth'?

15   Where did canasta originate?

16   What are the two winning numbers made with two dice in craps?

17   Who opened Les Quat' Saisons in 1977?

18   If you follow FINA rules which sport do you practise?

19   How many dominoes are there in a double six set?

20   Southampton boast of having the first sports area of what type in the country?

21   Which sport would interest you if you followed the work of the ACS?

22   Ellem in Scotland is the oldest club of what type?

23   In the Role-Playing Game known as D&D, what does the second D stand for?

24   Where do cycle races called criteriums take place?

25   If you spent your leisure time in a sulky where would you. be?

26   If you were spelunking in the US what would you be doing?

27   In 1976 the NBA and the ABA merged in which sport?

28   In sepek takrow you can hit the ball with any part of the body except which?

29   General Choi Hong Hi is responsible for the development of which martial art?

30   What position does the canoeist adopt in Canadian canoeing?

1   Who composed the opera The Bartered Bride?
2   Who won the 1972 Olympic pentathlon title?
3   In the film The Baltimore Bullet which game was featured?
4   How old was Henry III when he became King?
5   Who said, "I look upon the world as my parish"?
6   In which performing art was Beryl Grey famous?
7   Where in Egypt did Cleopatra's needle originally stand?
8   The Silk Road ancient trade route ran between China and where?
9   Micky Finn played bongos in which pop group?
10 Whose only UK Top Ten Hit was Mad Passionate Love from 1958?
11 Deuteroscopy is the common name for what?
12 Which actor links Awakenings, Toys and Cadillac Man?
13 Who was the first admiral to pass through the Northwest Passage?
14 Who is the elder – Nicholas Lyndhurst or Gary Lineker?
15 Daniel Ortega was President of which country from 1981-1990?
16 Where was the Encyclopaedia Britannica first published?
17 Why is Chinge Hall in Lancashire famous?
18 What name is given to the Runic alphabet?
19 What are affected by nystagmus?
20 What was Bobby Brown's first UK Top Ten hit?
21 Where were Frost Fairs held in London until 1831?
22 Which illustrator created the girls of St Trinians?
23 Where were the Russians defeated by the Germans from 26-30th August 1914?
24 Which creature is represented in the year the Chinese call 'ma'?
25 In which decade was pop superstar Mick Hucknall born?
26 Crockford's is a register of what?
27 Italy and Germany formed a military alliance in 1939 called what?
28 Who won the Best Director Oscar in 1992 for Unforgiven?
29 What is Dusty Springfield's real name?
30 What's the English name of the constellation Vulpecula?

1 In whose stately home was the Tarzan film Greystoke filmed?

2 What was Sharon Stone's first film, in 1980?

3 Uncle Buck was the debut of which movie star?

4 May Day was the Bond girl in which film?

5 What was the occupation of Madame Sousatzka in the Shirley Maclaine film?

6 Who had a lead role in the movie version of Rising Damp who wasn't in the TV sitcom?

7 Who did Alan Rickman play in Die Hard?

8 Who are the two letter writers in 84 Charing Cross Road?

9 Which son of a pop star appears as Jackson's friend in Moonwalker?

10 In which film did Jack Nicholson say the catchphrase "Here's Johnny"?

11 Who played Mrs La Motta in Raging Bull?

12 Which film all but bankrupted United Artist in 1980?

13 Which ailing actor's voice was dubbed by Rich Little in Curse of the Pink Panther?

14 Who played Meryl Streep's eccentric friend in Plenty?

15 Who won an Oscar for his first major role in 1982?

16 Who was Glenn Close's character in Dangerous Liaisons?

17 Which film included the song It Might Be You?

18 Who was the only Cambodian Oscar winner of the 80s?

19 Who was the only winner of an Oscar and a BAFTA for Platoon?

20 Who was nominated as Best Supporting Actress for The Color Purple?

21 In the film A Royal Love Story, who played Princess Diana?

22 The Color of Money recreated the character from which film?

23 Which father and son appeared in Wall Street?

24 Which role did Kevin Kline play in A Fish Called Wanda?

25 Which. presidential candidate's cousin won an Oscar for Moonstruck?

26 Apart from Music and Visual Effects, which other Oscar did E.T. win?

27 Who directed Psycho III?

28 Whose music features on the soundtrack of When Harry Met Sally?

29 Whose novel was Warren Beatty's Reds based on?

30 Who was the aerobics instructor in Perfect?

1 Who set up the production company Ardent?

2 Which duo first presented the breakfast show on GMTV?

3 Who appeared in a Tesco ad chasing chickens around France?

4 Who tore up a picture of the Pope on US TV in 1993?

5 Which character said, "You might very well think that, but I couldn't possibly comment"?

6 Who originally appeared in cabaret as the Menopause Sisters?

7 Who had a small role in Bergerac before starring in Heat and Dust?

8 Which play told of Falklands casualty Robert Lawrence?

9 How is comedian Chris Collins better known?

10 Who designed the Blue Peter logo?

11 For which two series did Emma Thompson win best actress BAFTAs two years in succession?

12 Who duetted with Cher on I Got You Babe in 1994?

13 Which Hollywood actress played Lola Lasagne in Batman?

14 Who was Frank Ormand, the Pretzel man in The Simpsons?

15 What was the prison chief called in The Governor?

16 Which British entrepreneur once guested on Friends?

17 Who played Joanna in Dr Who and was the wife of a future Doctor?

18 Who said to Lord Archer, "There's no beginning to your talents, Jeffrey"?

19 Which pop band was Dani Behr a member of before her TV career?

20 What was Gladiator Warrior's real name?

21 Who wrote and presented a History of the Tory Party?

22 Who replaced Craig McLachlan as Ed in Bugs?

23 Which brothers were played by the McGanns in The Hanging Gale?

24 Which TV company was founded by Peter Cadbury?

25 Who wrote the controversial series The Lakes?

26 In which series did Eileen Downey find fame?

27 Ab Fab's Edina was based on which PR lady?

28 Who became narrator for Thomas The Tank Engine in the US in '98?

29 Who played Rhett Butler in the TV sequel to Gone With the Wind?

30 A comedy writing award was introduced in 1998 in whose memory?

1 Which Saint claimed to have seen the Loch Ness monster in the 6th century?
2 What was Brotherhood of Man's first UK Top Ten hit?
3 In which county did the battle of Edgehill take place?
4 Who directed the films Superman II and Juggernaut?
5 In which decade was TV presenter Eamonn Holmes born?
6 Which theatre foundations were discovered in London in 1988?
7 Who was lead in the films Man of the Moment and The Square Peg?
8 Which ruler led the 7th and 8th Crusades?
9 Which actor won Best Actor Oscar for On Golden Pond aged 76?
10 How many countries surround Botswana?
11 Barbara Trentham was the second wife of which English comic?
12 What is Bordeaux Mixture a blend of?
13 Which Spanish artist painted The Persistence of Memory?
14 Which military group's HQ is at Aubagne near Marseilles?
15 What is the middle name of knighted cricketer Gary Sobers?
16 What was Greta Garbo's last film?
17 The WWSU is the governing body of which sport?
18 What mass is measured in Criths?
19 In which city is the Verrazano Narrows Bridge?
20 Which profession did George Washington start out in?
21 Who was the leading lady in the films McLintock and Rio Grande?
22 Which African country won the 1996 Olympics gold medal for soccer?
23 What was the title of the only UK Top Ten hit for James Brown?
24 Who is the elder – Joanna Lumley or Maureen Lipman?
25 What does the abbreviation 'fz' mean in music?
26 Spaniard Francisco Pizarro founded which city?
27 When was the magazine Cosmopolitan first published?
28 Which city was the first to erect a monument to Lord Nelson in Britain?
29 What was Angel Beast an old type of?
30 What is the county emblem of Lincolnshire?

Answers

Euro Tour (See Quiz 164)
1 Italy. 2 Romania. 3 Tbilisi. 4 Vienna. 5 Gulf of Riga. 6 Brussels.
7 Austria. 8 Koper. 9 Italy. 10 Baltic. 11 Netherlands. 12 9 million.
13 Gulf of Finland. 14 Great Britain. 15 Mount Etna and Stromboli.
16 Grande Dizence in Switzerland. 17 Finland. 18 London. 19 Germany.
20 Liechtenstein. 21 Ormeli in Norway. 22 Belarus. 23 Assisi in Central
Italy. 24 Germany. 25 Italy. 26 Roman Catholic. 27 Corfu. 28 Tourism and
tobacco. 29 Spain. 30 Norway.

1 Which country is Europe's largest wine producer?
2 Tarom Airlines are based in which country?
3 What is the capital of Georgia?
4 Which capital is further north – Budapest or Vienna?
5 Which Gulf is to the west of Estonia and Latvia?
6 Where is the news agency Centre d'Information Presse based?
7 In which country is Kranebitten International airport?
8 What is the chief port of Slovenia?
9 The Pelagian islands belong to which European country?
10 Bornholm is an island in which Sea?
11 Hoge Veluwe National Park is in which country?
12 To the nearest million, what was the population of Moscow in 1995?
13 St Petersburg is at the head of which gulf?
14 What is the largest island in Europe?
15 Which two Italian volcanoes erupted in 1994?
16 What is the world's highest dam?
17 Which country is called Suomen Tasavalta in its own language?
18 Which capital is further north - Berlin or London?
19 Aero Lloyd Airlines are based in which country?
20 Which European country has the highest life expectancy for men and women?
21 What is the highest waterfall in Europe?
22 Brest is a major town in which country other than France?
23 In which town did an earthquake claim nine lives in 1997?
24 In which country is the city of Bochum?
25 To which country do the islands of Stromboli and Vulcano belong?
26 What is the prominent religion of Lithuania?
27 Which is the northernmost and second largest of the Ionian islands?
28 What are Andorra's two main industries?
29 In which country is Sondica International airport?
30 Hardangervidda National Park is in which country?

1   What is No in Japan?
2   Who is the elder – David Mellor or Andrew Lloyd Webber?
3   What is a tulwar?
4   Who, with Paul McCartney, composed the Liverpool Oratorio?
5   What were Charles Dickens' two middle names?
6   Which group's only UK Top Ten hit was Word Up from 1986?
7   In which city is Fettes College?
8   Where was the cloth used to make duffle coats first made?
9   On May 21st, 1927, who landed at Le Bourget airport?
10 Where did Joseph of Arimathea's staff take root and bud, in legend?
11 Which song did Frank Sinatra feature in the film Robin And The Seven Hoods?
12 What is a skimmer to an American?
13 What name is given to the Greek letter that is the equivalent of letter O?
14 Which gulf is between the heel and sole of Italy?
15 Which famous leader brought an end to the Pharaohs in Egypt?
16 Which HG Wells' novel is the musical Half a Sixpence based on?
17 To ten years, when was the magazine The Economist founded?
18 What is the final event in a Decathlon?
19 How many unions merged in 1993 to form UNISON?
20 What was Mariah Carey's first UK Top Ten hit?
21 What was Charles De Gaulle's wife known as?
22 Who was the first wicket keeper to claim 50 stumping victims in Tests?
23 Which character was Dustin Hoffman in the film Midnight Cowboy?
24 On which island is Bungee jumping said to have originated?
25 What were the Christian names of the showman Barnum?
26 In mythology what was the special power of Perseus' helmet?
27 Whose one and only hit was Little Things Mean A Lot in 1954?
28 Which monarch introduced the sedan chair into England?
29 What physical property lets a needle float on water?
30 Whom did Dido, the Queen of Carthage, love?

Answers - see page 633

1   Along with Archaeology, which subject did Prince Edward read at Cambridge?
2   Who became the Queen's Private Secretary in 1990?
3   What was Princess Michael of Kent's maiden name?
4   Who was the third great grandson of the Queen Mother's?
5   Which Royal had a financial interest in a chain of hamburger restaurants called Deal?
6   Who was the first unmarried Royal to announce her pregnancy in 1989?
7   Which school was attended by Prince Charles and Kerry Packer?
8   What did Peter Phillips study at Exeter University?
9   Who was portrayed as a school dinner lady on Spitting Image?
10 At whose home did Prince Andrew propose to Sarah Ferguson?
11 Who sang a Handel aria at Charles and Diana's wedding?
12 In a 16th birthday interview what type of music did Prince William say he preferred?
13 Who has the car registration plate K7?
14 Who was the first Royal bride to include her own family's coat of arms on her marital coat of arms?
15 Who retained the number plate 3 GXM for a new Rolls in 1972?
16 How many Princesses of Wales were there before Diana?
17 Who turned up with Pamela Stephenson at Annabel's on Prince Andrew's stag night dressed as police officers?
18 At which kindergarten did Diana Spencer work?
19 When did Prince Philip become Duke of Edinburgh?
20 The Duchess of Windsor employed a make up artist daily from which cosmetics house?
21 What is Princess Margaret's house on Mustique called?
22 Who did Diana's make up on her wedding day?
23 What was Diana's nickname for Camilla?
24 Who delivered Prince William?
25 What was William and Harry's first boarding school?
26 Why did the Queen change the Birthday Parade from Thursday to Saturday?
27 What part did Lady Penelope and St David play at Charles and Diana's wedding?
28 To which reporter did Diana admit her marriage was "a bit crowded"?
29 What were Prince Philip's parents called?
30 What was Prince William's first public duty?

Answers

Pot Luck 81 (See Quiz 165)
1 A type of theatre. 2 Lord Lloyd Webber. 3 A sword. 4 Carl Davis. 5 John Huffham. 6 Cameo. 7 Edinburgh. 8 Duffel in Belgium. 9 Charles Lindbergh. 10 Glastonbury. 11 My Kind Of Town. 12 A straw hat. 13 Omicron. 14 Gulf of Taranto. 15 Alexander the Great. 16 Kipps. 17 1843. 18 1500 metres. 19 Three. 20 Vision of Love. 21 Tante Yvonne. 22 Bert Oldfield (Australia). 23 Ratso Rizzo. 24 Pentecost Island. 25 Phileas Taylor. 26 Made him invisible. 27 Kitty Kallen. 28 James I. 29 Surface tension. 30 Aeneas.

1 The discovery of which plot led to the death of Mary, Queen of Scots?

2 What was Dina Carroll's first UK Top Ten hit?

3 Which Duke commanded the English troops at Culloden?

4 Which letter is one dot and one dash in Morse Code?

5 Which Minister was murdered in 1990 outside his home by an IRA bomb?

6 Which Battle was the first in the Hundred Years War?

7 What is served at a Thyestean feast?

8 Who wrote Goodbye to All That?

9 Who commanded the winning side at the Battle of Marathon?

10 Which eccentric artist is the central character in The Horse's Mouth?

11 Who is the elder – Desmond Lynam or Sir Paul McCartney?

12 In which year did Francis Drake complete the circumnavigation of the world?

13 How do you travel on the Devizes-Westminster race?

14 How old were both Anne Boleyn and Mrs Beeton when they died?

15 Who composed Easter Parade?

16 Which country gained independence in 1908 from Turkey?

17 What is the opening track on the Verve's Urban Hymns?

18 Which hymn was written by Augustus Toplady after sheltering from a storm?

19 In which decade was William Hague born?

20 Who wrote Dr Johnson's biography?

21 Who is the only English monarch to have won a flat race as a jockey?

22 Mary II died of which disease at the age of 32?

23 Whose only UK hit was Patches?

24 What is the correct name for the Ink blot test?

25 Which drill gets women and children into lifeboats first?

26 Which greyhound was the first to win the Greyhound Derby twice?

27 The Sea of Marmara lies between the Bosporus and what?

28 Who designed The Monument in London?

29 Which scale other than the Richter scale measures earthquakes?

30 Who first charted in the UK with Always On My Mind?

1 What was the first UK No 1 in which the title posed a question?

2 Which traditional song provided instrumental and vocal versions that charted for 94 weeks?

3 What was Roy Orbison's final chart topper from 1964?

4 Which 'Women' was the longest ever at No 1 for the Rolling Stones?

5 Graham Gouldman and Eric Stewart wrote which 70s classic No 1?

6 Which 1950s vocalist began singing with the Tony Pastor band?

7 What are the first three words of San Francisco?

8 How were the birds singing in the original title of the No 1 Why Do Fools Fall In Love?

9 Which 1986 No 1 was a cover of a 1970 No 1?

10 Which artist took over the title of the youngest No 1 hitmaker in 1972?

11 What is Ray Charles only UK No 1?

12 Which Canadian was next to No 1 after Paul Anka?

13 Which hit gave producer Norrie Paramour his 27th and final No 1?

14 Emile Ford shared his first week at No 1 with which artist?

15 Which Chuck Berry hit was No 1 at the same time in the UK and US?

16 Steve Miller's The Joker hit No 1 in 1990 but when was it recorded?

17 Which hit gave The Searchers their second No 1?

18 Who had a No 1 with the original version of Young Love?

19 Who wrote and produced Nancy Sinatra's These Boots Are Made For Walking?

20 Which John Leyton hit was covered in 1985 by Bronski Beat and Marc Almond?

21 Whose only UK hit was Here Comes Summer?

22 Who wrote See My Baby Jive?

23 What film theme gave Danny Williams his only No 1 in 1961?

24 What was the first instrumental No 1 after the Shadows Foot Tapper?

25 What was the Kinks' third and final No 1 hit in the summer of 1966?

26 What was the only Cliff Richard & the Shadows No 1 double-A-side?

27 Which 1968 No 1 was revived in the.film Good Morning Vietnam?

28 What was Wonderful in the Shadows hit which stayed longest at No 1?

29 Which 1971 No 1 was re-released in 1992 as a tribute to its singer?

30 What was Cilla Black's only US Top 40 hit?

1 Which language do the words kiosk, tulip and caviar come from?
2 Whose Drum can be seen at Buckland Abbey in Devon?
3 Where is the Queen's bank account?
4 What do the initials stand for in the name of ghost story writer M.R. James?
5 Which actor played Major Gowen in Fawlty Towers?
6 In which decade was Lloyd Grossman born?
7 Whose hymn book was first published in 1873?
8 A durmast is a variety of what?
9 Whose only UK Top Ten Hit was Blue Is The Colour from 1972?
10 Which Europeans discovered Lake Tanganyika in 1858?
11 Who said, "I never hated a man enough to give him his diamonds back"?
12 Achulophobia is the fear of what?
13 Which brass instrument is wrapped around the player's body?
14 What colour appears with white and green on the Afghanistan flag?
15 In which US state was there a nuclear accident at Three Mile Island in 1979?
16 Who was the first woman to swim the English Channel in 1926?
17 What is the capital of Angola?
18 Where were a set of rules for football drawn up in 1848?
19 What is indium?
20 Who is the elder – Paul Merton or Richard Madeley?
21 Who lived at No. 1, London?
22 Where are the Aventine, Viminal and Quirinal Hills?
23 What nationality was Sir Robert Helpmann?
24 What is a clerihew?
25 To 10 miles, how far was Piper Alpha off Wick when it exploded?
26 In which European country is the province of Brabant?
27 Where, in the Keats' poem, did Ruth stand "in tears"?
28 What was David Cassidy's first UK Top Ten hit?
29 Where did Kun's Red Terror exist in 1919?
30 Who, in 43 AD, led the resistance against the Romans?

Answers

Olympics (See Quiz 170)
1 Alberto Juantorena. 2 Ice hockey. 3 Yachting. 4 St Moritz. 5 Bars and beam. 6 Michael Johnson. 7 Long jump. 8 Al Oerter. 9 Five. 10 Two. 11 Retained 10,000m and won 5,000m and marathon. 12 Evander Holyfield. 13 Lake Lanier. 14 Simone Jacobs. 15 Michelle Smith. 16 Izzy. 17 Seoul. 18 Allan Wells. 19 Spain. 20 Soling. 21 Poland's Renata Mauer. 22 Tim Henman & Chris Broad. 23 Jayne Torvill. 24 4 x 400m relay. 25 1900. 26 Quarantine laws. 27 Denise Lewis. 28 Montreal. 29 Robin Cousins. 30 Japan.

LEVEL 3

1   Who won 400m and 800m gold at the '76 Olympics?

2   At which sport did future tennis star Drobny win a medal in 1948?

3   Windsurfing is included in the Olympics as part of which sport's events?

4   Where were the Winter Olympics held in 1928 and 1948?

5   On which apparatus did Nadia Comaneci score perfect tens in 1976?

6   Who was the first man to win Olympic gold at 200m and 400m?

7   In which event did Carl Lewis win his ninth and final gold medal?

8   Who won the first of four discus golds in Melbourne in 1956?

9   How many silver medals did skier Raisa Smetanina win with her four golds and one bronze?

10   How many gold medals did Mark Spitz win in his first Olympics?

11   Which amazing treble did Emil Zatopek achieve at the 1952 Games?

12   Who carried the torch into the stadium at the Atlanta games?

13   On which lake did Steve Redgrave win his record breaking fourth gold medal?

14   Who was the only British woman sprinter to compete in all Olympics between 1984 and 1996?

15   Under what name did Mrs Erik de Bruin win gold at Atlanta?

16   What was the name of the Olympic mascot in Atlanta?

17   Where did Linford Christie run his first Olympic race?

18   Who was the oldest Olympic 100m champion when he won in 1980?

19   Who won women's gold in hockey in Barcelona?

20   Which is the only Olympic yachting event for three person crews?

21   Who won the first medal at the Atlanta games?

22   Who won Britain's first tennis medal since 1924 in Atlanta?

23   Who replaced her partner Michael Hutchinson before winning gold in 1984?

24   Other than 400m hurdles for which event did Sally Gunnell win a medal in Barcelona?

25   In which year did women first complete in the Olympics?

26   Why were equestrian event held in Sweden in 1956 when the Games were held in Australia?

27   Who was Britain's only female medallist at the Atlanta games?

28   Where did Daley Thompson compete in his first Olympics?

29   Which son of a former Millwall goalie won gold in the USA in 1980?

30   What was the first Asian country to have stage the Winter Olympics?

1 Who did the Spice Girls sack as their manager in early 1998?
2 What is a porbeagle?
3 Which bandleader married both Ava Gardner and Lana Turner?
4 What was the family name of artists Jacopo and his sons Gentile and Giovanni?
5 Scottish solicitor William Mitchell drew up the rules for which sport?
6 Which group had a 70s hit with Kiss You All Over?
7 Who was Prince Philip's mother?
8 What two colours go with black and yellow in printing's four-colour process?
9 What did Diana Princess of Wales describe as "a shameful friend"?
10 Who is the elder – Robin Cook or David Blunkett?
11 What was Bad Manners' first UK Top Ten hit?
12 What is a belvedere?
13 In which month is the feast day of St Cuthbert?
14 In which country are the mountains called the Stirling Range?
15 What is tufa?
16 Which soccer club has been managed by both Jimmy Armfield and Brian Clough?
17 Whose one and only hit was Float On in 1977?
18 Who was the first Prime Minister of Israel?
19 Where is New York's Metropolitan Museum of Art?
20 In what year did the London Stock Exchange go computerised?
21 What is a gibus?
22 Who was the first man to hold the post of Astronomer Royal?
23 In which decade was Lord Charles Spencer Churchill born?
24 Who founded the record label Anxious Records?
25 Which Michelangelo statue is in Florence?
26 Vera Caslavska was Olympic and World Champion in which sport?
27 In which year was Wimbledon first televised?
28 Where was the first woman MP to enter the Commons born?
29 Who ceased to be queen when Victoria became queen?
30 What do you do if you siffle?

1 What is the range of numbers on a roulette wheel?

2 Where would you watch FC Jazz and what would they be doing?

3 FIDE is the governing body of which game?

4 If you were watching the Queen's horse race, what colour sleeves would the jockey have?

5 In athletics how much does a hammer weigh?

6 Where is the Guggenheim Museum?

7 In abseiling what are karabiners?

8 Who first appeared in a strip cartoon 'in the Land of the Soviets'?

9 Which UK tourist attraction is on the site of an 8th century fortress?

10 Where in Normandy would you visit Monet's garden?

11 If you collected Bizarre pottery whose work would you have?

12 Paintball is a simulation of what?

13 How many zones does an archery target have?

14 In which London street was the first artificial ice rink opened?

15 In shinty what is the curved stick called?

16 Which radio star appeared in films such as The Wrong Box?

17 In which sport does a match last for a certain number of heads?

18 John Gold was the owner of which night club for over 30 years?

19 Which activity has two main types, tomiki and uyeshiba?

20 How many more people are there in an outer handball team than there are in an indoor one?

21 John Tomlinson is credited with starting which hobby?

22 Which form of flying was perfected by Francis Rogallo in the 70s?

23 In which mountains is the Brockenbahn steam railway?

24 Which restaurateur owned Daphne's and founded The Collection?

25 In cyclocross what do you do with your bike when you're not riding it?

26 Where is the Liseberg theme park?

27 Who opened the Braeval restaurant in Scotland in 1986?

28 In which activity do you 'dive for the horizon'?

29 Wing Chun is a popular form of which art?

30 In which Botanic Gardens was the tulip first introduced in 1594?

1   Bernard Webb was a pseudonym used by which famous song writer?
2   In which country is the royal family the House of Bernadotte?
3   Acrophobia is the fear of what?
4   In which country is the city of Abidjan?
5   What was the only No 1 UK hit for the Clash?
6   What colour is the circle on the Bangladesh flag?
7   A Brazilian Huntsman is a type of what?
8   Who played director Ed Wood in the 1994 film biography?
9   A Nutmegger is an inhabitant of which American state?
10 In which decade did South Africa resign from the Commonwealth?
11 How many locks are there on the Suez Canal?
12 What was the name of Vivienne Westwood's second shop opened in '82?
13 Who composed Rhapsody on a Theme of Paganini for Piano?
14 What was the number of the British Armoured Division nicknamed the 'Desert Rats'?
15 In which year did James Cook land at Botany Bay, Australia?
16 What is the correct form of address to begin a letter to a Baron?
17 In snooker in which year did the Lada Classic have two champions?
18 Who is the elder – Caroline Quentin or Linda Robson?
19 What was Neneh Cherry's first UK Top Ten hit?
20 What was the Christian name of aeroplane manufacturer Mr Boeing?
21 In which European country are the provinces of Sofiya and Burgas?
22 What size is A4 paper in millimetres?
23 Australia hosted the 1956 Olympics but equestrian events were held in which other country?
24 In which decade was Gary Glitter born?
25 Which artist painted The Watering Place in 1777?
26 What are the initials G.B.E an abbreviation of?
27 Who wrote the novel The Last Testament of Oscar Wilde in 1983?
28 Which magazine has been guest edited by Damien Hirst?
29 Clarence House was built for which monarch when he was still Duke of Clarence?
30 What is the capital of Bahrain?

1   Who played Mike Channel in KYTV?
2   Who is the smallest Teletubby?
3   Who found fame as Egg in This Life?
4   Who first hosted The Radio Times Show on Sky?
5   Who is the largest Teletubby?
6   Where did the first outside broadcast on Grandstand come from?
7   Who is Postman Pat's wife?
8   In which docu soap did Emma Boundy find fame?
9   Which Casualty character played a midwife in Spice World?
10 Which two words has Nicole uttered to advertise Renault?
11 What was the name of Wayne Sleep's 80s TV show which he later adapted for the stage?
12 Which TV presenter made the cake when Jemima Goldsmith married Imran Khan?
13 What was Michael Barrymore's talent spotting TV show called?
14 Who replaced Anneka Rice on Carlton's Capital Woman?
15 What was the name of the David Furnish directed documentary about Elton John?
16 Who played the Englishwoman in Parnell and the Englishwoman?
17 In which series did Lynda La Plante introduce Dolly Rawlings?
18 Who was the first woman presenter of Grandstand?
19 Who. replaced Richard Baker as the presenter of the Proms?
20 Who presented Channel 4's religious series Canterbury Tales?
21 How is TV playwright Romana Barrack better known?
22 In which show was Harry S Truman the sheriff?
23 In which town would you read The Daily Slate?
24 The music from Raging Bull was used to advertise which lager?
25 Whose magic ray transformed Supergran?
26 Who had a pet octopus called Aristotle?
27 Who played the title role in Alan Bleasdale's The Monocled Mutineer?
28 Anthea Turner was replaced at GMTV by whom?
29 Where did the Musters live?
30 On a Friday, on children's TV who were Jenny & Willy?

1 In which decade was actor John Cleese born?
2 After which American General were sideburns named?
3 Freetown is the capital of which country?
4 Who played Test cricket aged 52 years 165 days?
5 Who directed the 1967 film The Dirty Dozen?
6 What is the main language of Angola?
7 What happened to the Olympic flame during the 1976 games?
8 Hartford is the capital of which American State?
9 Which 18th Century artist painted Peasant Girl Gathering Sticks ?
10 To five years, when was the News Of The World founded?
11 What, other than Amazing Grace, was a top ten hit for Judy Collins?
12 A fear of the cold is known as what?
13 In which county is the Rude Man of Cerne?
14 Which country has the dalasi as its currency?
15 What was done in an apodyterium?
16 Emperor Nero was the adopted son of which other emperor?
17 What is the international car index mark for a car from Libya?
18 The spice annatto is made from which part of a plant?
19 Other than Buckingham Palace, which venue sees the daily Changing of the Guard?
20 What is the administrative centre for the Scottish Western Isles?
21 What was the Commodores' first UK Top Ten hit?
22 Who is the elder – George Michael or Anthea Turner?
23 Painter Georges Seurat was born, died and worked in which city?
24 What name is given to elements with atomic numbers 93 to 112?
25 What two colours appear with yellow on the Cameroon flag?
26 Who was the first woman to qualify for the Indy 500 motor race?
27 Which Latin phrase means, 'Let the buyer beware'?
28 In which year did women gain the vote in Switzerland?
29 In which country is the city of Bamako?
30 As a child Jonathan Ross appeared in an ad for which food product?

1   Which Barry Levinson film was used to satirise the US presidency during the Lewinsky crisis?
2   Who is the subject of Love is the Devil?
3   Which tough guy directed Christmas in Connecticut?
4   Who died during the filming of Dark Blood in 1993?
5   Which war is depicted in Land and Freedom?
6   Who was Lyon Gaultier in AWOL?
7   In which film did Tom Hanks make his directorial debut?
8   Which film's initial title was $3,000?
9   Who or what is Andre in the film of the same name?
10   Who was Leonardo DiCaprio's mother in This Boy's Life?
11   Who is Leslie Nielsen in the Naked Gun films?
12   What is Jim Carrey's job before he finds the mask in the hit movie?
13   Who was Tinkerbell when Spielberg met JM Barrie?
14   Who was the butler in Princess Caraboo?
15   What was director Tony Richardson's final film?
16   Which US presidents does Gump meet in Forrest Gump?
17   Who was the voice of Mufasa in The Lion King?
18   Muriel is a fan of which band in Muriel's Wedding?
19   Who did Woody Allen cast as his ex wife in Deconstructing Harry?
20   What was Hugh Grant's first Hollywood movie?
21   Who was Oscar winning best screen writer for Sense and Sensibility?
22   Who was John Goodman's mother in law in The Flintstones?
23   What is Macaulay Culkin's full name in the Home Alone movies?
24   Who designed The Riddler's costume in Batman Forever?
25   In which movie did Tom Jones sing It's Not Unusual?
26   In which film did Kate Winslet have her first nude scene?
27   Who played rat catcher Caesar in Mousehunt?
28   Who was the author in The Muppet Christmas Carol?
29   Which film was Gary Oldman's directorial debut?
30   In which comic did Sylvester Stallone's '95 futuristic police character appear?

1   What is another name for the North American nightjar?

2   Where is the world's greatest discharger of radioactive nuclear waste?

3   How is the disease trypanosomiasis also known?

4   What is meant by a haemorrhage which is 'occult'?

5   Which protein is present in a hair?

6   What does it mean if a cell is haploid?

7   In addition to tea and coffee where is caffeine found?

8   Where is the flexor carpi radialis?

9   What is an erythrocyte?

10   How is the sand hopper also known?

11   Guano is used as fertiliser but what is it made from?

12   Cranes are found on all continents except which two?

13   What is an alternative name for leptospirosis?

14   Carragheen is a type of what?

15   Where is a caterpillar's spinneret?

16   Which bird flies highest?

17   What is an insect's Malpighian tubes?

18   How does a mamba differ from a cobra?

19   Which part of the brain controls muscular movements, balance and co-ordination?

20   Which bird can swim as fast as a seal?

21   An urodele is another name for which reptile?

22   Which bird builds the largest nest?

23   The world's largest spider is named after which Biblical character?

24   What is a bird's furcula?

25   Disulfiram is used in the treatment of what?

26   What is a hairstreak?

27   On which island would you find the bee hummingbird?

28   Which bird produces the largest egg in relation to its body size?

29   Why should you avoid a chigger?

30   How many hearts does an earthworm have?

1   Who was the first person to receive a heart transplant?
2   In which European country are the counties of Viborg and Aarhus?
3   Who composed the music for the ballet The Wooden Prince?
4   Who played the lead role in the film Two A Penny?
5   Which country has the lek as its unit of currency?
6   Who was Vice President when Ronald Reagan was President?
7   Which animal head represents the Hindu god Ganesa?
8   Who is the elder – Julie Walters or Twiggy?
9   In which country is the city of Adana?
10 Which type of fish gives its name to a particular patterning of the sky?
11 In which year did Roy Plomley last present Desert Island Discs?
12 The first men's hockey club in England was founded in which London suburb?
13 Which bird stands in the centre of the national flag of Dominica?
14 In which decade was Michael Gambon born?
15 What was Randy Crawford's first UK Top Ten hit?
16 What are the initials BSE an abbreviation of?
17 How many seconds are there in half a day?
18 What was the nationality of the astronomer Nicolaus Copernicus?
19 Geri Halliwell became a UN ambassador specialising in what?
20 Who wrote the novels London Fields and Time's Arrow?
21 How is the letter S formed in Morse Code?
22 Who is the patron Saint of television?
23 Which public figure was shot dead by John Bellingham?
24 Bandleader Quincy Jones chiefly plays which instrument?
25 Changed in 1868 what was the former name of Tokyo?
26 What do you suffer from if you have acromegaly?
27 The yacht Black Magic won the America's Cup for which country?
28 A Hoosier is an inhabitant in which American state?
29 Who had hits with Stool Pigeon and I'm A Wonderful Thing, Baby?
30 Haphephobia is the fear of what?

Answers

Living World (See Quiz 177)
1   Whippoorwill. 2   Sellafield. 3   Sleeping sickness. 4   Internal. 5   Keratin.
6   Single set of chromosomes. 7   Kola nuts. 8   Human's forearm. 9   Red blood
cell. 10   Beachflea. 11   Bird droppings. 12   South America & Antarctica.
13   Weil's disease. 14   Seaweed. 15   Head. 16   Ruppell's vulture.
17   Excretory organs. 18   Not hooded. 19   Cerebellum. 20   Penguin.
21   Salamander. 22   Male malle fowl. 23   Goliath. 24   Wishbone.
25   Alcoholism. 26   Butterfly. 27   Cuba. 28   Kiwi. 29   Harvest mite
(which bites). 30   Ten.

1 Who was known as the 'father of the Soviet H-bomb'?
2 In which shipyards did Lech Walesa work before becoming Polish president?
3 Terry Waite was the envoy of which Archbishop of Canterbury when he was kidnapped?
4 Who founded the Police Memorial Trust after PC Yvonne Fletcher's death?
5 Who was the first US Ambassador in London?
6 Who recorded with the Hot Five and the Hot Seven in the 1920s?
7 Who became the youngest ever member of the GLC in 1969?
8 Who was the 20th Prince of Wales?
9 Who succeeded Len Murray as TUC general secretary in 1984?
10 Who was the first Archbishop of Canterbury to be appointed by the Church Crown Appointments Commission?
11 Which children's author was Russian correspondent for the Daily News during WWI and the Revolution?
12 Which advocate of black rights left the US to live in England in the late 50s?
13 Who was the last British monarch to refuse royal assent of a Bill through Parliament?
14 Who was UK Deputy PM between 1942 and 1945?
15 Which UK PM was responsible for the purchase of US Polaris missiles?
16 Who did Douglas Hurd replace as Foreign Secretary in 1989?
17 Who became President of the ANC in 1997?
18 Which Chancellor of the Exchequer introduced old age pensions?
19 Which Fine Gael candidate did Mary McAleese defeat in the 1997 election for Irish President?
20 Which invention improved on Alexander Cummings invention a century earlier?
21 What was Mikhail Gorbachev's wife called?
22 Who founded Standard Oil in 1870?
23 How was entrepreneur Roland Fuhrhop better known?
24 Which son of Findlaech was killed at Lumphanan?
25 Who was the first Archbishop of Canterbury?
26 Which former Enfield MP has the middle names Denzil Xavier?
27 The name of which UK PM was Ronald Reagan's middle name?
28 Who was shot at a rally in the US in 1972 while campaigning for the Democrats?
29 Which Baron began a continental pigeon post in 1849?
30 Who was German foreign minister during WWII?

1 The spice cayenne is made from which part of a plant?
2 Lincoln is the capital of which US state?
3 What was the only UK Top Ten hit from 1992 for Crowded House?
4 What was special about Robert Pershing Wadlow?
5 How many singles had Take That released before their first No 1 Pray?
6 What is the international car index mark for a car from Botswana?
7 In which decade was Sir David Frost born?
8 Who was the Roman God of fire?
9 What is the administrative centre for the Welsh county of Clwyd?
10 Mathematically speaking, what is an ALU?
11 In the 1920s who wrote The Land That Time Forgot?
12 How many stripes are on the national flag of Estonia?
13 Who is the only British prime minister to have been born outside the UK?
14 Which artist painted Le Jardinier in 1906?
15 In which year was the Battle of Edgehill?
16 Who directed the 1990 film Dick Tracy?
17 A Chief Constable is responsible for which uniformed force other than the police?
18 Lusaka is the capital of which country?
19 When does an MP apply for the Chiltern Hundreds?
20 What was Terence Trent D'Arby's first UK Top Ten hit?
21 What is the correct form of address to begin a letter to a Duke?
22 In which year did Frank Bruno first fight with Mike Tyson?
23 In which country is the city of Banjarmasin?
24 Who painted The Rake's Progress and A Bigger Splash in the 1960s?
25 Saint John Fisher was martyred during the reign of which English king?
26 Who is the elder – Lester Piggott or Michael Heseltine?
27 What's the English name of the constellation Pavo?
28 What size is A5 paper in millimetres?
29 What is the main language of the Republic of Benin?
30 Miles Davis is associated with which musical instrument?

Answers

Who Was Who? (See Quiz 179)
1 Andrei Sakharov. 2 Gdansk. 3 Robert Runcie. 4 Michael Winner.
5 John Adams. 6 Louis Armstrong. 7 Jeffrey Archer. 8 The future Edward VIII. 9 Norman Willis. 10 Robert Runcie. 11 Arthur Ransome. 12 Paul Robeson. 13 Queen Anne. 14 Attlee. 15 Macmillan. 16 John Major.
17 Thabo Mbeki. 18 Asquith. 19 Mary Bannotti. 20 Flushing toilet.
21 Raisa. 22 John D Rockefeller. 23 Tiny Rowland. 24 Macbeth. 25 St Augustine. 26 Michael Portillo. 27 Wilson. 28 George Wallace. 29 Paul Julius Reuter. 30 Joachim von Ribbentrop.

Quiz 181 Rockers

LEVEL 3

1 What was Eddie Cochrane's next UK single after Three Steps To Heaven?
2 Who played Jerry Lee Lewis in the 1989 biopic of his life?
3 How does Roger Peterson figure in rock history?
4 What was Billy Fury's first UK Top Ten hit from 1960?
5 In which city were R.E.M. formed?
6 As a teenager Morrissey ran a fan club for which group?
7 Who wrote the Holly classic It Doesn't Matter Anymore?
8 Which Elvis No 1 is the only one written solely by Lieber and Stoller?
9 Which hard-rock band did the Scottish Young brothers form in Australia?
10 Rock Around The Clock came out on which label?
11 Who did Keith Richard work for before coming a full-time Stone?
12 Which Slade hit was No 1 when US soldiers left Vietnam in 1973?
13 What did Rick Allen of Def Leppard lose in 1984?
14 What did an electrician fitting a burglar alarm find in Seattle in 1984?
15 Who first charted with Rip It Up?
16 James Jewel Osterberg took the stage under which name?
17 At which studio did the 'Million Dollar Quartet' get together in the 50s?
18 In which month did Jim Morrison die in 1971?
19 Where in London was the Sex Pistols first concert?
20 Which Dickie Valentine hit replaced Rock Around The Clock at No 1?
21 Which place used to form part of The Stranglers name?
22 Who was Francis Rossi's school mate and long time bass player in Status Quo?
23 How were the Rolling Stones billed for their first live concert?
24 Which Jerry Lee Lewis hit is the only version of the Ray Charles' classic to reach the British charts?
25 Who ran the Clovis, New Mexico studio where Buddy Holly recorded?
26 Who was Phil Lynott's father in law?
27 Who recorded the album Ma Kelly's Greasy Spoon?
28 Which Led Zeppelin drummer died in 1980?
29 Who ran the Chelsea clothes shop called Let It Rock?
30 Which 1955 Glenn Ford movie featured Rock Around The Clock?

1 Which part of the UK does not receive Channel 4?

2 In the 1980s, who wrote the novel A Twist in the Tale ?

3 What is the Parliament of Sark called?

4 What colour appears with white and red on the Faroe Islands flag?

5 In 1995 Hugh Grant got into trouble for performing a lewd act with whom?

6 What is the capital of Belize?

7 The North American Nebula is a region in which constellation?

8 What was The Damned's one and only UK Top Ten hit?

9 To the nearest thousand, how many different species of ant are there?

10 What is a golomyanka?

11 What are the initials GCVO an abbreviation of?

12 Bombay, Chartreux and Japanese bobtail are all types of what?

13 Which war is Stephen Crane's novel The Red Badge of Courage set in?

14 In which country is the city of Alma-Ata?

15 The writer Thomas Keneally comes from which country?

16 In which decade was actor Colin Firth born?

17 Prithwi Narayan Shah was the first King of which kingdom?

18 Where were William Hague, Jesse Owens and Pele brought together?

19 Homichlophobia is the fear of what?

20 Who is the elder – Patricia Hodge or Judy Finnigan?

21 Who or what was a piggin?

22 In which year was the Women's International Bowling Board formed?

23 Which media presenter left his wife Carol McGiffin in 1993?

24 Which band had a 70s UK hit with The Devil Went Down to Georgia?

25 Among which hills does Chequers lie?

26 Who composed the opera Noye's Fludde?

27 Who wrote Decline and Fall?

28 Under which name did Leslie Charles sail to pop success?

29 Which city has the oldest stock exchange in the USA?

30 What does the musical term 'giocoso' mean?

Quiz 183 Hobbies 3

Answers - see page 652

LEVEL 3

1   CIPS regulates which sport?
2   Where were Haagen-Daz ice creams first sold?
3   Where is Rick Stein's famous seafood restaurant?
4   What is octopush?
5   Where is the world's largest nightclub, Gilley's Club?
6   Who jointly opened La Gavroche in 1967?
7   Which venue was designed by George London and Henry Wise?
8   What colour might your balls be in croquet?
9   What is the nearest town to the Lightwater Valley Theme Park?
10 Which game was originally called Lexico?
11 The Toucan Terribles are prolific champions at what?
12 What is the name of England's smallest pub in Bury St Edmunds?
13 Which UK town has the longest shopping mall?
14 Where was the Grand National run during WWI?
15 Who founded the London restaurants Quaglino's and Mezzo?
16 In judo which Dan grades are awarded a red belt?
17 How many points is the gold circle on an archery target worth?
18 In 1848 William Mitchell drew up the rules to which modern game?
19 In shinty what is the opponent's goal called?
20 Which musical instrument was the creation of Charles Wheatstone?
21 Which soccer club has a fanzine called Fly Me to the Moon?
22 Who opened his first restaurant Harveys in 1987?
23 In paddle tennis what is the ball made from?
24 Which game was derived from baggataway?
25 What is important dress code at France's Domaine de Lambetran?
26 What is a gricer?
27 Where is the UK's largest amusement park?
28 What name is given to the circular target in curling?
29 What is Denmark's Rutschebahnen?
30 What do you wear on your feet in street hockey?

1 Who directed the 1992 film Bram Stoker's Dracula?
2 Robert Banks Jenkinson was British PM under which title?
3 Which cemetery is to the south of the Valley of the Kings?
4 What is Nick Faldo's middle name?
5 Which artist painted The White Horse in 1819?
6 The Lake Pontchartrain Causeway links Mandeville, Louisiana with where?
7 The spice coriander is made from which part of a plant?
8 When was The Sun newspaper founded?
9 Brown, Cornell and Dartmouth are all members of what?
10 What is the international car index mark for a car from Taiwan?
11 Neil Diamond started to train – but didn't qualify – as what?
12 Who is the elder – Liz Hurley or Yasmin Le Bon?
13 What type of musical instrument is the Japanese koto?
14 Who was Vice President when Jimmy Carter was President of USA?
15 Which British composer died on the island of Ischia in 1983?
16 Who was the last person to be executed by beheading in the UK?
17 In which decade did Agatha Christie die?
18 What was Doris Day's first UK Top Ten hit?
19 In quoits, what name is given to the target at which the rings are thrown?
20 Which country had a guerrilla group whose name translated as 'Alfaro lives, dammit'?
21 In cycling what is the first major classic of the season?
22 Which England cricketer lost four toes in a swimming accident while touring the West Indies?
23 In which island group is Guadalcanal?
24 Prince Charles, Prince Edward and Prince Philip were all head boys at which school?
25 What appears in the centre of the national flag of Ghana?
26 How many symphonies did Brahms compose?
27 What was the title of Dr. Feelgood's only Top Ten hit?
28 Which South American city has a name meaning 'fair winds'?
29 Alexander Gordon 1743-1827 gave his name to what?
30 In which country is the city of Antananarivo?

Hobbies 3 (See Quiz 183)
1 Angling. 2 New York. 3 Padstow, Cornwall. 4 Underwater hockey.
5 Houston, Texas. 6 The Roux Brothers. 7 Hampton Court maze. 8 Blue, red, yellow or black. 9 Ripon. 10 Scrabble. 11 Marbles. 12 The Nutshell.
13 Milton Keynes. 14 Gatwick. 15 Terence Conran. 16 9th to 11th.
17 10. 18 Bowls. 19 Hail. 20 Harmonica. 21 Middlesborough.
22 Marco Pierre White. 23 Sponge. 24 Lacrosse. 25 None (it's a naturist site). 26 Trainspotter. 27 Blackpool. 28 House. 29 Roller coaster.
30 Roller skates.

Answers

1 What is the real name of Renault's Nicole?
2 Mrs Peter Hook is best known on TV as whom?
3 Who co presented The Big Breakfast with Zoe Ball?
4 Who played Kadi Toura in the drama series Roots?
5 Who was the antiques dealer in the Paddington stories?
6 Who used to say, "The next Tonight will be tomorrow night"?
7 Which was the English port in the Triangle drama series?
8 Mrs Robert Powell was a member of which famous dance group?
9 Who was the first Teletubby to have its alter ego sacked?
10 Who composed the Barcarolle which advertised Bailey's Irish Cream?
11 In which series did Charles Dance play Guy Perron?
12 Who does the daughter of Band of Gold's creator play in Coronation Street?
13 Who directed a documentary called Genderquake after leaving a top soap?
14 Who followed Phillip Schofield as link man on Children's BBC?
15 Whose final TV role was as Daniel Reece?
16 In May to December what was Zoe's name before she married Alec?
17 Who composed the music for ITV's coverage of Grand Prix racing?
18 Who are the parents of Live & Kicking's first female presenter?
19 What is the profession of Postman Pat's Mrs Goggins?
20 Which series took place in Lochdubh?
21 Who was Bamm Bamm's dad?
22 What was Alan B'Stard's constituency?
23 Which magazine did Amanda work for in Girls On Top?
24 Who were Father Ted's colleagues?
25 Which disgraced ex MP is the uncle of Jack Davenport from This Life?
26 What did Angela Rippon dance to on The Morecambe and Wise Show?
27 George Baker aka Inspector Wexford appeared as which special agent in Up Pompeii?
28 What were the goldfish on Playschool called?
29 Who played Liz Shaw in Bodyguards?
30 What did Peter do in The Peter Principle?

1   Where is Baltasound Airport?
2   Who is the elder – Bob Monkhouse or Princess Margaret?
3   Grand Duke, Stanley and Lombard are all varieties of which fruit?
4   In which country is the city of Cali?
5   Who wrote The Alexandria Quartet novels?
6   Against which country did David Platt make his first full England appearance?
7   What is the correct form of address to begin a letter to a Lady Lord Mayor?
8   What was Frank Sinatra's first UK No 1?
9   Demophobia is the fear of what?
10 Which creature is represented in the year the Chinese call gou?
11 What is the most southerly London borough?
12 Anne Bonney and Mary Read famously carried out which trade?
13 Who composed the opera Death In Venice?
14 What have you had if you've just had a dog's nose?
15 During which decade did the Orient Express first run?
16 The Court of Arches is the chief court of whom?
17 Which country has the austral as a unit of currency?
18 Who was the ship Cutty Sark named after?
19 Emanuel Lasker was undisputed world champion for over 26 years at what?
20 What is the summer equivalent of hibernation?
21 Whose one and only UK Top Ten hit was Kung Fu Fighting?
22 What are the initials IPA an abbreviation of, as well as being an ale?
23 Which part of the London Underground is called the Drain?
24 The landau carriage takes its name from a town in which country?
25 Who wrote the novel A Time to Dance?
26 Talia Shire is the sister of which film director?
27 What have you got with a plateful of Pisum satvium?
28 Which country left the Commonwealth in 1949?
29 In music what does the abbreviation VS stand for?
30 Which two colours appear on the national flag of Honduras?

1   Who has been an Irish international and the head of HJ Heinz?
2   In which decade of which century did the first league varsity match take place?
3   In which city were Barbarians RFC founded?
4   Which was the first league side to score 1,000 points in a season?
5   Who was Wales' youngest ever captain?
6   Rob Andrew is qualified in what profession?
7   Where did Brian Moore begin his career?
8   How old was Will Carling when he played for Terra Nova Under 11s?
9   Against which side did Jeremy Guscott make his international debut?
10   Which league side was the first to win all its league games in a season?
11   Which of Wigan's 1994-5 trophies is no longer played for?
12   In 1986 St Helens beat Carlisle 112-0 in which competition?
13   Who was the first union player to kick eight penalties in an international?
14   What was Jason Leonard's first club?
15   Who were the beaten finalists in the first league Knockout Trophy?
16   Who captained Ireland in their centenary season?
17   Who did the All Blacks beat 106-4 in 1987?
18   Where was the first floodlit rugby union match played?
19   What name was given to the breakaway clubs from the Rugby Union in 1895?
20   Which club won the first Middlesex Sevens at Twickenham?
21   What position did J.J. Williams play for Llanelli?
22   Who in 1998 held the world record for the most capped hooker?
23   Who recorded the then highest score draw 46-46 in 1994?
24   Who sponsored the rugby league before Courage?
25   In which country was the first rugby league World Cup held?
26   Who was the first UK rugby league club side to play in Australia?
27   Who played a record 17 appearances on five tours with the British Lions?
28   What was the score when Salford beat Wigan's unbeaten 43 game run?
29   Who made the lowest score (0-0) in the BBC's Floodlit Rugby League competition?
30   Who were the first Scottish rugby union club champions?

1   Which country has the forint. as its unit of currency?
2   A fear of dreams is known as what?
3   What was Stephen 'Tin Tin' Duffy's only Top Ten hit?
4   How long is the Suez Canal?
5   In the military, what is an AFV?
6   Which UK No 1 was written by Red Dwarf creators Robert Grant and Doug Naylor?
7   Which letter is two dot in Morse Code?
8   In which decade was Rory Bremner born?
9   Mbabane is the capital of which country?
10 What popular pub name comes from the title held by soldier John Manners?
11 What colour are the stars on the national flag of the Republic of Iraq?
12 What does the Latin deo volente mean?
13 Which actor is married to actress Sarah Jessica Parker?
14 Raleigh is the capital of which US state?
15 What size is B4 paper in millimetres?
16 Which artist painted Christ of St John of the Cross in 1951?
17 Where was the Prince's Trust charity Party In The Park held in 1998?
18 What is the administrative centre for the Welsh county of Powys?
19 Who is the elder – Jimmy Nail or Liam Neeson?
20 Where in Westminster Abbey was the Stone of Scone?
21 What is the international car index mark for a car from Chile?
22 To five years when was the magazine Country Life founded?
23 Who directed the 1990 film Gremlins 2: The New Batch?
24 In which country is the city of Dalian?
25 Who was the Roman God of death?
26 Whose top hat sold for £22,000 at Sotheby's in 1988?
27 The spice fenugreek is made from which part of a plant?
28 What was Dollar's first UK Top Ten hit in 1979?
29 In the film Ace Ventura: Pet Detective Ace is hired to find what?
30 Who was known as 'Joltin Joe' and 'the Yankee Clipper'?

LEVEL 3

1   What is the currency of Bolivia?
2   Between which two rivers does Manhattan lie?
3   To the nearest million, what was the population of Seoul in 1995?
4   In which country is the city of Curitiba?
5   What is the capital of Brunei?
6   In which country is the deep-water port of Lobito?
7   The islands of Taipa and Coloane are part of which possession?
8   Pluna Airlines are based in which country?
9   Which capital is further north – Khartoum or Addis Ababa?
10 What is the official language of Bhutan?
11 In which country is Kakadu National Park?
12 Which country is due north of Uruguay?
13 Which two countries border Morocco?
14 Which desert lies between the Kalahari and the Atlantic Ocean?
15 Where is the news agency Colprensa based?
16 What is Madison Square Garden situated over?
17 On which island is Nassau, the capital of the Bahamas?
18 In which US state was the first National Park?
19 How is Denali in Alaska also known?
20 The Negev desert tapers to which port?
21 Who designed New Delhi?
22 What is the third longest river in Africa?
23 Which country has the largest oil resources in Africa?
24 To the nearest million, what was the population of the largest US city in 1994?
25 In which country is the city of Medan?
26 What is the capital of Burundi?
27 What is South Africa's judicial capital?
28 What is the most north-eastern US state?
29 SAHSA Airlines are based in which country?
30 Which island is situated between Sumatra and Bali?

1   Which 30s classic was originally called Night Bus?

2   Who does James Stewart play in Harvey?

3   Who did Carol Reed replace at the last minute on Oliver!?

4   In which 40s classic did Edward Gwenn play Kris Kringle?

5   Katharine Hepburn bought the rights to a Philip Barry play to make which movie?

6   What was the Marx Brother's first film for MGM?

7   Who played Mr Miniver in the Greer Garson Oscar winner?

8   Which film producer who died in 1997 co produced Chariots of Fire?

9   Who played Bill Sikes when Alec Guinness was Fagin?

10   What was the first Western to win a Best Picture Oscar after a 60 year gap?

11   Who directed the first Terminator films?

12   Who choreographed 42nd Street?

13   Titanic overtook which movie as the most costly ever made?

14   Which actor kidnapped Harrison Ford in Air Force One?

15   Which palace was used for Kenneth Branagh's Hamlet?

16   What is the name of Ralph Fiennes' character in Schindler's List?

17   Whose songs were on the soundtrack of Philadelphia?

18   Which 50s film cost $4 million, twice the maximum of the time?

19   Which film begins with "No man's life can be encompassed in one telling"?

20   Which star of The Exorcist also used the name Edna Rae?

21   Which film has the quote, "It wasn't the airplanes. It was beauty killed the beast"?

22   Where were Butch Cassidy and Sundance finally tracked down?

23   What is the most famous TV role of actress Agnes Moorhead?

24   The composer of the only Oscar nominated song from Grease was from which famous quartet?

25   John Mollo won an Oscar in Star Wars for what?

26   Who was the only woman to have top billing in A Bridge Too Far?

27   Who was originally sought for the role of Shears in The Bridge on the River Kwai?

28   Hattie McDaniel was the first black actress to win an Oscar, but for which role?

29   Which movie did Titanic overtake as a record UK earner?

30   The ex GI is in Paris to learn what in An American in Paris?

Quiz 191 Pot Luck 93

Answers - see page 660

LEVEL 3

1   Both Emma Bunton's dad and Robert Redford's dad worked as what?
2   London's Royal College of Music is in which regal sounding road?
3   Which actress starred in Thelma and Louise and Lorenzo's Oil?
4   In which European country are the regions of Kitaa and Tunu?
5   In which decade was Lord Archer born?
6   What name is given to the Greek letter that is the equivalent of letter M?
7   What is the Scottish equivalent of the Countryside Commission in England?
8   Who joined the European Union in 1995 with Finland and Sweden?
9   Which sea would you cross if you sailed from Corfu to Cephalonia?
10 Who is the elder – Paula Yates or the Duke of York?
11 What are the initials KCVO an abbreviation of?
12 What was Celine Dion's first solo UK Top Ten hit?
13 Which US state is called the Bullion State?
14 What name did former Mayfair hairdresser Nigel Davies adopt in the 1960s ?
15 What colours appear with black and red on the Jordanian flag?
16 In which year did Dennis the Menace first appear in the Beano?
17 Which British army officer invented shells containing bullets to inflict more casualties?
18 Who was the longest serving British PM?
19 What is a cutty sark according to Robert Burns?
20 What is the capital of Djibouti?
21 Which English seaside resort is associated with Count Dracula?
22 What was Donny Osmond's last UK No 1?
23 Who wrote Chicken Soup With Barley?
24 Doraphobia is the fear of what?
25 What was the pirate Blackbeard's real name?
26 What is the name Blimp derived from in the character Colonel Blimp?
27 Which fund pays the Queen's private expenses as sovereign?
28 What is tattooed on Robert Mitchum's knuckles in the film The Night of the Hunter?
29 Where was Captain James Cook killed in 1779?
30 Who composed the opera Billy Budd?

Answers

Plant World (See Quiz 86, page 318)
1 Ginkgo. 2 Oxalic. 3 Callus. 4 Cherokee leader. 5 It dissolves blood corpuscles. 6 Italy. 7 Rockies. 8 North & South Carolina. 9 Blue. 10 Ferns & mosses. 11 Pacific coast of North America. 12 Stalk. 13 African violet. 14 From insects. 15 It loses its green colour. 16 Matchbox bean. 17 Rose of Jericho. 18 Fungi. 19 Cactus. 20 Poppy. 21 General Sherman. 22 Lettuce. 23 On dung. 24 Sierra Nevada. 25 Belladonna. 26 Stalk. 27 By the sea. 28 Silver Fir. 29 Praslin & Curiense. 30 Giant waterlily.

Quiz 192 Plant World

Answers - see page 659

LEVEL 3

1   How is the maidenhair tree also known?
2   Which acid makes rhubarb leaves poisonous?
3   What is a tissue which forms on a damaged plant surface called?
4   The Sequoia takes its name from what?
5   What makes the death cap mushroom so toxic?
6   Which European country produces more than half of Europe's rice?
7   Where would you find the home of the bristlecone pine?
8   The Venus flytrap is found naturally in which US states?
9   A meadow clary has flowers of what colour?
10 What sort of plants are cryptogams?
11 The world's tallest tree is native only to where?
12 If a leaf is sessile what is missing?
13 What is another name for the Saintpaulia?
14 How does a bladderwort receive its nourishment?
15 If a plant suffers from chlorosis what happens to it?
16 How is the entada known in Australia?
17 What is the only plant which can change its shape?
18 What does a mycologist study?
19 What type of plant is a saguaro?
20 To which family does the greater celandine belong?
21 The largest known giant redwood is named after whom?
22 How is the plant lactuca sativa better known?
23 If something is coprophilous where does it grow?
24 The tree sometimes known as Wellingtonia is native to which mountains?
25 Atropine is derived from which plant?
26 Which part of the flax plant is used to make linen?
27 If a plant is halophytic where does it grow?
28 Which tree is the tallest native to Europe?
29 On which two islands would you find the sea coconut?
30 Which plant has the largest leaves?

LEVEL 3

1   A sentence containing all the alphabet's letters is known as a what?
2   What is the international car index mark for a car from Singapore?
3   Who is the elder – Terry Wogan or Bill Wyman?
4   What are Tony Blair's middle names?
5   In which decade did Fiji leave the Commonwealth?
6   Who wrote the novel The Pathfinder?
7   Columbus is the capital of which US state?
8   Who directed the 1991 film The Silence of the Lambs?
9   What was Duran Duran's first UK Top Ten hit?
10 Which post was held by William Gilbert at the courts of Elizabeth I and James I?
11 Which poet was awarded an Order of Merit in 1953, three years before his death?
12 A fear of dust is known as what?
13 Which river was explored by Scotsman Mungo Park?
14 Bill Robertie became the first person to win which World Championship twice?
15 Mogadishu is the capital of which country?
16 Where did the married Princess Elizabeth live before she came to the throne?
17 In music what does the expression 'pesante' mean?
18 Who was the Greek goddess of victory?
19 On the first of which month is Canada Day celebrated?
20 What is the title of the head of the College of Arms?
21 Which mathematician wrote the book The Elements?
22 Which TV character drove a yellow car called Bessie?
23 In which country is the city of Douala?
24 Whose only UK Top Ten hit was Jeans On?
25 For which film did Geena Davis first win an Oscar?
26 In 1860 Willie Park became the first winner of which sporting trophy?
27 What is the correct form of address to begin a letter to a Rabbi?
28 What colour separates the black, red and green bands on the Kenyan flag?
29 What part of your body is initialised as the ANS?
30 Which artist painted Dancer at the Bar around 1900?

Quiz 194 Music Stars

Answers - see page 661

LEVEL 3

1　What did the Rolling Stones sing to close their 1981 USA shows?
2　Who replaced Cliff Richard in the West End Musical Time in 1987?
3　Who wrote I'm A Believer for The Monkees?
4　From which film was Elvis Presley's 1962 No 1 Return to Sender?
5　What was Elton John's first solo hit on his own Rocket label?
6　Which Leo Sayer hit gave the Chrysallis label their first No1?
7　In which decade did Barbra Streisand first make the UK charts?
8　Which hit was the first to be No 1 over two separate Christmases?
9　Which singer/songwriter penned the lines, "The carpet, too, is moving under you"?
10　How many consecutive UK No 1 hits did the Beatles have?
11　Who duetted with Peter Gabriel on Games Without Frontiers?
12　What was Abba's only No 1 in the USA?
13　Which opera does Pavarotti's anthem Nessun Dorma come from?
14　Which of the Gibb brothers wrote their first UK No 1 Massachusetts?
15　Which David Bowie hit was his fourth UK and second US No 1 in '83?
16　Who replaced Diana Ross when she left The Supremes?
17　What was Elvis Presley's penultimate UK No 1 hit?
18　Stephen Bray and Patrick Leonard have both co-written No 1s with which singer?
19　Michael Jackson's Thriller and Bad came out on which label?
20　When did Tony Bennett first record I Left My Heart In San Francisco?
21　Which group singer put out a solo album called Primitive Cool?
22　A John Lennon song gave which group their only UK No 1?
23　Which singing superstar once had a trial for Brentford FC?
24　Pete Townshend first No 1 as a producer was for which group?
25　Who sang the theme song to the film Beauty and the Beast?
26　What was the final No 1 by any of the Osmond family?
27　Who conducted the Three Tenors for their Italia 90 concert?
28　Who is the only group to appear in the charts in every year of the 70s?
29　Which Springsteen song was a hit for Manfred Mann's Earth Band?
30　Which David Essex hit was the sound track for That'll Be The Day?

Answers

Pot Luck 94 (See Quiz 193)
1 Pangram. 2 SGP. 3 Bill Wyman. 4 Charles Lynton. 5 1980s. 6 James Fenimore Cooper. 7 Ohio. 8 Jonathan Demme. 9 Girls On Film. 10 Royal Physician. 11 Walter de la Mare. 12 Amathophobia. 13 River Niger. 14 Backgammon. 15 Somalia. 16 Clarence House. 17 Heavy, ponderous. 18 Nike. 19 July. 20 Earl Marshall. 21 Euclid. 22 Dr Who. 23 Cameroon. 24 David Dundas. 25 The Accidental Tourist. 26 Golf's British Open. 27 Dear Sir. 28 White. 29 Autonomic Nervous System. 30 Edgar Degas.

1   Which US state is called the Gopher State?
2   From which musical is the song June is Bustin' Out All Over?
3   In which decade was Frankie Dettori born?
4   The French physician Laennec invented which medical aid?
5   Nelophobia is the fear of what?
6   Who wrote Death In The Afternoon?
7   In which country is the city of Fortaleza?
8   Which French rugby union player holds the record for the most tries for his country?
9   Which tree appears on the Lebanese flag?
10 What's the English name of the constellation Dorado?
11 Whose only UK Top Ten hit was The Final Countdown?
12 Who is the most photographed person to attend Riddlesdown High school, Croydon?
13 In which country are the regions of Liguria and Calabria?
14 Which artist painted the famous painting The Ambassadors?
15 The majority of tourists to the USA are from which country?
16 Who composed the opera The Golden Cockerel?
17 What type of roses were in Lady Diana Spencer's wedding bouquet?
18 Which country has the ngultrum as a unit of currency?
19 Who is the elder – Ruby Wax or Victoria Wood?
20 How old was James Herriot when he began writing books?
21 Which King of Spain was known as Charles the Mad?
22 Who joined the European Union in the same year as Portugal?
23 What is the Swedish plattar?
24 Which media celeb founded a magazine called Passing Wind?
25 Who wrote the novel The Sound and the Fury?
26 What was Earth, Wind and Fire's first UK Top Ten hit?
27 The wall, bar and frog are all part of a horse's what?
28 What is the capital of the Dominican Republic?
29 What is Julie Andrews' full real name?
30 In which decade was the first Archery World Championship?

1 Who played John McCarthy in Hostages?
2 Which emergency service did Anthea Turner work for before her media career?
3 Who played the scheming city council chief in GBH?
4 Who did Andrew Lloyd Webber appear on Top of the Pops with in 1998?
5 What was the caterpillar called in Dangermouse?
6 Who founded Rutland Weekend Television?
7 Which company did Colin work for in Colin's Sandwich?
8 In a Comic Strip Hollywood spoof of the miners' strike Peter Richardson played which actor supposedly playing Arthur Scargill?
9 What did Crossroads change its name to in 1987?
10 Which show had a punk dog called Spit?
11 In The Darling Buds of May what was Charley's real name?
12 To The Manor Born was set in which village?
13 Who played Joe Maplin in Hi De Hi!?
14 What strolled across the opening title in Northern Exposure?
15 How was the US series Card Sharks known when it transferred to the UK?
16 Who played Lucinda in Grange Hill?
17 What was the name of the pub in Minder?
18 Who left the employ of Mohammed Fayed to host a daytime chat show on satellite TV?
19 Who hosted That Was the Week That Was in the US?
20 What record did Roy Castle break on the very first Record Breakers?
21 What was Zoe and Alec's baby called in May to December?
22 Which father of a former Corrie barmaid wrote The Lovers?
23 In Lovejoy who bough Felsham Manor after Lady Jane left?
24 Who replaced Foggy Dewhurst when Michael Aldridge joined the Last of the Summer Wine cast?
25 Which TV actress became President of the Dyslexia Institute?
26 Which series was based on Germany's File XY Unsolved?
27 Which company did Terence 'Twiggy' Rathbone own in Hot Metal?
28 In which series were jungle sequences shot in Norfolk and desert scenes in Sussex?
29 What colour hair did Crystal Tipps have?
30 Which actor was digging an allotment to advertise BT?

Quiz 197 Pot Luck 96

Answers - see page 666

LEVEL 3

1   In which country is the city of Ibadan?
2   What do the initials for the chemical DDT stand for?
3   Who directed the film trilogy Lethal Weapon?
4   Arthur Scargill and the Duchess of York were removed from where in 1996?
5   What was Pigmeat Markham's only UK Top Ten hit?
6   What is the main language of the Republic of Chad?
7   Douroucouli, de Brazza's guenon and red colobus are types of what?
8   Which artist painted Black Paintings in the 1820s?
9   Who invented the word 'frabjous'?
10 Salem is the capital of which US state?
11 What is Robson Green's middle name?
12 In which decade was Comtesse Raine de Chambrun born?
13 Windhoek is the capital of which country?
14 A fear of fear is known as what?
15 What invaded the town of San Antonio de los Caballeros in June '98?
16 What was Rod Stewart's last UK No 1?
17 Who was the Roman goddess of horses?
18 What does the green pentacle on the Moroccan flag depict?
19 What is the international car index mark for a car from Burundi?
20 What did the M stand for in J.M.W. Turner's name?
21 Where are the headquarters of the French Foreign Legion?
22 What is the drug thiopental used for?
23 Desmond Tutu's middle name is Mpilo, which means what?
24 How is Patricia Andrejewski better known?
25 Who had an 80s hit with She Means Nothing To Me?
26 Fergie was made Chancellor of which university?
27 In 1998 Tommy Dixon was arrested at home after what was mistaken for a gunshot?
28 In which city is the 305 metre long cable braced Erskine bridge?
29 The spice sassafras is made from which part of a plant?
30 Who is the elder – Earl Spencer or Sinead O'Connor?

Performing Arts (See Quiz 198)
Answers
1 French & English. 2 Michael Crawford. 3 English National Ballet.
4 A cappella. 5 Cell Mates. 6 Vanessa Mae. 7 Louis B Mayer. 8 John
Ogdon. 9 Rowan Atkinson. 10 Quintet du Hot Club de France. 11 Dash.
12 Mississippi. 13 Placido Domingo. 14 Phil Collins. 15 Popcorn.
16 Maureen Lipman. 17 Laurence Olivier. 18 Bournemouth Sinfonietta.
19 Tony Richardson. 20 Jerome Robbins. 21 Alan Ayckbourn. 22 Napoleon
III. 23 Jim Steinman. 24 Steve Coogan. 25 Jim Davidson. 26 Hello Dolly.
27 Arpeggio. 28 Leslie Bricusse. 29 South Pacific. 30 Sir Peter Hall.

1 In which languages did Irishman Samuel Beckett write his plays?
2 Who performed his one man show EFX in Las Vegas?
3 Princess Diana was patron of which ballet company?
4 Which type of singing means 'in the style of the chapel'?
5 Which play did Stephen Fry walk out of in 1995?
6 Who went on a Red Hot world tour in 1996?
7 Who founded the American Academy of Motion Picture Arts and Sciences?
8 Who won the 1962 Tchaikovsky competition with. Ashkenazy?
9 Who, in '81, became the youngest star of a West End one-man show?
10 Grappelli and Reinhardt were leaders of which Quintet?
11 What was the name of Wayne Sleep's 1980 dance company?
12 Tennessee Williams was born in which US state?
13 Which opera singer sang with Sarah Brightman in Requiem?
14 Who played the Artful Dodger in the first stage production of Oliver!?
15 Which Ben Elton novel was the first to be adapted into a West End play?
16 Who had a one woman show called Live and Kidding?
17 Who shared management of the Old Vic between 1944 and 1950 with Ralph Richardson?
18 With which orchestra did Simon Rattle make his professional debut?
19 Who established the English Stage Company with George Devine at the Royal Court in 1955?
20 Who choreographed West Side Story and Fiddler on the Roof?
21 Who was in the Guinness Book of Records for having five plays running in the West End at one time?
22 Which leader is the subject of the play L'Aiglon by Edmond Rostand?
23 Who wrote the lyrics for Lloyd Webber's Whistle Down the Wind?
24 Whose was the star of The Man Who Thinks He's It?
25 Who became the youngest comedian to appear at the London Palladium, in 1977?
26 Thornton Wilder's The Matchmaker was made into which musical?
27 Which musical term means 'like a harp'?
28 Who wrote the songs for Doctor Dolittle?
29 Sean Connery's first West End appearance was in which chorus line?
30 Who founded the RSC aged 30?

1. In which Hawaiian island is Pearl Harbor?
2. What was Cliff Richard's first 1980s No 1?
3. JF Kennedy was one of how many children?
4. Under what name did Helen Porter Mitchell sing her way to success?
5. What was John Schlesinger's first US film?
6. In which month is the US holiday President's Day?
7. In which European country are the areas of Telemark and Troms?
8. Joe Fagin's 80s hit was a theme tune for which TV series?
9. Which country has the pula as a unit of currency?
10. What is the correct form of address to begin a letter to an Earl?
11. Which US state is called the Bay State?
12. Who is the elder – Michael Flatley or Stephen Fry?
13. Hypegiaphobia is the fear of what?
14. Who did Joe Louis beat to first become world heavyweight champ?
15. What was Eva Braun working as when she met Adolf Hitler?
16. What does the second S stand for in the initials SSSI?
17. Which Battle was the last in the Hundred Years War?
18. Who joined the European Union in the same year as UK and Denmark?
19. Who composed the opera Punch and Judy?
20. What was American hero Paul Revere's day job?
21. Who founded the Pakistan People's Party?
22. In which country is the city of Guayaquil?
23. What was the name of the Queen's first corgi?
24. Who played Sally Bowles in the 1955 film I am a Camera?
25. What did Rajiv Gandhi study at the University of Cambridge?
26. Kurt Weill and Henrik Ibsen were born in which month?
27. Who was the first Austrian to top the UK charts?
28. Which country has the only national flag which is not rectangular?
29. Who played the lead role in the film Finders Keepers?
30. To five either way, how many weeks did Sinatra's My Way spend in the UK charts between 1969 and 1971?

1 Who were tennis's 'Four Musketeers'?

2 Which tennis player appeared in Octopussy?

3 Who had the car number plate X CZECH?

4 Who won the first US Men's Open?

5 Who, in 1986, became the youngest woman semi finalist at Wimbledon for 99 years?

6 Who won the inaugural Grand Slam Cup in Munich in 1990?

7 What was Monica Seles's first Grand Slam title?

8 Who was the first Australian woman to win the Wimbledon Singles?

9 How does a Golden Grand Slam differ from a Grand Slam?

10 With whom did Billie Jean Moffitt win her first Wimbledon Doubles title?

11 What year was the world's first Open tournament?

12 Who was the first German to win the Wimbledon Men's Singles after reunification?

13 At Wimbledon who won an unseeded Men's final in the 90s?

14 Which brothers asked to wear England shirts on Centre Court during the 1996 championships?

15 Which brother and sister won the Wimbledon Mixed Doubles in successive years in the 90s?

16 Who was the first woman to win $1 million in prize money?

17 Who gave Virginia Wade her trophy when she won Wimbledon?

18 Which new competition was included in the Wimbledon championships in 1884 along with the Women's Singles?

19 Which Grand Slam title has Boris Becker never won?

20 Who did Miss Kiyomura beat in the Wimbledon Junior Final in 1973?

21 In 1992 John McEnroe won the Wimbledon Doubles title with whom?

22 Who replaced Martina Hingis as World No 1 in October 1998?

23 Who did Boris Becker beat to become Wimbledon's youngest Men's Singles winner?

24 Who did Greg Rusedski sack as his coach during Wimbledon 98?

25 Who won his first Open title in 1985 two years after winning the Junior Grand Slam?

26 Which mentor of Pete Sampras died in May 1996?

27 Who was the last British man before Tim Henman to reach a Wimbledon quarter final?

28 Where was Martina Hingis born?

29 How is Wimbledon semi finalist Mrs Lampard better known?

30 Which Helena won two titles in one day at Wimbledon 96?

1 What was the christian name of chocolate founder Mr Cadbury?
2 In which country is the city of Gwangju?
3 Bill Perks the son of a bricklayer became known as who?
4 What does the Latin mea culpa mean?
5 Which creature is represented in the year the Chinese call 'long'?
6 Which country has the rufiyaa as a unit of currency?
7 Who was Willie Vernon to James Cagney?
8 Where does the Symphony of the Stars take place annually in Hollywood?
9 What was Foreigner's first UK Top Ten hit in 1981?
10 Who is the elder – Bob Geldof or Nigel Kennedy?
11 Which Hitchock film title ties in with his father's field of work?
12 Which three colours make up the Sultanate of Oman flag?
13 Whose nickname was 'Stormin' Norman'?
14 Who directed the 1987 film Good Morning Vietnam?
15 Columbia is the capital of which US state?
16 What is a honey locust?
17 Born Marie Grosholtz, under what name is this French lady remembered?
18 Who were Waiting For a Train in their only UK Top Ten hit?
19 Which saints share their names with three of the five inhabited Scilly Isles?
20 Maputo is the capital of which country?
21 What does the medical term D & C stand for?
22 A fear of floods is known as what?
23 Which artist painted Toledo Landscape around 1610?
24 How is the letter O formed in Morse Code?
25 How many square chains make one hectare in surveying?
26 In which county was Sir Humphry Davy, inventor of the miner's safety lamp, born?
27 What did Terry Wogan study at Belvedere College, Dublin?
28 Who was the Greek god of vegetation and re-birth?
29 Which seasonal rose is from the genus Helleborus?
30 What is the international car index mark for a car from Lebanon?

1 Whose stately home is Shugborough Hall?

2 Lord McAlpine is Lord of where?

3 What is the first name of the person who preceded Eddie George as Governor of the Bank of England?

4 Who is known to his family as 'Yog'?

5 Who became Mrs Taylor Hackford in 1997?

6 Who changed his name from Jim Moir so it didn't clash with the BBC's Head of Light Entertainment?

7 Why was Cliff Richard banned from entering Singapore in 1972?

8 How is the former Miss Katharine Worsley better known?

9 In whose family home did Charles and Diana spend the first night of their honeymoon?

10 Who was Margaret Thatcher's Press Secretary when she resigned?

11 Who aged 19 who married fellow drama student Doorn van Steyn?

12 Who founded the Chelsea Design Company in 1976?

13 Which Leeds born chef won three Michelin stars by his early thirties?

14 Who opened the punk boutique Seditionaries in the 70s with Vivienne Westwood?

15 Who has children called Betty Kitten, Harvey Kirby and Honey Kinny?

16 How were Issy Van Randwyck, Dillie Keane and Adele Anderson known collectively?

17 Who was Mohammed Fayed's first wife and Dodi Fayed's mother?

18 Who is London's largest landowner?

19 Who is the son of former rugby league international Danny Wilson?

20 Who was raised by his grandmother Olga Winogradsky?

21 Which former editor is Lady Lucinda Lambton's third husband?

22 Who are the parents of George, Harry, Tobias and Angus?

23 Who has '100% Blades' tattooed on his left arm?

24 William Hague's father's business produced what?

25 In '98 Stella McCartney designed for which fashion house?

26 What relation is Natasha Richardson to Jemma Redgrave?

27 After who or what did Lady Helen Taylor (nee Windsor) name her first son?

28 Which Hamlet ran off with his mother Gertrude in 1995?

29 Where was Michael Heseltine born?

30 Who succeeded John Galliano at Givenchy in 1996?

1   Which occupation was shared by the fathers of Roger Moore and Burt Reynolds?
2   What are the two colours of the national flag of Pakistan?
3   Who is the elder – Liam Gallagher or Ryan Giggs?
4   What is Gerald Ford's middle name?
5   What was the profession of escapologist Harry Houdini's father?
6   Over 700 people died in Greece in July 1987 due to what?
7   Who composed the opera The Rape of Lucretia?
8   What are the initials TARDIS an abbreviation of?
9   Whose one and only UK hit which reached No 1 was Float On ?
10 Which writer is actress Rudi Davies' mother?
11 Which prince was born in the year Ted Hughes became Poet Laureate?
12 If a wine is said to be flabby what does it lack?
13 What is the capital of Greenland?
14 In music, what does the expression 'strepitoso' mean?
15 For a role in which film did Vanessa Redgrave shave her head?
16 Which country has the lev as a unit of currency?
17 For what offence did Sophia Loren spend 17 days in prison in 1982?
18 In which decade was Richard Branson born?
19 In which European country are the regions of Beja and Guarda?
20 Which playwright was born in Whiston on Merseyside in 1947?
21 Which American state is called the Hawkeye State?
22 Which vitamin is also known as biotin?
23 Astraphobia is the fear of what?
24 What common factor links children of Cheryl Baker and children of Mollie Sugden?
25 Who played Ron Jenkins in Coronation Street?
26 DJ Jimmy Young was what sort of instructor in the army?
27 Which hit got to No 2 simultaneously in November 1995 with two separate groups?
28 Who created The Simpsons on TV?
29 Who in Gilbert and Sullivan is 'a dealer in magic and spells'?
30 Which soccer side does Eamonn Holmes support?

Screen Greats (See Quiz 204)

Answers

1 None. 2 Betty Grable. 3 Peter Lorre. 4 Goldfinger. 5 Errol Flynn. 6 20th Century Fox. 7 Charles Bronson. 8 Tony Curtis. 9 Barbara Stanwyck's. 10 Bela Lugosi. 11 Gene Kelly. 12 Audrey Hepburn. 13 Marlon Brando. 14 Ingrid Bergman. 15 Rita Hayworth. 16 Rebecca. 17 Sophia Loren. 18 One Night in the Tropics. 19 Dustin Hoffman. 20 George C Scott. 21 Julie Andrews. 22 Lola-Lola. 23 His wife Carole Lombard. 24 Ginger Rogers. 25 Charlotte Bronte. 26 Twenty. 27 Anchors Aweigh. 28 The Big Broadcast. 29 The Barkleys of Broadway. 30 Making A Living.

1 What is the total number of Oscars won by Errol Flynn, Peter Cushing and Richard Burton?

2 Who once had her name changed to Frances Dean by Goldwyn?

3 Who is mentioned by name in Al Stewart's song The Year of the Cat?

4 Which Bond film did Sean Connery make prior to Hitchcock's Marnie?

5 Eric Porter played Soames on TV but who played Soames in That Forsyte Woman?

6 Which was the first US studio Richard Burton worked for?

7 Who is known in Italy as 'Il Brutto'?

8 Who changed Bernie for Tony in his first film Criss Cross?

9 Bette Midler recreated whose 30s role in Stella?

10 Which screen great did Martin Landau play in Ed Wood?

11 Who was lent to Columbia by MGM for Cover Girl?

12 Sean Ferrer was the son of which Hollywood Oscar winner?

13 Whose first Oscar was for playing Terry Malloy in a 50s classic?

14 Who was the mother of actress Isabella Rossellini?

15 Whose pin up was pinned to the atomic bomb dropped on Bikini?

16 What was Hitchcock's first Hollywood film?

17 Who was the first performer to win an Oscar for a performance entirely in a foreign language?

18 What was Abbot and Costello's first feature film?

19 Who played Sean Connery's son in Family Business?

20 Who was the first actor ever to refuse an Oscar?

21 Who was the first British born British actress of British parents to win an Oscar?

22 What was the name of Marlene Dietrich in The Blue Angel?

23 Whose death in 1942 spurred Clark Gable to join the US Air Corps?

24 Whose first film was Campus Sweethearts with Rudy Vallee?

25 Which author did Olivia de Havilland play in Devotion?

26 How old was Debbie Reynolds when she made Singin' in the Rain?

27 What was the first film which teamed Gene Kelly with Frank Sinatra?

28 In which film did Bob Hope find his theme tune?

29 In which 1949 film were Rogers and Astaire reunited after a 10 year break?

30 In which film did Chaplin make his screen debut, in 1914?

LEVEL 3

1 What was the last ruling dynasty of China?
2 The Isle of Man belonged to which two countries before it came under UK administration in 1765?
3 What name meaning 'achievement of universal peace' is given to the reign of Emperor Akihito?
4 How did the former Princess Alix of of Hessen meet her death?
5 Who did not seek re election as Austrian President in 1991 after revelations about his activities in WWII?
6 Who was the first President of Israel?
7 How many days after Waterloo did Napoleon resign?
8 Which governor of Sumatra was responsible for the founding of Singapore?
9 What did the Rarotonga Treaty secure in 1987?
10 What does Rasputin mean, as a name given to Grigory Efimovich?
11 Where were all but six French kings crowned?
12 Which country had a secret police force called the securitate which was replaced in 1990?
13 Which President Roosevelt was Republican?
14 What name was given to the incorporation of Austria into the Third Reich?
15 What did Haile Selassie's title Ras Tafari mean?
16 Who was Nazi minister of eastern occupied territories from '41-44?
17 Who was secretary of state to Kennedy and Johnson?
18 Who was the first president of an independent Mozambique?
19 In which country was the Rosetta Stone found in in 1799?
20 What name was given to the socialist movement which carried out the Nicaraguan Revolution?
21 Which Conference drew up the United Nations Charter?
22 Where was the explosive Semtex manufactured?
23 Which city has the oldest university in the world?
24 Who succeeded Ian Smith as Prime Minister of Rhodesia which then became known as Zimbabwe?
25 Where was the first Marxist state in Africa created?
26 Where was the Maoist guerrilla group Sendero Luminoso active in the 80s?
27 Who became New Zealand PM in December 1997?
28 Who was joint secretary general of the ANC with Mandela in 1964?
29 Who were the first three states to break away from Yugoslavia in '91?
30 Where did the Hundred Flowers Movement encourage government criticism in the 50s?

1 Which two versions of the same song were in the Top Ten simultaneously in December 1987?
2 Which football team does Des Lynam support?
3 Pierre is the capital of which American State?
4 Which actress was also known as Lucille Le Sueur?
5 Which member of the Coronation Street cast has sung in the chorus of an Italian opera company?
6 Which reptiles come from the family Boidae?
7 Who produced a fitness video called Ultimate Fat Burner?
8 Who was the first female winner of the BBC Sports Personality of the Year?
9 How did fashion empress Laura Ashley die?
10 A fear of heaven is known as what?
11 Which singer's real name is Benjamin Earl Nelson?
12 What is the international car index mark for a car from Monaco?
13 Which artist painted La Desserte in 1908?
14 What colour appears with white on the State of Qatar flag?
15 What is the full name for the medical condition known as ME?
16 Where in the UK did Bob Hope have a theatre named after him?
17 Who directed the 1992 film Hook?
18 Bamako is the capital of which country?
19 Who is the elder – Barry Humphries or Eddie George?
20 Who duetted with David Essex on True Love Ways in 1994?
21 Whose first book was How to Cheat at Cooking?
22 Who is taller – Terry Waite or Frank Bruno?
23 Which country has the ouguiya as a unit of currency?
24 What was the christian name of shipowner Cunard?
25 Where was Patsy Gallant going from in her 70s UK Top Ten hit?
26 Which children's author appeared on the cover of Sergeant Pepper?
27 In which country is the city of Kaohsiung?
28 What is the nationality of writer and chef Ken Hom?
29 Testament of Friendship is about Vera Brittain's friendship with which author?
30 What is 13 cubed?

World History (See Quiz 205)
1 Manchu or Qing ('Ching'). 2 Norway & Scotland. 3 Heisei. 4 Shot with her husband Tsar Nicholas II. 5 Kurt Waldheim. 6 Chaim Weizmann. 7 Four. 8 Thomas Stanford Raffles. 9 Nuclear-free South Pacific. 10 Dissolute. 11 Reims. 12 Romania. 13 Theodore. 14 Anschluss. 15 Lion of Judah. 16 Alfred Rosenberg. 17 Dean Rusk. 18 Samora Machel. 19 Egypt. 20 Sandanista. 21 San Francisco Conference. 22 Czechoslovakia. 23 Cairo (El Azhar). 24 Bishop Abel Muzorewa. 25 Congo. 26 Peru. 27 Jenny Shipley. 28 Walter Sisulu. 29 Slovenia, Macedonia & Croatia. 30 China.

Quiz 207 Who's Who?

Answers - see page 676

LEVEL 3

1   Who starred with Steve Coogan on The Dead Good Show?
2   Who was the real life husband of the first girl in the famous Nescafe commercials?
3   How was comedy writer Gerald Wiley better known?
4   Who found fame with Emma Thompson playing Danny McGlone?
5   Who starred in and produced a mini series called Sins?
6   Who was a regular in Crown Court as barrister Jeremy Parsons QC?
7   In which series has Philip Franks been a tax inspector and a policeman?
8   Who stormed out of a TV interview when Robin Day called him a "here today gone tomorrow politician"?
9   Whose first pop TV series was called The Power Station?
10 Which Moll Flanders lost husband Ralph to Francesca Annis?
11 Who was the first male presenter of Live & Kicking?
12 What was Lenny Henry's Rastafarian community police officer called?
13 Who came to fame as 'Q' of The Little Ladies?
14 Who was Cherie Lunghi's character in The Manageress?
15 Who played Fletch's son Raymond in Going Straight?
16 Who runs the Amy International production company with wife Susan George?
17 Who are the two youngest. McGann brothers?
18 Who was the first female presenter of Top Gear?
19 Who wrote the Magic Roundabout scripts when they were first broadcast in the UK?
20 Which actresses created The House of Eliot?
21 Who appeared in Dixon of Dock Green aged 10 and found fame as Mrs Theodopolopoudos?
22 What is the real name of the comedian who had a No 1 with a cover version of Tommy Roe's Dizzy and wanted a One-2-One with Terry-Thomas?
23 Which EastEnders star used to be better known by his catchphrase 'Terr-i-fic'?
24 Who played Marjory in The Outside Dog in the Talking Heads series?
25 Who won New Faces and went on to present it?
26 Who is the real life mum of Grace and Henry Durham?
27 Who left Sherwood Forest for oil in Denver?
28 Who adapted his novel of the same name into Men Behaving Badly?
29 Who played the seventh Doctor Who?
30 Who was the only female presenter at the Live Aid concert?

Quiz 208 Pot Luck 101

Answers - see page 675

1   What is Lauren Bacall's full real name?
2   About whom did Cliff Richard say, "She really is a woman just like my Mum"?
3   Who wrote the poem The Idylls of the King?
4   What was the profession of fizzy drinks maker Jacob Schweppes?
5   Who is the elder – Harvey Goldsmith or Sir Elton John?
6   Saint Mary's airport serves which Isles?
7   What is the international car index mark for a car from Madagascar?
8   Who opened Europe's longest suspension bridge in 1998?
9   What was the Gap Band's first UK Top Ten hit?
10 What is the capital of Guinea?
11 Who did Kasparov beat to become world chess champion in 1985?
12 What is a kelim?
13 What was the by-name for the B24 bomber?
14 Which countries fought the Pacific War in the 19th century?
15 On which river does the US city of Cherokee lie?
16 What or who does UNICEF benefit?
17 Which political party did Mrs Pankhurst join in 1925?
18 Who was the first Archbishop of Canterbury to meet a Pope since the 16th century?
19 The first Bodyshop opened in which town?
20 Who was Elizabeth I's first stepmother?
21 What was Leif Garrett made for in his only UK Top Ten hit from 1979?
22 Which husband and wife team had a hit with A Song I'd Like to Sing?
23 What was the first text to be 'bowdlerised' by Thomas Bowdler?
24 Which American state is called the Pine Tree State?
25 Who is taller – Mick Jagger or Phil Collins?
26 Which country has the kyat as a unit of currency?
27 What colour appears with red and blue on the Romanian flag?
28 What make of raincoat did Harold Wilson popularise?
29 In which European country are the counties of Arad, Arges and Cluj?
30 Which duo got to No 30 with the hit Diamond Lights in 1987?

Answers

Who's Who? (See Quiz 207)
1 Caroline Aherne. 2 Trevor Eve. 3 Ronnie Barker. 4 Robbie Coltrane.
5 Joan Collins. 6 Richard Wilson. 7 The Darling Buds of May, Heartbeat. 8
John Nott. 9 Chris Evans. 10 Alex Kingston. 11 Andi Peters. 12 PC Ganja.
13 Rula Lenska. 14 Gabriella Benson. 15 Nicholas Lyndhurst. 16 Simon
MacCorkindale. 17 Mark & Stephen. 18 Angela Rippon. 19 Eric Thompson.
20 Jean Marsh & Eileen Atkins. 21 Pauline Quirke. 22 Jim Moir (Vic Reeves).
23 Mike Reid. 24 Julie Walters. 25 Marti Caine. 26 Victoria Wood.
27 Michael Praed. 28 Simon Nye. 29 Sylvester McCoy. 30 Janice Long.

1 What was Bob Geldof's TV production company called?
2 What is Kerry Packer's media company called?
3 Which mag did Jennifer Saunders and Joanna Lumley guest edit?
4 What was the first INR radio station?
5 Kelly's Directories catalogue what?
6 What is the signature tune of the BBC World Service?
7 What was the first magazine in the UK in 1691?
8 In which magazine did the Addams Family first appear?
9 Which American syndicated a newspaper column called 'My Day'?
10 Who founded the Daily Mail?
11 Where is the newspaper ABC from?
12 Which two UK national newspaper were founded in 1990?
13 Apart from the Tribune, which other US newspaper has Chicago in its name?
14 Which press agency has the abbreviation IRNA?
15 Which newspaper proprietor was born Jan Ludvik Hoch?
16 In '89 Richard Murdoch bought a 50% stake in which Hungarian tabloid?
17 Which Sunday Times editor made headline news himself regarding details of his affair with Pamella Bordes?
18 Lloyd Grossman was restaurant critic of which magazine in the 80s?
19 Who took over The Observer in 1981?
20 Apart from the Guardian, which other newspaper did James Naughtie work for before joining the BBC?
21 What type of correspondent for the BBC was Michael Cole before he went. to work for Mohammed Fayed?
22 Who was chairman of Saatchi & Saatchi when they took over the Tory Party account?
23 Which agency did the Saatchi brothers found in 1995?
24 Which famous columnist is married to Lady Camilla Harris?
25 Whose affair with David Mellor brought media man Max Clifford into the public gaze?
26 Which media man's sons all have the middle name Paradine?
27 Which soccer side does Tony Blair's press Secretary support?
28 Which co founder of TV am was married to a future Leader of the House of Lords?
29 What was Ted Turner's family business before he turned to TV?
30 Which media magnate has owned AC Milan and been his country's PM?

Quiz 210 Pot Luck 102

LEVEL 3

Answers - see page 677

1   What two colours appear on the flag of San Marino?
2   Male is the capital of which country?
3   In which century was Dame Barbara Cartland born?
4   What is the international car index mark for a car from Barbados?
5   Who directed the 1992 film A Few Good Men?
6   What did Paul Gambaccini sell at auction in 1997?
7   Which Persian word means 'pleasure garden'?
8   Which film production company began as the Famous Players Film Company?
9   In which country is the port of Lubango?
10 Which painting did Arthur Scargill choose as his luxury on Desert Island Discs?
11 Which vocalist had Top Ten hits with Shake Your Love and Foolish Beat?
12 Which country has the tugrik as a unit of currency?
13 Who was President of the USA before Richard Nixon?
14 In which Canadian province is the novel Anne of Green Gables set?
15 What was painter Tintoretto's real name?
16 Who is the elder – Patsy Kensit or Ulrika Jonsson?
17 Which Sea, after the Coral Sea, is the largest in area in the world?
18 From which countries do the Mende people originate?
19 Who was the Greek Goddess of the rainbow?
20 What does BUPA stand for?
21 What trade did playwright Brendan Behan learn on leaving school?
22 Who played Paul Verlaine in the film Total Eclipse. to Leonardo DiCaprio's Rimbaud?
23 What is the only US state to have been an independent republic?
24 In monetary and banking terms, what do the initials SIB stand for?
25 The Gladys Porter Zoo in Texas is noted for its collection of what?
26 Thalassophobia is a fear of what?
27 What was Peter Gabriel's first UK Top Ten hit?
28 Which actress is the mother of actress Beatie Edney?
29 Who wrote the screen play for the 1963 film Tom Jones?
30 What is the main language of the Dominican Republic?

The Media (See Quiz 209)
1 Planet 24. **2** Consolidated Press. **3** Marie Claire (UK). **4** Classic FM.
5 Towns and cities. **6** Lilliburlero. **7** Compleat Library. **8** New Yorker.
9 Eleanor Roosevelt. **10** Lord Northcliffe. **11** Madrid. **12** The Independent on Sunday & The European. **13** Chicago Sun-Times. **14** Islamic Republic News Agency. **15** Robert Maxwell. **16** Reform. **17** Andrew Neil. **18** Harpers and Queen. **19** Tiny Rowland. **20** The Scotsman. **21** Royal. **22** Tim Bell. **23** M & C Saatchi. **24** Nigel Dempster. **25** Antonia de Sancha. **26** David Frost. **27** Burnley. **28** Peter Jay. **29** Advertising. **30** Silvio Berlusconi.

Answers

Quiz 211 Who's Music?

Answers - see page 680

LEVEL 3

1 Who was knocked off No 1 position by Wannabe?

2 Whose record has the longest playing time of any to make No 1?

3 Who was Mike McGear's famous elder brother?

4 Whose one hit wonder replaced Honky Tonk Women at No 1 in US and Britain?

5 Which singer left school in 1961 to appear in the film It's Trad, Dad?

6 Which No 1 singer was born Arnold George Dorsey in Madras?

7 Which top musician produced Shakin' Stevens Merry Christmas Everyone?

8 Who sang lead vocal on the chart topper Babe?

9 Who wrote the lines, "All alone, without a telephone"?

10 Who has recorded singles with Paul McCartney, Julio Iglesias and Diana Ross?

11 Who was the first drummer with The Stone Roses?

12 Joyce Vincent and Thelma Hopkins were the girls in which 70s group?

13 Who joined Wendy Richard in the No 1 from 1962 Come Outside?

14 Which female singer did Peter Skellern ask to join his Oasis in 1983?

15 Which chart topper started life at Leigh, Lancashire as Clive Powell?

16 Who set up the DEP record label?

17 Which 60s artist was the first British born artist with three No 1 hits?

18 How is James Michael Aloysious Bradford better known?

19 Who wrote Chain Reaction for Diana Ross?

20 Who joined the Beatles on their first hit to enter the charts at No 1?

21 Who recorded the 1993 No 1 written and produced by Shaw and Rogers?

22 Which actor was talking to the trees on the B side of Wand'rin' Star?

23 Who was No 1 in the UK and US singles and album charts at the same time in 1971?

24 Who covered the Searchers' No 1 Sweets for My Sweet in 1994?

25 Which Creation Records boss signed Oasis?

26 Which duo made up the Righteous Brothers?

27 Who joined the Beautiful South after being roadie for The Housemartins?

28 Whose death moved Don McLean to write American Pie?

29 The Beatles apart, who first took a Lennon & McCartney song to No 1, with the Dakotas?

30 In the 1950s who was the first instrumentalist to achieve two No 1s?

Quiz 212 Pot Luck 103

LEVEL 3

1   Which country has the ports of Buchanan and Grenville?
2   Who wrote Chips With Everything?
3   Who were the first English team outside London to claim the European Cup Winners' Cup?
4   In Scrabble what would the word DOG score without any bonus points?
5   What was sewn into the hem of Princess Diana's wedding dress for luck?
6   Who co-wrote The Changeling with William Rowley around 1622?
7   Theophobia is the fear of what?
8   Which American state is called the Last Frontier?
9   "For whom the bell tolls" is a quote from whom?
10 What was Gabrielle's first UK Top Ten hit?
11 What did Olivia Newton-John's grandfather win a Nobel Prize for in 1954?
12 In which European country are the regions of Vigo and Murcia?
13 What type of animal is a kudu?
14 Who composed the opera Mask of Orpheus?
15 In which year did Michelin produce the first of its Red Guides?
16 Which detective novel did A A Milne write in 1922?
17 How many stripes are there on the Thai flag?
18 Whose first UK Top Ten hit was Swing Your Daddy?
19 What does ECSC stand for in European Community Organisations?
20 What is Charles Bronson's full real name?
21 What is the international car index mark for a car from Morocco?
22 Where had Jim Rockford been in the years preceding The Rockford Files?
23 What name is given to the Greek letter that is the equivalent of letter R?
24 What is Remembrance Sunday called in the US?
25 What does 'tai chi chuan' mean in Chinese?
26 Who is the elder – Princess Michael of Kent or Felicity Kendal?
27 In which country is the city of Maputo?
28 Which cricket commentator was awarded the Military Cross in WWII for his 'cheerfulness under fire'?
29 Who wrote the opera The Knot Garden?
30 Which soccer side does actor Robert Lindsay support?

Quiz 213 Who's Sport?

Answers - see page 682

LEVEL 3

1 Who beat Jahangir Khan's five year unbeaten record in 1986?
2 Who had the car number plate 1 CUE?
3 How was Walker Smith better known?
4 What was boxer Paul Ryan's nickname?
5 Who won the Oaks and the St Leger for the Queen in 1978 on Dunfermline?
6 What was the nickname of baseball player Ty Cobb?
7 Which woman was undefeated over 400m between 1977 and 1981?
8 Which horse did Willie Shoemaker ride in his last race?
9 Who was the only person to beat Sugar Ray Leonard in a professional fight?
10 Which athlete was nicknamed 'The Flying Finn'?
11 Who beat Babe Ruth's long standing record of 714 home runs in '74?
12 Who was the first jockey to saddle more than 8,000 winners?
13 Who was the first skier to overtake Pirmin Zurbriggen's four overall world championship titles?
14 Which American football player was nicknamed 'Sweetness'?
15 Who in 1985 was the first man for 30 years to hold the 1500m and 5000m world records at the same time?
16 Whose Triple Jump World Record did Jonathan Edwards break?
17 Who was the first South African to win the Benson & Hedges Masters snooker title?
18 Where did Nelson Piquet win his first Grand Prix?
19 Who did Giancarlo Fisichella drive for in 1998?
20 Who won the Moto Cross des Nations for the first time in 1975?
21 Who was dubbed the Louisville Lip?
22 Whose record of 24 Grand Prix wins was broken by Jim Clark?
23 Who was the first non European to win the Tour de France?
24 Who won the 1988 Jesse Owens Award as the year's most outstanding athlete?
25 Fiona May represents which country at which sport?
26 Who won the Fosters World Doubles with Stephen Hendry in 1989?
27 Which French cyclist's nickname means 'The Badger'?
28 Gene Tunney was only beaten once, by whom?
29 Who was the first Australian to win the Women's World Open Snooker Championship?
30 Who was the first racing driver to win 500 points in. Formula 1?

1   What's the most number of raised dots in a single letter of Braille?
2   Which 'E' number is used to represent riboflavin in products?
3   Who was actress Jane Seymour's first father in law?
4   In which country is the city of Maracaibo?
5   In which decade was Mohammed Fayed born?
6   Who, on the cover of Sergeant Pepper, was known by his three names?
7   Picasso's Guernica is a comment on what?
8   What is the correct form of address to begin a letter to a Roman Catholic Archbishop?
9   Which two colours form the background for the Vatican City flag?
10 What is the capital of the American state of Wisconsin?
11 Who was Henry IV's father?
12 Who has larger feet – Gladiator Hunter or Nick Faldo?
13 A fear of the number thirteen is known as what?
14 Which Spice Girl once appeared as an extra in Emmerdale?
15 What's the English name of the constellation Pictor?
16 What was Blondie's last UK No1?
17 Which country has the dirham as a unit of currency?
18 What is the main food of baby whales?
19 What is the international car index mark for a car from Tanzania?
20 In which US state is a university endowed by Cornelius Vanderbilt?
21 Which comedian played Tollmaster in Doctor Who in 1987?
22 What is the main language of Ethiopia?
23 Who played the black film detective Shaft?
24 Which Nobel Prize was won in 1975 by Andrei Sakharov?
25 Who had a No 1 UK hit with Seven Tears in 1982?
26 Who is the elder – Jemima Khan or Kate Moss?
27 Who wrote the Leatherstocking Tales?
28 Tegucigalpa is the capital of which country?
29 What was the Christian name of frozen food man Mr Birdseye?
30 Who directed the 1991 film JFK?

1   What is chiefly grown in Alabama's Canebrake country?
2   The Julian and Dinaric Alps extend into which two countries?
3   The Amur river forms much of the boundary between which two countries?
4   What is the Maori name for New Zealand?
5   Which two main metals are found in the Atacama Desert in Chile?
6   What is the currency of Malaysia?
7   Which country has the highest density of sheep in the world?
8   Which African country takes its name from the Shona for 'House of Stone'?
9   Which volcanic peak is west of Cook inlet in Alaska?
10 San Miguel is the main island of which group?
11 What is the capital of the Lazio region of Italy?
12 What is the former name of the capital of Dominica?
13 Which Brazilian state is the centre of Amazonian tin and gold mining?
14 Aqaba is which country's only port?
15 On which island of the Philippines is Manila?
16 What is the world's flattest continent?
17 Which former fort in New York State is the home of the US Military Academy?
18 Which US state capital lies on the river Jordan?
19 In which country is Africa's lowest point?
20 What is the largest primeval forest left in Europe?
21 The Red Sea is the submerged section of which valley?
22 Regina in Saskatchewan was originally called what?
23 How many countries do the Andes pass through?
24 In which country do the Makua live?
25 What is the highest peak of the Apennines?
26 Which city south east of St Malo was the old capital of Brittany?
27 Which Alps lie north east of the Sea of Showers?
28 Robben Island is a prison in which Bay?
29 What is Malawi's largest city?
30 Which south American port's name means River of January?

LEVEL 3

1 Where was Paddy Ashdown born?

2 How does a marimba differ from a xylophone?

3 In which country is the city of Surabaya?

4 Who composed the opera The Ice Break?

5 Which comic strip character was played by Warren Beatty?

6 Whose first UK Top Ten hit was Baby Baby ?

7 What would you drink from a cha-no-yu?

8 Whose theories did Jeffrey Masson attack in Against Therapy?

9 How many stripes are there on the Ugandan national flag?

10 What did the last emperor of China Hsuan Tung ask to be called after he was deposed?

11 In which war was the Battle of Inkerman?

12 What is Doris Day's full real name?

13 Which American state is called the Sunflower State?

14 Which letter is two dashes and two dots in Morse Code?

15 Who preceded Lal Shastri as Prime Minister of India?

16 What are the initials LVO an abbreviation of?

17 According to the Bonzo Dog Doo-Dah Band's The Intro and the Outro what is Princess Anne playing?

18 The Pulitzer Prize is awarded in which three categories?

19 In which European country is the region of Anatolia?

20 Phasmophobia is the fear of what?

21 Which country has the koruna as a unit of currency?

22 Who is the elder – Elaine Paige or Lily Savage?

23 Who is the male hero of the children's book Where the Wild Things Are?

24 What is cassata a type of?

25 What is the capital of Oman?

26 In the first Pink Panther film what was the professional jewel thief called?

27 In which country is the sculpture Monument to the Equator?

28 In Japan what type of entertainment is bunraku?

29 Pyelitis affects which organ of the body?

30 Which king of England was crowned on Christmas Day?

1　What was the name of Helen Sharman's space craft?
2　Over which part of Paris was the first successful balloon flight?
3　What was Boeing's first sea plane made from?
4　Who built the oil tanker Jahre Viking?
5　In which craft did Kenneth Warby set a water speed record in 1978?
6　The space probe Magellan went into orbit where in 1990?
7　What are the terminal cities of Japan's Hikari trains?
8　Why were Britain's first traffic lights built?
9　Which was the last country in Europe to change from driving on the left to the right?
10　Who produced the first mass produced four wheel drive saloon car?
11　The world's highest railway line runs between which countries?
12　Who designed and owned the eight engine Spruce Goose in the '40s?
13　What are the two termini of the Volga-Baltic Waterway?
14　Where is Narita airport?
15　In which craft did Charles Yeager first break the sound barrier in the air?
16　Who built Concorde with BAC?
17　What was the first ocean-going oil tanker called?
18　What was the first space station called?
19　Who built the B17 Flying Fortress in WWII?
20　How many passengers did the first hovercraft carry?
21　What was the name of the first nuclear powered ship?
22　Where was the Volkswagen factory before WWII?
23　In which country was the launch site of the European Ariane rocket?
24　How many people can ride a Frankencycle?
25　What was the cruise ship Norway called before a Norwegian bought it?
26　How many capital cities do you pass through on the Pan American Highway?
27　What was the name of the first balloon to cross the Atlantic?
28　If you took the India Pacific train where would you be?
29　Where did the Hindenberg explode in May 1937?
30　What was the first ship launched by Queen Elizabeth II?

Quiz 218 Who's Movies?

Answers - see page 685

1 Who duetted with Joan Jett on Light of Day in 1986?
2 Which two actors rejected Bridge on the River Kwai before Alec Guinness got the lead role?
3 How is actor/director Nobby Clarke better known?
4 Who played the first cinema vampire in Nosferatu?
5 Who was Daniel Day-Lewis' actress mother?
6 Who has a production company called Edited?
7 Which TV hero played a movie villain in Beethoven?
8 Who walked off the set of 10 and gave Dudley Moore a movie break?
9 Who did Schwarzenegger's love interest in Twins marry after the movie was made?
10 Who links TV's Yes Minister and the film Nuns on the Run?
11 Who was the voice of Zazu in The Lion King?
12 Whose legs were insured for more – Fred Astaire's or Betty Grable's?
13 Who did Val Kilmer replace as Batman?
14 Who had the title role in the remake of The Absent Minded Professor?
15 Which director was an amateur lightweight boxing champion in the early 20s?
16 In which film did Bing Crosby first play Father O'Malley?
17 Who adapted the play Cyrano de Bergerac into the movie Roxanne?
18 Who appeared in her father's Godfather Part III?
19 Who directed the first two films in which Dianne Wiest won Oscars?
20 After landing a weekend with this actor the winner said she really wanted the second prize of a fridge.
21 Who did Kristin Scott Thomas beat to win the role in The Horse Whisperer?
22 Who adapted Agatha Christie's Evil Under the Sun for the big screen?
23 Which production company was set up by Hugh Grant and Elizabeth Hurley?
24 Who is the president played by Anthony Hopkins in Amistad?
25 Who played Prinny in The Madness of King George?
26 Which 60s activist was the godfather of Winona Ryder?
27 Which actress's husband designed the Olympic Gateway in LA. '84?
28 Who played Streisand's son in Prince of Tides?
29 Who won supporting actor Oscar for Jerry Maguire?
30 Who directed Mrs Doubtfire?

Answers

1   In which country is the city of Srinagar?
2   Who wrote the novel *Rites of Passage*?
3   What was the first British Top Ten hit for Johnny Nash?
4   How many sides has an endecagon?
5   Carson City is the capital of which US state?
6   Which cathedral's 800th anniversary was marked by a 1989 set of stamps?
7   What is the only English anagram of ALIENATOR?
8   Who first manufactured barbed wire?
9   Belau and Kusac are in which island group?
10 To within five, how many league games did Gazza play for Newcastle?
11 Which electronics firm featured in the TV series "Making Out"?
12 What are the odds of rolling double one in dice-throwing?
13 What star sign links Michael Brunson and John Craven?
14 In Monopoly, if you were on Liverpool Street Station and got double four, where would you land?
15 What was the name of the outlaw nicknamed the Sundance Kid?
16 Hargenger and Spivoy are types of what?
17 In which sport was John Dennis Cronshey famous?
18 On TV, what was the name of Spender's wife?
19 Which US state is directly west of Colorado?
20 From which language does the word "sherbet" originate?
21 The airline Ladeco was formed in which country?
22 What was Artemus Ward's real name?
23 Who did Lynda Bellingham play in "General Hospital"?
24 Which female driver was the 1992 Indy 500 Rookie of the Year?
25 Which statesman won the Nobel Prize for Literature in 1953?
26 What kitchen aid did Charles Strite invent?
27 In which country was the TV Presenter Bob Holness born?
28 What did the people who appeared in "The Duty Men" work for?
29 Who had a hit in 1982 with "Pass the Dutchie"?
30 What is the approximate distance of Cairo airport from London in miles?

Transport (See Quiz 685)
1 Soyuz TM-12. 2 Bois de Boulogne. 3 Spruce. 4 Japan. 5 The Spirit of Australia. 6 Venus. 7 Tokyo & Osaka. 8 To make access easier to the Palace of Westminster. 9 Sweden. 10 Audi. 11 Peru & Bolivia. 12 Howard Hughes. 13 Astrakhan to St Petersburg. 14 Tokyo. 15 Bell X-1 rocket plane. 16 Aerospatiale. 17 Gluckauf. 18 Salyut 1. 19 Boeing. 20 Three. 21 Lenin. 22 Wolfsburg. 23 French Guiana. 24 Four. 25 France. 26 17. 27 Double Eagle II . 28 Australia. 29 Lakehurst, New Jersey. 30 Britannia.

Answers

HOW TO SET UP YOUR OWN

PUB QUIZ

It isn't easy, get that right from the start. This isn't going to be easy. Think instead of words like; 'difficult', 'taxing', 'infuriating' consider yourself with damp palms and a dry throat and then, when you have concentrated on that, put it out of your mind and think of the recognition you will receive down the local, imagine all the regulars lifting you high upon their shoulders dancing and weaving their way around the pub. It won't help but it's good to dream every once in a while.

What you will need:

- A good selection of Biros (never be tempted to give your own pen up, not even to family members)
- A copy of *The Biggest Pub Quiz Book Ever!*
- A set of answer sheets photocopied from the back of the book (there are two sets for each round)
- A good speaking voice and possibly a microphone and an amp
- A pub
- At least one pint inside you
- At least one more on your table
- Your table

What to do:

Choose your local to start with, there is no need to get halfway through your first quiz and decide you weren't cut out for all this and then find yourself in the roughest pub in Christendom 30 miles and a long run from home.

Chat it through with the landlord and agree on whether you will be charging or not, if you don't then there is little chance of a prize for the winners other than a free pint each and this is obviously at the landlord's discretion – if you pack his pub to bursting then five free pints won't worry him, but if it's only you and a couple of others then he may be less than unwilling, as publicans tend to be.

If you decide on a payment for entry to the quiz, keep it reasonable. You don't want to take the fun out of the quiz; some people will be well aware that they have very little hope of winning and will be reluctant to celebrate the fact by mortgaging their house.

Once location and prize are all sorted then advertising the event is paramount, get people's attention, sell, sell, sell or, alternatively, stick up a gaudy looking poster on the door of the bogs. Be sure to specify all the details, time, prize and so on – remember you are selling to people whose tiny attention span is being whittled down to nothing by alcohol.

After this it is time for the big night, if you are holding the event in the 'snug' which seats ten or so you can rely on your voice, if not you should get hold of a good microphone and an amplifier so that you can boom out your questions and enunciate the length and breadth of the pub (once again, clear this with the landlord and don't let liquid anywhere near the electrical equipment). Make sure to practice,

and get comfortable with the sound of your own voice and relax as much as possible. Try not to rely on alcohol too much or "round one" will be followed by "rown' too" which will eventually give way to "runfree". Relax your voice so that you can handle any queries from the teams, and any venomous abuse from the 'lively' bar area.

When you enter the pub make sure you take everything listed above. Also, make sure you have a set of tie-break questions, that you instruct everybody who is taking part of the rules – and be firm. It will only upset people if you start handing out impromptu solutions and let's face it the wisdom of Solomon is not needed when you are talking pub quiz rules; 'no cheating' is a perfectly healthy stance to start with. Keep people happy by double-checking your questions and answers, the last thing you need is a mix up on the prize-winning question.

Finally, keep the teams to a maximum of five members, hand out your answer papers and pens and, when everybody is good and settled, start the quiz. It might not be easy and it might not propel you to international stardom or pay for a life of luxury but you will enjoy yourself. No, really.

ANSWERS   Round One

1 _____

2 _____

3 _____

4 _____

5 _____

6 _____

7 _____

8 _____

9 _____

10 _____

11 _____

12 _____

13 _____

14 _____

15 _____

16 _____

17 _____

18 _____

19 _____

20 _____

21 _____

22 _____

23 _____

24 _____

25 _____

26 _____

27 _____

28 _____

29 _____

30 _____

ANSWERS

1 _____

2 _____

3 _____

4 _____

5 _____

6 _____

7 _____

8 _____

9 _____

10 _____

11 _____

12 _____

13 _____

14 _____

15 _____

16 _____

17 _____

18 _____

19 _____

20 _____

21 _____

22 _____

23 _____

24 _____

25 _____

26 _____

27 _____

28 _____

29 _____

30 _____

ANSWERS

1 _____

2 _____

3 _____

4 _____

5 _____

6 _____

7 _____

8 _____

9 _____

10 _____

11 _____

12 _____

13 _____

14 _____

15 _____

16 _____

17 _____

18 _____

19 _____

20 _____

21 _____

22 _____

23 _____

24 _____

25 _____

26 _____

27 _____

28 _____

29 _____

30 _____

ANSWERS   Round Two

1 _____

2 _____

3 _____

4 _____

5 _____

6 _____

7 _____

8 _____

9 _____

10 _____

11 _____

12 _____

13 _____

14 _____

15 _____

16 _____

17 _____

18 _____

19 _____

20 _____

21 _____

22 _____

23 _____

24 _____

25 _____

26 _____

27 _____

28 _____

29 _____

30 _____

ANSWERS   Round Three

1 _____

2 _____

3 _____

4 _____

5 _____

6 _____

7 _____

8 _____

9 _____

10 _____

11 _____

12 _____

13 _____

14 _____

15 _____

16 _____

17 _____

18 _____

19 _____

20 _____

21 _____

22 _____

23 _____

24 _____

25 _____

26 _____

27 _____

28 _____

29 _____

30 _____

ANSWERS Round Three

1 _____

2 _____

3 _____

4 _____

5 _____

6 _____

7 _____

8 _____

9 _____

10 _____

11 _____

12 _____

13 _____

14 _____

15 _____